Eminent Creativity, Everyday Creativity, and Health

Publications in Creativity Research
Robert S. Albert, Series Editor
(formerly Creativity Research Monographs
as edited by Mark A. Runco)

Achieving Extraordinary Ends: An Essay on Creativity, by Sharon Bailin, 1994

Beyond Terman: Longitudinal Studies in Contemporary Gifted Education, edited by Rena Subotnik and Karen Arnold, 1994

Counseling Gifted and Talented Children, edited by Roberta M. Milgram, 1991

Creative Thinking: Problem-Solving Skills and the Arts Orientation, by John Wakefield, 1992

Creativity and Affect, edited by Melvin P. Shaw and Mark A. Runco, 1994

Creativity in Government, by Thomas Heinzen, 1994

Divergent Thinking, by Mark A. Runco, 1991

E. Paul Torrance: The Creativity Man (An Authorized Biography), by Garnet W. Millar, 1995

Eminent Creativity, Everyday Creativity, and Health, edited by Mark A. Runco and Ruth Richards, 1997

Fostering the Growth of High Ability: European Perspectives, edited by Arthur J. Cropley and Detlev Dehn, 1996

Genius and Creativity: Selected Papers, by Dean Keith Simonton, 1997

Genius Revisited: High IQ Children Grown Up, by Rena Subotnik, Lee Kassan, Ellen Summers, and Alan Wasser, 1993

More Ways Than One: Fostering Creativity, by Arthur J. Cropley, 1992

Nurturing and Developing Creativity: The Emergence of a Discipline, edited by Scott G. Isaksen, Mary C. Murdock, Roger L. Firestien, and Donald J. Treffinger, 1993

Perspectives on Creativity: The Biographical Method, by John E. Gedo and Mary M. Gedo, 1992

Problem Finding, Problem Solving, and Creativity, edited by Mark A. Runco, 1994

Top of the Class: Guiding Children Along the Smart Path to Happiness, by Arline L. Bronzaft, 1996

Understanding and Recognizing Creativity: The Emergence of a Discipline, edited by Scott G. Isaksen, Mary C. Murdock, Roger L. Firestien, and Donald J. Treffinger, 1993

Why Fly? A Philosophy of Creativity, by E. Paul Torrance, 1995

In preparation:

The Person Behind the Mask: A Guide to Performing Arts Psychology, by Linda H. Hamilton

Creativity in Performance, by R. Keith Sawyer

Eminent Creativity, Everyday Creativity, and Health

edited by
Mark A. Runco
and
Ruth Richards

Ablex Publishing Corporation
Greenwich, Connecticut
London, England

Cover art by Lauren Richards-Ruby at 6 years of age.

Copyright © 1997 by Ablex Publishing Corporation

Printed in the United States of America

Library of Congress Cataloging-in-Publication Data

Eminent creativity, everyday creativity, and health / edited by Mark
  A. Runco, Ruth Richards.
     p.   cm. — (Creativity research)
   Includes bibliographical references and index.
   ISBN 1-56750-174-5 (cloth). — ISBN 1-56750-175-3 (pbk.)
   1. Creative ability.   2. Adjustment (Psychology).   3. Creative
ability—Social aspects.   I. Runco, Mark A.   II. Richards, Ruth.
III. Series.
BF408.E47   1997
153.3'5—DC20   96-5371
                                                  CIP

Ablex Publishing Corporation   Published in the U.K. and Europe by:
55 Old Post Road #2   JAI Press Ltd.
P.O. Box 5297   38 Tavistock Street
Greenwich, CT 06830   Covent Garden
                                London WC2E 7PB
                                England

Contents

v

Part III. Psychological Health and Creativity

Part IV. Societal Health and Creativity

Preface

Creativity and health? Of course. Creativity is good. Health is good. We should all be creative. We should all draw some pictures, sing a song.

This may be some people's view of creativity. As with many views, this one may be true in its place. Indeed, it is an important part of the picture. Yet when you look further, you see that the picture goes on and on, and becomes a great deal more complex. Here too you find issues of illness, pain, trauma and creativity. Of suffering and deprivation. Of creativity achieved at great personal expense. Of mood swings and thought disorder. Of creativity and the abuse of substances. And of creativity itself abused—creativity turned to socially destructive rather than socially useful ends.

Must some of these troubles arrive, at least in part, to anyone who chooses to create? Or is the picture somehow different for a few eminent and exceptional creators than for the rest of us?

Indeed, when we speak of creativity, of what exactly do we speak? We do not for a minute intend to minimize the importance of eminent and exceptional accomplishments, particularly in the arts and the sciences, which many people identify first with "creativity." In their very rarity and exceptionality, these achievements can touch us all fundamentally— through distillations of meaning, truth, beauty, or scientific essence that may do for us what we cannot. At times, they may lift us to higher realms than we ever imagined. This volume will consider such exceptional contributions, along with some of their costs.

Yet we look beyond these as well, to creativity as a general style of thinking, even of living. Of the essence of *originality* brought to the tasks of everyday life. Of creativity as an essential tool for adaptation to our environment and, indeed, to a changing world. Creativity, when viewed this way, becomes an essential survival tool, and not just for a few people, but for everyone. It is a force in our own personal development and in the evolution of society. In fact, from where we stand now, as a species, perhaps we can only begin to sense its fullest evolutionary potential.

When it is so framed, one may not be at all surprised to find that creativity can be good for one's health. The everyday practice of originality may enhance physical as well as psychological well-being. Surely there is a powerful message here. To do, to grow, to risk, to change, to know oneself, and the world about us—and also to dare to know what one does *not* know—can be healthy and good, and even lifegiving.

Yet if our own inner natures are sending us such a clear and objective message, why can this message be so hard to hear? This book also looks at some forces arrayed against creative growth—and these surely impact our everyday and individual creative growth, as well as more public accomplishments. Why might we at times personally throw in our lot with forces against creativity? Might we do so even when the well-being of our children, our employees, our students, our constituents, our friends, or our own selves is at stake? Do we also find that there can be too much of a good thing? One may consider if there is a dialectic here, an emergent balance for individuals as well as for cultures, which moderates between resistance and change, convention and innovation, order and chaos. If so, is there also a balance point—and perhaps an optimal balance point at a given time—which could promote our greater "health"?

What indeed of the evolution of *creativity*? This generative process might be considered in terms of (for better or for worse, concerning its results for our own perceived interests) an *evolution of information*. Such an evolution certainly would not occur in a vacuum, but rather in the context of a range of forces at the level of individuals and families, fields of endeavor, whole societies, and world culture, and through the myriad interactions of varied forms of exceptional and everyday creativity. Finally, all of these various forces might ultimately be defined as relatively more or less healthy by certain criteria—or at least this case may be argued.

Creativity, as an evolution of information, should also be shaped, and limited by, aspects of our biological and genetic endowment. As the saying goes, we can "do no more than is humanly possible." But what exactly does this mean? An evolving creative process could, at best, rapidly fuel what has been called our *conscious evolution*, speeding a process of learning and change that could move us rapidly forward as a species, despite the sluggishness of species change on a genetic basis. We can perhaps not imagine where such an evolution of mind could take us in another twenty, fifty, or one-hundred years. Yet we can readily see, without appealing beyond today's discoveries, how an evolution so-defined can outpace our biological evolution (with which it also interacts), and can hopefully alert us to global-scale hazards and personal possibilities which increase our changes for survival in the next century and beyond.

If this book seems to be taking on a great deal, be assured that you are right. It does so by pulling together, for the first time, a wide range of contributions by key researchers and thinkers, representing diverse strands in the creativity and health argument. Some contributions are newer, some older. The *Creativity Research Journal* has been a major vehicle for a number of these. The collection does not guarantee to answer all questions within the wide picture of creativity and health. Yet it raises a great many of these questions, and offers some strong indications of where we might look next.

Introduction

The creativity–health interface has been debated for a long, long time. *Eminent Creativity, Everyday Creativity, and Health* contains what we think is a representative sample of the most important recent research on that topic.

The range of approaches to the study of creativity and health is truly impressive. Given that wide range, numerous arrangements for the chapters were possible. We chose to organize the volume into five parts. Issues concerning individuals are contained in Parts I–III and issues concerning social context are contained in Parts IV and V. There is of course some overlap: Several chapters describe how the social context influences the individual, and others describe how the individual has an impact on social contexts. The separation of individual and social issues is, then, primarily a convenience and should not be taken too generally.

This Introduction will describe some of the themes that run through the individual chapters. This should justify the organization of the volume. It will also place the chapters and topics in context. The last chapter of the book, Part VI, presents a comprehensive discussion of the connections among chapters, but this Introduction will function as an advanced organizer. Most important are the bridges between the chapters of this volume, on the one hand, and the issues and controversies in the field, on the other. Here are some of the bridges.

Eysenck describes *psychoticism* and contrasts it with *psychosis*, and Andreasen, Jamison, Ludwig, Schuldberg, Richards and Kinney, and Flach each describe research on affective disorders. These chapters suggest a consensus about the specific affective disorders that are particularly relevant to creativity. The chapters herein are quite precise about these disorders, and similarly precise about possible relationships with different phases or expressions of creativity. This research takes us beyond previous vague questions about "the creative genius" and "mad scientists" (cf. Becker, 1992).

Interestingly, Andreasen, Jamison, Ludwig, and Rothenberg each examined creative writers (the latter two in a comparative way, along with others artists). It may be that there is something specific about the profession, although Ludwig makes the important point about differences among the various kinds of writing (also see Runco & Chand, 1994). Ostwald presents a convincing argument about the uniqueness (and healing power) of music.

Flach's work bridges Parts II and III. He describes the disruptive–reorganization process of creativity and describes his *resilience hypothesis.* This is in part a psychobiological resilience—which supports Hoppe and Kyle's, Penenbacker's, and Eisenman's theories of biological substrates and manifestations. It is also entirely consistent with Gardner and Moran's theory of adaptability and creativity. Part III also contains Gedo's chapter on "The Healing Power of Art." Gedo suggests that for some individuals—especially those in the "restitutional phase of chronic psychosis"—the creation of artwork can help restore health. The basic argument here is that art (and its creation) offers meaning to the creator. Gedo supports his argument with biographical data about the Belgian artist, John Ensor (1860–1949). In addition to its clinical significance, Gedo's article is a fascinating example of the *Biographical Method* for studying creativity. More precisely, it exemplifies one particular technique, for the biographical approach includes a surprising number of methodologies. These are discussed in detail by Gedo and Gedo (1992). The Gedos even discuss an investigation which is somewhat like a case study, but which allows for input by the subject him- or herself! Like Gedo, Ostwald explores the benefits of art, though as just mentioned, Ostwald focused on music.

Cropley, Eisenman, and Richards each address the issue of creativity in the real world. Cropley reports several specific examples of such creativity (i.e., women working on crafts, 10- to 12-year-old soccer players, and jazz musicians). Richards follows this line of thought and concludes that the study of the creativity in the natural environment allows us to better appreciate the behavior of noneminent individuals.

The idea of real-world creativity is in this sense related to the larger issue concerning appropriate methods for creativity research. Some researchers have argued that we can be objective about creativity only by studying eminent individuals. There is something to this view; Gedo's study of John Ensor and Rothenberg's study of John Cheever both show just how useful in-depth studies of eminent individuals can be. On the other hand, several chapters in Part III of the present volume (e.g., Cropley, Rhodes, Runco, Ebersole, and Mraz) suggest that we are also learning a great deal by studying noneminent instances of creativity. A detailed examination of the issues was presented by Runco (1990).

Rhodes and Runco, Ebersole, and Mraz focus on nonclinical populations. They also look at health per se, namely self-actualization, rather than health problems and disorders. This side of health is too often overlooked, perhaps because—as noted just above—the theories of the "mad genius" or eccentric artist are quite common. As Carl Rogers and Abraham Maslow suggested 20 years ago, creativity may be a integral facet of personal growth and self-actualization. Healthy individuals can be quite creative.

Part III also contains Hoppe and Kyle's work on hemispheric specialization and creativity. This work is noteworthy in part because hemispheric specialization—and one of its corollaries, namely handedness—has become a popular topic in the research *and* in the popular press (Al-Sabaty & Davis, 1989; Burke, Chrisler, & Sloan, 1989). Burke et al. (1989), for instance, suggested that left-handed individuals experience more frustration than right-handed individuals, and consequently have more opportunity to learn creative ways of coping with the environment. This argument is of course relevant to the research described above on anxiety and frustration.

Hoppe and Kyle suggest that great care must be taken when discussing "the dual brain." Perhaps most significant is Hoppe and Kyle's argument about the "bilateral integration of cerebral functions." This has clinical and practical significance and is important because too often when studying hemispheric specialization, it is assumed that one hemisphere can be used while the other somehow disconnected or "turned off." Katz (in press) and Runco and Okuda (1993) specifically addressed the abuse of the concept of "split brains."

The last section of Part III contains three chapters dealing with developmental issues. Smith and van der Meer, for example, discuss creativity, illness, and aging. They employ a unique methodology which relies on the *Identification Test* and the *Creative Functioning Test*—two projective, percept-genetic tests. This research is timely given how common it is these days to grow older (see Preston, 1984) and how common it is to explore alternatives to "growing old" (Langer, & Rodin, 1976; Runco, 1990–91; Skinner, 1983). Interestingly, projective techniques like those used by Smith and van der Meer (and Smith, Carlsson, & Andersson, 1989) seem to be gaining popularity. For example, Dudek and Verreault argue that divergent thinking tests can be used to reveal primary process ideation. They demonstrated that creative children projected highly libidinal interpretations (compared to the aggressive interpretations of less creative children), and were very effective in their use of *regression in the service of the ego.*

Gardner and Moran focus on the family. This chapter can be taken as a reminder of the large literature showing an association between family background and creativity. Gardner and Moran also present research with ramifications for the controversy between early adversity theories (Goertzel & Goertzel, 1962; Runco, 1993) and early stimulation theories (Harrington, Block & Block, 1987; Runco & Gaynor, 1993).

Part IV of the present volume turns the focus away from the individual issues and toward social issues. Part IV features an article on "Political Pathology and Societal Creativity" by Dean Keith Simonton, with seven Commentaries and a Rejoinder. In the feature article, Simonton offers a strong case for studying the relationship between creativity and health on the societal level. Put briefly, in his view, civil disturbances, war, and political instability may each be predictive of societal creativity. The Commentaries which follow Simonton's article emphasize the value of—and the questions uncovered by—the study of societal determinants of creativity. Taken together, these seven Commentaries reiterate my point that there is great variety in how creativity and health are defined and studied.

In Part V Barron and Bradley offer a discussion of how certain personality traits and attitudes may play a role in public policy. They ask, are certain attitudes more healthful than others? Are there attitudes which will help solve global problems? Gruber addresses similar questions, only his emphasis is on moral decisions and dilemma. This area has begun to attract a great deal of attention (e.g., Gruber, 1993; Richards, 1993; Schwebel, 1993) and has significant implications for education (Haste, 1993) and for our understanding of the nature of creativity (Runco, 1993).

Finally, Part VI contains the chapter by Richards that pulls the volume together.

MULTIDIMENSIONALITY

At this point it should be clear why I started the way I did. There is indeed an extremely wide variety of approaches being used to study creativity and health. Part of the variety can probably be explained by the fact that *health* and *creativity* are each multidimensional concepts. Studying both is therefore like rolling two dice, each with a large number of faces: The number of possible "health x creativity" combinations is incredibly large.

Is the range of approaches *that* wide? Just above frustration, aging, bipolar disorders, adaptation, hemisphericity, and self-actualization were mentioned, and the chapters themselves also cover stress, specific physical illnesses, psychoeconomics, art and literature, socialization and education psychopathology, and so on. Consider also the variety of methodologies: interviews, experimental manipulations, correlations, and projective tests are each used, along with archival, historiometric, psychometric, and biographical data. The variety may be the most apparent when considering the question about the direction of effect: Does creativity allow an individual to attain and maintain health, or does health facilitate a creative life? This volume contains various answers about the possible directions.

The variety of approaches attests to the importance of the topic of health and the importance of creativity. Some might call it an example of supply (of research) and demand (pressing issue and concerns). The variety can also be viewed as indicative of the evolution of the field, for it represents a diversity from which selections may be made. Granted, evolution does not guarantee progress (Gould, 1989), but the variety certainly will allow those of us conducting research in the area to be selective. In this light, the variety offers potential, and will presumably allow researchers and theoreticians to follow the most worthwhile directions.

The heterogeneity of the approaches should facilitate our finding the important issues and assumptions in this area (see Simonton's Rejoinder in Part IV and the concluding chapter, Part VI, by Richards), and it may stimulate creativity by virtue of contrast. Using the vernacular, the points of contrast may contribute to a type of *asynchrony* (Gardner & Wolf, 1989), or in the extreme case, an *essential tension* (Kuhn, 1977). Using the evolutionary model once again, the variety may supply the variations noted by Campbell (1960) and Simonton (1988; also see Albert [in press], Runco [1990a]) as necessary for the creative process. The variety can undoubtedly lead to a fresh perspective, like that acquired by individuals when they change from one field to another (Langer, 1989; Runco, 1990b) or take advantage of sociocultural or professional *marginality* (Simonton, 1988).

And beyond all of this, the variety makes for very good reading.

REFERENCES

Albert, R. S. (in press). The achievement of eminence as an evolutionary strategy. In M. A. Runco (Ed.), *Creativity research handbook* (vol. 2). Cresskill, NJ: Hampton Press.

Al-Sabaty, I., & Davis, G. A. (1989). Relationship between creativity and right, left, and integrated thinking styles. *Creativity Research Journal, 2,* 111–117.

Burke, J., & Chrisler, J. (1989). *Creativity Research Journal, 2.*

Campbell, D. (1960). Blind variation and selective retention in creative thought as in other knowledge processes. *Psychological Review, 67,* 380–400.

Gardner, H., & Wolf, C. (1988). The fruits of asynchrony: A psychological examination of creativity. *Adolescent Psychiatry, 15,* 106–122.

Gedo, J. E., & Gedo, M. M. (in press). *Perspectives of creativity: The biographic method.* Norwood, NJ: Ablex Publishing Corporation.

Gould, S. J. (1989). *Wonderful life: The Burgess shale and the nature of history.* New York: Norton.

Heinzen, T. (1989). On moderate challenge increasing creativity. *Creativity Research Journal, 2,* 223–226.

Jausovec, N. (1989). Affect in analogical transfer. *Creativity Research Journal, 2,* 99.

Kuhn, T. S. (1977). *The essential tension.* Chicago, IL: University of Chicago Press.

Langer, E. J., & Rodin, J. (1976). The effects of enhanced personal responsibility for the aged: A field experiment in an institutional setting. *Journal of Personality and Social Psychology, 34,* 191–198.

Preston, S. H. (1984). Children and the elderly in the U.S. *Scientific American, 251* (6), 44–49.

Rubenson, D. L. (1990). The accidental economist. *Creativity Research Journal, 3.*

Runco, M. A. (1990a). Genius and creativity. [A review of D. K. Simonton's *Scientific genius: A psychology of science.*] *Imagination, Cognition and Personality, 10,* 201–206.

Runco, M. A. (1990b). Mindfulness and personal control. [A review of E. Langer's *Mindfulness.*] *Imagination, Cognition and Personality, 10,* 107–114.

Simonton, D. K. (1988). *Scientific genius: A psychology of science.* Cambridge, MA: Harvard University Press.

Smith, G. J. W., Carlsson, I., & Andersson, G. (1989). Creativity and the subliminal manipulation of projected self-images. *Creativity Research Journal, 2,* 1–16.

Smith, K. L. R., Michael, W. B., & Hocevar, D. (in press). Performance on creativity measures with examination-taking instructions intended to induce high or low levels of test anxiety. *Creativity Research Journal, 3.*

Wallach, M. A., & Kogan, N. (1965). *Modes of thinking in young children.* New York: Holt, Rinehart & Winston.

PART I

EMINENT CREATORS: PSYCHOLOGICAL PROBLEMS AND CREATIVITY

Part I

Introduction

Creativity and psychological problems? Despite the popular belief in a link between these, and despite quite a bit of older literature—even going back to writings of Plato and Aristotle—many people have been reluctant to consider there might be some truth behind the belief. This book presents the modern studies that woke many people up. The subjects of these studies are "eminent creators," those well-known individuals who have received widespread public acclaim for their contributions to society. They have been selected by society at large, or by people in their particular fields of endeavor, for unusual distinction. Often, these are creators in the arts, or the sciences. Sometimes they hold leadership positions. Here one finds the renowned novelists, artists, playwrights, poets, scientists, mathematicians, statespersons. These are the people who have had an impact on our lives, who have made a difference.

It is important to emphasize that there are many routes to creativity—this is a critical point. Nonetheless, disorders of mood do seem to come up, in particular, among these creators, as do various historical adversities certain creators were forced to overcome.

Just how healthy are these eminent creators? Let us look at some people in the arts. Nancy Andreasen found that 80% of her eminent creative writers had a history of a major mood disorder. Eighty percent—that's four out of five people. It almost starts to sound as if a mood disorder is prerequisite to creative writing! It is important to know that subjects were carefully diagnosed, more rigorously, in fact, than in any study previous to this one. In addition, in Kay Redfield Jamison's work, over one-third of her British artists and writers had sought treatment for a mood disorder—treatment of a psychiatric condition for which only about a third of sufferers seek treatment to begin with. Not to mention that certain creators fear treatment will somehow rob them of their sources of inspiration. (As we shall see, the opposite is more likely the case; treatment of mood disorders can be highly effective, and may at once decrease suffering and release even more creative potential. Treatment appears to be to everyone's benefit.)

One may note with interest that bipolar disorder is found emerging throughout this picture. In Andreasen's work, over half the writers were diagnosed with a bipolar disorder, the majority with a "bipolar II" disorder. This is typified by mild or hypomanic mood elevations, along with potentially severe depressions. In Jamison's work, almost 9 out of 10 creators had experienced intense creative states, often two weeks in length, related to productive hypomanic-like periods. This last is a "state" rather than "trait" issue; it concerns transitory states of mind, rather than ongoing characteristics. There will be more to say about this. Indeed, it may be a key to the complex question of a "creative advantage" in face of personal difficulty.

One should recall that these are artists exclusively—not people in all lines of work—nor are these subjects necessarily representative of all artists. Will results be different for other creators, working in other areas of endeavor? Arnold Ludwig has made major strides in addressing this. Not only was his psychohistorical approach different than earlier methods, but Ludwig went to the library to read about his eminent creators! Everyone who had been written about, therefore, was fair game, and no one could refuse to take part. Furthermore, Ludwig didn't stop with artists, but looked at eminent creators across 18 different professions. Considering all this, it is interesting indeed that Ludwig's results with creators in the arts was relatively consistent with Andreasen and Jamison's findings.

By contrast, Ludwig found that creators in a range of other endeavors were—and let's pinpoint scientists here, for a moment—greatly less apt to carry such psychiatric diagnoses. Scientists were relatively healthy. A great many possibilities underlie this finding. For one, Ludwig's work leaves unanswered the question of the importance of (a) milder mood states one might experience—his methodology couldn't always capture this information—or of (b) a positive family history—is there more bipolar disorder, or more unipolar disorder, perhaps, in families of these eminent scientists? Might there be some more subtle or even *positive* expression of this clinical risk in the creators themselves? This is a question of *compensatory advantage* and it is also taken up later in this volume.

Rothenberg deals primarily with alcohol and literary creativity in his chapter, and he found alcohol abuse of negative value, in general, to actual creating. This was based both on group interview data and an in-depth study of the life of John Cheever. Rothenberg did find drinking more common at the end of day, after creating was over, in order to contain anxiety. One should also not forget the high comorbidity of alcoholism and mood disorders—as seen for instance in Andreasen's chapter. Mood disorders may be relevant to these phenomena. In the last section, Richards summarizes work including other data of Ludwig's, from publications not included in this book, which clarifies direct and indirect patterns of alcohol abuse both helping and hurting creativity. This is a more refined portrayal. Nonetheless, the harmful effects of alcohol remain the most prominent result. In general, drinking and creating don't seem to mix.

Chapter 1

Creativity and Mental Illness: Prevalence Rates in Writers and Their First-Degree Relatives*

Nancy C. Andreasen

People have wondered whether there is a relationship between creativity and mental illness, or "genius and insanity" in popular parlance, at least since classical times (Aristotle, 1953). In the nineteenth century the influence of Lombroso led to speculations that genius was a "hereditary taint" transmitted in families along with mental illness (Galton, 1892; Hirsch, 1896; Lange-Eichman, 1931; Lombroso, 1891). In the twentieth century this association has been supported by several techniques commonly used to examine familial transmission of various illnesses, including evaluation of first-degree relatives of creative individuals and examination of biological and nonbiological adoptive relatives of creative individuals adopted at birth (Andreasen & Canter, 1974, 1975; Ellis, 1926; Holden, 1986; Juda,

*From "Creativity and Mental Illness: Prevalence Rates in Writers and Their First-Degree Relatives," by N. C. Andreasen, 1987, *American Journal of Psychiatry, 144*(10), pp. 1288–1292. Copyright © 1995 American Psychiatric Association. Adapted with permission.

1949; McNeil, 1971). The striking number of suicides by contemporary writers has also led to renewed interest in this association. The following are only some of the writers who have died by suicide during the twentieth century: Ernest Hemingway, Sylvia Plath, John Berryman, Anne Sexton, and Virginia Woolf.

In spite of the considerable interest in this topic, quantitative studies have been sparse, and none of the published studies (apart from my own early work) has used modern diagnostic techniques developed to improve the reliability of psychiatric assessment, such as structured interviews and diagnostic criteria. Many studies have relied primarily on anecdotes; only a few have used direct personal interview of a systematically defined sample of recognized creative individuals.

Crucial questions include the following: Do creative individuals have a higher rate of mental illness? Do their first-degree relatives (parents, siblings, and offspring) have a higher rate of mental illness? Do these relatives have a higher rate of creativity? If there is a relationship between creativity and mental illness, is it a specific type of mental illness, such as schizophrenia, affective disorder, or alcoholism?

The present investigation attempted to answer some of these questions by systematically evaluating a sample of creative writers at the University of Iowa Writers' Workshop. The workshop is the oldest and most widely recognized creative writing program in the United States. Students and faculty have included such well-known writers as Philip Roth, Kurt Vonnegut, John Irving, Robert Lowell, Flannery O'Connor, and John Cheever. Since well-known writers are brought in for a semester or two each year as visiting faculty members, they represent a reasonably valid cross-section of contemporary American writers.

RESEARCH DESIGN

During the past 15 years, 30 faculty members at the workshop were evaluated with a structured interview designed by me in order to determine their patterns of creativity, their history of mental illness, and the prevalence of these traits in first-degree relatives. (This interview was developed before more recent standard interviews such as the Schedule for Affective Disorders and Schizophrenia [SADS]. It is available from me on request.) Confidentiality about the subjects' identity was a condition for participation in this study.

Twenty-seven men and three women were studied. Their mean age was 37.47 (SD = 11.49) years. The writers were matched for age, sex, and educational status to an occupationally varied sample of control subjects (hospital administrators, lawyers, social workers, etc.). The control subjects were not personally known to me and were selected because they provided a good sociodemographic match. Their mean age was 37.90 (SD = 12.20) years. Psychiatric diagnoses of the probands were made according to the Research Diagnostic Criteria (RDC; Spitzer, Endicott, & Robins, 1978), and diagnoses of first-degree relatives were made according to the Family History Research Diagnostic Criteria (Andreasen, Endicott, Spitzer, et al., 1977). Cognitive function and style were evaluated in a subset of 15 writers and control subjects with the Raven Progressive Matrices (advanced set; Raven, 1977) and the WAIS.

FINDINGS

Table 1.1 summarizes the principal finding concerning the rate of psychiatric illness in the writers and the control subjects. The rates are lifetime prevalences and therefore indicate whether the subjects had *ever* had a period of mental illness. the reliability of such lifetime estimates has been evaluated and found to be very good when structured interviews and diagnostic criteria are used (Andreasen, Grove, Shapiro, et al., 1981).

Contrary to some previous speculations about a relationship between schizophrenia and creativity (Heston, 1966; Karlsson, 1970), these results suggest a strong association between creativity and affective illness instead. Schizophrenia was conspicuous by its absence, while the rate of affective disorder (i.e., manic-depressive illness) was strikingly high. Eighty percent of the writers had had an episode of affective illness at sometime

Table 1.1. Lifetime Prevalence of Mental Illness in Writers and Control Subjects

RDC Diagnosis	Writers (n = 30)		Control Subjects (n= 30)		χ^2 (df = 1)[a]	p
	n	%	n	%		
Any affective disorder	24	80	9	30	13.20	.001
Any bipolar disorder	13	43	3	10	6.90	.01
Bipolar I disorder	4	13	0	0		n.s.
Bipolar II disorder	9	30	3	10	2.60	n.s.
Major depressive disorder	11	37	5	17	2.13	n.s.
Schizophrenia	0	0	0	0		n.s.
Alcoholism	9	30	2	7	4.01	.05
Drug abuse	2	7	2	7		n.s.
Suicide	2	7	0	0		n.s.

[a]Entries with no chi-square value had expected frequencies less than 5; Fisher's exact test was used in these cases.

in their lives, compared with 30% of the control subjects. A surprising percentage of the affective disorder was bipolar in nature; 43% of the writers had had some type of bipolar illness, in comparison with 10% of the control subjects. Both of these differences were statistically significant. In addition, the writers had significantly higher rates of alcoholism (30%, compared with 7% in the control subjects).

No statistically significant differences were noted in specific subtypes of affective disorder when the writers were compared with the control subjects, perhaps because the sample size was relatively small and nonparametric statistics have limited power. The differences that were statistically significant were nevertheless clinically important. Bipolar I disorder is a severe, although intermittent, illness characterized by episodes of depression alternating with excessive euphoria, increased energy, and poor judgment (and sometimes delusions or hallucinations as well); it almost invariably requires hospitalization and long-term treatment with somatic therapy. Bipolar II disorder, characterized by milder periods of euphoria that alternate with periods of despondency and depression, also produces an instability of mood that many find painful and that usually requires somatic treatment. Major depression, the mildest of the affective disorders, is also a potentially severe illness. Two-thirds of the ill writers had received psychiatric treatment for their disorders. Further supporting the clinical importance of these affective disorders in writers is the fact that two of the 30 committed suicide during the 15 years of the study. Issues of statistical significance pale before the clinical implications of this fact.

The rates of illness for the writers were substantially higher than one might expect. The rates for the control subjects were somewhat higher than those found in epidemiologic population studies (Robins, Helzer, Weissman, et al., 1984). Rates for the control subjects were not, however, strictly comparable with those in such epidemiologic studies, since the controls, having been sociodemographically matched to the writers, represented an educationally and occupationally advantaged sample. An association has been reported between bipolar disorder and occupational achievement (Woodruff, Robins, Winokur, et al., 1971), which might have led to a relatively higher rate of bipolar disorder in the control sample (and in the writers as well). The RDC definition of bipolar II disorder is also quite broad, which partially accounts for the high rate of bipolar II disorder.

Lombroso (1891), Ellis (1926), and many others (Galton, 1892; Hirsch, 1896; Lange-Eichman, 1931) have argued that creativity and mental illness run in families and that both tendencies are hereditary. Table 1.2 examines the rate of mental illness in the first-degree relatives of the writers and the control subjects according to the family history technique. This technique, which involves collecting information about the family directly

Table 1.2. Mental Illness in First-Degree Relatives of 30 Writers and 30 Control Subjects

Family History RDC Diagnosis	All Relatives						Parents						Siblings					
	Of Writers (n = 116)		Of Control Subjects (n = 121)		χ² (df = 1)[a]	p	Of Writers (n = 60)		Of Control Subjects (n = 60)		χ² (df = 1)[a]	p	Of Writers (n = 56)		Of Control Subjects (n = 121)		χ² (df = 1)[a]	p
	n	%	n	%			n	%	n	%			n	%	n	%		
Any affective disorder	21	18	3	2	14.21	.001	10	7	1	2	6.41	.001	11	20	2	3	6.35	.01
Bipolar disorder	4	3	0	0		.056	1	2	0	0		n.s.	3	5	0	0		n.s.
Major depression	17	15	3	2	9.84	.01	9	5	1	2	5.35	.05	8	14	2	3		.05
Alcoholism	8	7	7	6	0.01	n.s.	5	8	4	7		n.s.	3	5	3	5		n.s.
Suicide	3	3	0	0		n.s.	2	3	0	0		n.s.	1	2	0	0		n.s.
Any illness	49	42	10	8	34.77	.0001	25	42	5	8		.00003	24	43	5	8	17.00	.001

[a]Entries with no chi-square value had expected frequencies less than 5; Fisher's exact test was used in these cases.

from the proband, rather than by interviewing all relatives personally, has respectable sensitivity and specificity (Andreasen, Rice, Endicott, et al., 1986). Nevertheless, some "cases" will not be identified through this method because of lower sensitivity, thereby leading to lower prevalence estimates. These lower prevalence estimates are presumably equally lower in relatives of writers and in relatives of control subjects, however, thereby permitting valid comparisons between the two groups of relatives. As Table 1.2 indicates, the first-degree relatives of the writers had a disproportionately higher frequency of mental illness, particularly affective disorder. The rate of major depression was significantly higher for siblings, parents, and all relatives pooled. In addition, a higher frequency of bipolar disorder approached statistical significance when all relatives were pooled.

Since rates of affective disorder were higher for the writers, one would also expect them to be higher for their first-degree relatives, since affective disorders have a well-established familial pattern of transmission. In order to address the issue of whether affective disorder and creativity are intertwined, we must look at patterns of creativity in family members as well. This issue is addressed in Table 1.3. Information was collected concerning occupations, hobbies, and creative professional success among all first-degree relatives. Relatives were classified as "+creative" if they pursued

Table 1.3. Prevalence of Creativity in First-Degree Relatives of 30 Writers and 30 Control Subjects

Relatives' Creativity[a]	Relatives of Writers		Relatives of Control Subjects		χ^2 $(df = 1)$[b]	p
	n	%	n	%		
All relatives	116	100	121	100		
+Creative	20	33	11	18		n.s.
++Creative	12	20	5	8	4.85	.05
Total creative	32	53	16	27	9.10	.01
Parents	60	100	60	100		
+Creative	5	8	3	5		n.s.
++Creative	7	12	2	3		n.s.
Total creative	12	20	5	8	2.47	n.s.
Siblings	56	100	61	100		
+Creative	15	27	8	13	2.64	n.s.
++Creative	8	14	3	5	2.01	n.s.
Total creative	23	41	11	18	6.44	.01

[a]+Creative = somewhat creative; ++creative = well-recognized level of creative achievement.

[b]Entries with no chi-square value had expected frequencies less than 5; Fisher's exact test was used in these cases.

occupations that would be considered somewhat creative, such as jour-
nalism or teaching music or dance. Relatives were classified as "++ creative" if they had a well-recognized level of creative achievement, such as
writing novels, dancing in a major company, performing as a concert
artist or in a major symphony, or making a major scientific contribution
such as an invention.

The total number of creative relatives was significantly higher for the
writes, and it is particularly noteworthy that, when all relatives were
pooled together, the difference was contributed primarily by the number
of relatives who were in the ++ creative category. Most of the difference
between the writers and the control subjects was contributed by the siblings; 41% of the siblings of the writers displayed some creativity, compared with 18% of the control siblings. The rate for parents was 20%
versus 8%; whereas the rate among the parents of writers was higher, the
difference did not achieve statistical significance. Table 1.4 portrays the
intertwining of creativity and affective illness in the family members,
showing the rates of creativity and illness in the families of each of the
writers and control subjects. It indicates clearly that the families of the
writers were riddled with both creativity and mental illness, while in
the families of the control subjects much of the illness and creativity
seemed to be randomly scattered.

It is perhaps noteworthy that the types of creativity observed in the relatives of the writers were far broader than literary creativity. Some relatives of creative writers were indeed also in literary fields, but many were
creative in other areas, such as art, music, dance, or mathematics. This
suggests that whatever is transmitted within families is a general factor
that predisposes to creativity, rather than a specific giftedness in verbal
areas. Further, whenever traits are transmitted familially, it is of interest
to determine whether the transmission is due to social learning and modeling or to more purely genetic factors. While family studies cannot dis-
entangle this issue to the same extent that adoption studies can, the
variability in creativity in these families does suggest the possibility of
some form of genetic transmission. If social learning were the sole factor
involved, one would expect a preponderance of literary creativity in the
families of writers. The relatively higher rate of creativity among siblings
is also very slight evidence against the effect of role modeling based on
parental interests and behavior.

What is the relationship between intelligence and creativity? Several
studies have suggested that intelligence may be a necessary, but not sufficient, cause of creativity but that very high intelligence and high creativity are not necessarily the same (MacKinnon, 1965; Terman & Oden,
1947). Date concerning the intelligence of the writers and the control
subjects are summarized in Table 1.5. The WAIS IQ is based on an ex-

Table 1.4. Patterning of Mental Illness and Creativity in 30 Writers, 30 Control Subjects, and Their Families

Subject Number	Writer			Writer's Family		Control Subject		Control Subject's Family	
	Affective Disorder	Bipolarity	Alcoholism	Mental Illness	Creativity	Affective Disorder	Alcoholism	Mental Illness	Creativity
1	Yes	Yes		Yes	Yes				
2	Yes	Yes	Yes		Yes				
3				Yes					Yes
4	Yes	Yes	Yes	Yes	Yes	Yes			
5	Yes	Yes		Yes	Yes	Yes			
6	Yes			Yes	Yes				
7	Yes	Yes		Yes	Yes			Yes	
8	Yes	Yes	Yes	Yes	Yes			Yes	
9	Yes	Yes	Yes	Yes	Yes				
10	Yes	Yes	Yes	Yes	Yes				
11	Yes	Yes		Yes	Yes				Yes
12	Yes	Yes		Yes	Yes				Yes
13	Yes			Yes			Yes		
14	Yes			Yes				Yes	
15	Yes	Yes	Yes	Yes	Yes	Yes			Yes
16	Yes	Yes		Yes					
17	Yes	Yes	Yes	Yes					
18	Yes					Yes			
19	Yes				Yes				
20	Yes				Yes				
21	Yes	Yes	Yes	Yes	Yes	Yes			
22	Yes			Yes	Yes	Yes	Yes	Yes	
23	Yes			Yes					
24	Yes					Yes			
25						Yes		Yes	Yes
26	Yes	Yes						Yes	
27				Yes					
28						Yes			Yes
29	Yes		Yes	Yes	Yes				
30	Yes			Yes		Yes		Yes	

trapolated estimate from four subtests: similarities, vocabulary, picture completion, and block design. These were selected because two of these tests, similarities and vocabulary, are considered to be strong tests of verbal intelligence, while the other two, picture completion and block design, are strong tests of nonverbal visual intelligence. The Raven Progressive Matrices (advanced set) is a nonverbal IQ test designed to be culture free; it involves pattern perception of visual shapes.

As Table 1.5 indicates, there was no difference between the writers and the control subjects on most of these measures of intelligence. The writers scored significantly higher on the vocabulary subtest of the WAIS, but this would be expected given the fact that their life work involves a preoccupation with words. The most interesting data in Table 1.5 are the many nonsignificant differences. Both the writers and the control subjects were intellectually talented, with full-scale IQs usually over 120. Except for their differential excellence in vocabulary, the writers performed equally well on all the WAIS subtests. They did not seem to have a preferential giftedness in verbal intelligence, although they did have a nonsignificant decrement in verbal minus performance IQ. In general, they performed equally well in all aspects of intelligence assessment.

The data from the Progressive Matrices are particularly interesting, because this is a purely nonverbal test consisting of 36 different patterns that must be "solved." This test is considered by neuropsychologists to be extremely difficult, and perfect scores are thought to be very infrequent. In this relatively gifted sample of individuals, however, several achieved perfect scores, including both writers and control subjects. IQ equivalents for the Raven test are not available, since the test is not adequately

Table 1.5. *Scores on Intelligence Tests of 15 Writers and 15 Control Subjects*

	Score					
	Writers		Control Subjects			
Test	Mean	SD	Mean	SD	χ^2 (df = 1)	p
WAIS	123.7	9.3	121.2	7.1	0.82	n.s.
Verbal IQ	126.4	10.6	122.8	3.5	1.25	n.s.
Performance IQ	116.9	13.5	116.1	13.7	0.16	n.s.
Verbal minus performance	9.5	16.6	6.7	13.4	0.51	n.s.
Similarities scale	13.8	2.4	14.3	1.7	−0.61	n.s.
Vocabulary scale	15.3	1.8	13.1	1.2	3.89	.0006
Picture completion scale	12.4	2.7	12.0	1.6	0.49	n.s.
Raven Progressive Matrices (advanced set)	25.3	7.1	25.6	7.3	−0.11	n.s.

normed, but scores of 25 are probably more or less comparable with IQs in the 120–130 range.

These results indicate that the relatively higher rate of affective illness in the writers and their first-degree relatives was probably not an effect of intelligence, nor was the higher creativity in the relatives of writers due to higher intelligence in the writers. Apart from the factor of creativity, the writers and control subjects were closely matched on cognitive measures.

DISCUSSION

This study has several limitations. The investigator was not blind to the status of the sample with respect to creativity, thereby raising the possibility of biased estimates for the relatives of the writers. When the study was initially undertaken, however, it was designed to test the hypothesis of an association between schizophrenia and creativity, since an association between creativity and affective disorder was not even suspected at that time. The observed findings were contrary to those hypothesized at the outset, a fact that enhances their credibility even though it does not eliminate the possibility of a "halo effect." The failure to directly interview all first-degree relatives is also a limitation, since direct interview usually is considered to be more valid than the family history method. This limitation is likely to produce random noise across both the writer and control samples, however. Nevertheless, the possibility must be considered that the writers were more sensitive reporters of affective illness and creativity in their first-degree relatives, since they possessed these traits themselves. A third limitations is that the study was limited to writers; the findings are not necessarily generalizable to other types of creativity.

Overall, this investigation indicated that there is a close association between mental illness and creativity, as assessed in a sample of creative writers. Contrary to earlier hypotheses about a relationship between creativity and schizophrenia, the type of mental illness was predominantly affective disorder, with a possible tendency toward the bipolar subtype. Earlier hypotheses about a relationship with schizophrenia were based on the recognition that schizophrenia often leads to unusual perceptions, which could predispose to creativity; in most instances, however, perceptions in schizophrenia tend to be more bizarre than original, and many schizophrenic patients suffer from cognitive impairments that are likely to inhibit creativity (Andreasen & Powers, 1974). Schizophrenia also tends to be a chronic illness, whereas affective disorder is usually episodic, leaving most people with long periods of normality. Most writers reported that they tended to write during these normal periods rather than during highs or lows.

Reasons for the relationship between affective disorder and creativity need further exploration. Nevertheless, these results do suggest that affective disorder may produce some cultural advantages for society as a whole, in spite of the individual pain and suffering that it also causes. Affective disorder may be both a "hereditary taint" and a hereditary gift.

REFERENCES

Andreasen, N. C., & Canter, A. (1974). The creative writer: Psychiatric symptoms and family history. *Comprehensive Psychiatry, 15*, 123–131.

Andreasen, N. C., & Canter, A. (1975). Genius and insanity revisited: Psychiatric symptoms and family history in creative writers. In R. Wirt, G. Winokur, & G. Roth (Eds.), *Life history research in psychopathology, Vol. 4*. Minneapolis, MN: University of Minnesota Press.

Andreasen, N. C., Endicott, J., & Spitzer, R. A., et al. (1977). The reliability and validity of the family history method using Family History Research Diagnostic Criteria. *Archives of General Psychiatry, 34*, 1229–1235.

Andreasen, N. C., Grove, W., & Shapiro, R. W. (1981). Reliability of lifetime diagnosis: A multicenter collaborative perspective. *Archives of General Psychiatry, 38*, 400–405.

Andreasen, N. C., & Powers, P. S. (1974). Creativity and psychosis: A comparison of cognitive style. *Archives of General Psychiatry, 32*, 70–73.

Andreasen, N. C., Rice, J., & Endicott, J., et al. (1986). The family history approach to diagnosis: How accurate is it? *Archives of General Psychiatry, 43*, 421–429.

Aristotle. (1953). *Problemata* (vol. 2). (Trans. W. S. Hetts). Cambridge: Cambridge University Press.

Ellis, H. A. (1926). *A study of British genius*. London: Houghton-Mifflin.

Galton, F. (1892). *Hereditary genius*. London: Macmillan.

Heston, L. L. (1966). Psychiatric disorders in foster home reared children of schizophrenic mothers. *British Journal of Psychiatry, 112*, 819–82.

Hirsch, W. (1896). *Genius and degeneration*. New York: Appleton.

Holden, C. (1986). Manic depression and creativity. *Science, 233*, 725.

Juda, A. (1949). The relationship between highest mental capacity and psychic abnormalities. *American Journal of Psychiatry, 106*, 296–307.

Karlsson, J. L. (1970). Genetic association of giftedness and creativity with schizophrenia. *Hereditas, 66*, 177–182.

Lange-Eichman, W. (1931). *The problem of genius*. London: Kegan Paul, Trench, & Trubner.

Lombroso, C. (1891). *The man of genius*. London: Walter Scott.

MacKinnon, D. W. (1965). Personality and the realization of potential. *American Psychologist, 20*, 273–281.

McNeil, T. F. (1971). Prebirth and postbirth influence on the relationship between creative ability and recorded mental illness. *Journal of Personality, 39*, 391–406.

Raven, J. C. (1977). *Advanced Progressive Matrices.* New York: Psychological Corporation.

Robins, L. N., Helzer, J. R., Weismann, M. M., et al. (1984). Lifetime prevalence of psychatrich disorders in three sites. *Archives of General Psychiatry, 41,* 949–958.

Spitzer, R. L., Endicott, J., Robins, E. (1978). Research diagnostic criteria: Rationale and reliability. *Archives of General Psychiatry, 35,* 773–782.

Terman, L. M., & Oden, M. H. (1947). *Genetic studies of genius.* Stanford, CA: Stanford University Press.

Woodruff, R. A., Robins, L. N., Winokur, G., et al. (1971). Manic-depressive illness and social achievement. *Acta Psychiatr. Scand., 47,* 237–249.

Chapter 2

Mood Disorders and Patterns of Creativity in British Writers and Artists*

Kay Redfield Jamison

Several research strategies exist for examining the relationship between affective illness and creativity. The first, *historical and biographical studies,* focuses on life study investigations of prominent individuals (e.g., Ellis, 1904; Jamison, 1990; Juda, 1949; Lange-Eichbaum, 1932; Lombroso, 1891; Nisbet, 1912; Tasanoff, 1949; Wittkower & Wittkower, 1963). These biographical studies have provided strong, suggestive but as yet anecdotal clues to significantly increased rates of mood disorders and suicide in eminent writers and artists.

The second strategy, *studies of creative ability in affectively ill patients,* provides a different perspective but corroborating evidence. DeLong and Aldershof (1983) found an unusually high incidence of special ability (for example, outstanding artistic and mathematical talent) in a sample of children with manic-depressive illness. Richards et al. (1988) found

*From "Mood Disorders and Patterns of Creativity in British Writers and Artists," by K. R. Jamison, 1989, *Psychiatry, 52,* pp. 125–134. Copyright © 1995 The Washington School of Psychiatry, Washington, D.C. Adapted with permission.

significantly increased creativity in manic-depressive and cyclothymic patients, as well as their normal first-degree relatives, when compared with control subjects.

The third major strategy involves *systematic diagnostic and psychological studies of living writers and artists* (e.g., Andreasen, 1995; Andreasen & Canter, 1974; Andreasen & Powers, 1974). This chapter concerns research of the latter type. Andreasen and her colleagues, using modern diagnostic techniques, were the first to systematically study the relationship between creativity and psychopathology. They found an exceptionally high rate of affective illness, especially bipolar, in their sample of writers from the University of Iowa Writers' Workshop. Fully 80% of the 30 writers studied met Research Diagnostic Criteria (Spitzer, Endicott, & Robins, 1978) for an episode of affective illness at some time during their lives; 43% met criteria for bipolar illness (Andreasen, 1995). First-degree relatives of the writers also demonstrated a disproportionate rate of affective illness, especially major depressive disorder.

METHOD

Subjects

The poets, playwrights, novelists, biographers, and artists in the study were selected on the basis of having won at least one of several specified prestigious prizes painters and sculptors, for example, were either royal Academicians or Associates of the Royal Academy. Literary prizes used a selection criteria included the Queen's Gold Medal for Poetry and the Hawthornden, Booker, and James Tait Black Memorial Prizes. In addition, 9 of the 18 poets in the study sample were already represented in *The Oxford Book of Twentieth Century English Verse.* Of the 8 playwrights, 6 were winners of the New York Drama Critics Award or the Evening Standard (London) Drama Award; several had won both, had won one of these awards more than once, or had received Tony Awards.

Participants in the study were either British subjects (87%) or citizens of the British Commonwealth or the Republic of Ireland (13%). Most were men (87%), and the majority were Protestant (77%); 15% were Catholic, and 7% were agnostic or had no religious affiliation. The means age of the sample was 53.2 years (*SD* = 12.9). Demographic characteristics for the subgroups—poets, playwrights, novelists, biographers and artists—are summarized in Table 2.1. There were no significant differences between subgroups, except that the poets were disproportionately Protestant (94%) and the novelists disproportionately Catholic or agnostic (50%).

Table 2.1. Demographic Characteristics of Sample and Subgroups

Group	N	Mean Age	% Male	% Protestant
Poets	18	50.8	89	94
Playwrights	8	48.5	88	75
Novelists	8	55.0	88	50
Biographers	5	61.6	80	80
Artists	8	56.5	88	63
Total Sample	47	53.2	87	77

Procedures

All subjects ($N = 47$) were asked detailed (open-ended and scaled) questions about history and type of treatment, if any, for affective illness; observed, if any, diurnal and seasonal patterns in their moods and productivity; behavioral, cognitive, and mood correlates of their periods of creative work; and the perceived role of very intense moods in their work. Specific diagnostic criteria were not used in this study as the primary aim was to ascertain actual rates of treatment, a more stringent criterion for severity of affective illness. Extensive personality and attitudinal data, to be reported in a future paper, were also collected. As partial compensation for the considerable amount of time involved in participating, subjects were promised copies of all published reports resulting from the study.

RESULTS

History of Treatment for Affective Illness

The artists and writers were asked whether they had received treatment, and the nature of that treatment, for a mood disorder. The results are shown in Table 2.2. A very high percentage of the total sample (38%) had been treated for an affective illness; three-fourths of those treated had been given antidepressants or lithium, or had been hospitalized. Poets were most likely to have required medication for their depression (33%) and were the only ones to have required medical intervention (hospitalization, electroconvulsive therapy, lithium) for mania (17%). Fully one-half of the poets had been treated with drugs, psychotherapy, or hospitalization for mood disorders. The playwrights had the highest total rate of treatment for affective illness (63%), but a relatively large percentage of those treated (60%) had been treated with psychotherapy

Table 2.2. History of Treatment for Affective Illness in Total Sample and Subgroups

	% Treated for Bipolar Illness (Hospitalization lithium, ECT, etc.)	% Treated with Antidepressants for Depression	% Treated with Psychotherapy Alone for Depression	Total % Treated for an Affective Illness
Poets	16.7	33.0	5.5	55.2
Playwrights	0.0	25.0	37.5	62.5
Novelists	0.0	25.0	0.0	25.0
Biographers	0.0	20.0	0.0	20.0
Artists	0.0	12.5	0.0	12.5
Total Sample	6.4	23.4	8.5	38.3

alone. It is unclear whether this was due to a difference in severity of illness or in treatment preference.

With the exception of the poets, the subjects reported being treated for depression, not mania or hypomania; the design of the study did not allow systematic diagnostic inquiry into hypomanic or manic episodes. As Table 2.3 shows, however, about one-third of the writers and artists reported histories of severe mood swings, essentially cyclothymic in nature, and one-fourth reported histories of extended, elated mood states. Novelists and poets more frequently reported the prolonged, elated states; playwrights and artists, on the other hand, were more likely to report severe mood swings. The relatively low rate of treatment for affective illness in those who are creative in predominantly nonverbal fields (painting and sculpture) is interesting and may be due to the fact that artists are less inclined than writers to seek psychiatric help (especially if psychiatric treatment is perceived of as primarily verbal in nature). It is as likely, however, that mood disorders may not convey to visual artists the same experiential and cognitive advantages that are useful to writers, and that neuropsychological differences between those with and without affective illness (i.e., greater difficulties with right hemispheric functioning; see Goodwin & Jamison, 1990; Sackheim & Steif, 1988) may make visual artists a lower risk group. Interestingly, the biographers—who provided a comparison group by being outstanding but perhaps less creative writers—reported no history of mood swings or elated states.

Similarities Between Hypomanic and Creative States

Virtually all subjects (89%) reported having experienced intense, highly productive and creative episodes (100% of the poets, novelists, and artists; and 88% of the playwrights; but, consistent with the results re-

Table 2.3. History of Severe Mood Swings and Extended, Elated Mood States

	Severe Mood Swings	Extended, Elated Mood States
Poets	28%	33%
Playwrights	50%	25%
Novelists	13%	38%
Biographers	0%	0%
Artists	38%	13%
Total Sample	30%	26%

ported earlier, only 20% of the biographers). The modal duration of these episodes was two weeks (35%); 55% of the episodes lasted 1–4 weeks, and 25% continued for longer than a month. One-fifth of the episodes lasted 24 hours or less. The episodes were characterized by increases in enthusiasm, energy, self-confidence, speed of mental association, fluency of thoughts, elevated mood, and a strong sense of well-being (see Figure 2.1). A comparison with *DSM-III* criteria for hypomania reveals that mood and cognitive symptoms showed the greatest degree of overlap between intensely creative and hypomanic episodes. Several of the more behavioral changes typically associated with hypomania (hypersexuality, talkativeness, spending of money) were reported by only a minority of subjects.

Subjects were asked about changes in sleep and mood occurring just prior to these intense creative episodes. Almost all of the writers and artists (89%) reported a decrease in the need for sleep; 28% spontaneously reported waking abruptly at 3 or 4 A.M. and being unable to return to sleep. Changes in mood were profound. One-half of the subjects reported a sharp increase in mood just prior to the beginning of an intensely creative period e.g., ("excited, anticipatory, energetic"; "I have a fever to write, and throw myself energetically into new projects"; "elated," "euphoric"; "ecstatic"). Dysphoria preceded enhanced creativity in 28% of the subjects e.g., ("more anxious"; "near suicide"; "fearfulness, general mood of distress and slight paranoia"). Finally, approximately one-fourth (22%) of the sample reported mixed mood changes and psychomotor restlessness ("mixture of elation together with some gloominess, feeling of isolation, sexual pressure, fast emotional responses"; "restlessness"; "low ebb bordering on despair often precedes good phase when work will flow almost as though one is a medium, rather than an originator"; "restless, dissatisfied").

When the subjects were asked specifically about the importance of very intense feelings and moods in the development and execution of their work, 90% stated that such moods and feelings were either integral and

MOOD DISORDERS AND CREATIVITY

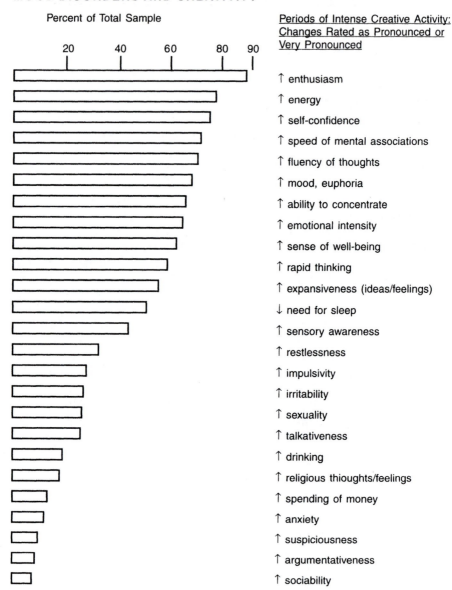

Percent of Total Sample

Periods of Intense Creative Activity: Changes Rated as Pronounced or Very Pronounced

20   40   60   80   90

↑ enthusiasm
↑ energy
↑ self-confidence
↑ speed of mental associations
↑ fluency of thoughts
↑ mood, euphoria
↑ ability to concentrate
↑ emotional intensity
↑ sense of well-being
↑ rapid thinking
↑ expansiveness (ideas/feelings)
↓ need for sleep
↑ sensory awareness
↑ restlessness
↑ impulsivity
↑ irritability
↑ sexuality
↑ talkativeness
↑ drinking
↑ religious thioughts/feelings
↑ spending of money
↑ anxiety
↑ suspiciousness
↑ argumentativeness
↑ sociability

Figure 2.1.   Mood, cognitive and behavioral changes reported during intense creative episodes.

necessary (60%), or very important (30%). Consistent with their rate of treatment for affective illness, more poets than any other group regarded these moods as essential to what they did and how they did it.

Seasonal Patterns of Moods and Productivity

Subjects were asked to rate their moods and productivity for 36 months. Many of the writers and artists relief upon extensive notes and journals to assist them in making their ratings. Figure 2.2 presents the mood and productivity curves for those subjects reporting no history of treatment for affective illness; Figure 2.3 shows the curves for subjects with a history of treatment for affective illness. Very different seasonal patterns emerged. Those in the history of treatment group demonstrated inversely related curves for summer productivity and moods, while those in the no history of treatment group showed mood and productivity curves more directly covarying. In the treatment group the peaks for productivity preceded and followed the mood peak by three to four months.

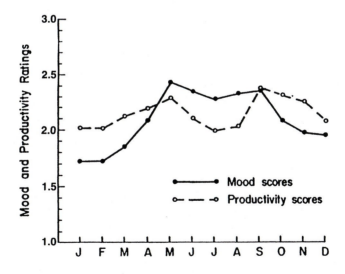

Figure 2.2. Mean mood and productivity ratings (36 months) in writers and artists with no history of treatment for affective illness (N = 32).

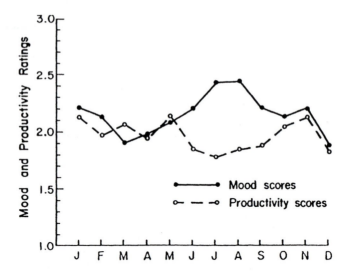

Figure 2.3.   *Mean mood and productivity ratings (36 months) in writers and artists with a history of treatment for affective illness (N = 15).*

DISCUSSION

Rates of Treatment for Affective Illness

The rate of treatment for affective illness (38%) was strikingly high in this sample of outstanding British writes and artists. Lifetime prevalence rates for bipolar and unipolar disorders in the general population are 1% and 5%, respectively. The proportion of individuals who actually seek or receive treatment, even though they meet the formal diagnostic criteria for affective illness, is far smaller. Therefore, rates in this study represent a conservative estimate of the actual prevalence of affective illness in the sample. Weissman, Myers, and Thompson (1981), for example, found that only 20% of persons with a current psychiatric disorder had seen a mental health professional in the previous year, and Shapiro et al. (1984) concluded that only one-third of affectively ill patients actually make a mental health visit. Likewise, although lithium is the treatment of choice for a minimal 1% of the general population, utilization rates determined by McCreadie and Morrison (1985) were only 0.77 per 1000, and by Escobar et al. (1987), 0.15%; both studies clearly indicated a gross underutilization of lithium relative to the established prevalence of mania. Antidepressants, more frequently prescribed, were used by 2.5% of the Epidemiological Catchment Area community sample ($N =$ 14,998) as reported by Escobar et al. These drug treatment figures are in marked contrast to the current sample of British writers and artists, 6.4% of whom reported the use of lithium (16.7% of the poets) and 23.4% the use of antidepressants. The contrast in rates is even more pronounced if one considers that antidepressant use is far more common in women than men, yet the sample of writers and artists was predominantly male (87%).

These surprisingly high rates of treatment for affective illness re, however, comparable to those reported by Andreasen and her colleagues. In an update of earlier work done with the well-known University of Iowa Writers' Workshop, Andreasen (1995) found that 80% of her sample of 30 writers (90% males) had experienced an episode of affective illness; 43% had had manic or hypmanic episodes. Possible explanations for the elevated rates of mood disorders in successful writers are discussed in details elsewhere (Andreasen & Powers, 1974, 1975; Jamison, 1990; Jamison et al. 1980; Prentky, in press; Richards, 1981) and can be only briefly reviewed here. Profound changes in mood, cognition, personality, sleep, energy and behavior characterize both altered mood and creative states. Cognitive changes occurring during hypomanic states—for example, the increase in speed, associational fluency and flexibility of thought—are likewise critical to creativity. For writers and artists, who draw so deeply from their lives and emotions for their work, the wide range, intensity, fluctuation, and variability of emotional experience brought about by mood disorders can work to the advantage, as well as disadvantage, of original composition. Too, what hypomania generates in enthusiasm and excess, the more critical and obsessive eye of depression often effectively judges and edits.

Similarities Between Hypomanic and Creative States

The study revealed many overlapping mood, cognitive, and behavioral (especially sleep) changes between hypomania and intense creative states, despite the fact that questions about both states were asked independently of one another and in a manner designed to minimize possible effects of suggestion. Cognitive and mood changes shared far more overlap than behavioral ones, perhaps indicating that the milder forms of hypomania may represent illness. The continuum that ranges from normal state to mildly (or, controllably) "hypomanic," to clinical hypomania and mania is an enormously important but poorly understood one. It remains unclear whether the overlap in cognitive and mood changes represents etiologically related syndromes or phenomenologically similar but causally unrelated patterns of expression. It also remains unclear the extent to which writers and artists are simply more sensitive than the general population to their own mood states and therefore more able to articulate and report them.

Seasonal Patterns of Mood and Productivity

There were significant differences in seasonal mood and productivity patterns between those writers and artists with a history of treatment for affective illness and those without; in the former group the peaks for productivity preceded, and followed, the mood peaks by three to four months; in the no-treatment group, the peaks for mood and productivity covaried. Several explanations are possible. First, high productivity associated with elevated mood is less likely to lead to treatment-seeking behavior than low productivity associated with high mood. Second, the elevated mood of the treatment group probably reflects more "true" hypomania (i.e., greater distractibility and dysphoria, and increased stimulus-seeking behavior) which might well lead to less productivity in the acute phase. In the no-treatment group, the periods of increased mood and productivity may represent a milder spectrum form of hypomania, or intensified normal functioning, resulting in more simultaneous peaks for mood and productivity. For both groups the summer peak in moods is consistent with what is known about seasonal patterns for hypomania, mania, and depression (Goodwin & Jamison, 1990; Rosenthal et al. 1984).

Writers and artists frequently express concerns about the effects of psychiatric treatment on their ability to create and produce; these concerns are particularly pronounced around issues of taking medication. Clearly, not all of these fears are realistic, but some may be. Early researchers were well aware of problems created by lithium's effects on certain productive and enjoyable qualities of manic-depressive illness (Polatin & Fieve, 1971; Schou, 1968; Van Putton, 1975); more recent studies demonstrate that missing certain positive features of hypomania is an important reason for lithium noncompliance.

The short- and long-term effects of lithium, carbamazepine, and the antidepressants on productivity and creativity remain unclear. Marshall, Neumann, & Robinson (1970) and Schou (1979) studied a total of 30 artists, writers, and businessmen taking lithium. Three-quarters of the subjects reported no change, or an increase in their productivity while on lithium. One-quarter reported a decrease, and 17% refused to continue lithium because of its effect on their work and lives. Studies of lithium's effect on cognitive processing, which conflict in their findings, are reviewed elsewhere (Goodwin & Jamison, 1990). Two studies of particular relevance for artistic creativity also conflict in their results. Judd et al. (1977) found no effects of short-term lithium treatment on creativity in normal subjects. A recent study using bipolar patients as their own controls, however, found substantial, detrimental effects of lithium on associational processing (Shaw et al. 1986). Differences in results may be in part due to the fact that lithium's effect on cognition is probably quite different in manic-depressive patients and normal volunteers (Pons, Nurnberger, & Murphy, 1985). Individual differences in the severity, frequency, and type of affective illness; sensitivity to cognitive side-effects; serum lithium levels; and clinical state also clearly affect the degree to which an individual will experience impairment in intellectual functioning, creativity, and productivity. Artists, writers, and the many others who rely upon their initiative, intellect, emotional intensity, and energy for their life's work underscore the need for a re-examination of this problem.

Artists and writers represent a group at high risk for affective illness and should be assessed and counseled accordingly. Ideal treatment requires a sensitive understanding of the possible benefits of mood disorders to creativity, as well as the severe liabilities, including the risk of suicide and of untreated depression and mania; use of available medications with awareness of side effects potentially damaging to the creative process; minimization, whenever possible, of drug (especially lithium) levels; the recongiton and sophisticated use of seasonal patterns in moods and productivity (for example, through self-charting of moods with a visual analogue scale); and sensitivity to the possible role of alcohol and drugs in inducing, maintaining, or exacerbating mood states.

Yet another implication stemming from the close relationship between mood disorders and creativity in the arts is a societal one. Genetic research is progressing to the stage where ethical issues will, in due course, arise about amniocentesis and early identification and treatment of individuals at high risk for affective, especially bipolar, illness. It becomes particularly important under these circumstances, and especially when dealing with treatable disorders, to have at least some broad notion of the individual and societal costs and benefits of making such decisions. Meyerson and Boyle (1941), in a study of manic-depressive psychosis in socially prominent American families, discussed at length possible social consequences of sterilization, an extreme procedure but relevant in many of the issues it raises. In analyzing one prominent family they noted:

> If sterilization had been done ... two psychotic individuals would have been eliminated from the American scene, patients with manic-depressive psychosis, but there would have gone with them a man internationally known, whose writings still remain as a source of inspiration and life orientation for many people, whose school of thought is still to be reckoned with and who is frequently cited as a figure unique in America and uniquely American. The group who clustered around this man left their influence on the whole of America. His descendants are still extremely eminent and also still send patients to hospitals for mental disease. (p. 18)

REFERENCES

Andreasen, N. C. (1997). Creativity and mental illness: Prevalence in writers and their first degree relations. In M. A. Runco & R. Richards (Eds.), *Eminent creativity, everyday creativity, and health.* Greenwich, CT: Ablex (original publication 1987).

Andreasen, N. C., & Canter, A. (1974). The creative writer: Psychiatric symptoms and family history. *Comprehensive Psychiatry, 15,* 123–131.

Andreasen, N. C., & Powers, P. (1974). Overinclusive thinking in mania and schizophrenia. *British Journal of Psychiatry, 125,* 452–456.

Andreasen, N. C., & Powers, P. (1975). Creativity and psychosis: An examination of conceptual style. *Archives of General Psychiatry, 32,* 70–73.

DeLong, G. R., & Aldershof, A. (1983). Associations of special abilities with juvenile manic-depressive illness. *Annals of Neurology, 14,* 362.

Ellis, H. (1904). *A study of British genius.* London: Hurst & Blackett.

Escobar, J. I., Anthony, J. C., Canino, G., et al. (1987). Use of neuroleptics, antidepressants, and lithium by U.S. community populations. *Psychopharmacology Bulletin, 23,* 196–200.

Goertzel, M. G., Goertzel, V. & Goertzel, T. G. (1978). *Three hundred eminent personalities.* San Francisco, CA: Jossey-Bass.

Goodwin, F. K., & Jamison, K. R. (1990). *Manic-depressive illness.* Cambridge: Oxford University Press.

Jamison, K. R. (1990). Manic-depressive illness, creativity, and leadership. In F. Goodwin and K. Jamison (Eds.), *Manic-depressive illness.* (pp. 332–367). Cambridge: Oxford University Press.

Jamison, K. R., Gerner, R. H., Hammen, C., & Padesky, C. (1980). Clouds and silver linings: Positive experiences associated with primary affective disorders. *American Journal of Psychiatry, 137,* 198–202.

Juda, A. (1949). The relationship between high mental capacity and psychic abnormalities. *American Journal of Psychiatry, 106,* 296–307.

Judd, L. L., Hubbard, R. B., Janowsky, D. S., et al. (1977). The effect of lithium carbonate on the cognitive functions of normal subjects. *Archives of General Psychiatry, 34,* 355–357.

Koestler, A. (1975). *The act of creation.* London: Pan.

Lange-Eichbaum, W. (1932). *The problem of genius.* New York: Macmillan.

Lombroso, C. (1891). *The man of genius.* London: Walter Scott.

McCreadie, R. G., & Morrison, D. P. (1985). The impact of lithium in Southwest Scotland. I. Demographic and clinical findings. *British Journal of Psychiatry, 146,* 70–74.

Marshall, M. H., Neumann, C. P., & Robinson, M. (1970). Lithium, creativity, and manic-depressive illness. *Psychosomatics, 11,* 406–408.

Meyerson, A., & Boyle, R. D. (1941). Incidence of manic-depressive psychosis in certain socially important families. *American Journal of Psychiatry, 98,* 11–21.

Nisbet, J. F. (1912). *The insanity of genius.* London: Stanley Paul.

Polatin, P., & Fieve, R. R. (1971). Patient rejection of lithium carbonate prophylaxis. *Journal of the American Medical Association, 218,* 864–866.

Prentky, R. (in press). Creativity and psychopathology: Gambolling at the seat of madness. In J. A. Glover, R. R. Ronning, & C. R. Reynolds (Eds.), *Handbook of creativity: Assessment, research and theory*. Plenum.

Richards, R. L. (1981). Relationships between creativity and psychopathology: An evaluation and interpretation of the evidence. *Genetic Psychology Monographs, 103*, 261–324.

Richards, R. L., Kinney, D. K., Lunde, I., Benet, M., & Menzel, A. P. C. (1988). Creativity in manic-depressives, cyclopthymes, their normal relatives, and control subjects: A preliminary report. *Journal of Abnormal Psychology, 97*, 281–288.

Rosenthal, N. E., Sack, D. A., Gillin, J. C., et al. (1984). Seasonal affective disorder: A description of the syndrome and preliminary findings with light therapy. *Archives of General Psychiatry, 41*, 72–80.

Sackheim, H. A., & Steif, B. L. (1988). Neuropsychology of depression and mania. In A. Georgotas & R. Cancro (Eds.), *Depression and mania*. Elsevier.

Schou, M. (1968). Special review of lithium in psychiatric therapy and prophylaxis. *Journal of Psychiatric Research, 6*, 67–95.

Schou, M. (1979). Artistic productivity and lithium prophylaxis in manic-depressive illness. *British Journal of Psychiatry, 135*, 97–103.

Shapiro, S., Skinner, E. A., Kessler, L. G., et al. (1984). Utilization of health and mental health services: Three epidemiologic catchment area sites. *Archives of General Psychiatry, 4*, 971–978.

Shaw, E. D., Mann, J. J., Stokes, P. E., & Manevitz, A. Z. A. (1986). Effects of lithium carbonate on associative productivity and idiosyncrasy in bipolar outpatients. *American Journal of Psychiatry, 143*, 1166–1169.

Spitzer, R. L., Endicott, J., & Robins, E. (1978). Research diagnostic criteria: Rationale and reliability. *Archives of General Psychiatry, 35*, 773–782.

Tsanoff, R. A. (1949). *The ways of genius*. Harper.

Van Putten, T. (1975). Why do patients with manic-depressive illness stop their lithium? *Comprehensive Psychiatry, 16*, 179–182.

Weissman, M. M., Myers, J. K., & Thompson, W. D. (1981). Depression and treatment in a U.S. urban community—1975–1976. *Archives of General Psychiatry, 38*, 417–421.

Wittkower, R., & Wittkower, M. (1963). *Born under Saturn: The character and conduct of artists*. Random House.

Woody, E., & Claridge, G. (1977). Psychoticism and creativity. *British Journal of Social and Clinical Psychology, 16*, 241–248.

Chapter 3

Creative Achievement and Psychopathology: Comparison Among Professions*

Arnold M. Ludwig

This study addresses two major issues: (a) whether members of the so-called creative professions display higher rates of mental disturbances over the course of their lives than those in other professions, and (b) whether there is a meaningful relationship between the creative achievement of individuals, regardless of their professions, and mental disturbance.

These issues have been debated since antiquity. Plato (1952), in his *Phaedrus*, described four types of divine madness: poetic, prophetic, ritual, and erotic. Aristotle (1979), though noting the predisposition of great artists and poets to melancholia, conceived of creativity as a rational process, originating from natural sources. Clinical and scientific studies over the years have not resolved this controversy. Consistent with the

*From "Creative Achievement and Psychopathology: Comparison among Professions," by A. M. Ludwig, 1992, *American Journal of Psychotherapy*, XLVI(3), pp. 330–354. Copyright © 1995. Adapted with permission.

"madness" position, earlier reports indicate higher rates of schizophrenia, "degeneracy," or "psychopathy" (an older term for "neurotic-type" symptoms) among eminent or creative individuals (Juda, 1949; Karlsson, 1970, 1978; Kretchmer, 1931; Lange-Eichbaum, 1932; Prentky, 1980), and later ones demonstrate higher rates of bipolar (manic-depressive) disorder, depression, and alcoholism (Akiskal & Akiskal, 1988; Andreasen, 1987; Andreasen & Glick, 1988; Ellis, 1926; Jamison, 1990, 1995; Richards, Kinney, Lunde Binet & Menzel, 1988). Consistent with the "natural" position, other reports and writings document the relative mental health of "geniuses" and eminent individuals (Cattell & Butcher, 1968; Galton, 1892; Goertzel & Goertzel, 1962; Goertzel, Goertzel, Goertzel, 1978; MacKinnon, 1962; Oden, 1968; Rothenberg, 1983; Shapiro, 1968; Terman, 1925–1959). Unfortunately, comparisons across studies become difficult because of differences in sampling techniques, psychiatric diagnostic criteria, measures of creativeness, eminence or genius, and methods of data analysis and interpretation.

Because of formidable conceptual and methodological problems surrounding the study of creativity, numerous strategies, each with inherent advantages and disadvantages, have been adopted to clarify its nature (Amabile, 1983; Brown, 1989; Hocevar, 1981; Hocevar & Bachelor, 1989; Michael & Wright, 1989; Mumford & Gutafson, 1980; Richards, 1981; Richards, Kinney, Benet & Menzel, 1988; Simonton, 1984, 19888, 1991). These strategies include the use of personality and attitude inventories, measures of "creative" thought and problem-solving, biographical inventories, expert judgments of products works of performances, ratings of self-reported creative activities and achievements, and evaluations of eminence as indicated by the space devoted to individuals in standard biographical dictionaries, membership in select professional societies, literature citations, or numbers of publications. The approaches adopted tend to be based on the issues under investigation and the sources of information available.

From a strategic standpoint, a likely place to search for answers to the seemingly elusive nature of creativity and its potential relationship to mental illness should be in eminent individuals whose lifetime accomplishments have withstood the test of time, and whose public and personal lives have been the objective of scholarly investigation. Access to this type of information is available through expert works and biographical studies devoted to these persons.

The present investigation uses assorted biographical material for the assessment of psychopathology and the creative accomplishments of eminent individuals. While there are potential disadvantages to the use of biographical data (e.g., biographer bias in the selection and interpretation of facts, the reliance on written material, the inability to question subjects directly, and the retrospective nature of the information) (Ludwig, 1990; Spence, 1982) they can be offset when scholarly works and criteria of plausibility are used (Nadel, 1984; Runyan, 1984), by the richness of the material, often gathered from multiple sources over the course of a lifetime (e.g., memoirs, autobiographies, personal interviews, observations by others, intimate accounts, judgments by authorities, and so on), and by the placement of lives within a cultural context.

Based on the disparate results of past studies, this investigation was designed to test the following null hypotheses:

1. No significant differences should exist among various professional groups with respect to psychopathology, nor should those representing the "creative arts" show more emotional difficulties than those in other vocations;

2. No significant differences should exist among various professional groups with respect to creative achievement, nor should those in the "creative arts" demonstrate greater accomplishments than those not; and

3. No form of psychopathology should prove to be related to creative achievement, irrespective of profession.

METHOD

Sample

The sample consisted of all individuals whose biographies were reviewed in *The New York Times Book Review* (NYT-BR) over a 30-year period (1960 to 1990) and who met the following inclusion criteria: (a) lived at least some portion of their lives in the 20th century; (b) a member of Western civilization; (c) deceased; and (d) the availability of at least one scholarly, well-documented, biographical source (not necessarily the one reviewed in the NYT-BR). Exclusion criteria were the following: (a) the availability of only autobiographical sources, collected letters, diaries, critiques or topical analyses, biographies written by relatives or unreliable, biographical materials; (b) biographies on individuals who had overcome a handicap, adversity, illness, drug addiction, or which dealt with the roles individuals played in catastrophes, wars, or other sensational events; and (c) books on "notorious" individuals or con artists. These selection criteria resulted in a total study sample of 1,028 subjects. Information about the different nationalities represented and where most subjects spent their preschool years is given in Table 3.1.

Table 3.1. Distribution of Subjects (N = 1,028)

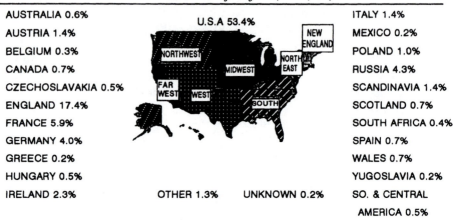

AUSTRALIA 0.6%	U.S.A 53.4%	ITALY 1.4%
AUSTRIA 1.4%		MEXICO 0.2%
BELGIUM 0.3%		POLAND 1.0%
CANADA 0.7%		RUSSIA 4.3%
CZECHOSLAVAKIA 0.5%		SCANDINAVIA 1.4%
ENGLAND 17.4%		SCOTLAND 0.7%
FRANCE 5.9%		SOUTH AFRICA 0.4%
GERMANY 4.0%		SPAIN 0.7%
GREECE 0.2%		WALES 0.7%
HUNGARY 0.5%		YUGOSLAVIA 0.2%
IRELAND 2.3%	OTHER 1.3% UNKNOWN 0.2%	SO. & CENTRAL AMERICA 0.5%

Preschool Years: New England 5.5%; Northeast 16.4%; South 8.1%; West 2.1%; Northwest 0.6%; Midwest 15.6%; Far West 2.3%; Foreign 48.4%; Not Noted 1.2

In order to determine the representativeness of this sample, the subject of all biographies in the *Book Review Digest* (BRD; 1964, 1969, 1974, 1979, 1984, 1989), which contains citations of all current English-language works of fiction and nonfiction that have been published in the United States, England, or Canada and have been reviewed by at least two of its approximately 75 periodicals or journals, were sampled over a one-year period for each of six comparison periods. Of those subjects in the *BRD* who met the selection criteria, the following percentages were included in the study: 79% for 1964, 73.3% for 1969, 61.6% for 1974, 58.5% for 1979, 59.4% for 1984, and 69% for 1989. In other words, the sample of names obtained from *The New York Times Book Review* represented an average of 66.8% of the names of all individuals about whom biographies were written and reviewed in at least two of the many journals sampled by the *BRD* for these time periods. In addition, of the 510 subjects included in the Goertzel studies (Goertzel & Goertzel, 1962; Goertzel, Goertzel, & Goertzel, 1978) who met the selection criteria, 68% were also on the master list. Of the 217 individuals listed in the *Biographies of Creative Artists: An Annotated Bibliography* (Stievater, 1991) 76.5% were included in the study. Of the 309 qualifying persons in the *St. James Guide to Biography* (Shellinger, 1991), which selects entrants on the basis of their contributions to their professions, the fame they achieved in world history, and the number of biographies written on them, 85% were in the study. And lastly, in the 1990 listing by *Life* magazine (1990) of the "100 most influential people of the 20th century," 68% of the 79 individuals who met the selection criteria were included in the sample (N.B.: The remaining 21 were still alive). These various measures indicated that the study sample could be regarded as representative of all suitable individuals who have been the subjects of published biographies.

After inclusion in the study, subjects were classified according to their primary and, if appropriate, secondary professions. When classification was unclear, encyclopedia and biographical dictionary entries were used for this determination. Professional designations generally conformed to those listed in the *Dictionary of Occupational Titles*, compiled by the U.S. Department of Labor (1977). Subjects were assigned among 19 general professional categories (see Table 3.2). Because of suggestive evidence in the literature that expository writers, poets, and fiction writers differ with respect to psychopathology (Akiskal & Akiskal, 1988; Jamison, 1995), they were assigned to separate groups. The "Unclassified" category (23 subjects) represented a heterogeneous wastebasket category and was excluded in subsequent analyses, resulting in a final study sample of 1,005 subjects. Selected demographic characteristics are given in Table 3.3. Initial chi-square analyses with regard to gender and race indicated significant differences among the various groups ($\chi^2(17) = 169.4$ and 122.1, respectively; $p < .000$).

Data Collection

Comprehensive information forms were used to record all relevant biographical data, pertaining not only to subjects but, when available, to their immediate relatives as well. Project personnel received extensive training and supervision with regard to the recording of appropriate biographical materials. Appropriate materials pertained mainly to "hard data": behavioral observations and judgments based on scientific evidence or expert sources. Opinions and interpretations by the biographers or others for which there was no documented evidence were ignored. When important information was missing, sketchy, or confusing in the primary biographical source (usually the book mentioned in the *New York Times Book Review*), other independent sources were used. Depending upon the adequacy of the primary source, from one to four complete biographies were read on every subject, also supplemented by entries from encyclopedias or biographical dictionaries. For the entire sample, information from a total of 2,184 biographical sources was obtained.

Based on the extensive material contained in the information forms, a data form, consisting of 240 items, was filled out for each subject. An Instruction Manual provided detailed guidelines for the interpretation and recording of information (see Ludwig, 1992).

Table 3.2. Primary Professions of Sample

	Count	%		Count	%
Architecture/Design (AD)	23	2.2	Social Activism (SA)	61	5.9
Architect	10	1.0	Human Rights Advocate	29	2.8
Commercial artist	6	0.6	Labor Leader	6	0.6
Designer	7	0.7	Persuader	5	0.5
Art (AR)	70	6.8	Revolutionary	21	2.0
Painter	54	5.3	Social Figure (SF)	30	2.9
Photographer	11	1.1	Collector, Aesthete	5	0.5
Sculptor	5	0.5	Host(ess)	9	0.9
Business/Entrepreneur (BU)	70	6.8	Museum/Film Curator	2	0.2
Advertiser, Publicist	2	0.2	Patron	11	1.1
Banker/Businessman	42	4.1	Philanthropist	3	0.3
Manager/Agent	3	0.3	Spouse/Lover (SL)	19	1.8
Producer	11	1.1	Social Science/Academics (SS)	73	7.1
Publisher	12	1.2	Anthropologist	13	1.3
Exploration (EH)	11	1.1	Economist	2	0.2
Adventurer	5	0.5	Educator	6	0.6
Explorer	6	0.6	Historian	7	0.7
Games/Athletics (GA)	19	1.8	Philosopher	12	1.2
Athlete	12	1.2	Political Theorist	3	0.3
Game Expert	0	0.0	Psychologist	14	1.4
Manager/Coach	4	0.4	Sociologist	6	0.6
Game, Other	3	0.3	Theologian	10	1.0
Musical Composition (MC)	48	4.7	Theater (TH)	70	6.8
Choreographer	5	0.5	Actor	57	5.5
Composer	38	3.7	Broadcaster	2	0.2
Conductor	5	0.5	Director	11	1.1
Musical Performance (MD)	47	4.6	Writing, Expository (WE)	64	6.2
Dancer	8	0.8	Biographer	3	0.3
Instrumentalist	12	1.2	Critic	11	1.1
Singer	27	2.6	Editor	7	0.7
Military (MO)	20	1.9	Essayist	16	1.6
Soldier	19	1.8	Journalist	27	2.6
Spy	1	0.1	Writing, Fiction (WF)	180	17.5
Public Official (PO)	108	10.5	Fiction Writer	127	12.4
Policy Advisor	2	0.2	Lyricist	2	0.2
Elected Official	51	5.0	Multimedia Writing	27	2.6
Judge/Lawyer	20	1.9	Playwright/Screen Writer	24	2.3
Appointed Public Official	19	1.8	Writing, Poetry (WP)	53	5.2
Religious Official	7	0.7	Unclassified (UC)	23	2.2
Royalty	9	0.9	Criminal	1	0.1
Physical Science (PS)	39	3.8	Dictator/Underling	14	1.4
Inventory	12	1.2	Prodigy/Other	6	0.6
Physicist/Mathematician	7	0.7	Traitor	2	0.2
Scientist/Naturalist	20	1.9	Total	1,028	100.2

Table 3.3. Selected Demographic Characteristics (Sample Size = 1,005)

	% Male	% White	% USA	Life Span	% ACC.	% NAT.	% SUI.	% ?
					Cause of Death*			
Architects (N = 23)	69.6	100.0	60.9	75.9	4.3	95.7	0	0
Artists (N = 70)	80.0	100.0	48.6	69.8	2.9	90.0	5.7	1.4
Businessmen (N = 70)	94.3	100.0	71.4	73.4	2.9	91.4	5.7	0
Explorers (N = 11)	81.1	100.0	54.5	51.4	36.4	45.5	0	18.2
Athletes (N = 19)	89.5	73.7	84.2	60.2	15.8	78.9	5.3	0
Composers (N = 48)	93.8	94.2	22.9	65.1	10.4	89.6	0	0
Musicians/Dancers (N = 47)	59.6	70.2	63.8	57.2	14.9	76.6	8.5	0
Military Officers (N = 20)	100.0	100.0	55.0	67.9	25.0	70.0	5.0	0
Public Officials (N = 108)	93.5	98.1	62.0	72.3	6.5	93.5	0	0
Physical Scientists (N = 39)	92.3	94.9	59.0	71.5	0	92.3	5.1	2.6
Social Activitists (N = 61)	59.0	90.2	45.9	66.0	27.9	67.2	1.6	3.3
Social Figures (N = 30)	26.7	96.7	56.7	74.4	6.7	93.3	0	0
Spouses/Lovers (N = 19)	5.3	100.0	47.4	75.1	0	89.5	5.3	5.3
Social Scientists (N = 73)	78.1	97.3	34.2	72.3	6.8	87.7	4.1	1.4
Actors/Directors (N = 70)	62.9	97.1	71.4	63.4	12.9	78.6	7.1	1.4
Expository Writers (N = 64)	71.9	100.0	68.8	70.6	1.6	93.8	1.6	3.1
Fiction Writers (N = 180)	75.0	96.7	47.2	66.1	8.3	87.2	3.9	0.6
Poets (N = 53)	75.5	100.0	45.3	59.6	7.5	69.8	18.9	3.8

*Cause of Death (Acc. = Accidental/incidental; Nat. = Natural Causes; Sui. = Suicide; ? = Unknown)

Reliability checks were conducted for each stage of the information-processing and coding procedures prior to data entry in the computer. In order to determine the adequacy of information transferred from a standard biographical source to the information form, all four raters independently read the same biographies on six different individuals and filled out separate information forms, each consisting of 116 general categories of information. Each form was then independently coded on a categorical basis as to whether or not it contained the requisite information. Crosstabulations were then performed to determine the extent of agreement among raters. Cohen's Kappa statistic, which ranged from .69 to .75 (mean = .71), indicated high levels of agreement. Percentage agreement between pairs of raters ranged from 81.9% to 88.4% (mean = 86.3%).

To determine the extent to which bias or error potentially affected the coding of material from the information form to the data form, four raters independently filled out data forms on 8 different subjects, using the same information forms on each. Because the 228 designated items represented a mixture of nominal, ordinal, and fixed interval data, inter-rater reliability was determined on the basis of percentage agreement between pairs of raters. These values ranged from 84.2% to 87.4% (mean = 85.0%). An automatic verification program was used during double data entry in the computer to detect and eliminate errors.

Creative Achievement Scale

For the purposes of this study, ti seemed appropriate to bypass the controversy about the nature of creativity by focusing instead on "creative achievement," a construct that can be operationalized and rated, utilizing criteria usually attributed to creativity. To this end, Creative Achievement Scale (CAS) scores were obtained for each subject. The CAS (Ludwig, 1992) consists of 11 rated items, included under three weighted categories, which yield a Total Score, ranging from 0 to 78. The first grouping of items, regarded as "major" criteria, pertained to degree of posthumous recognition, the universality of the contribution, the anticipation of social or future needs, influence on contemporary and subsequent professionals, the originality of the work or product, and the extent of innovative accomplishments over the person's adult lifetime. The second group of items, regarded as "intermediate" criteria, pertained to degree of versatility, productivity, and public fame. The third grouping of items, regarded a "minor" criteria, pertained to degree of professional competence and skill, and involvement in nonvocational, creative pursuits. Detailed instructions and examples for the rating of each item were provided in the Instruction Manual and were reproduced in Ludwig (1992).

The CAS appears to be a reliable and valid instrument. Internal consistency among scale items are high. Scale validity was demonstrated by correlating CAS Total Scores for two separate samples (n^s = 12 and n = 50) with the number of lines allotted to each subject in the *Encyclopaedia Brittanica* (r = .64, $p < .05$ and r = .40, $p < .01$, respectively) and the *Encyclopedia Americana* (r = .65, $p < .05$ and r = .29, $p < .05$, respectively). In subsequent analyses, comparable correlations with 150 randomly selected subjects also were statistically significant (r = .59, $p < .00$ and r = .42, $p < .00$, respectively). In addition, the four trained raters' scores were correlated with the average ratings of a panel of 10 expert judges from different professions for 12 designated subjects (Pearson r values ranged from .86 to .92, $p < .05$ for all values).

The distribution of CAS scores for subjects in the current study is depicted in the histogram in Table 3.4.

Psychopathology Ratings

Based on the available biographical material, the presence of various symptom clusters was recorded as being "definite," "probable," or "absent" before or after age 40. The criteria for the different categories of psychopathology corresponded in general to appropriate Glossary descriptions in the *Ninth Revision of the International Classification of Disease* (1978) (see Appendix). For the purpose of statistical analyses, the "definite" and "probable" categories were collapsed into one. Certain other symptom clusters that pertained to more enduring lifetime patterns, such a marked personality attributes, excessive gambling or sexual perversions, were noted as well. Because of the nature of the data, no attempt was made to establish formal psychiatric diagnoses for subjects.

Psychopathology was designated on a cross-sectional rather than longitudinal basis; that is, it pertained to a relatively stable clustering of symptoms at a given period in a person's life. So, if individuals displayed depression at one time in their lives and mania at another, they would be rated as positive both for depression and mania rather than given a longitudinal diagnosis of bipolar disorder. However, psychopathology for which there was a definite physical basis was recorded elsewhere as a medical or neurological condition.

In addition to these individual items, a variety of composite or additive scores were later constructed to assess susceptibility to different combinations of symptom clusters either before or after age 40 or over an entire lifetime.

Inter-rater reliability was high with regard to identification of the specific forms of psychopathology based on the available, biographical materials. The Kappa statistic between pairs of raters for the 24 items ranged

Table 3.4. Histogram of Creative Achievement Scale Scores

Frequency	Bin Center	
34.00	5.00	**
90.00	15.00	****
142.00	25.00	******
260.00	35.00	************
252.00	45.00	***********
132.00	55.00	******
88.00	65.00	****
7.00	75.00	

Bin width: 10.00. Each star: 22 cases

from .51 to .76 (mean = .65). Percentage agreement between pairs of raters ranged from 87.4% to 96.3% (mean = 91.7%).

Psychiatric-Type Therapies

The exposure of subjects to psychiatric-type therapies was recorded as present or absent. The different categories of therapy were as follows: Forced Treatment = the subject being pressured or forced to get help against his or her will; Voluntary Hospitalization = total mental health care provided in a psychiatric hospital, sanitarium, or spa at subject's own initiative; Outpatient Psychiatric Care = outpatient psychiatric care, with or without medications; Psychotherapy = exposure to a course of psychotherapy, psychoanalysis, or counseling; Unorthodox Therapy = exposure to quasi-therapeutic approaches, off-beat movements, fads, "cults," naturopathy, etc.; and Other Therapy = exposure to any approach designed to relieve emotional distress, which is not indicated above (e.g., Christian Science, religious healings).

Statistical Procedures

Aside from the specific analyses described above for evaluating interrater reliability, other statistical procedures were used to test the general hypotheses under investigation.

Differences among the groups for dichotomous variables were analyzed by using chi-square statistics on the raw data. Posthoc tests for significant chi-squares between individual pairs of groups were undertaken only if the overall chi-square (i.e., 2 × 18 contingency table) proved statistically. significant. Between-group comparisons were interpreted as meaningful only if one group differed significantly from at least two others. In instances when the proportion of responders was too small for chisquare analysis, Fisher's exact test was used. Multivariate analyses were based on logistic regression models that estimate the probability that an event occurs in relation to various categorical variables.

One-way analyses of variance were used to compare mean responses among professions for interval-level variables. Posthoc tests for significant F ratios were based on Scheffe's multiple comparison procedure and were undertaken only if the omnibus ANOVA proved statistically significant. Multivariate analyses were based on either three-way analyses of variance (i.e., gender, race, profession as independent variables) or multiple regression models.

A hierarchical cluster analysis of mean psychopathology scores was run on a posthoc basis to test the legitimacy of the a priori separation of professions into those comprising the "creative arts" and those not, as well as to assess the relative independence of groups at different stages of the agglomeration schedules.

RESULTS

Time Course

Chi-square contingency analyses for categorical variables were performed to determine whether differences existed among the 18 groups with respect to the prevalence of any psychiatric syndrome before age 13, between ages 13 and 20, between ages 21 and 40, between ages 41 and 60, and after age 61. Because of death, the sample size after age 40 decreased to 922 and after age 60 to 707. Chi-square analyses yielded statistically significant result among the professions after age 13 (Pearson's chi-square = 54.7, 146.4, 100.1, and 65.4, respectively, df = 17, $p < .000$) (see Figure 3.1). Between the ages of 13 and 20, between-group differences are initially noted for poets, fiction writers, and musical performers compared mostly to at least two of the following groups: businessmen, military personnel, politicians, social figures, and social scientists (chi-square values range from 4.4 to 16.9, df = 1, $p < .05$). After age 21, these more symptomatic groups are joined by artists, composers, expository writers, theater personnel, and, interestingly, by athletes. The significantly less symptomatic groups are joined by social activists, physical scientists, spouses/lovers of famous people, and by architects/designers (chi-square values range from 3.9 to 56.1, df = 1, $p < .05$). Except for minor shifts among the groups, comparable significant findings pertain throughout the remaining time periods.

The results also can be displayed as additive scores across all time periods, roughly representing a longitudinal measure of the extent to which subjects exhibit psychopathology over the entire course of their lives. Univariate analyses of variance yielded highly significant results among all 18 groups ($F (17, 987) = 8.7$, $p < .000$) with between-group comparisons (done by Scheffe tests) indicating significant symptomatology in fiction writers, poets, and theater personnel compared to at least two other groups.

Psychopathology

Chi-square analyses (18 × 2 tables) were performed to determine whether the presence of alcohol-related problems, substance abuse, depression,

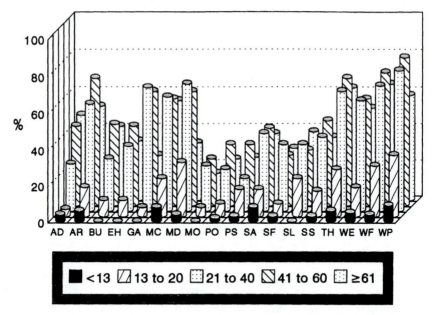

Figure 3.1.   Prevalence of psychopathology among professions different time periods.
Key: AD = Architecture; AR = Art; BU = Business; EH = Exploration; GA = Games; MC = Musical
Composition; MD = Musical Performance; MO = Military; PO = Public Office; PS = Physical Science; SA =
Social Activism; SF = Social Figure; SL = Spouse/Lover; SS = Social Science; TH = Theater; WE =
Exposition; WF = Fiction; WP = Poetry.
Percentages (rounded off) of subjects with psychopathology.

mania, psychosis, anxiety disorders, somatic-type disorders, adjustment
problems, and suicide attempts differed significantly among the various
professions. These particular forms of psychopathology were also used to
construct a composite Total Psychopathology Score. In addition, cross-
tabulation analyses also pertained to the presence or absence of any persistent memory disturbances, gambling problems, sexual perversion, or
other unspecified emotional problems. The results of these analyses are
given in Table 3.5. When overall chi-square analyses were statistically significant (i.e., $p \leq .05$, two-tailed test), 2×2 between-group comparisons,
employing a Pearson's chi-square coefficient (and Fisher's Exact Test
were appropriate), were undertaken. Space considerations preclude the
listing of the large number of significant results. Only those for which
one group differed significantly from at least two others are indicated in
Table 3.6.

Since gender and race differed significantly among the professions, logistic regression analyses were performed to determine if the differences
held after adjusting for these variables. Only in those instances when a
large proportion of the cells contained fewer than five subjects did logistic regression analyses fail to support the prior significant effects for pro-

Table 3.5. Prevalence of Psychopathology by Profession[*][#][§]

		AD	AR	BU	EH	GA	MC	MD	MO	PO	PS	SA	SF	SL	SS	TH	WE	WF	WP	χ^2
Alcohol	<40	13	21	10	18	21	21	40	5	6	0	7	10	11	6	50	16	37	30	132.3
	≥40	17	24	16	33	25	16	25	11	14	3	9	10	13	9	60	27	39	24	106.2
Drugs	<40	4	7	3	0	0	8	32	0	2	0	7	7	5	6	21	8	14	13	70.5
	≥40	0	6	6	0	0	7	22	0	1	0	6	14	0	4	17	8	13	12	45.5
Depression	<40	9	34	14	0	16	35	30	5	13	13	23	17	21	25	24	41	47	57	102.7
	≥40	17	44	24	0	13	41	19	5	17	11	30	14	25	21	28	41	47	66	96.8
Mania	<40	9	9	6	0	0	6	6	0	3	3	3	3	0	1	17	8	8	13	32.0
	≥40	13	6	5	0	0	7	8	5	3	3	6	3	0	1	13	10	7	7	21.3
Psychosis	<40	0	3	1	0	5	8	4	0	0	0	2	3	0	1	4	2	3	11	28.3
	≥40	4	5	3	0	6	9	3	0	0	0	6	3	5	3	5	9	6	17	29.6
Anxiety	<40	0	11	1	0	0	4	4	5	1	3	7	7	5	3	11	9	11	6	28.7
	≥40	9	8	3	0	0	2	6	5	2	5	4	3	0	7	10	10	7	10	14.9
Adjustment	<40	4	21	7	18	47	25	21	25	12	8	23	20	32	23	24	33	27	25	40.9
	≥40	13	21	22	22	25	27	11	5	19	34	28	7	19	23	18	24	31	27	23.9
Somatic	<40	9	6	7	0	5	6	15	5	3	0	12	10	5	6	6	11	10	13	19.4
	≥40	13	11	9	0	0	11	11	0	3	3	15	3	6	4	7	9	11	12	21.2
Suicide	<40	0	4	1	0	5	8	15	0	1	3	7	10	11	1	14	5	9	13	37.8
	≥40	9	6	5	0	6	2	8	5	0	5	6	3	6	0	12	5	6	20	33.7
Memory	<40	0	0	0	0	0	0	2	0	0	0	0	0	0	0	0	0	0	0	20.4
	≥40	13	0	10	0	6	7	3	0	4	0	4	3	13	1	8	5	5	0	22.0
Sex Disorder		0	1	0	0	5	0	4	5	1	5	3	3	0	3	1	0	3	2	12.9
Gambling		0	0	10	9	5	4	6	0	1	0	0	0	0	0	3	3	3	8	33.5
Other		0	6	4	0	11	4	13	0	1	13	3	3	11	8	9	3	4	4	25.0

*Key: AD = Architecture; AR = Art; BU = Business; EH = Exploration; GA = Games; MC = Musical Composition; MD = Musical Performance; MO = Military; PO = Public Office; PS = Physical Science; SA = Social Activism; SF = Social Activism; SF = Social Figure; SL = Spouse/Lover; SS = Social Science; TH = Theater; WE = Exposition; WF = Fiction; WP = Poetry

#Percentages are rounded to whole number

§Underlined X² value (Pearson) indicates $p < .05$

Table 3.6. Major Forms of Psychopathology Shown Within "The Creative Arts"

	AD	AR	MC	MD	TH	WE	WF	WP
ALCOHOL		▦■	▦	▦■	▦■	■	▦■	▦■
DRUGS				▦■	▦■		▦	▦
DEPRESSION		▦■	▦■	▦		▦■	▦■	▦■
MANIA					▦			▦
PSYCHOSIS								▦■
ANXIETY		▦			▦		▦	
ADJUSTMENT		▦				▦	▦	
SOMATIC								
SUICIDE				▦	▦■		▦	▦■

▦ = <40 or ■ = ≥40 if significantly greater than at least two other groups

Key: AD = ARCHITECTURE; AR = ART; MC = COMPOSITION; MD = PERFORMING; TH = THEATER; WE = ESSAYS; WF = FICTION; WP = POETRY

fession (i.e., mania, psychoses, and suicide attempts). This appeared to reflect the relatively low rate of these problems among most of this professions with a high rate only in a few.

As an alternative way to evaluate psychopathology, univariate analyses of variance were performed on all composite scores that summed particular forms of psychopathology over time periods or across relevant conditions. For example, Total Alcohol ("Lifetime") scores indicated whether alcohol problems were present both before and after age 40, with potential scores being 0, 1, 2. Total Substance Use/Abuse scores pertained to the composite abuse of either alcohol or illicit drugs, with the additive scores ranging from 0 to 4; likewise with Total Mood Disorder scores, which included the presence of depression or highs both before and after age 40. Total Neurosis scores included the presence of anxiety disorders, adjustment problems, and excessive somatic complaints over both time periods, with the scores ranging from 0 to 6. And Total Psychopathology scores included all of the above categories, along with the potential presence of psychoses or suicide attempts, the scores ranging from 0 to 18. Mean scores for these and comparable measures re given in Table 3.7 along with the results of between-group comparisons as determined, when indicated, by Scheffe tests. Though the number of significant findings is less, the results tend to be consistent with those for individual psychopathology items.

Table 3.7. Composite Mean Psychopathology Scores Among Groups

	AD	AR	BU	EH	GA	MC	MD	MO	PO	PS	SA	SF	SL	SS	TH	WE	WF	WP	Total	F	p≤
Alcohol	0.3	0.4	0.3	0.5	0.4	0.4	0.6	0.2	0.2	0.0	0.1	0.2	0.2	0.1	_1.0_	0.4	_0.7_	0.5	0.4	8.4	0.000
Drugs	0.0	0.1	0.1	0.0	0.0	0.1	_0.5_	0.0	0.0	0.0	0.1	0.2	0.1	0.1	0.4	0.2	0.3	0.2	0.2	4.3	0.000
Substance Use	0.3	0.6	0.3	0.5	0.4	0.5	1.1	0.2	0.2	0.0	0.3	0.4	0.3	0.2	_1.4_	0.6	_1.0_	0.7	0.6	9.0	0.000
Depression	0.3	0.8	0.4	0.0	0.3	0.7	0.4	0.1	0.3	0.2	0.5	0.3	0.4	0.5	0.5	0.8	_0.9_	_1.1_	0.6	7.7	0.000
Mania	0.2	0.1	0.1	0.0	0.0	0.1	0.1	0.1	0.1	0.0	0.1	0.1	0.0	0.0	0.3	0.2	0.1	0.2	0.1	1.6	0.068
Mood	0.5	0.9	0.5	0.0	0.3	0.9	0.6	0.2	0.4	0.3	0.6	0.4	0.4	0.5	0.8	1.0	_1.1_	_1.3_	0.7	6.1	0.000
Psychosis	0.0	0.1	0.0	0.0	0.1	0.2	0.1	0.0	0.0	0.0	0.1	0.1	0.0	0.0	0.1	0.1	0.1	0.2	0.1	1.9	0.015
Anxiety	0.1	0.2	0.0	0.0	0.0	0.1	0.1	0.1	0.1	0.1	0.1	0.1	0.1	0.1	0.2	0.2	0.1	0.1	0.1	1.3	0.154
Adjustment	0.2	0.4	0.3	0.4	0.7	0.5	0.3	0.3	0.3	0.4	0.5	0.3	0.5	0.5	0.4	0.5	0.6	0.5	0.4	1.9	1.017
Somatic	0.2	0.2	0.2	0.0	0.1	0.2	0.2	0.1	0.1	0.0	0.2	0.1	0.1	0.1	0.1	0.2	0.2	0.2	0.2	1.2	0.248
Neurosis	0.5	0.8	0.5	0.4	0.7	0.7	0.6	0.5	0.4	0.5	0.8	0.5	0.6	0.6	0.7	0.9	0.9	0.8	0.7	2.3	0.002
Suicide	0.1	0.1	0.1	0.0	0.1	0.1	0.2	0.1	0.1	0.1	0.1	0.1	0.2	0.0	0.2	0.1	0.2	0.3	0.1	3.0	0.000
Memory	0.1	0.0	0.1	0.0	0.1	0.1	0.0	0.0	0.1	0.1	0.0	0.0	0.1	0.0	0.1	0.0	0.1	0.0	0.0	1.2	0.201
Psychopathology	1.4	2.4	1.4	0.8	1.6	2.4	2.6	0.8	1.0	0.9	1.8	1.5	1.5	1.4	_3.2_	2.6	_3.2_	_3.3_	2.1	9.6	0.000
Total Time	1.2	1.8	1.2	0.9	1.4	1.8	1.7	0.7	0.9	0.9	1.3	1.0	1.2	1.3	_1.9_	1.8	_2.2_	_2.1_	1.5	8.6	0.000
Any Treatment	0.3	0.3	0.2	0.1	0.2	0.3	0.3	0.0	0.1	0.2	0.2	0.3	0.2	0.3	0.3	0.3	_0.4_	0.4	0.3	4.2	0.000

Underline = $p < .05$ compared to at least one other group

Key: AD = Architecture; AR = Art; BU = Business; EH = Exploration; GA = Games; MC = Musical Composition; MD = Musical Performance; MO = Military; PO = Public Office; PS = Physical Science; SA = Social Activism; SF = Social Figure; SL = Spouse/Lover; SS = Social Science; TH = Theater; WE = Exposition; WF = Fiction; WP = Poetry

Analyses of variance procedures also were run for each dependent variable, utilizing the sequential sum of squares method to adjust for the potential confounding effects of gender and race. Adjustment for these independent variables did not alter any of the significant differences previously noted for profession alone.

Psychiatric-Type Therapies

Cross-tabulation analyses were run to determine whether significant differences existed among the various professions with regard to treatment for emotional problems. The results, listed in Table 3.8, reveal significant differences in rates of forced hospitalization (higher for theater members and poets compared to businessmen and public officials), voluntary psychiatric hospitalization (higher for theater members, fiction writers, and poets compared mostly to public officials, physical scientists, and social activists), outpatient psychiatric care (higher for theater members and fiction writers compared mainly to public officials and social scientists) and psychotherapy (higher in social scientists, theater personnel, and expository and fiction writers compared mostly to public officials, businessmen, and social activists).

As a general indicator of the relationship between the extent of psychopathology and its duration in subjects, along with their exposure to any therapy, Pearson product-moment correlations, using the mean scores for each of the 18 professions, revealed highly significant relationships among these three variables ($r = .82$ to $.97$, $p < .000$). These relationships are depicted graphically in Figure 3.2.

"Creative Arts" versus "Other Professions"

As additional analyses of interest, all professions traditionally comprising the "creative arts" (i.e., art, architecture/design, musical, composition, musical performance, theater, expository writing, fiction writing, and poetry) were compared with the other 10 professions as a whole with regard to individual and composite psychopathology scores and exposure to psychiatric therapy. Chi-square analyses and univariate analyses of variance, as appropriate, yielded significantly higher rates and levels of psychopathology and treatment for virtually all dependent variables among persons in the creative arts versus the others. The results are given in Table 3.9. Logistic regression analyses for individual item scores and multiple regression analyses for composite scores did not reveal any appreciable alteration in the results when gender and race were factored in.

Table 3.8. Percentage Receiving Treatment for Mental Disorders

	AD	AR	BU	EH	GA	MC	MD	MO	PO	PS	SA	SF	SL	SS	TH	WE	WF	WP	SQUARE*	p ≤
Forced Hospitalization	8.7	2.9	0.0	0.0	5.3	6.3	6.4	0.0	0.0	0.0	1.6	3.3	0.0	2.7	11.4	1.6	7.8	11.3	36.8	0.004
Voluntary Hospitalization	8.7	10.0	11.4	0.0	5.3	16.7	19.1	0.0	2.8	5.1	4.9	13.3	5.3	13.7	18.6	7.8	20.6	24.5	45.5	0.000
Outpatient Psychiatric Care	4.3	10.0	8.6	0.0	5.3	8.3	8.5	0.0	0.0	5.1	6.6	6.7	10.5	4.1	20.0	9.4	15.0	15.1	38.8	0.002
Psychotherapy	8.7	7.1	4.3	0.0	0.0	12.5	4.3	0.0	1.9	5.1	1.6	16.7	5.3	16.4	17.1	15.6	14.4	11.3	41.9	0.000
Unorthodox Therapy	0.0	7.7	1.4	0.0	0.0	4.2	6.4	0.0	0.9	0.0	3.3	3.3	0.0	1.4	2.9	3.1	2.8	5.7	15.4	0.569
Other Treatment	0.0	4.3	1.4	0.0	0.0	0.0	4.3	0.0	0.9	5.1	6.6	0.0	0.0	0.0	1.4	3.1	4.4	5.7	18.3	0.369

Key: AD = Architecture; AR = Art; BU = Business; EH = Exploration; GA = Games; MC = Musical Composition; MD = Musical Performance; MO = Military; PO = Public Office; PS = Physical Science; SA = Social Activism; SF = Social Figure; SL = Spouse/Lover; SS = Social Science; TH = Theater; WE = Exposition; WF = Fiction; WP = Poetry

Table 3.9. Creative Arts (n=555) Versus Other Professions (n=450):
Prevalence of Psychopathology and Mean Composite Scores

Individual Item	% Create	% Oth	χ^2	p=	Composite Score	X̄ Create	X̄ Oth	dif = 1,1003	p=
Time (Yrs.)									
<13	5.6	2.4	6.1	.01	Time	1.92	1.07	113.5	.00
13–21	24.0	10.7	29.9	.00	Alcohol	.60	.19	83.4	.00
22–40	65.0	33.9	102.8	.00	Drugs	.24	.07	35.0	.00
41–60	67.9	39.4	75.2	.00	Depression	.76	.34	72.9	.00
>61	56.3	30.7	46.8	.00	Mania	.17	.05	17.4	.00
Alcohol					Psychosis	.10	.03	13.0	.00
<40	31.0	7.3	85.7	.00	Anxiety	.15	.06	13.0	.00
40	32.6	12.2	53.7	.00	Adjustment	.42	.38	4.6	.03
Drugs					Somatic	.19	.11	7.4	.00
<40	13.9	3.3	33.2	.00	Suicide	.16	.06	22.0	.00
40	11.4	3.5	19.8	.00	Memory	.05	.04	0.0	.99
Depression									
<40	38.7	16.4	60.3	.00					
40	41.2	18.8	53.9	.00					
Mania									
<40	9.5	2.7	19.5	.00					
40	8.2	2.8	12.5	.00					
Psychosis					Substance Abuse	.84	.26	91.0	.00
<40	4.3	1.1	9.2	.00					
40	7.4	3.5	6.6	.00					
Anxiety					Mood Disorder	.93	.40	72.7	.00
<40	8.6	2.9	14.5	.00					
40	7.4	3.5	6.6	.00					

Adjustment	<40	24.9	17.8	7.3	.00
	40	24.3	21.6	1.0	.32
Somatic	<40	9.4	5.6	5.1	.05
	40	10.5	5.4	7.9	.00
Suicide	<40	9.2	3.1	15.2	.00
	40	7.6	2.8	10.4	.00
Memory	<40	0.2	0.0	0.8	.36
	40	4.8	4.7	0.0	.92
Sex Disorder		2.0	1.8	0.1	.81
Gambling		3.2	2.2	1.0	.32
Other		5.2	4.9	0.1	.81
Neurotic Disorder		.81	.55	18.5	.00
Psychopathology		1.26	.67	127.8	.00
Ant Therapy		.33	.16	40.7	.00
Treatment					
Forced		7.1	1.1	20.8	.00
Voluntary		16.9	7.1	21.9	.00
Outpatient		12.8	4.4	21.0	.00
Psychotherapy		12.4	5.8	12.9	.00
Unorthodox		4.0	1.3	6.3	.01
Other		3.4	1.8	2.6	.11

Key: Create = Creative Arts; Oth = Other. χ^2 = chi square; $\bar{X}$ = mean. Substance Abuse = Alcohol + Drugs; Mood Disorder = Depression + Mania; Neurotic Disorder = Anxiety + Adjustment + Somatic; Psychopathology = All above + Suicide attempt

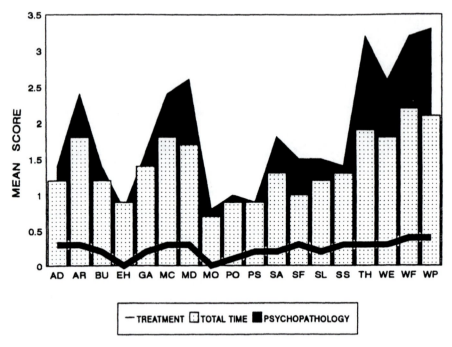

Figure 3.2.   Comparison of amount and time of psychopathology with treatment.
Key: AD = Architecture; AR = Art; BU = Business; EH = Exploration; GA = Games; MC = Musical Composition; MD = Musical Performance; MO = Military; PO = Public Office; PS = Physical Science; SA = Social Activism; SF = Social Figure; SL = Spouse/Lover; SS = Social Science; TH = Theater; WE = Exposition; WF = Fiction; WP = Poetry

In addition, in order to identify homogeneous groups, a hierarchical cluster analysis of 13 mean composite psychopathology scores (*see* Table 3.7) was run on a posthoc basis to test the legitimacy of the a priori grouping of professions into those comprising the creative arts and those not. The two-cluster solution, as depicted by the icicle plot in Figure 3.3, offer strong support for this division. Except for the architect and artist groups, the remaining six creative-arts professions remain distinct from the rest.

Despite these two groupings, the cluster analysis also suggests that the patterns of psychopathology among the creative-arts professions are relatively different. It is not until Stage 12 in the 17-stage agglomeration schedule that three of these groups cluster together and Stage 15 before all six groups do.

Creative-Achievement-Scale Scores

A univariate analysis of variance revealed significantly higher Creative Achievement Scale (CAS) Total Scores between those in the creative arts

```
W  W  T  M  W  M  P  P  M  E  S  S  S  G  S  B  A  A
P  F  H  D  E  C  S  O  O  H  S  L  A  A  F  U  R  D

 1 +XXXXXXXXXXXXXXXXXXXXXXXXXXXXXXXXXXXXXXXXXXXXXXXXXXXXX
 2 +XXXXXXXXXXXXXXX   XXXXXXXXXXXXXXXXXXXXXXXXXXXXXXXXXXX
 3 +XXXXXXXXXXXXXXX   XXXXXXXXXX   XXXXXXXXXXXXXXXXXXXXXXXX
 4 +XXXXXXX   XXXXXX   XXXXXXXXXX   XXXXXXXXXXXXXXXXXXXXXXXX
 5 +XXXX   X   XXXXXX   XXXXXXXXXX   XXXXXXXXXXXXXXXXXXXXXXXX
 6 +XXXX   X   XXXXXX   XXXXXXXXXX,   XXXXXXXXXX   XXXXXXXXXX
 7 +XXXX   X   X   XXXX   XXXXXXXXXX   XXXXXXXXXX   XXXXXXXXXX
 8 +XXXX   X   X   XXXX   XXXXXXX   X   XXXXXXXXXX   XXXXXXXXXX
 9 +XXXX   X   X   XXXX   XXXXXXX   X   XXXXXXX   X   XXXXXXXXXX
10 +XXXX   X   X   XXXX   XXXXXXX   X   XXXX   X   X   XXXXXXXXXX
11 +XXXX   X   X   XXXX   XXXX   X   X   XXXX   X   X   XXXXXXXXXX
12 +X   X   X   X   XXXX   XXXX   X   X   XXXX   X   X   XXXXXXXXXX
13 +X   X   X   X   XXXX   XXXX   X   X   XXXX   X   X   X   XXXXXX
14 +X   X   X   X   XXXX   X   X   X   X   XXXX   X   X   X   XXXXXX
15 +X   X   X   X   XXXX   X   X   X   X   X   X   X   X   X   XXXXXX
16 +X   X   X   X   X   X   X   X   X   X   X   X   X   X   X   XXXXXX
17 +X   X   X   X   X   X   X   X   X   X   X   X   X   X   X   XXXX
```

Figure 3.3.   Complete icicle plot for cluster analysis.

Key: AD = Architecture; AR = Art; BU = Business; EH = Exploration; GA = Games; MC = Musical Composition; MD = Musical Performance; MO = Military; PO = Public Office; PS = Physical Science; SA = Social Activism; SF = Social Figure; SL = Spouse/Lover; SS = Social Science; TH = Theater; WE = Exposition; WF = Fiction; WP = Poetry

as a whole (n = 555; mean + / - s.d. = 44.0 + / - 11.4) and the others (n = 450; mean + / - s.d. = 31.4 +/ - 16.1) (F (1003, 1) = 208.5, p < .000). Analyses of variance also were run to determine whether CAS Total Scores differed among the professions. The results are given in Table 3.10, along with the depiction of between-group differences determined, when appropriate, by Scheffe tests. Musical composers, physical scientists, artists, and architects/designers obtained the highest CAS scores and social figures, spouses/lovers, and explorers/adventurers the lowest. To adjust for the potential effects of gender and race, an analysis of variance was run with the sequential sum of squares method. Differences among the professions remained significant (F (17, 955) = 43.04, p < .000) despite adjustments for these variables.

Relationship of Psychopathology to Creative Achievement

In order to determine the relationship of psychopathology to creative achievement across all professions, a stepwise multiple regression analysis was run (PIN = .05; POUT = .10), utilizing the CAS Total Score as the dependent variable and all individual and composite psychopathology scores as independent variables. Beta coefficients and significance values for this analysis are given in Table 3.11. Total (Lifetime) Depression

Table 3.10. Means and Standard Deviations for CAS Total Scores
with Comparisons Between Groups

	BU 27.3 (12.9)	EH 25.2 (10.7)	GA 28.0 (7.2)	MO 27.7 (9.5)	PO 28.8 (12.5)	SA 30.7 (12.4)	SF 16.9 (10.5)	SL 7.0 (6.4)
AD 48.7 (10.8)	□	□	□	□	□	□	□	□
AR§ 46.7 (13.6)	□	□	□	□	□	□	□	□
MC§ 53.1 (9.8)	□	□	□	□	□	□	□	□
MD 42.3 (10.1)	□				□		□	□
PS§ 51.9 (14.1)	□	□	□	□	□	□	□	□
SS 44.0 (14.5)	□		□	□	□	□	□	□
TH 41.1 (9.2)	□	□			□		□	□
WE 35.8 (7.9)			□		□		□	□
WF 44.5 (11.4)	□		□		□	□	□	□
WP 43.5 (11.4)	□				□	□	□	□

TOTAL SAMPLE (F = 43.9; $p < .000$)   □ = $p < .05$
38.3
(15.0)

§AR, MC & PS are also significantly greater than WE ($p < .05$)

Key: AD = Architecture; AR = Art; MC = Musical Composition; MD = Musical Performance; PS = Physical Science; SS = Social Science; TH = Theater; WE = Exposition; WF = Fiction; WP = Poetry

scores and Total (Lifetime) Anxiety scores were found to significantly predict the level of creative achievement across professions but the variance contributed by these variables was low.

Table 3.11. Stepwise Multiple Regression Equation for CAS Total Score as Dependent Variable and Psychopathology Items and Composite Scores as Independent Variables

	Variables in the Equation					
Variable	B	SE B	BETA	R2	T	p =
Lifetime Depression	3.43	.76	.17	.04	4.54	.00
Lifetime Anxiety	3.96	1.68	.09	.04	2.36	.02
(Constant)	(36.45)	(.70)			(51.91)	

DISCUSSION

The results of the various analyses indicate that each of the three null hypotheses be rejected. Differences were found among the various professional groups, with those in the creative arts being at greater risk for psychopathology. Differences also were found among the various professions with respect to creative achievement, with those in the creative arts as a whole scoring higher than those not. Further, a significant relationship was found between certain measures of psychopathology and creative achievement. Each of these general findings, however, requires elaboration and qualification.

With regard to the first hypothesis, members of the so-called creative arts demonstrate higher rates of psychopathology, especially so when the eight creative-arts groups are collapsed into one and compared with the remaining ten groups. Those in the creative arts not only experience emotional difficulties earlier in life and over a longer time span but they also display greater rates of alcoholism, drug abuse, depression, mania, somatic problems, anxiety, psychoses, and adjustment disorders, and, consequently, undergo most forms of psychiatric therapy more often.

What needs emphasis, though, is that these general findings obscure those that pertain to differences among the individual professions with regard to the extent, time course, and patterns of symptomatology. This observation tends to be supported by the results of cluster analysis. Though Type 1 errors may account for certain results, they are unlikely to account for the preponderance, given the large number and consistent pattern of significant findings, as well as the conservative criterion of judging between-group comparisons meaningful only when one group differed significantly from at least two others.

Interpretation of the results, as a whole, indicates that members of the theatrical profession, all categories of writers, artists but not architects/designers, and musical performers and composers experience significantly more psychiatric difficulties over the course of their lives in comparison mostly to public officials, military personnel, social scientists, physical scientists, and, in some instances, businessmen. These psychiatric difficulties are not the same for all groups. Members of the theatrical profession demonstrate higher rates of alcohol and drug abuse, manic episodes, anxiety disorders, and suicide attempts but, surprisingly, not depression. Among the writers, the essayists/expository writers appear different from the others, and on some measures, as anticipated (Andreasen & Glick, 1988; Rothenberg, 1990), the poets and fiction writers diverge. Expository writers appear mostly prone to adjustment problems before age 40, alcohol-related problems after age 40, and depression throughout the course of their lives. Writers of fiction and poets share certain types of psychopathology (i.e., alcohol and drug abuse, depression and suicide attempts) and differ on others (i.e., poets show significantly more mania before age 40 and psychoses over their entire lives, and fiction writers show more anxiety and adjustment problems before age 40). Artists, in distinction, display a different pattern. In comparison to certain groups, they have significantly more alcohol-related problems and depression over their entire lives and anxiety and adjustment problems before the age of 40. Musical performers demonstrate more alcohol and drug abuse over the course of their lives and depression and suicide attempts below the age of 40, while musical composers display mostly high rates of alcohol-related problems before age 40 and histories of life-long depression. Within the creative professions, architects/designers show the least psychopathology. Stated differently, the results indicate that the prevalence of different forms of psychopathology is high for different groupings of these professions.

Among those not in the creative arts, athletes tend to experience the highest rates of adjustment problems before age 40, businessmen/entrepreneurs are more likely to be heavy gamblers, and social scientists undergo psychiatric therapy significantly more often than certain other groups.

While the presence of psychopathology is important, so too is its relative absence. For the most part, public officials and military personnel, joined at times by physical scientists, social scientists, and businessmen, appear to be the most emotionally "stable." This raises the question as to whether the existence of certain forms of psychopathology may be advantageous for certain professions and not for others.

These different patterns of response suggest that certain of the creative arts professions either attract predisposed individuals to them, aggravate their latent problems as a consequence of special stresses, particular life styles and professional status, or foster the cultivation of certain psychopathology as a vehicle for fame and success. Musicians, for instance, may be drawn to alcohol and drugs not only because of a possible biological predisposition or the belief that drugs enhance performance or the calming or stimulating properties of those substances but also because they are pressured to do so by their immediate circle of friends. Poets not only may be susceptible to affective disorders, psychoses, and suicide, but they also may be influenced by the cultural expectation that they are supposed to struggle with their *angst*. In contrast, public officials and military officers who are accountable to their public or their superiors are less likely to be successful if they show obvious signs of mental instability or social deviance. While they may experience private distress, their public *persona* must be such that psychopathology cannot be revealed. Otherwise, they are unlikely to gain the kind of public trust and approval essential for most leadership positions. Although a certain proportion of these individuals suffer from mental illness, professions that operate in the public domain tend to be selective for individuals who are reasonably stable or who have the capacity to hide their psychopathology, perhaps even from themselves. This also pertains to social scientists/academicians, and physical scientists. Because of the demands for perseverance, rigor, impartiality, and often painstaking, laborious experimentation within the scientific and academic disciplines, persons who experience certain psychiatric disturbances may be relatively disadvantaged with respect to professional success.

With regard to the second hypothesis, we need to note that while members of the creative arts on a whole display significantly greater creative achievement than those of other professions, they do not hold a monopoly on creative achievement. Physical scientists, in fact, rank next to highest among all the professions, and social scientists/academicians, as a group, rank higher than expository writers, musical performers, poets and those in the theater. This suggests that it is not so much the attributes of innovativeness, originality or even "creativeness" which distinguish members of the creative arts from those in scientific and academic professions but rather the formal requirements of their vocations, with perhaps more personalized, stylistic, or private media of expression associated with the former.

With regard to the third hypothesis, the demonstration that lifetime depression and lifetime anxiety significantly predict creative achievement for the sample as a whole indicates that there may be some truth to the age-old belief in a relationship between psychopathology and genius. However, what the results also reveal is that the relationship, though statistically significant, is exceptionally weak and likely not meaningful.

Even though the results of this investigation suffer from certain limitations associated with biographical data and cannot necessarily be generalized to individuals of lesser eminence or renown, they help resolve some of the prior confusion to date about the presumed relationship between psychopathology and creative achievement. Since no single profession or grouping of professions hold a monopoly on creative achievement and since substantial creative achievement can occur in the relative absence of emotional problems and since no given pattern or time course of psychopathology is characteristic for all the creative arts, the age-old issue about whether "madness" and creativity are allied in an either-or manner appears to encourage procrustean answers to fit discrepant observations and facts. Rather, as the findings of this study indicate, the more appropriate issue seems to be what types of psychopathology, if any, tend to be associated with which particular professions, and with what degree of creative achievement within these professions, and during what time periods in these individuals' lives. When the issue is formulated in this fashion, the intricacies of this mysterious relationship can be better understood.

ACKNOWLEDGEMENTS

The following colleagues provided valuable critiques: Kay R. Jamison, Victor Hesselbrock, and Albert Rothenberg, Richard Kryscio, and John V. Haley, provided statistical consultation. Karen Cooke, Gregory Guenthner, Linda House, Janis Saylor, and Donald Jones served as research assistants over the years.

REFERENCES

Akiskal, H. S., & Akiskal, K. (1988). Reassessing the prevalence of bipolar disorders: Clinical significance and artistic creativity. *Psychiatrie & Psychobiologie, 3,* 29s–36s.

Amabile, T. (1983). *The social psychology of creativity.* New York: Springer-Verlag.

Andreasen, N. C. (1987). Creativity and mental illness: prevalence rates in writers and their first-degree relatives. *American Journal of Psychiatry, 144,* 1288–1292.

Andreasen, N. C., & Glick, I. D. (1988). Bipolar affective disorder and creativity: Implications and clinical management. *Comprehensive Psychiatry, 29,* 207–217.

Aristotle. (1979). *Metaphysics* (H. G. Apostle, Trans.). Iowa: Peripatetic.

Book review digest (1964, 1969, 1974, 1979, 1984, 1989). New York: H. W. Wilson Co.

Brown, R. T. (1989). Creativity: What are we to measure? In J. A. Glover, R. R. Ronning, & C. R. Reynolds (Eds.), *Handbook of creativity* (pp. 3–32). New York: Plenum.

Cattell, R. B., & Butcher, H. J. (1968). *The prediction of achievement and creativity.* Indianapolis: Bobbs-Merrill.

Dictionary of occupational titles (4th ed.). (1977). Washington, DC: U.S. Printing Office.

Ellis, H. (1926). *A study of British genius.* Boston, MA: Houghton-Mifflin.

Galton, F. (1892). *Hereditary genius.* London: Macmillan.

Goertzel, V., & Goertzel, M. G. (1962). *Cradles of eminence.* Boston: Little, Brown.

Goertzel, V., Goertzel, M. G., & Goertzel, T. G. (1978). *Three hundred eminent personalities.* San Francisco: Jossey-Bass.

Hocevar, D. (1981). Measurement of creativity: review and critique. *Journal of Personality Assessment, 45,* 450–464.

Jamison, K. R. (1990). Manic-depressive illness, creativity and leadership. In F. K. Goodwin & K. R. Jamison (Eds.), *Manic-depressive illness* (pp. 332–367). New York: Oxford University Press.

Jamison, K. R. (1997). Mood disorders and patterns of creativity in British writers and artists. In M. A. Runco & R. Richards (Eds.), *Eminent creativity, everyday creativity, and health.* Norwood, NJ: Ablex.

Juda, A. (1949). The relationship between highest mental capacity and psychic abnormalities. *American Journal of Psychiatry, 106,* 296–307.

Karlsson, J. L. (1970). Genetic association of giftedness and creativity with schizophrenia. *Heriditas, 66,* 177–182.

Karlsson, J. L. (1978). *Inheritance of creative intelligence.* Chicago: Nelson-Hall.

Kretchmer, E. (1931). *The psychology of men of genius.* London: Kegan Paul.

Lange-Eichbaum, W. (1932). *The problem of genius.* New York: Macmillan.

Life (1990). Fall.

Ludwig, A. M. (1990). Who is someone? *American Journal of Psychotherapy, 44,* 516–524.

Ludwig, A. M. (1992). The creative achievement scale. *Creativity Research Journal, 5.*

MacKinnon, D. W. (1962). The nature and nurture of creative talent. *American Psychology, 17,* 484–495.

Michael, W. B., & Wright, C. R. (1989). Psychometric issues in the assessment of creativity. In J. A. Glover, R. R. Ronning, & C. R. Reynolds (Eds.), *Handbook of creativity* (pp. 32–52). New York: Plenum.

Mumford, M. D., & Gustafson, S. B. (1980). Creativity syndrome: Integration, application and innovation. *Psychological Bulletin, 103,* 27–43.

Oden, M. (1968). The fulfillment of promise: 40-year follow-up of the Terman Gifted Group. *Genetic Psychology Monographs, 77,* 3–93.

Plato. (1952). *Phaedrus* (R. Hackworth, Trans.). Indianapolis: Bobbs-Merrill.

Prentky, R. A. (1980). *Creativity and psychopathology: A neurocognitive perspective.* New York: Praeger.

Richards, R. L. (1981). Relationship between creativity and psychopathology: An evaluation and interpretation of the evidence. *Genetic Psychology Monographs, 103,* 261–324.

Richards, R. L., Kinney, D. K., Lunde, I., Benet, M., & Merzel, A. P. C. (1988). Creativity in manic-depressives, cyclothymes, their normal relatives and control subjects. *Journal of Abnormal Psychology, 97,* 281–288.

Richards, R. L., Kinney, D. K., Benet, M., & Merzel, A. P. C. (1988). Assessing everyday creativity: characteristics of the lifetime creativity scales and validation with three large samples. *Journal of Personality and Social Psychology, 54,* 476–485.

Rothenberg, A. (1983). Psychopathology and creative cognition. *Archives of General Psychiatry, 40,* 937–942.

Rothenberg, A. (1990). *Creativity and madness.* Baltimore: Johns Hopkins University Press.

Runyan, W. M. (1984). *Life histories and psychobiography.* New York: Oxford University Press.

Schellinger, P. E. (Ed.). (1991). *St. James guide to biography.* Chicago: St. James Press.

Shapiro, R. J. (1968). The creative research scientist. *Psychologia Africana,* Mono Suppl. 4.

Simonton, D. K. (1984). Scientific eminence historical and contemporary: A measurement of assessment. *Scientometrics, 6,* 169–182.

Simonton, D. K. (1988). *Scientific genius.* New York: Cambridge University Press.

Simonton, D. K. (1991). Latent-variable models of posthumous reputation: A quest for Galton's G. *Journal of Personality and Social Psychology, 60,* 607–619.

Spence, D. P. (1982). *Narrative truth and historical truth: Meaning and interpretation in psychoanalysis.* New York: W. W. Norton.

Stievater, S. (1991). *Biographies of creative artists: Annotated bibliography.* New York: Garland.

Terman, L. M. (1925–1959). *Genetic studies of genius* (vols. 1–6). Stanford, CA: Stanford University Press.

World Health Organization. (1978). *Mental disorders: Glossary and guide to their classification in accordance with the ninth revision of the international classification of disease.* Geneva: Author.

Appendix

ABBREVIATED CRITERIA FOR PSYCHIATRIC SYNDROMES

Alcohol Dependence/Abuse

Evidence of physical, vocational, personal, interpersonal, or legal problems related to compulsive, excessive and/or sustained drinking.

Drug Dependence/Abuse

Evidence of physical, vocational, personal, interpersonal, or legal problems related to compulsive, excessive and/or sustained licit or illicit drug use.

Depression/Melancholia

At least one sustained episode of severe depression, characterized by sad mood, sleep disturbance, increased or decreased appetite, lack of energy, dread, futility, social withdrawal, morbid thoughts, or suicidal preoccupation and attempts. "Probable" indications of depression include descriptions of moodiness, unhappiness, pessimism and general dysphoria. Often, no obvious precipitating cause is noted.

Mania/"Highs"

At least one sustained episode of elation, grandiosity, excessive energy, poor judgment, racing thoughts, social intrusiveness, prolonged insomnia, excessive buying or overcommitment. "Probable" indications of mania include major mood swings with periods of heightened well-being, marked irritability, diminished sleep, lapses in judgment, and increased physical activity.

Psychosis/Schizophrenia

At least one sustained episode, characterized by auditory or visual hallucinations, delusions of persecution, inappropriate affect, ideas of reference, incoherent communications, bizarre behaviors or impaired ability to care for one's self in the context of clear consciousness. This category also includes symptomatology consistent with such syndromes as schizophreniform, schizoaffective, affective psychotic or paranoid disorders.

Anxiety/Panic

A sustained period or episodes of fearfulness, apprehensiveness, agitation or panic with no adequate physical or psychological basis. This symptom complex may also be associated with obsessive-compulsive disorder, major phobias, post-traumatic stress responses and "nerves."

Adjustment Reactions

Maladaptive but usually reversible responses to stress or trauma out of proportion to what is normal or expected and usually associated with a decreased ability to cope and accompanied by such symptoms as depression, agitation, fearfulness or work paralysis, etc. In distinction from melancholia, there is always a triggering situation.

Somatic/Psychosomatic Disorders

Evidence of prolonged and excessive preoccupation with bodily functions or somatic dysfunctions for which there is no physical basis or, conversely, for which there is a likely psychological cause. This category also pertains to instances of emotionally induced paralyses, dramatic, attention-gaining symptomatology, conversion hysteria, hypochondriasis or related psycho-somatic bodily disorders, and older diagnoses or "nervous exhaustion," nervous debility or "neuresthenia."

Suicide (Attempts)

Any successful and unsuccessful attempt or serious threat to terminate life. Unless indications of impulsiveness, severe pain, psychosis or exceptional circumstances, underlying depression is also assumed.

Sexual Disorder/Perversion

Evidence of voyeurism, exhibitionism, transsexualism, transvestitism, pedophilia, sadism, masochism or other "perversions."

Excessive Gambling

Evidence that betting or gambling is excessive or "addictive" as manifested by an inability to stop despite occupational, social, familial, economic, and legal consequences.

Memory Disorder/Dementia/Senility

Instances of brain disease or dementia, such as Alzheimer's disease, senility, multiple strokes, etc., with evidence of severe memory impairment, confusion, delirium, disorientation, aphasia, and deterioration in functioning.

Other/Unspecified

This category serves as a wastebasket for all mental disorders not included above that cause emotional, behavioral or social impairment and for which the available descriptions are imprecise or nonspecific. Examples include "nervous breakdown," "shell shock," etc.

4

Creativity, Mental Health, and Alcoholism*

Albert Rothenberg

This analysis of the relationship between mental health and the creative process is based on empirical findings from a 25-year research project on psychological processes involved in creativity in the arts and sciences. I first briefly describe these findings and then discuss their general pertinence to mental health and creativity. A concrete example of mental illness' effects on creativity will occupy the remainder of this chapter; this will illustrate the effects of alcoholism on the literary creative process chiefly through discussion of primary data derived from interviews with John Cheever.

The empirical findings consist primarily of special types of cognitive, motivational, and affective processes operating at all phases of the creative process. Discovered initially through intensive and extensive research interviews with highly creative research subjects, not patients in therapy, they have been further demonstrated through objective psychological and quantitative analyses of creative works in progress, and

---

*From "Creativity, Mental Health, and Alcoholism," by A. Rothenberg, 1990, *Creativity Research Journal*, 3(3), pp. 179–201. Copyright © 1995 Ablex Publishing Corporation. Adapted with permission.

through a series of experiments involving creative persons and controls (Rothenberg, 1969, 1971, 1972, 1979a, 1979b, 1983b, 1988a, 1988b). Research subjects have consisted of Nobel Prize Laureates in science and literature, awardees of distinctions such as the Pulitzer Prize, National and American Book Award, National Gold Medal, Bowdoin Poetry Prize, and other literary prizes, membership in United States and British institutes and academies of arts and sciences, or science alone, as well as neophyte and potentially creative persons from a wide age range.

Initially, this research consisted of multiple series of intensive interviews with highly outstanding American novelists, poets, and playwrights during a period of their lives when they were actively engaged in some particular creative work. Located throughout the continental United States, these people were offered pay for participation in the project, and they agreed to submit to me their ongoing manuscript work in progress prior to out sessions. We met regularly on a weekly or biweekly basis for periods of more than two years in many cases (from the inception to the time of publication of the work) and our sessions focused directly on work in progress. Starting with the manuscript material, we discussed the following: the nature and source of revisions, themes, fantasies, and inspirations; dreams and life experience connected with the work; and affects, thought processes, and conflicts occurring during composition and in the interim periods. Although current psychological processes were in the forefront of the research interview, childhood background, previous writings, and other past information also became pertinent. We met regularly, whether or not manuscript material was produced, and I assured the subjects of anonymity and confidentiality (subsequent to participating in the research project, some subjects granted me permission to disclose their names in connection with specific material and reports). A similar but modified research design was also applied later to creative people in the visual arts, physical sciences, and technology. More than 95 such subjects have been interviewed for a total of more than 2,100 hours.

The experimental studies were based on hypotheses developed during the interview studies; one experimental series, to be described more fully below, involved presentation of specially constructed visual stimuli, and the other involved the administration of word-association tasks. Subjects ranging from highly talented college students to Nobel Laureates in physics, chemistry, and medicine were tested, or exposed to experimental manipulations, and intergroup and intragroup control comparisons were made. More than 1,000 people have been subjects in these experiments and results have confirmed specific hypotheses and supported interview findings.

HOMOSPATIAL PROCESS

One of these findings is the homospatial process (Greek: *homoios* = same). This process consists of actively conceiving two or more discrete entities occupying the same space, a conception leading to the articulation of new identities (Rothenberg, 1979a). In the course of creating literary characters, metaphors, complete works of art, or scientific theories, creative people actively conceive images and representations of multiple entities as superimposed within the same spatial location. These sharply distinct and independent elements may be represented as discrete colors, sounds, and so on, organized objects such as knives and human faces, or more complex organizations such as entire landscape scenes, or else a series of sensory patterns or written words together with their concrete or abstract meanings. This conception is figurative and abstract in the sense that it represents nothing that has ever existed in reality; it is one of the bases for constructive and creative imagination.

One of the tenets known for universal sensory experience is that two objects or two discrete entities can *never* occupy the same space. Nor can more than two. The creative person, however, brings *multiple* entities together in a mental conception for the purpose of producing new and valuable ideas, images, sound patterns, and metaphors.

Because of the difficulty in maintaining multiple elements in the same spatial location, the homospatial conception is frequently a rapid, fleeting, and transitory mental experience. Although this form of cognition often involves the visual sensory modality, and like all constructive imagination is probably easiest to describe in visual terms, the superimposed entities may be derived from any one of the sensory modalities. There may be entities and sensations of the gustatory, olfactory, auditory, kinesthetic, or tactile type.

The homospatial process is a special type of secondary process cognition; it is neither primary process thinking nor a form of "regression in the service of the ego" (Kris, 1952). Nor is it a form or modification of primary process condensation (combining multiple diverse elements) or displacement (shifting onto something smaller or less significant) despite the sharing of superficial similarities such as the breaking of spatial restrictions. It is a specific ego function that produces creative and adaptive results.

Unlike primary process condensation, the homospatial process involves no spatial substitutions or compromise formations, but sensory entities are consciously and intentionally conceived as occupying an identical spatial location. Because consciously superimposed discrete spatial elements cannot be held in exactly the same place, this produces a hazy and unstable mental percept rather than the vivid images characteristically due to primary process From this unstable image, a new identity is then articulated in the form of a metaphor or other type of aesthetic or scientific unity. Also, whereas in the primary process condensation aspects of various entities are *combined* in the same spatial area in order to represent all of those entities at once, the homospatial process involves no combinations but rather whole images *interacting and competing* for the same location. For example, a patient's dream about a man named Lipstein was reported by Grinstein (1983, p. 187) and shown to be a clear-cut instance of a condensation of the names Grinstein and Lipschutz. Rather than such a compromise formation in a mental image that necessarily involves change or transformation of one or both of the elements entering into the compromise, the homospatial process operating with these same name elements would instead involve mental images of the full names Grinstein and Lipschutz as neither combined, nor modified, nor adjusted, but visualized unchanged within exactly the same mentally depicted space.

Although the homospatial process involves sensory images and the alteration of ordinary perceptual experience, it is primarily a conscious, deliberate, and reality-oriented mode of cognition. Ordinary perceptual experience is consciously manipulated and mentally transcended in order to create new and valuable entities. The homospatial process is a type of logic-transcending operation that I have called a "translogical process" (Rothenberg, 1978–1979, 1979b). Such a process deals with reality by improving on it. As reality-oriented, reality-transcending, and deliberate, it is a part of the secondary process mode.

Examples of this process are a poet research subject's superimposition of the mental image of a horse together with the mental image of a man. This complex concatenation of images led to a central creation in a poem concerning the alienation of modern man. Constructed as a metaphorical description and poetic "image," this central creation presented the horse and rider as virtually fused, as follows: "Meadows received us, heady with unseen lilac./ Brief, polyphonic lives abounded everywhere./With one accord we circled the small lake" (author's name withheld). Also, playwright Arthur Miller told me, in the course of a research interview, that his initial conception of the play "Death of a Salesman" consisted of superimposed mental images of a man occupying the same space as the inside of his own head. Novelist Robert Penn Warren indicated that he created the character Jack Burden in his famous novel *All the King's Men* from a mental superimposition of his self-image or self-representation on the mental images or representations of a young man he had known. A Nobel Laureate microbiologist reported that he visualized himself superimposed on an atom in an enzyme molecule in the process of constructing a new scientific theory. From another source than my own researches, Pyle (1982, p. 50) reported that the scientist Fuller Albright developed innovative and useful formulations of cellular mechanisms "by thinking of himself as a cell."

The experimental assessment of the creative effect of the homospatial process has been carried out by means of an externalized concrete representation of the mental conception consisting of transilluminated superimposed slide images (Rothenberg, 1986, 1988b; Rothenberg & Sobel, 1980, 1981; Sobel & Rothenberg, 1980). In one experiment, the function of the process in literary creativity was assessed. Ten pairs of slide images, especially constructed to represent literary themes of love, animals, war, aging, and so on, were projected superimposed and side by side, respectively, to an experimental and matched control group of creative writers. Subjects in both groups were instructed to produce short literary metaphors inspired by each of the projected images. Results were that metaphors produced in response to the superimposed images, representing externalizations of the homospatial conception, were "blindly" rated significantly more highly creative by independent writer judges than the metaphors produced in response to the side-by-side images. By shortening the time of exposure of the projected images and encouraging mental imaging in another identically designed experiment with other creative writer groups, results were produced that supported the conclusion that creative effects were due to *mental superimposition* of imagery.

In order to trace connections between the visually stimulated homospatial conception and a visual creative result, and to replicate the findings in another domain of creativity, another experiment was carried out with visual artists (Sobel & Rothenberg, 1980). Subjects were asked to create pastel drawings in response to either superimposed or side-by-side slide images under the same experimental conditions as in the literary experiment. Independent artists and art critic judges rated the products, and the superimposed image presentation resulted in significantly more highly creative drawings. Also, specific features of line, color, and so on, of the drawings themselves gave evidence that they were produced from superimposed mental representations.

Another experiment was carried out with highly talented award-winning artists to assess whether the findings of all the previous experiments could have been the result of stimulus presentation effects (Rothenberg, 1986). Single images were constructed to represent composite foreground–background displays of the same slide pairs used in transilluminated superimposition. This experiment also showed significantly higher rated created products in response to the superimposed images. All the experiments together indicate a distinct connection between consciously constructed superimposed images representing the homospatial conception and the production of creative effects.

JANUSIAN PROCESS

The term I have used for another creative function derives from the qualities of the Roman god, Janus. This god, a very important one in the Roman religion, had faces that simultaneously looked in diametrically opposite directions. As the god of entryways and doorways, he was able to look both inside and outside at once. Very likely this function became symbolically elaborated because he also was the god of beginnings who looked both backwards and forwards—commemorated by the calendar use of his name in the month January—and in several myths he was considered the creator of the world. Although he is often depicted as having two faces (*Janus bifrons*), Roman doorways were multifaceted, having four or even six entryways, and in Roman literature he is described variously as having two, four, or six faces, all looking in opposite directions (Holland, 1961). On the basis of this feature, and his mythological importance, I have used his name for another empirical finding, the Janusian process.

The Janusian process consists of actively conceiving multiple opposites or antitheses *simultaneously*. During the course of the creative process, opposite or antithetical ideas, concepts, or propositions are deliberately and consciously conceptualized side by side or as coexisting simultaneously. Although seemingly illogical and self-contradictory, these formulations are constructed in clearly logical and rational states of mind in order to produce creative effects. They occur as early conceptions in the development of artworks and scientific theories and at critical junctures at middle and later stages as well. Because they serve generative functions during both formative and critical stages of the creative process, these conceptions usually undergo transformation and modification and are seldom directly discernible in final created products. They are formulated by the creative thinker as central ideas for a plot, character, artistic composition, or as solutions in working out practical and scientific tasks.

Simultaneity of the multiple opposites or antitheses is a cardinal feature. Opposite or antithetical ideas, beliefs, concepts, or propositions are formulated as simultaneously operating, valid, or true. Firmly held propositions, for example, about the laws of nature, the functioning of individuals and groups, and the aesthetic properties of visual and sound patterns are conceived as simultaneously true and not true. Similarly, multiple opposite or antithetical propositions are formulated a concomitantly operative. A person running is both in motion and not in motion at the same time, a chemical is both boiling and freezing, or kindness and sadism operate simultaneously. Previously held beliefs or laws are still considered valid but opposite or antithetical beliefs and laws are formulated as equally operative or valid as well.

These formulations within the Janusian process are way stations to creative effects and outcomes. They interact and join with other cognitive and affective developments to produce new and valuable products. One of these developments may be a later interaction with unifying homospatial process effects. Others may be the use of analogic, dialectic, inductive, and deductive reasoning to develop theories, inventions, and artworks. The Janusian process usually begins with the recognition and choice of salient opposites and antitheses in a scientific, cultural, or aesthetic field, progresses to the formulation of these factors operating simultaneously, and then to elaborated creations. For example, in an interview with a poet research subject carried out shortly after he had begun the earlier mentioned poem concerning the alienation of modern man, he described to me a germinating idea involving the formulation that a horse was simultaneously both a beast and not a beast, and also both human and not human. This formulation developed from his chance encounter some time earlier with a horse in Arizona's Monument Valley that evoked thoughts regarding separation and opposition between human and animal species. Over the following several weeks, he engaged in various types of thinking—including the construction of other homospatial and Janusian formulations—and constructed a five stanza poem in which the initial idea was transformed and elaborated. The final lines of the poem referred to that initial idea in the following way: "About the ancient bond between her [the horses] kind and mine/Little more to speak of can be done."

Numerous other research subjects have also described central formulations and breakthroughs for novels, plays, and scientific discoveries that manifested simultaneous antithesis or opposition. Arthur Miller told me that his initial idea for the play "Incident at Vichy" consisted of conceiving both the beauty and growth of modern Germany and Hitler's destructiveness simultaneously. In science, Nobel Laureate Edwin McMillan's formulation of "critical phase stability" leading to his development of the syndrocyclotron (later called the synchrotron) was derived from a sudden realization involving simultaneous opposition. The synchrotron is a high-energy particle accelerator that has allowed for the discovery of a number of new particles and other nuclear effects. McMillan described the sequence of events to me in the following verbatim transcription:

It was in the month of July. I think it was the month of July. I didn't put down the date—I should record these things. It was night. I was lying awake in bed and thinking of a way of getting high energy and I was thinking of the cyclotron and the particle going around and encountering the accelerator field—the right phase each time around. And I thought of what will happen if the resonance is wrong, if the period is wrong, what will happen? And I sort of analyzed in my mind that it's going around it's being accelerated, and it's getting heavier; therefore, it's taking more time to get around, and it will fall out of step. Then it gets behind and it gets the opposite sense. It gets pushed back again, so it will oscillate. It's going to oscillate back and forth, be going at too high and too low energy. Once I realized that, then the rest was easy. If the timing is wrong, it's not going to fall completely out of step, but it will overshoot and come back. Phase stability, I call it phase stability. The very next day I called it phase stability. Phase is the relation—time relation—of what you're worried about. Stability implies that it clings to a certain value. It may oscillate about, but it clings to a certain fixed value.

Here, McMillan described the formulation of a critical concept that led to the construction of the synchrotron. He conceived the simultaneously opposite states of too high and too low energy. Realizing that out-of-step particles would fall back in the accelerator field, he grasped the idea that these particles would be forced to accelerate. Consequently, they would oscillate and be both too high and too low in energy with respect to the overall accelerator field. They would be lower in energy because they were heavier and out of phase and would be also higher in energy because they would overshoot. Consequently, they would be stable overall with respect to the field. As McMillan told me in further elaboration:

Once you have an oscillation, you have the element of stability. The things will stay put. They will wiggle around, but they won't get away from you. Then all you have to do is to vary your frequency, or vary the magnetic field, either one or both, slowly, and you can push this thing anywhere you want. That all happened one night, and the next day I started to write down the equations for that and proved that it would work.

Other research subjects in both art and science have also described such Janusian formulations. Outside of data from my direct investigations with living creative people, I have also presented detailed documentary evidence indicating that both Albert Einstein and Niels Bohr used a Janusian process in the development of the general theory of relativity and the theory of complementarity, respectively (Rothenberg, 1987). For Einstein, the key formulation providing the "physical basis" of the general theory—what he called "the happiest thought of my life"—consisted of the idea that a person falling from the roof of a house was both in motion and in rest at the same time. For Niels Bohr, his initial formulation of complementarity—the theoretical construct on which quantum physics is based—was that light and electrons possessed antithetical wave and particle features simultaneously.

A tendency or capacity for the use of the Janusian process, manifested by rapid opposite responding on word association tasks, has also been experimentally identified (Rothenberg, 1973a, 1973b, 1983a). Standard Kent–Rosanoff Word Association Tests were individually administered to rated-as-creative college students and business executives and to Nobel Laureates in science. Control groups consisted of matched but rated-less-creative students, business executives, and high IQ psychiatric patients. Test instructions were go give the first word that came to mind in response to a standardized list of word stimuli. Both speed and content of response were electronically recorded. The experimenters made special attempts to reduce any anxiety related to testing in order to ensure spontaneous and valid associational responses. After factoring out any tendency to give common and popular types of responses, results indicated a significantly higher number of rapid opposite responses given by creative subjects than by subjects in any of the control groups. Speed of opposite responding among creative subjects in these experiments was extremely rapid, averaging 1.1 to 1.2 seconds from the time the experimenter spoke the stimulus word, suggesting the formulation of virtually simultaneous opposite associations.

THE CREATIVE PROCESS AND MENTAL ILLNESS

Both the Janusian and homospatial processes are unusual types of thinking and both play a major role in creativity. Because they differ significantly from everyday types of conceiving, particularly logical stepwise ones, they may be mistaken for psychotic and other types of psychopathological thinking and behavior. That something is both true and not true at the same time is highly illogical and, on the surface, quite irrational. That two or more elements can occupy the same space is beyond the dictates of our experience, and it may seem a formulation of the incredible, bizarre, and fantastic. Persons in the throes of mental illness do indeed have such conceptions as these, believe literally in them, and allow them to guide their behavior. Creative people who have been psychotic or suffering from other types of severe psychopathology surely have also literally believed in such conceptions and therefore been unable to use them in a creative way.

Although the demarcation between psychopathological thinking and creative thinking is superficially thin, the underlying psychological dynamisms are worlds apart. Both homospatial and Janusian processes are active, intentional operations that are employed for purposes of producing creations. They therefore appear during the course of a creative process after the person has developed a particular creative goal, such as writing a novel, constructing a sculpture, or developing a scientific theory. At this point, truly creative people are oriented toward producing something outside of themselves, are rational, and are completely aware of logical distinctions. Their emotional energy is not directed toward themselves, as in most forms of psychopathology, and they knowingly formulate unusual conceptions in order to improve on reality and to create. They are able to take mental risks and formulate the seemingly illogical and incredible because they re relatively free of anxiety and can assess reality well.

At those moments, their thinking is unhampered by emotional interference. Rather than the unusual and sometimes bizarre thinking that develops because of the person's inability to tolerate extreme anxiety, thinking that seems to serve a defensive function, the creative process requires an ability to tolerate high levels of anxiety and a relative lack of defensiveness in order to proceed. In sum, although creative people may suffer from psychosis and other types of thought distorting psychopathology at various periods of their lives, or even at various times during a day or week, they cannot be psychotic or use psychopathological thought processes *at the time they are engaged in a creative process* or it will not be successful. Homospatial and Janusian processes are healthy ones.

Creative work, however, can be risky. Although Janusian, homospatial, and other creative operations derive from healthy functions, they generate mental conflict and tension. In addition to the mental strain induced by these translogical modes of thinking, anxiety is generated because these modes also function to unearth unconscious material during the course of the creative process. Although sometimes causing difficulties for their users, they lead to the gratifying achievement of lasting works of art, novels, poems, and scientific theories. To clarify these assertions and illustrate the unearthing of unconscious material specifically, I shall consider the specific type of psychopathology associated with alcohol dependency and abuse. I first discuss some general issues and then in some detail present material from my research interviews with the highly creative alcoholic writer, John Cheever. The verbatim material presented indicates Cheever's use of homospatial and Janusian processes as well as the manner in which alcoholic illness interfered with his creativity. Finally, I apply the findings regarding the creative work of this author to the general case of alcoholism in relation to creativity.

ALCOHOLISM AND WRITING

Heavy use of alcohol among highly creative people, especially writers, is surprisingly frequent. In the United States, five of the eight writers who won the Nobel Prize in literature all suffered at some time from severe alcohol abuse or dependency, and many writers in other parts of the world have also had this difficulty (Koski-Jännes, 1983b). Various lists add or subtract some notable figures depending on the information available, but there is now relative certainty about the alcohol abuse of the following major writers: James Agee, Charles Pierre Baudelaire, Louise Bogan, James Boswell, Truman Capote, John Cheever, Stephen Crane, Theodore Dreiser, William Faulkner, F. Scott Fitzgerald, Lilliam Hellman, Ernest Hemingway, Victor Hugo, Samuel Johnson, Ring Lardner, Sinclair Lewis, Jack London, Robert Lowell, Malcolm Lowry, John O'Hara, Eugene O'Neill, Edgar Allen Poe, William Sydney Porter (O. Henry), Edwin Arlington Robinson, John Steinbeck, Dylan Thomas, Tennessee Williams, and Thomas Wolfe. It is worth noting also that, among painters, Mark Rothko, Arshile Gorky, Jackson Pollock, and Willem de Kooning have been famous alcohol abusers as well (see also Roe, 1946, regarding alcohol use in painters).

Although this is a striking list, it proves nothing by itself. If we drew up a list of all the great writers throughout history and placed it side by side with this group, we would very likely find that the number of non-alcoholic writers and even of abstainers far, far outnumbers this relatively small assemblage. Two recent U.S. Nobel Laureates, Isaac Bashevis Singer and Saul Bellow, show no indication of alcohol abuse, nor, for that matter, did other greats such as Thomas Mann, Marcel Proust, or Shakespeare. Nevertheless, the qualitative information that so many really good writers used alcohol to excess raises questions such as whether the alcohol drug itself actually facilitates the creative process or whether, now that genetic factors have been suggested to be operating in alcoholism, there is some biological propensity connecting creativity and drinking.

Let us take up first the question of the influence of alcohol on the creative process itself. Experimental investigations of the influence of alcohol on creative thinking have yielded equivocal results. A study of the influence of different amounts of alcohol on results of the Torrance Tests of Creative Thinking showed little variation and effect, except that individuals who thought they had received alcohol evaluated their own creative performances more highly than those who believed they had no received any (Lang, Verret, & Watt, 1984). Experimental studies done in Finland have reported both increase and nonreduction of creativity with the use of alcohol in some instances but criteria and measures of creativity used were very variable or unclear (Koski-Jännes, 1983a).

In a systematic assessment I carried out of available pertinent bio-graphical and autobiographical material regarding each of the writers listed, reports indicated that very few did their actual writing, or even their thinking about writing, while under the influence of alcohol. More-over, their writing was seldom successful when it was done under the in-fluence of alcohol and, at various points in their lives, drinking absolutely interfered with their capacity to do any creative work. F. Scott Fitzgerald, denying the newspaper reports about his drinking said, "As a matter of fact I have never written a line of any kind while I was under the glow of so much as a single cocktail" (LeVot, 1983, p. 117). Ring Lardner, in the more pithy style for which he was famous, said, "No one, ever, wrote anything as well after even one drink as he would have done without it" (Lardner, Jr., 1976, p. 165). In a serious reflective way, the poet Robert Lowell said, "Nothing was written drunk, at least nothing was perfected and finished," and added, "but I have looked forward to whatever one gets from drinking, a stirring and a blurring" (Hamilton, 1983, p. 389).

Lowell's afterthought is worthy of some note because it points to some nuances and complications about the relationship between drinking and the creative process. Other authors reputedly have actually used alcohol as the kind of stimulant to inspiration that Lowell indicated. Hemingway, at one point in his life, reportedly awakened regularly at four-thirty in the morning and started to write standing up, "with a pencil in one hand and a drink in the other" (Meyers, 1985, p. 426), and Fitzgerald also appar-ently used alcohol as a stimulant later in his life. Short story writer William Sydney Porter (O. Henry) wryly boasted, "Combining a little or-ange juice with a little scotch, the author drinks the health of all maga-zine editors, sharpens his pencil and begins to write. When the oranges are empty and the flask is dry, a saleable piece of fiction is ready for mail-ing" (Davis & Maurice, 1931, p. 361).

Such reports and public statements must be considered cautiously. Writers make statements and give reports such as these in order to add to what they think should be a writer's public image. This image factor, as I shall explain below, even plays a role in the motivation to drink in the first place. In reality, the picture is quite mixed in many ways. Al-though some may indeed use alcohol to stimulate inspiration or, more ac-curately, to reduce inhibition, by far the majority find it to be an interference. Even Malcolm Lowry, who wrote about alcoholism and drank himself to death, was directly observed to work in the following way: "Lowry drank in order to avoid writing, sobered up in order to write, then drank in order to avoid writing" (Day, 1973, p. 30). Thomas Wolfe, who also almost destroyed himself with drink, was similarly directly ob-served as follows: "If he was sick or mentally upset or having trouble with his work, he would often use liquor as a kind of cureall or escape" (Nowell, 1960, p. 109).

Overall, the pattern of alcohol use in all the writers studied was the same as for the ordinary alcohol abuser. By and large, they did not use alcohol while they were actually engaged in working and writing, but tended to drink when they were finished for the day. Early in the course of their illness, they only drank regularly during after-work or evening hours. As the volume of their alcohol consumption increased, they became increasingly uncomfortable, irritable, and anxious during periods of the day when they were not drinking, including times ordinarily set aside for work. Then, in order to sedate themselves, they began to drink during work-alloted hours. This pattern of drinking for sedation and relaxation, followed by jutteriness and anxiety when stopping and subsequently drinking again to produce sedation for those effects, is typical for any alcoholic ranging from the skid-row derelict to the closet drinker in the executive suite. One possible distinguishing feature for a writer—or for any artist—is that unlike other kinds of work activity, creative pursuits are often carried out in solitude. On the one hand, working alone may be a lonely affair, and on the other the artist is free to drink without interference or detection from others. This self-enforced loneliness and freedom may enhance the proclivity to drink.

Among the materials that I gathered, here is a fairly typical account given by John O'Hara to the columnist Earl Wilson about heavy drinking in relation to writing. It pertains to the creation of one of his most successful pieces, *Pal Joey*:

My wife and I were . . . living at . . . 93rd and 5th [New York City]. . . . I had an idea for a story. I said to my wife I'd go to Philadelphia. Hole up in the Hotel Ben Franklin a couple of days, lock myself in, eat on room service. Just work. . . . But the night before, we went out, and I got stiff. I got up next morning to start to the station, and I am dying. Now as we got to the Pierre, at 60th Street, I said to the cab, 'Stop here.' I went in. After a drink or two, I feel what-the-hell. Better take a nap. I check in. Then began a real beauty. Just getting stiff and passing out. I started Thursday. By Saturday morning I'd drunk myself sober. I picked up the phone and said, 'What time is it?'

The girl says, 'Quarter after seven.'

I asked her, 'A.M. or P.M.?' The girls said, 'A.M. and the day is Saturday.' They knew me there.

At that point remorse set in. I asked, 'What kind of a God-damned heel am I? I must be worse'n anybody in the world.' Then I figured, 'No, there must be somebody worse than me—but who?' Al Capone, maybe. Then I got it—maybe some nightclub masters of ceremonies I know. . . .

That was my idea. I went to work and wrote a piece about a nightclub heel in the form of a letter. I finished the piece by 11 o'clock. I went right home. . . .

The New Yorker bought the story the same day, ordered a dozen more, and then came the play and the movie.

That was the only good thing I ever got out of booze, but mind you, Wilson, I wasn't on a bender at the time I wrote. I was perfectly sober! Have you got that down in your notebook? (Bruccoli, 1977, pp. 181–182)

O'Hara describes the typical sequence of having to drink the next day after starting the previous night and then continuing into the time of work. Certainly he had been motivated to write a story early in this particular sequence but, except for inducing his guilt, one could not say that the alcohol intake itself facilitated the writing. O'Hara himself makes the point that he couldn't work while drinking. Even writers who have characteristically used small amounts of alcohol while working have eventually gotten into a pattern of drinking, then guilt, and then abstinence in order to write. William Faulkner could not drink at all when writing later in his life.

The O'Hara account also illustrates what might be considered a causative—perhaps it would be better to say instigating—factor in writes' and other artists' heavy use of alcohol. In many cultures, especially the modern American one, a certain tough guy or macho image is associated with heavy drinking and the so-called ability to "hold one's liquor." O'Hara's boasting manner to Wilson, along with a later comment by Wilson himself from this same account describing O'Hara as "a pretty good boy with the juice," illustrates such an image. It is not clear what has led to this macho image related to alcohol in this and other cultures, nor is it clear why writers and other artists might be attracted to it. An idea of achievement in the face of disability or bravery in the face of danger may be involved. For male writers and other artists, there may be a particular need to counter widespread cultural images of effeteness or effeminacy or, in some cases, to deny actual latent homosexual tendencies. Sociologist Room (1984) pointed out that many of the Nobel laureates who were alcohol abusers were born in the late 1880s and 1890s and were part of a rebellious "lost-generation" literary subculture of the time.

Particular ethnic cultural factors may also be involved. For example, many successful 20th-century writers in modern times have come from Irish backgrounds and there is a rather high incidence of alcoholism in that cultural group. Interestingly, drinking and masculinity are especially linked in Irish culture, a social factor some theorists have construed to be an overcompensation against the culturally enforced long period of Irish sons' dependence on their mothers. Several of the 20th-century writers on the earlier stipulated list have Irish backgrounds—John O'Hara, F. Scott Fitzgerald, Malcolm Lowry, Louise Bogan, James Agee, and other heavy drinkers such as James Joyce and Brendan Behan could be included as well. (There is, however, no simple way to connect Louise Bogan to the macho image.) These social explanations are only a small part of the picture; they do not adequately account for the individual factors in heavy alcohol use among so many highly creative people. Also they do not explain how alcohol hinders or facilitates the creative process. To clarify those matters and to depict some of the earlier mentioned variable effects of mental illness on the literary creative process and the role of homospatial and Janusian processes, I now focus on the research data I have collected in my work with the author John Cheever.

JOHN CHEEVER: CREATION OF A NOVEL

Cheever wrote more than 300 short stories and five novels. Known primarily as a modern master of the short story, he composed fantasies and satirical social commentaries about the people and life of modern suburbia. He won the National Book Award, the Pulitzer Prize, the Howells Medal, and the National Gold Medal, and was a member of the National Institute of Arts and Letters. Although he had been nominated for the Nobel Prize in literature several times, this award ultimately escaped him. Despite his reputation as a short story writer, his novel *Falconer* was recognized as outstanding and came close to earning him that highly coveted prize. He received the Pulitzer Prize for his collection of short stories the year after *Falconer* was published because, it is generally acknowledged, of that novel's boost to his reputation.

Born the son of a shoe salesman and the proprietress of a gift shop in Quincy, Massachusetts, Cheever always claimed to be a descendant of an illustrious and legendary New England schoolmaster—a claim that has recently been disputed (Donaldson, 1988). He had one sibling, an older brother, and very little formal education. Expelled from Thayer Academy, a preparatory school, because of poor grades, he never went on to college despite his wide and intense intellectual interests. His first literary success was a short story entitled "Expelled," which he publicly affirmed to be a thinly fictionalized account of his own prep-school experience. This was not, however, the case; the boy in the story was expelled for smoking infractions rather than poor academic performance.

The course of Cheever's writing career was quite erratic. Although hailed for his stories, and supported comfortably by the income from them, he sought for a more substantial literary reputation by the writing of novels. His first, *The Wapshot Chronicle*, was a wide success, and the second, *The Wapshot Scandal*, was less so. The third, *Bullet Park*, was not at all well received. During the period of his life in which he was writing these novels, Cheever used alcohol to great excess. He had numerous extra-marital affairs, and his marriage to Mary Winternitz was under constant strain. Although his diaries indicate that he also struggled with conscious homosexual impulses throughout this time and had occasional homosexual encounters, he did not engage openly in a homosexual affair until close to the end of his life. As for his alcoholism, he stopped drinking completely before writing, or more accurately, before completing his fourth novel, *Falconer*. My interviews with him took place during the year after *Falconer* was published and are directly pertinent to both his abstinence and his creative achievement.

Cheever struggled with alcoholism for most of his life. How he got started is not clear, but what is clear is that he was exposed to a good deal of drinking by his parents. That his father was an alcoholic and a work failure is fairly well known, but what is not generally known is that his mother also drank excessively despite her more responsible employment history. This is how Cheever described his mother's death to me:

> At the age of 82, it was discovered that she had diabetes and drank herself to death, quite obviously. I tried to stop her from it but she said, "No." She was fully intending to die, and to die as soon as possible, a very sensible girl. She would have had to have an amputation; she was quite put out by it. Absolutely pissed at finding out she had diabetes. The last thing she asked for was Old Crow, her dying words. . . . She absolutely loved bourbon; she called the grocer and ordered a case of bourbon whisky. Someone called me from Boston and said, "Your mother is drinking herself to death." So I immediately flew down and went to see her. And I said, "You're drinking yourself to death." And she said, "Yes." And I said, "You can't do this . . . you know life's a very splendid mystery, and it isn't in your power to take it." And she said, "You must go to church a great deal." And I said, "Yes." And she said, "High or low?" And I said, "Low." And she said, "Humph, the family was always high." They were practically her last words. . . . Her last request—I moistened her lips, although I was a little embarrassed, with a little bourbon.

Although it was somewhat difficult for me to know whether every part of this story was true, given the ironic pun on the word "high" (i.e., alcoholic "high" or "high" Episcopal and Cheever's tendency to tell stories with tongue in cheek), there seems little question that the substance regarding his mother's drinking was valid, and that alcohol therefore pervaded this author's family background. Although we have not yet come to understand all the factors—genetic, dynamic, and educational—connecting parental alcoholism to alcoholism in children, we can say with certainty that, in Cheever's case, his background did severely influence his own alcohol abuse. This alcohol abuse intermittently interfered with his work throughout his life until it threatened to kill him three years before our interviews.

In the 1960s, Cheever's reputation was at a very high level. He had been on the cover of *Time* magazine, had won the prestigious Howells Medal, and had a successful movie made from one of his stories. After publishing the unsuccessful *Bullet Park* in 1969, his writing output dwindled markedly, and he drank more and more heavily. Then, in 1973, he suffered a heart attack while mowing his lawn. Although he vowed never to drink after this heart attack and was told by his doctors that he would die if he did, he soon returned to his old patterns. He went to the University of Iowa Writers' Workshop for a semester and, together with his teaching activities and a number of heterosexual affairs, his drinking increased. Finally, in the autumn of 1974, he accepted an invitation to teach writing at Boston University. He had started the novel that was to become *Falconer*, but his experience in Boston at that point turned out to be, in his own words, "a dreadful mistake." He drank regularly and steadily, and finally required hospitalization to dry out.

From the hospital in Boston he was transferred to the Smithers Alcoholism Rehabilitation Unit of St. Luke's-Roosevelt Hospital in New York City. His experience in this unit led to his recovery from alcoholism and complete abstinence from then on. He described that experience to me in the following way:

Cheever:	I have no use for a psychiatrist who assumes he can cure drug addiction or alcoholism. It's truly ridiculous, I think, and it's totally irresponsible.
Rothenberg:	What made you stop [drinking]?
Cheever:	Self-confinement to an alcohol and drug rehabilitation place. Hospital room, beds—
Rothenberg:	How did they help you?
Cheever:	Made me chill out. They got me away from the bottle. Can't get out—confined for, oh, 33 days, something like that.
Rothenberg:	Oh, it's a cold turkey kind of thing?
Cheever:	Yeah, it was cold turkey. It was cold turkey in an A.A. branch and the A.A. was right at hand. You were lectured on the A.A...
Rothenberg:	Just 33 days and you never took anything again?
Cheever:	I still smoke. And if I have to give that up, and I may—if I have more trouble with the spot on my lung, I will go to them. They have a nicotine cure, you sign up for two weeks and here again they beat

you over the head with sticks and you cry a lot. . . .
Smithers . . . worked for me and a friend of mine, a
woman. . . .

It was originally to have been, I think, for sort of
upper-crusts, terribly, expensive. And Medicare or
Medicaid, of course, has opened it up for anybody
who claims to have an alcoholic problem and you
share a room about this big [indicates a small room]
with five other men, one bathroom. Some folks may
have hallucinations during the course of the incarceration, it's absolutely hell. But it seems to work.

This woman was very wealthy and you might say,
a spoiled woman. . . . Truman Capote is, as far as I
know, in there now at my insistence. And I think he's
been there two weeks, if he's alive. I haven't been in
touch with him since I've been on tour. . . .

The letters that I got were tremendously important in getting me through it. It's like the army, or
being in a far-away country. Mail, even though your
wife mails it over, is rally your only—

You can't telephone, there's a pay phone, but—

Through this experience, Cheever became a devoted member of Alcoholics Anonymous, attended their meetings regularly, and followed
their procedures. In addition to the constant support of the organization,
it appeared that, as a religious person throughout this life, he also benefited from their spiritual or religious focus.

What other reasons were there for the success of this treatment for
Cheever at this point in his life? He was 63 years old at the time, had by
then consulted numerous psychiatrists about his problem and, he told
me, had previously been very scornful of the Alcoholics Anonymous organization. When I asked him directly about his motivation to stop drinking at that particular point, he stated that he had had a heart attack and
knew he would die if he continued. Although this certainly may have
been a reason at some time, it was inadequate as a real explanation because the heart attack had occurred three years previously and, rather
than becoming abstinent, he had actually increased the use of alcohol following his serious brush with death. Confinement with its care and removal from availability of alcohol itself was surely a help, of course, but
without motivation, confinement alone would have had little effect. I
found that the real clue to his stopping and the events of that period of
his life came from other material in our sessions and pertained to factors
in his writing at the time.

The explanation pertains to the novel *Falconer*, the work Cheever completed during the year after he gave up drinking. This novel takes place in the fictional Falconer State Prison and concerns a university professor/drug addict named Farragut who is incarcerated after having murdered his brother. He is subjected to brutalizing treatment by the other inmates, and there is much elaboration of both loving and sadistic homosexual prison relationships. Deeply poignant and meaningful human strivings are also enacted. After having given up his drug addiction in the prison, Farragut escapes by substituting himself in the shroud of a dead cellmate. Totally evading all pursuers, he finds himself finally at an ordinary laundromat and nearby bus stop and, in that banal setting, he experiences a new sense of compassion and freedom. Clearly, it is a tale of resurrection and redemption.

Prior to the interview excerpt that I am about to quote, Cheever and I had been talking about Sing Sing—the prison that was near his home in Ossining—and some successful teaching experiences he had had with convicts there. Because *Falconer* was set in a prison, I asked the following question:

Rothenberg: The idea for that novel . . . was that a gradual development? Did you have a particular initial idea? Can you remember? Or was the going to Sing Sing part of thinking about the idea of such a novel?

Cheever: I had not set the novel in prison until—it's a brother conflict—I had written about the brother conflict, since the beginning. . . . Out of about, what, some 300 published stories . . . I think there must be 20 stories about brothers. Brothers or men generally run trough my whole work. This is simply another run-through of the scene. But this is the only one in which a murder takes place. In the other stories, one brother hits the other over the head as a rule—or strikes him in some way, or tries in some way to wound him. And very often unsuccessfully. This was the only time—and this was presumably a sum of the experience which is part of my life (as if fiction can bring order to experience). It was emotional in this way [pause]—I've always been close to my brother [Fred].

Rothenberg: Is your brother younger or older?

Cheever: He was seven years older than I. He died about this time last year.

Rothenberg:	He was an only brother?
Cheever:	He was an only brother, yes. We were very close. It was . . . probably, speaking structurally, the broadest and deepest love in my life.

Somewhat later, he answered my question here about the specific thought that instigated the novel, as follows:

"[It consisted of] a falcon, a bird of prey but confined within the—confined within the discipline of the Falconer."

And with respect to his creation of the main character in the novel, Farragut, he later also described the following mental conception:

"[I thought of myself as] . . . on board a sailboat, with which [I was] . . . very familiar, but . . . sailing towards a coat totally unknown, and the man beside [me was] . . . a total stranger in every way. But [my] . . . brother [was] . . . sitting [there too]."

The latter two conceptions for the novel, it should be noted, were instances of Janusian and homospatial processes, respectively. The first of these, the instigating idea for the novel regarding the falcon, was a conscious and rational positing of a simultaneous opposition. The falcon was conceived by Cheever as simultaneously predatory and confined, both as an aggressively uncontrolled creature and as aggressively controlled by a falconer, and that Janusian conception intsigated the writing of this novel about amrudering professor. The second series of deliberate thoughts describes the characterization of Farragut himself as emerging from a homospatial conception involving the mental image of a stranger sitting beside the author superimposed on an image of his brother.

With respect to the specific content of his commentary, his very first response to my question regarding the genesis of the novel had alluded directly to his brother Fred, and his brother had also been represented in the homospatial conception involved in the creation of the main character. Clearly, therefore, his feelings and thoughts about Fred were connected in an important way with the writing of *Falconer*. It is of further interest, then, that he returned in another interview to a discussion of his brother as follows:

Cheever:	It was the strongest love of my life, certainly the most rewarding. Very strong.
Rothenberg:	Did you do things together a lot?
Cheever:	Yes, I adored him. And then, when he went away to college, I didn't see him. He came back and left—I don't know what crossed his mind. I think he saw that I was in trouble; my parents weren't speaking to one another, and he managed to be everything for

Rothenberg: me. . . . When I was about 19, I realized how unnatural this love was and how poignant—
Rothenberg: Why do you call it unnatural?
Cheever: Um, because it was; it was quite unnatural. And—I
mean not homosexual, but we really had very little
at that point to give to one another.

At that juncture in the session, Cheever went on to tell me about how, during a period that they lived together in Boston, he and his brother would accompany each other on dates. On one occasion, there was a crisis when a girl wanted to spend time with the brother but Fred would not leave John's side. Irately, the girlfriend told John that he was ruining his brother's life. Then, Cheever told me with a flat tone in his voice, he decided to move out of the house the same night. He continued:

Cheever: She was really pissed off.
Rothenberg: Jealous?
Cheever: I'm very grateful to her, actually.
Rothenberg: Why?
Cheever: I think I would have left anyhow. Boston was easily
accommodated us as brothers, it's an eccentric soci-
ety. And we were the Cheever brothers; it would have
been dreadful as far as I was concerned.

Here, Cheever was directly indicating his mixed feelings about his brother; staying together, he said, would have been dreadful for him. What has this to do with the novel and with Cheever's alcoholism? It is difficult to pinpoint all of the connections, but consider what the author had to say when I asked him about his experiences with therapy. He had seen three different psychiatrists, none of whom had, he thought, helped him. I asked him why:

Cheever: It's rather hard to say. I don't think I was ever cooperative. My principal concern, as I say, was alcohol.
And they would say, 'Well, alcohol is simply symptomatic.' [However] . . . I was never able to get . . .
[name of psychiatrist], I was never able to get either
. . . [name of psychiatrist] or . . . [name of another
psychiatrist] to go into my brother in depth. I would
say, 'Look, you know, if there was any problem I
would like to discuss it would be my brother.' And
they would say, 'Well, we'll come to that.' And then

> I would say something polite like, 'You mean six thousand dollars later we will come to my brother?' And neither ... [name of psychiatrist] nor ... [name of other psychiatrist] were terribly interested. And I'd say, 'Well I love him dearly and I've missed him more painfully than I've missed anybody else in my life.' They'd say: 'Well, we'll go into that later. We'll mind that later.' Maybe there wasn't much to say, I don't know.

Rothenberg: You missed him; this is before he died?

Cheever: This love of my brother was mutual. He loved me also very much. We went to Europe together—uh—when I was 17, I think. And then he went to Europe when I was 18 and I was miserable. I was completely miserable without him. More miserable, I think, than I would have been, you know, with the removal of another person in my life.

Rothenberg: Did he marry and have a family of his own?

Cheever: Oh yes, he married, and unfortunately, he married an old girl of mine.

Regardless of whether the sessions with the psychiatrists were so extremely off the mark as Cheever described, it was clear that he himself felt that he had not been helped to work on a problem that was very important to him. Also, as his own sequence of comments indicates, he connected the problem with his brother directly to his alcoholism.

I attempt to present both the answer to the question about why this author stopped drinking at the time he did and the connections with his work, specifically with his creativity. With respect first to the writing, Cheever himself stated that he had written several stories about men or brothers, and they had seldom hurt each other seriously. With emphasis, he told me that never did a brother murder a brother. However, in *Bullet Park*, the novel he wrote before his most serious bout with alcoholism a brutal murder almost does take place. The character Paul Hammer attempts to murder the young son of a man with whom he is inextricably linked, Elliot Nailles. Not only are Hammer and Nailles linked together by name, but also by their identities which are inextricably intermingled in a manner reminiscent of Cheever's description of his relationship with his brother.

This novel was, as stated earlier, not well received by the public and the critics, and some observers have proposed that Cheever's ensuing deterioration resulted from that failure. He subsequently went to teach at

Boston University and there drank to enormous excess until he was totally unable to function and required hospitalization. Regarding this period, his daughter Susan, in her biography of her father, quoted him as saying that the suicide of fellow writer Ann Sexton had upset him terribly, and he could not go on (Cheever, 1984, p. 191). Sexton taught in the same program as Cheever, and they had been frequent companions up to the time of her death. Upsetting as her suicide must have been, very likely a more important difficulty of this period was that Cheever's brother Fred was also living in Boston at that time. While living in an apartment in the same city, he and his brother saw each other more than they had done for many, many years.

My explanation for these events in Cheever's life and work is this: The creative process, as I have described in detail previously, involves a gradual unearthing of unconscious processes (Rothenberg, 1979b, p. 35 ff). Writers, as well as other creative people, use both the Janusian and homospatial processes as a means of attaining partial insight into their own unconscious contents. To summarize the means by which this comes about: Both of these processes operate as templates that reverse the disguising operations of primary process cognition. This type of cognition uses the particular mechanisms of condensation, displacement, equivalence of opposites, and others in order to allow disguised discharge of unconscious material. Because Janusian and homospatial processes are conscious, and because they bear a superficial *formal* resemblance to the disguising mechanisms of primary process cognition, they serve to reverse and undo the disguise progressively as they are used. They thereby bring unconscious material partially into consciousness and produce partial insight. It is important to emphasize that this is not an eruption of unconscious material into consciousness nor a regression in the service of the ego as described by Kris (1952). A burst of unconscious material does not initiate the creative process, but the unconscious is gradually unearthed in part during the progression. The creative person embarks on an activity leading to discovering and knowing himself or herself in a very fundamental way. This was seen in Cheever's case, as I clarify further, with the initial homospatial and Janusian conceptions pertaining to his brother and to killing bird of prey in writing the novel, *Falconer*.

Such an unearthing process is fraught with a good deal of anxiety as it unfolds. Also, anxiety and strain arise from carrying out very high-level performance and the especially demanding work of creative accomplishment. There is conscious cognitive strain in the use of unusual logic-defying Janusian and homospatial processes. Such leaps of thought are often mentally difficult to experience and employ.

The gradual unearthing of unconscious processes and the progression toward insight are invariably tenuous and may go awry. Because they occur without any real support or help from another person, the un-earthing and progression may both fall far short of the goal. Not con-sciously, or in actuality, a form of therapy, only partial rather than full insight ever occurs. Even when such a process of inner self-discovery is pursued in the collaborative circumstance of therapy, it may all too easily be diverted or go aground.

It appears that Cheever did go aground on his own in the writing of *Bullet Park*. Intermixed with love for his brother was intense antagonism, jealousy, hostility, and unconscious murderous feelings and, in the writ-ing of that novel, he had come closer than ever before to full unearthing of the latter. Rather than a murder of a brother—or a brotherlike fig-ure—however, he depicted the attempted murder of the symbolic brother's young son. It is likely, therefore, that at that point he ap-proached recognition of his hidden homicidal emotions toward his brother but could not actually acknowledge them to himself.

The descent into alcoholism during the period in Boston, then, seems to be primarily connected to the close association with his brother and the intensification of his guilt over his constant but unacknowledged hos-tile and murderous feelings. With his recovery, there is distinct evidence of some acknowledgement and acceptance of these feelings. It is difficult to determine whether Cheever achieved insight regarding these impulses and wishes directly from improved creative functioning following his ab-stinence, whether he achieved it in some other way and then both absti-nence and creativity followed, or whether some other sequence was involved. It is clear, however, that his conflict about his feelings toward Fred both intensified his alcoholism and blocked his creativity.

The important facts supporting this conclusion are that Cheever was able to return to work on *Falconer* after he left the Smithers Alcohol Re-habilitation Unit and that the novel itself portrays an intellectual man who kills his brother. At the beginning of the novel, Farragut has been sentenced to prison because of fratricide. That this plot idea, derived from the Janusian falcon conception, represented Cheever's own wish and fantasied punishment was dramatically suggested by the following comments to me about a visit his brother made to Cheever after he had completed *Falconer*. "He [Fred] was ... 70. ... He hurt his hip in a mo-torcycle spill and went into the hospital for an operation and was dis-charged as having too weak a heart for the operation. He immediate came here [to see me] and said, 'I think you ought to know that while I was in the hospital I had delirium tremens—this is withdrawal from two glasses of sherry." And I said, 'Thank you very much for telling me.' And I had completed *Falconer* and I said, 'Oh, I killed you in the book.' And he said, 'Oh, did you? Oh, good.' "

At another time Cheever told me that, when two-thirds through the novel, he developed the idea that Farragut was going to get out of prison successfully. This was early spring, he said, and he actually ran out of his house shouting, "He's out, he's out. He's going to get out". Thus, the events in the novel seemed to recapitulate or represent the dynamics of this author's own psychological struggle. Set in a prison, the novel contained a representation both of the site of his recent teaching successes and of his own confinement at Smithers. In describing to me the experience at Smithers he had explicitly called it an incarceration and indicated that, in all respects, it was like being in a prison. Feeling punished as well as cared for, his guilt about his hostile wishes began to be absolved just as the homospatially conceived brother and self leading character (a substance abuser) in the novel experienced punishment and the beginning of absolution for the actual crime of fratricide. The ensuing story of incarceration, eventual freedom, and redemption of this character, then, was driven by Cheever's own struggle with guilt over his murderous wishes for his brother. His running out of his house shouting about the escape and redemption of Farragut was, it seems, in part a manifestation—temporary or permanent—of his own personal relief and sense of redemption from culpability.

A final example of Cheever's use of the Janusian process illustrates the working of the overall uncovering and discovery process. Speaking to me of the Greek myth regarding the satyr Marsyas and the god Apollo, Cheever described the following thoughts during the creation of the novel:

> Marsays sang beautifully, or wrote beautiful poetry. And at one point, he thought himself better than Apollo. Do you know this myth? He was put to death by having his skin removed in very small pieces until he was still alive but quite without flesh. . . . I've been fascinated by [this story] and in *Falconer* [I conceived] . . . a scene where the Cardinal takes an escaped criminal into Saks Fifth Avenue and buys him a suit rather than turn him in. You give the beggar the skin . . . the skin [is] the same device as clothes.

[Note: In the novel the Cardinal and his choir had visited Falconer prison to give prisoners their diplomas for having religious instruction. One convict had escaped by masquerading as one of the Cardinal's choir members. When he was discovered, the Cardinal protected him as Cheever described it.]

In this complicated Janusian formulation, Cheever simultaneously conceived the lowly satyr having his skin *removed* by the god Apollo and the downtrodden escaped prisoner having his clothes (figurative skin) *put on* by the religious figure, the Cardinal. This consciously formulated simultaneous opposition generated a portion of the novel and, on an unconscious level, it very likely represented Cheever's self-inflicted punishment—the tearing away of his own skin or figurative covering and exposing his murderous hostility to his brother in the novel—and the hoped-for redemption of being given new clothes (skin) by a religious authority figure. Both of these types of feelings, the hostility and the redemption from guilt, became more conscious for the author as he proceeded with the literary creative process.

Cheever's creative and alcoholic course was therefore as follows: In his writings, he had returned again and again to the theme of hostility to a brother, and his struggle to unearth and deal with his own unacceptable feelings was one of the dynamics that gave power to his work. When finally hostility and homicidal feelings toward his brother came close to the surface and threatened to overwhelm him, as they did with the writing of *Bullet Park* and assumedly also with other events in his life, he turned increasingly to alcohol for sedation and relief. This produced a typical alcoholic vicious cycle in which the physical and psychological effects of using the drug required continuation and increasing amounts to produce desired sedation effects. Finally, he went into a treatment program that helped him to stop drinking and also to continue the threatening confrontation with his feelings toward his brother in the writing of *Falconer*. The triumphant, more healthy struggle involved in the creative process with the continuing use of homospatial and Janusian processes produced a successful work of art.

CHEEVER, ALCOHOLISM, AND WRITING

The use of alcohol in this account of Cheever's struggle appears to be broadly representative. Most writers do not actually suffer from the same degree of alcohol dependence and abuse as Cheever, but that is a separate matter that I clarify later. What does seem to be an important issue, and one that applies to several writes, is the need to use alcohol to cope with the anxiety that is generated by the creative process itself. Because the creative process, when it is successful, involves the use of homospatial and Janusian processes and the creative person's unearthing some unconscious material, there is always a measure of anxiety. Depending on a writer's stability and proclivities, he or she may cope with such threatening discomfort in various ways. It has long been widely and reliably known that writers and other artists are highly irritable during intense periods of work or for sometime afterward. Some writers become depressed, some engage in flamboyant and eccentric behavior, some engage in philandering, some use the other relaxing outlets that the rest of us do, and some drink. Drinking alcohol has a gratifying sedative effect, and given the social reasons that have made it acceptable among writers and other creative people, it may even have become the mode of choice for writers particularly to deal with the anxiety generated by the creative process.

This is not to say that alcohol use and dependence are the inevitable penalties for creative life. Most creative people are like the majority of the population who use alcohol in moderation. In each case the development of alcoholism depends on personality and personal background. In Cheever's instance, I do not possess detailed data about the critical factors entering into his illness. That both parents were alcoholics and had a difficult marriage in which they involved Cheever as well as Cheever's intensely ambivalent relationship with his brother (and very likely, his father) were all probable causative factors. In cases in which both parents are alcoholics, identification and the need to repeat traumatic experiences of childhood, as well a simple availability and acceptance of alcohol in the house, have effects as important as any postulated genetic factors. Also, Cheever distinctly had a great deal of lifelong conflict about his bisexuality. Such conflicts incorporating problems about homosexuality, passivity, and dependency often have causative effects in alcoholism. These are, however, general factors that may or may not relate directly to his creative work.

Factors that do seem to connect Cheever's alcoholism with his writing have some general applicability to alcoholism in other creative people. Living with parents who were frequently in a withdrawn, inebriated state, Cheever as a child felt helpless and unable to communicate with them. His turning to writing seemed to serve as a way to bring order into a chaotic, disorganized experience and, in a sense, as a way to get his parents to hear him. The writing may also have become a means of compensating for his own feelings of weakness and loss. His first short-story success turned his expulsion from Thayer Academy for poor grades and failure into an arbitrary expulsion by mindless authorities for smoking a cigarette.

Cheever was loved and preferred by his mother. Although his father was weak and ineffective, Cheever seemed to have nevertheless identified with him in adopting his more severe alcoholism. This identification with the father very likely served as a way of being closer to his mother, a woman who was attracted both to an alcoholic person and to the alcohol drug itself. As observed clinically and in Alcoholics Anonymous, people who become alcoholic over and over again adopt the patterns of someone loved by their own specially beloved parent, whether it be that parent's own alcoholic father, mother, lover, or spouse. Although the psychodynamics are detailed here for the case of alcoholism in writers, factors of helplessness and inability to communicate with parents, competition and acquiescence with a same-sex parent, and other general matters stipulated very likely also apply to alcoholism in creative visual artists, scientists, and others. Alcoholism is not, however, the handmaiden of creative life. Mental health increases the creative person's capacity to use Janusian and homospatial processes and to cope with the anxieties generated by the creative process. Maintaining and improving mental health are critical facilitators of creativity.

REFERENCES

Bruccoli, M. J. (1977). *An artist is his own fault. John O'Hara on writers and writing.* Carbondale, IL: Southern Illinois University Press.

Cheever, S. (1984). *Home before dark.* Boston: Houghton Mifflin.

Davis, R. H., & Maurice, A. B. (1931). *The caliph of Baghdad: Being Arabian nights flashes of the life, letters and work of O. Henry.* New York: D. Appleton.

Day, D. (1973). *Malcolm Lowry: A biography.* New York: Oxford University Press.

Donaldson, S. (1988). *John Cheever: A biography.* New York: Random House.

Grinstein, A. (1983). *Freud's rules of dream interpretation.* New York: International Universities Press.

Hamilton, I. (1983). *Robert Lowell: A biography.* New York: Random House.

Holland, L. A. (1961). *Janus and the bridge.* Rome: American Academy.

Koski-Jännes, A. (1983a). Juoda ja/Vai Luoda? (To drink and/or to create). *Alkoholipolitiikka, 48,* 68–78.

Koski-Jännes, A. (1983b). Alcohol and literary creativity: Finnish experience. *Alkohloipolitiikka, 38,* 263–274.

Kris, E. (1952). *Psychoanalytic studies of art.* New York: International Universities Press.

Lang, A. R., Verret, L., & Watt, C. (1984). Drinking and creativity: Objective and subjective effects. *Addictive Behaviors, 9,* 395–399.

Lardner, R., Jr. (1976). *The Lardners: My family remembered.* New York: Harper and Row.

LeVot, A. (1983). *F. Scott Fitzgerald: A biography.* Garden City, NY: Doubleday.

Meyers, J. (1985). *Hemingway: A biography.* New York: Harper and Row.

Nowell, E. (1960). *Thomas Wolfe: A biography.* Garden City, NY: Doubleday.

Pyle, E. B. (1982). Fuller Albright's inimitable style. *Harvard Medical Alumni Bulletin, 56,* 46–51.

Roe, A. (1946). Alcohol and creative work. *Quarterly Journal of Studies on Alcohol, 6,* 415–467.

Room, R. (1984). "A reverence for strong drink": The lost generation and the elevation of alcohol in the American culture. *Journal of Studies on Alcohol, 45,* 540–546.

Rothenberg, A. (1969). The iceman changeth: Toward an empirical approach to creativity. Journal of the American Psychoanalytic Association, 17, 549–607.

Rothenberg, A. (1971). The process of Janusian thinking in creativity. *Archives of General Psychiatry, 24,* 195–205.

Rothenberg, A. (1971). Poetic process and psychotherapy. *Psychiatry, 3,* 238–254.

Rothenberg, A. (1973a). Word association and creativity. *Psychological Reports, 33,* 3–12.

Rothenberg, A. (1973b). Opposite responding as a measure of creativity. *Psychological Reports, 33,* 15–18.

Rothenberg, A. (1978–1979). Translogical secondary process cognition in creativity. *Journal of Altered States of Consciousness, 4,* 171–187.

Rothenberg, A. (1979a). Homospatial thinking in creativity. *Archives of General Psychiatry, 33,* 17–26.

Rothenberg, A. (1979b). *The emerging goddess: The creative process in art, science and other fields.* Chicago: University of Chicago Press.

Rothenberg, A. (1983a). Psychopathology and creative cognition. A comparison of hospitalized patients, Nobel laureates, and controls. *Archives of General Psychiatry, 40,* 937–942.

Rothenberg, A. (1983b). Janusian process and scientific creativity: The case of Niels Bohr. *Contemporary Psychoanalysis, 19,* 101–119.

Rothenberg, A. (1986). Artistic creation as stimulated by superimposed versus combined-composite visual images. *Journal of Personality and Social Psychology, 50,* 370–381.

Rothenberg, A. (1987). Einstein, Bohr and creative thinking in science. *History of Science, 25,* 147–166.

Rothenberg, A. (1988a). *The creative process of psychotherapy.* New York: W. W. Norton.

Rothenberg, A. (1988b). Creativity and the homospatial process: Experimental studies. *Psychiatric Clinics of North America, 11,* 443–459.

Rothenberg, A., & Sobel, R. S. (1980). Creation of literary metaphors as stimulated by superimposed versus separated visual images. *Journal of Mental Imagery, 4,* 77–91.

Rothenberg, A., & Sobel, R. S. (1981). Effects of shortened exposure time on the creation of literary metaphors as stimulated by superimposed versus separated visual images. *Perceptual and Motor Skills, 53,* 1007–1009.

Sobel, R. S., & Rothenberg, A. (1980). Artistic creation as stimulated by superimposed versus separated visual images. *Journal of Personality and Social Psychology, 39,* 953–961.

PART II

EVERYDAY CREATORS: PSYCHOLOGICAL PROBLEMS AND CREATIVITY

Part II

Introduction

Here are the creators we all know so well—they're everywhere around us. Indeed, they *are* us. Everyday creativity is the originality of everyday life, the doing of something new in the course of one's activity at work or at leisure. One person does gourmet cooking, another does accomplished journal keeping, another a superb job of child rearing, another the management of a complex office, another many ingeneous home and automobile repairs. In every case, the activity involves innovative elements which are also meaningful to others—two common criteria for creativity.

Would we expect this everyday type of creativity to bear the same relationship to mood disorders? To adversity or disruption? This group is fundamentally different than the eminent and exceptional few who receive general acclaim, and hence the question is a different question. If most people who were writers had brown eyes, we wouldn't expect all people with brown eyes to be writers. Even if *all* eminent creators had a mood disorder (in this tiny percentage of all people with mood disorders) we wouldn't expect all people with mood disorders to be creative, and would certainly not expect them to be eminent. If we want to answer the question of everyday creativity and mood disorders, we've still got a long way to go.

The present selections prominently raise the questions of *state* versus *trait* effects. Even if everyday creators are often depressed (if they are!), it still doesn't mean they are more creative *when* depressed. Eisenman's study of psychotic inpatients doesn't convince us that severe or chronic psychosis is the magic key. Several studies, including Eysenck's, Schuldberg's, and that of Richards, Kinney, Benet, Merzel and Lunde, speak more to *intermediate* mood states, and what Richards et al. termed the "inverted-U" hypothesis.

Notably this latter study was the first research on broad-based real-life everyday creativity in a general population. To this end, and over a number of years, the researchers developed and validated The Lifetime Creativity Scales. Indeed, if originality can come out anywhere, the researcher must always be waiting at the door it chooses to use when it uses it. Fashion, teaching, singing, basketball, social activism. Whatever it may be. The creativity may not come out anywhere else and the true relationship with mood disorders will be diluted by the omission. Here is where we may worry more about *false negatives* than *false positives*. What is the creativity that was missed?

The importance of *hypomania* or a mild state of mood elevation, is found in the papers of Schuldberg and Richards et al., and this fits as well with the findings of Andreasen, and of Jamison's findings with eminent creators. Furthermore, Eysenck concludes that an intermediate state of his "psychoticism" dimension is important. We may ask if Eysenck's findings also reflect an elevation of *mood,* and/or the subtle forms of unusual *thought* reported here as well by Schuldberg, and/or reflect something else. Eysenck, elsewhere, suggests that "overinclusion" is key, and in fact, in 1974, Andreasen and colleagues showed similarities in overinclusion between manics (but not schizophrenics) and creative writers. Richards addresses this and other points above in this volume's conclusion.

It does appear, especially with eminent creativity in the arts, that eminent creativity is related to psychopathology. Everyday creativity may be somewhat more tied to health and more subtle manifestations of mental states. This is underlined by findings of Richards et al. that the psychiatrically *normal* relatives of bipolars also have a creative advantage, by Schuldberg's findings with normal college students, and by Eysenck's results with general research subjects. In Richards et al.'s work, the creative advantage was not shared by normal control subjects who did not have a bipolar family history. Hence, we have a more subtle phenomenon going on here. We may wonder again about groups such as Ludwig's creative scientists, who do not show major psychopathology. We are also put on alert to think hard before we call something a psychiatric *disorder.* Where creativity is concerned *abnormal* does not necessarily mean *pathological.*

5

Creativity, Preference for Complexity, and Physical and Mental Illness*

Russell Eisenman

What is the relationship between creativity on the one hand and physical and mental health on the other? This chapter reports two studies, both having to do with creativity, and both involving preference for complexity as an indicator of creativity. One study was on creativity and mental illness, and also involved ratings of stories written by psychotics. The other study, on creativity and physical health, relied on the preference for complexity measure. Preference for complexity has been shown to be a good indicator of creativity (Barron, 1963) and the specific measures utilized here have been found to indicate that schizophrenics may be less creative than nonschizophrenics (Eisenman, 1965). For mental illness, it may be that highly creative people are sometimes helped in their creativity by mental illness, but noncreative people may be hindered by such a disorder. Following this line of thinking, physical illness, though less obvious in its effects, might tend to reduce creativity in the average person by creating stress that makes the person focus on his or her negative feelings and not produce anything of an imaginative or original nature.

*From "Creativity, Preference for Complexity, and Physical and Mental Illness," by R. Eisenman, 1990, *Creativity Research Journal*, 3(3), pp. 231–236. Copyright © 1995 Ablex Publishing Corporation. Adapted with permission.

STUDY 1

There is currently a strong belief in a positive link between creativity and mental illness (Flach, 1990; Schuldberg, 1990). However, a look at what makes up mental illness (American Psychiatric Association, 1987) reveals a host of characteristics that would seem to reduce creativity. For example, thinking disorder, inappropriate emotions, and anxiety would make creativity unlikely. Schizophrenics are unable to screen out and assimilate percepts effectively (McReynolds, 1960) and may have a brain disorder (Levin, Yurgelun-Todd, & Craft, 1989). Thus, a variety of deficits are associated with being schizophrenic, which is one kind of psychosis (Harrow & Quinlan, 1986; Robey, Cohen, & Gara, 1989). These views are consistent with previous investigations of schizophrenics that show them to resist racial integration in a state mental hospital (Eisenman & Coyle, 1965) and to prefer simple polygons, which are the kinds of shapes preferred by noncreative people (Eisenman, 1965, 1966). If inability to screen out perceptions leads to a high arousal level, this too could impair creativity (Martindale, 1981).

The purpose of the present study was to confirm that schizophrenics prefer simple shapes, and to see if the same holds true of other psychotics (manic-depressives and psychotic depressives). Also, an additional creativity measure was used, namely, stories written by the patients that were rated for creativity. This additional measure, if consistent with the preference for complexity–simplicity measure, would further strengthen the view that creativity is related to mental health.

RESEARCH DESIGN

The subjects were 37 hospitalized patients diagnosed as schizophrenic, manic-depressive (bipolar disorder), or psychotic depressive. All were committed to a state mental hospital. A control group consisted of 37 hospital employees: attendants, cooks, housekeeping staff, and part-time employees. An attempt was made to select a control group that would be similar in social-class background to the psychotics, most of whom were from lower or lower middle-class backgrounds. The mean age of the patients was 37.5 years, and the mean age of the hospital staff control group was 35.8 years. Fifteen patients and 15 employees were female.

Measures and Procedure

For the first creativity measure, all subjects were shown 12 cards, each card containing the photograph of a polygon. Three of the 12 polygons were symmetrical shapes of 4, 8, or 10 points, taken from Birkhoff (1933). The other nine polygons were asymmetrical shapes with three each having 4, 12, or 24 points. They were previously used by Vanderplas and Garvin (1959) and had originally been constructed by randomly connecting points on a 100 × 100 grid (Attneave & Arnoult, 1956). Subjects chose their three most preferred polygons.

For the second creativity measure, all subjects were instructed to write three imaginative stories. Imagination was briefly explained and questions answered. The stories were scored for creativity by two professionals with experience in creativity research. The stories were rated on 1–7 scales both for originality and for usefulness, and scorers were allowed to further consider the overall creativity or noncreativity of the story in their final overall global rating of creativity. There was 85% agreement between the two scorers on their final creativity ratings, and differences were resolved by further discussion.

RESULTS

There were no differences among the different diagnostic categories and no sex differences, so the data were pooled. The mean number of points preferred by the psychotics on the polygons was 15.1, and the mean number of points preferred by the hospital employees was 20.5 ($t(72) = 3.84$, $p < .001$). For the stories, 5 of the 37 in the patient sample were judged creative, and 28 of the 37 were judged creative in the employee sample. This is significant beyond the .01 level with Fisher's Exact Test, as obtained by extrapolating from the tables in Siegel (1956). Ratings from the stories and complexity scores were significantly correlated ($r = .55$, $p < .05$).

DISCUSSION

The findings did nothing for the view that mental illness is associated with creativity. Schizophrenic, manic-depressive, and psychotic depressive patients scored less creatively than the control group on both measures. Although it could be argued that their mental disorders make story telling a difficult task, the preference for shapes is a nonverbal task, and they scored low (noncreatively) there as well.

Compared to previous samples (Eisenman, 1965, 1966; Eisenman & Coyle, 1965), the polygon scores of both the patients and the employees were in the direction of preference for simplicity. Thus, from the polygon data, one might conclude that both samples were relatively noncreative.

How then did the raters find that a majority of the control group wrote creative stories? Because care was taken so that the raters would not know whether the stories came from psychotic or control-group samples, experimenter bias would not seem applicable. It is, however, possible that psychotics revealed themselves in some fashion by their writing. What is perhaps more likely is that the raters, even though experienced, felt obligated to rate a reasonable percentage of the stories as creative. According to this explanation, the stories from the hospital employees may have been clearly better than those from the patients, but perhaps not truly creative.

In any event, the results are consistent with previous findings (Eisenman, 1965, 1966) in which samples of schizophrenics were found to prefer simple polygons, suggesting low creativity. Perhaps there is some connection between mental illness and creativity in normal, highly creative subjects (Flach, 1988). But the current study and those of Eisenman (1965, 1966) suggest that serious mental illness is associated with low creativity.

STUDY 2

The findings of Study 1 suggest a negative relationship between creativity and mental illness. Would physical illness also have a negative effect on creativity? Stress can be harmful to the person and make it difficult to cope (Christian, 1963; Holmes & Rahe, 1967; Martindale, 1981; Selye, 1956). On the other hand, people often show remarkable strength in the face of diversity (Affleck, Tennen, Croog, & Levine, 1987; Scheier & Carver, 1985, 1987; Silver, Boon, & Stones, 1983; Taylor, 1983). Thus, it is not clear how one would react to physical illness.

In the present investigation, three kinds of physical illness were investigated: influenza, diabetes, and herpes. All are serious illnesses, but influenza is relatively temporary. In addition, herpes is a genital disease and in our society has the negative consequences associated with having a sexual disease. Diabetes is a blood-sugar disorder, with the most negative consequences of the three. The question was, "Would creativity increase, decrease, or remain the same after being diagnosed as having one of the three above-mentioned illnesses?"

RESEARCH DESIGN

The subjects were patients in a large health maintenance organization in an urban setting. They had previously been part of a larger sample tested for creativity. With their consent and that of their doctors they were requested to retake the creativity test when they were diagnosed with a new illness. This possibility of being retested on creativity had not been mentioned when they were first tested for creativity, as it was not originally intended. The present sample included all those who agreed to be tested: 20 subjects with diabetes, 20 subjects with herpes, and 40 with influenza. Those who refused to participate in the follow-up measurement of creativity included four subjects diagnosed as having diabetes, six diagnosed as having herpes, and four diagnosed as having influenza.

Measure and Procedure

As a measure of creativity, subjects were shown a photograph of 12 polygons differing in complexity–simplicity, as defined by the number of points or turns. Subjects took the initial measure aimed at assessing creativity and then took the follow-up measure after being diagnosed. The time between these testings varied greatly, depending on whether a new illness was diagnosed (the range was three months to two years). The follow-up testing took place within two weeks of the diagnosis of the physical illness. At each assessment, subjects chose their three most preferred polygons.

RESULTS

Data from males and females have been combined, as their numbers were nearly equal and no significant sex differences were found on any variables.

For subjects with diabetes or herpes, there was no significant change in creativity scores, as measured by complexity–simplicity preference. In both instances, 10 subjects increased their complexity score on the second testing and 10 decreased. Almost all the changes were minor variations from their original choices, the range being from an increase of 12 points to a decrease of 18 points. However, among the influenza subjects, 30 of the 40 subjects decreased in complexity preference, preferring simpler polygons once their influenza had been diagnosed. Ten increased in complexity preference. The 30-out-of-40 result yielded a χ^2 of 10 ($df = 1$, $p < .01$). Thus, influenza subjects significantly decreased in creativity. Many of the changes, especially the decreases, were of a major magnitude. The range of the decreases was from 10 to 40 polygon points.

DISCUSSION

It is not surprising that experiencing an illness such as influenza would cause a person to show a decrease in many abilities, including creativity. Perhaps a person plagued by uncomfortable feelings strives for the simplest possible environment, perceptions, experiences, and so on. However, this explanation would be stronger if corresponding decreases were found for the herpes and diabetes sample. Perhaps the smaller number of the subjects in these samples made significant results less likely. Or perhaps influenza, although running its course eventually, is a more debilitating illness, at least physically, in its initial onset than herpes or diabetes. Herpes symptoms can range from mildly painful blisters to very painful blisters and fever. Thus, some herpes sufferers might not be in great physical pain at the time of the diagnosis. The same could be true for the diabetics. Still, some people cope with illness better than others, and different coping styles are used at different times and by different people (Gannon & Paride, 1989; Miller, Brody, & Summerton, 1988). Thus, it is often difficult to say what effects a disorder will have on a person's ability to function.

The results of the two studies suggest that creativity can be decreased by mental illness (Study 1) or by a physical illness (Study 2). There may, of course, be instances in which a mental or physical illness somehow aids in the development of creativity, but we should certainly not automatically assume that creativity and illness are always positively related. The two studies reported in this article showed a negative relationship between creativity on the one hand and mental or physical illness on the other.

REFERENCES

Afflect, G., Tennen, H., Croog, S., & Levine, S. (1987). Causal attribution, perceived benefits and morbidity following a heart attack: An eight-year study. *Journal of Consulting and Clinical Psychology, 55,* 29–35.

American Psychiatric Association. (1987). *Diagnostic and statistical manual of mental disorders* (3rd ed., rev.). Washington, DC: Author.

Attneave, F., & Arnoult, M. D. (1956). Methodological considerations in the quantitative study of shape and pattern in perception. *Psychological Bulletin, 53,* 452–471.

Barron, F. (1963). *Creativity and psychological health.* Princeton, NJ: Van Nostrand.

Birkhoff, G. D. (1933). *Aesthetic measure.* Cambridge, MA: Harvard University Press.

Christian, J. (1963). The pathology of over-population. *Military Psychologist, 128,* 571–603.

Eisenman, R. (1965). Aesthetic preferences of schizophrenics. *Perceptual and Motor Skills, 20,* 601–604.

Eisenman, R. (1966). The effect of disapproval on aesthetic preferences of schizophrenics. *Journal of General Psychology, 75,* 315–318.

Eisenman, R., & Coyle, F. A., Jr. (1965). Reaction to racial integration as a function of certain actuarial variables in hospitalized southern mental patients. *Journal of Psychology, 61,* 289–293.

Flach, F. (Ed.). (1988). *The creative mind.* Buffalo, NY: Bearly Limited.

Flach, F. (1990). Disorders of the pathways involved in the creative process. *Creativity Research Journal, 3,* 158–165.

Gannon, L., & Pardie, L. (1989). The importance of chronicity and controllability of stress in the context of stress-illness relationships. *Journal of Behavioral Medicine, 12,* 357–372.

Harrow, M., & Quinlan, D. M. (1985). *Disordered thinking and schizophrenic psychopathology.* New York: Gardner.

Holmes, T. H., & Rahe, R. H. (1967). The social readjustment rating scale. *Journal of Psychosomatic Research, 11,* 213–218.

Levin, S., Yurgelun-Todd, D., & Craft, S. (1989). Contributions of clinical neuropsychology to the study of schizophrenia. *Journal of Abnormal Psychology, 98,* 341–356.

Martindale, C. (1981). *Cognition and consciousness.* Homewood, IL: Dorsey.

McReynolds, P. (1960). anxiety, perception and schizophrenia. In D. D. Jackson (Ed.), *The etiology of schizophrenia* (pp. 248–292). New York: Basic Books.

Miller, S. M., Brody, D. S., & Summerton, J. (1988). Styles of coping with threat: Implications for health. *Journal of Personality and Social Psychology, 54,* 142–148.

Robey, K. L., Cohen, B. D., & Gara, M. A. (1989). Self-structure in schizophrenia. *Journal of Abnormal Psychology, 98,* 436–442.

Scheier, M. F., & Carver, C. S. (1985). Optimism, coping and health: Assessment and implications of generalized outcome expectancies. *Health Psychology, 4,* 219–247.

Scheier, M. F., & Carver, C. S. (1987). Disposition optimism and physical well-being: The influence of generalized outcome expectancies. *Journal of Personality, 55,* 169–210.

Schuldberg, D. (1990). Schizotypal and hypomanic traits, creativity, and psychological health. *Creativity Research Journal, 13,* 219–232.

Selye, H. (1956). *The stress of life.* New York: McGraw-Hill.

Siegel, S. (1956). *Nonparametric statistics for the behavioral sciences.* New York: McGraw-Hill.

Silver, R., Boon, C., & Stones, M. (1983). Searching for meaning in misfortune: Making sense of incest. *Journal of Social Issues, 39,* 81–102.

Taylor, S. E. (1983). Adjustment to threatening events: A theory of cognitive adaptation. *American Psychologist, 38,* 1161–1173.

Vanderplas, J. M., & Garvin, E. A. (1959). The association value of random shapes. *Journal of Experimental Psychology, 57,* 147–154.

6

Creativity and Personality: Word Association, Origence, and Psychoticism*

Hans J. Eysenck†

Eysenck (1983, 1989, 1993) suggested that the personality trait of *psychoticism* (Eysenck & Eysenck, 1976; Eysenck, 1992) underlies creativity, as measured by the usual tests (e.g., divergent thinking, unusual word associations, Barron–Welsh Art Scale "origence" responses). There is good evidence that both the Word Association Test and the Barron–Welsh Scale measure creativity, as shown in real-world achievement. With respect to the Word Association Test, the work of MacKinnon (1962a, 1962b) and Gough (1976) may be mentioned. The Barron–Welsh Scale also has been subjected to similar validity tests (Barron, 1953; Gough, 1994; Welsh, 1975). Correlations with such a criterion as rated originality in architects is about .50 for both measures; oddly enough, although both tests were

---

*From "Creativity and Personality: Word Association, Origence, and Psychoticism," by H. J. Eysenck, 1994, *Creativity Research Journal*, 7(2), pp. 209–216. Copyright © 1995 Ablex Publishing Corporation. Adapted with permission.

†I am indebted to P. Barrett for assistance with the analysis of the data.

used on the same population, the actual correlation between them, or the multiple *R* with rated originality, has never been published.

Psychotism is a dispositional trait variable that renders a person psychosis-prone; it is *not* synonymous with psychosis. There is good evidence that highly creative people are high on psychopathology but not actually psychotic (at least not at the time when they perform successfully). The evidence presented by Andreasen and Canter (1974), Jamison (1993), Prenky (1980), Richards (1981), Schuldberg (1990), and many others supports such a view, as does the early work of MacKinnon (1962a, 1962b, 1965, 1978). Psychoticism, as represented by the P scale of the Eysenck Personality Questionnaire (Eysenck & Eysenck, 1975), measures this underlying psychopathology that forms such a large part of the creativity literature. The aim of this study was to test the theory that psychoticism is correlated with word-association unique responses and with Barron–Welsh preference for complexity. Other personality test scores (e.g., extraversion, neuroticism, impulsivity, venturesomeness, empathy) were available and were included in the analysis, although only impulsivity was strongly linked with creativity in the past.

There is good evidence that word association tests, scored for unusual responses, give positive correlations with psychoticism (Hundal & Upmanyu, 1981; Merten, 1992, 1993; Upmanyu & Kaar, 1986). Particularly impressive are two recent studies by Merten (1992, 1993), carried out in Germany; they show a much more rigorous methodology than most previous studies, many of which are subject to criticisms such as those voiced by Schwartz (1978a, 1978b, 1982). Merten used several different methods of testing word association parameters, and it is important to look at the differential results for these different methods in order to be able to integrate the results within a theoretical framework. Beginning with Mannhaupt's (1983) norms for verbal reactions, Merten constructed six word lists of 25 words each, carefully equated for the categories of words used (e.g., tools, insects, musical instruments). Norms were established in the usual free-association mode, and associations were described a frequent, medium, and rare.

Subjects were tested along several different lines: (a) Free association—respondent answered with the first word that came to mind; (b) Individual response condition—respondent was asked to give responses that were unusual; and (c) Usual responses—respondent was asked to give responses that most people would give. There is a fair literature concerning these different types of response requirements (e.g., Jenkins, 1959; Lisman & Cohen, 1972; Rothberg, 1967; Routh & Schneider, 1970). The fourth method was an original one in which respondents were offered a usual, a middling frequent, and an unusual response, and were required to indicate which was which.

In addition to these different tests, questionnaires and IQ tests were administered, including Sullwold's and Huber's (1986) Thinking and Speaking scales, the Brief Psychiatric Rating scale (Overall & Gorham, 1962), and the Eysenck Personality Questionnaire (Eysenck & Eysenck, 1975).

Subjects were 46 healthy persons, 43 schizophrenics, and 15 manic-depressive patients. The main results were as follows. There were no differences between acute and chronic schizophrenics. Manic-depressive patients were not differentiated from schizophrenics, except for the individual response condition, where they were close to the normal group. Most important, normals with *high* P scores gave more unusual answers in the free- and usual-association conditions, very much like the psychotics; in the individual-association condition they gave more original and hence better answers. This is in good agreement with the theory that high P normals are more original but can also judge appropriateness well. High L scorers (Lie scale, indicative of conformity) did poorly on the individual-association condition, tending to give unoriginal answers. This finding is in good agreement with Horton, Marlowe, and Crowne (1963), who found high L scale scorers giving less unusual responses, and Routh (1971) who found high "schizoid" subjects able to give more unusual responses in a free test, but also able to give even less usual responses on instruction.

Merten's (1993) second article took up the search for the relation between unusual responses and personality, particularly P and L. Using 46 normal subjects, he found *negative* correlations between P and response commonality in free-, common-, and individual-response conditions. He concluded, "that means that they present the 'psychosis-like' associative disturbance in the free and common response condition, and yet fulfill the individual response condition better since it is precisely in that condition that idiosyncratic responses are really demanded" (Merten, 1993, p. 838). Again, therefore, we find original response creation joined with control of relevance, with the former linking the high P response activity with that of schizophrenics and the latter forming a crucial difference. Similarly, high P scorers did not fail to react appropriately to questions about the commonness or uncommonness of their own associations; they clearly were aware, as schizophrenics were not, of responding more individually on the word association test than did the majority.

L scorers show a high positive correlation with the individual-association condition; in other words even when asked to give unusual responses, they were loath to do so. They generally fail to respond appropriately, confirming the usual interpretation of high L scores as indicative of conformity. L correlates, as usual, negatively with P; $r = -.30$. These two studies are in good agreement with the theory of psychoticism.

There is direct evidence concerning the Barron–Welsh scale and P (Eysenck & Furnham, 1993), and the correlations published by Welsh (1975) with a variety of traits suggests that similar correlations with P might be found. The theory to be tested, therefore, predicts that high scores on psychoticism, unusual responses on the Word Association Test, and preferences for complex drawings on the Barron–Welsh Scale should go together. It was also predicted that differences in IQ would play little part in this "creativity" group of tests.

Additional predictions were made about a variety of personality measures other than psychoticism. As has often been found, creative people, as defined in terms of rated achievement, tend to combine psychopathology (high psychoticism) with ego strength (Barron, 1969; Barron & Harrington, 1981); this emphasis on ego strength suggests that creativity, as measured by the three tests mentioned above, would be negatively correlated with neuroticism, which is in many ways the opposite of ego strength.

Dellas and Gaier (1970) and Barron and Harrington (1981) gave lists of personality traits that have been found to correlate with creativity, and based on the general tenor of these lists scales measuring impulsivity, venturesomeness, and extraversion, which were predicted to correlate *positively* with creativity, and scales measuring social desirability (conformity), which was predicted to correlate *negatively* with creativity were included. Also included was an empathy scale for which no prediction was made, although its known negative correlation with psychoticism would suggest a negative correlation with creativity.

The prediction, then, is of a clearly defined pattern, with high psychoticism, high word-association uniqueness of responses, high preference for complex designs on the Barron–Welsh Scale, impulsivity, venturesomeness, and extraversion on the one side, and neuroticism, conformity (as measured by the Lie scale), and common-word-association responses on the other. Previous work suggested that intelligence would not enter into this picture (Welsh, 1975). It was decided that the best test of a predicted profile or configuration would be provided by *dimensional scaling* (smallest space) analysis, and accordingly this was chosen as the method to be employed.

METHOD

The population tested consisted of 100 adult nonacademic subjects (mean age = 34) of whom 37 were male and 63 were female. They were originally reached by adverts, word of mouth, and notices left at the Labour Exchange; all had taken part in earlier studies of intelligence and personality as related to psychophysiological measures of averaged evoked potential. Hence their IQ (verbal and performance) on the Jackson (1985) scales were known, as well as their personality test scores on the EPQ-R (Eysenck, Eysenck, & Barrett, 1985) and the I_7 (Eysenck & Eysenck, 1992), a test that contains scales of impulsiveness, venturesomeness, and empathy. The EPQ-R contains scales of psychoticism, neuroticism, and extraversion, as well as a lie scale that serves as a measure of conformity when subjects are not motivated to dissimulate. The personality measures were repeated on the occasion of the experiment to be described, two years after the original testing, so that test-retest correlations could be calculated. The IQ test was not repeated, so the values were obtained two years prior to the actual experiment.

The sample is a convenience one, varying widely in socioeconomic status and education, although neither appeared to affect results very much as Runco and Albert (1986) suggested; contrary to the view that creativity tests are correlated with IQ in samples with IQs below 120, they found no such correlation in samples with IQs below 120.

Central to the experiment was the Barron–Welsh Art Scale, which is part of the Welsh Figure Preference Tests (Welsh, 1949), but was given as a separate test. This consists of 86 drawings, some of which are *simple* and some *complex*. Subjects are required to say "like" or "dislike" for each drawing; the complexity score is made up of the number of complex drawings liked plus the number of simple drawings disliked. Liking for complexity has been found to be correlated with creativity (Barron, 1953; Welsh, 1975).

For the Word-Association Test the Kent–Rosanoff (1910) stimulus words were used, with the usual instructions to respond with the first word that came into mind. Scoring was based on the norms derived from the subjects themselves, because there were no population norms that could be applied to this group. Three scores were derived: A—the number of times the subject gave the *most frequent* response; B—the number of times the subject gave the *least frequent* response; and C—the number of times the subject gave a response that had been made by two or three others (i.e., a rare but not unique response).

RESULTS

Table 6.1 gives means and standard deviations for all relevant variables. The IQ tests failed to show any correlations of interest or significance; verbal IQ correlated .70 with performance IQ, which is fairly typical considering the available range of talent. On the personality side, test-retest correlations were quite high, considering the two-year gap: P = .86;

Table 6.1. Means and Standard Deviation
of Variables Used

	M	SD
Word Association		
A Responses	48.19	10.19
B Responses	7.24	6.75
C Responses	8.90	3.96
Barron–Welsh		
Like Response	13.07	6.94
Dislike Response	7.73	7.92
Total Score	20.80	12.79
IQ		
Full IQ	110.03	12.12
Verbal	111.00	12.38
Performance	108.61	13.64
Personality, second testing		
Psychoticism	6.16	4.36
Extraversion	15.05	5.81
Neuroticism	11.74	5.81
Lie Scale	6.49	4.00
Impulsiveness	8.02	4.63
Venturesomeness	8.35	4.51
Empathy	13.35	3.84

Note. A responses represent the number of the most frequent responses; B responses represent the number of least
frequent responses; and C responses represent rare but not
unique responses.

E = .89; N = .82; L = .86; Impulsivity = .85; Venturesomeness = .85, and
Empathy = .78. For the Barron–Welsh Scale, the correlation between L
(like) and D (dislike) was .37; $p < .01$. Some of the scales were clearly
heavily skewed; inspection of the scatter diagrams suggested that any observed correlations were not due to outliers.

Results for the Word-Association Test are given in some detail in Table
6.2. It will be seen that correlations between odd and even items, except
for C, were reasonable: A = .64; B = .76; and C = .33. A correlated negatively with B and C, while B and C correlated positively throughout.
Adding odd and even item scores, A_T correlated $-.74$ with B_T, and $-.70$
correlated with C_T; B_T correlated .49 with C_T, where the subscript refers
to total (odd and even) scores. These data suggest that all the tests be-
haved lawfully and in a manner similar to that observed in previous
studies.

For a consideration of the between-test correlations, Table 6.3 shows
correlations between personality and word association. As predicted, psychoticism correlated very significantly with A (negatively) and with B

Table 6.2. Correlations Between Frequent, Rare,
and Unique Item Scores for Odd and Even Words
on the Word-Association Test

		Odd items			Even items	
		A	B	C	A	B
Odd Items	A					
	B	−.71				
	C	−.55	.39			
Even Items	A	.64	−.60	−.35		
	B	−.55	.76	.35	−.66	
	C	−.51	.42	.33	−.64	.32

(positively); the positive correlation with C was significant on a one-tail test. Impulsiveness showed a similar pattern, although here the correlation was with C rather than with B.

Table 6.4 shows the results for the relationship between personality variables and the Barron–Welsh Art Scale. Psychoticism correlated significantly with the L score, but only on a one-tail test with the total score. Extraversion showed a curious discrepancy between L and D scores that makes interpretation hazardous. Venturesomeness was very significantly correlated with preference for complexity. Correlations for impulsiveness, neuroticism, and conformity (Lie scale) were usually in the predicted direction, but very low. Altogether correlations were nearly always as predicted, but they cannot be said to be high enough to give strong support to the theory; a more inclusive test is indicated.

Concerning the major test of the theory, namely the multidimensional scaling (smallest space) analysis, the initial matrix of Pearson correlations gave a stress value of 0.15, and the two-dimensional figure is given below.

Table 6.3. Correlations Between Personality
and Word-Association Tests

	A	B	C
P	−.25**	.27**	.17
E	−.14	−.06	.17
N	.07	.02	.02
L	.04	−.03	−.09
Venturesomeness	−.12	.01	.07
Impulsiveness	−.21*	.14	.26**
Empathy	.04	−.02	−.00

$*p < .05.$ $**p < .01.$

Table 6.4. Correlations Between Personality
and the Barron–Welsh Art Scale

	Like	Dislike	Total
P	−.20*	.06	.16
E	.35**	−.11	.13
N	−.17	.01	−.09
L	−.11	.05	−.03
Venturesomeness	.39**	.16	.32*
Impulsiveness	.19	.04	.13
Empathy	−.10		−.06

$*p < .05.$ $**p < .01.$

It is somewhat dangerous to interpret the dimensions of such an analysis, but Dimension 1 clearly separates the postulated creativity measures— Barron-Welsh Scale, word-association unique and rare responses, psychoticism, impulsiveness, venturesomeness, and extraversion—from the noncreative measures—common association on the Word-Association Test, conformity, neuroticism (low ego strength), and empathy.

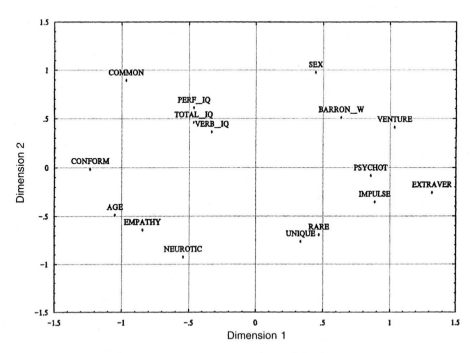

Figure 6.1.   Multidimensional scaling analysis of test scores.

The IQ test measures were quite separate from all the other measures; on a three-dimensional solution, they would vanish into the third dimension. The profile furnished by multidimensional scaling thus supports the main predictions made on the basis of previous studies of the general theory linking personality and creativity (Eysenck, 1993). Many of the correlations are quite small, suggesting that P, the Word-Association Test, and the art scale determine somewhat different inputs of creativity; a combination of these measures with divergent thinking measures might give a much better picture of creativity than any of them by themselves, If, as the literature indicates, the Word-Association Test and the Barron–Welsh Scale individually correlate .50 with creative achievement in architects, and if, as the present data suggest, the correlation between the measures is fairly low, the multiple R should be around .70. Future research will have to determine how realistic such a prediction may be.

CONCLUSIONS

The predictions made at the beginning of the experiment were that connections would be found between *personality* variables, particularly high psychoticism scores, low neuroticism scores, low conformity scores, and high impulsivity, and venturesomeness, on the one hand, and recognized measures of *creativity*, such as preference for complexity on the Barron–Welsh Art scale, and rare and unique responses on the Word-Association Test on the other hand. It is clear from the multidimensional-scaling analysis that these predictions are all borne out by the results. Although individual correlations are not high, the pattern of relations turned out very much as predicted. It was also predicted, and found, that measures of intelligence would not form part of the patterns, and indeed intelligence did not correlate significantly with any of our measures of personality or creativity.

Sex and age were included in the analysis, and *maleness* and *youth* were found to form part of the creativity complex. Because neither formed part of the prediction, and because sex and age were included in the analysis only as a precaution, these results should not be taken too seriously, although of course they align with the frequent observation that creativity in science and the arts seem to be observed most frequently in young people and that males are represented to an overwhelming extent among creative geniuses.

Predictions and results must be viewed against the background of the general theory of creativity that was suggested elsewhere (Eysenck, 1993), based on the argument that creativity is not an *ability* variable, but a *personality* one (Eysenck, 1983, 1989). The data presented here appear to support this view. As predicted, the personality trait of psychoticism was found to be linked with two acknowledged measures of creativity, namely Word-Association Uniqueness and Barron–Welsh Complexity Preference. The correlations are not very high, but of course the population tested did not include any highly creative subjects. In spite of this, the pattern of relations that was found was very much in line with current theories.

REFERENCES

Andreasen, N. C., & Canter, C. C. (1974). The creative writer: Psychiatric symptoms and family history. *Comprehensive Psychiatry, 15*, 123–131.

Barron, F. (1953). Complexity-simplicity as a personality dimension. *Journal of Abnormal and Social Psychology, 48*, 163–172.

Barron, F. (1969). *Creative person and creative process.* New York: Holt, Rhinehart & Winston.

Barron, F., & Harrington, D. M. (1981). Creativity, intelligence, and personality. *Annual Review of Psychology, 32*, 435–476.

Dellas, M., & Gaier, E. L. (1970). Identification of creativity: The individual. *Psychological Bulletin, 73*, 55–73.

Eysenck, H. J. (1983). The roots of creativity: Cognitive ability or personality trait? *Roeper Review, 5*, 10–12.

Eysenck, H. J. (1989). Die Bewertung der Kreativitat mit Hilfe des Psychotizismus-Wertes. In R. Lindner (Ed.), *Einfallsreiche Vernunft-Kreativ durch Wissen oder Gefuhl?* Zurich: Edition Interfraun.

Eysenck, H. J. (1992). The definition and measurement of psychoticism. *Personality and Individual Differences, 13*, 757–785.

Eysenck, H. J. (1993). Creativity and personality: Suggestions for a theory. *Psychological Inquiry, 4*, 147–178.

Eysenck, H. J., & Eysenck, S. B. G. (1975). *Manual of the Eysenck personality questionnaire.* London: Hodder & Stoughton.

Eysenck, H. J., & Eysenck, S. B. G. (1976). *Psychoticism as a dimension of personality.* London: Hodder & Stoughton.

Eysenck, H. J., & Eysenck, S. B. G. (1992). *The Manual of the EPQ-R and the impulsiveness, venturesomeness and empathy scales.* London: Hodder & Stoughton.

Eysenck, S. B. G., Eysenck, H. J., & Barrett, P. (1985). A revised version of the Psychoticism scale. *Personality and Individual Differences, 6*, 21–29.

Eysenck, H. J., & Furnham, A. (1993). Personality and the Barron-Welsh Art Scale. *Perceptual and Motor Skills, 76*, 837–838.

Gough, H. (1976). Studying creativity by means of word association tests. *Journal of Applied Psychology, 61*, 348–353.

Gough, H. (1994). In A. Montuori (Ed.), *Unusual associates.* Cresskill, NJ: Hampton.

Horton, D. L., Marlowe, D., & Crowne, D. P. (1963). The effect of instructional set and need for social approach on commonality of word association responses. *Journal of Abnormal and Social Psychology, 66,* 67–72.

Hundal, P. S., & Upmanyu, V. V. (1981). Nature of emotional indicators elicited by Kent-Rosanoff wrod association test: An empirical study. *Personality Study and Group Behavior, 1,* 50–61.

Jackson, D. N. (1985). *The multidimensional aptitude battery.* Port Huron: Research Psychologists Press.

Jamison, K. R. (1993). *Touched with fire.* New York: Free Press.

Jenkins, J. J. (1959). Effects on word-association of the set to give popular responses. *Psychological Reports, 5,* 94.

Kent, G. H., & Rosanoff, A. J. (1910). A study of association in insanity. *American Journal of Psychiatry, 67,* 37–96.

Lisman, S. A., & Cohen, B. B. (1972). Self-editing deficits in schizophrenia: A word-association analogue. *Journal of Abnormal Psychology, 79,* 181–188.

MacKinnon, D. W. (1962a). The nature and nurture of creative talent: *American Psychologist, 17,* 484–495.

MacKinnon, D. W. (1962b). The personality correlates of creativity: A study of American architects. In G. S. Nielsen (Ed.), *Proceedings of the Fourteenth International Congress of Applied Psychology* (Vol. 2, pp. 11–39). Copenhagen: Munksgaard.

MacKinnon, D. W. (1965). Personality and the realization of creative potential. *American Psychologist, 20,* 273–281.

MacKinnon, D. W. (1978). *In search of human effectiveness.* Buffalo, NY: Creative Education Foundation.

Mannhaupt, H. R. (1983). Produktions normen fuer verbale Reaktionen zu 40 gelaufigen Kategorien. *Sprache Kognition, 2,* 264–278.

Merten, T. (1992). Wortassoziation und Schizophrenic: Eine empirische Studie [Word association and schizophrenia: An empirical study]. *Der Nervenarzt, 63,* 401–408.

Merten, T. (1993). Word association responses and psychoticism. *Personality and Individual Differences, 14,* 837–839.

Overall, J. E., & Gorham, D. R. (1962). The brief psychiatric rating scale. *Psychological Reports, 10,* 799–812.

Prenky, R. A. (1980). *Creativity and psychopathology.* New York: Praeger.

Richards, R. L. (1981). Relationship between creativity and psychopathology: An evaluation and interpretation of the evidence. *Genetic Psychological Monograph, 103,* 261–324.

Rothberg, M. A. (1967). The effect of "social" instructions on word-association behaviour. *Journal of Verbal Learning and Verbal Behaviour, 6,* 298–300.

Routh, D. K. (1971). Instructional effects on word-association commonality in high and low "schizophrenic" college students. *Journal of Personality Assessment, 35,* 139–147.

Routh, D. K., & Schneider, J. M. (1970). Word-association and ink blot responses as a function of instructional sets and psychopathology. *Journal of Projective Technique and Personal Assessment, 34,* 113–120.

Runco, M. A., & Albert, R. S. (1986). The threshold theory regarding creativity and intelligence: An empirical test with gifted and non-gifted children. *Creative Child and Adult Quarterly, 11*, 212–218.

Schuldberg, D. (1990). Schizotypal and hypomanic traits, creativity, and psychological health. *Creativity Research Journal, 3*, 218–230.

Schwartz, S. (1978a). Do schizophrenics give rare word-associations? *Schizophrenia Bulletin, 4*, 248–251.

Schwartz, S. (1978b). Language and cognition in schizophrenia: A review and synthesis. In S. Schwartz (Ed.), *Language and cognition in schizophrenia* (pp. 257–276). Hillsdale, NJ: Erlbaum.

Schwartz, S. (1982). Is there a schizophrenic language? *Behaviour and Brain Science, 5*, 579–588.

Sullwold, L., & Huber, G. (1986). *Schizophrene Basisstörungen* [Basic schizophrenic disturbance]. Berlin: Springer.

Upmanyu, V. V., & Kaar, K. (1986). Diagnostic utility of word association emotional indicators. *Psychological Studies, 32*, 71–78.

Welsh, G. (1949). *Barron-Welsh art scale.* Palo Alto, CA: Consulting Psychologists Press.

Welsh, L. (1975). *Creativity and intelligence: A personality approach.* Chapel Hill, NC: University of North Carolina Press.

Chapter 7

*Creativity in Manic-Depressives, Cyclothymes, Their Normal Relatives, and Control Subjects**

Ruth Richards
Dennis K. Kinney
Inge Lunde
Maria Benet
Ann P. C. Merzel

*A version of this article was presented at the 93rd annual meeting of the American Psychological Association, Los Angeles, August 1985.

We are grateful to Paul Wender, Seymour Kety, Fini Schulsinger, and David Rosenthal for permission to use the present sample and interview data base for this study of creativity, and to the Spencer Foundation for its support of the further development and refinement of the Lifetime Creativity Scales. We wish to thank Seymour Kety, Steven Matthysse, Sandow Ruby, and Christine Waternaux for their helpful suggestions. Sincere thanks are also extended to Beth Gerstels and Carol Paik for their assistance in making creativity assessments, and to Heidi Daniels and Karen Linkins for work on data analysis and preparation of tables.

Bipolar manic-depressive illness (MDI) tends to run in families. Adoption and twin studies support a marked genetic contribution to this familial pattern (e.g., Bartelsen, 1979; Mendlewicz & Ranier, 1977; Wender et al., 1986). In this study we investigated whether manic-depressive pathology might be associated with positive behavioral characteristics that run in the same families. Such a *compensatory advantage* to genes that increase vulnerability to illness has been proposed for behavioral disorders such as schizophrenia (e.g., Kinney & Mathysse, 1978). A rough analogy may be drawn to sickle cell anemia, although the genetics of affective disorder are likely more complex. In the sickle-cell case, individuals homozygous for the mutant gene typically have severe anemia with clinical complications and often suffer an early death. In contrast, the much larger number of heterozygous carriers of the gene are frequently asymptomatic and have the advantage of increased resistance to malaria.

The present study asks whether there is a familial compensatory advantage to bipolar illness involving creativity. By analogy with the sickle cell example, creativity was hypothesized to be less prominent in manic-depressives themselves than in their better functioning relatives. The present research is, to our knowledge, the first to advance this hypothesis. It is also the first study to group subjects solely by psychiatric diagnosis and then to consider their overall creative accomplishments. Using the Lifetime Creativity scales (LCS; Richards, Kinney, Benet, & Merzel, 1988), we compared manic-depressives, cyclothymes, and their first-degree normal relatives with psychiatrically normal and ill controls.

Previous studies have reported both familial and individual associations between creativity and major affective disorders (for reviews, see Andreasen, 1978; Richards, 1981). However, it is difficult to generalize from these previous studies to the typical family with bipolar members. First, these studies typically did not consider creative accomplishments unless they were socially recognized, and these studies were often constrained to certain traditionally creative areas involving the arts or sciences. Second, subjects were initially selected for high creativity, and their individual or family psychopathology was then assessed rather than the other way around.

Keeping in mind these limitations, in existing studies of families, one finds a higher prevalence of endogenous psychosis (MDI, schizophrenia, and undetermined psychosis) in the relatives of artists and scientists than in the general population (Juda, 1949), and one finds a higher prevalence of major affective disorder in the relatives of creative writers than in the relatives of controls (Andreasen & Canter, 1974).

One researcher did begin with index cases identified by psychopathology rather than creativity (Karlsson, 1970) and found greater social recognition for artistic or scientific work in the families of psychotic probands than in the families of controls. However, diagnoses were not determined for these socially recognized relatives. No conclusions could therefore be drawn about creativity and psychiatric status in the same individuals. Relatives of manic-depressives seem to have contributed more to this pattern of familial recognition than the relatives of schizophrenics (Andreasen, 1978; Richards, 1981). In an associated examination of extensive family trees (Karlsson, 1968, 1970), the same family branches were found to be high in both psychosis and social recognition.

Only one adoption study has focused on the familial relation between creativity and psychopathology. McNeil (1971) found an association between the adoptees' level of socially recognized creativity and the prevalence of psychopathology in their biological—but not adoptive—parents. Thus, genetic factors are implicated. Affective disorder appeared to be particularly important to this creativity-psychopathology relation (Richards, 1981).

We now turn to studies of creativity and psychopathology in the same individual. Among McNeil's (1971) adoptees, there was a significant relation between creativity and the overall prevalence of psychopathology. McNeil found personality disorders among adoptees, but no major mood disorders or psychosis. Other investigators, however, found elevated levels of psychosis (Juda, 1949) and major affective disorder (Andreasen & Canter, 1974; Jamison, in press) compared with control or general population levels, findings that are also supported by data from some uncontrolled studies (see Andreasen, 1978; Richards, 1981). However, in all but one study (see Andreasen & Canter, 1974), the typical creator either carried a milder diagnosis or was considered psychiatrically normal.

In fact, there is good reason to expect that a number of milder psychiatric disorders may have been missed in most previous research; only Andreasen and Canter's (1974) study used direct personal interviews to determine diagnosis. In addition, no previous study has considered family psychiatric history along with the creator's own psychiatric condition; family history might have been of particular interest for the less-disordered creator.

It has been argued that affective disorder may carry particular advantages for creativity but that these benefits may be greater in affective disorder's milder rather than more severe forms. Several potential advantages of a mild hypomanic state are given (Richards, 1981). In the third edition of the *Diagnostic and Statistical Manual of Mental Disorders* (*DSM-III*; American Psychiatric Association, 1980), two of the criteria for the hypomanic phase of cyclothymic personality disorder involve sharpened and unusually creative thinking and increased productivity. Cyclothymic personality was a frequent second diagnosis in Andreasen and Canter's (1974) study of eminent creators, and hypomanic symptomatology was also found frequently in Jamison's (in press) sample. There is evidence that cyclothymia may represent a milder manifestation of bipolar liability; cyclothymic personality is more prevalent, for instance, in relatives of manic-depressives than in relatives of unipolar depressives and controls (Weissman, et al., 1984). Richards (1981) proposed that in some psychiatrically normal creators, creativity may be facilitated by subclinical factors related to a family history of major psychiatric disorder.

In the present study we examine whether creativity is an inverted-U function of the degree of manifest bipolar psychopathology in individuals at risk for manic-depressive illness: (a) Individuals with frank manic-depressive illness were expected to manifest an intermediate mean level of creativity, (b) cyclothymes to have the highest mean creativity, and (c) the psychiatrically normal first-degree relatives of manic-depressives or cyclothymes to show intermediate creativity. (Although normal relatives who carried genetic liability for bipolar disorder were expected to be particularly creative, our sample of normal relatives was assumed to be heterogeneous for such liability; it is unlikely that all of these relatives would have inherited genes conferring such liability.) In addition, these three index groups taken together were expected to show higher creativity than a group of control subjects who lacked any personal or family history of major affective disorder.

We also hypothesized that the inverted-U pattern would persist after the effects of age, education, and intelligence were partialed out of the creativity scores. Variables related to education and intelligence were expected to show positive associations with creativity (Barron, 1969; Barron & Harrington, 1981; Richards & Casey, 1979); such factors may enhance the realization of creative potential and should not be regarded merely as nuisance variables. However, the projected differences in creativity between groups, if meaningful, should not be fully explained by such factors (e.g., Getzels & Jackson, 1962). Previous studies of associations between creativity and psychopathology have not taken these variables into account.

Thus the present study is distinguished in several respects from most previous research on creativity-psychopathology relations. In addition to providing the first general study of creativity in subject groups defined solely by psychiatric diagnostic criteria, the present research considers together the individual and the family psychiatric history of subjects, and it uses data from personal interviews as the basis for assessing both psychiatric status and creativity of the primary study subjects. Use of a new and broad-based measure with high interrater reliability and multiple indications of construct validity—the LCS—allowed for assessment of adult creative accomplishment among these diverse subjects. Finally, appropriate controls were instituted for variables such as education and intelligence.

METHOD

Sample and Diagnostic Data

The 77 subjects in this study all met our diagnostic criteria among those previously interviewed as part of a Danish adoption study of affective disorder conducted by Wender, et al. (1986). Wender et al.'s subjects were the biological and adoptive relatives of 72 index adoptees (diagnosed as having manic-depressive illness, unipolar depression, neurotic depression, or affect reaction, the latter a Danish diagnosis) and 72 control adoptees, matched on age, sex, age at adoption, and socioeconomic status of the adoptive family. Relatives of the adoptees were identified via thorough searches of centralized Danish registers. Greater detail on this adoption study is found elsewhere (Wender, et al. 1986). A total of 174 subjects, or 23% of the sample of biological and adoptive relatives previously identified by Wender et al., had been personally interviewed, providing a basis for assessing creativity, psychiatric diagnosis, and other variables in the present study. We based diagnoses for the remaining relatives in the sample on formal hospital and clinic records as described by Wender, et al. (1986). To meet the requirements of the present study, it was necessary to modify the design of Wender, et al.'s original adoption study. Each subject's family psychiatric history was as complete as possible, based not only on the adoptee to whom the subject was biologically related but also on all of the subject's other identified biological relatives in the entire sample.

For the interviewed subsample, blind consensus diagnoses were made by Wender, et al. (1986), after interview material had been edited to remove potentially biasing information. Also, a primary and a secondary diagnosis were recorded for each subject using criteria of *DSM-II* (American Psychiatric Association, 1968). (Some *DSM-III* diagnoses were also available [Wender, 1986], but they were based only on hospital records, not interview data, they lacked the added sensitivity of primary and secondary diagnoses, and they were less, rather than more, conservative for our major diagnostic categories—most notably the *DSM-II* vs. *DSM-III* diagnosis for unipolar depression.)

For the present study, we included subjects in the manic-depressive group if they received primary or secondary diagnoses of definite or possible manic-depressive illness. This raised the likelihood of being able to distinguish a spectrum, or range, of disorders, including some of the less severe cases. The secondary diagnosis for each of these subjects usually involved another form of affective disorder. Subjects were considered cyclothymic if they received this as a primary or secondary diagnosis; nearly all of these cases had no other recorded psychopathology. Some individuals who might receive research diagnoses of bipolar II disorder (included under atypical bipolar disorder in *DSM-III*) might have been included in this group. Our sample of normal relatives was composed of interviewed subjects who received no primary or secondary psychiatric diagnosis whatsoever and who were first-degree biological relatives of either manic-depressives or cyclothymes as defined previously.

Our control subjects were composed of all those biological and adoptive relatives of the psychiatrically normal control adoptees, previously identified by Wender, et al. (1986), who also satisfied our additional screening criteria. These criteria included having neither a personal nor a family history of (a) major affective disorder or cyclothymia, (b) possible variants of bipolar disorder (acute schizophrenia, schizoaffective disorder), or (c) schizophrenia or suicide. These procedures yielded a sample of 17 manic-depressives, 16 cyclothymes, 11 psychiatrically normal first-degree relatives, 15 control subjects diagnosed as normal, and 18 controls carrying a diagnosis other than those just noted. These groups are characterized demographically in Table 7.1.

Data Base, Data Preparation, and Measures

Subjects were interviewed by Inge Lunde, a Danish psychiatrist who is fluent in English as well as Danish. Lunde was blind to relatives' relationships to probands. The typical interview lasted several hours and included the taking of a general history for diagnostic and other purposes. Subjects were asked in an open-ended way about their major formal and informal occupational and avocational activities during childhood, adolescence, and, particularly, adulthood. Results of the interviews were reported in English, in detailed narrative form. Information on lifetime vocational and avocational history was used to assess creativity, as required by our creativity measure. Vocational history was reported for every subject, typically as a chronological description of activities; avocational information was available for 81% of the immediate study sample of 77 subjects. (Avocational information was unavailable for 5 manic-depressives, 2 cyclothymes, 2 normal relatives, 3 psychiatrically normal controls, and 3 controls carrying a diagnosis.)

Prior to the rating of creativity variables, all potentially biasing information was edited out of the interview report by a member of the research team other than the rater. This editor eliminated any references to positive or negative aspects of personality, intellectual functioning, family psychiatric history, or the subject's own psychiatric diagnosis. Age, sex, and educational level were recorded directly at this point. Diagnostic data were recorded independently, along with a global intelligence estimate

Table 7.1. Creativity and Demographic Variables on Five Diagnostic Groups

Group	N	Peak creativity[a]		Adjusted peak creativity[b]		Age		Educational level		Intelligence estimate	
		M	SD	M	SD	M	SD	M	SD	M	SD
Manic-depressives											
Males	5	2.60	0.89	2.30	.72	42.0	16.4	12.20	5.76	1.40	.55
Females	12	2.08	0.90	2.08	.74	47.3	16.1	9.83	2.79	0.92	.29
Both sexes[c]	17	2.30	0.87	2.20	.72						
Cyclothymes											
Males	8	3.13	0.83	2.78	.62	51.6	15.4	9.38	3.70	1.63	.52
Females	8	2.50	0.53	2.37	.56	52.0	19.0	9.38	3.02	1.13	.35
Both sexes	16	2.79	0.69	2.55	.57						
Normal relatives											
Males	7	3.29	0.49	3.00	.36	46.3	17.0	11.71	4.31	1.44	.53
Females	4	2.25	0.96	2.22	.88	38.5	7.2	10.25	1.89	1.00	.00
Both sexes	11	2.83	0.72	2.63	.59						
Normal controls											
Males	5	2.80	1.30	2.73	.75	48.8	21.1	10.60	2.51	1.20	.84
Females	10	2.10	0.74	1.97	.79	54.3	25.6	8.80	2.90	1.20	.42
Both sexes	15	2.38	0.92	2.27	.77						
Controls with a diagnosis											
Males	10	2.30	.67	2.29	1.07	53.7	20.7	9.02	3.40	1.20	.63
Females	8	2.25	.89	2.22	.73	56.9	18.0	8.00	1.07	1.13	.35
Both sexes	18	2.23	.78	2.21	.93						

aRaw scores.

bScores were adjusted for the effects of age, education, and intelligence.

cThe effects of sex have been partialed out.

that was made on a 3-point scale (1 = above-average, 2 = *average*, and 3 = *below-average intelligence*) based on a standard psychiatric determination. (Because subjective ratings of intelligence may be inflated by observed creativity [Barron & Harrington, 1981], it is possible that creativity variance could be erroneously removed when intelligence is partialed out of creativity scores. However, this should not affect the relative—rank-order—standing of the psychodiagnostic groups in this study.)

Lifetime Creativity Scales

Characteristics of the LCS are summarized here and described in greater detail elsewhere (Richards, et al., 1988). The LCS conceptualization of creativity departs from more restrictive views of creative accomplishment, for example, that such accomplishment has occurred only rarely throughout history (as in the work of a Beethoven or Einstein) or that it occurs more broadly but only in traditionally creative fields such as the arts and sciences. In contrast, in the present study creativity is viewed as a quality or capability that varies broadly in the general population and may be manifested in a wide variety of outcomes involving virtually any field of endeavor (see Richards, et al., 1988). This perspective at once bears similarities to the views on creativity expressed by humanistic psychologists, such as Maslow (1968) or Rogers (1961), and to the concept of phenotypic plasticity underlying human inventiveness and adaptability that has been described by evolutionary biologists (e.g., Dobzhansky, 1962).

The empirical rationale for broad-based assessment of creativity is based on evidence for a disposition toward originality and core characteristics of the individual associated with creativity across diverse fields of endeavor (Barron, 1955, 1969; Barron & Harrington, 1981). Assessment of creativity by the LCS is based on subjects' real-life vocational and avocational activity. This approach had been taken in several previous studies of creativity and psychopathology (Andreasen & Canter, 1974; Heston, 1966; McNeil, 1971). However, we extended this approach to nonpsychiatric populations, considered all creative activities over the adult years rather than present activities only, and removed any requirement that endeavors be socially recognized.

Seven scales make up the LCS. These pertain to the quality or quantity of creative accomplishment over the adult lifetime. Peak creativity and extent of creative involvement are each assessed separately for vocational and for avocational activity. We distinguished between creativity at work and leisure in order to examine expected group differences in emphasis between these two areas. Of relevance here are suggestions (e.g., Akiskal, Hirschfeld, & Yerevanian, 1983) that subjects at risk for bipolar disorder may concentrate their energies disproportionately on work. The LCS also contain summary measures for peak creativity and extent of creative involvement as well as a measure of overall creativity.

Peak measures are designed to identify the strongest real-life reflections of an underlying disposition toward originality (Barron, 1955, 1969), capturing those occasions during the adult years when personal and environmental conditions for creativity are optimal. The extent-of-involvement scales identify the relative importance of creative versus other activity during the lifetime and are seen as more responsive to environmental conditions that help or hinder creativity.

The overall-peak-creativity measure was viewed a priori as providing the best test of any fundamental intergroup differences in creative capability, while minimizing the effects of the environment. It reflects the maximum level of creativity at either work or leisure. As such, it does not represent a simple combination of peak vocational and avocational indexes. Patterns between subjects will differ. (For example, a "workaholic" with a relatively low peak creativity at leisure could have high overall creativity, reflecting the dominance of a high level of peak vocational creativity in his or her life.) Overall peak creativity was therefore the focus of this study; vocational and avocational peak creativity served as supplementary measures.

Following Barron (1969), we used two general criteria to identify creative outcomes: (a) that an unusual or novel element be involved (originality criterion) and (b) that outcomes be meaningful to others (criterion of adaptation to reality) rather than bizarre and idiosyncratic. Peak-creativity assessments were each made on 6-point scales (1 = *insignificant,* 2 = *minor,* 3 = *some,* 4 = *moderate,* 5 = *high,* and 6 = *exceptional creativity*), where the level of *some creativity* was taken as a normative average. Only major enterprises or ongoing areas of creativity were considered (e.g., building a house or designing an advertising campaign), so creative efforts are more likely to reflect true capability rather than chance fluctuations. The significance of innovative elements to a total enterprise is based on the departure of this enterprise from more typical products and practices. When elaborative detail is lacking (typically the case for vocational activity in this sample), alternative ratings may be assigned on the basis of detailed standard descriptions of the activity (Kolstrup, 1982; U.S. Department of Labor, 1977). Two consultants on Danish culture helped formulate methods that were valid for a Danish population. A rating guide provides specific criteria for each rating level (see Table 7.2), along with multiple examples. (The guide is available for research purposes to the interested investigators.) Tables 3 and 4 provide some abbreviated sample descriptions of subjects at three levels of peak vocational and avocational creativity.

Table 7.2. Definitions of Levels of Two Types of Creativity Scales

Level	Definition
	Levels for peak creativity
Not significant (0)	Routine or prescribed endeavors with negligible innovative aspects
Minor degree (1)	Small unexceptional departures from routine or prescribed endeavor
Some (2)	Greater innovativeness, but not unusual in the population
Moderate (3)	Presence of central innovative elements that stand out in the population, although not markedly; these may involve major modifications of common practices or products
High (4)	Presence of markedly distinctive innovative elements that set endeavors well part from others in the population
Exceptional (5)	Radical departures from the commonplace; these may require conceptual reorganization to be assimilated
	Levels for extent of creative involvement
Not Significant (0)	Highly prescribed or routine patterns of lifetime activity
Minor Degree (1)	Prescribed or routine patterns, broken by brief, rare instances of innovative activity
Some (2)	Greater extent of innovative activity than above, but not unusual in the population, and other activity tends to predominate
Moderate (3)	Notable innovative activity in a pattern that tends to admix this with other forms of endeavor
High (4)	Markedly distinctive emphasis on innovation—a dominant life theme and primary commitment
Exceptional (5)	Intense, pervasive, and perhaps compulsive preoccupation with innovative activity over time to the virtual exclusion of other emphases

Validation data for the LCS were based on three large independent samples, as described further in Richards, et al. (1988). The first two validation samples were large, representative control samples (Ns = 173 and 209) from Danish psychiatric adoption studies. Subjects were drawn from all over Denmark and represented a wide range of other demographic factors. The third validation sample was the full interviewed adoption study sample (N = 174), from which the present study subjects were drawn. In each case, data distributions were approximately normal for all scales, consistent with the broad definition of creativity and our norm-referenced assessment method. Interrater reliability ranged from good to excellent. It was calculated for 10 randomly selected subjects from each sample. There were four, seven, and three raters, respectively, for the affective, Copenhagen, and Danish provincial samples; interrater reliability was calculated between all pairs of raters in each case. For the affective sample, the mean reliability for vocational creativity measures was .76 (SD = .21); for avocational measures, .83 (SD = .40); and for overall measures, .89 (SD = .33). Corresponding figures for the Copenhagen sample

Table 7.3. *Abbreviated Examples of Subjects at Three Rating Levels*
of Peak Vocational Creativity

Example 1	Example 2
No significant creativity	
Mixed and carried mortal for local brick layer for 20 years, then inherited a large income-paying trust fund and retired to a passive life on a country estate.	Washed store windows for 3 years under foreman's supervision, spent 5 years on assembly lines in two factories, and, for the past 11 years, has done routine quality-control tasks in a brewery.
Moderate peak creativity	
Longtime owner and manager of a small dairy farm who, after 10 years of producing cheese and other dairy products, expanded and began marketing through a local distributor.	Optician who spent 4 years selling optical items, then acquired a small optical shop, and now grinds lenses to prescription while managing the retailing of standard optical products.
High peak creativity	
Former avant garde dancer and choreographer who developed and directed a variety of unusual productions for several dance companies, but, postwar, has worked solely as a hotel clerk	Entrepreneur who advanced from chemist's apprentice to independent researcher of new products before starting a major paint manufacturing company, and whose operation surreptitiously manufactured and smuggled explosives for the Danish Resistance during World War II.

Note. The primary distinction between avocational and vocational activities is whether the activity was financially compensated. The following points are pertinent to both avocational and vocational measures: (a) peak creativity is based only on the level of the most creative major enterprise, (b) appreciation of others' creativity is not credited on these scales, and (c) social recognition is not required as a criterion for higher creativity. Examples have been altered to protect subjects' confidentiality.

were, for vocational creativity measures, .90 (SD = .10); for avocational measures, .86 (SD = .05); and for overall measures, .81 (SD = .14). For the Danish provincial sample, the reliabilities were, for vocational measures, .87 (SD = .08); for avocational measures, .91 (SD = .04); and for overall measures, .88 (SD = .07).

Several lines of validity evidence are available. They involve (a) sampling or content validity, (b) hypothesis testing with correlates of adult creativity suggested by the research literature (childhood creativity, fantasy, appreciation of creativity, and Holland's (1973) primary interest styles), and (c) factor analyses of LCS and other variables showing the structure of the creativity domain and discriminant validity from selected control variables (Richards, et al., 1988).

Factor analyses for all three samples involved a principal-components

Table 7.4. *Abbreviated Examples of Subjects Falling at Three Rating Levels of Peak Avocational Creativity*

Example 1	Example 2
No significant creativity	
Once read movies magazines intensively, but now spends most evenings with the new family television. Also does much needlepoint following specified patterns and, on weekends, watches spouse play handball.	Often reads in spare time, has a standing subscription to the local theatre, belongs to a health club, has been going daily for directed group calisthenics, attends a social club to watch weekly television sporting events with friends, and occasionally attends local soccer games.
Moderate peak creativity	
Active church member who has ushered at church services for over 20 years, has sung for the last 10 years in the alto section of the church choir, and who recently has been volunteering on a committee designed to expand parish membership.	Avid reader and sports fan/spectator who previously completed a night-school journalism course and now gives brief accounts of sporting events for a monthly community newspaper. On weekends, also volunteers as an assistant coach for a children's swim team.
High Peak Creativity	
Amateur archaeologist who for years has spent summers and other free time seeking new sites, initiating archaeological digs with professionals from a nearby university, researching artifacts, reconstructing aspects of primitive societies, and collaborating in articles on this work.	Invests much spare time in working with own handicapped child and once, over several years, designed and constructed a complex apparatus to help this child with locomotion, gross changes of posture, and fine motor manipulation of objects. Now works as a volunteer teacher twice a week to help other handicapped children use this invention.

solution with varimax rotation, with each analysis yielding similar results on key points. Regarding creativity factors, the first analysis was viewed as exploratory and the second and third as confirmatory. Each showed (a) the distinctness of the vocational and avocational creativity measures, each of which defined an orthogonal factor; (b) a strong relation between peak creativity and the involvement scales within the vocational, avocational, and summary measures; and (c) the distinctness of creativity from control variables including socioeconomic status, educational level, and intelligence, which tend to define other factors. (These variables still showed the predicted positive, but moderately low, correlations with creativity variables. For more detailed information on validity, including associations of LCS scores with predictors of creativity reported by other investigators, see Richards, et al., 1988).

In summary, the results support the choice of overall peak creativity as the summary variable and vocational and avocational peak creativity as two different dimensions of this peak creative accomplishment. Peak measures were superior to extent measures for our purposes because they explain much of the extent variance while minimizing the effect of environment in the estimate of underlying creative capability.

RESULTS

Preliminary Analyses

Residual peak creativity scores were derived by partialing out the effects of age, education, and intelligence from the measure of overall peak creativity. This was done for male and female subjects separately by using all subjects of each sex in the interviewed sample of 174 subjects. Adjusted raw and residual scores were derived for male and female subjects by adding back the grand mean of creativity for each sex. A preliminary 2 × 5 analysis of overall peak creativity, with diagnostic group and sex as independent variables, showed no significant Sex × Diagnosis interaction, $F(4, 67) = 0.68$, $p < .60$, making it possible both to partial out a significant main effect of sex, $F(1, 67) = 8.90$, $p < .005$, which favored male subjects, and to combine male and female subjects for subsequent analyses of both raw and adjusted creativity scores. Descriptive statistics on overall peak creativity and on the covariates are shown by group in Table 1. There was no significant diagnostic Group × Sex interaction for either vocational or avocational creativity. Interestingly, there was another significant main effect of sex for vocational creativity, $F(1, 63) = 5.76$, $p < .02$, but not for avocational creativity.

Major Results: Overall Peak Creativity

Four statistically independent orthogonal contrasts, derived from our hypotheses, tested whether creativity was (a) higher in all index subjects (manic-depressives, cyclothymes, and normal first-degree relatives combined) than in control subjects lacking risk for affective disorder; (b) higher in cyclothymes than in other index subjects (i.e., than in manic-depressives and normal relatives combined), consistent with our inverted-U configuration; (c) different in normal relatives versus manic-depressives (with no significant difference expected for this contrast, in accord with the inverted-U hypothesis); and (d) different in the psychiatrically normal controls versus those controls who had a diagnosis (again, no difference was expected). We used one-tailed tests for the first two contrasts because the direction of the effect had been hypothesized, and we used two-tailed tests for the last two hypotheses. Results re portrayed graphically in Figure 7.1.

The first contrast was significant ($t = 1.78$, $p < .05$), and the third was suggestive ($t = 1.70$, $p < .10$), whereas the second and fourth contrasts were nonsignificant. Thus, between control groups (i.e., the psychiatrically normal controls and those carrying a diagnosis), there was no significant difference. However, the combined index subjects (manic-depressives, cyclothymes, and normal relatives) were significantly higher on overall peak creativity than all control subjects combined. Interestingly, first-degree normal relatives of manic-depressives and cyclothymes were suggestively higher on creativity than the manic-depressive subjects, whereas cyclothymes did not show the significantly higher creativity that was expected when compared with manic-depressives and normal relatives combined. Inspection of Figure 7.1 suggests the interesting reason behind this: Normal relatives and cyclothymes were both comparably high on creativity compared with other groups.

When the effects of age, education, and intelligence were partialed out, index subjects remained suggestively higher on creativity than did controls ($t = 1.31$, $p < .10$). The ranking of group means remained very similar to that in the original analysis (Spearman rank-order correlation of .90, $p < .02$); notably, normal relatives and cyclothymes still showed the highest creativity (see Figure 7.1).

When the specific areas of creative activity of all index subjects with moderate or higher creativity scores were examined, we found that vocational activity was divided more or less equally among the arts, sciences, humanities and social sciences, and organizational and leadership roles. In contrast, avocational activity was almost entirely confined to crafts and the fine arts—perhaps because such hobbies have traditionally been emphasized in Denmark. Activities involving visual content were nearly as prevalent as those involving language, music, and movement combined. A similar pattern appeared in creative controls.

Supplementary Analyses: Vocational and Avocational Peak Creativity

Adjusted scores were gain used in these analyses. Using the same orthogonal contrasts, normal relatives scored significantly higher than manic-depressives on avocational peak creativity ($t = 2.57$, $p < .05$), with cyclothymes falling in between. Thus, avocational peak creativity tended to vary directly with degree of psychological health. However, on vocational peak creativity, cyclothymes were significantly higher than the other two index groups combined ($t = 1.69$, $p < .05$, one-tailed).

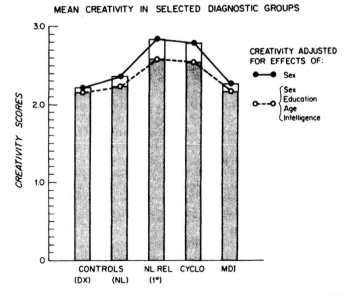

Figure 7.1.   Mean Overall Peak Creativity scores for (a) controls with a diagnosis (DX), normal controls (NL), (c) normal first-degree biological relatives of cyclothymes and manic-depressives (NL REL), (d) cyclothymes (CYCLO), and (e) manic-depressives (MDI).

DISCUSSION

A modification of the original inverted-U hypothesis can be proposed. Overall peak creativity may be enhanced, on the average, in subjects showing milder and, perhaps, subclinical expressions of potential bipolar liability (i.e., the cyclothymes and normal first-degree relatives) compared either with individuals who carry no bipolar liability (control subjects) or individuals with more severe manifestations of bipolar liability (manic-depressives). Indeed, some normal relatives might have been *hyperthymic* (Akiskal, 1983). Supplementary results suggest the cyclothymes and normal relatives may tend to realize their creative potential in different ways. In avocational activities (perhaps because they tend to involve fewer external structures, rewards, or constraints than occupational activities), creativity in subjects at risk for bipolar disorders may vary directly with the level of personal functioning; here, normal relatives showed the highest creativity. In vocational activity, the high creativity of cyclothymes, and the notable differential between vocational and avocational creativity for manic-depressives compared with other groups, complement previous research reporting that a driven, work-oriented temperament may be associated with risk for manic-depressive illness (Akiskal, et al., 1983).

Among normals, it is a subject's relationship to a manic-depressive or cyclothyme, not psychiatric normalcy per se, that predicts heightened creativity. There may be a positive compensatory advantage (Kinney & Matthysee, 1978) to genes associated with greater liability for bipolar disorder. The possibility that normal relatives of manic-depressives and cyclothymes have heightened creativity may have been overlooked because of a medical-model orientation that focused on dysfunction rather than positive characteristics of individuals. Such a compensatory advantage among the relatives of a disorder affecting at least 1% of the population could affect a relatively large group of people.

The finding of enhanced creativity in cyclothymes is consistent with results on creative persons (Andreasen & Canter, 1974; Jamison, 1990) and extends this association to the general population. Previous work can be interpreted to suggest a higher prevalence of bipolar disorder Type II (Andreasen & Canter, 1974; Jamison, 1990) as well as Type I (Juda, 1949) among eminent creators. The present findings on manic-depressives do not contradict this, for the present study as the first to investigate relations between creative accomplishment and psychopathology in subjects initially identified by psychodiagnostic criteria rather than by creativity—a very different research design (Richards, 1981). Moreover, different forms of bipolar disorder (e.g., those varying in frequency and severity of manic and depressive phases) may carry different consequences for creativity.

It is noteworthy that eminent artists and writers have described hypomanic symptomatology during intense creative periods (Jamison, 1990) and that manics and hypomanics have attributed both immediate and lasting effects on creativity to hypomanic episodes (Jamison, Gesner, Hammen, & Padesky, 1980; Kinney, Richards, Daniels, & Linkins, 1988). It will be important to distinguish between potential state versus trait characteristics that may enhance creativity. It would be fortuitous if one such trait led to discovery of a biological marker that could track inherited bipolar liability through a pedigree in clinically unaffected as well as affected relatives. In addition, there would be major clinical implications if genotype-environment interactions could be identified that lead to enhanced creativity. Positive intervention might then not only prevent the development of bipolar disorders but also foster creative talent and productive contribution to society.

REFERENCES

Akiskal, H. S. (1983). The bipolar spectrum: New concepts in classification and diagnosis. In L. Grinspoon (Ed.), *Psychiatry update: The American psychiatric association annual review* (Vol. II, pp. 271–292). Washington, DC: American Psychiatric Press.

Akiskal, H. S. Hirschfeld, R. M. A., & Yerevanian, B. I. (1983). The relationship of personality to affective disorders. *Archives of General Psychiatry, 40,* 801–810.

American Psychiatric Association. (1968). *Diagnostic and statistical manual of mental disorders* (2nd ed.). Washington, DC: Author.

American Psychiatric Association. (1980). *Diagnostic and statistical manual of mental disorders* (3rd ed.). Washington, DC: Author.

Andreasen, N. C. (1978). Creativity and psychiatric illness. *Psychiatric Annals, 8,* 113–119.

Andreasen, N. C., & Canter, A. (1974). The creative writer: Psychiatric symptoms and family history. *Comprehensive Psychiatry, 15,* 123–131.

Barron, F. (1955). The disposition toward originality. *Journal of Abnormal and Social Psychology, 51,* 478–485.

Barron, F. (1969). *Creative person and creative process.* New York: Holt, Rinehart & Winston.

Barron, F., & Harrington, D. (1981). Creativity, intelligence, and personality. *Annual Review of Psychology, 32,* 439–476.

Bartelsen, A. (1979). A Danish twin study of manic-depressive disorders. In M. Schou & E. Stromgren (Eds.), *Origin, prevention, and treatment of affective disorders* (pp. 227–239). Orlando, FL: Academic Press.

Dobzhansky, T. (1962). *Mankind evolving.* New Haven, CT: Yale University Press.

Getzels, J. W., & Jackson, P. W. (1962). *Creativity and intelligence: Explorations with gifted students.* New York: Wiley.

Heston, L. L. (1966). Psychiatric disorders in foster home reared children of schizophrenic mothers. *British Journal of Psychiatry, 112,* 819–825.

Holland, J. L. (1973). *Making vocational choices: A theory of careers.* Englewood Cliffs, NJ: Prentice-Hall.

Jamison, K. R. (1990). Manic-depressive illness and accomplishment: Creativity, leadership, and social class. In F. K. Goodwin & K. R. Jamison (Eds.), *Manic-depressive illness* (pp. 332–367). Oxford: Oxford University Press.

Jamison, K. R., Gesner, R. H., Hammen, C., & Padesky, C. (1980). Clouds and silver linings: Positive experiences associated with primary affective disorders. *American Journal of Psychiatry, 137,* 198–202.

Juda, A. (1949). The relationship between highest mental capacity and psychic abnormalities. *American Journal of Psychiatry, 106,* 296–307.

Karlsson, J. L. (1968). Genealogic studies of schizophrenia. In D. Rosenthal & S. S. Kety (Eds.), *The transmission of schizophrenia,* (pp. 85–94). New York: Pergamon Press.

Karlsson, J. L. (1970). Genetic association of giftedness and creativity with schizophrenia. *Hereditas, 66,* 177–181.

Kinney, D. K., & Matthysse, S. (1978). Genetic transmission of schizophrenia. *Annual Review of Medicine, 29,* 459–473.

Kinney, D. K., Richards, R. L., Daniels, H., & Linkins, K. (1992). Everyday creativity and bipolar and unipolar affective disorder: Preliminary study of personal and family history. *European Psychiatry 7,* 49–52.

Kolstrup, H. C. (Ed.). (1982). *Hvad kan jeg blive?: Erhvervsvejledning* [What can I do?: A guidebook to vocations]. Copenhagen, Denmark: Politikens Forlag.

Maslow, A. H. (1968). *Toward a psychology of being.* New York: Van Nostrand.

McNeil, T. (1971). Prebirth and postbirth influence on the relationship between creative ability and recorded mental illness. *Journal of Personality, 39,* 391–406.

Mendlewicz, J., & Ranier, J. D. (1977). Adoption study supporting genetic transmission in manic-depressive illness. *Nature, 268,* 327–329.

Richards, R. L. (1981). Relationships between creativity and psychopathology: An evaluation and interpretation of the evidence. *Genetic Psychology Monographs, 103,* 261–324.

Richards, R. L., & Casey, M. B. (1979). Predictors of achievement in a model two-year college. *Community Junior College Research Quarterly, 4,* 205–214.

Richards, R. L., Kinney, D. K., Benet, M., & Merzel, A. P. C. (1988). Assessing everyday creativity: Characteristics of the Lifetime Creativity Scales and validation with three large samples. *Journal of Personality and Social Psychology, 54,* 476–485.

Rogers, C. R. (1961). *On becoming a person.* Boston: Houghton-Mifflin.

U.S. Department of Labor. (1977). *Dictionary of occupational titles* (4th Ed.). Washington, DC: U.S. Government Printing Office.

Weissman, M. M., Gershon, E. S., Kidd, K. K., Prusoff, B. A., Leckman, J. F., Kibble, E., Hamovit, J., Thompson, W. D., Pauls, D. L., & Guroff, J. J. (1984). Psychiatric disorders in the relatives of probands with affective disorders. *Archives of General Psychiatry, 41,* 13–21.

Wender, P. H., Kety, S. S., Rosenthal, D., Schulsinger, F., Ortmann, J., & Lunde, I. (1986). Psychiatric disorders in the biological and adoptive families of adopted individuals with affective disorders. *Archives of General Psychiatry, 43,* 923–929.

Chapter 8

Mood Swings and Creativity*

Ruth Richards[†]
Dennis K. Kinney

A positive mood can affect how we process information; it may even increase our creativity (e.g., Isen, Daubman, & Nowicki, 1987; Snyder & White, 1982). In this chapter, we ask whether this phenomenon may have special significance for people at risk for bipolar mood disorders. The answer may have implications for a large number of people, including the 4%–5% of the population that may develop bipolar "spectrum" disorder (Akiskal & Mallya, 1987), and their unaffected relatives. From the time of Plato and Aristotle, people have linked mood disorders with creativity (Becker, 1978; Jamison, 1990; Richards, 1981). In the first part of this chapter, we evaluate recent evidence for the link between bipolar *diag-*

*From "Mood Swings and Creativity," by R. Richards & D. K. Kinney, 1990, *Creativity Research Journal*, *3*(3), pp. 202–217. Copyright © 1995 Ablex Publishing Corporation. Adapted with permission.

[†]The authors are grateful to Jonathan Cole, M.D. and members of the Manic-Depressive and Depressive Association for their assistance with this study, and to Karen Spritzer for her help with the data analysis.

nosis and creativity. In the second part, we look at preliminary data suggesting particular bipolar mood *states* that may best enhance creativity. This chapter considers a range of bipolar spectrum (Akiskal & Mallya, 1987) mood disorders including (a) the severe mood elevations and depressions of manic-depressive illness or *bipolar disorder type I*, (b) the milder "hypomanic" highs and severe depressions of *bipolar disorder type II*, (c) the milder highs and lows of *cyclothymia*, and (d) the "hidden" situation called *bipolar disorder type III* in which a person subjects to depression becomes hypomanic, or mildly high, after taking antidepressant medication (Akiskal & Akiskal, 1988). (The bipolar disorders will henceforth be called bipolar I, II, and III disorders.) Multiple other features also accompany these mood changes (see American Psychiatric Association, 1987; Jamison, 1990; Keller, 1987).

Even within diagnostic categories, wide variations occur in the frequency and amplitude of mood swings. People with mood disorders may also be perfectly normal between episodes, sometimes even for years. Bipolar disorders have a significant genetic component (Bertelsen, 1979; Wender et al., 1986). They are fortunately very treatable with medication (Andreasen & Glick, 1988; Goodwin & Jamison, 1990).

WHAT IS THE ASSOCIATION BETWEEN CREATIVITY AND BIPOLAR MOOD DISORDERS?

The answer depends on how one frames this question, as well as one's criteria for creativity. This chapter distinguishes between research on *eminent* and *everyday* creativity.

Eminent Creativity

In this sort of study, creativity is identified using one of a number of criteria of social recognition, such as prizes, awards, or citations. Older studies in this area have shown a wide range of methodological problems (Richards, 1981). Nonetheless, as a group, these studies converge in supporting higher levels of psychopathology, including mood disorders, among eminent creators or their relatives (for reviews, see Andreasen, 1987; Jamison, 1990; Richards, 1981). There is more information available on artistic than scientific creativity. Diagnostic problems in these studies leave the actual rates of the disorders uncertain.

Two newer and more rigorous studies show surprisingly high rates of mood disorders among eminent creators in the arts. A full 80% of Andreasen's (1987) 30 faculty from the famed *Iowa Writer's Workshop* had a mood disorder, over half with a bipolar disorder. (Only two subjects approached refused to take part in the research [Andreasen, personal communication, 1989]; hence, the high-risk figure could only be slightly affected by self-selection.) Approximately two-thirds of these bipolar writers had bipolar II disorder, showing the relatively milder hypomanic mood elevations (lacking serious incapacitation) and full depressive lows. The remainder showed the severe manic-depressive mood swings of bipolar I disorder.

We should not overlook Andreasen's (1987) unipolar depressed writers. Unfortunately, we do not know how many had bipolar disorder in their family. In a preliminary study (Richards, Kinney, Daniels, & Linkins, 1992), the level of creativity was found to be significantly higher in depressives with a bipolar family history than in depressives lacking this history. Some of Andreasen's depressive writers could, for instance, have been diagnosable as bipolar III, with latent tendencies toward hypomania.

In the second study (Jamison, 1989, 1990) 47 outstanding British artists and writers, all recipients of major honors, and recruited through a mailing, were interviewed about factors important to their creativity. Approximately one in three agreed to participate in the study (Jamison, personal communication, 1989)—a good response rate. Psychopathology was never mentioned as a focus. Thirty-eight percent of the subjects in this study were found to have been treated for a mood disorder. The figure is impressive, given that other studies (see Jamison, 1989) suggest that one third or less of affectively ill people tend to seek help. The actual rate of affective disorder in Jamison's sample was probably much higher. Also of key importance, 89% of Jamison's artists and writers had experienced intense creative episodes that share many features with clinical hypomania. Thus, some of these creators could have had bipolar II disorder or cyclothymia.

As important as this work is in understanding our eminent artistic creators, it tells us little about (a) the reverse question—whether the millions of people with mood disorders in the population at large in turn show elevated creativity, and (b) the broader question—whether a creative advantage extends beyond eminent artistic or scientific work to *everyday creativity* in the multitudinous facets of daily life. The present study addresses these questions and provides some interesting answers. But we must first address what basis exits for comparing these different types of creativity.

Issues in Comparing Different Types or Levels of Creativity

Domain of creativity

Specific factors may be distinguished in creative activities. Linguistic, mathematical, or musical "intelligences," for instance (e.g., Gardner, 1983), may be necessary for certain creative endeavors. Having talent in one area in no way guarantees having it in another. However, these capacities are not necessarily the defining ingredients that give creativity its flavor (Tardif & Sternberg, 1988). For instance, one can produce exceptionally skilled but basically unimaginative artwork, or technically simple yet dramatically original compositions.

One research approach is to simultaneously examine creativity in a number of areas, effectively collapsing across more domain- or task-specific factors while seeking a common quality that might remain. Such a general quality might be especially prominent where mood disorders are concerned. Andreasen (1987), for instance, found greater creativity among the relatives of eminent writers than control subjects, and this creativity embraced a variety of enterprises, not just literary ones.

In our research, we have employed a broad-based measure of everyday creativity, the *Lifetime Creativity Scales* (Richards, Kinney, Benet, & Merzel, 1988). Virtually any endeavor can be assessed for creativity if it meets the two widely accepted criteria (after Barron, 1969) of originality and adaptation to reality. Everyday creativity, so defined, can run the gamut from the commonplace to the notable accomplishments that may lead (among other things) to eminence—reflecting the many ways in which people realize their creative potentials. This rationale draws in part on evidence for a "disposition toward originality" and "core" personality traits associated with creativity across fields (Barron, 1969, 1988; Barron & Harrington, 1981). This central quality in creativity might also be compared to what Amabile (1983) termed creative *task attitudes*, rather than her other two components of creativity, *innate skills* and *learned abilities*.

The notion of everyday creativity is also based in the concept from evolutionary biology of "phenotypic plasticity" (Dobzhansky, 1962). This involves the basic capacity of human beings—indeed of all living things—to adapt flexibly to changing environments (also see Sinott, 1959). Everyday creativity, in this view, might even be considered a generic form of creativity, with other forms representing special cases. Defined in terms of adaptive capacity, such creativity logically pertains to many types of activities at many levels of complexity; it serves, after all, as a basis for human survival. Different endeavors, then, should certainly bear some common points for comparison.

Level of creativity

Some authors have distinguished two types of creativity, *major* and *minor* (e.g., Arieti, 1976; Mumford & Gustafson, 1988). Major creativity requires a significant change in one's own conceptual framework. In minor creativity, one applies existing strategies to new tasks. For example, few would argue that Pasteur, in developing the germ theory of disease, totally changed how he (and we) think about the origins of infection. Most would say this contribution was more creative than the—nonetheless difficult and innovative—job of developing new antibiotics against particular organisms.

However, the real question is whether there are forms of creative process so qualitatively different that one cannot conceivably shade into the other. And if so, then why are there just two levels of creative outcome, and not three or four? Increasingly, researcher are finding many similarities in mental strategies employed at different levels of cognitive and creative complexity (e.g., Gardner, 1988; Perkins, 1981; Simonton, 1988; Weisberg, 1986). As Perkins (1981) stated, "These same resources of selection explain masterly and more ordinary creating. The master will notice more, remember more, exercise better critical judgment, and so on, but the processes involved are the same in kind" (p. 287).

The *Lifetime Creativity Scales* presuppose that, on rather crude (six-point) scales, one can meaningfully compare the innovation (or effort) characterizing a wide range of creative accomplishments—even at the extremes of everyday and eminent creativity. These creativity scales have demonstrated multiple indications of construct validity (Richards, Kinney, Benet, & Merzel, 1988). The simplicity of these measures also need not detract from the unique and multidimensional detail of specific products of creation, which would require much more complex modes of description.

EVERYDAY CREATIVITY

We conducted the first study of overall creativity in subjects chosen only by diagnostic criteria. This turned the research design usually used for studying creativity and psychopathology around; it meant assessing creativity wherever we found it, no matter what a person's interests and activities, and whether their work had received social recognition. We asked if bipolar I (manic-depressive) subjects, cyclothymes, or their first-degree normal relatives would show higher everyday creativity than two groups of control subjects—either psychiatrically normal controls or those carrying other diagnoses (Richards, Kinney, Lunde, Benet, & Mer-zel, 1988).

Our results were different from those for the eminent and exceptionally creative. We looked at "Peak Creativity," based on the most original major enterprise of a subject's adult lifetime, and found bipolar I subjects showed no special advantage (or disadvantage) in levels of everyday creativity. The creative advantage was found in the cyclothymes and, very interestingly, in the psychiatrically normal relatives of bipolars. Results supported our *inverted-U* hypothesis, that an optimal manifestation of an underlying bipolar risk may be a better predictor of creativity than a stronger manifestation (as in bipolar I disorder) or a lack of bipolar risk (as in the psychiatric normalcy of controls lacking a family history of bipolarity). Creativity might serve as a *compensatory advantage* rot he risk for bipolar disorder, somewhat similar perhaps to the heterozygote advantage seen in carriers of sickle cell anemia, namely, resistance to malaria. A compensatory advantage to bipolar mood disorders might even help explain the persistence of this genetically influenced spectrum of conditions down through the generations.

A familial compensatory advantage could even go beyond creativity to include accomplishment in general. Coryell et al. (1989) found that first-degree relatives of bipolar I and II subjects excelled in occupational or educational achievement over the relatives of unipolar subjects. (The depressed and the bipolar I and II subjects themselves did not differ.) In work with the eminent, Jamison (1990) also addressed leadership and socioeconomic advantages linked to bipolar disorder.

It is important to modify our *inverted-U* position a bit. It appears that intermediate levels of mood *elevations* may "count" more for creativity than the milder forms of the depressive phase (Richards & Kinney, 1989). Indeed, our cyclothymes, who were diagnosed using an earlier diagnostic scheme, may have included subjects who would now be diagnosed as bipolar II (Richards, et al., 1988). In more recent work (Kinney, et al., 1989; Richards, et al., 1992), bipolar II subjects showed a high level of vocational creativity, similar to the cyclothymes in our previous work (Richards, et al., 1988), and bipolar I subjects fell closer to typical values for vocational creativity in several previous control samples. Akiskal and Akiskal (1988) also found higher artistic creativity in a group of patients diagnosed bipolar II and III (those with milder or latent mood elevations, along with full major depressions) than in a group of bipolar I and schizoaffective subjects.

Thus, the overall severity of illness does not appear to be the key variable, nor one inversely related to creativity. Bipolar II disorder in particular can be a very disabling condition. In one follow-up study, bipolar II patients had made more suicide attempts than bipolar I or unipolar patients (Keller, 1987). Rather, mood elevations may be more important than depressions where creativity is concerned, with mildly elevated mood states more important than extreme elevations.

From this perspective, we may now attempt to bridge the gap between results for eminent versus everyday creativity and bipolar disorders.

Reconciling Patterns for Everyday Versus Eminent Creativity

Is there even a basis for reconciliation?

Judging from past research, major mood disorders appear more common and serious among eminent than everyday creators. Yet comparisons between the two types of studies are limited by design differences (Richards, 1981). These includes use of creativity as the dependent rather than independent variable, and assessment of the wide range of endeavors and levels of complexity of everyday creativity, rather than the relatively more homogeneous results of eminent creativity in a specific domain. Future work will separate meaningful differences from methodological artifacts. But some speculations now might help guide that inquiry.

Significance of similarities between studies

Whether we consider eminent or everyday creativity, it is still not the extreme disabilities or mood states that are most strongly linked with creativity. This is especially clear for mood elevations. Bipolar II disorder is perhaps emerging as particularly important, both among eminent creators (Andreasen, 1987; Jamison, 1989), and everyday creators (Akiskal & Akiskal, 1988; Richards, et al., 1988; Richards, et al., 1992).

We would re-emphasize the variety of presentations within (as well as between) bipolar diagnoses, including the presence of high-functioning periods. High-creators may spend significant time at this more functional end of the mood state spectrum. One hopeful possibility is that creative behavior may work in the service of health, and can sometimes aid coping and help preserve this functional state (Richards & Kinney, 1989). From another perspective, pharmacological treatment of bipolar disorders can modulate mood states, increase functional control, and often enhance creativity (e.g., Andreasen & Glick, 1988; Schou, 1979).

Significance of differences between studies

We still need to understand how as many as four out of five eminent creators (Andreasen, 1987) could show a major mood disorder, but everyday creators appear relatively healthy. This latter finding makes sense, at least, if everyday creativity, as we have defined it, is an essential part of health, adaptation, growth, and human survival.

Various hypotheses have been advanced regarding the value of creativity of major mood disorders (e.g., Akiskal & Akiskal, 1988; Andreasen & Glick, 1988; Jamison, 1990; Jamison, Gerner, Hammen, & Padesky, 1980; Richards, 1981; Richards & Kinney, 1989). As one explanation, the mood-disordered experience may provide material to enrich and motivate artistic creative expression. Beyond this, we would suggest that certain facets of bipolar illness may pertain more to *motivation* than creative process; they may raise the chance of "eminent" recognition when creative talent is already present (Richards & Kinney, 1989).

First we note the possible results of the combination of driven, work-focused tendencies and bipolar potential to think in broad (if not grandiose) terms. Akiskal, Hirschfeld, and Yerevanian (1983) noted a hard-driven work-orientation among bipolar individuals. The work tendency is supported by our own research, where it was the cyclothymes who showed the highest vocational creativity, and normal relatives of bipolars excelled in leisure-time creativity (Richards, et al., 1988). Interestingly, manic-depressive children have also demonstrated, in addition to some special talents, obsessive interests and what has been called an "attention excess disorder" (DeLong & Aldershof, 1988). An obsessive drive, turned toward the vocational arena, would be more likely to affect others, even society at large, and could consequently raise the chance of social recognition. Recognition of important creative strengths could also provide needed external validation for persons with a fluctuating experience of themselves.

Secondly, we note a sense of "standing apart" which the bipolar person, as well as others with physical or psychiatric disorders, may experience (Richards & Kinney, 1989). This explanation is adapted from Richards' (1981) typology of interactions between psychopathology and creativity, and is consistent with Gardner and Wolf's (1988) "asynchrony hypothesis." A creator who innovates at a socially significant level may well need to oppose societal norms and negotiate public resistance to change. This is also the case for innovative leadership. A person who already "stands apart," and who has the other strengths and talents necessary for creating, may have less difficulty assuming this challenger role than someone whose path has been more conventional. Some more rebellious or iconoclastic creators may even seek this role out.

Thus we posit that the risk for bipolar disorder may enhance the creative process in a variety of ways for both eminent and everyday creativity. But the arena of expression, as well as its motivation, may differ between groups and help account for high rates of mood disorders among some eminent writers and artists.

Now we focus more closely on the mood *states* that may facilitate creativity.

WHICH BIPOLAR MOOD STATES MAY ENHANCE CREATIVITY?

Richards (1981; Richards & Kinney, 1989) suggested that there are cognitive, affective, and motivational advantages of a mild hypomanic state for creativity. (One may note that the hypomanic or mildly elevated mood state is found in all of *hyperthymia, cyclothymia,* and *bipolar II disorder,* conditions that differ most markedly at the depressive pole). Potential advantages of hypomania include a richer associative and cognitive process, heightened emotional awareness, and energizing potential. It is interesting that the third edition of the *Diagnostic and Statistical Manual of Mental Disorders* (APA, 1980) even gave one criterion for clinical hypomania as "sharpened and unusually creative thinking." The most detailed information relevant to this point is given by Jamison (1989), who reported that 89% of her eminent artists and writers had brief creative episodes reminiscent of hypomania. These episodes had a modal duration of two weeks. She identified over two dozen features with some degree of association of these episodes, including enthusiasm, confidence, energy, and speed of mental association.

Jamison et al. (1980) also looked at the perceived effects of a hypomanic state on a patient population, and found that subjects felt more creative and productive during those episodes. However, Jamison did not compare normalcy (euthymia) and other mood states. It was during periods of normal functioning, according to Andreasen (1987), that her eminent writers tended to be most creative. We could straddle this fence by citing our own finding of heightened everyday creativity among the psychiatrically *normal* relatives of bipolars. The creative advantage among people at risk for bipolar disorder may not translate into a particular symptom picture, and could even be more of a trait, than state, phenomenon. However, we suspect that some of the normal relatives in our research may have been somewhat *hyperthymic* (Richards, et al., 1988), that is, showing a recurrent tendency to milder mood elevations or hypomania, but lacking the depressive lows (Akiskal & Mallya, 1987).

In the present study, we therefore: (a) compared patients with bipolar I and II disorders and unipolar mood disorders regarding the moods during which they felt most creative, asking about mild and extreme mood states, as well as normalcy. We also (b) asked patients about the importance to their experience of everyday creativity of the 23 mood, cognitive, and behavioral features Jamison (1989) studied in eminent artists and writers during their intense creative episodes. We asked if these would be more relevant for bipolar patients whose creative experience peaked during mood elevation that for those for whom normalcy was the most creative state. We also (c) asked if there was a smaller number of factors or dimensions underlying these features of creative experience that might help us better understand them.

RESEARCH DESIGN

Attendees at a local chapter meeting of the national Manic-Depressive and Depressive Association (MDDA), a self-help and support group, were asked to complete a voluntary and anonymous questionnaire about "moods and personality." These subjects included people with bipolar or unipolar mood disorders and their relatives. MDDA members were selected because of their high-functioning characteristics, including the potential for a range of creative experiences, and a very high personal awareness of the nature and features of their illnesses.

Questionnaire items were typically of checklist form. Included were background questions on demographics and personal and family psychiatric history. Diagnoses provided included major depression, bipolar I and II disorders, and "other," with brief definitions of these. In addition, one experimenter reviewed in detail the relevant diagnostic categories with the group, as per the *Diagnostic and Statistical Manual* (DSM-III-R), and answered questions. Because MDDA members tend to be sophisticated patients, are in psychiatric treatment, and have regular exposure to information on mood disorders, this brief lecture was viewed as only supplementary, to aid the subjects in reporting their own diagnoses.

Subjects then completed two tasks. First, they checked off their most typical mood states at the times they experienced the highest levels of five characteristics (adapted from Jamison et al., 1980): sensitivity/alertness, productivity, creativity, good judgment, concentration. A five-point scale was used: *extremely depressed, somewhat depressed, normal mood, somewhat elevated, very elevated.* Creativity was defined as "the ability to produce new or original ideas that could be used for doing things better, solving problems, making things, helping people." Only the creativity results will be reported here.

Subjects next indicated the degree of relevance of 23 characteristics to their "most creative period" (during whichever mood state that happened to represent for them), using another five-point scale: *much less, somewhat less, about the same, somewhat more, and much more than usual.* We focused on the patient experience for two reasons: First, because self-reports of personality and creativity can be notably accurate measures (e.g., Hocevar, 1981), and second, because the experience of heightened or lessened creativity is in itself crucial for understanding mood-disordered patients, their self-concept, potential, expectations, and attitudes toward treatment.

Results

Definition of groups

Ninety-one percent (75) of the MDDA attendees turned in their questionnaire. This included 49 subjects who reported a clear bipolar or unipolar mood disorder. Twelve subjects had unipolar depression, all but one lacking a family history of bipolar disorder; these 11 were designated the unipolar depressed group for later analysis. Twenty-eight subjects had bipolar I diagnoses, and were considered a group. Nine others had a history of mood swings with hypomania, two with cyclothymia and the remainder with bipolar II disorder; they were all grouped together as well. Of these 48 subjects, 94% (all but two unipolar and one bipolar II subject) indicated their diagnosis was one that a clinician had communicated to them. There were 20 females and 28 males. A chi-square test showed no significant effect of sex on diagnosis for these three groups. Age ranges had been used, rather than actual ages, to further protect subjects' anonymity. The modal age range was 36–45 years for each group, ranging from a minimum of 18–25 to grater than 65 years. As expected, subjects were highly educated, with a minimum of a high school education, and modal educational level of 18, 16, and 17 years for the depressives, bipolar I, and bipolar II subjects, respectively.

Primary Analyses

1. **Do bipolar subjects experience the highest creativity when their mood is mildly elevated, and are such mood elevations less important for unipolar depressive subjects (here, unipolars lacking bipolar family history)?** Table 8.1 shows the "most creative mood state" for three groups: depressives, bipolar subjects with severe mood elevations, and bipolar subjects with milder mood elevations (mania and hypomania, respectively). We termed these groups bipolar I and II for convenience, but recognized the two cyclothymes in the latter group. For analysis, the subjects were collapsed into a 2 × 2 structure, as shown in Table 8.1. A one-tailed fisher's Exact

Table 8.1. Most Creative Mood State for Unipolar Depressed Subjects and for Bipolar Subjects with Hypomanic and Manic Mood Elevations

	Mood When Most Creative				
Diagnosis	Very Depressed	Mildly Depressed	Normal	Mildly Elevated	Very Elevated
Unipolar, Depressed, No Bipolar Family	1	1	4	2	3
Bipolar with Mania (Type I)	1	0	6	15	6
Bipolar with Hypomania) (Type II*)	1	0	0	4	4

*and two subjects with Cyclothymia

Test showed a significant link (p=.045) between the presence or absence of mood elevation when most creative (a mood elevation of any degree), and bipolar/unipolar status.

It is also evident that *mild* elevations may be key to the exper-ience of creativity for *bipolars*. A notable 54% and 44% of the bi-polar I and II groups (showing mania and hypomania, respectively) experienced the greatest creativity when mildly high, as compared with only 18% of the depressives. A one-tailed Fisher's Exact Test for mild mood elevation versus all other mood states, for all bipolar versus unipolar subjects, yielded a result that is surely an underestimate (p = .052). This is because the actual percentage of bipolar II subjects reporting their creative peaks during submanic mood elevations is more likely to have been 89% (mildly elevated plus very elevated mood state) than 44% (mildly elevated, only). For bipolar II subjects, even their highest mood elevations are, by definition, in the "milder" category. (For this reason, we did not further test the Bipolar Type I and II differences. Clinician assessment of mood states could be included in future work as one way around this difficulty.)

2. **Are different features important to the experience of creativity for bipolars who differ in their "most creative mood state"?** Table 8.2 shows the 34 bipolar subjects for whom complete data were available. Seven reported *normal* mood, 20 *mildly elevated* mood, and 7 *very elevated* mood, when experiencing the greatest creativity. Bipolar I and II subjects appeared in roughly equal proportions in each group (6 and 1, 15 and 5, and 5 and 2 subjects, respectively). One sees that many of these features—previously reported in eminent artists and writers—appear as well in this noneminent patient population. Furthermore, the pattern of findings is quite similar (except for low need for sleep) for the mildly elevated and very elevated mood groups.

The similarity disappears, however, when the *normal* mood group is compared to the *elevated* mood groups. In Table 8.2, the first 10 features (associative speed, ease of thinking, new ideas, energy, euphoria, expansiveness, impulsivity, low need for sleep, sociability, and talkativeness) were set apart to illustrate a pattern of features most clearly tied to *elevated* mood states. These variables were not tested statistically because of the small sample size. However, the main point is not the particular distinguishing variables but, rather, the general possibility that mood elevations may influence the character of one's most creative experiences.

3. **Is there a smaller number of meaningful clusters of these 23 mood, cognitive, and behavioral features of subjects' "most creative" states?** Tables 8.3 and 8.4 show descriptive statistics and intercorrelations on the 23 variables for 71 MDDA attendees, the

Table 8.2. *Percentage of Bipolar Subjects Reporting Either Mild or Pronounced Levels of 23 Characteristics During Their Most Creative Mood State*

Feature	"Most Creative" Mood State		
	Normal Mood (n=7)	Mildly Elevated (n=20)	Very Elevated (n=7)
Expansiveness	0	72	86
Impulsivity	17	79	86
Need for Little Sleep	29	50	100
Interest in Socializing	33	89	86
Rapid Thinking	40	85	100
Ease of Thinking of New Ideas (Fluency)	40	95	86
Speed of Mental Associations	43	85	86
Talkativeness	50	84	100
Energy	57	90	100
Euphoria (High, Pleasant Mood)	57	85	86
Religious Thoughts or Feelings	17	26	33
Sexual Interests	20	45	43
Sensitivity to Sensations	29	55	43
Irritability	33	63	57
Spending of Money	33	50	43
Anxiety	33	40	43
Suspiciousness	33	26	33
Argumentativeness	33	50	57
Restlessness	50	80	86
Positive Sense of Well-Being	67	79	83
Self-Confidence	71	89	86
Intensity of Feelings	71	80	71
Enthusiasm	71	95	86

Note. The first 10 features are set apart to illustrate a pattern of stronger association with creative experience during mood elevations than during a normal mood state.

largest subject group to complete this portion of the questionnaire. All available data were used for each calculation; missing data sometimes lowered the sample size further, as seen in Table 8.3. Nearly all of these MDDA members may be considered at risk for a mood disorder because they either actually had such a disorder or were related to someone who did.

Table 8.5 shows a factor analysis of the 23 variables; the results should be viewed as preliminary because of small sample size for this variable set. A principal components solution produced six factors with eigenvalues greater than one, accounting for 72% of the variance; these factors were rotated to the varimax criterion. (Notably, a factor analysis for the smaller subsample of unipolar and bipolar patients produced a similar solution.)

Table 8.3. *Means and Standard Deviations*
on 23 Features of the Most Creative Mood State
for Subjects at Risk for a Mood Disorder

Feature	n	M	SD
Enthusiasm	71	4.15	0.82
Energy	71	4.20	0.90
Emotional Intensity	70	3.80	1.03
Confidence	69	4.13	0.89
Expansiveness	63	3.87	0.81
Associative Speed	71	3.96	0.92
Fluency	69	4.04	0.81
Well-Being	68	3.88	1.00
Sleep Need	70	2.49	1.10
Euphoria	68	4.00	0.91
Sociability	69	3.80	0.87
Talkativeness	68	3.99	0.82
Rapid Thinking	68	3.88	0.99
Impulsivity	68	3.78	0.94
Restlessness	70	3.59	1.14
Irritability	68	3.18	1.35
Sensory Awareness	70	3.51	0.96
Sexuality	68	3.46	0.89
Spending	69	3.49	0.83
Anxiety	70	2.74	1.28
Suspiciousness	67	2.69	1.25
Argumentativeness	69	3.13	1.14
Religious Thoughts	67	3.07	1.00

Note. Features were rated using a 5-point scale. All
available data were used for each variable.

From the variables that load most strongly on them, the factors
might be named: (I) Intense Energy/Cognition; (II) Restless Impulsivity; (III) Anxious Paranoia; (IV) Sleeplessness; (V) Sensory
Stimulation; (VI) Religiosity. The 10 features of creative states that
best distinguish the normal from elevated mood groups in Table
8.2, above, come primarily from Factors I and II. But, interestingly,
not all of the features loading on Factors I and II appear to be as
important in distinguishing the normal from elevated mood groups.

DISCUSSION

Elevated mood has been shown to enhance creativity in a nonpsychiatric
population (e.g., Isen et al., 1987). But for people with bipolar disorders,
elevated moods may carry added potential. Significantly, it is a *milder* mood

Table 8.4. Intercorrelations Between 23 Features of the Most Creative Mood State for 71 Subjects at Risk for a Mood Disorder

Feature	1	2	3	4	5	6	7	8	9	10	11	12	13	14	15	16	17	18	19	20	21	22	23
1 Enthusiasm		52	16	39	43	33	58	28	-51	35	32	40	11	25	05	-14	29	18	16	-31	-12	-03	04
2 Energy			28	52	44	72	53	56	-39	60	53	36	17	25	15	-11	24	43	16	-22	-14	-05	05
3 Emotional Intensity				31	17	34	33	10	00	24	16	09	20	11	13	08	26	03	-03	00	06	20	-16
4 Confidence					46	55	64	48	-44	59	40	58	33	46	16	-08	30	25	34	-18	-03	22	12
5 Expansiveness						56	46	33	-56	44	52	45	51	41	21	-06	27	26	26	-24	00	22	05
6 Associative Speed							75	50	-35	63	56	39	37	31	30	-04	39	35	31	-21	-05	15	-03
7 Fluency								41	-31	55	42	46	35	50	28	-13	44	30	20	-26	-01	21	09
8 Well-being									-29	57	50	28	03	08	-10	-04	52	49	31	-20	-14	05	-09
9 Sleep need										-34	-28	-51	-24	-37	-22	08	-15	-08	-23	14	10	-06	09
10 Euphoria											49	38	12	26	05	-15	30	36	27	-30	-24	00	21
11 Sociability												52	08	20	05	-10	20	34	19	-30	-29	06	-19
12 Talkativeness													34	46	20	15	15	25	39	-03	-03	32	12
13 Rapid thinking														56	51	24	18	14	24	20	42	48	07
14 Impulsivity															55	27	17	12	23	12	16	48	13
15 Restlessness																42	05	-05	33	41	48	65	15
16 Irritability																	-08	-04	20	38	45	48	-02
17 Sensory awareness																		43	44	-07	11	15	-04
18 Sexuality																			21	-26	-12	00	01
19 Spending																				05	28	35	14
20 Anxiety																					57	37	07
21 Suspicious																						59	14
22 Argumentative																							03
23 Religious thought																							

151

Table 8.5. Factor Analysis of Features of Most Creative State
for 71 Subjects at Risk for Bipolar or Unipolar Disorders

	Factor						
Features	I	II	III	IV	V	VI	h²
Enthusiasm	78						71
Energy	81						74
Emotional Intensity	72					35	78
Confidence	68			42			78
Expansiveness		64		38			67
Associative Speed	62	45					75
Fluency	62	52			32		77
Well-Being	54			37	51		77
Sleep need	−38			−73			76
Euphoria	67			35			64
Sociability	43	34		32	−50		72
Talkativeness	43	45		59			81
Rapid Thinking		83					79
Impulsivity		80					72
Restlessness		66	50				77
Irritability		71					59
Sensory Awareness					81		73
Sexuality					67		55
Spending				64	56		81
Anxiety			68		−37		63
Suspicious			75				68
Argumentative		64	46			−32	75
Religious Thoughts							84

Note. Loadings of .30 or higher are reported. Decimal points are omitted. Factors are tentatively named: (I) Intense Energy/Cognition, (II) Restless Impulsivity, (III) Anxious Paranoia, (IV) Sleeplessness, (V) Sensory Stimulation, and (VI) Religiosity.

state, not an extreme one—that appears most facilitative. Findings are consistent with our hypothesized *inverted-U* relationship (Richards, et al., 1988) between manifestations of bipolar risk and creativity, that is, with our notion of an optimal level, at least as far as mood *elevations* are concerned.

These results do not directly explain our previous finding (Richards, et al., 1988) of enhanced creativity in the psychiatrically *normal* relatives of bipolars. One might posit a trait rather than state phenomenon, consistent with nonclinical phenomena, in which subclinical factors related to bipolar risk (rather than some obvious modulation of symptoms) enhance creativity. But we would again suggest that some members of our "normal" group may have been clinically *hyperthymic* (Akiskal & Mallya, 1987). The question might then involve what range a "mild" mood elevation might assume (from how subtle to how severe, and also perhaps how short or long) to best facilitate creativity.

We should also keep in mind those subjects who *do* create best during normalcy, or enduring severe depressions. There is no one single pattern to the relationship between mood and creativity. Much more detail about an individual's course of mood swings (their frequency and amplitude over time), and the totality of their illness is needed to get the full picture. The domain of their creative activities and the level of creativity (e.g., everyday vs. eminent) might also be important. Depressive lows, for instance, might well be spurs for certain forms of drama or poetry for some people.

We next turn to reasons *why* a particular mood state might enhance creativity. Characteristics reported during intense creative episodes by Jamison's (1989) eminent artists and writers seem to be applicable to a patient population. The greatest number of these features, once again, apply to subjects who feel most creative during mood elevations. This study can only demonstrate association between mood states and creativity, and does not show causality. Nonetheless, these characteristics pertain to *cognition* (e.g., rapid thinking), *affect* (e.g., euphoria), as well as factors influencing *motivation* (e.g., energy), and show face validity as enhancers of creativity.

There is also a more limited subset of features (e.g., sense of well-being, confidence, intense feelings, and enthusiasm) that applies equally well to subjects who report creativity during "normal" mood states. An underlying hyperthymia may be less likely in these subjects who de-emphasize features such as energy, little sleep, talkativeness, and euphoria. These features may reflect "true" creative normalcy, existing as a transient state in this mood-disordered group and perhaps also as an ongoing condition in more healthy individuals. Such features need to be studied in nonpsychiatric as well as psychiatric samples, and in unipolar as well as bipolar subjects and their relatives. Factor analysis can also help simplify the dimensions of interest. Finally, actual creative accomplishment needs to be assessed as a function of these perceived creativity-enhancing (and less creativity-enhancing) internal conditions. Because our sample of MDDA members encompasses a variety of occupations and interest, one might posit that the mood, cognitive, and behavioral changes studied are *not* domain-specific; they could facilitate a broad range of actual creative endeavors.

In conclusion, there do indeed appear to be associations between the risk for bipolar disorders and both eminent and everyday creativity. Although patterns are sure to be more complicated, with much individual variation, mildly elevated mood states may have the most overall advantages when one is actively creating. However, there is much yet to be learned.

Finally, we would re-emphasize the importance of the affective dimension to creativity in general, especially in an era when "on-line" studies of cognitive process are becoming highly sophisticated (see Gardner, 1988; Tardif & Sternberg, 1988). Integration of affective variables into such studies could be very revealing. Emotions can serve as subjects or mediums of creative expression, as strong motivating forces, and as close companions to cognition in the identification of problems to explore (e.g., Sternberg, 1988), chanelling ongoing inquiry and decision-making (e.g., Perkins, 1981), or evaluating a creation's success, elegance, or esthetic fit (e.g., Barron, 1969, 1988). The fact that enhanced creativity is connected with psychiatric mood disorders should perhaps, finally, underline the importance of mood for all of us.

REFERENCES

Akiskal, H. S., & Akiskal, K. (1988). Reassessing the prevalence of bipolar disorders: Clinical significance and artistic creativity. *Psychiatry and Psychobiology, 3*, 29–36.

Akiskal, H. S., Hirschfeld, R. M. A., & Yerevanian, B. I. (1983). The relationship of personality to affective disorders: A critical review. *Archives of General Psychiatry, 40*, 801–810.

Akiskal, H. S., & Mallya, G. (1987). Criteria for the "soft" bipolar spectrum: Treatment implications. *Psychopharmacology Bulletin, 23*, 68–73.

Amabile, T. (1983). *the social psychology of creativity.* New York: Springer-Verlag.

American Psychiatric Association (1980). *Diagnostic and statistical manual of mental disorders* (3rd ed.). Washington, DC: Author.

American Psychiatric Association (1987). *Diagnostic and statistical manual of mental disorders* (3rd ed., revised). Washington, DC: Author.

Andreasen, N. C. (1987). Creativity and mental illness: Prevalence rates in writers and their first-degree relatives. *American Journal of Psychiatry, 144,* 1288–1292.

Andreasen, N. C., & Glick, I. D. (1988). Bipolar affective disorder and creativity: Implications and clinical management. *Comprehensive Psychiatry, 29,* 207–216.

Arieti, S. (1976). *Creativity: The magic synthesis.* New York: Basic Books.

Barron, F. (1969). *Creative person and creative process.* New York: Holt, Rinehart & Winston.

Barron, F. (1988). Putting creativity to work. In R. Sternberg (Ed.), *The nature of creativity* (pp. 76–98). New York: Cambridge University Press.

Barron, F., & Harrington, D. M. (1981). Creativity, intelligence, and personality. *Annual Review of Psychology, 32,* 439–476.

Becker, G. (1978). *The mad genius controversy.* Beverly Hills, CA: Sage.

Bertelsen, A. (1979). A Danish twin study of manic-depressive disorders. In M. Schou & E. Stromgren (Eds.), *Origin, prevention, and treatment of affective disorders* (pp. 227–239). Orlando, FL: Academic.

Coryell, W., Endicott, J., Keller, M., Andreasen, N., Grove, W., Hirschfeld, R. M. A., & Scheftner, W. (1989). Bipolar affective disorder and high achievement: A familial association. *American Journal of Psychiatry, 146*, 983–995.

DeLong, G. R., & Aldershof, A. L. (1988). An association of special abilities with juvenile manic-depressive illness. In L. Obler & D. Fein (Eds.), *The exceptional brain* (pp. 387–395). New York: Guilford Press.

Dobzhansky, T. (1962). *Mankind evolving.* New Haven, CT: Yale University Press.

Gardner, H. (1983). *Frames of mind.* New York: Basic.

Gardner, H. (1988). Creativity: An interdisciplinary perspective. *Creativity Research Journal, 1*, 8–26.

Gardner, H., & Wolf, C. (1988). The fruits of asynchrony: A psychology examination of creativity. *Adolescent Psychiatry, 15*, 96–120.

Goodwin, F. K., & Jamison, K. R. (1990). *Manic-depressive illness.* New York: Oxford University Press.

Hocevar, D. (1981). Measurement of creativity: Review and critique. *Journal of Personality Assessment, 45*, 450–464.

Isen, A. M., Daubman, K. A., & Nowicki, G. P. (1987). Positive affect facilitates creative problem solving. *Journal of Personality and Social Psychology, 52*, 1122–1131.

Jamison, K. R. (1989). Mood disorders and patterns of creativity in British writers and artists. *Psychiatry, 52*, 125–134.

Jamison, K. R. (1990). Manic-depressive illness and accomplishment: Creativity, leadership, and social class. In F. Goodwin & K. R. Jamison (Eds.), *Manic-depressive illness* (pp. 332–367). New York: Oxford University Press.

Jamison, K. R., Gerner, R. H., Hammen, C., & Padesky, C. (1980). Clouds and silver linings: Positive experiences associated with primary affective disorders. *American Journal of Psychiatry, 137*, 198–202.

Keller, M. B. (1987). Differential diagnosis, natural course, and epidemiology of bipolar disorders. In R. E. Hales & A. J. Frances (Eds.), *American Psychiatric Association Annual Review* (Vol. 6, pp. 10–31). Washington, DC: American Psychiatric Association.

Kinney, D. K., Richards, R., Daniels, H., & Linkins, K. W. (1989). *Influences of moods on creativity in bipolar, unipolar, and cyclothymic patients.* Unpublished manuscript.

Mumford, M. D., & Gustafson, S. B. (1988). Creativity syndrome: Integration, application, and innovation. *Psychological Bulletin, 103*, 27–43.

Perkins, D. N. (1981). *The mind's best work.* Cambridge, MA: Harvard University Press.

Richards, R. (1981). Relationships between creativity and psychopathology: An evaluation and interpretation of the evidence. *Genetic Psychology Monographs, 103*, 261–324.

Richards, R., & Kinney, D. K. (1989). Creativity and manic-depressive illness (letter). *Comprehensive Psychiatry, 30*, 272–273.

Richards, R., Kinney, D. K., Daniels, H., & Linkins, K. (1992). Everyday creativity and bipolar and unipolar affective disorder: Preliminary study of personal and family history. *European Psychiatry, 7*, 49–52.

Richards, R., Kinney, D. K., Benet, M. & Merzel, A. P. C. (1988). Assessing everyday creativity: Characteristics of the Lifetime Creativity Scales and validation with three large samples. *Journal of Personality and Social Psychology, 54,* 476–485.

Richards, R., Kinney, D. K., Lunde, I., Benet, M., & Merzel, A. P. C. (1988). Creativity in manic-depressives, cyclothymes, their normal relatives, and control subjects. *Journal of Abnormal Psychology, 97,* 281–288.

Schou, M. (1979). Artistic productivity and lithium prophylaxis in manic-depressive illness. *British Journal of Psychiatry, 135,* 97–103.

Simonton, D. K. (1988). *Scientific genius: A psychology of science.* New York: Cambridge University Press.

Sinott, E. W. (1959). The creativeness of life. In H. H. Anderson (Ed.), *Creativity and its cultivation* (pp. 12–29). New York: Harper & Row.

Snyder, M., & White, P. (1982). Moods and memories: Elation, depression, and the remembering of the events of one's life. *Journal of Personality, 50,* 149–167.

Sternberg, R. (1988). A three-facet model of creativity. In R. Sternberg (Ed.), *The nature of creativity* (pp. 125–147). New York: Cambridge University Press.

Tardif, T. Z., & Sternberg, R. J. (1988). What do we know about creativity? In R. J. Sternberg (Ed.), *The nature of creativity* (pp. 429–440). New York: Cambridge University Press.

Weisberg, R. W. (1986). *Creativity, genius, and other myths.* New York: W. H. Freeman.

Wender, P. H., Kety, S. S., Rosenthal, D., Schulsinger, F., Ortmann, J., & Lunde, I. (1986). Psychiatric disorders in the biological and adoptive families of adopted individuals with affective disorders. *Archives of General Psychiatry, 43,* 923–929.

Chapter 9

Schizotypal and Hypomanic Traits, Creativity, and Psychological Health*

David Schuldberg†

The connection between genius and madness was initially investigated biographically. Although many creative people have led traumatic lives, suffered great adversity, and at one time or another exhibited deviant be-

*From "Schizotypal and Hypomanic Traits, Creativity, and Psychological Health," by D. Schuldberg, 1990, *Creativity Research Journal*, 3(3), pp. 218–230. Copyright © 1995. Ablex Publishing Corporation. Adapted with permission.

†Assistance was provided by the University of Montana Office of Research Administration and a grant from Montanans on a New Track for Science (MONTS). The author also gratefully acknowledges the support of a NIMH Postdoctoral Fellowship in Clinical Research, Department of Psychiatry, Yale University School of Medicine and the Clinical Science Research Center in Psychiatry, Yale University (Grant # 5 P50 MH 30929), as well as discussions with Drs. Donald M. Quinlan, William S. Edell, Sidney J. Blatt, John Strauss, and Courtenay Harding. The author also wishes to thank Drs. David Strobel, Kendall Bryant, Mark Runco, two anonymous reviewers, Jim Allen, Carol Blum, Jeanette Heberle, Rosemary Toomey, Jeff Arntson, James Boone, Russell Feist, Katie Fitzpatrick, Tim Hepburn, Jill Jeakins, Paul Jensen, Leah Lescantz, David Means, John Menello, Dan Normandeau, Bob Norton, Laura Ross, Linda Schultz, Myrna Heinrich Terry, Laurie Toner, and Randy Winstead.

Portions of this article were presented at the 50th annual meeting of the Society for Personality Assessment, New York, April 13–15, 1989.

havior, the study of the life histories of the creative and eminent has the potential for retrospective bias, and typically lacks appropriate contrast groups (Goertzel, Goertzel, & Goertzel, 1978; Prentky, 1980). Nevertheless, schizophrenia, affective disorder, organic pathology, antisocial behavior, and alcohol and substance abuse have also emerged in empirical research with creative populations, and some nonnormative behavior may occur almost by virtue of the definition of creativity.

Studies of the relatives of schizophrenics indicate that along with a higher incidence of "schizophrenia spectrum" disorders, these relatives also show greater degrees of creativity and achievement (Karlsson, 1970). Heston (1966) found that about half of the foster-home raised offspring of the schizophrenic mothers he studied had successful adaptations, with imaginative and artistic talents not found in control children. McNeil (1971) reported somewhat elevated rates of mental disorder in both highly creative individuals and their relatives. Other researchers have uncovered overlap in cognitive styles of creative individuals and schizophrenics (Andreasen & Powers, 1975; Hasenfus & Magaro, 1976; Keefe & Magaro, 1980; Prentky, 1980) and noted similarities between schizophrenic thought disorder and creative divergent thinking (Guilford, 1967). There also appears to be a higher incidence of affective disorder, particularly bipolar affective disorder and hypomania, in writers and other creative or eminent individuals (Andreasen & Canter, 1974; Andreasen & Glick, 1988; Jamison, 1989, 1990).

Psychometric studies have found deviant, antisocial, and abrasive traits, but also traits of health and ego strength in creative groups (Barron, 1972; Cross, Cattell, & Butcher, 1967; Drevdahl & Cattell, 1958; MacKinnon, 1961). The relationship between specific personality traits and specific creative endeavors remains a topic of systematic exploration (Richards, 1981). Overlap as well as disjunction in the characteristics of creativity and psychopathology can occur in the areas of perception, cognition, affect, motivation, behavior, and interpersonal relationships.

This overlap suggests a two-factor model of creative functioning (Barron, 1968; Richards, 1981). The critical factor differentiating genius from madness may be *ego strength* (Barron, 1953; Frank, 1967), referring to resiliency, stress-resistance, a sense of physical and mental well-being, and facility for controlling one's primary process productions. Ego strength is a multifaceted trait, including sexual interest, and emotional, cognitive, and physical well-being (Barron, 1953; Stein & Chu, 1967). A two-factor model of creativity and psychopathology may be expanded to include interactions of psychopathological and healthy processes in the separate areas of perception, cognition, affect, motivation, behavior, and interpersonal relationships. Psychological well-being would result from the coordination of excesses and deficits in each of these areas, from strengths in one domain counteracting deficits in another, or from a dialectical alternation of phases of inspiration and consolidation.

To date, research has focused on overlap in the characteristics of extraordinary groups, on "diagnosed" eminence and "diagnosed" psychopathology. However, both creative and psychopathological traits may be viewed as continua (Person, 1986) and their interrelationship studied in ordinary, nonclinical populations. Although this approach may restrict the range of both creativity and psychopathology and raise questions regarding the ecological validity of work with normal and noneminent subjects, the processes resulting in unusual experiences or in a creative product are relevant to ordinary life and to healthy functioning. Everyday life demands improvisation, flexibility, and originality, not only in response to crises but in day to day living; a well-lived life is a result of creative processes. Previous research with some of the same instruments used in the present study found that college students who reported higher levels of psychoticlike experiences also received higher scores on some, but not all, creativity tests (Schuldberg, 1988; Schuldberg, French, Stone, & Heberle, 1988).

Using another nonclinical and noneminent group, this chapter describes an expanded investigation of the relationship between pencil-and-paper measures of deviant traits and creativity in perceptual, cognitive, affective, motivational, and behavioral areas. It includes the Hypomanic Traits Scale (Eckblad & Chapman, 1986), as well as a measure of ego strength. The contribution of this research is to treat both creativity and subclinical symptomatology as continuous and multifaceted traits, and to study their relationships in normal subjects.

The Perceptual Aberration-Magical Ideation (Per-Mag) and Impulsive Nonconformity Scales appear to represent subclinical expressions of positive symptoms (Andreasen, 1985; Andreasen & Olsen, 1982). The Hypomanic Traits Scale was specifically developed to measure submanic affective symptoms. A positive relationship is hypothesized between the Per-Mag Scale, Impulsive Nonconformity, and Hypomanic Traits, on the one hand, and creativity test scores on the other. The Physical Anhedonia Scale, and, to a lesser extent, the Schizoid Taxon Scale, appear to measure subclinical deficit or negative symptoms. These measures are expected to show a negative relationship to creativity test scores.

RESEARCH DESIGN

Data were gathered from 625 undergraduate students who participated to satisfy a portion of the requirements of an introductory psychology class. Subjects who signed up for the study were administered the creativity tests, the Ego Strength and Hypomanic traits Scales, a vocabulary test, and a number of other instruments in a single classroom testing session lasting between one and one half and two hours. A substantial number of the subjects (n = 524) had previously completed the scales of hypothetical psychosis-proneness as part of ongoing testing of the subject pool near the beginning of each academic quarter.

The sample was composed of 268 males and 357 females, with a mean age of 21.4 (SD = 5.4; range = 17.9–52.3). The subjects were predominantly Caucasian (89%), with 7% Native Americans, and about 4% from other ethnic groups. Due to constraints on testing time, in the latter phases of the study one group of subjects was given the Remote Associates Test but not Alternate Uses, the Revised Art Scale, or the How Do You Think Test.

Instruments

Scales of hypothetical psychosis-proneness

The Perceptual Aberration/Magical Ideation Scale is composed of two of the Wisconsin Scales of Hypothetical Psychosis-Proneness. The Perceptual Aberration Scale (Chapman, Chapman, & Raulin, 1978) measures distortions of perceptual experience, particularly regarding one's own body. A sample item is: "My hearing is sometimes so sensitive that ordinary sounds become uncomfortable." The Magical Ideation Scale (Eckblad & Chapman, 1983) taps superstitious and perhaps minidelusional beliefs, some of which have cultural or subcultural support. A sample item is "Some people can make me aware of them, just by thinking about me." In the present investigation, these two scales were combined into the Perceptual Aberration-Magical Ideation (Per-Mag) Scale (the sum of the subject's standard scores on the two individual scales). The Physical Anhedonia Scale (Chapman, Chapman, & Raulin, 1976) measures lack of experienced pleasure, a different aspect of schizotypal-like functioning associated with social withdrawal and lack of sexual interest. A sample item is "The beauty of sunsets is greatly overrated." The Impulsive Nonconformity Scale (Chapman, Chapman, Numbers, Edell, Carpenter, & Beckfield, 1984) was developed to measure a different aspect of psychosis-proneness and has been used to refine Per-Mag risk groups in other research. The items on this scale inquire about attitudes and beliefs relevant to impulsive or acting-out behavior (e.g., "It is important to save money" [keyed false]).

Hypomanic traits (Eckblad & Chapman, 1986) is a newer scale measuring experiences of being "up" or "hyper." An example is, "I often get so happy and energetic that I am almost giddy." The scales are intended to define hypothetically psychosis-prone high-scoring groups. In concurrent validation work, the Wisconsin researchers and others using the scales have found that high scorers perform deviantly on a wide variety of tasks (Edell

& Chapman, 1979). Work is beginning to appear on the scales' predictive validity, indicating that high scorers on some scales may be at somewhat increased risk for mental disorders (Chapman & Chapman, 1985, 1987).

The Golden and Meehl (1979) Schizoid Taxon Scale is based on responses to seven Minnesota Multiphasic Personality Inventory (MMPI; Hathaway & McKinley, 1967) items derived through a complex taxonometric procedure to detect "schizotaxia," a presumably inherited predisposition to schizophrenia or related disorders (Meehl, 1962).

Creativity tests

Creativity tests include the Revised Art Scale (Welsh & Barron, 1963), a set of 60 figures or drawings to which the subject responds with either "Like" or "Dislike." This scale was empirically derived using a variety of creative groups and appears to measure perceptual preferences that are associated with creativity, such as liking for complexity. Alternate Uses (Guilford, Christensen, Merrifield, & Wilson, 1978) measures divergent thinking, a cognitive component of creativity (Guilford, 1967). The present study uses Harrington's (1975) modification of the test, in which the instructions define creative solutions as both "unusual" and "worthwhile" and the subject is instructed to "be creative." The Remote Associates Test (RAT; Mednick, 1967), based on Mednick's (1962) associative theory of the creative process, was given to a subset of the subjects in the later testing groups. In this test, subjects are given three words and asked to provide a fourth word that is related to all three, often in different ways. The How Do You Think Test (Davis, 1975; Davis & Subkoviak, 1975) taps beliefs, attitudes, traits, and behaviors associated with creativity. The items on this instrument sample affective and motivational aspects of creativity, as well as the respondent's real-life creative activities. The Gough (1979) Creative Personality Scale (CPS) of the Adjective Check List (ACL: Gough & Heilbrun, 1980) measures personality traits associated with creative functioning. Subjects' Adjective Check Lists were also scored for Domino's (1970) Creativity Scale.

Other measures

The 68 items comprising Barron's (1953) Ego Strength Scale were also administered. This scale, originally developed as a predictor of success in insight-oriented psychotherapy, provides a general measure of psychological health and intactness. It largely measures *non*endorsement of psychological and physical complaints. The scale has been criticized as a negative indicator and as a global "absence of pathology" measure (Frank, 1967), and the patterns of responses to the scale have changed in the years since it was developed (Colligan & Offord, 1987). Nevertheless, the scale has played an important role in the study of both creativity and health.

The Quick Word Test (Borgatta & Corsini, 1964) provides an estimate of the subjects' verbal intelligence and was administered as a speeded test with a 10-minute time limit (Martin & Chapman, 1982). This particular test was chosen for its brevity and ease of administration in a group situation and was included to evaluate the positive relationship observed between IQ and creativity measures in previous research. Various forms of psychopathology have also been found to be associated with cognitive deficits, and the Quick Word Test scores allow an examination of the relationship between verbal intelligence and both the schizotypy and creativity constructs.

RESULTS

Means and standard deviations of the measures are presented in Table 9.1. The Pearson product-moment correlations of the creativity and psychopathology measures are presented in Table 9.2. Partial correlations

Table 9.1. Means and Standard Deviations of the Measures of Psychosis-Proneness and Creativity

	M	SD	n
Psychosis-Proneness			
Per/Mag Scale	.64	1.81	501
Physical Anhedonia	11.00	6.42	501
Schizoid Taxon	.34	.28	583
Impulsive Nonconformity	16.74	7.37	501
Hypomanic Traits	19.93	8.05	595
Creativity			
Alternate Uses	15.92	4.80	437
B-W Art Scale	29.42	13.24	439
How Do You Think	307.04	39.71	441
ACL CPS	47.87	8.58	517
Remote Associates	10.66	4.93	177
Other			
Barron Ego Strength	41.71	6.27	595
Quick Word Test	35.81	11.42	451

Note. The Per-Mag Scale is the sum of standard scores on the Perceptual Aberration and Magical Ideation Scales. The maximum possible scores for the other scales are: Physical Anhedonia, 61; Impulsive Nonconformity, 51; Hypomanic Traits, 48; Alternate Uses, 36; Revised Art Scale, 60; Remote Associates, 30; Ego Strength, 68; and Quick Word Test, 100. The Schizoid Taxon Index varies between 0 and 1. How Do You Think Scores can range from 100 to 500. The ACL CPS Score is a *T*-Score: $M = 50$, $SD = 10$.

Table 9.2. Intercorrelations of Test Measures of Psychosis-Proneness and Creativity

| | Psychosis-Proneness | | | | | Creativity Measures | | | | |
| | Schizotypal | | | Acting Out | | | | | | |
	Per-Mag	Physical Anhedonia	Schizoid Taxon	Impulsive Nonconformity	Hypomanic Trait	Alternate Uses	B-W Art Scale	How Do You Think	ACL[a] CPS	Remote[b] Associates
Schizotypal										
Per Mag	1.00	-.18*	.15**	.40**	.45**	.10	.06	.28**	-.03	-.17
Physical Anhedonia		1.00	.14**	.14**	-.23**	-.17**	-.06	-.38**	-.21**	-.08
Schizoid Taxon			1.00	.21**	.10*	.03	.01	-.06	-.22**	.11
Acting-Out										
Impulsive Nonconformity				1.00	.46**	.06	.10	.26**	-.09	-.07
Hypomanic Traits					1.00	.17**	.11	.61**	.25**	-.10
Creativity										
Alternate Uses						1.00	.08	.33**	.12	—
B-W Art Scale							1.00	.20**	.05	—
How Do You Think								1.00	.50**	—
ACL CPS									1.00	.04
Remote Associates										1.00

Note. Correlations left blank are for tests that were not given together. Overall $N = 675$. In individual analyses, $N = 358$–583, except as noted.
[a] $n = 334$–517; [b] $N = 132$–175; $*p \leq .01$; $**p \leq$. (One-tailed tests of significance)

were computed to statistically control verbal intelligence. Correlations are also reported between the measures and Quick Word Test and Barron Ego Strength Scores. As explicit relationships are hypothesized between the measures, one-tailed tests of significance were used. Finally, in order to summarize the interrelationships of the variables, a Principal Components Analysis (with Varimax rotation) was conducted with a subgroup of the tests.

Physical Anhedonia (measuring   set of symptoms distinct from the other schizotypal-like traits) was negatively correlated with both the Per-Mag and Hypomanic Traits Scales, a finding in agreement with other work (Chapman, Chapman, & Miller, 1982; Eckblad & Chapman, 1986). Impulsive Nonconformity and the Schizoid Taxon were positively correlated with all of the measures of deviant traits, except that the Schizoid Taxon was only slightly correlated with Hypomanic Traits. The correlations among the creativity tests themselves vary from substantial to weak. The last column of Table 9.2 contains several blank entries; because of time constraints, the RAT was never given to subjects who received Alternate Uses, the Revised Art Scale, or the How Do You Think Test.

The rectangle in the center of Table 9.2 presents the overlap between deviant traits and creativity test scores. The correlations are generally small in magnitude; they tended to increase when the effects of verbal intelligence are partialled out, although this does not change the pattern of results. As expected, the Per-Mag Scale was positively correlated with the How Do You Think Scores, although it was virtually uncorrelated with the Revised Art Scale. Physical Anhedonia was negatively correlated with the creativity test scores; the Schizoid Taxon was also negatively correlated with the ACL Creative Personality Scale. When analyses were conducted using Domino's (1970) Creativity Scale for the Adjective Check List, very similar results were obtained. However, Domino's scale was more related to Impulsive Nonconformity, Alternate Uses, the RAT, and the Quick Word Test than the CPS, and the nonsignificantly correlated with the Schizoid Taxon.

Impulsive Nonconformity and Hypomanic Traits were both positively correlated with scores from the How Do You Think Test; Hypomanic Traits Scores were also correlated with several other creativity tests. The Alternate Uses test was weakly positively correlated with Hypomanic Traits and negatively correlated with Physical Anhedonia. No significant correlations occurred between the psychopathology measures and the Remote Associates Test. Because the How Do You Think Test contains a diverse set of items, some of which overlap in content with the Per-Mag Scale, a subset of items was constructed with nonoverlapping content; the results remained unchanged.

Ego Strength (see Table 9.3) was significantly negatively correlated

Table 9.3. *Correlation of Measures of Psychosis-Proneness and Creativity with Barron's Ego Strength Scale and Quick Word Test Scores*

	Barron Ego Strength	Quick Word Test
Psychosis-Proneness		
Per/Mag	−.33**	−.12
Physical Anhedonia	−.01	−.10
Schizoid Taxon	−.39**	.06
Impulsive Nonconformity	−.21**	−.17**
Hypomanic Traits	−.24**	−.05
Creativity		
Alternate Uses	.06	.27**
B-W Art Scale	−.04	−.01
How Do You Think	.12*	.17**
ACL CPS	.27**	.12*
Remote Associates	.16	.67**
Other Tests		
Barron Ego Strength	—	.18**

*$p \leq .01$; **$p \leq .001$ (One-tailed tests of significance) $n = 135–595$.

with all of the deviant trait measures except Physical Anhedonia and positively correlated with the Creative Personality Scale and the How Do You Think Test.

In general, the psychopathology indicators were uncorrelated or mildly negatively correlated with verbal intelligence. All of the creativity tests, with the exception of the Revised Art Scale, were significantly and positively correlated with the Quick Word Test, substantially so for the Remote Associates Test ($r = .57$, $p < .0005$).

In order to summarize the interrelationships of the variables, a principal components analysis with Varimax rotation was conducted with a subset of the measures. The Remote Associates Test, given with few of the other tests, was omitted to maximize the number of subjects. Three factors were derived, accounting for 57% of the variance in the measures (Table 9.4).

Factor I was a general behavioral "acting out" and psychopathology factor, with large loadings with Hypomanic Traits, the Per-Mag Scale, Impulsive Nonconformity, and the How Do You Think Test. Factor II, named "Ego Strength/Creative Personality," had large positive loadings with the Barron Ego Strength Scale and the Adjective Check List Creative Personality Scale, a large negative loading with the Schizoid Taxon Scale, and a moderate positive loading with the How Do You Think Test. Factor III, named "differentiation and Complexity (Affective, Perceptual, and Ideational)," had a large negative loading with Physical Anhedonia,

Table 9.4. *Factor Analysis: Measures of Psychosis-Proneness, Health, and Creativity*

	Factor			
	I	*II*	*III*	
		Personality:	*Differentiation:*	
		"Ego	*"Complexity:*	
	Behavior:	*Strength/*	*Affective/*	
	"Pathology/	*Creative*	*Perceptual/*	
Variable	*Acting-out"*	*Personality"*	*Cognitive"*	*Communality*
Per/Mag	**0.74**	−0.21	0.05	0.59
Physical Anhedonia	−0.04	−0.02	**−0.77**	0.60
Schizoid Taxon	0.16	**−0.65**	0.04	0.44
Impulsive Nonconformity	**0.75**	−0.17	−0.21	0.63
Hypomanic Traits	**0.79**	0.09	0.27	0.70
Barron Ego Strength	−0.33	**0.73**	−0.04	0.65
Alternate Uses	0.17	0.16	**0.56**	0.37
B-W Art Scale	−0.12	−0.24	**0.52**	0.33
How Do You Think	**0.55**	**0.44**	**0.54**	0.79
ACL CPS	0.23	**0.70**	0.21	0.59
Variance accounted for by the factor	0.23	0.18	0.16	

Note. Total percent variance accounted for = 57%.
Loadings (≥ 0.40) used in naming the factor are in bold print.

and moderate positive loadings with the Barron-Welsh Art Scale, How Do You Think Test, and Alternate Uses.

When factor scores based on the principal components analysis were computed for each subject, Factor I ("Behavior: Pathology/Acting Out") was surprisingly uncorrelated with the Quick Word Test. However, Factor II ("Ego Strength/Creativity") was correlated .17 ($p = .01$) with the vocabulary scores, and Factor III ("Differentiation and Complexity: Affective/Perceptual/Cognitive"), also tapping pleasure and energy and loaded with the Alternate Uses Test, was correlated .13 ($p = .05$) with the Quick Word Test.

DISCUSSION

An important question concerns the relative contributions of intellectual, stylistic, and personality factors to creativity and psychological well-being (Sternberg, 1988). The present work emphasizes the role of stylistic and personality factors. To what extent do fluid cognition, hypomania, flat affect, and creative personality traits separately account for the overlap and disjunction of health, creativity, and symptoms? Several distinct types of motivational and emotional factors were assessed in the present study: impulsivity and hypomania, anhedonia or flat affect, and several aspects of the "creative personality." The findings point to the primary importance of subclinical symptoms of hypomania and impulsivity; affective symptoms may be more important than primary process thinking in determining generativity within a normal population. This contrasts with previous work (e.g., Andreasen & Powers, 1975; Hasenfus & Magaro, 1976; Keefe & Magaro, 1980; Suler, 1980) that emphasized the similarity between creativity and schizophreniclike cognition, but it fits with recent work on affective symptomatology (Andreasen & Canter, 1974; Andreasen & Glick, 1988; Jamison, 1989, 1990; Jamison, Gerner, Hammen, & Podesky, 1980). In addition, current work on disordered cognition (e.g., Harrow & Quinlan, 1985) has found that "thought disorder" occurs in affective and other disorders as well as schizophrenia. The present study raises the possibility that creative cognition is more akin to manic "flight of ideas" than to schizophrenic "loose associations."

Both creativity and deviant traits are heterogeneous constructs (Barron & Harrington, 1981; Dellas & Gaier, 1970). A useful approach for future research will consist of transferring the distinction between positive and negative psychotic symptoms from the study of psychopathology to research on subclinical deviant functioning, creativity, and psychological health. If positive and negative symptoms are considered as behavioral or psychological excesses and deficits rather than as symptoms per se, the distinction becomes a useful one for classifying healthy processes of resilience, resourcefulness, and creativity. The Physical Anhedonia Scale and Schizoid Taxon Scale appear to measure subclinical negative or deficit symptoms (Andreasen, 1985; Andreasen & Olsen, 1982; Strauss, Carpenter, & Bartko, 1974) and were negatively related to creative functioning. The Per-Mag Scale, Impulsive Nonconformity, and Hypomanic Traits appear to tap, respectively, perceptual/cognitive, behavioral, and affective aspects of positive symptoms; these are associated with higher scores on the creativity tests. Surprisingly and in contrast with previous work (Schuldberg, 1988; Schuldberg et al., 1988), the Revised Art Scale was uncorrelated with the Per-Mag Scale in this group of subjects.

The results of the principal components analysis further clarify these areas of overlap and contrast. Factor I tapped behavioral characteristics, including high levels of energy and unconventionality. Factor II was loaded on measures of the healthy and creative personality, and had negative loadings on the Schizoid Taxon Scale. Factor III measured several forms of differentiation as well as energy and perseverance. The Physical Anhedonia Scale had a negative loading on this factor. Deficit symptomatology appears to be at one end of a continuum, with measures of creativity or creative potential at the other. The fact that Alternate Uses was most highly loaded with this factor suggests that divergent thinking, in addition to being a facet of intelligence (Guilford, 1967), also contains an affective and motivational component related to *"joie de vivre"* and energy.

The How Do You Think Test split its loadings across all three factors, indicating that they are all related to creative functioning. The strong findings involving the How Do You Think Test suggest an important role for the assessment of real-life achievements (e.g., Davis, 1975; Holland & Astin, 1962) and attitudes about creativity in research on psychological well-being. Further work remains to be done on separating the components of creativity and creative potential measured by this instrument.

The measures of psychosis-proneness and deviant traits differ in the breadth of symptoms or behaviors measured. The Schizoid Taxon, despite its brevity, appears to be a global measure of subclinical schizotypal traits or a predisposition to psychopathology, although less related to bipolar affective symptoms. Healthy functioning is also a heterogeneous domain. As observed in past research, the Barron Ego Strength Scale is a nonspecific absence of pathology indicator, negatively correlated with all of the schizotypal traits except the deficit symptoms of the Physical Anhedonia Scale. Ego Strength was also significantly positively correlated with two of the creativity scales.

This study's emphasis on affect raises questions regarding the role of motivation in creativity test performance. Many authors have acknowledged the sensitivity of these tests to motivational factors. The timed tests in this study (Alternate Uses, the Quick Word Test, and Remote Associates) appear to include a motivational component related both to speed and to perseverance in the testing session. The significant negative correlation of the Quick Word Test and the Impulsive Nonconformity Scale supports this interpretation for the vocabulary test scores.

Nevertheless, the significant correlations between the creativity tests and the Quick Word Test are relevant to the ongoing question of the extent to which creativity tests can be differentiated from more traditional intelligence measures (Getzels & Jackson, 1962; Welsh, 1975). The creativity measures in this study are "contaminated" by verbal abilities as well as motivation. Ego strength, which includes energy and a sense of well-being, is likely to involve these factors as well. Verbal scores, however, were virtually unrelated to the schizotypy measures, with the exception of Impulsive Nonconformity, and perhaps negatively related to perseverance in timed tasks. Importantly, the *relationships* among the schizotypy and creativity instruments were largely independent of verbal ability and changed little when Quick Word Test Scores were partialled out.

Behavioral excesses in the areas of energy and cognitive complexity are associated with both psychopathology and healthy functioning. The affective deficits tapped by the Physical Anhedonia Scale and possibly the Schizoid Taxon are negatively associated with both creativity and psychological well-being. Although the present work has little positive to say about subclinical negative symptoms, current research is also turning toward the adaptive aspects of negative symptomatology (e.g., Strauss, Rakfeldt, Harding, & Lieberman, 1989). Narrative accounts of the process of creation often contain descriptions of alternating phases of withdrawal and productivity, depression and energy. Granting the essentially biphasic and possibly dialectical nature of the creative process, psychological deficits akin to negative symptoms may also have their place in generative work.

In conclusion, this research argues for the utility of including creativity tests in the assessment of psychological health and resourcefulness. These instruments are unique in measuring positively evaluated aspects of unconventionality and in detecting healthy adaptations even in the context of experiences and symptoms often considered pathological. The present study finds a qualified degree of overlap in creative and psychopathological processes, emphasizes the role of affective factors, and argues for the relevance of these processes to "ordinary" life. It also points to specificity in the relationships between creative processes and psychopathology; future work will benefit from an examination of the specific "symptoms" of psychopathology and of creativity in a variety of endeavors.

REFERENCES

Andreasen, N. C. (1985). Positive vs. negative schizophrenia: A critical evaluation. *Schizophrenia Bulletin, 11*, 380–389.

Andreasen, N. C., & Canter, A. (1984). The creative writer: Psychiatric symptoms and family history. *Comprehensive Psychiatry, 32*, 70–73.

Andreasen, N. C., & Glick, I. D. (1988). Bipolar affective disorder and creativity: Implications and clinical management. *Comprehensive Psychiatry, 29*, 207–217.

Andreasen, N. C., & Olsen, S. (1982). Negative vs. positive schizophrenia: Definition and validation. *Archives of General Psychiatry, 39*, 789–794.

Andreasen, N. C., & Powers, P. S. (1975). Creativity and psychosis: An examination of conceptual style. *Archives of General Psychiatry, 32*, 70–73.

Barron, F. (1953). An ego-strength scale which predicts response to psychotherapy. *Journal of Consulting Psychology, 5*, 327–333.

Barron, F. (1968). *Creativity and personal freedom.* Princeton, NJ: Van Nostrand.

Barron, F. (1972). *Artists in the making.* New York: Seminar Press.

Barron, F., & Harrington, D. M. (1981). Creativity, intelligence, and personality. *Annual Review of Psychology, 32*, 439–476.

Borgatta, E. F., & Corsini, R. J. (1964). *Quick word test manual.* New York: Harcourt, Brace & World.

Chapman, L. J., & Chapman, J. P. (1985). Psychosis-proneness. In M. Alpert (Ed.), *Controversies in schizophrenia: Changes and constancies* (pp. 157–174). New York: Guilford.

Chapman, L. J., & Chapman, J. P. (1987). The search for symptoms predictive of schizophrenia. *Schizophrenia Bulletin, 13,* 498–503.

Chapman, L. J., Chapman, J. P., & Miller, E. N. (1982). Reliabilities and inter-correlation of eight measures of proneness to psychosis. *Journal of Consulting and Clinical Psychology, 50,* 187–195.

Chapman, L. J., Chapman, J. P., Numbers, J. S., Edell, W. S., Carpenter, B. N., & Beckfield, D. (1984). Impulsive nonconformity as a trait contributing to the prediction of psychotic-like and schizotypal symptoms. *Journal of Nervous and Mental Disease, 172,* 681–691.

Chapman, L. J., Chapman, J. P., & Raulin, M. L. (1976). Scales for physical and social anhedonia. *Journal of Abnormal Psychology, 85,* 374–382.

Chapman, L. J., Chapman, J. P., & Raulin, M. L. (1978). Body-image aberration in schizophrenia. *Journal of Abnormal Psychology, 87,* 399–407.

Colligan, R. C., & Offord, K. P. (1987). Resiliency reconsidered: Contemporary MMPI normative data for Barron's Ego Strength scale. *Journal of Clinical Psychology, 43,* 467–472.

Cross, P. G., Cattell, R. B., & Butcher, H. J. (1967). The personality patterns of creative artists. *British Journal of Educational Psychology, 37,* 292–299.

Davis, G. A. (1975). In frumious pursuit of the creative person. *Journal of Creative Behavior, 9,* 75–87.

Davis, G. A., & Subkoviak, M. J. (1975). Multidimensional analysis of a personality-based test of creative potential. *Journal of Educational Measurement, 12,* 37–43.

Dellas, M., & Gaier, E. L. (1970). Identification of creativity: The individual. *Psychological Bulletin, 73,* 55–73.

Domino, G. (1970). Identification of potentially creative persons from the Adjective Check List. *Journal of Consulting and Clinical Psychology, 35,* 48–51.

Drevdahl, J. E., & Cattell, R. B. (1958). Personality and creativity in artists and writers. *Journal of Clinical Psychology, 14,* 107–111.

Eckblad, M., & Chapman, L. J. (1983). Magical ideation as an indicator of schizotypy. *Journal of Consulting and Clinical Psychology, 51,* 215–225.

Eckblad, M., & Chapman, L. J. (1986). Development and validation of a scale for Hypomanic Personality. *Journal of Abnormal Psychology, 95,* 214–222.

Edell, W. S., & Chapman, L. J. (1979). Anhedonia, perceptual aberration, and the Rorschach. *Journal of Consulting and Clinical Psychology, 47,* 377–384.

Frank, G. H. (1967). A review of research with measures of ego strength derived from the MMPI and the Rorschach. *Journal of General Psychology, 77,* 183–206.

Getzels, J. W., & Jackson, P. W. (1962). *Creativity and intelligence.* New York: Wiley.

Goertzel, M. G., Goertzel, V., & Goertzel, T. G. (1978). *Three hundred eminent personalities.* San Francisco, CA: Jossey-Bass.

Golden, R. R., & Meehl, P. E. (1979). Detection of the schizoid taxon with MMPI indicators. *Journal of Abnormal Psychology, 88,* 217–233.

Gough, H. G. (1979). A creative personality scale for the Adjective Check List. *Journal of Personality and Social Psychology, 39,* 1398–1405.

Gough, H. G., & Heilbrun, A. B. (1980). *The Adjective Check List manual.* Palo Alto, CA: Consulting Psychologists Press.

Guilford, J. P. (1967). *the nature of human intelligence.* New York: McGraw-Hill.

Guilford, J. P., Christensen, P. R., Merrifield, P. R., & Wilson, R. C. (1978). *Alternate Uses: Manual of instructions and interpretations.* Beverly Hills, CA: Sheridan Psychological Services. [Currently published by Consulting Psychologists Press, Palo Alto, CA.]

Harrington, D. M. (1975). Effects of explicit instructions to "be creative" on the psychological meaning of divergent thinking test scores. *Journal of Personality, 43,* 432–454.

Harrow, M., & Quinlan, D. M. (1985). *Disordered thinking and schizophrenic pathology.* New York: Gardner.

Hasenfus, N., & Magaro, P. (1976). Creativity and schizophrenia: An equality of empirical constructs. *British Journal of Psychiatry, 129,* 346–349.

Hathaway, S. R., & McKinley, J. C. (1967). *Minnesota Multiphasic Personality Inventory: Manual* (Rev. ed.). New York: Psychological Corporation.

Heston, L. L. (1966). Psychiatry disorders in foster home reared children in schizophrenic mothers. *British Journal of Psychiatry, 112,* 819–825.

Holland, J. L., & Astin, A. W. (1962). The prediction of the academic, artistic, and social achievement of undergraduates of superior scholastic aptitude. *Journal of Educational Psychology, 53,* 132–143.

Jamison, K. R. (1989). Mood disorders and patterns of creativity in British artists and writers. *Psychiatry, 52,* 125–134.

Jamison, K. R. (1990). Manic-depressive illness and accomplishment: Creativity, leadership, and social class. In F. K. Goodwin, & K. R. Jamison (Eds.), *Manic-depressive illness* (pp. 332–367). New York: Oxford University Press.

Jamison, K. R., Gerner, R. H., Hammen, C., & Padesky, C. (1980). Clouds and silver linings: Positive experiences associated with primary affective disorders. *American Journal of Psychiatry, 137,* 198–202.

Karlsson, J. L. (1970). Genetic association of giftedness and creativity with schizophrenia. *Hereditas, 66,* 177–182.

Keefe, J. A., & Magaro, P. A. (1980). Creativity and schizophrenia: An equivalence of cognitive processing. *Journal of Abnormal Psychology, 89,* 390–398.

MacKinnon, D. W. (1961). The study of creativity and creativity in architects. In *Conference on the creative person.* Berkeley, CA: University of California, Institute of Personality Assessment and Research.

Martin, E. M., & Chapman, L. J. (1982). Communication effectiveness in psychosis-prone college students. *Journal of Abnormal Psychology, 91,* 420–425.

McNeil, T. F. (1971). Prebirth and postbirth influence on the relationship between creative ability and mental illness. *Journal of Personality, 39,* 391–406.

Mednick, S. A. (1962). The associative basis of the creative process. *Psychological Review, 69,* 220–232.

Mednick, S. A. (1967). *Remote Associates Test* Boston, MA: Houghton Mifflin.

Meehl, P. E. (1962). Schizotaxia, schizotypy, and schizophrenia. *American Psychologist, 17,* 827–838.

Person, J. B. (1986). The advantages of studying psychological phenomena rather than psychiatric diagnoses. *American Psychologist, 41,* 1252–1260.

Prentky, R. A. (1980). *Creativity and psychopathology: A neurocognitive perspective*. New York: Praeger.

Richards, R. L. (1981). Relationships between creativity and psychopathology: An evaluation and interpretation of the evidence. *Genetic Psychology Monographs, 103*, 261–324.

Schuldberg, D. (1988). Abstract: Perceptual-cognitive and affective components of schizotaxia and creativity in a group of college males. *Journal of Creative Behavior, 22*, 73–74.

Schuldberg, D., French, C., Stone, B. L., & Heberle, J. (1988). Creativity and schizotypal traits: Creativity test scores, perceptual aberration, magical ideation, and impulsive nonconformity. *Journal of Nervous and Mental Disease, 176*, 648–657.

Stein, K. B., & Chu, C. (1967). Dimensionality of Barron's ego-strength scale. *Journal of Consulting Psychology, 31*, 153–161.

Sternberg, R. J. (1988). A three-facet model of creativity. In R. J. Sternberg (Ed.), *The nature of creativity: Contemporary psychological perspectives* (pp. 125–147). New York: Harvard University Press.

Strauss, J. S., Carpenter, W. T., and Bartko, J. J. (1974). The diagnosis and understanding of schizophrenia: Part III. Speculations on the processes that underlie schizophrenic symptoms and signs. *Schizophrenia Bulletin, 1*(11), 61–69.

Strauss, J. S., Rakfeldt, J., Harding, C. M., & Lieberman, P. (1989). Psychological and social aspects of negative symptoms. *British Journal of Psychiatry, 155*(Suppl. 7), 128–132.

Suler, J. R. (1980). Primary process thinking and creativity. *Psychological Bulletin, 88*, 144–165.

Welsh, G. S. (1975). *Creativity and intelligence: A personality approach*. Chapel Hill, NC: Institute for Research in Social Science.

Welsh, G. S., & Barron, F. (1963). Barron-Welsh Art Scale. Palo Alto, CA: Consulting Psychologists Press.

PART III

PSYCHOLOGICAL
HEALTH
AND CREATIVITY

PART III

Introduction

Freud said creativity derived from unconsious conflict, disguised and transmuted into more a universal creative expression, this in pursuit of a more settled homeostasis. By contrast, Maslow, and other humanists, argued for ongoing growth motives involving curiosity, personal development, and movement toward self-actualization, with creativity emerging as part of an ongoing process of personal evolution and an ultimate expression of health. Does eminent creativity at times derive more from the former, conflictual origins, and everyday creativity more from the less conflicted latter (Richards, 1981)? In either case it is notable that creativity tends to work in the service of health and may at times transform illness into health.

In any case, creativity needn't be unitary in motivation any more than in its expression. In the present section, we look at some varied dimensions—involving first the overcoming of adversity, and then personal growth. Next we look at neurological and immunological factors (and touch on issues of overcoming traumatic experience), along with varied issues which arise over the lifespan.

It may not seem surprising to some that visual artistic expression, or musical creativity, may be greatly healing, and inspring in other ways as well in the greater development of oneself in the world. This emerges in different ways in the contributions of John Gedo on visual art and Peter Ostwald on music. Frederick Flach reminds us how any creative advance, whatever the motive, requires the destruction and reorganization of the contents of one's own mind, along with changes in the external world. This need hardly be tragic, and with proper preparation, can be seen as a step in an ongoing, and *natural* process of growth.

There may in fact be ambiguity, anxiety, distress—and even great fear—in having one's thoughts jostle about in creative disarray. Yet an ultimate resolution can bring in turn deep satisfactions and joy. For each of us, in overcoming the stresses of life, our creative effort may fuel a tremendously powerful *resilient* force. How important this can be. Yet we must not therefore romanticize the stress or forget, for a moment, that not everyone *does* overcome. With the advent of more flexible creative attitudes—through seeing the world and oneself as part of a dynamic process in motion—we may all become more cheerfully resilient, and find this process a more natural one than we sometimes do now.

This is not to suggest that *all* creativity is necessarily good or healthy. Here is an area that still needs much study. But one may cheer with Cropley at his delineation of a healthily divergent and novelty-seeking cognitive style—a creative way of being which can become characteristic of one's personality over time. One may feel greatly encouraged by Rhodes who nicely develops Maslow's move from "deficiency" to "being" needs in the context of creativity. Here one may naturally evolve (*if* and when various blocks are addressed and removed, we might add) from a more self-involved and corrective orientation in creativity to a more expansive, joyful, and universally oriented position. Mark Runco et al. remind us of the limited research in this critical area, but this chapter happily contributes a positive, if modest, association between measures of creative personality and self-actualization.

In a picture of evolving creative self and world, we may not find it surprising that an intact brain, with richly interconnected hemispheres, is most fruitful for creativity. This is Hoppe and Kyle's contribution. Or be surprised that by creatively addressing one's traumas, as in Pennebaker et al.'s research, one may not only experientially open up rich new mental pathways, but increase one's immune responsiveness, general health status, sense of well-being, and, indeed, perhaps the potential to live on and to continue this good work.

Benefits of creativity can accrue from cradle to grave, as with Dudek and Verrault's child subjects, whose creative advantages include a richer primary process, flexible ego controls and, quite interestingly, a lessening of aggressive themes compared to libidinal one. It does recall the slogan, "make love, not war." The home environment of creative children, Gardner and Moran tell us, tends to be open and accepting of their individuality, whether or not it is conflictual. (But we should not forget—perhaps especially for eminent creators—that it may also have tended to be conflictual or troubled.) Meanwhile, the creative older person, facing inevitable illness and death, shows related qualities: being less negative and defensive about aging, and more flexible and emotional. In fact, as Ellen Langer, in her book *Mindfulness,* and others have shown, older people who are more actively involved may be less apt to get sick and, in fact, even live a longer life.

Chapter 10

Disorders of the Pathways Involved in the Creative Process*

Frederic Flach

Is creativity a sign of mental health or illness? When we examine the biographies of those famous for their creative accomplishments, we cannot help but be struck by the frequent occurrence of emotional and behavioral disturbances. The poet, Edgar Allen Poe; the painter, Vincent Van Gogh; and the writer, Ernest Hemingway, are only three examples of that connection. Small wonder, then, that a powerful link between outstand-

---

*From "Disorders of the Pathways Involved in the Creative Process," by F. Flach, 1990, *Creativity Research Journal*, 3(2), pp. 158–165. Copyright © 1995 Ablex Publishing. Adapted with permission.

ing creative achievement and mental illness has been so widely presumed. Only recently, Andreasen (1987) reported that writers—and event heir families—showed a significantly higher incidence of affective disorder, especially of the bipolar type, than a carefully matched group of control subjects. She employed as a measure of creativity the ability to produce the written word in such a way as to form characters and plots that would win critical and perhaps commercial acceptance. Lack of creativity was represented by the pursuit of careers in law, hospital administration, and social work, that, on the whole, involved more pedestrian, conventional, and structured forms of activity.

However, counterpositioned to those impressions, other investigators have found the very opposite, namely an inverse relationship between creative ability and maladjustment. For example, Schubert (1988) tested a group of college students using the Minnesota Multiphasic Personality Inventory and Guilford's standardized tests of creative performance. Those students who tested high on the creative performance tests scored low on all scales of personality dysfunction; moreover, they were less likely to fail or drop out of school than were the low-creativity performers. In fact, they were above-average achievers, significantly more autonomous and resistant to the pressure of their environment, and less bound by traditional and stereotyped responses. Other investigators, including Barron (1963), Cashden and Welsh (1966), and MacKinnon (1965), arrived at similar conclusions, finding a large number of ego-strength traits among creative men and women. Such coping abilities include: a high level of autonomy, a low likelihood of blindly incorporating external demands of society into self-image, the capacity to et one's own personal goals, verbal fluency, curiosity, openness to stimuli, intuition, social poise, a wide range of interests, a strong sense of responsibility, dedication to self-chosen purposes, originality, a blending of traits conventionally attributed to the more masculine or feminine side of the personality, and a strong sense of personal destiny.

At first glance, those points of view would seem to be diametrically opposed. Some highly creative individuals demosntrte a great deal of emotional instability, whereas others seem to possess the very characteristics that should provide unique strength to deal successfully with the stresses that commonly trigger emotional and behavioral disorders.

FORM VERSUS ESSENCE

One explanation for this seeming contradiction undoubtedly lies in the *form* of the creative process rather than its *essence*. When the creative act assumes a form that is, by consensus, an outstanding work of genius—be it a great painting, inspiring musical composition, or profoundly moving novel—many complex factors beyond creativity alone come into play. Not only is something new created, but the creator must also possess a singular talent that he or she has developed through practice and study. The creator's vision of the world around him or her and of the human experience must be unique and original. He or she must be strongly motivated to express talents creatively, considering the obstacles that must often be overcome and the discipline that must be exercised with regularity. Such motivation often represents a way to resolve internal conflicts or a protection against the disorganizing and immobilizing potential of such conflicts (Storr, 1972). With a few notable exceptions, da Vinci being one, such creative geniuses tend to be intensely one-sided; their creative efforts are made at the expense of many other dimensions of ordinary living, thus setting up a condition of relative deprivation. Finally, they must have the means and the opportunity to engage in their creativity; shortage or absence of such resources readily induces ongoing frustration. Therefore, their apparent susceptibility to emotional disturbances may rest as much in the conditions required for their creative expressions in their creativity itself.

It may be no less important to define the arena in which an individual's exceptional level of creativity operates. Cattell and Butcher (1970) surveyed the lives of eminent scientists and concluded that the typical research scientists of genius appeared to be more introverted and stable and less prone to behavioral illness than creative artists. Hudson (1968) also noted that scientists seemed less likely than artists to experience mental and emotional disorders. He referred to the scientists as "convergers," whose personalities were more tightly structured and controlled from early life, and used the term "diverger" to describe the make-up of artists, whose personality structures were more loosely knit and who revealed more emotion and instability.

ORIGINALITY

Another aspect of creative greatness is originality. To be original implies that one is able to look at something in a way that is meaningfully different from the way in which the object is ordinarily considered. Einstein's theory of relativity falls into this category. In his doctoral thesis research, C. Flach (personal communication, 1986) uncovered a clue as to the roots of originality. He studied visual information processing styles in relation to personality profiles and performance on standardized tests of creative problem solving. Those subjects whose preferential form of information processing could be called "central" and whose scores on psychological testing showed strong field independence, appeared to be more introverted and less responsive to external stimulation or vulnerable to its diversionary and prejudicial influences. They also scored significantly higher on tests of originality; therefore, one can hypothesize that an inherent part of originality in the creative process depends on a long-standing—perhaps even life-long—tendency to be more or less perceptually cut off from, or independent of, environmental input, less susceptible to adopting conventional wisdom, and hence freer to form one's own perception of reality.

This suggests an interesting difference between the requirements of scientific and literary creativity. The mind in search of new mathematical formulations can easily benefit from being divorced from ordinary environmental stimuli. The writer, attempting to bring creative originality to bear on his or her perception of human events, must continually shift between a state of contact with and observation of the world (which necessarily has an impact while he or she does so) and still remain sufficiently detached to permit singular interpretation of events that are to be expressed in the written produce. Moreover, we can even speculate that the writer's relationship with the people he or she creates on the page may well assume such power and reality in his or her own mind that he or she may become vulnerable to the kind of depression that originates within interpersonal contexts (Klerman & Lubin, 1988).

THE DISRUPTIVE-REINTEGRATIVE NATURE
OF THE CREATIVE PROCESS

When we look beyond the form that creativity takes to the essence of the creative process itself, its nature assumes much broader dimensions. Whether one is engaged in searching for a new scientific theory or attempting to solve one of life's seemingly unsolvable problems, the underlying process involves the disruption of existing mental, emotional, interpersonal, or environmental structures, and the subsequent building of new, more suitable and more adaptive ones.

Kubie (1958) defined creativity in the broadest possible terms. Creativity, he stated, implied invention—the uncovering of new facts or new relationships among new and old data. "This is not the whole of creativity," he wrote, "but an essential part of the process without which there can be no such thing as creativity" (p. 50). Wertheimer (1959) defined creative thinking as "the process of destroying one gestalt in favor of a better one." He viewed the phenomenon within Gestalt theory, involving closure and the ability to shift from one whole to another.

Stein (1988) described the fundamental process of creativity in this way: "At the start of the creative process the creative individual experiences a state of disequilibrium. His psychological condition is marked by disturbed homeostasis—tension arising from a lack of perceptual closure and a lack of emotional satisfaction with the existing state of affairs. This total state may be traceable to the creative person's own doing . . . or he was uniquely predisposed and sensitive to the disequilibria already existing in his environment" (pp. 53–54). The creator may be acting or reacting to internal or external conditions. As he or she works his or her way forward, the capacity to tolerate ambiguity is manifest. To quote Stein, "to exist in a state in which he does not necessarily comprehend all that he perceives or feels" (p. 54). Such lack of structure inevitably generates emotional distress,which usually takes the form of anxiety or depression, but not infrequently with a disorganizing quality.

During the creative act, access to many levels within the individual's personality is required. Memories, perceptions, anticipations, and imaginations commingle; the situation is not unlike the episodes of regression and reduced intrapsychic structure seen in the course of psychoanalytic psychotherapy, the so-called "regression in the service of the ego." Gradually, new ideas and combinations of ideas emerge until one or more takes shape; that illumination and synthesis is commonly associated with a sense of joy and even exhilaration. In the end, closure takes place. The new insight or vision is then ready for critical scrutiny. If its validity is established, its actualization usually calls for further dedicated, persistent effort of a highly organized nature.

In this sense, the term creativity can be applied to any form of human discovery, however personal, regardless of whether it is great, original, or socially recognized as innovative. Is not the child who destroys one perception of himself or herself in favor of a new one—as in discovering that mastery of motor skills imparts control over the environment—engaged in a creative act? Is not the patient who gains a remarkably new insight, such as a radically different way to view his or her family relationships, fulfilling Kubie's definition of creativity as "the uncovering of new facts or new relationships among new and old data?" Has not the person who is engaged in reorganizing the bits and pieces of a life shattered by economic reversals, divorce, or the death of a loved one embarked on a journey that demands creativity for its successful completion? Don't these require the formation of a new Gestalt? In fact, would it not be more accurate to state that any significant change in the organization of one's personality, or in the meaningful structure of one's life, demands activation of the creative process? This would seem to be a necessary prerequisite for proceeding from the demise of things as they have been to the construction of things as they re becoming and will be.

The need for disruption and reintegration of one's personality structure and surrounding environmental conditions recurs throughout the natural life cycle. The degree to which this will be true of any one person depends greatly on the conditions of his or her life. As Butler (1957) wrote in *The Way of All Flesh*: "In quiet, uneventful lives, the changes internal and external are so small that there is little or no strain in the process of fusion and accommodation; in other lives there is great strain, but there is also great fusing and accommodating power. A life will be successful or not, accordingly as the power of accommodation is equal or unequal to the strain of fusing and adjusting internal and external changes" (pp. 296–297).

Moving from childhood to adolescence, from young, single adulthood to being married and becoming parents, reaching middle age, and moving beyond into later life—each shift requires some forfeiting of both intrapsychic self-perceptions and external landmarks that had been established in prior phases of life but that no longer apply to present circumstances. Additional stresses, such as accidents, unexpected illnesses, divorce, the death of a child, serious financial reversals, and even high levels of success and achievement, also mandate a period of psychobiological disruption to set the stage for reintegration and the formation of a new, more differentiated psychic structure. The essence of the creative process must come into play repeatedly in everyday events in the lives of people whenever and wherever they must abandon old ways of looking at things in favor of new ones; when they shed obsolete responses in favor of new skills, acquire important insights, or rebuild the conditions of their lives.

CREATIVITY AND THE RESILIENCE HYPOTHESIS

The recurring need for disruption and reintegration forms the basis of the view I have called the *resilience hypothesis* (Flach, 1988b). Psychobiological resilience is that combination of psychological, biological, and environmental elements that must be present for the successful transit of stress-induced episodes of disorganization and reorganization. Not surprisingly, one of the central attributes of resilience is the ability to think and act creatively.

In fact, instead of asking whether creativity is a sign of mental health or illness, we would better inquire: *Does mental illness represent an abnormality or dysfunction in the normal process of creativity or various processes that serve as the basis of creativity?*

As a first step in answering that question, we must be willing to redefine the nature of mental and emotional illness. Psychiatric diagnosis has evolved in a systematic manner through the identification of clusters of psychological and behavioral symptoms that seem to fit together into coherent patterns and follow more or less predictable clinical courses. But psychiatric diagnosis suffers from serious limitations. As with the nature of creativity, form must be distinguished from essence. Symptom clusters are little more than a matter of form. The essence of the turbulent, disorganizing event itself—whatever traditional symptomatologic profile it assumes—is something else, and a wide variety of states of emotional disturbance that clinicians presume to represent illness may in fact not warrant such a conclusion at all.

Consider depression. Is the experience of depression evidence of illness in and of itself? The common denominator in many episodes of depression is that they are triggered by stressful events, such as the loss of someone or something valued, or more specifically the loss of a vital influence that supports one's identity and self-esteem (Kaplan, 1987). If we examine the elements that go into a diagnosis of affective disorder, we find that illness depends not so much on the melancholic mood itself but rather on the phenomenology of how the mood is experienced, and on the resources that should enable the depressed person to recover effectively from a depressive episode in a reasonable period of time.

What is true of depression is no less true of other forms of behavioral distress, from anxiety to disorganizing panic. It is not so much the painful emotional state nor the extent of personality disorganization that indicates illness, but how the episode of disruption is managed, how it is interpreted by the patient, and how well and quickly reintegration follows.

THREE OPPORTUNITIES FOR ILLNESS

According to the resilience hypothesis, there are three opportunities for illness. The first lies in the inability of the person to experience disruption when confronted with stresses or changes that demand it. The presence of a rigid, inflexible personality organization and the pervasive use of such defensive mechanisms as denial—however well such a person may function in the world—represents at the very least a special vulnerability to illness. Lack of personal growth and the failure to learn advanced adaptational abilities render such persons less and less able to deal with change in themselves or others. They can also give rise to a personality structure that, if ruptured by extreme stress, can lead to overwhelming disorganization and the tendency for such disorganization to persist with the same tenacity that once sustained the original inflexible structure. Furthermore, recent evidence suggests that such inflexibility sets the stage for a variety of psychosomatic illnesses, and even cardiovascular disease or cancer, particularly when it is associated with a high level of hostility or learned helplessness, respectively (Eysenck, 1987).

Such people are reminiscent of Koestler's (1974) description of the plight of Australia's koala bear, overly organized and too specialized in its organization. "that charming and pathetic creature, the koala bear," Koestler wrote, "which specializes in feeding on the leaves of a particular variety of eucalyptus tree and on nothing else; and which, in lieu of fingers, has hook-like claws, ideally suited for clinging to the bark of the tree—and for nothing else" (p. 281).

The second opportunity for illness lies in the manner in which the individual experiences disruption. Anxiety and depression are the norm rather than the exception at such times. Should disruption be associated with auditory or visual hallucinations, one may conclude that the form it has taken is unhealthy. But even then, one cannot be sure. For example, the difference between a state of anxiety and depression that can be successfully managed and one that propels itself into a state of utterly disorganizing panic can lie not so much in the level of health of the patient as in the nature of his or her environmental support systems. Not infrequently, moderately depressed individuals confronted with rejecting and unempathic husbands or wives can be driven to a degree of chaos that would never have occurred had they had spouses who sensed their suffering and could reach out to them caringly (Flach, 1986).

Successful management of the disruptive phase of the normal response to stress involves the ability to tolerate ambiguity, a characteristic cited earlier by Stein (1988) as describing one of the unique qualifications for the creative act. It is this phase in the cycle that I believe that Andreasen (1988) was referring to when (in her response to my letter about her article in the *American Journal of Psychiatry* [Flach, 1988a]) she wrote, "I suspect that creative people have a characteristic underlying cognitive style that predisposes them to be both creative and vulnerable to fluctuations in mood ... characterized by curiosity and adventuresomeness ... and a willingness to take risks. This style is likely to generate more positive and negative life events, more subjective experiences of both happiness and sadness, and a fresh and innovative approach to almost any task that is undertaken" (p. 772).

The third opportunity for illness lies in the failure to reintegrate—when living on the edge becomes a life style. There, the chronic form of behavioral illness comes in. If one persists in a condition of disorganization, anxiety and depression will necessarily endure and closure will not take place. What begins as a healthy response to stress becomes disabling.

Again, the reintegrative stage of the resilience cycle involves psychological, biological, and environmental parameters. Certain patients whose distress and disability persist over time lack adequate biological resilience.

Among depressed patients, resilience is a function that can often be restored by means of psychopharmacologic agents such as the antidepressants. Certain so-called schizophrenic patients with a tendency to relapse into disruption may be said to lack adequate social and vocational skills to support their lives in the community, a situation that can often be corrected through training and education (Liberman & Engel, 1989).

PSYCHIATRIC ILLNESS AS A DISORDER OF CREATIVITY PROCESSES

The appearance of emotional and behavioral instability among highly gifted and creative individuals could be seen as indicative of an inevitable marriage between creative accomplishments and illness. However, it seems more logical to view the connection as a reflection of a disorder that specifically involves the ability to successfully engage in the cycle of disruption and reintegration provoked by stress and disequilibrium.

In other words, the essence of the creative process—regardless of what form it assumes—is present, either actually or potentially, within most human beings. In that sense, it is akin to any other psychological process, such as memory or intelligence. Thus, certain forms of mental illness, primarily those that are commonly precipitated by stress (as in the case of affective disorders) represent a disorder of the essential mechanisms that underlie the operation of creativity. They include the abilities to recognize and reject incorrect or maladaptive personality or environmental structures, to tolerate the uncertainty of living—for a while—without such structures, and finally, to synthesize and construct new structures that are more appropriate and usually of a higher degree of organization than those that went before.

THERAPEUTIC IMPLICATIONS

Envisioning certain forms of psychiatric illness as disorders that involve the psychobiological pathways of the creative process has an important implication of patient care. In ordinary clinical assessments, the therapist can assess the creative skills of each patient with an eye toward the role those skills can play in furthering the patient's recovery. Usual psychometric tests can be supplemented with those that evaluate various aspects of creative ability (Davis & Kaltsounis, 1977; Hocevar, 1981).

Many highly creative individuals fear psychotherapy and biological treatment less their original output level be diminished. That is not an entirely spurious concern, because inappropriate psychotherapy strategies can inadvertently interfere with creativity in an effort to "normalize" the patient. Repositioning emotional dysfunction caused, in part, by disordered creative process can set the stage for compliance.

This concept of creativity can also enhance restoration of a patient's morale, seen by Frank (1974) as the heart of psychotherapeutic healing. For example, if a patient can view his or her illness partly as a natural response to overwhelming stresses as well as one that promises the possibility of a more effective level of adaptation afterwards—or when the recovering patient can look on a period of resurgent distress as part of a learning experience rather than simply as a relapse—both hope and motivation for therapy can be strengthened. In addition, certain negative countertransference reactions can be mitigated.

One of the more difficult aspects of therapy is the challenge patients represent to therapists' sense of their own emotional health. Even as therapists seek a frame of reference within which to evaluate the distressed persons consulting them, how can they not help but position themselves within a similar context? If episodes of emotional distress—even to the point of dysfunction—are regularly seen as signs of illness rather than reflecting a stage in the creative experience, what conclusions can therapist draw with regard to their own feelings of uncertainty, anxiety, and futility?

The skilled therapist must be the master of ambiguities. As such, he or she must be steeped in knowledge about and experience with creativity.

REFERENCES

Andreasen, N. C. (1987). Creativity and mental illness: Prevalence rates in writers and their first-degree relative. *American Journal of Psychiatry, 144*, 1288–1292.

Andreasen, N. C. (1988). [Letter to the editor]. *American Journal of Psychiatry, 145*, 771–772.

Barron, F. (1963). *Creativity and psychological health.* New York: Van Nostrand.

Butler, S. (1957). *The way of all flesh.* New York: Dutton. (Original work published 1903)

Cashden, S., & Welsh, G. S. (1966). Personality correlates of creative potential in talented high school students. *Journal of Personality, 34*, 445–455.

Cattell, R. B., & Butcher, H. J. (1970). Creativity and personality. In P. E. Vernon (Ed.), *Creativity* (pp. 313–315). Harmondsworth, England: Penguin.

Davis, G. A., & Kaltsounis, B. (1977). Testing instruments useful in studying creative behavior and creative talents. In S. J. Parnes, R. B. Noller, & A. M. Biondi (Eds.), *Guide to creative action* (pp. 278–285). New York: Charles Scribner.

Eysenck, H. J. (1987). Personality as a predictor of cancer and cardiovascular disease, and the application of behaviour therapy in prophylaxis. *European Journal of Psychiatry, 1*, 29–41.

Flach, F. (1986). *The secret strength of depression* (rev. ed.). New York: Bantam.

Flach, F. (1988a). [Letter to the editor]. *American Journal of Psychiatry, 145,* 771–772.

Flach, F. (1988b). *Resilience.* New York: Fawcett Columbine.

Frank, J. D. (1974). Psychotherapy: The restoration of morale. *American Journal of Psychiatry, 131,* 271–274.

Hocevar, D. (1981). Measurement of creativity: Review and critique. *Journal of Personality Assessment, 45,* 450–464.

Hudson, L. (1968). *Frames of mind.* London: Methuen.

Kaplan, H. B. (1987). Social identities and psychological distress. *Directions in Psychiatry, 7,* Lesson 22.

Klerman, G. L., & Lubin, L. (1988). Interpersonal psychotherapy and depression: Approach and treatment. *Directions in Psychiatry, 8,* Lesson 2.

Koestler, A. (1974). *Act of creation.* New York: Macmillan.

Kubie, L. S. (1958). *Neurotic distortion of the creative process.* Lawrence: University of Kansas Press.

Liberman, R. P., & Engel, J. (1989). Rehabilitation of the seriously mentally ill. *Directions in Psychiatry, 9,* Lesson 4.

MacKinnon, D. W. (1965). Personality and the realization of creative potential. *American Psychologist, 20,* 273–281.

Schubert, S. P. (1988). Creativity and the ability to cope. In F. Flach (Ed.), *The creative mind* (pp. 97–114). Buffalo, NY: Bearly.

Stein, M. I. (1988). Creativity: The process and its stimulation. In F. Flach (Ed.), *The creative mind* (pp. 51–75). Buffalo, NY: Bearly.

Storr, A. (1972). *The dynamics of creation.* New York: Atheneum.

Wertheimer, M. (1959). *Productive thinking* New York: Harper & Row.

Chapter 11

The Healing Power of Art: The Case of James Ensor*

John E. Gedo

A selection of aesthetically successful examples from the Prinzhorn Collection of art produced by socially disabled, chronically hospitalized "psychotics" recently circulated through North America. This work impresses the contemporary viewer through its disturbing iconography. Clearly, it was produced during the lengthy phase of attempted restitution that generally follows any acute disorganization that necessitates hospitalization. As such, effective efforts to organize a pictorial gestalt may play an important role in reconstituting islands of integrated behavior, usually by trying to attribute some arbitrary meaning to the basically incomprehensible experience of the acute illness.

*From "More on The Healing Power of Art: The Case of James Ensor," by J. E. Gedo, 1990, *Creativity Research Journal*, 3(1), pp. 33–57. Copyright © 1995 Ablex Publishing. Adapted with permission.

The naïve style employed by every artist represented in the exhibit has been attributed to lack of artistic training. Yet major artists whose technical skills left nothing to be desired, like James Ensor, produced series of works using formal means closely similar to those of "psychotic art." The subject matter of this segment of Ensor's oeuvre also resembles that of the Prinzhorn material. Although Ensor was never completely disabled psychologically, he was greatly disturbed for about a dozen years at the very apex of his career. His successful adaptation thereafter testifies to the beneficial effect of his revolutionary art on his integration. The fact that for almost 50 years Ensor kept on replicating the works of his great period of turmoil renders it probable that the specific imagery he evolved helped to buttress his self-organization. Thus, Ensor's example suggests that the formal characteristics of "psychotic art" may optimally serve specific expressive aims and should not be dismissed as a matter of naïveté.

I know of no better description of the relationship of the artist to his public than that of Migeul de Cervantes in his book of morality tales, *Novelas Ejemplares.* Cervantes called the artist "the man of glass"—a translucent repository of riches to satisfy the curiosity of a rabble attracted by his apparent madness. Should the unfortunate performer ask to be taken seriously, however, Cervantes predicted an abrupt loss of interest in his message. The national attention devoted to the touring exhibition of selections from the Prinzhorn Collection demonstrates that the passage of 400 years has scarcely altered the general preference for equating creativity and madness. There is something unseemly about our avidity to violate the privacy of the unfortunates who produced these objects for their private purposes, rather than intending them as aesthetic communications to posterity.[1] If we are to justify our unauthorized intrusion upon these personal tragedies, we are under obligation to make optimal use of this unearned privilege, *pro bono publico.*

What, then, can we learn from such an exhibition? Does it have anything to tell us about the "art of the insane"? Alas, very little—only that, if such a collection is surveyed with sufficient care by aesthetically trained selectors, it will yield a modest number of examples of undoubted artistic merit. But this is scarcely a surprise, given our familiarity with the vicissitudes of great artists active in madhouses and prisons, from Torquato Tasso through the Marquis de Sade and Vincent van Gogh, to Jean Genet and Ezra Pound. In this connection, it may suffice to recall August Strindberg's reaction to the news of Friedrich Nietzsche's mental collapse: With

---

[1]These works were obtained by the psychiatrists at the University of Heidelberg under circumstances that, by present-day American ground rules, would constitute malpractice or violation of patients' civil rights. Moreover, the revelation of the actual identities of these patients, albeit long dead, is an outrage that should recall to us that some Heidelberg professors participated in the judicial murder of psychotics under the Nazi regime.

exquisite empathy and insight, Strindberg sent his farewells to is fallen comrade through the ancient Hellenic salutation—"Come, let us be mad together!" Can there by anyone left in the civilized world who believes that psychosis deprives people of their humanity?

Hans Prinzhorn's impression that chronic psychotic illness is more likely to interfere with the capacity to produce written documents than imagery is almost certainly a result of haphazard sampling in collecting his materials. In fact, the single most powerful piece of "psychotic art" produced in the 20th century is a written memoir, that of his nervous illness, by the Saxon jurist, Daniel Paul Schreber (1955). Sigmund Freud (1958) used this document to illustrate his theory about the psychology of paranoid delusions. His conclusions about Schreber's creation are, I believe, entirely applicable to the subject matter of the works from the Prinzhorn Collection.

Freud pointed out that the creative activity of the psychotic patient begins after the subsidence of the acute phase of the illness—and indeed, in most cases the artists in the exhibition started to produce many years after their initial hospitalization. The product is an effort on the part of the victim of a personal catastrophe to make some sense of the incomprehensible experience of a loss of integration. The banal consequences of faulty neural wiring or disordered metabolism are thus transformed into events of portentous, even cosmic significance. The works are replete with imagery expressing megalomania, erotomania, or delusions of persecution and bizarre religious ideas—the full lamentable panoply through which a modicum of sense is wrought out of senselessness.

In the past 60 years, in large measure because of the direct influence of the Heidelberg archives on major avant-garde figures such as Max Ernst, Paul Klee, Richard Lindner, and Jean Dubuffet, subject matter of this kind has entered the mainstream of contemporary art—incidentally, nowhere more vigorously and with greater emotional power than on the Chicago scene. Yet it would be a major error to confuse the sophisticated and ironic work of subtle commentators on modern life such as the Chicago imagists, or the Continental intellectuals who preceded them, with the direct efforts of schizophrenics and manic-depressives to organize their chaotic experiences in terms of coherent visual perceptions. In the art of the insane, there is no conscious intention to communicate with an audience by means of some shared language of signs, and *our* ability to extract aesthetic pleasure from their hermetic private language is clearly the result of the work of the masters of Surrealism and *l'art brut*, which constitutes our Rosetta stone for the decipherment of these mad hieroglyphs.

As a consequence, we are now in a position to consider whether the undeniable aesthetic power of most of the works in the Prinzhorn exhibition may not stem from the formal choices made by these particular patients.

The question would be easier to answer if we had been offered a more representative sample of the collection, instead of the crème de la crème. The catalog (1984) accompanying the exhibit stated that the style of these works is entirely characteristic of naïve art, produced by amateurs without formal training. This statement is a gross oversimplification. The formal means employed in this body of work is not so much naïve—it is, rather, characteristic of the varied graphic production of Central Europe in the early 20th century.[2] Another way to approach the matter is to recollect that artists without academic training are well able to mater the formal vocabulary of any particular style if it suits their expressive purposes: Witness such erstwhile amateurs as Paul Gauguin or Yves Tanguy—or, on the other side of the stylistic divide, the determined effort to the Douanier Rousseau to retain *his* unique pseudonaïve style in his finished works, often based on sketches competently executed in that of his Impressionistic predecessors.

I believe we may be able to define the sources of the affective impact of the Prinzhorn exhibit by comparing it to a segment of the work of a major artist, one capable of using a *variety* of styles with equal effectiveness. A painter and etcher who produced art of the greatest emotional power using formal means similar to those of our sampling of "psychotic art" was the Anglo-Belgian pioneer of fantastic art, James Ensor, whose greatest creative achievements occurred a full generation before the works in the exhibit were produced. Ensor was a native of Ostende, a port city on the North Sea where Flanders becomes the meeting place of the civilizations of France, Holland, and England. His father was an educated Englishman settled in Belgium, his mother a Fleming of petit bourgeois background. The future artist was born in 1860, while his father and namesake was in America seeking his fortune. Defeated by the outbreak of our Civil War, the latter was back in Belgium by 1861 and never again made a serious effort to earn a living. The Ensors lived on the proceeds of the souvenir shop owned by the mother's family—an emporium filled with the masks, shells, and bric-a-brac that are apparent in the painter's images.

Ensor lived until the age of 89; in late life, he conveyed to his biographers a nostalgic and idealized version of his childhood, complete with a reprise of Leonardo's infantile "memory" about being visited in the cradle by a magical bird. It has been widely recognized that Ensor's persona was intended to mislead the public: The Belgian scholar Francine-Claire Legrand (1971) describes him as an impostor who hid his inner emptiness by assuming masks or hiding within shells. Consequently, we have little reliable information about his private life, and almost none about his

---

[2] I owe this insight to Professor Theodore Reff, of Columbia University, who viewed the Prinzhorn exhibit during its installation at the Smart Gallery of the University of Chicago (March and April, 1985).

mother. We do know that Ensor's only sibling, his sister Mitsche, was only 16 months his junior. A maternal aunt joined the household, allegedly to help with the boy's upbringing, but the dominant figure was apparently his maternal grandmother, whom he later described as "hardened with age" (de Ridder, 1930, p. 25). Ensor's devastating image of "Sloth" in a late etching (Figure 11.1) was seemingly his conception of his grandmother as a hardfaced hag, but she is uniformly described as an "authoritarian" person. The earliest memory reported by the artist involved a daytime visit to the madame of a neighboring brothel in the company of his grandmother—this is our only hint that he disapproved of her character. We do possess a photograph of Ensor at age 5 in a dress, melting into his father's form. In later life, he recalled his father as sensitive, intellectual, handsome, and prodigiously strong, but he also remembered that his mother had tried to turn him against his father. The boy learned instead to mistrust every member of his family. The family atmosphere was so rancorous that Ensor was consciously afraid to marry lest he himself blunder into such a hell.

It is hardly surprising that as a child the future artist is said to have been shy, easily scared or hurt, oversensitive, irreverent, and prone to aggressive outbursts. In some ways he was apparently overindulged, especially with food by his mother, and so-called freedom by his father—and he was not sent to school until the age of 13. At that point, the boy was unable to adjust to the usual requirements, stayed but two years, and later claimed that he educated himself by reading the classics. His talent for art

Figure 11.1. J. Ensor, Sloth, 1902. Etching.

was recognized early, and private art lessons were arranged for him until he could go to Brussels at the age of 17 to study at the Académie des Beaux-Arts. He received solid training there, made excellent contacts both in the art world in the narrower sense and in the important intellectual circles of the capital, so that it is entirely unclear why at the age of 20 he decided to return to Ostende, set up his studio under his parents' roof, and live out his life as their dependent. Libby Tannenbaum (1952) believed that the painter was simply unable to separate from his family.

To be sure, being away from Brussels did not interfere with Ensor's career; he was able to participate fully in Belgian artistic life and was soon recognized as a leading avant-garde painter. Yet his mother and sister refused to acknowledge his success: They regarded his work as worthless and silly and assailed the artist for his failure to earn money. During the 1880s, while his work was going from strength to strength, Ensor witnessed his father's deterioration as a consequence of alcoholism—a tragedy duplicated in the next generation by his sister. The elder James Ensor finally died in 1887, as a result of exposure while in an alcoholic stupor. Thenceforth the artist was continuously preoccupied in an obsessive manner with his own death. But Ensor's psychological difficulties had already manifested themselves several years earlier when he was 24, in the form of dyspepsia and nervousness. The biographer Paul Haesaerts (1957) asserted that he also had a panic fear of crowds. In view of the fact that he produced a series of drawings on the theme of the Passion at the time of this crisis, it may not be excessively speculative to attribute the outbreak of this illness to the increasing public mockery of Ensor's father by malicious townspeople as the unfortunate alcoholic's behavior deteriorated. At the time of his father's actual demise, the painter became incapacitated for several months.

A tender drawing of his dead father (Figure 11.2) attests to the profound attachment between Ensor and his parents. The magnitude of his sense of loss may be gleaned from his numerous subsequent self-portrayals as a creature in decay. It would seem that the painter was able partially to restore his equilibrium by identifying with aspects of his father's behavior: for example, it is said that he would provoke the Ostende fishwives by jeering them; when they replied with streams of abuse or threw a fish at him, he appeared to be delighted. His entire existence in this period was characterized by mockery and self-hatred: Ensor became a debunker and a caricaturist, a wounded combination of gravity and buffoonery and (as I shall try to demonstrate shortly) his work was impregnated with pain, terror, and impotent rage.

This paranoid experience of human relations did not spare Ensor's professional life: He felt abused by his artistic associates in Les Vingts, the Brussels arena for progressive exhibitions. Although an occasional work

Figure 11.2.   J. Ensor, The Artist's Father in Death, 1887. *Conté crayon. Koninklijk Museum voor Schone Kunsten, Antwerp.*

of Ensor's failed to gain acceptance by this group, these lapses in the support they provided were in no way comparable to Ensor's own efforts to blackball certain potential exhibitors (like Whistler), his unreasonable demands for special treatment at the expense of artists such as Toulouse-Lautrec, his insensate charge that a fellow-member, the eminent symbolist Fernand Khnoff was plagiarizing his work, and his savage depreciation of every potential rival for artistic eminence. According to both Legrand (1971) and Delevoy (1981), Ensor fabricated a paranoid myth about opposition to his participation in these exhibitions.

In 1888, Ensor became linked with Augusta Boogaerts, a young shopgirl who remained his lifelong companion. Characteristically, the painter mocked his mistress by calling her La Sirène, and he was careful never to live with her. Marriage was allegedly out of the question because of his family's opposition. La Sirène gained more and more personal influence over him nonetheless; ultimately, she literally directed him in his moment-to-moment activities, as a nursemaid might control a bewildered child, and she did not hesitate to chastise Ensor caustically. The establishment of this symbiotic mode of adaptation was accompanied, as we might expect, by a gradual loss of Ensor's artistic power. Some critics (including Legrand) detect the onset of this falling off as early as 1893, when Ensor was but 33 years of age. In view of the continued excellence of Ensor' etchings for several years thereafter, these judgments may be too severe, but there is general agreement about the fact that after 1898, the artist produced few works that merit serious attention. One exception (Figure 11.3) is his portrayal of his mother on her deathbed in 1915. I believe the flavor of this powerful painting conveys to us the difference in Ensor's feelings toward mother and father.

In any event, there is no doubt that after 1890 Ensor produced less, his personal behavior became more aggressive and isolated, and he was filled with righteousness and a sense of persecution. Despite increasingly favorable attention from critics, the appearance of Demolder's monograph on his work in 1892, the influential patronage of the industrialist Franck, and purchase of some of his works by museums, Ensor's artistic self-confidence was shattered: He began to replicate his own past achievements. His prices rose, he had an exhibition in Paris—in 1903, he was decorated by the Belgian government—but he knew himself to be artis-

Figure 11.3.   J. Ensor, The Artist's Mother in Death, 1915. Oil on canvas. Stedelijk Museum, Ostende.

tically bankrupt and devoted the rest of his life to self-promotion and the impersonation of a great man. Psychologically sophisticated biographers, like Legrand, stress the lack of authenticity of the persona Ensor assumed after 1900; as I mentioned, she calls this masquerade a bit of bravado hiding the tragedy of inner emptiness. So pervasive was Ensor's self-contempt that he could not even believe in the sincerity of critical acclaim for his work.

To recapitulate the personality portrait I have culled from the standard Ensor biographies: The future artist was raised in a stressful and destructive family atmosphere, by a confusing and warring set of caretakers, none of whom provided a model of healthy adaptation. Throughout life, Ensor seemed unable to separate himself from this family matrix; his early history suggests that he had a school phobia, and the premature termination of his studies in Brussels betokens a failure to transcend adolescence and to achieve the status of an autonomous adult. Around the age of 24, in the context of his father's descent into alcoholism, Ensor's adjustment began to break down: His hypochondriasis was the ominous forerunner of worse disorganization to come. This catastrophe supervened with the father's shocking demise; it took the form of paranoia and depression. But this emotional crisis produced the artist's most powerful and original creations. Ensor's disorganization was halted short of an overt psychosis and the understanding of supportive friends permitted him to pursue his art in relative isolation until his personal storm had blown over. But the success of this healing process also brought a diminution of aesthetic power and the self-contempt of an ambitious man whose time of accomplishment had passed.

Let us now turn to the evidence of Ensor's artistic production to fill out the testimony of his biographers. In his first period of activity, from 1880 to 1883, Ensor produced over 125 paintings, starting with a traditional style and gradually adopting a manner influenced by Manet. In 1881, Ensor painted *Russian Music*,[3] a major genre scene incorporating portraits of Mitsche and a fellow-artist; by 1882, with *Woman in Distress*, he began to focus on the troubled psychological atmosphere of the Ensor household, for the model for this painting was also the artist's sister. The first reference to the fate of the elder Ensor appears in the powerful yet sympathetic canvas of 1883, *The Drunkards*. Most commentators believe that *The Scandalized Masks*, also painted in that year, depicts the relationship of the artist's parents in the trappings of revelers in the Carnival: The man is surrounded by empty bottles and the woman seems ready to

---

[3]For illustrations of this work and others mentioned in the text but not reproduced here, consult Haesaerts (1957) and the exhibition catalog of the Prinzhorn Collection (1984).

chastize him with her stick. Yet the painting is generally regarded as a genre scene and *not* a portrayal of the world of Ensor's imagination, as the later pictures of masks are thought to be.

Ensor mastered the craft of painting by the age of 23: he was able to use the medium through the full range of stylistic alternatives available in the early 1880s. The production of the next several years is more difficult to assess, for Ensor often reworked these pictures at a later time but pretended to have crated their final versions on his first attempt. Presumably he wished to exaggerate his originality by creating a myth about having reached his full potential earlier than was in fact the case. The *Self-Portrait in a Flowered Hat*, dated 1883, is one example of this chicanery. The painting was first conceived as a conventional self-depiction; the stunning 17th-century headgear, borrowed from a Rubens' self-portrait, was added later, presumably at a time when the quality of Ensor's work gave him hope of equaling the achievements of the last giant of Flemish art.

Another picture that went through the same process of change is the *Girl with Doll*, dated 1884. In its original version, this painting must have been a sentimental genre scene, similar to Ensor's *Russian Music*, done three years before. After the onset of his psychological crisis, the artist radically transformed this image by introducing a series of ectoplasmic apparitions into the scene—the so-called doll the child is cuddling is a miniature monster of this kind; a second gnome is lurking behind her; and we cannot ascertain whether a number of visages in the background form part of the wallpaper or flat in the air like hallucinations. Ensor's visions are strikingly similar to an image of a spook from the Prinzhorn exhibit. With both works, one gains the conviction that the artist is setting down an actual *perception*, the reality of which he cannot quite decide.

A third painting Ensor is thought to have transformed in the same manner is *Skeleton Studying Chinoiseries* (1885). Presumably the artist originally portrayed himself surrounded by some of the exotic possessions of his family; after the onset of the most severe phase of his illness, he changed his head into a skull, thus creating one of the grisliest images of the subjective experience of psychological death—only to be equaled by Kafka's *Metamorphosis*. However, by 1885 much of Ensor's work was impregnated by this ominous spirit, so that his self-depiction qua skeleton may actually date from that year or very soon thereafter. Its menace is echoed by the feeling conveyed by *Rooftops of Ostend*, painted in the same year—for me, this might be the setting for a drama of Gothic horror. I am not alone in this opinion: Paul Haesaerts (1957, p. 188) perceived these paintings as images of a foundering world. A townscape from the Prinzhorn Collection seems to radiate a similar sense of cosmic anxiety, through comparable stylistic expedients.

Tannenbaum (1952) noted that, in Ensor's mature images employing masks as prominent elements, the victim whom the maskers intend to terrify is never shown. But the earliest image in this series, an 1885 drawing entitled *Haunted Furniture*, showed a child terrified by a combination of skeletons and masks. de Ridder (1930) asserted that the child (a girl!) stands for the artist himself. A second version of *Haunted Furniture* shows Ensor in his own guise as both the terrified victim and the apparition from the spirit world who would terrify us. From the evidence of this drawing, I infer that by 1886 the artist was in the throes of his supreme emotional crisis. Tannenbaum also noted that the year 1886 marks the beginning of Ensor's maximal stylistic freedom and diversity.

I think there is little doubt that Ensor's illness was precipitated by the deterioration of his father. The artist was identified with his disintegrating namesake, and—like so many of the patients represented in the Prinzhorn exhibit—he equated the suffering of both with the Passion of Christ. One example of this identification is a drawing of 1886, *Alive and Radiant: Entry into Jerusalem.* This work is related to Ensor's masterpiece, the enormous canvas *Entry of Christ into Brussels, 1888,* painted two years later, and translated into the medium of etching in 1895 (Figure 11.4). It has been generally understood that the contemporaneous Belgian Christ in this image could only be a self-reference, but it has been assumed that the theme alludes to the fate of the avant-garde artist among the Pharisees. Such an interpretation is probably valid enough; in his etching of

Figure 11.4. J. Ensor, The Entry of Christ into Brussels, 1985. Etching.

1886, *The Cathedral,* Ensor showed a multitudinous rabble turning its back on this great artistic edifice, as Tannenbaum rightly noted. But the more personal determinants of Ensor's greatest work have also been noted: Delevoy (1981) pointed out that the chief drummer in the mocking band celebrating the martyrdom of Jesus is a portrait of Ensor's implacable grandmother. Hence I conclude that this supreme effort on the part of the artist commemorates the demise of his idealized father. And the effects of the loss of this beloved parent are recorded in numerous other works. If the martyrdom of the elder James Ensor caused his son's psychological death, I wonder whether the astonishing *Fireworks* of 1887 may not mark the moment of the artist's collapse—a delusion of the end of the world—for today the painting suggests not so much a festive *feu d'artifice* as the detonation of a nuclear device.

To demonstrate the ubiquitousness of the foregoing themes in the mental life of individuals in psychological extremis, let me return to a work from the Prinzhorn exhibit (Figure 11.5) depicting scenes from the Passion of Christ. Here we find the same *horror vacui,* the same flattening of figures, and the same violent color contrasts as in Ensor's great canvas.

Figure 11.5.   Moog, Untitled, 1919. Pencil, colored pen, and tempera. Prinzhorn Collection, University of Heidelberg.

This is not naïve art, but a return to medieval practices in order to express the fervent convictions of an *imitatio Christi*, and a representation from the Prinzhorn exhibit of a fearsome change of body image (Figure 11.6) reminds us of Ensor's self-depictions in the guise of a skeleton as well as the caricatural style he began to employ in the *Entry of Christ into Brussels*.

It should never be forgotten that, in parallel with the expressionist works for which he is best known, Ensor continued to paint tranquil and glowing pictures, like the joyous still life in Figure 11.7, also dated 1888. But his predominant mood, as reflected in his paintings, is sadistic and scatological, as Tannenbaum (1952) correctly stated. If, as Tannenbaum would have it, we are able to view many of these works as metaphysical inquiries into evil, portrayals of mankind as its most vile, such images gain their power to convince because, at the same time, they express the artist's paranoid resolution of the disorganizing experience of his family crisis. The work in which the paranoia comes across most directly is an 1888 drawing of a swarm of demons teasing the artist (Figure 11.8). The image Ensor used 10 years later for the poster of his Paris exhibition is a reprise of the original in which this terrifying per-

Figure 11.6.   L. Berthold, Untitled. Pencil. Prinzhorn Collection, University of Heidelberg.

Figure 11.7. J. Ensor, **Still Life with Fish and Shells,** *1888. Oil on canvas. Art Institute of Chicago.*

secution has been transformed into a game (Figure 11.9). I believe that this gradual taming of raw emotion through repetition gives us an indication of one mechanism through which the practice of art exerts its healing power.

By coincidence, there were severe disturbances in Ostende in 1888—a desperate strike put down with considerable brutality. These events provided an external focus around which Ensor's bitterness and rage could crystallize, and he produced a series of works that can be regarded as an art of social protest. Yet I believe that Ensor, whose subsequent life proves to have been entirely without political convictions, may have produced these provocative paintings in order to bring about on the stage of actuality the persecution he was experiencing in his inner life: These scurrilous pictures were not accepted for exhibition in Brussels, and this rejection set in motion Ensor's rancorous battles with his erstwhile artistic allies. *Belgium in the 19th Century,* a drawing of 1889, exemplifies Ensor's mordant spirit. In this caricatural work, the artist skirted the limits permissible under the laws of his time and place. *The Gendarmes,* exe-

*Figure 11.8.   J. Ensor, Demons Teasing Me, 1888. Pencil and black chalk.
Art Institute of Chicago.*

cuted in 1892, harks back to the violent repression of the Ostende strike, and *The Good Judges* of 1891—transformed into an etching of 1894—extends Ensor's savage satire by means of the deliberate crudity of his style. But the artist's contempt spared almost nobody: Witness his savage depiction of the crowds in *Ostende Beach*, an etching of 1899. And his un-provoked depreciation of other artists, as in his mocking picture of a Wagner performance *At the Conservatory* (undated) is sheer nastiness, without possibility of rational justification.

Ensor's productivity began to decline as early as 1890, a circumstance that he himself attributed to his family difficulties. Can we understand the artist's canvas *Adam and Eve Expelled from Eden*, painted in 1887, as an expression of the feeling that his own childhood was coming to its end with the death of his father? And is *The Fall of the Rebel Angels* of 1889 an avowal of his own disintegration after the loss of his infantile paradise? In any case, the supernatural beings Ensor depicted in such painting recur again and again in the Prinzhorn material, as in one drawing (Figure 10.10) of a personage as if from another planet. After the resolution of the acute crisis of 1887–1888, the loose style of Ensor's paintings of cos-

Figure 11.9.   J. Ensor, Poster for "La Plume," 1898. Colored lithograph.

mic catastrophe disappears from his work: The mise-en-scène tends to focus on studio interiors, and the forces of disorganization are represented symbolically, through the presence of a myriad masks, rather than by formal means alone. These masks are like the shards of a shattered personality in the 1889 canvas *Attributes of the Studio*, as well as the *Old Woman with Masks* of the same year (Figure 11.11). This painting was rejected by the sitter who commissioned it; to our eyes, it is an empathic portrait of a desperate effort to erect a false front in order to hide one's inner emptiness or despair. The Prinzhorn material includes a similar image of a masklike face (Figure 11.12).

Through the years of declining artistic vigor that followed, Ensor's most impressive works continued to deal with this very theme: His self-depictions fluctuated between masquerade and a living death. One of his powerful etchings, *Death Pursuing a Flock of People* (1896), located the conflict on the Ostende street of Ensor's domicile, and a painting of that same date, *Skeleton Painter in His Atelier*, made the autobiographical meaning of this representation explicit by surrounding the protagonist with Ensor's own works. The usual masked carnival of figures are present in

Figure 11.10.   Pohl, Untitled, *c. 1909–1916. Crayon. Prinzhorn Collection,
University of Heidelberg.*

the foreground: Ensor was by this time ready to embark on the course of self-parody and self-plagiarism that marked the last 50 years of his life. This was the grinning mask that the artist himself wore to disavow his sense of inner emptiness. In *Skeletons Trying to Get Warm* (1897), these figures of decomposition assumed the jauntiness that was to characterize Ensor, the international celebrity. In 1899, in a work that may have been his last major success, *Self-Portrait with Masks*, Ensor acknowledged, by representing himself in the costume of Rubens, that his pose as the successor of Flanders' *premier peintre* is the façade that hides his true self, that of the living dead. Perhaps the luscious *natures mortes* he had produced for two decades convey the same message: Is the cold fish, staring at us in such a human way in *Still Life with Ray* (1892: Figure 11.13), dead or alive?

By stressing the pathological implications of Ensor's iconography, I have for the moment neglected the most important consequence of the decade of artistic activity that followed his father's death. Far from succumbing to the disintegrative forces that threatened his stability, he was able increasingly to confine the sickness to the subject matter of his work. Although the mast of celebrity and "Baron of Painting" concealed

Figure 11.11.   J. Ensor, Portrait of Old Woman with Masks, *1889. Oil on canvas. Museum voor Schone Kunsten, Ghent.*

the scars of his great crisis of 1887, by dint of sheer repetition it became the prevailing actuality of Ensor's existence. Through his work, the artist largely healed himself. Although his mistress tried to control him, he was well able to fend her off through passive resistance. As if conscious of the power of his imagery to encapsulate his illness,[4] Ensor increasingly restricted his production to new versions of his preceding works.

Ensor lost his artistic self-confidence as early as 1892. He acknowledged that he had been brought to his knees in a canvas painted in the style of the contemporary Dutch artist Thorn Prikker. This work is en-

---

[4]Elsewhere I have tried to show that Cézanne, another great artist with depressive and paranoid propensities, made use of a radically different adaptive device, that of gradually excluding his personal conflicts from his overt subject matter, using them instead to invest powerful, novel formal solutions (Gedo, 1983 [pp. 187–193], 1986).

*Figure 11.12.   Neter, Witch, c. 1919. Pencil. Prinzhorn Collection,
University of Heidelberg.*

titled *The Consoling Virgin.* Ensor, holding his palette, kneels in front of
his easel, which holds an image of the *virgo lactans.* Like the angel of
the Annunciation, Ensor's model stands erect before him, costumed as
the Queen of Heaven. The consoling virgin is not the girl posing in
Ensor's studio but the work of art he himself has created. It is no mere
etymological quibble to remind ourselves that Galatea is "maiden white
as milk," the *virgo lactans:* Every artist is a Pygmalion who creates is own
sustenance.

Ensor's art proved to be an effective antidote for his incipient psychosis, in part by gaining him recognition as one of the great men of
the glorious tradition of Flanders. Thus it provided him with the sense
of union he had apparently needed in relation to his father, by linking
him with powerful progenitors such as Rubens, Breughel, and Bosch. As
Ensor's equilibrium gradually stabilized, the work of his great period inevitably assumed for him the status of Flemish classics. I believe this is

Figure 11.13.   J. Ensor, Still Life with Ray, 1892. Oil on canvas.
Musées Royaux des Beaux Arts de Belgique, Brussels.

the significance of his 1902 painting, *The Antiquarian.* Although this is ostensibly a portrait of one of Ensor's friends, the fact that the artist reproduces the Renaissance paintings that occupy most of the picture plane in his own brilliant palette introduces an unmistakable self-reference into this postscript to his brief but meteoric career as *chef d'école* of Northern painting. By the age of 40, James Ensor had truly become an antiquarian.

The patients whose artistic products Hans Prinzhorn collected did not succeed in healing themselves to the same degree. Perhaps, after all, the power of image-making to stabilize mental functioning may depend on the appreciative response of a significant public. We are told that the patient who produced the gouache of a *Witch's Head* (Figure 10.14) only began to make art in the 14th year of his hospitalization. He also "served the institution as a competent mechanic"—surely a sign of partial recovery. The daemon of his psychosis is writ large at the center of this image—yet it is, at the same time, a quasi-naturalistic depic-

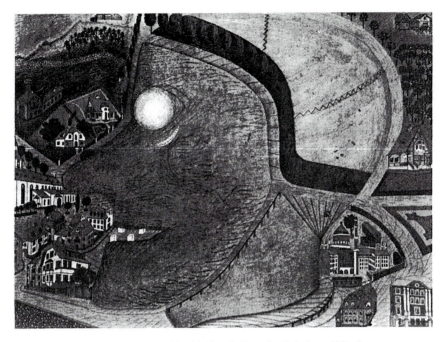

Figure 11.14.   *Neter,* **Witch's Head.** *Gouache. Prinzhorn Collection,
University of Heidelberg.*

tion of a bucolic landscape, rendered from a bird's eye perspective. At
first blush the work seems naïve, but (like similar works in Ensor's oeuvre)
it uses this style knowingly to express the primitive quality of psychotic
experience.

REFERENCES

Delevoy, R. (1981). *Ensor.* Antwerp: Mercatorfonds.
Demolder, R. (1892). *James Ensor.* Brussels: Lacomblez.
de Ridder, A. (1930). *James Ensor.* Paris: Rieder.
Freud, S. (1958). Psycho-analytic notes on an autobiographical account of a case
    of paranoia (dementia paranoides). *Standard Edition* (vol. 12, pp. 9–82).
    London: Hogarth. (Original work published 1911)
Gedo, J. (1983). *Portraits of the artist.* New York: Guilford.
Gedo, J. (1986). Paul Cézanne: Symbiosis, masochism, and the struggle for per-
    ception. *Psychoanalytic perspectives on art* (vol. 2, pp. 187–201). Hillsdale, NJ:
    Erlbaum.

Haesaerts, P. (1957). *Ensor.* London: Thames & Hudson.

Legrand, F. C. (1971). *Ensor cet inconnu.* Brussels: La Renaissance du Livre.

Prinzhorn Collection. (1984). *Selected work.* Urbana-Champaign, IL: University of Illinois.

Schreber, D. (1955). *Memoirs of my nervous illness.* In I. Macalpine & D. Hunter (Eds.). London: William Dawson & Sons. (Original work published 1911)

Tannenbaum, L. (1952). *James Ensor.* New York: Museum of Modern Art.

Chapter 12

The Healing Power of Music: Some Observations on the Semiotic Function of the Transitional Objects in Musical Communication

Peter Ostwald

The extraordinary power of music in evoking feelings, conveying moods, and establishing emotional contacts between people has long been a subject of interest among scholars, musicologists, and scientists. You will recall the biblical story of young David, with his harp and beautiful singing voice, soothing the melancholic King Saul, who was said to have been afflicted by an 'evil spirit' (1 Samuel 16:14-23). That is one of history's first commentaries on music therapy, and there have been many others.[1] References to the healing potential of musical sounds can be found in Egyptian papyri, Arabic and Hindu medical writings, and the literature of ancient China, Greece, and Rome (Pratt & Jones, 1984).

213

HISTORICAL PERSPECTIVES

Particularly influential in the development of theory regarding the use of music as a therapeutic agent have been the contributions of Greek philosophers. (One must remember that for the ancient Greeks, the god *Apollo* governed the domains of both medicine and music.) Plato, for example, wrote that music can directly alter the human soul, which in turn affects the body. Galen, addressing the work of physicians more specifically, recommended that listening to music would improve a patient's health. Pythagoras began to investigate the physical properties of sound; he developed mathematical and cosmological theories about the nature of music. Descriptions of its curative properties can also be found in Greek myths and literature. Homer's *Iliad* tells how the singing of paeans relieved the afflicted Achaeans of the plague, while his *Odyssey* shows Odysseus with the help of musical charms, recovering from the wounds produced by a wild boar.

The ancient history of medicine records interest in the possibility of using music to cure specific disease states, including poisoning due to snake bites (said by Democritus to respond to music played on a flute), fevers, and painful conditions of the joints, muscles, or bones, especially if patients could be induced to dance. And of course there were reports about the effective use of music in treating melancholia, mania, hypochondriasis, hysteria, delirium, insomnia, and other mental disorders. In terms of its ability to bring about changes in behavior, music in all cultures and probably from the beginning of civilization has been observed to play a major role in funeral ceremonies, religious rites, military pageants, and other social manipulations of emotion.

The Renaissance brought with it a renewed interest in music as a healing influence, not only because of the study of Greco-Roman medical traditions, but also through Galileo's discoveries in acoustics, which were used as proof that music can cure diseases such as sciatica and epilepsy. In Italy, from the 15th century to the 17th it was believed that a folkdance known as the *tarantella* was a specific treatment for 'tarantism', a disease throught at the time to be caused by the mildly toxic bite of a spider but more likely a form of mass hysteria. During the last quarter of the 18th Century, numerous case histories appeared in both medical and popular journals about people who were supposedly cured by music, and in the 19th Century many practitioners of music—composers and performers—

---

[1]A modern history of music in medicine remains to be written, and several scholars are presently at work on such a project. Professor Rosalie Rebollo Pratt of Brigham Young University in Provo, Utah, in preparation for her definitive book, has already published a number of articles pertaining to this field. Another scholar, Gretchen Finney, is working on a book titled *The Philosopher's Stone: Music to Cure Disease—Medical Theories in Europe 1489-1840*.

tried in letters, diaries, or essays to explain what it might be about music that so deeply affects human behavior (Strunk, 1950).

Of course no one today would claim that music has the miraculous healing powers ascribed to it in the past. Theories about the causation of disease have changed dramatically as a result of discoveries in bacteriology, molecular biology, and other modern sciences, as well as advances in the fields of public health, nutrition, and preventive medicine. Modern medicine takes into account a patient's general vulnerabilities, as well as his or her defenses against specific disease, upon which the different pathogenic stresses (viral, bacterial, traumatic, metabolic, neoplastic, psychosocial, etc.) act in a variety of ways to bring about breakdowns in health (Wyngaarden & Smith, 1985). Whenever specific treatment interventions are contemplated, be they surgical, anti-toxic, anti-inflammatory, anti-neoplastic, or anti-psychotic, one must always consider the therapeutic effects of nonspecific health measures, including nutrition, rest, interpersonal relationships, and environmental factors. Music, along with the other arts, probably belongs in this latter category of health-maintaining influences.

There is yet another reason why it would be naive to subscribe with undue enthusiasm to any simplistic ideas about music as therapy. This has to do with the amazing versatility of music as an art form. As suggested by the following astute definition of music by Carl Seashore, a sophisticated psychologist as well as a gifted musician, this artistic medium seems to fulfill many human needs simultaneously as well as sequentially:

> From the beginning music, as the expression of emotional life not reducible to logical language, has been a medium for communicating ideals or urges as contrasted with ideas. It has been the language of mysticism, going far beyond the idealizations as expressed in poetry. It has expressed an attitude toward the gods and the spiritual world as a whole. As in the behavior of birds, it has expressed the sexual urge in all its rationalized and idealistic forms. As music for music's sake, it is a sort of dream language which carries the performer and the listener far beyond the routine of daily life. (Seashore, 1947, p. 305).

SCIENTIFIC POSSIBILITIES

The science of psychoacoustics, founded over a hundred years ago by the German musician and psychologist Hermann Helmholtz (1877) has been able to explain many of the physical properties of musical sound. But as Helmholtz himself recognized, it cannot fully account for the universal appeal of music, its ability to make people feel the most intense satisfaction, to stir up excitement, to foster patriotism, or to create unrest. A social approach to music has been proposed by Farnsworth (1958), taking into consideration personal preferences of listeners, cultural values, and public as well as private rules governing emotional expression. Moles (1968) has outlined an information theory of aesthetic perception based on mathematical principles. Meyer (1956), employing principles of Gestalt psychology has shed light on the problem by emphasizing that the musical ear detects patterns that demand closure. A number of specific, definable communicative actions appear to take place at the moment of musical enjoyment, creating symbolic links between the music-makers (composers and performers) with each other and their audience. What is called emotion and meaning in music can be accounted for, in part at least, by an anlysis of the auditory expectations set up when listeners are primed with specific patterns of anticipation. Tension rises with unexpected deviations or elaborations. Pleasure is enhanced by good continuations and satisfying completions.

Another approach, one that ought to have particular appeal for the semiotician, is cognitive psychology. For example, music and speech have been compared along the lines of a possible generative grammar that may underlie both of these symbolic systems. In his valuable book on the cognitive psychology of music, John Sloboda (1985) finds similarities between Chomsky's analysis of verbal language and Schenker's approach to musical forms. An organizational structure that accepts certain sequential arrangements of acoustical elements and prohibits others seems to characterize many musical forms. Indeed, the process of musical composition has been likened to a gradual generation of ever longer and more complex sound patterns, arranged horizontally (rhythms and melodies) as well as vertically (harmony and counterpoint). What seems to start such a process going is the imagined musical 'inspiration', almost like an hallucination spontaneously experienced by a composer. Music-in-action requires of course that composers find ways of sharing these ideas with audiences. One way this can be done is through 'improvisation', i.e. the composer elaborates his ideas while singing or performing on an instrument in the presence of listeners. The alternative, commonly, is for the composer to put his ideas into notational writing or some other form of instruction, making it possible for someone else to perform this music.

CLINICAL OBSERVATIONS AND INFANT DEVELOPMENT

My personal inclination in approaching the semiotics of music has been to combine an appreciation for this art form with deductions based on clinical and therapeutic experience (Ostwald, 1973a). This I look to the literature of clinical therapeutics and developmental psychology for helpful observations. For example, the musically sophisticated psychoanalyst Richard Sterba has written that "the gratification which music provides is based on a deep regression to the earliest states of extrauterine development" (1965, p. 111). Pinchas Noy, another clinician who has long been interested in this issue, observed that musical communication is rooted in the very earliest preverbal phases of psychological organization, when boundaries between self and reality are not yet distinct (1966, 1967). According to Noy, the mother's voice, with its tonal inflections in both speech and song, seems to provide many infants with their first experience of an auditory stimulus that can be described as having musical properties (1968). I have taken the position that opportunities for exposure to music-like sounds could exist even prior to birth (Ostwald, 1975). In the uterus, the fetus is surrounded by an aqueous medium that readily transmits both tactile and acoustical vibrations. And the mother's body is, as it were, a rhythmical engine, with pulsations of the heart and major arteries impinging on the womb. Whether the fetal auditory system has the capacity to respond to such stimuli is another question. Anatomical studies have shown an amazing maturity of the human ear at birth, and electroencephalographic tracings taken during the birth process suggest that there may, indeed, be some neurological responsiveness to sounds during gestation (Ostwald & Peltzman 1974).

The possibility that musical structures—tones and melodies as well as rhythms—may be incorporated into the mental life of an infant seems quite consistent with the theories formulated by Daniel Stern (1985), a psychoanalyst and developmental psychologist. Perception is probably an 'amodal' process for at least the first three months of life. Information received in one sensory realm, say audition, is readily converted into another realm, say vision. Thus musical stimuli are perhaps 'felt' throughout all the dimensions of an infant's physical and mental self. Somewhat later, from the third to the eighth month, an infant normally begins integrating its sensations and actions into experiences that belong to the 'core' self, i.e. the sense of being an agent or entity existing separately from the mother (or other care-giving persons). Later yet, from the eighth to the fifteenth month, the capacity for social interrelatedness is established. Now the infant begins to sense how others feel and how he or she feels about others. It may be during this developmental phase of the 'subjective' self that music can become a pleasure to be shared. And for the next two years, while acquiring language and the other code-structured systems for communication, the infant's 'symbolic' self undergoes maturation. This presents possibilities for using mental tools to transcend reality. Involvement with musical activities can thus achieve cultural dimensions, acquiring social meaning in addition to narcissistic gratification.

THE TRANSITIONAL OBJECT

An imaginative link between the psychological world of the infant and those adults (the mother, father, and other care-givers) who are vital for its survival and growth was forged by the British pediatrician and psychoanalyst Donald Winnicott (1953) when he outlined his theory of transitional objects and transitional phenomena. Winnicott observed how infants and mothers acquire the capacity for maintaining distance from one another. It is necessary for them to reduce anxiety and other intense feelings commonly associated with separation to a comfortable and nondisruptive level. For many mothers and infants a helpful ingredient of this necessary developmental process turns out to be some physical object the child can hold on to, an object that is customarily found within the nursery environment. Examples of such 'transitional objects' are a blanket, a pillow, a toy, a doll, or even just a piece of fluffy material from the baby's crib. Physical contact with such an object seems essential whenever the infant feels (or actually is) physically separated from its mother. The transitional object belongs to them both, feels, smells, and tastes familiar, and thus bridges the physical gap of the separation. In possession of the transitional object, an infant can feel tranquil, stop crying, and fall asleep, while the mother, knowing that her baby is content, can better tolerate the distance between them. Winnicott (1953) called the transitional object an infant's first 'not-me' possession, assigned it a special place in the realm of possessiveness, and suggested that it probably plays a crucial role in the development of a child's tastes, talents, and social behavior later on.

Some babies find it difficult if not impossible to let go of their transitional objects. We all know of such cases; remember the Peanuts cartoon of Linus who is always carrying his 'security blanket' and goes to pieces if anyone tries to take it away. Here the transitional object has becomes a more or less permanent fixture of the child's environment. The same primal terror of separation originally evoked by the mother's leaving is now experienced whenever physical separation from the transitional object is threatened. Why that should be is not quite clear. Normally, a child is expected to develop psychological resources, viz. fantasies, cognitive structures, and intellectual skills so that the transitional object and what it represents can remain in the mind when it is no longer present in the environment. In terms of Stern's (1985) concepts of self-development mentioned earlier, one might say that for an infant to free itself from the need for physical contact with a transitional object requires maturation through the stage of 'subjective' selfhood, when physical continuities between mother and child are still necessary (nine to fifteen months, approximately) into and beyond the stage of 'symbolic' selfhood, which allows for substitutive, symbolic self gratifications. Delays or failures in these maturational processes, i.e. the persistence of transitional object use into later childhood, adolescence, or even adulthood, have been postulated as possible etiological factors in the appearance of what psychiatrists call 'borderline' psychopathology (Morris, Gunderson, & Zanarani, 1986).

It should be strongly emphasized, however, that the retention of transitional objects beyond the necessary stage in early life when an infant's survival depends on physical contact with a mother can also be quite nonpathological. Healthy and constructive uses of transitional objects may even be important, if not essential, for the childhood development of creativity. Winnicott himself wrote a great deal about the function of creative play in mental development: The way a child toys with things, arranges and rearranges them in the crib or on the floor, pulls them apart, and reorganizes them, seems almost to foreshadow future promise of creative (and I should add destructive) abilities (Winnicott, 1971). Whether or not a child allows people in the environment to participate in this playful activity probably has some bearing on whether in the future his or her playfulness becomes solitary and more self-centered rather than socially inviting, pleasing, and entertaining.

Finally, the willingness of parents (as well as older children and other significant persons in the environment) to endure at infant's self-generated play, to be amused rather than annoyed by his or her transitional objects, and to encourage the child's more artistic inclinations through training and education, may have a bearing on the development of creativity.

In this connection there has been a host of studies suggesting various ways that transitional objects and phenomena may be precursors for adult creativity (as well as psychopathology) (Grolnick, Barkin, & Muensterberger, 1978). For example, the dream, which incorporates memory elements of the child's physical environment as well as the elaboration of this material in unconscious fantasies, has been considered from the purview of Winnicott's theory. Instead of focussing so exclusively on the content of dreams, Simon A. Grolnick suggested spending more time on the analysis of the process of exchanging dreams. It was found that the dream elements—e.g. images of important people from childhood, parts of the body, or physical activities such as masturbation—would then seem more concrete, or 'anthropomorphized' (Grolnick, 1978, pp. 211-231). Under these conditions, patient and analyst were able to experience playful and pleasurable emotions, a welcome contrast to their dryly intellectual exchanges earlier in the psychoanalysis. The essentially visual nature of dreaming lends itself readily to concretization, i.e. to talking about 'things and objects'.

Symbols that are communicated acoustically, such as poetry, music, or speech have also received attention; indeed, Winnicott (1971) had in-

cluded the infant's use of noises, sounds, and words within his earliest notions about transitional phenomena. Martin J. Weich (1978) proposed
that 'transitional language' may be a 'crucial developmental phase' in
language acquisition, occurring between the time of acquisition of one-
word and two-word utterances:

> In the early development of symbols, there is a stage where the distinction
> between the symbol and the referential object has not yet been clearly es-
> tablished . . . [the baby uses words as] protosymbols. These are transitional
> forms of both true objects and true symbols—in contrast to representa-
> tional symbols, where there is a separation between the symbolic vehicle
> and the referent . . . [A baby word such as] 'weeda' derives from the lan-
> guage sounds of the environment (i.e. mother), which are creatively trans-
> formed by the child, leading to an idiosyncratic significance. It is a
> precursor of the use of speech for symbolic communication. (p. 419)

Not surprisingly, the concept of transitional language, derived from
the observation that word sounds are used in a more fluid, relativistic way
during infancy, has also been applied to the study of poetry. Here the
connections between sound and meaning can be looser and more arbitrary than in conventional adult speech. For example, Emilie Sobel wrote

> that the protosymbolic function of language thrives in [Gerard Manley]
> Hopkins, and perhaps, to a greater or lesser degree, in all poets . . . Hopkins
> liked to build up groups of words into single linguistic units, combining ad-
> jectives, verbs, and nouns in an idiosyncratic array. The result is an entity
> possessing the functions of all the major parts of speech without their clear
> assignment to discrete words . . . At the same time, the strict bifurcation be-
> tween inner and outer realities, between action and subject, symbol and ref-
> erent that a more syntactical speech reflects, is eliminated (1978 p. 441).

MUSIC AS TRANSITIONAL OBJECT

Like the pillows, toys, or other things from the nursery environment that
many babies cling to as a way of maintaining a sense of security when they
are separated from their mother (or other caregivers), tunes, fragments
of songs, rhythms, and familiar noises may be taken along by a child in
its quest for independence, to be repeated while playing alone, during
moments of solitude, or while falling asleep (Ostwald & Morrison, 1988).
Children may also rearrange the sound and rhythms they have heard, a
kind of primitive interest in composing new pieces or decomposing old
ones. These activities seem to emerge during the separation-individuation
phase of infancy. Writing about 'transitional tunes and musical development', McDonald (1970) pointed out that:

Some children who have experienced music from birth onward as an integral part of the loving motherly and fatherly caretaking environment, might . . . find in music their special 'transitional phenomenon.' Some may even select from a musical repertory a special 'transitional tune' . . . [or create] his own special music, a transitional tune by transferring onto this 'creation' the musical properties of both himself and of his mother (or parents). (pp. 503-520).

As children grow older, certain aspects of music often continue to be mental links or reminders of earlier experiences that had been associated with feelings or states of security, closeness, pleasure, and intimacy. Once can observe this introspectively when familiar songs and musical pieces evoke strong memories and emotions of childhood situations. The process may be similar to that of mourning for something that has been lost forever. In that sense the transitional object becomes a kind of 'linking phenomenon' (see Volkan 1982). In clinical practice one also observes the function of music as a transitional or linking phenomenon in patients whose lives, at one time relatively normal, became complicated by traumatic events or diseases. Let me give two examples from personal observation:

a) A woman recalled that her otherwise quite normal childhood with loving parents had been marred by the sudden death of her father, and thereafter by repeated physical abuse at the hands of a series of stepfathers. During her adolescence, while living with foster-parents who were interested in the arts, she discovered that listening to music provided "the only tranquility which I could rely on." She learned how to play the flute and began socializing almost exclusively with "musical" people. As an adult, afflicted with recurring states of severe panic and suicidal depressiveness, she deliberately chose a therapist whom she knew to be a musician. Now in her thirties, the patient regards music as "a power that has made my life meaningful; the only thing which can give me any peace of mind."

b) A male patient remembered his childhood as essentially normal until age nine, when he began to suffer from disabling depressive episodes that have recurred periodically. During adolescence he discovered that playing the harpsichord was immensely satisfying, almost an 'orgiastic' pleasure. "Music was a life-saver for me, and without it, I don't know how I would have coped with my depressions." He sought psychiatric help after a physical injury of the hand made it impossible for him to enjoy playing his instrument, and he was on the verge of committing suicide.

The very nature of music seems conducive to its use as transitional or linking object.[2] Music is sonic experience: it proceeds in the dimensions of time and space; it feels all-embracing and all-encompassing; it has the immediacy of speech but does not require semantic knowledge; it emanates from within the body (when sung) or from parts of the body (when musical instruments are played), by way of the ears it literally enters the body. Thus various dimensions of music can become transitional. Take the musical instrument itself. For many families, a piano, violin, clarinet, or other instrument serves as a link between generations. Even when an instrument is not actually used for making music, members of the family may invest it with strong emotion and vivid imagery, occasionally associated with past generations or dead relatives. Wills have been known to be hotly contested when 'the piano grandma loved to play on' ended up in the wrong household. Here is an example, again from clinical observation, of a musical instrument used as linking object in a personal relationship.

> A chronically unhappy man, planning to separate from a close friend with whom he had lived for several years, moved everything except his piano into his new apartment. After staying there for two days, he developed insomnia, became despondent, started to drink heavily, and made a suicide attempt. Treated in a hospital, he found that playing the piano there was more uplifting than any of the medical treatments administered on the ward. Both he and his friend recognized the importance of the piano as a tangible link between them that could not be broken. How and when to move the instrument to the new location, who would pay for the move, and whether their friendship would continue after the move became important topics for psychotherapeutic discussion.

The history of music offers numerous examples of the transitional or linking properties of musical themes. Let me cite one from the biography of Robert Schumann (Ostwald, 1985). This composer, born in 1810, lost his mother as a nurturing object when he was less than two years old. She came down with a severe case of typhus and had to be quarantined. Schumann's mother had prided herself on being called a 'living book of arias'. She regularly sang to him while he was an infant. During their enforced separation he became overly attached to a neighborhood woman and later recalled with considerable emotion how painful it was for him to be separated from this 'second mother'. Here is an entry from his diary:

---

[2]This is not to suggest, of course, that music is the only art form which lends itself to transitional experience. Indeed, as we mentioned in the review of Winnicott's original ideas (1953), the human mind seems to have a capacity for using anything as a transitional object.

I couldn't sleep the night before moving out of [her] house, and I cried throughout the entire night. Once before [when she was away] I got up along during the night when she was to return and sat at the window, crying bitterly, so that early in the morning they found me, asleep, with tears rolling down my cheeks. (Ostwald, 1985, pp. 15-16).

In his teens Schumann began composing songs, mostly love-songs, a practice he took up again at age thirty, while having to endure a painful separation from his fiancee. During that stressful period he wrote a song titled '*Ich hab' im Traum geweinet*' ('I was crying in my dream.') (Schumann 1840, Opus 48).

Ich hab ïm Traum geweinet,	I was crying in my dream,
Mir träumte, du lägestim Grab.	I dreamt you lay in your grave.
Ich wachte auf, und die Träne	I woke up, and a tear
Floss noch von der Wange herab.	*Was still flowing* from my cheek.
Ich hab 'im Traum geweinet,	I was crying in my dream,
Mir träumt', du verließest mich.	I dreamt you had abandoned me.
Ich wachte auf, und ich weinte	I woke up, and yet I was still crying
Noch lange bitterlich.	For a long time, bitterly.
Ich hab' im Traum geweinet,	I was crying in my dream,
Mir träumte, du wärst mir noch gut.	I dreamt you still cared for me.
Ich wachte auf, und noch immer	I woke up, and none the less
Strömt meine Tränenflut.	A flood of tears was pouring forth.

The poetry of this song clearly evokes the imagery of someone in great pain who is yearning for a lost love object. Very striking is the similarity of these images and Schumann's childhood memories of separation from his mother. In the first stanza, the dreamer thinks that his beloved has died, and he wakes up crying.[3] The second stanza features a dream of abandonment, somewhat less devastating perhaps than the previous dream about death, but resulting in tears nevertheless when the dreamer, now awake, realizes that he is still alone. The final stanza contains the sort of bittersweet irony that characterizes much of Heine's poetry. This time the dreamer has a happy dream; the beloved still cares for the dreamer. Nonetheless he is flooded with tears, realizing perhaps that it was only a dream after all.

---

[3]Fantasies about the death of someone from whom one is separated have often been observed clinically; it is thought that such dreams and fantasies may reflect unconscious revenge directed against the lost love object. For further discussion of these and related phenomena, see Bowlby (1969).

The music of this song is in E flat minor, and the range of tones used by the singer is quite narrow, resembling a sad cry or moan. Each time the sad words '*Ich hab' im Traum geweinet*' are intoned, the phrase begins with five syllables repeated on the same note, creating a depressive monotony, followed by a melody rising and falling only a half-step on the remaining two syllables. So far the voice has been unaccompanied, emphasizing the dreamer's isolation and loneliness. Now the piano enters, also alone, with a funereal dotted rhythm. The dreamer wakes up (accented piano chord), and his tears (another chord) flow, (followed by two chords, and a pause). This pattern repeats itself in the second stanza, followed by sustained but equally funereal chords on the keyboard. Now the voice joins the piano, singing again, dolefully, about crying in the dream. The dreamer wakes up, on the same insistent note repeated monotonously, and a climax is reached on '*Tränenflut*', After a moment of dead silence, the piano enters alone, pianissimo, then further silence, followed by two ominous final chords.

Here then we have a beautiful example of music as transitional object. On a personal level, Schumann's song allows the forlorn, motherless child, by way of dreams, poetic imagery, and music to come to terms with the anxieties of a new painful reality, the unrequited yearning of the adult for his distant beloved. And on a public, or social level, Schumann's song serves as a semiotic link to future generations of empathic listeners who are able to experience the composer's anguish of separation and unfulfilled love.

Another example of music used as a linking phenomenon can be observed in the practice of composers sharing each other's ideas and playing or writing variations on each other's themes. This was done frequently in the salons and small concert halls of the 18th and 19th centuries. By taking up the theme of an older, established musician and incorporating it into his own work, an ambitious young composer could express admiration for the model and at the same time exhibit his own special talents to the audience.

One musician who was particularly influential in terms of stimulating future composers to write variations on his themes was the charismatic Italian violinist Niccolo Paganini. Born in 1782, Paganini had to endure extreme poverty and abuse as a child. He was frequently beaten by his father, a laborer who also starved the boy to get him to practice the violin. (Paganini's mother, even before he was born, had developed the firm conviction that God had chosen him to be the greatest violinist in the world.) He ran away from home in his teens, became an itinerant musician, a promiscuous lover, and a gambler. Later he also became an extraordinary virtuoso and a great composer. Paganini formed only one lasting relationship in his entire life, and that was with his son, Archille, who accompanied him on his many travels. Paganini was an incredibly successful showman, partly as a result of his unusual appearance—he was very thin, had slender, hyperextensible limbs (possibly due to a congenital disorder called Marfan's Syndrome, cf. Schoenfeld, 1978), and always dressed in black—and partly because he capitalized on a rumor that he was the devil in disguise.

Paganini's impact on other musicians was often overwhelming; Schumann, for one, decided after attending one of his concerts that he too must become a virtuoso. (He was a 20-year old college student at the time [1830], and still undecided about his future.) Soon Schumann was writing innumerable pieces for the piano, many of them expert copies of Paganini's famous *Caprices* for the violin. Thus one can observe musical themes being used as linking objects, helping a younger and less mature composer to achieve a sense of identification with the power and fame of an established musician.

Franz Liszt, too, was so taken by Paganini's playing that he not only copied his stage mannerisms—long hair, exotic dress, dramatic stage entrances, etc.—but also, like Schumann, used the violinist's *Caprices* as models for his own compositions. Liszt, born in 1811, was a glamorous and highly successful child prodigy until his adolescence, when his father suddenly died, leaving him bereft and stranded in the middle of a concert tour. He became severely depressed, thought constantly about death and religion, and swore never again to play the piano in public. He supported himself and his widowed mother by giving music lessons. Then he heard and saw Paganini. It was a revolutionary experience and gave Liszt the courage to re-enter the concert stage. To assure his own success, he composed numerous bravura *Etudes* and *Fantasies*, all based on Paganini's, themes. Interestingly, Liszt dedicated these brilliant and difficult works to Clara Wieck, the young piano prodigy who later became the wife of Robert Schumann, a composer Liszt greatly admired. Here then is further evidence for the power of musical themes as transitional objects in the semiotic linking of several musicians to a common theme.

Johannes Brahms, born in 1833, was a composer who frequently made connections between himself and other musicians by employing their themes. Raised in poverty by a very odd couple—his mother was 17 years older than his father—Brahms had to help support the family by playing the piano in taverns near Hamburg's red-light district. He became a solitary, introverted adolescent, fearful of women, and very involved in his composing. At age twenty-one he met Robert and Clara Schumann. After Robert became psychotic and had to be hospitalized, Brahms lived with Clara and entered into the role of a go-between for the estranged couple, visiting him and reporting back to her. He never married, but throughout his life he continued to play this sort of 'transitional' role between people, allowing them to communicate through him and not getting deeply involved with any of them (Ostwald, in press).

Brahms made much use of other composers' themes and ideas, which he incorporated with great skill and imagination into his own voluminous compositions. While Schumann was still alive, Brahms wrote a set of variations (opus 9) on a theme by the older composer and dedicated it to his wife. Like Liszt, he also composed piano variations (opus 35) on Paganini's 24th *Caprice*. Indeed, this violin piece continues to inspire composers to this day, and it will probably do so in the future, as a living example of musical themes linking generations of composers. For example, Sergei Rachmaninoff in 1934 composed his well-known *Rhapsody on a Theme by Paganini*, for piano and orchestra, and there have been other contemporary composers who have used the Paganini theme.

Finally, I would like to call attention to the *Piano Sonata* in F minor, opus 14, also called 'Concerto Without Orchestra', written by Robert Schumann, as a good example of a musical masterpiece that was generated by a linking object, viz. a theme composed by Clara Wieck, who was in love with Schumann and later married him. This work is one of four piano sonatas composed by Schumann during the decade in his twenties when he was writing exclusively for the keyboard. It was also the time when he was having great difficulties in his relationship with this young woman, whose father insisted that they be separated and violently opposed their romance. Having had little in the way of formal musical training, and possessing a great flair for improvisation, Schumann's success up to this point had been in composing short pieces in quickly shifting moods ('butterflies' as he often called them). These piano pieces did not require elaborate working out of any larger musical structure. But Schumann had ambitions to compose big works, operas, and symphonies. There had been almost no great piano sonatas written since the deaths of Beethoven and Schubert. One of Schumann's hopes was to remedy this situation, and he labored on his own piano sonatas for several years, revising and rewriting many of the movements while he was simultaneously working as a music critic and newspaper editor. He kept changing the names of these sonatas, for example calling the one in C major (opus 17) a '*Fantasie*' and the one in F minor a '*Concerto without Orchestra*' These compositions were not well received. Schumann himself could not play them, and Clara Wieck, the brilliant young virtuoso whom he relied on to perform his music, thought that the F minor sonata was too difficult and that it lacked audience appeal. Ignaz Moscheles, a famous older pianist to whim Schumann had dedicated the work, complained about its unorthodox harmonies and unusual rhythms. Hence the '*Concerto without Orchestra*' was never played in public during Schumann's lifetime, and even today very few pianist are willing to tackle it. The work has had its champions, however. Johannes Brahms recognized its merits immediately, used it as a model for his own great F minor Sonata, and gave Schumann's work its first performance in 1862, six years after the composer's death. More recently, the great Russian-born pianist Vladimir Horowitz has been playing this neglected musical treasure.

What makes Schumann's F minor Sonata so extraordinary is that it is in cyclic form, with each of the four movements constructed around a descending five-note theme written by Clara Wieck. (It appears in its original form at the beginning of the third movement.) Schumann opens the first movement with a bold statement of the theme in the bass, followed by various subtle transformations and reiterations throughout this very turbulent *Allegro*. The second movement also begins with Clara's theme, this time disguised as a jumpy *Scherzo* in dotted-rhythm, one of Schumann's specialties, and it occurs again, now more quiet and solemn, in the middle section (*Trio*). The third movement begins with Clara's *Andantino*, richly harmonized and followed by four magnificent variations by Schumann. The final movement presents her theme in a wildly turbulent toccata-like structure, a sort of perpetual motion piece that is marked to be played 'as fast as possible', then 'faster', and 'even faster'. This frenzied, 'hypomanic' ending mirrors a mood that Schumann often experienced before he would fall into a state of depression. It is likely that Clara Wieck's theme not only helped the composer in organizing his sonata, but also served as a symbolic linking object between him and the woman from whom he was separated.

SUMMARY

A semiotic approach facilitates the interconnection of various levels of analysis in the study of musical phenomena—the acoustical, the psychological, the social, and the historical—that ordinarily are held apart by necessarily rigid disciplinary boundaries. Starting from the observation that musical experience seems to contain a healing or therapeutic quality, this chapter has examined some of the causal explanations offered by scholars and scientists. Several examples of the meaning that music can assume in the lives of patients seeking professional help were offered.

Of special relevance is the concept of the transitional object, first utilized by psychoanalysts, but now more widely applicable in clinical investigation. It pertains first of all to the notion of linkages made by infants between the wordless realm of emotional gratification in the mother-child relationship and their growing capacity to achieve comfort when alone. Physical items from the earlier phase of development—pillows, toys, and other 'things'—permit links to be made with behavioral tasks required in subsequent phases of maturation, when language and symbolic behavior begin to serve as media for social communication. Secondarily, transitional objects (both in physical reality and as represented symbolically) may play an important function in creative activity and artistic behavior. Because it resembles language but has a relatively nonspecific semantic function, music may be particularly well suited for use as a transitional object. Examples were given of the sound of a child's lonely wail linked to the composition of a song, of a violin theme linking composers from different eras, and of a melody linking two musicians in love. It remains to be seen whether these concepts can also be applied to the understanding of broader semiotic phenomena such as the use of 'background' music in film and television, the manipulation of mass emotion through music at rallies, parades, memorial occasions, etc., and the popularization of different musical styles across linguistic and cultural barriers.

REFERENCES

Bowlby, J. (1969). *Attachment and loss.* New York: Basic.

Farnsworth, P. R. (1958). *The social psychology of music.* New York: The Dryden Press.

Grolnick, S. A. (1978) *Dreams and dreaming as transitional phenomena.* In Grolnick et al., 211–231.

Grolnick, S. A., Barkin, L., & Muensterberger, W. (eds.) (1978). *Between reality and fantasy—Transitional objects and phenomena.* New York: Jason Aronson.

Helmholtz, H. (1877) (Translation reprinted in 1954) *On the Sensations of Tone as a Physiological Basis for the Theory of Music.* Trans. Alexander J. Ellis from the fourth German edition, New York: Dover Publications.

McDonald, M. (1970). Transitional tunes and musical development. *Psychoanalytic Study of the Child* 25, 503–20.

Meyer, L. B. (1956). *Emotion and meaning in music.* Chicago: University of Chicago Press.

Moles, A. (1968). *Information theory and esthetic perception.* Trans. by J. L. Cohen, Urbana, Il: University of Illinois Press.

Morris, H., Gunderson, J. G., & Zanarini, M. C. (1986). Transitional object use and borderline psychopathology. *American Journal of Psychiatry* 143, 1534–38.

Noy, P. (1966, 1967). The psychodynamic meaning of music. *Journal of Music Therapy* 3, 126–34; 4, 7–23, 45–51, 81–94, 117–125.

Noy, P. (1968). The development of musical ability. *Psychoanalytic Study of the Child* 23, 332–47.

Ostwald, P. (1973a). *The semiotics of human sound.* The Hague: Mouton.

Ostwald, P. (1973b). Musical behavior in early childhood. *Developmental Medicine and Child Neurology* 15, 367–75.

Ostwald, P. (1985). *The inner voices of a musical genius.* Boston: Northeastern University Press.

Ostwald, P. (in press). Johannes Brahms—Music, Loneliness, and Altruism. In H. Karnel & G. Pollock (eds.), *Psychoanalytic and psychiatric studies of musicians*, New York: International University Press.

Ostwald, P., & Morrison, D. (1988). Music in the organization of childhood experience. In D. Morrison (ed.), *The development of imagination and cognition in childhood; the organization of early experience*. Farmingdale, NY: Baywood press.

Ostwald, P., & Peltzman, P. (1974). The cry of the human infant. *Scientific American* 230, 83–90.

Pratt, R. R., & Jones, R. W. (1984). Music and medicine: A partnership in history. In R. Sprintge & R. Droh (eds.), (pp. 307-318). *Second International Symposium on Music and Medicine*. Paris: Editions Roche.

Schoenfeld, M. R. (1978). Nicolo Paganini: Musical Magician and Marfan Mutant? *Journal of the American Medical Association 239*, 40–2.

Schumann, R. A. (1840). *Opus 48 Dichterliebe* (#3). Lyrics from Heinrich Heine's *Buch der Lieder*. Trans, by Peter Ostwald.

Seashore, C. (1947). *In search of beauty in music*. New York: Ronald Press.

Sloboda, J. A. (1985). *The musical mind—The cognitive psychology of music*. Oxford: Clarendon Press.

Sobel, E. (1978). Rhythm, sound and imagery in the Poetry of Gerald Manley Hopkins. In Grolnick *et al.*, 427–45.

Sterba, R. (1965). Psychoanalysis and Music. *American Imago, 22*, 96–111.

Stern, D. S. (1985). *The interpersonal world of the infant*. New York: Basic.

Strunk, O. (Ed.) (1950). *Source readings in music history from classical antiquity through the romantic era*. New York: Norton.

Volkan, V. (1982). *Linking objects and linking phenomena: A study of forms, symptoms, metapsychology, and therapy of complicated mourning*. New York: International Universities Press.

Weich, M. J. (1978). *Transitional language*. In Grolnick *et al.*, 413–23.

Winnicott, D. W. (1953). Transitional Objects and Transitional Phenomena. *International Journal of Psychoanalysis 34*, 89–97.

Winnocott, D.W. (1971). *Playing and Reality*. London: Tavistock Publications.

Wyngaarden, J. B., & Smith, L. H. Jr. (1985). *Cecil Textbook of Medicine*. Philadelphia: W. B. Saunders.

Chapter 13

Creativity and Mental Health in Everyday Life*

Arthur J. Cropley

HIGH CREATIVITY AND MENTAL ILLNESS

The idea that there is a relationship between creativity and mental health is one of psychology's oldest issues: Plato, for instance, concluded that poets are set aside from ordinary mortals by the fact that the gods speak through them. More than 2,000 years later, at the beginning of the era of modern psychology, Lombroso (1891) argued that genius and madness are closely allied. Over the years, this theme has repeatedly been the subject of research (e.g., Ellis, 1926; Juda, 1949; McNeil, 1971; Rothenberg, 1983). The idea of a connection between creativity and mental illness has

---

*From 'Creativity and Mental Health in Everyday Life,' by A. J. Cropley, 1990, *Creativity Research Journal*, *3*(3), pp. 167–178. Copyright © 1995 Ablex Publishing Corporation. Adapted with permission.

received renewed attention in the last few years. Broadly speaking, two approaches are to be seen: Some studies have examined highly creative individuals and have asked whether they display a significantly higher incidence of mental illness than ordinary members of the public (e.g., Andreasen, 1987/this volume). Others have studied people regarded as either "odd" (e.g., Weeks & Ward, 1988) or mentally ill (e.g., Richards, Kinney, Lunde, Bennet, & Merzel, 1988), and have asked whether they are unusually creative.

In seeking to explain the psychological connection between creativity and mental illness, Cropley and Sikand (1973) initially adopted a cognitive position, hypothesizing that the connection is best explained in terms of thinking and related processes. They showed that the members of a group of creative architects, writers, and musicians resembled a sample of patients diagnosed as schizophrenic in some aspects of the cognitive domain, and that both groups were significantly different from people who were neither creative nor schizophrenic. However, they also found that, despite the cognitive similarities between schizophrenics and creatives, there were substantial noncognitive differences between them: The creative individuals tended to be excited by unusual associations in their own thinking and tried to build on them, whereas the schizophrenics were frightened by them, and tried to avoid them. Thus, Cropley and Sikand concluded that the relationship between creativity and psychological disturbance is more a matter of affect than of different ways of thinking. Other early studies of creativity and schizophrenia are those of Heston (1966), Karlsson (1970), Schuldburg (this volume), and Walder (1965).

Holden (1987) described a study by Jamison of 47 British artists and writers who had all either won major awards or were members of the Royal Academy. Jamison found that 18 had been treated for manic-depressive conditions, a figure six times as high as would be expected in the general populace. Linking these data with observations of famous creative people from the past such as Byron, Shelley, Coleridge, and Poe—who were apparently able to work creatively only when their mood was elevated—Jamison concluded that mood "highs" are essential for creativity. Such "highs" are characterized by unusual fluency in thinking (i.e., cognitive processes), but also by high levels of motivation and an overwhelming feeling of self-confidence (affective variables) (see Holden, 1987). However, as both Holden (1987) and Andreasen (1987/this volume) emphasized, the connection between affective disorders and creativity may not be directly causal in nature at all: It is possible that wide mood swings, on the one hand, and rich imagination and high motivation to create, on the other hand, booth result from a common cause, without actually influencing one another directly. Such a common cause could be "emotional reactivity" (Holden) or possession of a particularly labile or "fine tuned" nervous system (Andreasen)—a tendency to react unusually strongly to external stimuli and internal mood signals. It is important to notice that, as Richards and Kinney (1990) concluded after examining the results of a number of studies in the area, florid psychosis does not seem to be a favorable condition for creative productivity; nonetheless, mild affective disorders may favor it, possibly through mechanisms such as those just outlined.

EVERYDAY CREATIVITY

The approaches just discussed have three important limitations: They have (even if implicitly rather than explicitly) understood creativity as professional and aesthetic (practical/scientific/artistic/literary) production; they have concentrated on people whose creative behavior reached a level of unusualness or rarity sufficient to bring public acclaim; and they have concentrated on mental illness. By contrast, the present article focuses on creativity as (a) an everyday phenomenon found in all people and (b) as a facet of personality capable of contributing to the maintenance of mental health.

Of particular interest in this context is the conceptualization of creativity as a *qualitative* aspect of mental functioning: About 20 years ago I described creativity as a "style" for applying intelligence, rather than as a separate ability (Cropley, 1969); more recently, Gardner (1983) referred to creativity as the highest *form of application* of intelligence, and Runco and Albert (1986) defined it as *intelligence in action*. Horn (1988) distinguished between two basic styles of reacting to novelty, one involving avoidance, the other attraction. In essence, the "style" approach argues that, *at all levels of ability*, people may deal with situations requiring intelligence either by trying to re-apply the already learned, concentrating on proven tactics, and relating the new situation to the familiar, or by searching for the novel, backing intuitions, taking a chance, and so on. For brevity's sake, I will call the first kind of tactic "convergent," and the second "divergent." In real life these are obviously stereotypes, as few people function permanently at the one or other extreme, most tending toward a greater or lesser degree of divergence/convergence according to the particular situation in question.

An early treatment of creativity as an aspect of day-to-day life was that of Nicholls (1972), in an article entitled "Creativity in the person who will never produce anything original and useful: The concept of creativity as a normally distributed trait." In essence, he argued that creativity need not be regarded as something that is present in a tiny group of exceptional people but absent in most, but as a quantitative property that is, in principle, possessed by all, even if to different degrees. More recently, Richards et al. (1988) reported on an investigation of creative activities carried out in everyday life by "ordinary" men and women without pretensions to fame as creators. At work, everyday creativity was divided about equally among the arts, the sciences, the humanities, the social sciences, organizational activities, and leadership. Leisure-time creative activities were, however, almost completely confined to the crafts and the fine arts. Among children and adolescents, Milgram (1990) reported on out of school and leisure activities in, among others, science, music, fine arts, writing, drama, and dance.

PSYCHOLOGICAL COMPONENTS OF EVERYDAY CREATIVITY

The connection between creativity as a psychological disposition and actual creative behavior in the forms investigated by Richards et al. (1988) or Milgram (1990) has been elucidated by Nečka (1986). He argued that people behave creatively when three psychological elements are present: special content related knowledge and skills (for instance, a carpenter must know how to use tools, a writer how to put words together to form sentences); special creativity facilitating abilities (the ability to get new ideas, see the unexpected, make new combinations, branch out from the known, and the like); and willingness to expend energy in producing some product or other (i.e., motivation). Only when all three prerequisites are fulfilled is there what I call "freely developing creativity." In other cases, where one or more element is missing, "incomplete" forms of creative behavior are seen. Nečka lists a few examples of only partially realized creativity: *abandoned creativity* (motivation is lacking), *frustrated creativity* (high levels of technical skill exist, but the spark involved in having new ideas, seeing the unexpected and the like is missing); or *juvenile creativity* (technical skills are missing—a person might wish to paint creatively and may have many novel ideas, but simply be incompetent in design or use of the brush). Of particular interest in the present context are the two psychological components—on the one hand, creative thinking, on the other, personal characteristics (motivation, personality).

COGNITIVE PROCESSES

The initial impulse in modern times in this area came from the work of Guilford. Early theorizing adopted a relatively undifferentiated approach (intelligence as convergent thinking, creativity as divergent thinking), but this has since been expanded by a number of authors. Torrance and Hall (1980), for instance, concluded that creativity involves: (a) uniting disparate ideas by putting them into a common context; (b) being able to imagine, at least as a theoretical possibility, almost anything; (c) enriching one's own thinking through the application of fantasy; and (d) adding spice to one's thinking through the use of humor.

Nečka's (1986) "triad" model of creativity went beyond a purely cognitive position. Nonetheless, the cognitive elements are of great importance; they involve original, inventive, effective thinking strategies, which are prerequisites for actual creative behavior in real-life settings, although not by themselves sufficient. These are essential tactics for processing information, and include: (a) forming associations, (b) recognizing similarities, (c) constructing metaphors, (d) carrying out transformations, (e) selectively directing the focus of attention, and (f) seeing the abstract aspects of the concrete.

Sternberg (1985) emphasized the importance of "metacognitive" processes through which people reflect upon their own thinking, evaluate it, choose new tactics, and differentiate between blind allies and promising approaches. Among the metacognitive processes that are important for creativity are: (a) recognizing the nature of the problem, (b) representing the problem internally, (c) determining which solution strategies are relevant and promising, (d) choosing and organizing cognitive resources, (e) combining thinking strategies, (f) evaluating progress towards the solution of a problem, and (g) identifying new lines of attack when old ones fail.

CREATIVITY AS A FACET OF PERSONALITY

Despite the importance of cognitive processes, creativity depends on more than thinking skills (Barron & Harrington, 1981). In fact, Farisha (1978) concluded that personality is consistently emphasized in the literature as a deciding factor in the emergence of creativity. People need to be willing to branch out and to break away from the conventional; to have confidence in themselves and their ideas; to be able to tolerate the anxiety resulting from questioning the commonplace; to be able to stand up to pressure to conform to the group; to be capable of living with the consequences of being divergent, of accepting and coming to terms with the "loneliness of the long distance runner" (cf. Rothenberg, 1990, this volume).

Many attempts have been made to give details of the association between creativity and personality. Earlier studies (e.g., Dellas & Gaier, 1970; Foster, 1971; Taft & Gilchrist, 1970) have, like the by now "classic" studies of Barron, Cattell, MacKinnon, Roe, and Torrance, suggested that persons such as artists and creative scientists have specifiable personality characteristics that differentiate them from the public at large. In summarizing some of the findings, Neff (1975, pp. 75–76) listed the main characteristics on which there is agreement. These include: (a) flexibility, (b) sensitivity, (c) tolerance, (d) sense of responsibility, (e) empathy, (f) independence, (g) positive self-image, (h) need for social contact, and (i) interest in getting ahead.

The list has been extended by Heinelt (1974, p. 29), who identified the following characteristics of creative school children: They: (a) are usually introverts, (b) are self-willed, (c) are not dependent on group support, (d) are intellectually active and ask many questions, (e) are extremely flexible in their thinking, (f) show wit and a sense of humor, (g) often remain aloof from their classmates, (h) prefer to work independently, (i) are often socially isolated, (j) feel superior to their classmates and tend to be arrogant, and (k) are not among the most popular in their class. In addition, certain traits seem to be seen less frequently in creative people than in noncreative, although there is some disagreement in the relevant literature on specifics (Neff, 1975). The list of "uncharacteristics" of creative individuals includes: (a) feeling of well being, (b) willingness to conform, (c) self-control, (d) desire to make a good impression, and (e) conformity.

CREATIVITY AND MOTIVATION

In addition to possessing certain personal traits, creative individuals are characterized by their willingness to expend effort. Some people seem to be able to tolerate high levels of uncertainty, or even to have a need for novelty (Cropley & Sikand, 1973; Dellas & Gaier, 1970). Associated with this is the willingness of some people to take risks, for instance, by abandoning previously held positions or trying strange or different tasks. These factors define "the courage to create" (Motamedi, 1982, p. 84). Finally, as Roe (1953) initially showed and later writers (e.g., Biermann, 1985) have confirmed, successful creative people as a group show high levels of persistence—they stick at something once they have started it. Treffinger, Isaksen, and Firestien (1983) developed the following list of key characteristics of creative individuals in the domain of motivation. Creative individuals display: (a) curiosity, (b) willingness to respond freely in stimulating situations, (c) openness to new or unusual experiences, (d) willingness to take risks, (e) sensitivity to problems and a desire to solve them, (f) tolerance for ambiguity, and (g) self-confidence.

In his model of creativity, Neçka, (1986) distinguished five classes of motives that energize creative behavior:

1. Instrumental motives: Creative behavior is a means to an end.
2. Playful motives: Creative behavior leads to a state of inner satisfaction. This kind of motivation is also an aspect of the process of self-actualization.
3. Intrinsic motives: Creative behavior is an end in itself. The value of creativity is regarded as self-evident, and creative behavior arises from a sense of duty or the feeling of having a mission.
4. Control motives: Creative behavior increases a person's level of competence or strengthens the feeling of having the external world under control.
5. Expressive motives: Creative behavior makes it possible to communicate one's own thoughts and feelings to other people.

In the case of actual creative achievements, these motives probably interact and combine rather than acting singly; for instance, a verbally gifted person might seek fame and fortune through the writing of novels (an instrumental motive), but at the same time have a strong sense of mission (intrinsic motivation) or a desire to "reach" other people (expressive motivation). It is also probable that different people show different combinations or patterns of motives, with different weightings of the various areas in different people. As a result, it is possible to speak of an individual structure of motives. Furthermore, it is likely that these structures change with the passage of time. The original profit motive of the novelist mentioned above could, for instance, eventually be replaced by the feeling of having something important to say to humanity.

The different kinds of motivation for creativity listed by Neçka (1986) include a mixture of external and internal factors. Amabile (1983), however, argued that extrinsic motivation (i.e., the desire to obtain rewards offered by the external world and consequent shaping of one's behavior in order to make it pleasing to external authorities, such as teachers) is deadly for creativity. According to her, the crucial element in creativity is intrinsic motivation; a certain activity is pursued because it provides internal satisfactions—it is fascinatingly interesting in itself for a particular person, satisfies some internal drive or need, or produces a feeling of pleasure or well-being. Amabile went so far as to argue that the real task in fostering creativity is helping children become immune to extrinsic motivation (see also Amabile, Goldfarb, & Brackfield, 1990).

SOCIAL FACTORS IN CREATIVITY

Newborns display many socially unacceptable behaviors. However, with the passage of time the hitherto asocial infant comes to confine itself to patterns of behavior acceptable to the people around it. Even "difficult" children may come, in adulthood, to stick rigidly to their society's way of doing things. A transformation occurs with the passage of time as children learn to conform to the rules of the society in which they live. Not only are specific forms of behavior learned, such as what to say when introduced to someone for the first time, but also more general values and standards. Children learn, for instance, that authority may or may not be questioned, that the good opinion of peers is or is not of supreme importance, that to stand alone is tolerable or intolerable, and so on. As Cropley (1973) put it, each society has a central core of behaviors that are totally taboo; public defecation would be an example from Western European–North American societies. Surrounding this is a shadow zone of behaviors that are barely acceptable and lead to public disapproval, but are not necessarily "fatal," and a further zone of mildly disapproved behaviors, and so on. The actual contents of the various zones differ from society to society, and even from social class to social class both within and across societies. Also, there are often discrepancies between what is officially frowned upon, for instance by virtue of being against the law, and what is publicly tolerated, accepted, or even regarded as brave or smart; an example of this is tax evasion. Despite the limitations just outlined, it remains true that the rules of society restrict freedom of ideas—naturally, no evil intention lies behind this; on the contrary, it is vital for all groups of people who share the same living space to agree on certain ground rules. The problem from the point of view of creativity, however, is that the rules may go far beyond what is needed for peaceful coexistence, and may become rigid and self-perpetuating. As Fromm (1980) put it, a society has "filters" through which not only behaviors, but also ideas must pass. Otherwise they are rejected; they become literally unthinkable. Amabile et al. (1990) referred to "surveillance," through which a society keeps watch on its members and makes sure that the rules are not broken.

The effects of social standardization of thinking on creativity raise questions about the whole relationship between creativity and nonconformity. To the extent that their divergent thinking is often accompanied by flamboyant nonconforming behavior, creative thinkers frequently show up as highly unconventional. According to Cropley (1973), creative people are in a certain sense social deviants, because they often behave in ways lying outside the usual or expected in their society, and thus represent "failures" of the socialization process. Cropley even speculated that creative individuals may "suffer" from a biologically determined learning disability, deriving from faulty uric acid metabolism (Cropley, Cassell, & Maslany, 1970). The notion of creativity as involving negative social characteristics has also been put forward by Albert and Runco (1986), who pointed out that changing things, behaving differently and independently, inherently involves being dissatisfied with the status quo: The creative person is "oppositional and discontented" (p. 337). This may lead to rejection by others and imposition of sanctions ranging from sarcastic or humiliating remarks, exclusion from important peer groups, even rejection as "weird" or "crazy," or ultimately incarceration. Thus, the creative individual runs the risk of becoming a "marginal" person (Wallace, 1985). For this reason, *creativity requires the capacity to diverge from the norm, but simultaneously to function within the society's rules* (Fromm, 1980). Unconventionality is one of the concomitants of creative thinking, but mere unconventionality does not by itself signal the presence of genuine creativity. In creative people social deviance is channelled into constructive activities.

One characteristic of highly divergent individuals that has struck many observers is their playfulness. They may, for example, be particularly good at making up humorous story titles, as was the case in the historically important study of Getzels and Jackson (1962). They often display a particularly lively sense of humor, and are frequently unusually alert to the funny side of life and especially good at making up humorous responses to tests. Creative people's playfulness may also manifest itself in the ability to play with the meanings of words so that they see new aspects to them that have not previously been seen. They may play with fundamental laws and principles and eventually arrive at unusual solutions to problems, or they may play with common objects until they see implications that have not previously been noticed. What such play involves, essentially, is the capacity to look at the familiar in a new light, and to break the set imposed by the stereotypical meaning of any particular stimulus (Gabriel, 1976). Many creative people, among them Einstein, have made this point about their own creativity. According to psychoanalytic theory, creative individuals are able to relax strict ego control and admit primary process material into consciousness (see Stein & Stein, 1984, who summarized the importance of play in a number of psychoanalytic models of creativity, including those of Freud, Kris, and Kubie).

CREATIVITY AND MENTAL HEALTH

As has been shown in preceding sections, creativity is connected with personal properties such as flexibility, openness, autonomy, humor, playfulness, willingness to try things, elaboration of ideas, realistic self-assessment, and similar characteristics. Generally, these properties have been ascertained in studies of highly creative people, and they are usually thought of as prerequisites for the emergence of creativity (i.e., as something out of which creativity arises, or whose absence makes creativity impossible). However, theory and research on normal personality development—with or without direct reference to creativity—also emphasize similar properties as core elements of the healthy personality. According to psychoanalytic theory, the ability to express drives and impulses without excessive use of defence mechanisms, or to admit primary process material into consciousness, for example in the form of humor, requires high ego strength. Ammon (1974) saw creativity as an ego function in itself. According to Hartmann (1958), ego autonomy permits freedom from blind obedience to instinct and freedom from dependence on immediate environmental events; high levels of autonomy make it possible for the individual to cope in a positive way with change, even with catastrophies in life. Anthony (1987) concluded that there is a cause and effect relationship between creativity and mental health and argued that because creativity is related to ego autonomy, and ego autonomy promotes the capacity to deal with life situations, creativity favors the development of resistance to psychopathology.

In humanistic psychology, concepts such as self and self-realization are at the heart of healthy personality development. Maslow (1954) and Rogers (1961), in their classic studies, emphasized the importance of openness, flexibility, and tolerance in the healthy personality. Krystal (1988) made the link between mental health and creativity even more specific in a study in which he also took the unusual step of studying extremely uncreative people. He found that they had considerable difficulties in the area of self: "Self-caring" is difficult for them, for instance, and they lack "self-coherence." Fostering creativity in these people would promote their mental health in the sense of self-realization. Cognitive approaches to creativity emphasize cognitive styles that involve openness to a wide range of environmental stimuli, flexible coding of information obtained from the environment, and ready accessibility of a variety of categories when information is called up from memory.Processing of this type requires assimilation of large amounts of information and necessitates frequent accommodation, if cognitive processes are to be rich, full, open, and flexible. Nearly 30 years ago Hudson (1963) made the point that convergers tend to be narrow and rigid in cognitive processes, achieving a sense of security in this way, but at the cost of healthy personality development.

Writing from a clinical point of view, Burkhardt (1985) offered a dramatic summary of the line of argument developed in preceding paragraphs. He defined the "right to be a unique individual" as one of the basic human rights. Although he did not refer directly to creativity, he wrote in much the same terms as in the present chapter, and saw what I have called "creativity" as an integral part of the personality of all human beings and an essential element in their dignity and individuality. However, he identified a "mass psychosis" of modern life that has at its core an "obsession with uniformity and sameness." Thus, he not only emphasized the importance of creativity as a healthy phenomenon in itself, but also identified an unhealthy anticreative "mass dogma," that he regarded as the result of mistaken understanding of the idea of equality and confusing the ideology of a particular age with ethics and morality.

FOSTERING MENTAL HEALTH

The following argument has emerged in previous sections: Creativity is connected with psychological characteristics such as openness, autonomy, playfulness, and flexibility. Creativity training procedures usually proceed from this point to ask whether it is possible to train such personal characteristics and thus increase creativity. More important for the present chapter, however, is that such properties are highly favorable to the maintenance of positive mental health. The practical question raised here is that of whether it is possible to emphasize "creativity" in everyday settings, and by doing this help people to show more openness, flexibility, and autonomy. In this way, without trying to create highly creative individuals, it would be possible to make a contribution to the maintenance of mental health in day-to-day life. Several small studies carried out in Hamburg in recent years cast some light on this question. The following paragraphs will briefly outline some of these. All of the projects focused on everyday life. They are all modest in scope and scientific rigor, but close to reality.

Schwarzkopf (1981) carried out a longitudinal study with nine adult women who met once a week and worked "creatively" on sewing, knitting, weaving, crocheting, and similar projects. Factors such as making unexpected combinations trying out new ideas, or seeing the familiar in a new way were emphasized. At the beginning of the year, each woman was rated on a number of personality traits by several relatives and close friends. These raters had no knowledge of the research project or its intentions. At the end of the year, the women were again rated and the more recent scores compared with those from a year earlier. There were significant differences in the ratings for a number of personality dimensions. In their day-to-day life, the women showed less anxiety in unfamiliar situations, were more playful, more self-critical, and less cautious. They were judged to be positively motivated by the need to make difficult decisions, more independent and lively, able to show more fantasy, more goal oriented, and able to show more task persistence.

Herrmann (1987) compared two soccer teams in a league for 10–12-year-old boys. One team was coached in an authoritarian way, and the other "democratically." Emphasis in the latter situation was on taking personal responsibility, spontaneously doing the unexpected, and even having fun. The democratically trained boys produced significantly more novel elements in a creativity test as well as making a significantly larger number of cross-relationships. Correlating these with data on a personality test, Herrmann concluded that the democratic training style in the sporting domain had fostered self-confidence and reduced anxiety. The democratically trained boys made significantly more humorous responses, and Hermann concluded that the creativity fostering training style had encouraged the expression of aggression in the form of humor rather than on-the-field violence.

Stranger (1987) worked with a group of 58 10–13-year-old boys and girls diagnosed as legasthenic, and showed that they produced the same number of responses on a divergent thinking test as "normal" readers. They also showed the same degree of originality. However, there was a large and significant difference between the two groups in the area of elaboration: Legasthenic children were as capable as the members of the control group of producing novel ideas, but they were inhibited in extending and carrying through these ideas. Stranger interpreted this as reflecting the effects of lack of self-confidence and negative self-evaluation, and recommended emphasis in instruction with legasthenic children on obtaining and elaborating ideas and developing personal (internal) criteria for their evaluation.

Scheliga (1988) tested a group of dedicated amateur jazz musicians—mainly playing in jazz cellars among the famous (or infamous) Hamburg Reeperbahn—with a paper-and-pencil creativity test. They scored significantly higher than a control group of lab technicians on dimensions such as spontaneity, wealth of ideas, power of association, willingness to take risks, and flexibility. An important conclusion by Scheliga was that "latent" creativity had been released by participation in music making, which offers (especially in the form of jazz improvisation) special psychological opportunities: expression of individuality, elimination of inhibitions, encouragement of fantasy, confrontation with one's own emotions, and use of nonverbal forms of expression. Nonetheless, the musician must remain within a particular framework—the product must be relevant to the main musical theme—so that blind unconventionality is not called for.

Of considerable importance in these studies is that a degree of personal development occurred. However, this took the form of a mirror image of the usual creativity training procedures: A "divergent" way of going about a real-life activity was judged to have promoted personal properties (e.g., self-confidence, fantasy, openness to new situations), whereas the conventional procedure involves attempting to "train" personal properties in a formal laboratory of classroom setting in order to produce divergent behavior. This suggests the need to encourage people to attack everyday situations in a creative way, rather than expose them to abstract "creativity training" programs: Real-life activities should be suffused with creativity enhancing elements. The result would be enhanced mental health.

REFERENCES

Albert, R. S., & Runco, M. A. (1986). The achievement of eminence: A model based on a longitudinal study of exceptional gifted boys and their families. In R. J. Sternberg & J. E. Davidson (Eds.), *Conceptions of giftedness* (pp. 332–357). New York: Cambridge University Press.

Amabile, T. M. (1983). *The social psychology of creativity*. New York: Springer.

Amabile, T. M., Goldfarb, P., & Brackfield, S. C. (1990). Social influences on creativity: Evaluation, coaction, surveillance. *Creativity Research Journal, 3*, 6–21.

Ammon, G. (1974). *Gruppendynamik der Kreativität* (Group dynamics of creativity). München, Germany: Kindler.

Andreasen, N. C. (1987) Creativity and mental illness: Prevalence rates in writers and their first degree relatives. *American Journal of Psychiatry, 144*, 1288–1292.

Anthony, E. J. (1987). Risk, vulnerability and resilience: An overview. In E. J. Anthony & B. J. Cohen (Eds.), *The invulnerable child* (pp. 3–48). New York: Guilford.

Aviram, A., & Milgram, R. (1977), Dogmatism, locus of control and creativity in children educated in the Soviet Union, the United States, and Israel. *Psychological Reports, 40*, 27–34.

Barron, F. X., & Harrington, D. M. (1981). Creativity, intelligence and personality. *Annual Review of Psychology, 32*, 439–476.

Biermann, K.-R. (1985). Über Stigmata der Kreativität bei Mathematikern des 17. bis 19. Jahrhunderts (Indicators of creativity in mathematicians of the 17th–19th centuries). *Rostocker Mathematik Kolloquium, 27*, 5–22.

Burkhardt, H. (1985). *Gleichheitswahn Parteienwahn* (Equality mania Conformity mania). Tübingen, Germany: Hohenrain.

Cronbach, L. J. (1968). Intelligence? Creativity? A parsimonious reinterpretation of the Wallach Kogan data. *American Educational Research Journal, 5*, 491–511.

Cropley, A. J. (1969). Creativity, intelligence and intellectual style. *Australian Journal of Education, 13*, 3–7.

Cropley, A. J. (1973). Creativity and culture. *Educational Trends, 8*, 19–27.

Cropley, A. J., Cassell, W. A., & Maslany, G. W. (1970). A biochemical correlate of divergent thinking. *Canadian Journal of Behavioural Science, 2,* 174–180.

Cropley, A. J., & Sikand, J. S. (1973). Creativity and schizophrenia. *Journal of Consulting and Clinical Psychology, 40,* 462–468.

Dellas, M., & Gaier, E. L. (1970). Identification of creativity: The individual. *Psychological Bulletin, 73–73.*

Ellis, H. A. (1926). *A study of British genius.* New York: Houghton Mifflin.

Farisha, B. (1978). Mental imagery and creativity: Review and speculation. *Journal of Mental Imagery, 2,* 209–238.

Foster, J. (1971). *Creativity and the teacher.* London: Macmillan.

Fromm, E. (1980). *Greatness and limitations of Freud's thought.* New York: New American Library.

Gabriel, J. (1976). Creativity and play. In W. R. Lett (Ed.), *Creativity and education* (pp. 156–172). Melbourne: Australian International Press and Publications.

Gardner, H. (1983). *Frames of mind: The theory of multiple intelligences.* New York: Basic Books.

Getzels, J. W., & Jackson, P. W. (1962). *Creativity and intelligence.* New York: Wiley.

Hartmann, H. (1958). *Ego psychology and the problem of adaptation.* New York: International Universities Press.

Heinelt, G. (1974). *Kreative Lehrer - kreative Sch244ler* (Creative teachers-creative students). Freiburg, Germany: Herder.

Herrmann, W. (1987). *Auswirkungen verschiedener Fußball-Trainingsstile auf Leistungsmotivation* (The effects of different football coaching styles on achievement motivation). Unpublished master's thesis, University of Hamburg, Hamburg, Germany.

Heston, L. L. (1966). Psychiatric disorders in foster home-reared children of schizophrenic mothers. *British Journal of Psychiatry, 112,* 819–825.

Holden, C. (1987). Creativity and the troubled mind. *Psychology Today, 21,* 9–10.

Horn, J. L. (1988, August). *Major issues before us now and for the next few decades.* Paper presented at the Seminar on Intelligence, Melbourne, Australia.

Horowitz, F. D., & O'Brien, M. (1986). Gifted and talented children: State of knowledge and direction for research. *American Psychologist, 41,* 1147–1152.

Hudson, L. (1963). Personality and scientific aptitude. *Nature, 196,* 913–914.

Juda, A. (1949). The relationship between highest mental capacity and psychic abnormalities. *American Journal of Psychiatry, 106,* 296–307.

Karlsson, J. L. (1970). Genetic associations of giftedness and creativity in schizophrenia. *Hereditas, 66,* 177–182.

Krystal, H. (1988). On some roots of creativity. *Psychiatric Clinics of North America, 11,* 475–491.

Lombroso, C. (1891) *The man of genius.* London: Scott.

Maslow, A. H. (1954). *Motivation and personality.* New York: Harper.

McNeil, T. F. (1971). Prebirth and postbirth influence on the relationship between creative ability and recorded mental illness. *Journal of Personality, 39,* 391–406.

Milgram, R. M. (1990). Creativity: An idea whose time has come and gone? In M. A. Runco & R. S. Albert (Eds.), *Theories of creativity* (pp. 215–233). Newbury Park, CA: Sage.

Motamedi, K. (1982). Extending the concept of creativity. *Journal of Creative Behavior, 16*, 75–88.

Neçka, E. (1986). On the nature of creative talent. In A. J. Cropley, K. K. Urban, H. Wagner, & W. H. Wieczerkowski (Eds.), *Giftedness: A continuing worldwide challenge* (pp. 131–140). New York: Trillium.

Neff, G. (1975). *Kreativität in Schule und Gesellschaft* (Creativity in school and society). Ravensburg, Germany: Maier.

Nicholls, J. G. (1972). Creativity in the person who will never produce anything original and useful: The concept of creativity as a normally distributed trait. *American Psychologist, 27*, 717–727.

Richards, R., & Kinney, D. (1990). Mood swings and creativity. *Creativity Research Journal, 3*, 203–218.

Richards, R., Kinney, D. K., Lunde, I., Bennet, M., & Merzel, A. (1988). Creativity in manic-depressives, cyclothymes, their normal relatives, and control subjects. *Journal of Abnormal Psychology, 9*, 281–288.

Roe, A. (1953). *The making of a scientist.* New York: Dodd, Mead.

Rogers, C. R. (1961). *On becoming a person.* Boston: Houghton Mifflin.

Rothenberg, A. (1983). Psychopathology and creative cognition: A comparison of hospitalized patients, Nobel laureates and controls. *Archives of General Psychiatry, 40*, 937–942.

Rothenberg, A. (1988). Creativity and the homospatial process: Experimental studies. *Psychiatric Clinics of North America, 11*, 443–460.

Rothenberg, A. (1990). Creativity, mental health, and alcoholism. *Creativity Research Journal, 3*, 179–201.

Runco, M. A., & Albert, R. S. (1986). The threshold theory regarding creativity and intelligence: An empirical test with gifted and nongifted children. *The Creative Child and Adult Quarterly, 11*, 212–218.

Scheliga, J. (1988). *Musik machen und die Förderung von Kreativität* (Making music and the fostering of creativity). Unpublished master's thesis, University of Hamburg, Hamburg, Germany.

Schwarzkopf, D. (1981). *Selbstentfaltung durch kreatives Gestalten* (Self-development through creative production). Unpublished master's thesis, University of Hamburg, Hamburg, Germany.

Simonton, D. K. (1988). *Scientific genius. A psychology of science.* Cambridge: Cambridge University Press.

Stein, A., & Stein, H. (1984). *Kreativität - psychoanalytische und philosophische Aspekte* (Creativity—psychoanalytic and philosophical aspects). München, Germany: Johannes Bermann.

Sternberg, R. J. (1985). *Beyond IQ: A triarchic theory of human intelligence.* New York: Cambridge University Press.

Stranger, A. (1987). *Lese- Rechtschreibschwäche und divergentes Denken* (Legasthenia and divergent thinking). Unpublished master's thesis, University of Hamburg, Hamburg, Germany.

Taft, R., & Gilchrist, M. B. (1970). Creative attitudes and creativity among students. *Journal of Education Psychology, 61*, 136–143.

Torrance, E. P., & Hall, L. K. (1980). Assessing the further reaches of creative potential. *Journal of Creative Behavior, 14*, 1–19.

Treffinger, D. J., Isaksen, S. G., & Firestien, R. L. (1983). Theoretical perspective on creative learning and its facilitation. *Journal of Creative Behavior, 17,* 9–17.

Walder, R. (1965). Schizophrenic and creative thinking. In H. M. Ruitenbeck (Ed.), *The creative imagination* (pp. 123–136). Chicago, IL: Quadrangle.

Wallace, D. B. (1985). Giftedness and the construction of a meaningful life. In F. D. Horowitz & M. O. O'Brien (Eds.), *The gifted and talented: Developmental perspectives* (pp. 361–385). Washington, DC: American Psychological Association.

Weeks, D.J., & Ward, K. (1988). *Eccentrics: The scientific investigation.* Stirling, Scotland: Stirling University Press.

Chapter 14

Growth from Deficiency Creativity to Being Creativity*

Celeste Rhodes[†]

When examining the spectrum of views regarding the connection between creativity and mental health (Richards, 1990), one can only be
struck by the variety of explanations for creative motivation. The following hypotheses reflect possible connections between creativity and psychological growth. They also support the need for research in creativity
using an interactive perspective (Feldman, 1982; Gruber & Davis, 1988):

*From "Growth from Deficiency Creativity to Being Creativity," by C. Rhodes, 1990, *Cre-
ativity Research Journal,* 3 (4), pp. 287–299. Copyright © 1995 Ablex Publishing Corporation.
Adapted with permission.

[†]The author wishes to thank Carolyn M. Callahan, Marcia Delcourt, and Harold Strang,
from the University of Virginia, and Lesley Novack and Ruth Porritt from Mary Baldwin College for their help with previous drafts of this article.

1. Creativity results from an interaction between inherited and environmental factors.
2. Creativity is manifested in some individuals because they were born with above-average intelligence and an introverted nature. These factors predispose them to both creative expression and an intense psychological response to life.
3. Introverted, intelligent individuals who grow up in repressive or deprived environments may be motivated by deficiency needs for love and affirmation to develop their creative gifts as a means of coping with conflict and as a potential force for growth.

This chapter examines the relationship between creativity and psychological health with particulai focus on creativity as an interactive process, as a coping mechanism that helps the individual deal with conflict, and as a force for growth. *Deficiency creativity* and *being creativity* are offered as new constructs for understanding the motivation for creativity. Illustrations of these constructs are provided as they apply to the lives of creative individuals. Salient individual factors in the development of creativity are discussed, including a problem-finding orientation, introversion, and childhood trauma. The interaction of these factors is presented as a base for understanding the use of deficiency creativity as a force for growth.

CREATIVITY AS AN INTERACTIVE PROCESS

Rogers's (1961) definition of the creative process is an interactive one that recognizes as the resolution of the process a novel product of artistic, scientific, or ideological content. Rogers also viewed the change in personality resulting from personal growth as a creative product, "growing out of the uniqueness of the individual on the one hand, and the materials, events, people, or circumstances of his life on the other" (p. 350).

Rogers (1961) indicated that this view of creativity does not include the evaluation of constructive or destructive creativity, acceptance of the product, or degree of creativity. The reason for this is that all of these require value judgments that he considered subject to too many unstable variables. Instead he explained that constructive creativity is dependent on the individual's ability to be open to his or her own experience. Individuals who deny or repress large amounts of their experience may be more subject to creative responses that are individually or socially destructive.

Delineating three inner conditions for constructive creativity, Rogers described the importance of: (a) openness to experience—which prevents a defensive distortion of awareness and allows for tolerance of ambiguity and conflict without premature closure; (b) an internal locus of evaluation—which recognizes that the ultimate source of judgment for the product is internal; and (c) the ability to toy with elements and concepts—which promotes a spontaneous playful approach to ideas, symbols, and elements, and leads to the transformation of the known and ordinary into the unknown and extraordinary.

Recognizing the creative process in this interactive manner acknowledges that creativity can be both a means for artistic or symbolic expression and a conscious or unconscious force for personal growth. Therefore, a person who has developed skill in the creative process might not only be unconsciously affected by the enaction of the process but also more able to use this kind of a process consciously in coping with and adapting to life. A paradox emerges here, however, because only those individuals who are open to their own experience seem to have use of creativity as a tool for growth. This same skill of creative expression can also cause pathologic symptoms for the sensitive individual. He or she may deal with both the performance anxieties associated with creative acts and the heightened vulnerability from access to unconscious thoughts and feelings (Rothenberg, 1990; Storr, 1972).

Rothenberg (1990) emphatically stated that creative people "cannot be psychotic or use psychopathological thought processes *at the time they are engaged in a creative process* or it will not be successful" (p. 186). Emphasizing that "the creative process requires an ability to tolerate high levels of anxiety and a relative lack of defensiveness in order to proceed," Rothenberg also acknowledged that creative work can be risky. He explained that anxiety is produced through the uncovering of unconscious material during the creative process itself. Although leading to the accomplishment resulting from significant creative works, "the gradual unearthing of unconscious processes and the progression toward insight are invariably tenuous and may go awry" (Rothenberg, 1990, p. 197).

Before further considering creativity as a force for growth, it is helpful to examine one of the most critical factors in creativity, namely motivation. Amabile (1989) defined intrinsic motivation as "the desire to do something for its own sake, because it is interesting, satisfying, or personally challenging" (p. 50). A review of the studies on motivation (Hennessey & Amabile, 1988) uncovered both the importance of the individual's perception and the impact of the environment. Although external constraints (i.e., deadlines and evaluations) and rewards decrease intrinsic motivation (Amabile, DeJong, & Lepper, 1976; Deci, 1972) and the perception of a reward as being contingent on a task results in a decrease in creativity on the task (Amabile, 1982; Lepper, Greene, & Nisbett, 1973), intrinsic motivation training can help subjects overcome the negative effects of reward and increase creative productivity (Hennessey & Amabile, 1988). Hennessey and Amabile concluded that characteristics of the perceiver of an environmental constraint directly influence the interpretation of the experience, making it unique for the individual.

Individual perceptions may be: (a) informational—when behavioral information is provided signifying competence with no associated pressure to perform; (b) controlling—when there is external pressure to perform; or (c) a motivational—when internal feelings of inadequacy and helplessness take over, signifying the individual's inability to perform (Deci & Ryan, 1985). These findings (Hennessey & Amabile, 1988) emphasize the significance of the individual as a mediating force in interpreting life experience. They therefore support the argument for studies of the creative individual that take an interactive perspective.

CREATIVITY AS A FORCE FOR GROWTH

It is useful to examine the third hypothesis of this chapter—that some individuals might be motivated by needs for love and acceptance to use their creativity as a force for survival and potential growth—within the context of previous theories. Freud's (1953–1964) sublimation theory views the creative response as a means of converting human instinctual drives into socially acceptable forms of behavior. The alternative perspective taken when examining the position of creativity vis-à-vis the health continuum is one that sees creativity as the expression of an optimally healthy individual. Maslow (1962) exemplified this view but focused on creativity to the growth potential within each person by defining "self-actualizing creativeness . . . as the universal heritage of every human being that is born, and which seems to covary with psychological health" (p. 127). Maslow distinguished this form of creativeness, which was humanly realized in a tendency to do anything creatively, from "special talent creativeness," which he acknowledged seemed "independent of goodness or health of character" (p. 158).

In his theory of human motivation, Maslow (1962) defined growth as a series of processes that move the person toward ultimate self-actualization. To achieve this highest form of growth, the individual progresses through Maslow's hierarchy by fulfilling deficiency needs first and then progressing through the growth needs to the final state of self-actualization. The lower level deficiency needs begin with physiological needs, move up to safety, love, and respect needs, and finally knowledge needs. Transcending the deficiency needs, growth needs include self-expression, integration, and creativity. The result is a self-actualized individual.

Deficiency Creativity and Being Creativity

Maslow applied this definition of creativity to the potential self-realization of the average human being, not the specially talented individual. If this conception of creativity and growth is applied to all human creativeness, a new understanding of creativity as a tool for human growth is revealed. By recognizing that some talented individuals use creative expression as a means of meeting their deficiency needs for love, acceptance, and respect, particularly when more common avenues of interpersonal and emotional expression are not available to them, two categories of creativity are suggested (using Maslow's identifiers): those forms that primarily arise from deficiency needs—D (deficiency) creativity—and those forms that primarily arise from being needs—B (being) creativity.

Maslow (1987) did acknowledge some exceptions to his needs hierarchy regarding the creative individual. He observed that there are some naturally creative individuals within whom the need to be creative takes precedence over other more basic needs. "Their creativeness might appear not as self-actualization released by basic satisfaction, but in spite of lack of basic satisfaction" (p. 26). This observation by Maslow stops short of an explanation as to how or why the creative individual might benefit or be harmed from a short circuiting of the needs hierarchy.

Although recognizing that some creative individuals expressed their creativity before their lower level needs were met, Maslow did not distinguish between D-creativity and B-creativity. However, he did make this distinction between deficiency and being when discussing D-love and B-love. Maslow (1962) described D-love as a selfish form of love. Motivated by the lower level deficiency needs, it has an addictive quality. B-love, however, is unselfish love for the being of another person and represents a higher form of maturation and growth.

Through this comparative approach, D-creativity can be defined as representation by creative forms and expressions that are essentially motivated by deficiency needs for acceptance, love, and respect. Although such products might not be as ultimately satisfying or "constructive" (Rogers, 1961) as those that are developed from a more unselfish, intrinsic perspective, they can serve the needs of the individual on many levels. By using their creative strengths to meet basic deficiency needs for affirmation, such individuals not only develop their talents but also receive both intrinsic and extrinsic rewards that may propel them further along the growth hierarchy to Being levels of creative expression.

B-creativity can be defined as motivation by higher level growth needs that may result in products and experiences that have intrinsic meaning for the individual and therefore bring a high level of transcendent satisfaction and understanding for both the originator and the audience. Arieti (1976) expressed this view as follows: "Although creativity is by no means the only way in which the human being can grow, it is one of the most important. The growth occurs not only in the creative person but in all those who are affected by the innovation" (p. 413).

Moving from D-Creativity to B-Creativity

By overlooking the distinction between D-creativity and B-creativity, Maslow could not help but omit a discussion of how creativity can meet deficiency needs. When lacking natural means of meeting basic deficiency love needs in an emotionally repressive or deprived environment, potentially talented individuals can make use of D-creativity as a vehicle for love, acceptance, and self-healing. This process can eventually lead these individuals to higher levels of creative expression–using B-creativity as greater skills are developed and as the necessary deficiency needs are met by basic D-creativity rewards. Creative expression then becomes a way for these individuals to turn their deprived environments into nurturing ones, all because of their independent actions.

Storr (1988b) supported this view in discussing the role of solitude in the lives of creative individuals. He made the point that in certain circumstances, "partial deprivation of interpersonal relationships encourages imagination to flourish" (p. 106). Storr described writers such as Saki, Wodehouse, Lear, Potter, and Trollope in his argument of how childhood experiences of loss, isolation, and deprivation can motivate gifted individuals to use their imagination "both as a retreat from the world, and also as an indirect way of making a mark upon it" (p. 119). Clearly this perspective supports the view that creative expression can be motivated by deficiency needs and lead to further development of creative skills. Reinforcing that idea, Storr stated, "The development of such highly complex imaginative worlds was the consequence of being cut off from the emotional fulfillment that children with more ordinary backgrounds experience in their relations with parents and other care-takers" (p. 119). He concluded that "what began as compensation for deprivation became a rewarding way of life" (p. 122).

In explaining the creative drive manifested by talented individuals with depressive illness and low self-esteem, Storr (1988a) again supported the view that creativity can become a force for meeting deficiency needs. "Success and public recognition can, in some degree, compensate for inner emptiness by providing recurrent injections of self-esteem from external sources. Depressives are dependent on frequent 'fixes' of recognition and success as are addicts on their drug" (p. 265).

Some might argue that D-creativity is motivated by extrinsic sources and therefore would result in products and experiences that are destructive or superficial. Although this may be true when the creative individual focuses solely on the external rewards of creative effort, it is also true that significant elements of intrinsic motivation are experienced by the individual through the D-creative process. Practicing creativity even when motivated extrinsically by deficiency needs can lead the individual to increasing levels of skilled control of both the environment and the symbol system used for expression; increasing opportunities for self-expression and self-discovery; and increasing levels of joy and satisfaction resulting from the creative experience itself. Although growth from D-creativity to B-creativity is by no means assured, the use of creativity as a spur for growth is possible if certain individual and environmental conditions are present.

Rothenberg (1990) supported this view that some talented individuals who grow in confusing or unresponsive environments may be driven to creative expression as a means of meeting the basic deficiency needs of love, affirmation, and self-respect. He illustrated this by describing the childhood environment of a writer, John Cheever, who eventually was able to control his problem of alcoholism:

> Factors that do seem to connect Cheever's alcoholism with his writing have some general applicability to alcoholism in other creative people. Living with parents who were frequently in a withdrawn, inebriated state, Cheever as a child felt helpless and unable to communicate with them. His turning to writing seemed to serve as a way to bring order into a chaotic, disorganized experience and, in a sense, as a way to get his parents to hear him. The writing may also have become a means of compensating for his own feelings of weakness and loss. (Rothenberg, 1990, p. 199–200)

When external rewards of attention, admiration, and praise are given for valuing the intrinsic rewards of the process of creativity, it is possible that the individual will continue to grow from D-creativity to B-creativity. This process would, in essence, be a natural form of intrinsic motivation training (Hennessey & Amabile, 1988) that would help the individual use external rewards as informational feedback.

THE DUAL ROLE OF CONFLICT IN CREATIVITY

Although the conflict experienced through childhood trauma can serve as the motivating force and content for creative expression, such conflict can also overwhelm the individual and stifle expression. The drama of intrapsychic and interpersonal conflict increases as the tension mounts between the competing personal emotional needs and the creative intellectual needs of the individual. At this point the individual has the choice of using creativity as a healthy defense leading toward potential growth (Arieti, 1976; Masterson, 1989; Roe, 1951; Storr, 1972) or as the conflict becomes too great to bear, the individual may become creatively blocked (Rothenberg, 1990; Storr, 1972). Acknowledging that the evidence points to a high incidence of psychopathology among creative people, Storr concluded: "They are also equipped with greater resources which help them to overcome their conflicts and problems. Psychiatrists experienced in treating creative people know it is only when their creative powers are paralyzed that they seek help" (1988b, p. 143).

Heightened conflict and the associated creative block might also be the propelling force for some individuals to indulge in self-destructive behavior, or attempt to control feelings and the environment in a destructive way. Storr (1972) described the creatively blocked individual as occasionally considering or attempting suicide when "the person's identity has become so completely embodied in the work that its success or failure is entirely substituted for personal success or failure in interpersonal relations" (p. 221). According to Storr, these vulnerable individuals did not feel sufficiently loved as children and had given up the hope of ever being loved. Other outcomes that may occur when the individual uses creativity as a means of self-justification or self-expression could range from significantly destructive to constructive results as in the D-creative efforts in the "will for power" (Rentchnick, 1989) of a Hitler or a Manson to the B-creative efforts of a Shakespeare or a Gandhi. This view of creativity supports the Rogers's (1961) perspective that creative products can be constructive or destructive depending on the creative individual's ability to be open to his or her experience.

Openness to conflict can provide significant motivating energy in the realization of creative potential. Roth (1976) stated that conflict is "one of the two great motivating forces for original work, the other being the desire for self-expression immanent in all of us" (Arieti, 1976, p. 378). Arieti (1976) distinguished between traumatic or neurotic conflict, which prevents individuals from transcending their personal view and expressing their ideas in a form that has universal meaning, from the nontraumatic or resolved conflict, which serves as the personal fuel for an objective depiction of experience and results in meaningful creative work.

Explaining the link between creativity and mental illness, Storr (1988a) emphasized that creative activity not only serves as an indirect means of communication for the individual but also is an essentially integrative act. Creative motivation then becomes the need to reconcile opposites and control the experienced conflict for the prevention of personal disintegration. "The motive force that impels a man or woman to embark upon the hazardous, often unrewarding task of endeavoring to make coherence out of the external world or out of their own inner selves often originates from alienation and despair" (Storr, 1988a, p. 267).

CREATIVITY AS A FORCE FOR HEALTH

This view of creative expression as a force for health and potential growth can be applied further to those creative individuals who have been identified as having mental illness. When considering the connection between psychopathology and the ability to do creative work, Horney (1950) concluded that "an artist . . . creates not because of this neurosis but in spite of it" (p. 332).

Although Horney (1950) believed that an artist's conflicts and search for an escape from them might provide the subject for creative expression, she also cautioned that the artist can only be productive "to the extent that his or her real self is alive" (p. 332). Because she viewed neurosis as an individual's alienation from the self, the neurotic individual's access to his or her own creative energy would be in serious jeopardy. Contrary to the belief that analysis would defuse the necessary motivation for creative expression, Horney argued that "an artist may retrieve his or her productivity when in analysis his or her desire for (his or her drive toward) self-realization is liberated" (p. 332).

Masterson (1989) observed that for individuals with personality disorders, creative expression can serve as a means toward growth. Although recommending psychotherapy as the preferred method toward recovery of the real self, he acknowledged that it is not the only method. "The artist uses the creativity of his or her real self to find a way of dealing with the feelings of abandonment and engulfment and to temper the abandonment depression's power to ruin his or her life" (p. 208). Masterson illustrated this point by describing how Sartre, Munch, and Woolfe defended themselves against the abandonment depression and expressed their real selves. Because each of these three—the philosopher, artist, and novelist—communicated his or her own abandonment depression experience, the creative works of each took on a universal perspective in expressing the powerful theme of developmental conflict.

Masterson hypothesized that these artists had disorders of the self that were controlled by and became the thematic focus for the emerging creativity of their real selves.

The following section describes the salient cognitive, personality, and developmental characteristics that may interact in some individuals to promote creativity. A discussion then follows of how these factors predispose some individuals to use D-creativity as a means of survival and potential growth.

A Problem-Finding Orientation

It may be that the problem-finding orientation is reinforced in some introverted individuals as a result of difficult childhood circumstances. In an environment where the emotional life of the child is not nurtured, although the creative and intellectual development is recognized, the child will develop in an asynchronous manner. Thus, individual development might occur within the creative intellectual context and not in the personal or interpersonal context (Storr, 1972). A paradox is presented as this individual becomes intensely invested in the displacement of emotional energy from identifying problems in the personal milieu to identifying and attempting to solve universal intellectual or aesthetic problems. Such emotional energy can become the motivation behind the hard work of creative productivity.

A problem-finding orientation is the cognitive ability to recognize critical issues in an area of study and to focus on these issues to the exclusion of others (Getzels & Csikszentmihalyi, 1976; Perkins, 1981; Sternberg, 1988). In addition to selecting potentially soluble problems of sufficient magnitude and scope, creative individuals also have the unique ability to break conventions, redefining problems and structuring them in a new way, thus enhancing their solubility and significance (Sternberg, 1988). This kind of problem-sensing ability appears to draw on the aesthetic strengths of the individual (Tardif & Sternberg, 1988).

Introversion and Creativity

Examining the personality factor of introversion will help to define the role of conflict in the life of an introverted creative person and explain the motivation of the introverted individual in using creative expression as a vehicle for coping or growth. The notion of introversion and extraversion as opposing psychological types was developed by Jung (1923). He described the introverted person as inwardly focused, subjectively oriented, and naturally moving away from others. The extravert, on the other hand, is outwardly focused, objectively oriented, and naturally gravitating toward others. In essence, then, the introvert is drawn to privacy and solitude, gaining energy from quiet solitary activities while quickly losing energy in social situations.

MacKinnon (1978) found several factors describing the creative person: above-average intelligence, alertness and adaptiveness in response to life, absence of repression and suppression, a theme of remembered unhappiness in childhood, a considerable amount of psychic turbulence, and a tendency toward introversion. MacKinnon's finding that two-thirds or more of each group participating in his research demonstrated a tendency toward introversion takes on even more significance considering that introverts comprise only one quarter of the general population (Kiersey & Bates, 1984).

Several other researchers found a high frequency of introversion occurring in creative individuals in both the arts and the sciences (Cattell & Drevdahl, 1955; Eysenck, 1983; Gotz & Gotz, 1979; Hudson, 1966; Roe, 1951, 1976). Sternberg (1988) identified the introverted psychological type as having an internal style of mental self-government. He described such individuals as task-oriented, aloof, and socially and interpersonally less aware than normal. Sternberg also emphasized that "some internal scope is needed, even in one's dealings with people, in order to display creativity" (p. 142). Eysenck and Eysenck (1985) pointed to the physiological base for introverted behavior. Using Pavlovian theory, Eysenck and Eysenck found that introverts showed better response to conditioning than extraverts. They argued that "introverts have a chronically higher level of cortical activity than extraverts and that introverts were more responsive to stimulation" (p. 234). And because the main activity of the cortex of the brain is the inhibition of the lower centers, the more aroused the cortex becomes and the more it inhibits behavior, resulting in an introverted response.

Eysenck (1982) found that introverts, being more sensitive to sensory stimulation, would tolerate sensory deprivation more readily than extraverts who would tolerate painful stimuli more readily. This observation by Eysenck could explain why introverted individuals might choose to avoid social situations and opt for quiet, private experiences: The nature of interactive experience might not only be too unpredictable for the introvert, but also too emotionally conflictive and painful to bear. Consequently, as the young introvert chooses early on to opt out of the social milieu, important interpersonal skills simply do not develop. The choice for time alone then becomes more of a necessity as the youth feels unequal to the task of social interaction.

Roe (1976) supported the view that this kind of creative individual might be more inclined to avoid interpersonal confrontation and retreat to symbolic forms of creative expression as follows: "they are markedly preoccupied with things and ideas not with people.... They dislike emotionally toned preoccupations outside of their own field ... and are especially sensitive to interpersonal controversy in any form" (p. 171). Because such individuals are hypersensitive to stimuli, it becomes understandable for the introverted individual to avoid emotional situations and interpersonal conflict, and choose forms of interaction and expression that are controllable and predictable, such as fantasy, art, and ideation.

Arieti (1976) described how this introverted pattern of choosing solitude might ultimately provide the individual with the necessary motivation for creative work. He suggested that "the introverted personality may not permit the young and gifted individual to savor life as much as he would like, and may instead predispose him to crave for something that he does not have or see.... It is by searching for this object that he will continue to grow and give an acceptable meaning to his life" (p. 30).

Introversion and Conflict

Tardif and Sternberg (1988) described the creative person as one in conflict, considering the many contradictory characteristics that describe such individuals. The overriding theme of conflict reflects the tension between the individual's needs for time alone and natural resistance to societal demands, with the competing needs for social acceptance and social interaction. This conflict between social isolation and social interaction is even more pronounced as the individual experiences a heightened sensitivity to life and empathy for others along with a competing need for distance from social constraints and expectations.

Marie Curie's personal discipline and precept of "disinterestedness" in aiming for scientific objectivity is an example of how a creative person can work toward the benefit of humanity while maintaining such a personal distance (Perkins, 1981). Einstein is another example of a creative person who was saintly, kind, and generous, with an active social conscience, but not very socially involved with other individuals (Storr, 1972).

Roe (1951) found high values for social status in the families of her scientist subjects, meaning that considerable value was placed on interpersonal relations. Because some of her subjects found such interaction difficult, they would use the psychologically sound principle of generalizing their personal problems to a larger context that "serves as a motivation for doing a good deal of work that may be extremely useful" (p. 91).

Childhood Trauma and Creativity

Childhood trauma appears to have an important impact on the individual's ability to use creativity as a force for coping and growth. MacKinnon (1978) acknowledged that creative persons share the experience of remembered unhappiness in childhood; however, he appeared to minimize this finding by stating that it comes from self-reports by individuals who are known for their openness to experience. Findings from several studies of eminent adults (Eisenstadt, 1989; Goertzel, Goertzel, & Goertzel, 1978; Roe, 1951) seemed to support the reality of a difficult childhood for eminant individuals. Some studies (Goertzel & Goertzel, 1962; Roe, 1951) showed a high percentage of eminent individuals had physically handicapping conditions during childhood. Other evidence of childhood trauma showed a higher frequency of early parent death of eminent and creative individuals than estimates from the general population (Eisenstadt, 1989; Roe, 1951).

Viewing the bereavement process as a trauma that might spur the child to assume increased responsibility in the family, Eisenstadt (1989) stated that once mastery of the stress of bereavement has occurred, a great motivational desire to excel may ensue. He reasoned, "if feelings of insecurity, inadequacy, emptiness and, especially, guilt can inhibit functioning by overwhelming the personality, then the mastery of these feelings may be a springboard of immense compensatory energy" (p. 26). He described creative effort as a restorative act with its deepest roots in the need to master the environment and the personal intense feelings of bereavement.

THE CREATIVITY GROWTH CONNECTION: A SYNTHESIS

The connection between creativity and growth becomes clearer as the following four points are considered:

1. *The Biological Base.* The factors inherent in the biological makeup of the individual of above-average intelligence and introversion, which contribute to a heightened experience of life, might be the raw materials that contribute to both creative expression and the ability to use creativity as a force for personal growth (Arieti, 1976).

2. *The Environmental Base.* The environmental factors of neglect, rejection, and deprivation may be catalysts for creative expression and ultimate growth for some individuals. Growing up in a difficult, painful, and confusing environment may reinforce problem-

finding behaviors in the sensitive and intelligent child as coping mechanisms. "Benign genes and happy childhoods are not our only allies in the struggle for adaptation, and the human ego grows in adversity as well as in prosperity" (Vaillant, 1977, p. 336). The human need to control, to self-justify, and to make meaning out of existence through creative activity "could be a major explanation for why so many injured people are drawn to create" (Briggs, 1988, p. 246).

3. *The Interactive Perspective of Creativity and Growth.* MacKinnon (1978) stated that our task in predicting creative behavior is to identify traits, situations, and their interactions. Such an interactive approach is taken in this chapter by examining the effect of an emotionally deprived environment on the development of some introverted individuals. A stressful setting can become the catalyst for potentially talented individuals to meet their deficiency needs for attention, love, and approval through D-creative efforts providing self-expression and rewards. Introverted individuals may be inclined to convert feelings of personal conflict into universal abstract creative forms and thereby develop skills in creative expression. Therefore, by using their creative skills to meet basic deficiency needs, these individuals also can develop their creative abilities so that D-creative energy, through its own momentum, can facilitate the movement to higher levels of B-creative expression and personal growth.

4. *The Upward Spiral of the Creativity Growth Process.* D-creativity, although primarily motivated by extrinsic sources, can result in the self-perpetuating personal growth process that fortifies the creative process. This potential upward spiral can fluctuate from creative growth to personal growth and back again. Thus, a growth spiral, initiated first through the "fix" of extrinsic rewards from D-creativity, can be reinforced by the more subtle intrinsic rewards of experiencing the control and shaping of symbols, systems, environments, and ideas, as well as the competence and effectiveness gained through skill development and self-discipline from the B-creative experience. Whether the growth process is allowed to progress undisturbed is dependent on the individual's ability to tune into the intrinsic rewards enough so that the external pressures and constraints do not distort or stifle the uniqueness of the individual's creative voice, resulting in a less satisfying creative experience and product. Ironically, the more able an individual becomes in tuning into his or her original voice, the more vulnerable such a person is when the unconscious material rises to the surface to challenge with further self-awareness or overwhelm with incapacitating anxiety.

CONCLUSIONS AND DIRECTIONS FOR FUTURE STUDY

Personal growth is dependent on the individual's willingness to heed the call of the hero's journey (Campbell, 1949). The uncovering of unconscious material that occurs in the creative process (Rothenberg, 1990) can loom as a giant dragon that the creative hero can choose to block out or challenge head on and ultimately use for future creativity and growth. The more the creative individual can make the courageous and painful choice for growth, the more personal awareness, depth, and richness such a person can bring to his or her creative work (Barron, 1988). Therefore, personal growth gained either independently through the D-creative process or through the helping psychotherapeutic relationship could only help the individual become more creative and increase the significance of his or her creative work.

Future research evolving from this theory includes the need for elaboration of the notion of D-creativity as a means for growth. A qualitative case study would offer the rich detail necessary to determine how such creative introverted individuals might use their abilities to meet deficiency needs.

Also recognizing that alcoholism and creativity are frequently linked, particularly in the lives of writers (Andreasen & Canter, 1974; Rothenberg, 1990), it appears that adult creativity and addictive behavior might occur in the same individual as a result of environmental conditions of deprivation. A naturalistic study examining the link between creativity and alcoholism might include extensive interviews and observations of a recovering alcoholic who is creative. Siblings could also be interviewed to determine the different adaptive life choices made by each individual and possible reasons for different behaviors.

REFERENCES

Amabile, T.-M. (1982). Children's artistic creativity: Detrimental effects of competition in a field setting. *Personality and social Psychology Bulletin, 8,* 573–578.

Amabile, T. M. (1989). *Growing up creative.* New York: Crown.

Amabile, T. M., DeJong, W., & Lepper, M. R. (1976). Effects of externally imposed deadlines on subsequent intrinsic motivation. *Journal of Personality and Social Psychology, 34,* 92–98.

Andreasen, N. C., & Canter, A. (1974). The creative writer: Psychiatric symptoms and family history. *Comprehensive Psychiatry, 15,* 123–131.

Arieti, S. (1976). *Creativity: The magic synthesis.* New York: Basic Books.

Barron, F. (1988). Putting creativity to work. In R. J. Sternberg (Ed.), *The nature of creativity* (pp. 76–98). New York: Cambridge University Press.

Briggs, J. (1988). *Fire in the crucible, the alchemy of creative genius.* New York: St. Martin's.

Campbell, J. (1949). *The hero with a thousand faces.* New York: Pantheon Books.

Cattell, R. B., & Drevdahl, J. E. (1955). A comparison of the personality profile of eminent researchers with that of eminent teachers and administrators. *British Journal of Psychology, 44,* 248–261.

Deci, E. (1972). Intrinsic motivation, extrinsic reinforcement, and inequity. *Journal of Personality and Social Psychology, 22,* 113–120.

Deci, E., & Ryan, R. (1985). *Intrinsic motivation and self-determination in human behavior.* New York: Plenum.

Eisenstadt, M. (1989). Parental loss and genius. In M. Eisenstadt, A. Haynal, P. Rentchnick, & P. De Senarclens (Eds.), *Parental loss and achievement* (pp. 1–34). Madison, CT: International Universities Press.

Eysenck, H. J. (1982). *Personality, genetics, and behavior selected papers.* New York: Praeger.

Eysenck, H. J. (1983). The roots of personality: Cognitive ability or personality trait? *Roeper Review, 5,* 10–12.

Eysenck, H. J., & Eysenck, M. W. (1985). *Personality and individual differences, a natural science approach.* New York: Plenum.

Feldman, D. H. (1982). A developmental framework for research with gifted children. In D. Feldman (Ed.), *New directions for child development: Developmental approaches to giftedness and creativity* (No. 17, pp. 31–45). San Francisco, CA: Jossey-Bass.

Freud, S. (1953–64). *The standard edition of the complete psychological works of Sigmund Freud.* In J. Strachey (Ed. and Trans.) Vols. 1–24. London: Hogarth.

Getzels, J. W., & Csikszentmihalyi, M. (1976). *Creative vision: A longitudinal study of problem finding in art.* New York: Wiley.

Goertzel, M. G., Goertzel, V., & Goertzel, T. G. (1978). *300 eminent personalities.* San Francisco, CA: Jossey-Bass.

Goertzel, V., & Goertzel, M. G. (1962). *Cradles of eminence.* London: Constable.

Gotz, K. O., & Gotz, K. (1979). Personality characteristics of successful artists. *Perceptiual and Motor Skills, 49,* 919–924.

Gruber, H. E., & Davis, S. N. (1988) Inching our way up Mount Olympus: The evolving-systems approach to creative thinking. In R. Sternberg (Ed.), *The nature of creativity.* New York: Cambridge University Press.

Hennessey, B. A., & Amabile, T. M. (1988) In R. J. Sternberg (Ed.), *The nature of creativity* (pp. 298–324). New York: Cambridge University Press.

Horney, K. (1950). Neurosis and human growth: The struggle toward self-realization. New York: W. W. Norton.

Hudson, L. (1966), *Contrary imaginations.* London: Methuen.

Jung, C. G. (1923). *Psychological types, the psychology of individualation* (H. G. Baynes, Trans.). London and New York: Harcourt, Brace & Company.

Kiersey, D., & Bates, M. (1984). *Please understand me.* Del Mar, CA: Prometheus Nemesis Book Company.

Lepper, M., Greene, D., & Nisbett, R. (1973). Undermining children's intrinsic interest with extrinsic rewards: A test of the "overjustification" hypothesis. *Journal of Personality and Social Psychology, 28,* 129–137.

MacKinnon, D. (1978). *In search of human effectiveness.* Buffalo, NY: Creative Education Foundation.

Maslow, A. H. (1962). *Toward a psychology of being.* Princeton, NJ: Van Nostrand.

Maslow, A. H. (1987). *Motivation and personality.* New York: Harper & Row.

Masterson, J. (1989). *The search for the real self.* New York: Scribners & Sons.

Perkins, D. N. (1981). *The mind's best work.* Cambridge MA: Harvard University Press.

Rentchnick, P. (1989). Orphans and the will for power. In M. Eisenstadt, A. Haynal, P. Rentchnick, & P. De Senarclens (Eds.), *Parental loss and achievement* (pp. 35–70). Madison, CT: International Universities press.

Richards, R. (1990). Everyday creativity, eminent creativity, and health. *Creativity Research Journal, 3,* 300–326 Norwood, NJ: Ablex.

Roe, A. (1951). *The making of a scientist.* New York: Dodd, Mead.

Roe, A. (1976). Psychological approaches to creativity in science. In A. Rothenberg & C. R. Hausman (Eds.), *The creativity question* (pp. 165–175). Durham, NC: Duke University Press.

Rogers, C. (1961). *On becoming a person.* New York: Houghton Mifflin.

Roth, N. (1976). Free association and creativity. *Journal of the American Academy of Psychoanalysis, 3,* 373–381.

Rothenberg, A. (1990). Creativity, mental health, and alcoholism, *Creativity Research Journal, 3,* 179–201 Norwood, NJ: Ablex.

Sternberg, R. J. (1988). A three-facet model of creativity. In R. J. Sternberg (Ed.), *The nature of creativity* (pp. 25–147). New York: Cambridge University Press.

Storr, A. (1972). *The dynamics of creation.* New York: Atheneum.

Storr, A. (1988a). *Churchill's black dog, Kafka's mice and other phenomena of the human mind.* New York: Grove.

Storr, A. (1988b). *Solitude, a return to the self.* New York: Ballentine Books.

Tardif, T. Z., & Sternberg, R. J. (1988). What do we know about creativity? In R. J. Sternberg (Ed.), *The nature of creativity* (pp. 429–440). New York: Cambridge University Press.

Vaillant, G. E. (1977). *Adaptation to life.* Boston, MA: Little, Brown & Co.

Chapter 15

Creativity and Self-Actualization *

Mark A. Runco
Peter Ebersole
Wayne Mraz†

CREATIVITY AND SELF-ACTUALIZATION

Self-actualized individuals should, according to theory, be creative. In Maslow's (1971) view, for example, self-actualization and creativity are functionally interdependent, with creativity facilitating self-actualization and self-actualization facilitating creativity. At one point Maslow went as far as to suggest that creativity and self-actualization "may turn out to be

*From "Self-Actualization and Creativity," by M.A. Runco, P. Ebersole, & W. Mraz, 1990, *Journal of Social Behavior and Personality*, 6, pp. 161–167. Copyright © 1995. Adapted with permission.

†The authors would like to express their gratitude to Celeste Diaz for her assistance with the data coding and preparation of the manuscript.

the same thing" (1971, p. 57). Similarly, in a discussion of motivation, Rogers (1961) suggested that "the mainspring of creativity appears to be the same tendency which we discover so clearly as the creative force in psychotherapy—man's tendency to actualize himself, to become his potentialities . . . the individual creates primarily because it is satisfying . . . because this behavior is felt to be self-actualization" (pp. 351–352).

Maslow (1971) and Rogers (1961) based their theories primarily on clinical observations. Two empirical projects have further tested the association between creativity and self-actualization. Mathes (1978) found very low correlations between self-actualization, assessed with the *Personal Orientation Inventory* (POI), and four measures of creativity. However, the creativity measures were highly verbal (e.g., the *Remote Associates Test*), with marginal reliabilities (ranging from .51 to .67) and unimpressive convergent validity coefficients (.01 < *r*s < .48) indicating poor construct validity. Murphy, Dauw, Harton, and Fredian (1976) used the more widely recognized *Torrance Tests of Creative Thinking* (TTCT), as well as the *Similies Preference* test. They reported that the elaboration index from the TTCT was significantly correlated with POI scores, but no coefficient was reported. The fluency and originality scores from the TTCT and the scores from the *Similies* test were unrelated to POI scores. Thus, aside from Maslow's and Rogers's own observations, there is very little support for an association between self-actualization and creativity.

This may be in part because creativity is very difficult to define and assess. Rogers (1961) wrote that "the very essence of the creative is its novelty, and hence we have no standard by which to judge it" (p. 351). Still, the link between self-actualization and creativity is sufficiently important to justify further investigation with alternative measures. In our view, the problem with earlier empirical attempts is that the creativity measures may not have been sensitive to the unique characteristics of self-actualized individuals. Most earlier measures of creativity have focused on creative products (e.g., solutions to problems or divergent thinking) rather than personality. As Maslow (1968) pointed out:

> SA creativeness stresses first the personality rather than its achievements, considering these achievements to be epiphenomena emitted by the personality and therefore secondary to it. It stresses characterological qualities like boldness, courage, freedom, spontaneity, perspicuity, integrity, self-acceptance, all of which make possible the kind of generalized SA creativeness, which expresses itself in the creative life, or the creative attitude, or the creative person. I have also stressed the expressive or Being quality of SA creativeness rather than its problem-solving or product-making quality. (p. 145)

There are clear parallels between the traits that characterize creative people and the traits found in self-actualized individuals. In addition to those mentioned in the quotation just above, when describing self-actualized people Maslow (1968) identified an acceptance of self, others, and nature, and detachment, a desire for privacy, autonomy, resistance to enculturation, problem-centering, and democratic character structure. Looking specifically at creativity, Runco and Bahleda (1986) identified confidence, intrinsic motivation, preference for aesthetic experiences, independence, energy, a wide range of interests, and tolerance for ambiguity (also see Albert, 1983).

Actually, some empirical support for the relationship we predicted was given by Buckmaster and Davis (1985). They found that a creativity factor accounted for the largest portion in an eight-factor solution of the *Reflections of Self and Environment* (ROSE) self-report, which was developed specifically to measure self-actualization. This creativity factor only accounted for 18.9% of the variance in the scores, and the ROSE total score was not as nearly as strongly correlated with the POI ($r = .26$) as it was with the measure of creativity, but again, these results are consistent with our predictions.[1]

The present investigation was conducted with two creativity measures that were thought to be entirely compatible with the theory of self-actualization. These are not measures of creative products, such as those used in earlier research, but rather are measures of creative traits, preferences, and attitudes. In addition, we employed a different measure of self-actualization than the previously used POI (Shostrom, 1963). The advantage of our choice—Jones and Crandall's (1986) *Self-Actualization Scale* (SAS)—over the POI lies in its brevity, unambiguous format, and provision of a single score. Unfortunately, it is so new as to have only preliminary validity. In a sense, the present investigation adds to what is known about the SAS.

Design of the Investigation

Three questionnaires were administered to 84 students from three introductory psychology classes. The students were asked to complete the

---

[1]As a matter of fact, Buckmaster and Davis (1985) also found a significant correlation ($r = .73$) between the ROSE and a measure of creative personality traits. It is unfortunate that we did not know of that investigation until ours was completed, but again, the findings of Buckmaster and Davis are entirely compatible with our own. We would have conducted our investigation regardless in order to test the predictions with a less select sample of subjects (Buckmaster and Davis studied students in a creativity course), with the SAS (rather than the POI and the ROSE) and the standardized measure of personality (the ACL). Even our HDYT scales differ from those of Buckmaster and Davis, although apparently there is overlap between the HDYT and their *What About You* test. We used Interests, Confidence and Flexibility, Energetic Originality, and Arousal and Risk Taking scales, along with the CPS scale from the ACL.

instruments on their own time, and return them during the next meeting of the class. Sixty-four students returned all three questionnaires (76% of the 84 students). They received research credit for doing so. Thirty-six (56.3%) of these students were females, and 28 (43.7%) were males. The average age was 19 years, with a standard deviation of 1.2 years.

The *How Do You Think Test* (HDYT; Davis & Subkoviac, 1975), the *Adjective Check List* (ACL; Gough & Heilbrun, 1980), and the *Self-Actualization Scale* (SAS; Jones & Crandall, 1986) were each administered. The SAS consists of 15 items modified from the POI and the *Personal Orientation Dimensions* scales. Unlike the forced-choice format of the POI, the SAS employs only one statement; the participant rates each statement on a continuum ranging from *strongly agree* to *strongly disagree*. The SAS with the six-choice format (printed at the end of the Crandall, McCown, and Robb [1988] article) was chosen in light of its test-retest reliability of .84 (Jones & Crandall, 1986) compared to .69 for the earlier four-choice format. The validation information, which was gathered only utilizing the four-choice format, was reasonable for a new instrument in that it was significantly and positively correlated with the POI, a measure of self-esteem, and rationality, and was negatively correlated with a measure of neuroticism. In addition, the measure correctly discriminated between individuals nominated as actualizing.

The HDYT contains 100 statements describing preferences, interests, and attitudes that are indicative of a creative personality and lifestyle. Each item has a five-level Likert type response option. It is highly reliable, and significantly correlated with other measures of creativity (Runco, Okuda, & Thurston, 1987). Four HDYT item clusters were identified a priori, based largely on the multidimensional scaling of Davis and Subkoviak (1975). (Davis and Subkoviak [1975] used a different form of the HDYT and six composites.) Composite scores for each were computed by averaging the item scores within each cluster. The *Interests* scale contained 24 items (e.g., "I have many hobbies," I am very conscious of aesthetic considerations"). The *Confidence and Flexibility* scale contained 37 items (e.g., "I am very independent," "I enjoy some amount of ambiguity in my life"). The *Energetic Originality* scale contained 18 items (e.g., "I am often inventive or ingenious," "I often become engrossed in a new idea"). Finally, the *Arousal and Risk Taking* scale contained 21 items (e.g., "I enjoy a job with unforeseeable difficulties," "I take a playful approach to most things").

The ACL was scored for the Creative Personality Scale (CPS), as described by Gough and Heilbrun (1980). The CPS score was standardized by calculating a ratio, with the raw score divided by the total number of adjectives checked (cf. Gough & Heibrun, 1980). Gough and Heilbrun

(1980) reported CPS interitem reliabilities of .76 and .77 for males and females, respectively, with test-retest coefficients of .74 and .75.

Reliabilities and Correlations

In our sample, the HDYT composites had interitem reliabilities of .67 (Interest Scale), .79 (Confidence and Flexibility Scale), .83 (Energetic Originality Scale), and .80 (Arousal and Risk Taking Scale). The interitem coefficient for the SAS was .58. Table 15.1 presents the product moment correlations for the creativity (HDYT and ACL) and SAS scales. Most important is that the HDYT Scales were each significantly related to the SAS scores. After taking the reliability of the HDYT composites into account (Nunnally, 1978), these coefficients were .32, .34, .42, and .46 for the Interest, Confidence, Energy, and Arousal Scales, respectively. The correlation between the SAS and the CPS scale from the ACL only approached statistical significance ($r = .22$, $p = .07$). This coefficient was .28 after adjusting for attenuation resulting from the reliability of the CPS.

A regression analysis indicated that the four HDYT composites together accounted for 18% of the variance in the SAS scores ($R = .42$, $p = .03$). When the composites were entered into the regression equation based on decreasing tolerance, the Energy Scale was pulled into the equation first and accounted for 12% of the SAS variance ($p < .01$). The other three HDYT scores each accounted for less than 4% of the remaining variance (R^2-changes $< .035$, ns). Hence, the Energy scale seemed to be the best predictor of SAS scores.

Table 15.1. Product-Moment Correlation Matrix

	Mean	SD	1	2	3	4	5
			Correlations				
1. SAS	62.7	(6.7)					
HDYT							
2. Interest	3.01	(0.42)	.24*				
3. Confidence	3.13	(0.41)	.28*	.60***			
4. Energy	3.24	(0.69)	.35**	.82***	.60***		
5. Arousal	2.88	(0.59)	.39***	.61***	.75***	.69**	
ACL							
6. CPS Ratio	0.037	(0.041)	.22	.38**	.39**	.45**	.28**

Note. The SAS is the *Self-Actualization Scale* (Jones & Crandall, 1986). The Interest, Confidence, Energy, and Arousal are scales from the *How Do You Think Test* (HDYT; Davis & Subkoviac, 1975). The CPS is the Creative Personality Scale from the *Adjective Check List* (ACL; Gough & Heilbrun, 1980). *$p < .05$, **$p < .01$, ***$p < .001$.

Self-Descriptions

Looking at the specific adjectives chosen as self-descriptive by the individuals whose SAS scores were in the top 25% of the subject sample (n = 16), 15 checked Adventurous, Alert, Appreciative, Clever, Dependable, Friendly, Helpful, Honest, and Loyal, and 14 checked Active, Adaptable, Capable, Easy Going, Formal, Humorous, Intelligent, Interests Wide, Kind, and Mature. None of the subjects in this subsample chose Commonplace, Conceited, Cruel, Despondent, Distrustful, Dull, Gloomy, Queer, Slipshod, Stolid, Sulky, Unintelligent, Unkind, or Unstable.

DISCUSSION

These results fit well with the descriptions given by Maslow (1971) and Rogers (1961) of the relationship between creativity and self-actualization. It also makes a great deal of sense that there would be an association, given that both creativity and self-actualization are signs of psychological health (Richards, 1990) and given that they share numerous traits. Still, the present results are inconsistent with the empirical findings of Mathes (1978) and Murphy et al. (1976). As mentioned above, this may reflect the difficulties involved in assessing creativity. The earlier projects did not utilize the HDYT or the ACL, nor any personality or attitudinal measure. Mathes (1978) specifically noted that his finding a nonsignificant association between creativity and self-actualization may have been because he used measures of creative products rather than personality.

Although the second regression analysis suggested that there was some multicollinearity (interscale redundancy) among the HDYT scales, the product moment correlation between the SAS and the HDYT composites were all significant (see Table 15.1). Importantly, Runco et al. (1987) demonstrated that the HDYT is one of the best criteria of creativity. In their research, HDYT scores were significantly related to—and thus predictive of—several other creativity indices. Future research on self-actualization should be conducted with other indices of creativity. Apparently, they should use measures of the creative personality rather than of creative products.

Future research should also be conducted with other subject samples. Because the participants in the present investigation were all college students, the range of scores may have been restricted, and the correlation coefficients thereby attenuated. It might even be argued that no highly self-actualized individuals participated in this project, for college students might lack the perspective or experience for self-actualization (cf. Rizzo & Vinacke, 1975; Schatz & Buckmaster, 1984). On the other hand, the range of scores was large enough, and the degree of self-actualization varied enough, to detect the expected relationship with creativity.

Unfortunately, we cannot infer the direction of effect from the correlational results. Although the correlations were significant, they do not indicate causality: Creativity may allow individuals to become self-actualized, or self-actualization may lead to creative behavior. This direction of effect problem is quite common in the research on creativity and health (Runco, 1990). When discussing self-actualization, there is also another option: Creativity and self-actualization may be correlated because they are each associated with a third general tendency or trait. For example, effective coping or adaptive skills might allow individuals to develop both self-actualization and creativity (Rhodes, 1990). Like self-actualized individuals, creative individuals seem to have effective coping skills (Burke, Chrisler, & Sloan, 1989; Rothenberg, 1990; Runco, 1994).

The quotation from Rogers (1961), given early in this chapter, implies that self-actualization and creativity both reflect an underlying motivational force, and one that might reflect the need for growth (Rhodes, 1990). In Maslow's (1971) terms, creative people are able to cope with the *emotional blocks* to being creative. Rubenson and Runco (1992) described these as the *psychic cost* of independent and original behavior, and they argued that such costs are notably lower for creative individuals than uncreative individuals.

The traits shared by creativity and self-actualization (e.g., autonomy, confidence) are suggestive of bidirectional effects. Still other traits have been identified by recent research. McLeod and Vodanovich (1991), for instance, looked to boredom, postulating a negative relationship between it and self-actualization. They reasoned that individuals who are easily bored have been portrayed as having low levels of frustration tolerance, a strong drive for immediate gratification, a tendency toward insecurity, conformity, eating disorders, and substance abuse, and a lack of creativity. The expected correlation between boredom and self-actualization was obtained. Flett, Hewitt, Blankstein, and Mosher (1991) found a negative correlation between the self-actualization and perfectionism. This was explained by the fact that the potential for self-actualization can be crushed by learning to expect disapproval from others. Flett, et al. suggested that expectations of disapproval can contribute to a compensating perfectionism. Ebersole and Humphreys (1991) reported a positive correlation between the SAS and the Purpose in Life test (PIL), the most widely accepted measure of depth of meaning in individuals' lives. The PIL was an especially appropriate measure because of the large number of studies supporting its validation, and because it is one of the few measures—in addition to the SAS—that purports to measure the best that individuals are capable of becoming.

Richard and Jex (1991) supported the relationship between the SAS and low levels of trait anxiety, and high levels of optimism and self-esteem. However, their factor analysis sounded a cautionary note by uncovering the need for further work on the conceptual clarification of the difference between self-actualization and self-esteem. Incidentally, the work of McLeod and Vodanovich (1991), Flett, et al. (1991), Ebersole and Humphreys (1989), and Richard and Jex (1991) has additional importance because it supports the use of the SAS. Granted, all is not well. There are, for example, criticisms being directed toward the conceptual foundations of self-actualization (Richard & Jex, 1991).

Cognitive style might also be considered. As a matter of fact, Kirton and Hammond (1980) predicted a relationship specifically between self-actualization and an "adaptors" cognitive style. In their research, adaptors were defined using Kirton's own measure, which identifies "innovators" as well as adaptors. Adaptors were expected to have higher self-actualization scores than innovators because they are thought to "operate within consensually agreed paradigms . . . [and are] more willing to adhere to accepted modes of thought and behaviour that will mould their image of themselves and so are capable of higher self-actualization; the converse might be true of innovators" (Kirton & Hammond, 1980, p. 1321). Product moment analyses did not support the hypothesis; however, a bivariate plot suggested a nonlinear relationship wherein both innovators and adaptors had lower levels of reported self-actualization in comparison to the subjects scoring in the middle range. So again, cognitive style might be brought into predictive equation, along with creative attitudes, for a better prediction of self-actualization.

Not all creative people are self-actualized. There seems to be an association, but there is also evidence that creativity can be destructive. This is "the dark side of creativity" described by McLaren (1993) and Richards (1993). In addition to creative but destructive inventions and discoveries (e.g., thermonuclear weapons), there is the possibility of self-destruction, as in the case of suicide (Domino, 1988; Mraz & Runco, 1993) or alcoholism (Rothenberg, 1990, this volume).

Conclusion

In conclusion, the theories of Rogers (1961) and Maslow (1971) suggest that creativity and self-actualization are related, and the present study found this to be the case. The present results also support the construct validation of the SAS. This validation, combined with the simpler format of the SAS, encourage its use in a wider range of studies than would be the case for the POI or its successor, the *Personal Orientation Dimensions* test (Knapp & Knapp, 1978). Creativity also has many challenges to it, such as the measurement difficulties noted earlier, some of which will be considered in future research.

REFERENCES

Albert, R. S. (Ed.). (1983). *The social psychology of genius and eminence.* England: Pergamon.

Buckmaster L., & Davis G. (1985). ROSE: A measure of self-actualization and its relationship to creativity. *Journal of Creative Behavior, 19,* 30–37.

Burke, B. F., Chrisler, J. C., & Sloan, A. (1989). The creative thinking, environmental frustration, and self-concept of left- and right-handers. *Creativity Research Journal, 2,* 279–285.

Crandall, R., McCown, D. A., & Robb, Z. (1988). The effects of assertiveness training on self-actualization. *Small Group Behavior, 19,* 134–145.

Davis, G. A., & Subkoviak, M. J. (1975). Multidimensional analysis of a personality-based test of creative potential. *Journal of Educational Measurement, 12,* 37–43.

Domino, G. (1988). Attitudes toward suicide among highly creative college students. *Creativity Research Journal, 1,* 92–105.

Ebersole, P., & Humphreys, P. (1991). The short index of self-actualization and purpose in life. *Psychological Reports, 69,* 550.

Flett, G. L., Hewitt, P. L., Blankstein, K. R., & Mosher, S. W. (1991). Perfectionism, self-actualization, and personal adjustment. *Journal of Social Behavior and Personality, 6,* 147–160.

Gough, H., & Heilbrun, A. B. (1980). *Adjective Check List manual.* Consulting Psychologists Press.

Jones, A., & Crandall, R. (1986). Validation of a short index of self-actualization. *Personality and Social Psychology Bulletin, 12,* 63–73.

Kirton, M., & Hammond, S. (1980). Levels of self-actualization of adaptors and innovators. *Psychological Reports, 46,* 1321–1322.

Knapp, R. R., & Knapp, L. (1978). Conceptual and statistical refinement and extension of the measurement of actualizing: Concurrent validity of the Personal Orientation Dimensions. *Educational and Psychological Measurement, 38,* 523–526.

Maslow, A. H. (1968). *Toward a psychology of being* (2nd ed.). New York: Van Nostrand Reinhold

Maslow, A. H. (1971). *The farther reaches of human nature.* New York: Viking.

Mathes, E. W. (1978). Self-actualization, metavalues, and creativity. *Psychological Reports, 43,* 215–222.

McLaren, R. (1993). The dark side of creativity. *Creativity Research Journal, 6,* 137–144.

McLeod, C. R., & Vodanovich, S. J. (1991). The relationship between self-actualization and boredom proneness. *Journal of Social Behavior and Personality, 6,* 137–146.

Mraz, W., & Runco, M. A. (1993). Suicide ideation and creative problem solving. *Suicide and Life-Threatening Behavior, 24,* 38–47.

Murphy, J. P., Dauw, D. C., Harton, R. E., & Fredian, A. J. (1976). Self-actualization and creativity. *Journal of Creative Behavior, 10,* 39–44.

Nunnally, J. C. (1978). *Psychometric theory* (2nd ed.). New York: McGraw Hill.

Rhodes, C. (1990). Growth from deficiency to being creativity. *Creativity Research Journal, 3,* 287–299.

Richard, R. L., & Jex, S. M. (1991). Further evidence for the validity of the short index of self-actualization. *Journal of Social Behavior and Personality, 6,* 331–338.

Richards, R. (1990). Everyday creativity, eminent creativity, and health: Afterview for CRJ issues on creativity and health. *Creativity Research Journal, 3,* 300–326.

Richards, R. (1993). Seeing beyond: Issues of creative awareness and social responsibility. *Creativity Research Journal, 6,* 165–183.

Rizzo, R., & Vinacke, E. (1975). Self-actualization and the meaning of critical experience. *Journal of Humanistic Psychology, 15,* 19–30.

Rogers, C. R. (1961). *On becoming a person.* Boston, MA: Houghton Mifflin.

Rothenberg, A. (1990). Creativity, mental health, and alcoholism. *Creativity Research Journal, 3,* 179–201.

Rubenson, D. L., & Runco, M. A. (1992). The psychoeconomic approach to creativity. *New Ideas in Psychology 10,* 131–147.

Runco, M. A. (1990). Creativity and health. *Creativity Research Journal, 3,* 81–84.

Runco, M. A. (1994). Creativity and its discontents. In M. P. Shaw & M. A. Runco (Eds.), *Creativity and affect* (pp. 102–123). Norwood, NJ: Ablex.

Runco, M. A., & Bahleda, M. (1986). Implicit theories of artistic, scientific, and everyday creativity. *Journal of Creative Behavior, 20,* 93–98.

Runco, M. A., Okuda, S. M., & Thurston, B. J. (1987). The psychometric properties of four systems for scoring divergent thinking tests. *Journal of Psychoeducational Assessment, 2,* 149–156.

Schatz, E. M., & Buckmaster, L. (1984). Development of an instrument to measure self-actualizing growth in preadolescents. *Journal of Creative Behavior, 18,* 263–272.

Shostrom, E. L. (1963). *Personal Orientation Inventory.* San Diego, CA: Educational and Industrial Testing Service.

Chapter 16

Dual Brain, Creativity, and Health*

Klaus D. Hoppe
Neville L. Kyle

Since the epochal work on split brain patients conducted by Nobel Laureate Roger Sperry and his associates (Sperry, Gazzaniga, & Bogen, 1969), the importance of the specialized functions of the right and left cerebral hemispheres has been recognized, with applications to education (Bogen, 1975) and brain research (Benson & Zaidel, 1985). The contributions of Bogen and Bogen (1969, 1977, 1988) and the clinical findings of Hoppe (1977, 1978, 1988, 1989) demonstrate the importance of the corpus callosum for creativity. Before describing connections be-

*From "Dual Brain, Creativity, and Health, by K.D. Hoppe & N. L. Kyle, 1990, *Creativity Research Journal*, *3*(2), pp. 150–157. Copyright © 1995 Ablex Publishing Corporation. Adapted with permission.

tween the dual brain, creativity, and mental health, a short summary should be given regarding our own clinical and experimental studies.

CLINICAL OBSERVATIONS AND EXPERIMENTAL STUDY

Stimulated by the original findings of Sperry et al. (1969) and Bogen (1985), Hoppe (1977, 1978) interviewed 12 commissurotomy patients and found that their dreams lacked condensation, displacement, and symbolization; their fantasies were unimaginative, utilitarian, and tied to reality; and their symbolizations were concrete, discursive, and rigid. Hoppe and Bogen (1977) independently rated these 12 commissurotomy patients on six of the eight key items from the Beth Israel Hospital Psychosomatic Questionnaire (Sifneos, 1973) and found a high degree of alexithymia, especially a lack of fantasy and of appropriate words to describe feelings.

In order to evaluate these clinical observations, an experimental study was performed by TenHouten, Hoppe, Bogen, and Walter (1985a, 1985b, 1985c, 1985d, 1986; TenHouten, Walter, Hoppe, & Bogen, 1987, 1988). Eight cerebral commissurotomy patients were paired with eight normal control subjects matched for age, sex, ethnic and linguistic background, and handedness. The stimulus in the experiment was a film with the title "Memories: If Truncated in Mourning," which was intended to symbolize loss and death. In the first scene a baby plays in its crib, surrounded by dolls and teddy bears and, over its head, by a large rotating white bird with black eyes. Then the crib is empty; the death of the baby is symbolized by a slowing of the piano music ("Somewhere Over the Rainbow") and of the rotation of the white bird over the empty crib. In the second scene, a boy is swinging in a park, kicks his ball away, and chases it into the street. A car approaches, the ball is seen rolling into the street, and then the street and playground are shown empty. The death of the boy is symbolized by the slowing of the piano music ("Raindrops Keep Falling on my Head") and by the slowing, empty swing, while the camera zooms towards the shadow under the swing.

There are no spoken words in the film. The meaning of the film is conveyed by music and by visual images alone; the major events in it are shown not directly but symbolically. If the significant meanings of the symbols are grasped by the subject, it is likely that the film will evoke feelings of loss, sadness, separation, and death.

The film was shown individually to each subject four times. After the first showing of the film, the subjects were asked about their general impression; after the second, to write four sentences about the film; after the third, to answer a series of questions about major symbols in the film (e.g., the white bird or the shadow under the swing); and after the fourth showing, to express their feeling about the film.

In addition to the examination of spoken and written responses, EEG recordings were performed on each subject during the whole period of the experimental study by placing gold-cup electrodes over the left (F3) and right (F4) frontal, left (C3) and right (C4) central, left (P3) and right (P4) parietal, and left (T3) and right (T4) temporal scalp locations, using the 10-20 electrode placement system (TenHouten et al., 1987, 1988).

Summarizing the results of this experimental study, we found that commissurotomy patients, in comparison with normal controls, used significantly fewer affect-laden words, a higher percentage of auxiliary verbs, and applied adjectives sparsely revealing a speech that was dull, uninvolved, flat, and lacking in color and expressiveness. Commissurotomy patients tended not to fantasize about, imagine, or interpret the symbols, and they also tended to describe the circumstances surrounding events, as opposed to describing their own feelings about these events.

Commissurotomy patients symbolized in a discursive, logically articulate structure, using mainly a secondary process, as opposed to a presentational structure as an expression of a predominantly primary process. They also showed a concreteness of symbolization, emphasized low rather than creative capacity, lacked a summary of the whole gestalt, showed a relatively impoverished fantasy life, and tended not to be able to convey symbolic meanings. In other words, the quality of their symbolization emphasized stereotyped denotation as opposed to being flexible and rich in symbols, images, ideas, and connotations.

We also found that commissurotomy patients showed a significantly higher level of a complex of shame- and total-anxiety in combination with hostility directed both inward and outward. In contrast, mutilation-separation anxiety and death-separation anxiety were most characteristics of the normal subjects when confronted with our film.

Comparing alexithymia, manifested in seven commissurotomy patients and one control subject, with expressiveness in seven control subjects and one commissurotomy patient, we found the following results:

1. In alexithymic subjects, the right temporal area (T4) was less activated, suggesting an inadequate grasp of the significance of visual images and music of the film.
2. In alexithymic subjects, the two language areas of the left hemisphere (F3—Broca, and T3—Wernicke) were less activated, suggesting a possible lack of inner speech. In addition, the higher left parietal (P3) activation might be interpreted as an inhibition of conducting inner speech between the two language areas.
3. Alexithymic subjects showed a higher coherence between the

right frontal (F4) and left parietal (P3) areas, suggesting a possible inter-hemispheric aspect of inhibition of expression. In contrast, expressive subjects had a higher coherence level between the right frontal (F4) and left temporal (T3) areas, which suggests a possible mechanism facilitating the transformation of the affective understanding in the right hemisphere into the verbal expression of the left hemisphere.

With regard to the results of item analysis, factor analysis, discriminant function analysis, Gottschalk-Gleser content analysis, and EEG-spectra analysis, see the original *Alexithymia and Split Brain* papers (TenHouten et al., 1985a, 1985b, 1985c, 1985d, 1986; TenHouten et al., 1987, 1988).

DUAL BRAIN AND CREATIVITY

The results of the experimental study described above illuminate several aspects of creative ability. The surgical disconnection of transcallosal interhemispheric exchange and of any access or communication between the two hemispheres resulted in a lack of creativity in commissurotomy patients. Their dull, uninvolved, and flat speech was lacking in color and expressiveness, indicated by their significantly infrequent use of affect-laden words and adjectives. There was also a high percentage of auxiliary verbs, which conveys a passive and indirect presentation of the self, as well as a high percentage of incomplete sentences in which the subject was often left out. This lexical alexithymia makes it clear that alexithymia is probably opposed to creative ability. The sentential-level results underscore this phenomenon: If one cannot fantasize about, imagine, or interpret symbols, so richly presented in the film, and if one is only describing the circumstances surrounding events but not one's own feelings about these events, then one lacks creativity, as commissurotomy patients do.

According to Langer (1942), discursive symbolization is articulated and needs a secondary thought process (or reality principle [Freud 1911/1958]). Presentational symbolization represents a logic of feelings, as expressed in fine art, mystical experiences, or music, and exhibited primary process attributes, such as condensation and displacement. In expressive-creative people, the presentational symbolization and imagery in the right hemisphere are available to the left hemisphere via the corpus callosum. The transformational process of verbalizing presentational symbols was called *symbollexia* by Hoppe (1985, 1986). This is depicted in Figure 1b. Commissurotomy-split-brain patients lack symbollexia. Their predominantly discursive symbolization in the left hemisphere corresponds with the alexithymia of people who have not been operated on but function in a similar way (*functional commissurotomy*, Hoppe, 1977, 1978, 1984b, 1985).

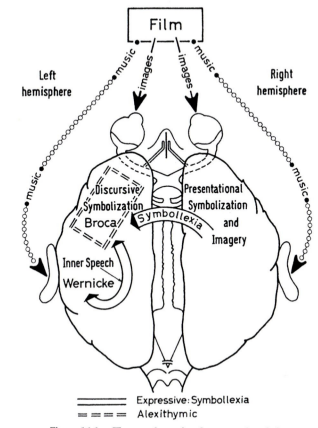

Figure 16.1. The transformational process of symbols

Creativity thus may depend in part on the transformational intercallosal process of symbollexia. The question remains: What facilitates the creative moment? What combines primary and secondary process to the "magic synthesis" of a "tertiary process" (Arieti, 1976)? By using Arthur Koestler's ingenious concept of bisociation (1964), we could call creativity a *hemispheric bisociation* (Hoppe, 1988, 1989). Whereas the left hemisphere follows the fixed set of rules, this code governs the matrix of an overwhelming possibility of choices expressed by the right hemisphere. The "magic synthesis" of the two cerebral planes is a creative process of hemispheric bisociation. As Koestler (1978) put it, "By living in both planes at once, the creative artist or scientist is able to catch an occasional glimpse of eternity looking through the window of time" (p. 146).

Interestingly, our EEG analysis supports this concept of hemispheric bisociation. Because the alexithymic person cannot fully grasp the significance of visual images and music of his right hemisphere, he or she is impeded in hemispheric bisociation and can only follow the fixed set of rules of his or her left hemisphere. The possible lack of inner speech between the two language centers of the left hemisphere further increases its fixed rules. In addition, the suggested interhemispheric inhibition of inner speech deprives the alexithymic person of the affective and symbolic understanding of his or her right hemisphere and thus from "looking through the window of time."

Hemispheric bisociation combines the view through the window of outside time (*erlebte Zeit* [Hoppe, 1978] or clock time [Loye, 1983]), registered in the left hemisphere, with the view through the window of inner time experience (*gelebte Zeit* [Hoppe, 1978] or spatial time [Loye, 1983]), experienced mainly in the right hemisphere. Hemispheric bisociation also makes use of homospatial and Janusian thinking (Rothenberg, 1979), which transcends space and time.

With regard to feelings, so much involved in creativity, it should be stressed that emotions, which are generated in the two closely linked limbic systems, are not simply lateralized to the right hemisphere. The cognitive representations of emotions (feelings and symbols) are also represented in both hemispheres. However, there exists experimental evidence suggesting that the right hemisphere plays a special role in perceptual judgment of a variety of affect-laden stimuli (see TenHouten et al., 1986). Bryden and Ley (1983) found that emotional stimuli are perceived more accurately when presented to the right hemisphere, which suggests that the right hemisphere has a special and prominent influence on the reception and expression of emotions.

In this context, the affects of anxiety and hostility—scored for the Gottschalk–Gleser content analysis scales (TenHouten et al., 1985d)— have to be considered with regard to creativity. The significantly higher level of the complex of shame- and total-anxiety in combination with hostility directed both inwardly and outwardly corresponds with superego-functions on a childhood level in commissurotomy patients (Hoppe, 1978). Their strict, punitive conscience directs hostility toward themselves; sometimes also in angry outbursts toward authority figures outside, and a fearful avoidance of sex and a submissive clinging to an external idealized figure indicate shame- and total-anxiety. Thus, the person who is restricted to the fixed set of rules of the left hemisphere and of early superego components cannot develop creativity, because he or she is deprived of symbollexia and of the access to symbolization and imagery of the right hemisphere. The individual can daydream about hostile revenge and sexual involvement (primary process) but is incapable of romantic or more elaborate and metaphoric fantasies.

In contrast, the expressive persons of our study verbalized mutilation-separation anxiety and death-separation anxiety due to their empathic identification and scenic understanding of the film. They were able to imagine the symbolically depicted death of the baby and the boy, to empathically experience pain, grief, and sorrow caused by it, and to express it creatively by being open to hemispheric bisociation. If we follow Bogen's (1975) speculation that "each hemisphere represents the other and the world in complementary mappings: the left mapping the self as a subset of the world, and the right mapping the world as a subset of the self" (p. 27), we appreciate the importance of our brain hemispheres for creativity. Open to the presentational matrix of self-asserting and self-transcending choices of the right hemisphere, combining it with the discursive power of the left hemisphere via symbollexia, we may experience our being in the world as an infinite act of creation.

CLINICAL APPLICATIONS

In a study by Hoppe and Kyle (1987), the "bilateral integration of cerebral function" was borne out of an experimental group of creative subjects. It was found, by comparison, that Catholic priests and non-priests in treatment tended to use right hemisphere approaches to problems more than creative subjects or normal priest-controls. This is in keeping with studies showing greater levels of anxiety and cognitive disruption among many pathology groups, that is, right-hemisphere disinhibition (Kyle, 1988). On the other hand, relatively *alexithymic* patients tended to draw more heavily on left-hemispheric functions. Although creative and control subjects indicated a more frequent use of left-brain-characteristics and coping strategies than patients in treatment, they also resorted to bilateral hemispheric usage more frequently than the patient group.

During the course of psychotherapy, according to their particular stage, our patients were asked to fill out the Brain/Mind Profile (Loye, 1983) and were subsequently informed about the results. This was followed by an attempt to work through marked imbalances between the two hemispheric styles and to stimulate more creative processes.

The realization of a predominant hemispheric style was not only helpful to patients but also useful to the understanding of the significant others in their lives. For example, a very creative female patient persistently complained about the lack of intellectual and emotional communication with her husband. After she had completed her profile, she took another home for her husband to fill out. The dramatic difference between her predominantly right-hemispheric profile and the predominantly left-hemispheric profile of her husband provided a basis for her understanding and tolerance for the different style of thinking, feeling, and communication between her and her spouse.

As mentioned above, presentational symbolization and imagery is closely linked with feelings. In contrast, exclusive discursive symbolization is prone to become arid, concrete, and rigid. Symbols are changed into signs that lose their emotional meaning and replace warm communications, vitality, and spontaneity. For example, one priest whose psychotherapy was described in detail (Hoppe, 1984a) was able to balance his right- and left-hemispheric thinking. By gaining insight and openness toward symbols and feelings, this patient was able to develop a vital balance between the cortical styles of his left and right hemispheres. He enjoyed his leisure time, the beauty of nature, and was living more according to his "inner time" experience. He developed communication with co-priests and parishioners and introduced symbolic elements into the church liturgy.

HEALTH AS A CORTICAL BALANCE

It is established that when we consider the "higher" intellectual functions of humans, including the capacity for synthesis, fantasy, and symbolization (i.e., their creativeness), some areas of the cortex may be demarcated (Arieti, 1976); however, the consensus also is that "the bilateral integration of cerebral function is most clearly exhibited by creative artists who typically enjoy intact brains" (Lezak, 1983, p. 63; see also Bogen, 1969). From a review of our own work and that of other investigators, it is clear that bilateral integration is also a central feature of mental health (Kyle, 1988). Conversely, it may be said that variations in lateralization result in variations in inhibitory and facilitative function of interhemispheric transcallosal communications as well as in the limbic and reticular formation. These are areas in which intentional and affective adaptive behavior are frequently involved. Several studies demonstrate the facilitative (or loss of left-inhibitory) effects from the right hemisphere when left-hemisphere damage occurs. These consist of over-arousal, anxiety, undue cautiousness, over-concern, over-sensitivity to impairment, and a tendency to exaggerate disabilities. By contrast, right-hemisphere lesions result in fewer self-dissatisfactions and may even show indifference or facetiousness toward difficulties and failures (Kolb & Taylor, 1981, p. 90).

It would appear, then, that decrements in callosal transmissions lead to decrements in emotional arousal and response. Damasio and Van Hoesen (1983) described patients with lesions of the right limbic frontal area, especially of the anterior cingulate gyrus, with "particularly lowered levels of emotional interest and drive to respond" (p. 94). Using the term coined by Hoppe (1977, 1978, 1984b, 1985), a *functional commissurotomy* may produce similar effects and is particularly likely when the lateralizing functions of the limbic-hypothalamus-reticular system are taken into account (Kyle, 1988). Under conditions of poor or absent transcallosal transformation, we would expect to see absent or deficient emotional responsiveness (i.e., a deficit of mental health). In contrast, expressive-empathic people represent their mental health via symbollexia and hemispheric bisociation, using fully the creative power of their dual brain.

REFERENCES

Arieti, S. (1976). *Creativity: The magic synthesis.* New York: Basic Books.

Benson, F., & Zaidel, E. (1985). *The dual brain: Hemispheric specialization in humans.* New York: Guilford.

Bogen, J. E. (1969). The other side of the brain: II. An appositional mind. *Bulletin of the Los Angeles Neurologic Society, 34,* 135–162.

Bogen, J. E. (1975). Some educational aspects of hemispheric specialization. *UCLA Educator, 17,* 24–32.

Bogen, J. E. (1985). The callosal syndromes. In P. M. Heilman & B. Valenstein (Eds.), *Clinical neuropsychology* (2nd ed., pp. 295–338). New York: Oxford University Press.

Bogen, J. E., & Bogen, G. M. (1969). The other side of the brain: III. The corpus callosum and creativity. *Bulletin of the Los Angeles Neurologic Society, 31,* 191–220.

Bogen, J. E., & Bogen, G. M. (1977, October). *Some further thoughts on the corpus callosum and creativity.* Seminar at the Chicago Institute for Psychoanalysis, Chicago.

Bogen, J. E., & Bogen, G. M. (1988). Creativity and the corpus callosum. In K. Hoppe (Ed.), *Hemispheric specialization* (pp. 293–301). Philadelphia, PA: W. B. Saunders.

Bryden, M. P., & Ley, R. G. (1983). Right-hemispheric involvement in the perception and expression of emotion in normal humans. In K. M. Heilman & P. Satz (Eds.), *Neuropsychology of human emotion* (pp.6–44). New York: Guilford.

Damasio, A. R., & Van Hoesen, G. W. (1983). Emotional disturbances associated with focal lesions of the limbic frontal lobe. In K. M. Heilman & P. Satz (Eds.), *Neuropsychology of human emotions* (pp. 85–110). New York: Guilford.

Freud, S. (1958). Formulations on the two principles on mental functioning. In J. Strachey (Ed. and Trans.), *The standard edition of the complete psychological works of Sigmund Freud* (Vol. 12, pp. 219–226). London: Hogarth. (Original work published 1911)

Hoppe, K. D. (1977). Split brains and psychoanalysis. *Psychoanalytic Quarterly, 46,* 220–224.

Hoppe, K. D. (1978). Split brain—Psychoanalytic findings and hypotheses. *Journal of American Academy of Psychoanalysis, 6,* 193–213.

Hoppe, K. D. (1984a). Psychoanalysis and Christian religion: Past views and new findings. *Bulletin of the National Guild of Catholic Psychiatrists, 30* 10–23.

Hoppe, K. D. (1984b). Severed ties. In S. A. Luel & P. Marcus (Eds.), *Psychoanalytic reflections on the holocaust: Selected essays* (pp. 94–111). New York: KATV, publishing house.

Hoppe, K. D. (1985). Mind and spirituality: Symbollexia, empathy and God-representation. *Bulletin of the National Guild of Catholic Psychiatrists, 31*, 10–23.

Hoppe, K. D. (1986). Dialogue of the future. In L. Robinson (Ed.), *Psychiatry and religion: Overlapping concerns* (pp. 120–132). Washington, DC: Monograph Series of American Psychiatric Press.

Hoppe, K. D. (1988). Hemispheric specialization and creativity. In K. Hoppe (Ed.), *Hemispheric specialization* (pp. 303–315). Philadelphia, PA: W. B. Saunders.

Hoppe, K. D. (1989). Psychoanalysis, hemispheric specialization, and creativity. *Journal of American Academy of Psychoanalysis, 17*, 253–269.

Hoppe, K. D., & Bogen, J. D. (1977). Alexithymia in twelve commissurotomized patients. *Psychotherapy-Psychosomatics, 28*, 148–155.

Hoppe, K. D., & Kyle, N. (1987). Hemispheric specialization and creativity in psychotherapy. In E. M. Stern (Ed.), *The psychotherapy patient* (Vol. 4, pp. 137–150). New York: Haworth.

Koestler, A. (1964). *The act of creation.* New York: Macmillan.

Koestler, A. (1978). *Janus.* New York: Random House.

Kolb, B., & Taylor, L. (1981). Affective behavior in patients with localized cortical excisions: Role of lesion site and side. *Science, 214*, 89–91.

Kyle, N. L. (1988). Emotions and hemispheric specialization. In K. Hoppe (Ed.), *Hemispheric specialization* (pp. 367–381). Philadelphia, PA: W. B. Saunders.

Langer, S. (1942). *Philosophy in a new key.* Cambridge, MA: Harvard University Press.

Lezak, M. D. (1983). *Neuropsychological assessment* (2nd ed.). Oxford: Oxford University Press.

Loye, D. (1983). *The sphinx and the rainbow.* Boulder, CO: Shambhala.

Rothenberg, A. (1979) *The emerging goddess.* Chicago: University of Chicago Press.

Rothenberg, A. (1990). Creativity, mental health, and alcoholism. *Creativity Research Journal, 3*, 179–201.

Sifneos, P. (1973). The prevalance of "alexithymic" characteristics in psychosomatic patients. *Psychotherapy-Psychosomatics, 22*, 255–263.

Sperry, R., Gazzaniga, M., & Bogen, J. (1969). Interhemispheric disconnection. In P. J. Vinken & G. W. Bruyen (Eds.), *Handbook of clinical neurology* (Vol. 4). Amsterdam: North Holland.

TenHouten, W., Hoppe, K., Bogen, J., & Walter, D. (1985a). Alexithymia and the split brain I: Lexical-level content analysis, *Psychotherapy-Psychosomatics, 43*, 202–208.

TenHouten, W., Hoppe, K., Bogen, J., & Walter, D. (1985b). Alexithymia and the split brain II: Sentential-level content analysis. *Psychotherapy-Psychosomatics, 44*, 1–5.

TenHouten, W., Hoppe, K. Bogen, J., & Walter, D. (1985c). Alexithymia and the split brain III: Global-level content analysis of fantasy and symbolization. *Pschotherapy-Psychosomatics, 44*, 89–94.

TenHouten, W., Hoppe, K., Bogen, J., & Walter, D. (1985d). Alexithymia and the split brain IV: Gottschalk-Gleser content analysis, *Psychotherapy-Psychosomatics, 44*, 113–121.

TenHouten, W., Hoppe, K., Bogen, J., & Walter, D. (1986). Alexithymia: An experimental study of cerebral commissurotomy patients and normal control subjects. *American Journal of Psychiatry, 143,* 312–316.

TenHouten, W., Walter, D., Hoppe, K., & Bogen, J. (1987). Alexithymia and the split brain V: EEG alpha-band interhemispheric coherence analysis. *Psychotherapy-Psychosomatics, 47,* 1–10.

TenHouten, W., Walter, D., Hoppe, K., & Bogen, J. (1988). Alexithymia and the split brain VI: Electroencephalographic correlates of alexithymia. In K. Hoppe (Ed.), *Hemispheric specialization* (pp. 317–329). Philadelphia, PA: W. B. Saunders.

Chapter 17

Disclosure of Traumas and Immune Function: Health Implications for Psychotherapy*

James W. Pennebaker
Janice K. Kiecolt-Glaser
Ronald Glaser

There is little doubt that psychotherapy reduces subjective distress and yields positive behavioral outcomes. In recent years, a small group of researchers has sought to learn whether psychotherapy can also reduce health problems. Two promising reviews have indicated that the use of

*We are indebted to Sondra Brumbelow, Steve Gordon, Jean Czajka, Kathleen Ferrara, Holly Williams, Hema Patel, Brad Richards, David Alexander, Richard Cole, and John Tiebout (at Southern Methodist University) and to Paula Ogrocki (at Ohio State University) for their help in conducting the research. Thanks are extended to Jonathon Brown and David Watson for comments on the manuscript.

Portions of this research were funded by National Science Foundation Grant BNS 8606764 and National Institutes of Health Grant HL32547 to James W. Pennebaker and by National Institute of Mental Health Grant MH40787 to Janice K. Kiecolt-Glaser and Ronald Glaser.

mental health services is associated with fewer medical visits, fewer days of hospitalization, and lower overall medical costs. In a summary of 15 studies published between 1965 and 1980, Mumford, Schlesinger, and Glass (1981) found that individuals who underwent psychotherapy evidenced a 13% decrease in medical utilization relative to nonpsychotherapy control subjects. Similarly, in a review of 13 studies of mental health services that were introduced into organizations, Jones and Vischi (1980) found that psychotherapy was associated with a 20% drop in medical utilization.

Although promising, these findings leave open the question of why medical use drops following psychotherapy. Kiesler (1983), for example, urged caution in blindly accepting a causal interpretation because we do not know if these effects generalize across practitioners and sites. Furthermore, individuals who seek psychotherapy in an organized health system, such as a Health Maintenance Organization (HMO), tend to be some of the highest users of the medical system (see also Tessler, Mechanic, & Diamond, 1976). Finally, these studies have not distinguished between actual health problems and unnecessary medical visits.

Ironically, in the fields of psychosomatics and health psychology, researchers have long known that psychological disturbance can lead to health problems. Alexander (1950), Selye (1976), and other pioneers have provided overwhelming evidence that psychological conflict, anxiety, and stress can cause or exacerbate disease processes. It follows that the reduction of conflict or stress should reduce illness.

An important predictor of illness is the way in which individuals cope with traumatic experiences. It has been well-documented that individuals who have suffered a major upheaval, such as the death of a spouse or a divorce, are more vulnerable to a variety of major and minor illnesses. However, the adverse effects of stress can be buffered by such things as a social support network (e.g., Cohen & Syme, 1985; Swann & Pridmore, 1985) and by a predisposition toward hardiness (Kobasa, 1982).

A common theme in the psychotherapy literature is that individuals tend to deal with trauma most effectively if they can understand and assimilate it. Indeed, Breuer and Freud (1895/1966), in their development of the cathartic method, emphasized the value of talking about the thoughts and feelings associated with upsetting events in the reduction of hysterical symptoms. To examine the links between confronting traumatic events and long-term health. Pennebaker and Beall (1986) asked healthy college students to write about either personally traumatic experiences or trivia topics for 4 consecutive days. Subjects who wrote about traumatic events were required to discuss either the relevant facts (trauma–fact condition), their feelings about the events (trauma–emotion), or both their thoughts and feelings (trauma–combination). In the months following the study, subjects in the trauma–combination condition visited the student health center for illness significantly less often than people in any of the other conditions.

Confronting a trauma may be beneficial from at least two perspectives. First, individuals no longer need to actively inhibit or hold back their thoughts and feelings from others. Indeed, several studies have indicated that actively inhibiting ongoing behavior is associated with both short-term autonomic activity (cf. Fowles, 1980; Gray, 1975) and long-term stress-related disease (Pennebaker & Susman, 1988). Confronting a trauma, then, may reduce the long-term work of inhibition. Second, by confronting the trauma, individuals may assimilate, reframe, or find meaning in the event (Horowitz, 1976; Meichenbaum, 1977; Silver, Boon, & Stones, 1983).

A major problem in evaluating the health effects of confronting a trauma is that most measures are relatively subjective or are susceptible to demand characteristics, such as self-reported symptoms or physician visits. Furthermore, studies such as these fail to identify the underlying mechanisms that influence health. Recent research in psychoneuroimmunology has indicated that the central nervous system can directly influence the functioning of the immune system. For example, the psychological stress associated with exams, loneliness, and divorce can lead to adverse immunological changes (e.g., Bartrop, Luckhurst, Lazarus, Kiloh, & Penny, 1977; F. Cohen, 1980; Kiecolt-Glaser, Garner, Speicher, Penn, & Glaser, 1984; Kiecolt-Glaser et al., 1987). Similarly, relaxation interventions can enhance some aspects of immunocompetence (Kiecolt-Glaser et al., 1985).

Although there is no single, general measure of immune function, many psychoimmunological studies have examined the lymphocyte (white blood cell) response to stimulation by substances foreign to the body, called *mitogens*. *Blastogenesis*, the measurement of the proliferation of lymphocytes in response to stimulation, is thought to provide an in vitro model of the body's response to challenge by infectious agents, such as bacteria or viruses. Because different mitogens stimulate different subpopulations of lymphocytes, two types of mitogens—phytohemagglutinin (PHA) and concanavalin A (ConA)—were used. Both PHA and ConA stimulate the proliferation of T-lymphocytes. Whereas PHA stimulates the proliferation of helper cells, ConA stimulates both helper and suppressor T-cells (e.g., Ader, 1981; Glaser et al., 1985; Reinherz & Schlossman, 1980).

The present project examined the effects of writing about a traumatic experience on immunological function and on other measures of distress. We predicted that individuals assigned to write about traumatic experience would demonstrate a heightened proliferative response to PHA and ConA assays relative to control subjects who merely wrote about superficial topics.

METHOD

Overview

Fifty healthy undergraduates were randomly assigned to write about either personal traumatic events or trivial topics for 20 min on each of 4 consecutive days. Lymphocytes, which were prepared from blood samples obtained the day before, the last day, and 6 weeks after writing, were assayed for their blastogenic response to PHA and ConA. Health center illness records, self-reports, autonomic measures, and individual difference measures were collected before and during the experiment.

Subjects

Thirty-six women and 14 men who were enrolled in undergraduate psychology courses participated as part of an extra-credit class option. Prior to agreeing to participate, all subjects were told that the experiment might require that they write about extremely personal material and that they have their blood drawn. All subjects participated in the pretest and in the 4 writing days. Two subjects missed the 6-week followup blood draw. Two subjects' immunological data were excluded from the analyses: 1 for taking cortisone, the other for pregnancy. In addition, three blood samples for the second draw and one for the third draw were lost during the assaying process.

Procedure

The day prior to the actual writing, subjects met as a group and completed a battery of questionnaires. During the session and after sitting quietly for at least 10 min, subjects' blood pressure levels, heart rates, and skin conductance levels were measured. At assigned times, subjects were escorted to the adjacent Student Health Center building where blood was drawn by the nursing staff. After the blood was drawn and all questionnaires were completed, subjects met individually with the first experimenter, who randomly assigned them to conditions with the provision that an equal ratio of men to women be in each of the two conditions. All subjects were told that they would be required to write about specific topics on each of the following 4 days. Subjects in the trauma condition were informed as follows:

> During each of the four writing days, I want you to write about the most traumatic and upsetting experiences of your entire life. You can write on

different topics each day or on the same topic for all four days. The important thing is that you write about your deepest thoughts and feelings. Ideally, whatever you write about should deal with an event or experience that you have not talked with others about in detail.

Those in the no-trauma condition were informed that they would be asked to write on an assigned topic during each of the 4 writing days. The experimenter emphasized that subjects were to describe specific objects or events in detail without discussing their own thoughts or feelings.

On each of the 4 writing days, subjects first met individually with the first experimenter, who reiterated the instructions. For subjects in the no-trauma cell, the specific writing topic was assigned. Depending on the day of the study, subjects were variously asked to describe their activities during the day, the most recent social event that they attended, the shoes they were wearing, or their plans for the remainder of the day. Each day, subjects were escorted to individual private rooms by an experimenter blind to condition, where they were given 20 min to write on their assigned topics. Immediately before and after writing, subjects completed a brief questionnaire that assessed their moods and physical symptoms. After writing only, subjects evaluated their day's essay. The questionnaires and writing samples were stapled and deposited in a large box by the subjects as they left.

After writing on the 4th day, blood pressure, heart rate, and skin conductance were measured before subjects went to the health center for the second blood draw. After the draw, subjects completed a brief questionnaire. Six weeks later, subjects returned to the health center, where autonomic levels and blood samples were collected for a third time. Subjects completed a postexperimental questionnaire and were extensively debriefed about the experiment.

At the conclusion of the study, the health center provided data regarding the number of visits each student had made for illness for the 5 months prior to the study and for the 6 weeks of the study. Approximately 3 months after the writing phase of the study, all subjects were mailed a final questionnaire in order to assess the possible long-term effects of the experiment. The long-term follow-up questionnaire included items assessing subjective distress and daily habits (e.g., smoking and exercise patterns) that had been completed earlier in the study. Of the 50 subjects, 2 did not receive the questionnaire (due to incorrectly listed mailing addresses) and 4 failed to return the questionnaire. All subjects were mailed a follow-up letter that provided the study's outcome, their own immune data, and interpretation of these data. All essays, physiological data, and self-reports included only subject numbers. Immune assays were collected, performed, and analyzed blind to condition.

Immune Assays

In the study, each subject's blood was drawn at the same time each day to control for possible diurnal variations. For each blood draw, whole blood treated with ethylenediominetetra-acetic acid (EDTA) to prevent clotting was collected from each subject. The blood samples were sent to the laboratory the following morning and assayed for their ability to respond to PHA and ConA (Kiecolt-Glaser et al., 1984). Lymphocytes were separated from whole blood samples on Hypaque-Ficall gradients.

The PHA and ConA were used at three different concentrations: 5, 10, and 20 *µg/ml for PHA and 2, 5, and 10* µg/ml for ConA. Each assay was performed in triplicate. Complete medium was used for baseline controls. One tenth milliliter of mitogen was added to 1×10^6 lymphocyte (in 0.1 ml medium) in 96 well plates and was incubated at 37 °C for 48 hr. Fifty microliters of tritiated thymidine (10 μCi/ml, specific activity 82 Ci/mM) were added to each well and the plates were incubated at 37 °C for 4 hr. Cells were harvested into GF11A filters. Radioactivity was measured using a Beckman LS7000 scintillation counter. The mean stimulation value (expressed in counts per minute) was subtracted from the control value and transformed to log (base 10).

RESULTS

Three general classes of data were collected: evaluations of and responses to the essays, long-term effects of the experiment, and individual differences mediating responses to the essays. Each will be discussed separately.

Parameters of Essay Writing

Subjects disclosed highly personal and upsetting experiences in the trauma condition. Overall, the primary topics of the essays were coming to college (19%), with 10% focusing on the loss and loneliness associated with leaving home; conflicts associated with members of the opposite sex (15%); parental problems (14%), including divorce (6%), family quarrels (6%), and family violence (2%); death (13%) of either a relative (6%), friend (4%), or pet (3%); injury or illness (12%), including eating disorders (4%), car accidents (4%), alcohol/drug abuse (2%), or other causes; sexual abuse (9%) by family member (4%) or stranger (5%); serious thoughts of suicide (6%); public humiliation (5%), such as learning that others suspected the subject of homosexuality; and miscellaneous concerns about religion (4%) and the meaning of life (3%).

Two independent judges rated each essay for the degree to which the content was personal, using a 7-point unipolar scale on which 7 = *personal.* Interjudge correlations across essays averaged .89. In addition, objective parameters of each essay were tabulated, including the total number of words, number of self-references (I, me, my, mine), and number of emotion words. An overall multivariate analysis of variance (MANOVA) was initially computed on the objective and self-ratings of the essays. As expected, a highly significant condition effect was obtained, $F(9, 40) = 72.31$, $p < .01$. As can be seen in Table 17.1, simple one-way analyses of variance (ANOVAs) indicated that trauma subjects' essays were rated as more personal than those of control subjects, $F(1, 48) = 215.94$, $p < .01$. Finally, relative to control subjects, trauma subjects wrote more words and included more self-references and more emotion words (every $p \leq .01$) on each essay.

After completing each writing session, subjects rated how personal they considered their essay to be, the degree to which they revealed emotions in their essay, and the degree to which they had previously held back telling others about the subject covered in their essay. Subjects rated each question along a 7-point unipolar scale on which 7 = *a great deal.* Averaging across the 4 days of writing, subjects in the trauma group considered their essays to be far more personal, $F(1, 48) = 279.89$, $p < .01$, and re-

Table 17.1. Parameters and Responses to Essays

	Condition	
	Trauma	*Control*
Variable	*(n = 25)*	*(n = 25)*
Essay parameter		
No. words/essay	465.8	388.8
No. self-references/essay	46.8	30.2
No. emotion words/essay	11.7	0.6
Personal rating	4.69	1.08
Self-report essay rating		
Personal	5.87	2.14
Revealing of emotions	5.18	1.34
Previously held back	4.58	1.52
Response to essay		
Physical symptoms		
Before writing	12.3	12.2
After writing	15.4	11.4
Negative moods		
Before writing	13.4	13.1
After writing	17.8	11.4

Note. Means for the two groups were all significantly different ($p \leq .01$) except for ratings of symptoms and moods before writing.

vealing of their emotions, $F(1, 48) = 266.73$, $p < .01$, than those in the control group As depicted in Table 17.1, subjects in the trauma group wrote about topics that they had previously held back from telling others relative to those in the control group, $F(1, 48) = 73.80$, $p < .01$.

Each day, immediately before and after writing, subjects completed a brief questionnaire assessing the degree to which they felt each of eight common physical symptoms (e.g., headache, pounding heart, tense muscles) and six negative moods (e.g., frustrated, guilty, depressed). The self-report items were summed to yield separate physical symptom and mood scales. The two scales were subjected to separate $2 \times 2 \times 4$ (Condition $\times$ Time [before vs. after writing] $\times$ Day) repeated-measures ANOVAs. Contrary to a simplistic catharsis or venting view, subjects in the trauma group reported higher levels of physical symptoms and negative moods following the writing compared with the control subjects. Significant Condition $\times$ Time interactions emerged for both symptoms, $F(1, 48) = 37.21$, $p < .001$, and negative moods, $F(1, 48) = 61.27$, $p < .001$. Although significant main effects for condition and time for the negative moods were obtained (each $p < .01$), these effects were attributable to the interaction. No other effects attained significance.

Long-Term Effects of Essay Writing

Four types of data assessed the long-term effects of disclosing traumatic experiences; mitogen responses, health center visits, self-reports of subjective distress, and autonomic changes. The immune, subjective distress, and autonomic data were collected the day before the experiment began (and before assignment to condition was made), approximately 1 hr after the final writing sample was collected, and 6 weeks after the conclusion of the writing portion of the study.

Immunological data

The blastogenic data for PHA and ConA stimulation were analyzed separately. A $2 \times 3 \times 3$ (Condition $\times$ Day $\times$ Concentration [of mitogen; 5, 10, and 20 $\mu g/ml$]) repeated-measures ANOVA was computed on the PHA data. Significant effects emerged for day, $F(2, 80) = 79.10$ $p < .001$, concentration, $F(2, 80) = 29.94$, $p < .001$, and Concentration $\times$ Day interaction, $F(4, 160) = 5.25$, $p = .001$. Most important, however, was the emergence of the Condition $\times$ Day interaction $F(2, 80) = 3.36$ $p = .04$, indicating that trauma subjects demonstrated an overall higher mitogen response following baseline in comparison with control subjects.

The writing phase of the experiment took place during the first week of February immediately prior to midterm exams. According to annual health center records, this period is marked by one of the highest illness rates of the entire school year. The follow-up blood draw, 6 weeks later, took place 4 days before the school's spring break vacation, a time when the incidence of illness visits is much lower. In short, the highly significant increase in immune response for the follow-up period may reflect, in part, both normal seasonal variation and normal fluctuations in the mitogen stimulation assays.

The ConA data, which were only available from the first two blood draws (due to a problem with the ConA preparation), were subjected to a 2 × 2 × 3 (Condition × Day × Concentration [mitogen stimulation level]) ANOVA. As with the PHA findings, significant day, concentration, and Day × Concentration effects emerged (each $p \leq .01$). Although it occurred in the same direction as the PHA means, the Condition × Day interaction did not attain significance, $F(1, 43) = 2.03$, $p = .16$. No other effects approached significance.

Health center data

The number of health center visits for illness were tabulated by the student health center over two time periods: from the beginning of the school year until the beginning of the study (covering a 4-month interval) and from the beginning of the study until the debriefing period (a 6-week interval). The number of health center visits was adjusted to reflect visits per month and was subjected to a 2 × 2 (Condition × Time) ANOVA.

Consistent with the Pennebaker and Beall (1986) findings, a significant Condition × Time interaction emerged for health center visits for illness, $F(1, 48) = 4.20$, $p < .05$. As depicted in Figure 17.1, trauma subjects evidenced a drop in visits relative to control subjects. No other effects

Table 17.2. Mean Lymphocyte Response to PHA Stimulation Over Sample Points in Counts per Minute, Log_{10}

Group	5 μg/culture	10 μg/culture	20 μg/culture
Trauma ($n = 20$)			
Before writing	4.93	4.99	4.90
After writing	4.96	5.00	4.94
6-week follow-up	5.43	5.42	5.34
Control ($n = 22$)			
Before writing	5.01	5.07	4.97
After writing	4.82	4.88	4.81
6-week follow-up	5.37	5.39	5.30

Note. PHA = phytohemagglutinin. Higher numbers reflect greater lymphocyte response. The writing period took place during the first week of February. Average standard deviation within mitogen concentration levels was .260 for the trauma group and .262 for the control group.

attained significance. As with the immune data, it is important to note that the apparent increase in illness visits for the control group probably reflects normal seasonal illness rates during the month of February.

Subjective distress

Questionnaires pertaining to the effects of the experiment were completed 1 hr after the last writing session, 6 weeks later prior to the final blood draw, and again at the end of the semester approximately 3 months after the writing phase of the study. Two general types of information were included on the questionnaires. The first included subjects' general attitudes about the experiment. The second focused on the health-related behaviors that had changed since the experiment.

Although the experiment was associated initially with some negative feelings among the trauma subjects, they were significantly happier than control subjects at the 3-month follow-up, $t(42) = 2.09$, $p < .05$. In response to the question, "Looking back on this experiment, to what degree has this experiment been valuable or meaningful for you?" trauma subjects were far more positive than control subjects, $t(42) = 4.50$, $p < .001$ (on a 7-point scale on which 7 = *a great deal*, trauma mean = 4.35, control mean = 2.33). Whereas subjects in the trauma group reported feeling more depressed than control subjects on the last day of writing, $t(48) = 2.81$, $p < .01$ (trauma mean = 3.80, control mean = 2.68), this difference disappeared by the follow-up questionnaire, $t = .09$ (trauma mean = 2.70, control mean = 2.67). No other simple effects attained significance.

A series of repeated-measures ANOVAs were computed on questions assessing the following health-related behaviors: cigarettes smoked per day, caffeinated and alcoholic beverages consumed per day, aspirin and sleeping pill use, and hours of strenuous exercise per week. No significant main effects or interactions approached significance. In short, the experiment did not appear to influence long-term behavior.

Other relevant data

Resting levels of systolic and diastolic blood pressure, heart rate, and skin conductance level were measured approximately 1 hr prior to each of the three blood draws. Repeated-measures ANOVAs on each autonomic index yielded no significant effects.

Finally, simple correlations were computed between changes in immune response and changes in health center visits and autonomic levels from the first to the final day of the study. Although PHA and ConA changes over the first 5 days of the study were correlated with each other, $r(43) = .88$, $p < .01$, changes in PHA and ConA were unrelated to all other variables. Similarly, changes in illness visits were unrelated to autonomic levels.

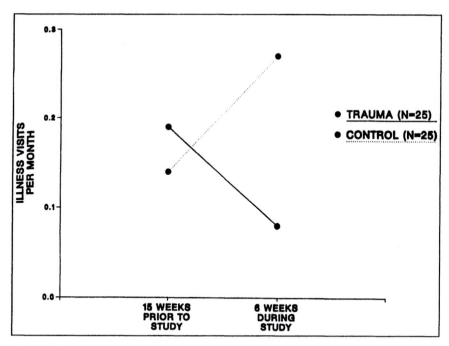

Figure 17.1.   Mean health center illness visits for the periods before and during the experiment. (Note that the standard deviation for visits per month ranged from .12 to .40, averaging .26 over the four observations.)

Who Benefits Most: Exploring Individual Differences

Do all individuals who write about a traumatic experience benefit equally? We have argued here and elsewhere (cf. Pennebaker, Hughes, & O'Heeron, 1987) that the failure to confront traumatic experience is stressful. A significant form of stress is associated with the work of inhibiting or actively holding back the disclosure of important traumas. All participants in the present study rated the degree to which they had written about an event that they had "actively held back in discussing with others" after each writing session. According to our conception, those individuals in the trauma condition who had addressed issues that they had previously held back should have benefited most.

To test this idea, subjects in the trauma condition were split at the median into two groups based on their mean response to the actively-holding-back question. Those who reported that they had written about topics that they had previously held back were labeled high disclosers (*n* = 11) and the remainder were labeled low disclosers (*n* = 14). A series of

ANOVAs was computed on the primary variables of interest using the three groups (trauma, high discloser; trauma, low discloser; control) as the between-subjects factor. Contrasts using the mean square error term compared high versus low disclosers.

Overall, high disclosers wrote significantly more words, $t(48)$ = 3.53, $p < .01$ (high mean = 505.3, low mean = 435.5) on each essay than low disclosers. Although high disclosers reported that their essays were more personal than low disclosers, $t(48)$ = 2.94, $p < .05$ (M = 6.13 vs. 5.68, respectively), independent judges rated the two groups equivalently, $t < 1.0$. No other significant essay characteristics emerged that separated high and low disclosers.

More interesting were the physiological correlates of disclosure. Analyses of the immune data indicated that, overall, high disclosers had a marginally higher response to PHA stimulation than low disclosers, $t(39)$ = 1.96, $p = .06$ (high mean = 5.18, low mean = 5.00). An ANOVA on the ConA data, on the other hand, yielded a significant Condition × Day × Concentration interaction, $F(4, 84)$ = 2.99, $p = .02$. As can be seen in Figure 17.2, high disclosers demonstrated an improved mitogen response across all mitogen concentrations relative to low disclosers and control subjects from before the study to the last day of writing (recall that follow-up ConA data were lost). No other interactions with the discloser variable attained significance for either PHA or ConA.

Although there were no initial differences in autonomic levels as a function of type of discloser or condition prior to the study, repeated-

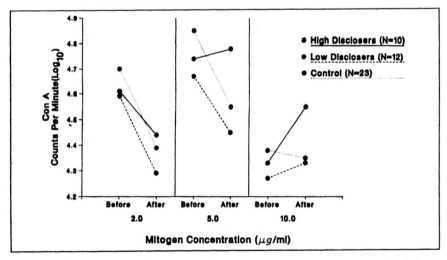

Figure 17.2.   Lymphocyte response to three levels of concanavalin A (Con A) stimulation before and after the writing sessions.

measures ANOVAs yielded Condition × Day effects for systolic blood pressure, $F(4, 84) = 2.68$, $p < .05$, and a marginal effect for heart rate, $F(4, 84) = 1.97$, $p = .10$. Indeed, from the beginning of the study to follow-up, high disclosers showed a greater decline than low disclosers in both systolic blood pressure, $t(44) = 3.42$ $p < .01$ (change from before study to follow-up: high disclosers = −5.8 mm/hg, low disclosers = 1.0 mm/hg). Similar nonsignificant trends were found for heart rate (high disclosers = −1.2 beats per minute, low disclosers = 1.1) and skin conductance (high disclosers = −2.6 μmhos, low disclosers = 0.3).

DISCUSSION

The results indicate that writing about traumatic experience has positive effects on the blastogenic response of T-lymphocytes to two mitogens, on autonomic levels, on health center use, and on subjective distress. The results are important in (a) supporting an inhibitory model of psychosomatics, (b) pointing to the effectiveness of using writing as a general preventive therapy, and (c) promoting an awareness that psychotherapy can bring about direct and cost-effective improvements in health.

Within psychology, it has been generally accepted that stress can increase the incidence of illness. We have proposed that one form of stress is associated with the failure to confront traumatic experience. Specifically, the inhibition or active holding back of thoughts, emotions, or behaviors is associated with physical work that, over time, can become manifested in disease. The present study supports this idea. Individuals who are forced to confront upsetting experiences in their lives show improvements in physical health relative to control subjects. More important, in our study the individuals who showed the greatest health improvements were those who wrote about topics that they had actively held back from telling others.

One important remaining question concerns the specific dimensions of writing that actively promote health. Based on previous work (e.g., Pennebaker & O'Heeron, 1984; Wegner, 1988), we believe that the failure to confront a trauma forces the person to live with it in an unresolved manner. Indeed, not disclosing a recent trauma such as the death of a spouse is associated with increased obsessions about the spouse. It follows, then, that actively confronting a trauma allows for the understanding and assimilation of that trauma.

In the present study, for example, several subjects who wrote about the same traumas day after day gradually changed their perspectives. One woman, who had been molested at the age of 9 years by a boy 3 years older, initially emphasized her feelings of embarrassment and guilt. By the third day of writing, she expressed anger at the boy who had victimized her. By the last day, she had begun to put it in perspective. On the follow-up survey 6 weeks after the experiment, she reported, "Before, when I thought about it, I'd lie to myself. . . . Now, I don't feel like I even have to think about it because I got it off my chest. I finally admitted that it happened. . . . I really know the truth and won't have to lie to myself anymore."

Clinical psychologists within the cognitive and psychodynamic traditions are currently addressing some of the processes underlying this confrontational strategy (Horowitz, 1976; Meichenbaum, 1977). Through writing or talking about an upsetting experience, the person can come to understand the causes and effects of the trauma better, which may ultimately eliminate the need for inhibition.

Although some therapists have asserted the value of writing about one's problems, such as in bibliotherapy (cf. Lazarus, 1984), very little systematic work has been done on it. Within the context of the present study, psychologically healthy individuals were initially upset about disclosing personal and upsetting experiences. That is, immediately after writing, trauma subjects reported more physical symptoms and negative moods. Writing about traumas, then, appears to be painful in the short run. Indeed, in a recent study by Lamnin and Murray (1987) comparing a writing therapy with a client-centered approach, clients were found to be more depressed immediately after each writing session than after a live therapy session.

There are clear disadvantages as well as advantages to writing versus talking with another person about traumas. Writing about intensely personal experiences does not allow for an objective outside opinion, support from others, or objective coping information. Alternatively, writing is tremendously cost-effective, allows people to confront traumas at their own rates, and encourages them to devise their own meaning and solutions to their problems. Above all, writing may provide an alternative form of preventive therapy that can be valuable for individuals who otherwise would not enter therapy.

Previous archival studies have indicated that medical use decreases once psychotherapy begins (e.g., Mumford, et al., 1981). Although encouraging, meta-analyses such as these have not been able to pinpoint the direct causal mechanisms. The present study offers experimental evidence linking the confronting of traumas with health improvement. Obviously, we have only examined the responses of a psychologically healthy population. Nevertheless, the present findings, along with those from conceptually similar experiments (e.g., Pennebaker & Beall, 1986), suggest that the disclosure of traumas is simultaneously associated with improvement in certain aspects of immune function and physical health.

REFERENCES

Ader, R. (1981), *Psychoneuroimmunology.* New York: Academic Press.

Alexander, F. (1950). *Psychosomatic medicine.* New York: Norton.

Bartrop, R. W., Luckhurst, E., Lazarus, L., Kiloh, L. G., & Penny, R. (1977). Depressed lymphocyte function after bereavement. *Lancet, 1,* 834–836.

Breuer, J., & Freud, S. (1966), *Studies on hysteria.* New York: Avon. (Original work published 1895)

Cohen, F. (1980). Personality, stress, and the development of physical illness. In G. C. Stone, F. Cohen, & N. E. Adler (Eds.), *Health psychology* (pp. 77–111). San Francisco: Jossey-Bass.

Cohen, S., & Syme, S. (Eds.). (1985). *Social support and health.* Orlando, FL: Academic Press.

Fowles, D. C. (1980). The three arousal model: Implications of Gray's two-factor theory for heart rate, electrodermal activity, and psychopathy. *Psychophysiology, 17,* 87–104.

Glaser, R., Kiecolt-Glaser, J. K., Stout, J. C., Tarr, K. L., Speicher, C. E., & Holliday, J. E. (1985). Stress-related impairments in cellular immunity. *Psychiatric Research, 16,* 233–239.

Gray, J. (1975). *Elements of a two-process theory of learning.* New York: Academic Press.

Horowitz, M. J. (1976). *Stress response syndromes.* New York: Jacob Aronson.

Jones, K., & Vischi, T. (1980). Impact of alcohol, drug abuse and mental health treatment on medical care utilization: A review of the literature. *Medical Care, 17* (Suppl. 2), 1–82.

Kiecolt-Glaser, J. K., Fisher, L., Ogrocki, P., Stout, J. C., Speicher, C. E., & Glaser, R. (1987). Marital quality, marital disruption, and immune function. *Psychosomatic Medicine, 49,* 13–34.

Kiecolt-Glaser, J. K., Garner, W., Speicher, C., Penn, G., & Glaser, R. (1984). Psychosocial modifiers of immunocompetence in medical students. *Psychosomatic Medicine, 46,* 7–14.

Kiecolt-Glaser, J. K., Glaser R., Williger, D., Stout, J., Messick, G., Sheppard, S., Ricker, D., Romisher, S. C., Briner, W., Bonnell, G., & Donnerberg, R. (1985). Psychosocial enhancement of immunocompetence in a geriatric population. *Health Psychology, 4,* 25–41.

Kiesler, C. A. (1983). Psychology and mental health policy. In M. Hersen, A. E. Kazdin, & A. S. Bellack (Eds.), *The clinical psychology handbook* (pp. 63–82). New York: Pergamon Press.

Kobasa, S. (1982). The hardy personality: Toward a social psychology of stress and health. In G. S. Sanders & J. Suls (Eds.), *Social psychology of health and illness* (pp. 3–32). Hillsdale, NJ: Erlbaum.

Lamnin, A. D., & Murray, E. (1987). *Catharsis versus psychotherapy.* Unpublished manuscript, University of Miami.

Lazarus, A. A. (1984). Multimodal therapy. In R. J. Corsini (Ed.), *Current psychotherapies* (3rd Ed., pp. 491–530). Itasca, IL: Peacock.

Meichenbaum, D. H. (1977). *Cognitive-behavior modification: An integrative approach.* New York: Plenum Press.

Mumford, E., Schlesinger, H. J., & Glass, G. V. (1981). Reducing medical costs through mental health treatment: Research problems and recommendations. In A. Broskowski, E. Marks, & S. H. Budman (Eds.), *Linking health and mental health* (pp. 257–273). Beverly Hills, CA: Sage.

Pennebaker, J. W., & Beall, S. (1986). Confronting a traumatic event: Toward an understanding of inhibition and disease. *Journal of Abnormal Psychology, 95,* 274–281.

Pennebaker, J. W., Hughes, C., & O'Heeron, R. C. (1987). The psychophysiology of confession: Linking inhibitory and psychosomatic processes. *Journal of Personality and social Psychology, 52,* 781–793.

Pennebaker, J. W., & O'Heeron, R. C. (1984). Confiding in others and illness rate among spouses of suicide and accidental death victims. *Journal of Abnormal Psychology, 93,* 473–476.

Pennebaker, J. W., & Susman, J. R. (1988). Disclosure of traumas and psychosomatic processes. *Social Science and Medicine.*

Reinherz, E. L., & Schlossman, S. F. (1980). Current concepts in immunology: Regulation of the immune response—Inducer and suppressor T-lymphocyte subsets in human beings. *New England Journal of Medicine, 303,* 370–373.

Selye, H. (1976). *The stress of life.* New York: McGraw-Hill.

Silver, R. L., Boon, C., & Stones, M. H. (1983). Searching for meaning in misfortune: Making sense of incest. *Journal of Social Issues, 39,* 81–102.

Swann, W. B., & Pridmore, S. C. (1985). Intimates as agents of social support: Sources of consolation or despair? *Journal of Personality and Social Psychology, 49,* 1609–1617.

Tessler, R., Mechanic, D., & Diamond, M. (1976). The effect of psychological distress on physician utilization. *Journal of Health and Social Behavior, 17,* 353–364.

Wegner, D. M. (1988). Stress and mental control. In S. Fisher & J. Reason (Eds.), *Handbook of life stress, cognition, and health* (pp. 685–699). London: Wiley.

Chapter 18

The Creative Thinking and Ego Functioning of Children

Stephanie Z. Dudek
Rene Verreault

An objective study of creative process requires that it be observed as the product is being created, over the time period devoted to its completion. Getzels and Csikzentmihalyi (1976) attempted to do this in their work with art students. They set up a still life situation and observed students as they arranged and rearranged objects prior to beginning drawing or painting. Getzels and Csikzentmihalyi labeled the initial process *problem finding*. The quality of the finished products, evaluated by a jury of artists, was highly correlated with the degree to which the students worked at restructuring the original still life. Photographs of the work in progress revealed a variety of procedures, varying from student to student.

Aside from direct observation of a creative process over time, there are at least two ways of studying its traces: (a) via creativity tests, and (b) via projective type material (e.g., Rorschach, TAT, literary products). Each approach requires that a mini-creative situation be set up from which a mini-creative product can emerge. When the stimulus consists of unstructured material, there are no obviously correct responses and the examinee is free to create something personal, and possibly unique. The product may be described as a *creative response* in the face of an externally presented problem. In the case of projective material, the "shape" of the response reveals also the process that gives it its specific form. In such a task, we are dealing with the externalized products of the initial phase of creativity. The projected contents and their verbalized justifications can only offer vague clues as to the possible further transformations that can follow the initial phase. These clues reside in the types of manipulation that the ego uses in its modulation of drive and imaginative energy (i.e., in its construction of a final acceptable form, whether verbal or figural). There is no guarantee that the final form will succeed in achieving the status of a fully creative product. Not all "created" products—even by persons of significant talent—are great works of art or science, but the process does not differ (Patrick, 1937).

THEORETICAL APPROACH

The goal of the present study is to gain a better understanding of how drive energy may be transformed into products that are identified as creative. Our approach to this problem makes use of *regression in the service of the ego* (Kris, 1952), in which the sources, or raw material, of creative production are crude untransformed drive affects. The contents of these affects are coded central nervous system representations of lived and felt experience. They emerge symbolically in the form of primary process ideation. This is a drive laden, pleasure-oriented, analogical mode of thinking. It is characterized by condensation, symbolisation, contradiction, and so on—forms of thinking that have no concern for reality. Primary process, expressed in verbal or figural form, offers evidence of drive affect to the extent that "drive material enters in a thematic or associative elaboration" (Holt, 1970a, p. 1). In order to transform primitive feelings into symbolic forms that are socially acceptable, the ego must call upon an array of mechanisms and thought forms that impose reality-oriented, secondary process thought. The emerging contents, however, bear the traces of the transformed drive and thus reveal the nature of the "inspiration."

The uniqueness of the present study resides in its attempt to infer creative process by studying the traces of source material in created products. It attempts to demonstrate that young children who differ significantly from their peers in the extent to which their divergent thinking abilities have been developed will demonstrate not only greater differences in accessibility to the raw material, but they will also show evidence of a greater ability to transform this material into socially acceptable products. The products in our experiment are the responses to the stimuli of the *Torrance Tests of Creative Thinking* (TTCT). The responses may be interesting, original, and richly elaborated, or sterile and banal. Their emotional tone may be neutral, well modulated; or it may be primitive and disturbing. The creative products are interpreted on two levels. First, they may be given objective scores—derived from Guilford's (1967) structure of intellect model (SOI) and extended by Torrance (1974)—and second they may be scored for primary process content according to the system developed by Holt (1970a, 1977) for assessing primary and secondary manifestations of primary process. Our contention is that the combination of the divergent thinking (Guilford, 1967; Torrance, 1974) and psychoanalytic models (Holt, 1970a; Kris, 1952) offers a novel methodology with which a greater understanding of transformative creative process may be achieved. The combination of these two approaches is possible to the extent that the responses elicited by Torrance's stimuli can be seen as a creative product. Each response is evaluated according to the two above mentioned systems.

EXAMPLES OF PRIMARY PROCESS

Primary process content is a normal component of every day speech and thought at all ages. It reflects drive affect. According to Holt (1970a), roughly 40% of our daily language consists of level 2 primary process— that is, socialized as opposed to crude level 1 content. The proportion of level 1 is greater in artists than nonartists.

The following is an example of primary process content. A response to the unstructured red and black areas of Card Two of the Rorschach is seen as "a bleeding body ripped open by an explosion." This reflects crude, violent, aggressive affect, and there is an implicit *demand for defense* (DD) against the anxiety which might lead a subject to feel or say, "it is my body, I feel destroyed." When the response is rationalized—that is, seen with some degree of distance, as a photograph reprinted in a magazine exposing the horrors of terrorist activity—it turns into a socially acceptable, even laudable story. This defensive activity by the ego assures us that there are processes at work to deal with the violence released. When a highly aggressive response is justified by the subject, as in the above case, by reference to a newspaper illustration, the explosive affect has been used in the service of the ego to create an acceptable story. We can infer that intact ego functions direct the expression of violence into appropriate channels (let the people know that violence is horrible). A constructive expression, here an interesting story, has been created out of potentially disorganizing affect, the sources of which lie within the subject. Something about the Rorschach stimulus triggered some personal sensitivity or conflict about aggression, and it emerged as a response showing the traces of the aggressive drive.

As clinicians we might infer that this subject knows how to deal with his or her aggressive conflicts. As story lovers we may find the content entertaining, the imagery perhaps exciting or morbid (each in terms of individual sensibilities). What is evident is that the response to the stimulus has been efficiently handled, revealing both crude affect and a socially constructive way of dealing with it.

An example of socialized, level 2 primary process in a Rorschach response would be to see two persons in Card Two yelling at each other in anger. This is a socially acceptable way of expressing strong anger; ripping a body up is not. That is why it had to be transformed into a socially acceptable "story."

CREATIVE PRODUCTS AND THE TTCT

The neutral stimuli of the TTCT are only minimally structured. They offer the subject an opportunity to project and thus reveal primary process ideation. For example, in Torrance's figural activity three, the series of two straight lines repeated 30 times may be transformed (with a few additional lines) into a high rise, a ladder, a fence, or a tree—all reasonably neutral contents with no evidence of primary process. On the other hand, the same two lines can be transformed—with no more effort than the above—into a coffin, a smokestack shooting fire, an exploding rocket, or a broken arm. All these drawings reflects degrees of aggressive affect that will be scored as primary process in the same way that Rorschach content is scored.

Freudian theory would lead one to postulate that there will be imbrication of drive energy in the development of divergent thinking. However it cannot be assumed a priori that these two facets of human motivation need necessarily be interwined. The relationship is undoubtedly as much a learned phenomenon as a natural association. Guilford's (1971) contention was that intelligence, of which divergent thinking is one form, is highly dependent on development in order to emerge in an adequately functional form. Organisms must learn to use their endowment. From a clinical perspective, primary process ideation, as evidence of a conflictive drive state, can be expected to be disruptive rather than facilitative if it is not directed into adaptive use by a sufficiently strong ego. (In schizophrenics, primary process is totally disorganizing.) The presence of divergent thinking skills is evidence of ego strength. It implies presence of tools which the ego can use in its service. But it can only do so with the cooperation of convergent thinking (that is, reality-oriented, facilitative thinking). In the Holt (1970) system, the defense effectiveness score reflects this controlling, modulating capacity. Such forms of self-conscious modulation are not likely to be evident at early ages.

PRIMARY PROCESS IN THE YOUNG CHILD

Primary process is by definition the young child's original mode of thinking. What must crystalize is secondary process thinking, reality-oriented, logical analytic, synthetic thinking opposed to primary process with its propensity to action. Most important, however, is the child's acquisition of the efficient modulation of the two. This capacity to adopt primitive contents in the service of the ego takes time.

Rorschachs of young children (e.g., kindergarten) are full of autistic logic, displacement, condensations, poor forms, disregard of time, place, and causality. Using data from Dudek's (1974) longitudinal study of maturation and learning, Rivard and Dudek (1977) demonstrated that between kindergarten and Grade 4 (age 9 years) considerable progress is made toward the elimination of formal deviations of thinking and toward the refinement and stabilization of secondary process thinking. Primary process content, on the other hand, remains in evidence in Grade 4 in proportions similar to that of young adults (39% vs 43%). It is now generally expressed in the more socialized level 2 form (Holt 1970a). Although blatant deviations of thinking tend to disappear in all children with time there are great differences among children in the degree to which they are open to their primary process, and in the degree to which they can learn to use it adaptively, as is true of adults.

REGRESSION IN THE SERVICE OF THE EGO

Creative adults acquire a variety of techniques to express or transform conflicting feelings: humor, satire, parody, displacement, rationalization, and cultural contextualization. These are seldom part of a young child's arsenal of tricks. It is therefore not surprising that although the majority of studies using adult populations were able to demonstrate regression in the service of the ego, those with children have yielded negative results (Dudek, 1975; Rabie, 1969; Rogolsky, 1968; Russ, 1988). Russ (1988) found a positive correlation between divergent thinking and *adaptive re-*

gression in the Rorschach, but only with fifth-grade boys. Rogolsky's (1968) study of creativity with third grade children offered a way out of the dilemma by presenting a different formula for the scoring of adaptive regression.

Holt's (1970a) formula for computing regression in the service of the ego is REGO = DD X DE/PPR, where DD is *defense demand* (crudity of response), DE is *defense effectiveness* (success of ability to attenuate its expression appropriately), and PPR is the total number of primary process responses. When this failed to differentiate the creative and uncreative groups, Rogolsky (1968) substituted the DE score with other forms of control and found the popular response to be the most effective substitute. (This formula only worked with boys.) Rogolsky interpreted it to mean that the creative young child is adapting more than regressing. Rogolsky's children were between the ages of 8 and 9 years, when primary process has diminished a great deal but is still not an abnormal mode of thinking. The popular response (on any test for children) can be seen as an index of greater socialization and therefore of greater maturity. As such it reflects acquired acceptable ways of dealing with drive—knowing the "right way" to do things. Whereas in adults the popular response is a sign of conventional thinking, in childhood it may be seen as a tool that gives the child an "edge," and greater "know-how" in effecting socially acceptable products.

In the present study, Rogolsky's formula (1968) was accepted as the most appropriate defense effectiveness measure for children. Furthermore, because the creative products of the TTCT were to be used to assess adaptive regression, (rather than administer an independent tool such as the Rorschach which is not a test of creativity but of adjustment), no sex differences were expected. The created products are examples of adaptive regression. If a child qualifies, on the basis of his or her products, for placement in the highly creative group, there is reason to assume that no sex differences will be found in adaptive regression.

THE LIBIDINAL FOCUS

To the extent that he developed it, Freud's theory of creativity suggests that it is libidinal energy that provides the contents for sublimation in creative work. Hart (1948) and Hartmann (1955) pointed out the importance and inevitability of sublimating aggressive energy as well. According to Freudian theory, there must be an excess of libidinal over aggressive energy because it is libido which maintains life, and which unites (i.e., creates). Aggression pulls apart and destroys. Aggression may supply the motive power and the rebellious will to form, but without a surcharge of libido, the subject will remain at the state of analysis (i.e., dissection or destruction) and hence it will be difficult to attain the constructive, creative phase.

The hypothesis that the presence of libidinal content should predominate over aggressive was supported in studies by Dudek (1968, 1984) and Gagnon (1977). Both analyzed the Rorschach content of a group of renowned creative artists and a control group of productive professional persons. Evidence of libidinal drive expresssed as primary process was indeed present in greater quantities than aggressive drive in the artists' responses to the Rorschach test, whereas both aggressive and libidinal content were present in equal amounts in the comparison group of nonartists. There was also a significantly greater degree of crudity and primitivity in the responses of the artists (i.e., a greater degree of regression). The greater accessibility to primary process and its transformation by a strong but flexible ego was already characteristic of the artists at the beginning of the creative cycle. Dudek and Chamberland-Bouhadana (1982) compared Rorschachs of young art students (between the ages of 18 and 25 years, and in their second and third years of art school) to mature, renowned artists. Both artists and art students obtained high divergent thinking scores on the TTCT. Moreover, Rorchachs of adolescents (ages 14–17 years), some of whom were seriously engaged in art activities, others for whom it was an important hobby, also showed the same primary process structure (Dudek, 1982). Finally, Dudek (1984) demonstrated that within a world class group of creative architects, the 36% ranked at the top of the group produced more libidinal (level 1) primary process content than the 36% ranked at the bottom of this exceptional group of eminent persons.

It must be noted that all "normal" persons retain varying degrees of access to primary process and inevitably show a capacity for adaptive regression. Where the creative person differs is in the degree to which level 1 primary process is projected, and in particular in the regressive quality or crudity of the affect. The creative person also shows significantly greater presence of level 1 formal thinking deviations. It is in the capacity to transform such transgressions of socialized thinking into creative production that the creative person demonstrates regression in the service of the ego.

CREATIVITY AS DIVERGENT THINKING

The adult studies of REGO (Holt, 1970a) were predominantly concerned with adults engaged in real-life creativity (poets, artists, musicians, actors, architects). They have all shown greater evidence of level 1, primary process ideation and greater capacity to regress in the service of the ego than normal controls. Our assumption is that their openness to primary process was not closed off in childhood. They only had to learn to use it effectively. We would also conjecture that their skills began to develop early. There is no way to verify these hypotheses with adults.

It is our contention that the imbrication of divergent thinking and drive energy in young children also begins early. Divergent thinking is seen as an index of creative potential, but cannot be compared to real life creativity in adults. Nor can children's creativity be judged by adult standards. It is unlikely that children can be truly creative until they have achieved some mastery over the formal operational stages of thinking, as defined by Piaget (Dudek, 1974). Young children's drawings are seen as creative by adults because they display virtually no tranformation of primary process. For adults, the goal is to remove its traces, to transform it consciously into something novel and valuable. The child does not have the slightest idea of what this implies. The child's created product breaks no boundaries, challenges no values, and inspires no unconscious fears. Its vocabulary is internationally known. The child's desire is to express energy, not to adapt it.

A study by Russ (1988) on play activity in first- and second-grade children lends support to our view that young children take pleasure in expressing primary process (which is a language that is "normal" to them) and are not yet aware of the need or desire to transform primary process in the service of the ego. Russ found a significant relationship between amount of primary process on the Rorschach (i.e., ease in expressing it) and frequency of affective as well as primary process expression in play. There was also a significant positive relationship between quantity of primary process in the Rorschach and quality of fantasy and imagination as well as comfort in play activity. On the other hand, the correlation between adaptive regression on the Rorschach and the Alternate Uses test as a measure of divergent thinking was a nonsignificant −.17. If affective play activity can be seen as expression of drive energy, the study by Russ may be interpreted as providing support for a psychodynamic conception of where sources of creative energy lie. The failure to demonstrate adaptive regression is consistent with our belief that young children (ages 7–8 years) have not yet discovered a need for regression in the service of the ego, and furthermore that defense effectiveness as used in the Holt (1970a) system is not an appropriate measure of what the child can use as control over unrestrained primary process expression.

For the purposes of the present study, it is not necessary (nor is it possible) to establish a child's creativity in a real world sense. Our goal is to demonstrate that the creative process attempts to fashion forms appropriate to the quality of the affect. What is important for our study is that a young child's mind show evidence of being versatile and alive, faculties that are virtually synonymous with high divergent thinking. Such a mind, with its fluidity and flexibility of processing, is expected also to be intimately in contact with drive energy. The combination of drive, skills, and opportunity translates into product. To demonstrate the imbrication of drive and divergent thinking, we only need to have access to a population of children manifesting high levels of divergent thinking.

In summary, the value of the present study lies in its attempt to lend support to the psychoanalytic postulate that drive energy is imbricated in the development of divergent thinking skills at an early age. This imbrication is necessary in order to effect expression of need in symbolic form. The originality of this study resides in its novel methodology which assesses both process and talent from the finished product. We have also hypothesized that representation of both sexes should be in approximately equal numbers in the creative versus the uncreative groups. Because sex differences on creativity tests have not been conclusively demonstrated in the research literature, we have further assumed that only the stereotypes about sexual differences—verbal superiority in females, greater aggressive drive in males—would apply to this group (Maccoby & Jacklin, 1974). An additional hypothesis (for which there is no available research) is that girls will give more libidinal as opposed to aggressive content, but boys are expected to show the reverse. This hypothesis assumes that the symbolic projections of the girls can be expected to be more tender than aggressive, and that those of boys can be expected to be more aggressive than tender. These inferences are based on prevailing social conditioning patterns which are still in effect despite considerable consciousness raising by the women's liberation movements.

Finally, our methodology allows us to test for the presence of sex differences in ability to use drive energy adaptively. Differences have been found consistently in favor of boys. Our hypothesis is that there will be no differences in regression in the service of the ego when a creative product is used to assess primary process, and when a more appropriate measure to evaluate defense effectiveness is applied (i.e., the popular response).

HYPOTHESES

H_1. More creative children will have more primary process and more popular responses than less creative children.

H_2. More creative children will show greater regression in the service of the ego.

H_3. The mode of control (i.e., the popular response) will alone distinguish the more creative from the less creative children.

H_4. There will be a greater incidence of populars and a smaller incidence of P% in more creative children.

H5.   The content of the primary process will be different in more as opposed to less creative children (i.e., libidinal will exceed aggressive responses in protocols of more creative children, with the opposite expected in less creative children).

H6.   There will be no significant differences on the total creativity score for boys and girls.

H7.   Girls will score higher on the verbal scale of the TTCT while boys will score higher on the nonverbal scale of the TTCT.

H8.   There will be no sex differences in the scores for regression in the service of the ego.

H9.   Girls will show more evidence of libidinal primary process content and less evidence of aggressive, with the reverse true for boys.

METHOD

Subjects

Dudek's original longitudinal study comprised 11 schools selected by the Protestant School Board as typical of high, middle, and low SES milieux. The sample consisted of 1,450 (50 classrooms) fifth- and sixth-grade children. The present study will deal only with data of 200 children: 100 identified as most creative and 100 as least creative on the basis of their TTCT protocols. Selection procedures were as follows:

Prior to selecting the creative and uncreative groups, a random selection of 509 TTCT protocols from the pool of 1,450 were drawn in order to establish norms for popular content responses. Some attempt was made to insure that all schools and classrooms were represented. This selection resulted in the following distribution. In terms of SES, there were 172 low, 140 medium, and 197 high subjects. Of these, 222 were girls and 287 were boys with 277 from Grade 5 and 232 from Grade 6.

Some 25,000 figural and verbal TTCT productions were analyzed for content to establish frequency of response categories. A list of populars was established according to the following criteria. In order to identify a response as popular, it had to be given at least once by 15% of the 509 subjects. Torrance gives no norms for popular responses, but his cut-off point for an original response is 5%. In the present study, 28 populars were identified. They were produced by between 17.5% and 66% of the population at least once.

The 509 protocols were then put back into the original sample. To generate a group with equal representation of sex, SES, and grade, a modified random selection was made resulting in a total of 504 subjects, with boys and girls equally represented. Two hundred subjects were drawn from this pool of 504 according to the criterion of 100 most and 100 least creative scores (total TTCT, combining verbal and figural). Neither sex, grade, nor SES were modifying variables in this selection.

The high and low creativity subjects were represented within the SES groups as follows. In the low SES group, there were 60 uncreative and six creative children. In the high SES group, there were 58 creative and nine uncreative children. The middle SES group was more balanced, with 36 creative and 31 uncreative subjects.

Measures

The experimental variables consist of the TTCT with the Holt (1970a) system of scoring primary process. The TTCT consists of two scales: verbal and figural. They show low intercorrelations (Torrance, 1974), and results are therefore presented separately. The verbal scale consists of seven activities. In the present study, only two of the seven verbal activites were used (Product Improvement and Just Suppose). All three figural activities were used. The tests were administered under timed conditions: 30 minutes for the figural tests and 20 minutes for the verbal. Torrance's scoring system, with fluency, flexibility, originality, and elaboration indices, does not take into consideration quality or appropriateness of product.

The Torrance tests generally show low correlations with intelligence, rarely exceeding .30 (Torrance, 1974). (The unevaluative nature of the scoring may explain the low correlations.) In Dudek's original study with a sample of 1,450 children, the correlation between TTCT and the B scale (intelligence) of the Children's Personality Questionnaire (Porter & Cattell, 1960) was not significant within classrooms nor within SES groups. However, when the SES groups were combined, the correlation between intelligence and the verbal scale of the TTCT was .38 ($p < .01$), but a nonsignificant .29 (n.s.) for the figural scale. Scoring of the TTCT is reported to have high interrater reliability and requires little training (Halpin & Halpin, 1974; Rosenthal, 1983; Torrance, 1974).

REGO and the Holt System

The Holt (1970b) system for assessing primary process is divided into four categories: (a) *Content,* intended to identify instinctual tendencies, with two *Levels of Content* (1 and 2); (b) *Deviations of Logical Thinking* (e.g., *condensation, displacement, symbolization*), with two *Levels of Deviation* (1 and 2); (c) *Controls and Defenses,* which reflect the way in which the individual defends him- or herself against the emergence of primary process with the activity of the ego; and (d) *Global Measures* which establish the force of the instinctual energy (its progressive pull and its intensity) and establish the efficiency of the defensive system. The final result of the interaction between instinctual drive and defensive system establishes whether it is adaptive or not (i.e., whether the regression is in fact in the service of the ego). It is more commonly referred to as Adaptive Regression (AR). The two terms will be used interchangeably.

Recall that the formula for REGO in Holt's (1970a) system is Defense Demand (DD) times Defense Effectiveness (DE) divided by the total number of Primary Process Responses (PPR). Defense Demand (DD) reflects the crudity of the response. In the present analysis of content, a four-point scale was used with four identifying the most crude primary process content and one the least. Defense effectiveness in our study is inferred by using the popular response, and our formula for REGO is thus DD X P/PPR.

The scoring of primary process was limited to content and scored for libidinal and aggressive drive and their derivatives only. Formal deviations of thinking in both TTCT verbal and pictorial productions are rare, except in the productions of seasoned artists (Loveless, 1978), and were therefore not scored. The scoring system yields 38 scores which break down into 20 global scores (see Holt, 1970a, 1977).

Interrater Agreement

The TTCT scoring was carried out by four of the individuals who administered the tests. They were trained by the first author and an administrative assistant. Each scorer was given the task of scoring for one index only: One person scored fluency, another flexibility, and so on. In this way, any existing bias was evenly distributed over all the protocols. Eighteen percent (260 protocols) were rescored by two other test scorers. The agreement varied between 85% and 99%.

For the present study the 200 protocols that were selected by a computer search were rescored by a trained scorer on two occasions, the second time after an interval of six weeks. The same procedure was used with the scoring of primary process. Interrater agreement for the TTCT was between 94% and 97%, and for the Holt scores it varied between 95% and 99%.

RESULTS

Intercorrelations among fluency, flexibility, and originality were extremely high, ranging from .65 to .96 in this sample. However, elaboration was unrelated to these indices (−.10 to .35) for both verbal and figural scales. This is consistent with Torrance's (1974) findings, but analyses were limited to the first three indices. The score limits of each scale varied considerably so that conversion to standard scores was effected when sum verbal and sum figural scales were the objects of analysis. However, the raw scores were used where the individual indices (fluency, flexibility and originality) were involved.

Before primary analyses, ANOVAs were performed and Tukey's test was applied where necessary. Tukey's test takes into account the size of the means in relation to each other. There were no significant Grade × Sex × SES interactions, so data were pooled.

Table 18.1 summarizes the results of an ANOVA for the TTCT scores of the creative and uncreative groups. The differences between the two groups are very great, as would be expected on the basis of the selection criteria.

The first four hypotheses are supported. Table 18.2 indicates that the creative children were more productive and gave significantly more popular responses, a lower P%, and more REGO than the uncreative children. The number of children giving zero responses are presented in Table 18.3.

Table 18.3 also summarizes differences between creative and uncreative groups on qualitative contents of primary process. In the interests of conserving space only significant differences are summarized in the table. The data in Table 18.3 support the part of hypothesis 5, which states that there will be more projection of libidinal as opposed to aggressive primary process content by the more creative children. However, the uncreative children did not project more aggressive than libidinal

Table 18.1. Fluency, Flexibility, and Originality for the Creative and Uncreative Groups (each n = 100)

	Creative		Uncreative		
	Mean	SD	Mean	SD	$F(1, 198)$
Verbal Scale					
Fluency	23.9	6.6	6.6	3.8	505.4**
Flexibility	13.9	3.3	4.3	2.5	520.6**
Originality	15.8	5.6	3.4	2.5	396.2**
Verbal Total					
Standard Scores	1.26	.81	−.99	.48	574.7**
Figural Scale					
Fluency	32.8	5.6	14.6	5.6	516.4**
Flexibility	23.3	4.0	11.2	3.4	513.4**
Originality	46.2	10.0	18.9	7.7	459.6**
Figural Total					
Standard Scores	1.01	.62	−1.07	.62	538.4**

**p < .01

Table 18.2. TTCT Productivity, P, P%, DD, and REGO for the Creative
and Uncreative Groups (each n = 100)

	Creative		Uncreative		
	Mean	SD	Mean	SD	F(1, 198)
Prod.	56.7	7.4	21.3	5.7	1,422.8**
P	12.6	3.6	5.8	2.8	219.2**
P%	22.0	6.0	28.0	12.0	14.5**
DD	29.5	11.4	11.5	7.1	176.3**
REGO	19.1	5.6	9.0	4.7	184.7**

**$p < .001$

content as predicted. The ratio of total aggressive (Ag 1 & 2) to total libidinal (Lib 1 & 2) for the creative children is 8.5:10.5 versus 3.5:3.7 in the uncreative. A t-test indicated that the projection of libidinal content over aggressive content was significantly greater ($t_{(198)} = 3.25$ $p < .01$).

When percentages of primary process content were used, an ANOVA revealed only a few significant differences between creative and uncreative groups. These were in the area of aggression. The uncreative children obtained higher scores on subject aggression (AgS)—that is, content where the subject is the aggressor ($F_{(1,198)} = 51.42$, $p < .01$).

Table 18.4 summarizes the findings relative to hypothesis 6. It is evident that there were no differences in total creativity between boys and girls, although girls tended to score higher on the various scales. This is

Table 18.3. Global Scores of Primary Process TTCT Content for the Creative
and Uncreative Groups (each n = 100)

	% Giving Zero Responses		Groups				
			Creative		Uncreative		
	Creat	UnCr	Mean	SD	Mean	SD	F-ratio
Oral Ag T	50	73	0.65	0.76	0.30	0.57	13.2*
Oral T	00	20	5.98	3.02	1.99	1.71	131.6*
Anal T	27	63	1.04	1.07	0.41	0.79	22.7*
Sexual T	51	80	0.85	1.31	0.23	0.56	18.4*
E-VT	06	23	2.55	1.56	1.05	0.97	66.2*
LM T	83	97	0.16	0.38	0.02	0.15	10.8*
Lib 1 + 2	00	1	10.59	3.89	3.77	2.42	221.7*
AgS T	01	00	5.36	3.56	2.44	1.96	51.4*
Ag 1 + 2	00	00	8.51	4.80	3.54	2.83	79.2*
PriPro 1	54	80	0.79	1.17	0.24	0.59	17.3*
PriPro 2	00	00	18.31	5.76	7.07	3.97	258.6*
PriPro 1 + 2	00	00	19.10	6.16	7.31	4.10	253.6*

*$p < .01$, df = 1,198

Table 18.4. Means and Standard Deviations of TTCT Scores
for Boys and Girls (each n = 100)

| | Girls | | Boys | |
	Mean	SD	Mean	SD
Verbal				
Fluency	16.34	9.86	14.42	10.47
Flexibility	9.69	5.59	8.71	5.73
Originality	10.60	7.63	8.89	7.52
Verbal Total				
Standard Scores	0.28	1.29	0.02	1.33
Figural				
Fluency	25.37*	10.53	22.42	10.66
Flexibility	18.21	7.09	16.52	7.18
Originality	33.73	16.70	31.66	16.05
Figural Total				
Standard Scores	0.09	1.22	−0.13	1.22
Verbal + Figural Total				
Standard Scores	0.18	1.13	−0.09	1.17

*Boys and girls differed significantly ($F_{1,188}$ = 3.89, p <.01)

contradictory to hypothesis 7. Table 18.5 summarizes the data pertaining to hypothesis 8.

There were no sex differences on scores for REGO, as predicted by hypothesis 8. Girls obtained significantly higher scores on production (Ms = 4.17 and 36.8, $F_{(1,198)}$ = 4.01, p < .05) and popular responses (Ms = 10.0 and 8.1, $F_{(1,195)}$ = 4.96, p < .05). Their lower scores on DD (Ms = 19.6 and 21.2) may explain why their REGO is not significantly higher.

Finally, Table 18.6 indicates that girls did in effect project more libidinal and less aggressive content than boys as per hypothesis 9. This is all the more interesting because the total amount of primary process content projected by both was the same. (The number of subjects giving zero responses was less than 1%).

Table 18.5. TTCT Prod, P, P%, and REGO by Sex (N = 200)

| | Girls | | Boys | | |
	Mean	SD	Mean	SD	F-ratio
Prod	41.7	18.2	36.8	19.3	4.01*
P	10.0	4.6	8.6	4.7	4.96*
P%	25.0	8.0	25.0	11.0	0.30
DD	19.6	12.8	21.2	12.2	1.76
REGO	14.5	6.8	13.7	7.6	0.55

*p < .05, df = 1,188

Table 18.6. Means and Standard Deviations for Boys and Girls on Categories
of Primary Process (N = 200)

| | Girls | | Boys | | |
	Mean	SD	Mean	SD	F-ratio
L10	0.22	0.51	0.09	0.32	4.47*
L20	3.87	3.23	2.94	2.60	5.20*
L20-Ag	0.28	0.51	0.45	0.67	4.46*
L2E-V	1.99	1.49	1.50	1.34	6.27*
Ag2S	2.98	2.57	4.49	3.37	16.24**
Oral T	4.49	3.44	3.58	2.87	4.25*
E-V T	2.07	1.52	1.58	1.45	5.58*
Lib T	8.01	4.86	6.50	4.49	6.04*
AgS T	3.02	2.64	4.62	3.47	16.99**
Ag T	5.21	4.31	6.69	4.84	7.61**
PriPro T	13.22	7.93	13.20	7.88	0.06

*$p < .05$, **$p < .01$, df = 1,188

There was a significant grade effect with children in Grade 6 tending to obtain both higher TTCT scores on the total verbal scale ($F_{(1,188)} = 19.37$, $p < .05$) and having higher primary process scores (PriPro 1 + 2, $F_{(1,188)} = 5.43$, $p < .05$). This is in keeping with expectations for the TTCT, and is consistent with psychoanalytic theory in that primary process should increase as adolescence approaches.

DISCUSSION

Both *divergent thinking* and *regression in the service of the ego* have proved useful in research on creativity in the liberal arts using adult populations. Both have demonstrated solid validity bases within their respective theoretical models having received substantive research support (Dudek, 1969, 1982, 1984; Dudek, Berneche, Berube, & Royer, 1991, 1989; Holt, 1970a; Huard, 1971; Martindale, 1986; Myden, 1959; Noy, 1969; Pine, 1959). For example, Martindale (1986) adapted Freud's concept of primary process to computer in his research on stylistic change in literature, music, and painting with impressive results. That research with children has yielded predominantly negative results in demonstrating a capacity for regression in the service the ego is not surprising when we consider the operational definition of adaptive regression.

Adaptive regression involves the massacre of desire in its full primitive longing for expression. As need emerges, the ego immediately intervenes to constrain, attenuate, or modulate in order not to completely repress expression. In short, it submits expression of drive to a stringent reality principle with the inevitable and considerable transformation of the original need into forms of expression that are socially acceptable and therefore accepted. In the case of the artist, the transformation finds symbolic form, is sublimated, and emerges as an object of art with the traces of the original drive animating it, giving it life and interest.

In the adult, adaptive regression implies a capacity to abandon the immediate pleasures of the impulse in order to achieve something of value. It implies long term goals, purposes, and a focus on skills and competencies that are needed for complex production.

The expressive creations of childhood reflect an unselfconscious creative process that seldom if ever achieves a creative product. This can be judged as creative only if placed at the lowest end of the creativity continuum—*expressive* as opposed to *emergentive* (Taylor & Getzels, 1975). From this vantage point is would have been surprising if the early studies using Holt's complex formula for REGO had yielded significant results with children. The popular response as an index of control, that is of more mature learned skills, is a more appropriate reflection of what helps a child to adapt needs to acceptable formulas for expression. Conventions are handy mechanisms in problem solving and in getting through the day. They reflect anything but unique, individual, idiosyncratic solutions. The child is constantly being taught how to "do it right," and not how to arrive at unique formulations. There is little encouragement to develop divergent thinking in the early years. It is our contention that the child who develops a capacity for high divergent thinking has retained contact with the chaotic primary process that follows no rules and no conventions. It is *perversely divergent.*

One is tempted to infer that children who show little development of divergent thinking and little access to drive are products of a repressive environment. Encouragement to think divergently and to retain contact with primary process depend on the type and severity of early family and school influences (Freud, 1926/1959). Repressive environments are likely to close off dynamic sources of life energy minimizing not only chances for personal happiness but social productivity as well. Torrance (1967) defined creativity in young children as anything that makes a young child more alive. Repressive environments are not likely to stimulate aliveness. Without further research, it is impossible to know the meaning of this apparent developmental arrest (if it may be seriously considered as such). This will be further discussed under the theme of fluency.

The results of our research indicate that high levels of divergent thinking and easy access to primary process are interrelated and may be interpreted as reflecting creative potential. Such potential may or may not be applied to creative production in later years. It is difficult to track the development of creativity, especially with the possibility of a U-shaped developmental curve (Johnson, 1985). Our findings do not pretend to be predictive. The actualization of creative potential depends on a complex variety of factors that high divergent scores cannot reflect anymore than a high IQ can predict high achievement in the real world. Prediction in the arts is a particularly difficult process. In fact, Dudek and Berneche (1989) found that only 35% of university students completing a three-year diploma course in the arts had made what they felt to be a lifetime commitment to creative production despite evidence of talent and interest. The others were waiting for life circumstances to help them make their decision.

Although the TTCT full scale score used in this study consists of the sum of fluency, flexibility, and originality, it may be more parsimonious to use high levels of fluency to identify creative children. Flexibility and originality depend on fluency, as the high intercorrelations indicate. This has been Wallach's (1970) carefully considered contention as well. Fluency has been shown to be independent of intelligence and of sex (Dudek, 1969; Hargreaves & Bolton, 1972; Raina, 1982; Wallach, 1970) and is a factor which by itself may be seen as a sufficient index of creative strength. This is especially the case with the present results suggesting that in an imaginative context high fluency will be accompanied by a high projection of primary process.

The present findings suggest that fluency may be considered as an index of openness, or low defensiveness, in view of the fact that higher fluency levels are accompanied by greater access to contents which are usually personal and private, if not taboo. Lower defensiveness has been shown to be a significant characteristic of more creative persons (Bowers, 1967). However, it does not follow that high fluency will necessarily be accompanied by high levels of primary process, and this fact may explain why some persons who are highly fluent may not be flexible, original, or creative. Why the two are not always associated remains to be more fully investigated.

Although low fluency scores on the TTCT normally suggest that we are dealing with personality types in which control, restraint, inhibition, and defensiveness are primary defenses—Freud's inhibited personality—other explanations are also possible. Low fluency might also reflect conscious resistance to testing, low motivation, situational blocking due to anxiety, or depression. Both low motivation and resistance to testing for reasons other than purely defensive (e.g., disinterest, poorly developed drawing skills) might both be factors that can result in low fluency. Furthermore, creativity tests are known to be sensitive to situational factors (Wallach & Kogan, 1965). However, such reasons alone cannot explain why some children under the same conditions do well, while others fail to produce. It is evident that reasons for low creativity scores may be complex. In the present case, low creativity scores were predominantly obtained by children in low SES schools (i.e., schools different from those that high and middle SES subjects attend) and it may be that different school philosophies are operating. Although all children were given the same instructions by well trained examiners, the situations may have been experienced differently in different school settings. In short, intrinsic motivation or habitual responses conditioned by a particular school setting may contribute to, or sabotage a positive response. The influence of SES factors on creativity are dealt with in Dudek and Strobel (1989).

Children who obtain high scores on divergent thinking tests appear to be emotionally open and free to express their individuality as judged by evidence of primary process content. Still, we should not conclude that children who score low on tests or divergent thinking need be emotionally closed off and uncreative. Caution seems warranted in view of the fact that when percentages of primary process content were computed, the less creative children did not differ significantly from the more creative. The only area in which significant differences were maintained was on responses scored as aggressive in content. On this basis, we might speculate that high aggressive content may be an index of blocked creativity if it is not exceeded by a significant proportion of libidinal content. As already indicated, research with creative artists reveals that creative persons project significantly more libidinal as opposed to aggressive content in imaginative productions (Dudek & Chamberland-Bouhadana, 1982; Dudek, 1984; Gagnon, 1977). According to psychoanalytic theory, it is the sublimation of libido that is crucial to creative production because it is *Eros* which unites (creates). Although the presence and sublimation of aggression is also essential, the aggressive drive is by definition destructive and in excess over the libidinal. It may lead to uses of energy (critical, analytic, stalemating) that are not in the service of creation. Such energy will be spent on criticizing and sabotaging rather than on creating.

Keep in mind that the use of percentages to interpret differences may be a dubious practice. Quantity beyond a certain point translates into a quality which no ratios can erase. Use of percentages where fluency is the limiting point eradicates important differences on a test such as the TTCT much as setting too low an upper limit would eradicate IQ differences.

The finding that boys give more aggressive content than girls is consistent with the sex differences reported in the literature on aggressive behavior (Maccoby & Jacklin, 1974). What is of more interest is that girls project significantly greater amounts of libidinal content (mainly oral, and exhibitionistic-voyeuristic). This supports the impression that girls continue to make (i.e., they appear to be more dependent and show greater secondary narcissism). Interestingly, the libidinal scores of the girls exceeded their aggressive (Ms = 8.0 and 5.2) whereas the boys were balanced (Ms = 6.5 and 6.7). There were 48 boys as opposed to 52 girls in the more creative group.

The girls scored higher on all the creativity scales, but this difference only reached significance on figural fluency. This was an unexpected finding. Where the more creative boys exceeded the more creative girls is on defense demand (DD) or crudity of the primary process content. The DD may be interpreted as an index of depth of regression. This would explain why the girls do not have a higher REGO score than boys although they score higher on production and higher on number of populars (Table 16.6) and show a more favorable libido to aggression balance. It is evident that the interactions leading to creative expression are more subtle and complex than quantitative scores can explain.

The present data indicate that the more creative child can be distinguished from the less creative by a number of factors, each operating independently as well as in concert: The TTCT scores (particularly the fluency score), the totals of primary process scores alone, the popular response alone, the DD alone, and the REGO all distinguish them. They are present in significantly different quantities in more versus less creative children's productions. Except for the REGO scores, all identify presence of ability rather than effective use. None of the scores alone or in concert can predict to what extent the potential will be used for real world creativity even when know-how is present.

The percentage of popular responses distinguishes less from more creative by its greater presence in the less creative group and as such it is an index of conventional thinking (perhaps stereotypy). This suggests that we are perhaps approaching the age where P as an index of adaptive regression may be questionable, and a more refined index of defense effectiveness may be needed. The most economical index of creative potential is fluency, but from a theoretical point of view, the extent to which the more creative child can put creative potential to productive use may perhaps be better determined by the REGO score, particularly as the child enters adolescence.

What is clear is that highly developed divergent thinking describes a more versatile and interesting mind. The numerous differences between the more and less creative groups are probably indicative of creative energy which has not yet crystallized. Perhaps the most parsimonious interpretation would be to infer that the more creative children are both cognitively more fluent and emotionally more open to their own sources of energy. They would therefore be in a better position to learn to use this energy creatively given at least a minimum of the proper environmental stimulation and support.

REFERENCES

Bowers, P. (1967). Effect of hypnosis and suggestion of reduced defensiveness on creativity test performance. *Journal of Personality, 35*, 311–312.

Dudek, S. Z. (1968). Regression and creativity. *Journal of Nervous and Mental Disease, 147* 535–546.

Dudek, S. Z. (1974). Creativity in young children: Attitude or ability. *Journal of Creative Behavior, 8,* 282–292.

Dudek, S. Z. (1975). Regression in the service of the ego in the young child. *Journal of Personality Assessment, 39,* 369–376.

Dudek, S. Z. (1982, October). *Rorschachs of adolescent students engaged artistic activities.* Invited colloquium, University of Montreal.

Dudek, S. Z. (1984). The architect as person: A Rorschach image. *Journal of Personality Assessment, 48,* 597–605.

Dudek, S. Z. & Berneche, R. Berube, H. & Royer, S. (1991). Factors determining commitment to the profession of art. *Creativity Research Journal, 11,* 367–391.

Dudek, S. Z., & Chamberland-Bouhadana, G. (1982). Primary process in creative persons. *Journal of Personality Assessment, 39,* 369–376.

Dudek, S. Z. & Hall, W. B. (1984). Some test correlates of high level creativity in architects. *Journal of Personality Assessment, 48,* 351–359.

Dudek, S. Z. & Strobel, M. G. (1989). *Effects of SES on divergent thinking measures.* Unpublished manuscript.

Freud, S. (1959). Inhibitions, symptoms, and anxiety. In J. Strachey (Ed. and Trans.) *The standard edition of the complete psychological works of Sigmund Freud* (Vol. 20). London: Hogarth. (Original work published 1926)

Gagnon, P. E. (1977). *Sublimation d'agressivit`e chez les artistes peintres.* Unpublished master's thesis, University of Montreal, Quebec, Canada.

Getzels, J. W. & Csikzentmihalyi, M. (1976). *The creative vision.* New York: Wiley.

Guilford, J. P. (1967). *The nature of human intelligence.* New York: McGraw-Hill.

Guilford, J. P. (1971). Some misconceptions regarding measurement of creative talent. *Journal of Creative Behavior, 5,* 77–87.

Halpin, G. & Halpin, G. (1974). Can self-trained scorers reliably score the Torrance tests of creative thinking. *Psychology in the Schools, 11,* 56–58.

Hargreaves, D. J. & Bolton, N. (1972). Selecting creativity tests for use research. *British Journal of Psychology, 63,* 451–462.

Hart, H. H. (1948). Sublimation and aggression. *Psychiatric Quarterly, 22,* 389–411.

Hartmann, H. (1955). Note on the theory of sublimation. *Psychoanalytic Study of the Child, 10,* 9–29.

Holt, R. R. (1970a). Artistic creativity and Rorschach measures of adaptive regression. In B. Klopfer, M. M. Meyer, F. B. Brawer & W. G. Klopfer (Eds.), *Developments in the Rorschach Technique* (Vol. 3, pp. 263–320). New York: Harcourt; Brace Jovanovich.

Holt, R. R. (1970b). *Manual for primary process manifestations in Rorschach responses* (10th ed.). New York: Research Center for Mental Health, New York University.

Holt, R. R. (1977). A method for assessing primary process manifestations and their control in Rorschach responses. M. A. Rickers-Ovsiankina (Ed.), *Rorschach Psychology* (pp. 375–420). New York: Krieger.

Huard, M. (1971). *Les processus primaires et secondaires chez les Musiciens de Jazz professionnels.* Thise de doctorat inedite, Universite de Montreal.

Johnson, L. D. (1985). Creative thinking potential: Another U-shaped development: *Creative Child and Adult Quarterly, 10,* 146–159.

Kris, E. (1952). *Psychoanalytic explorations in art.* New York: International Universities Press.

Loveless, R. (1977). *Relationship of primary process thinking to indices of creativity in Rorschach and Torrance tests.* Unpublished doctoral dissertation, University of Montreal.

Maccoby, E. T. & Jacklin, L. W. (1974). *The psychology of sex differences.* Stanford CA: Stanford University Press.

Martindale, C. (1984). Evolutionary trends in poetic style: The case of English metaphysical poetry. *Computers and the Humanities, 18,* 3–21.

Martindale, C. (1986). On hedonic selection, random variation, and the direction of cultural evolution. *Current Anthropology, 27,* 50–51.

Myden, A. (1959). Interpretation and evaluation of certain personality characteristics involved in creative production. *Perceptual and Motor Skills, 9,* 139–158.

Noy, P. (1969). A revision of the psychoanalytic theory of the primary process. *International Journal of Psychoanalysis, 50,* 155–178.

Patrick, C. (1937). Creative thought in artists. *Journal of Psychology, 4,* 35–73.

Pine, F. (1959). Thematic drive content and creativity. *Journal of Personality, 27,* 136–151.

Porter, R. & Cattell, R. B. (1966). *The Early School Personality Questionnaire.* Champaign, IL: Institute of Personality and Ability Testing.

Rabie, V. (1969). *A method for scoring TAT drive content with children.* Unpublished master's thesis, University of Montreal, Quebec, Canada.

Raina, T. N. (1982). Sex differences in creativity in India: A second look. *Indian Educational Review, 17,* 122–128.

Rivard, E. & Dudek, S. Z. (1977). Primary process thinking in the same children at two developments levels. *Journal of Personality Assessment, 41,* 120–131.

Rogolsky, M. M. (1968). Artistic creativity and adaptive regression in third grade children. *Journal of Projective Techniques and Personality Assessment, 32,* 53–62.

Rosenthal, A. (1983). Comparison of interrater reliability on the Torrance Tests of Creative Thinking for gifted and non-gifted children. *Psychology in the Schools, 20,* 20–40.

Russ, S. (1982). Sex differences in primary process thinking and flexibility in problem solving. *Journal of Personality Assessment, 52,* 539–548.

Russ, S. (1988). Primary process on the Rorschach, divergent thinking, and coping in children. *Journal of Personality Assessment, 52,* 539–548.

Russ, S. (1988). Primary process thinking on the Rorschach, divergent thinking, and coping in children. *Journal of Personality Assessment 52,* 539–548.

Taylor, I. A. & Getzels, J. W. (1975). *Perspectives in creativity.* Chicago, IL: Aldine.

Torrance, E. P. (1967). Guidance and measurement. In J. C. Gowan, G. D. Demos, & E. P. Torrance (Eds.), *Creativity: Its educational implications (pp. 220–224).* New York: Wiley.

Torrance, E. P. (1974). *Norms/Techical Manual.* Lexington, MA: Personnel Press.

Wallach, M. A. (1970). Creativity. In P. H. Mussen (Ed.), *Carmichael's mannual of child psychology (pp. 1211–1272).* New York: Wiley.

Wallach, M. A., & Kogan, N. (1965). *Modes of thinking in young children.* New York: Holt, Rinehart & Winston.

Chapter 19

Family Adaptability, Cohesion, and Creativity

Kathleen Green Gardner
James D. Moran III

A number of researchers have indicated that the family environment influences the development of the creative individual (see Guilford, 1964; Kennett, 1984). Family environments consist of varying levels of perceived adaptability and cohesion. Some researchers have defined adaptability as the ability of a marital/family system to "change its power structure, role relationships and relationship rules in response to a situational or developmental stress" (Olson, Sprenkle, & Russell, 1979, p. 12). Family cohesion has been defined as the "degree of emotional bonding family members have toward one another" (Olson et al., 1979, p. 5). These two dimensions may affect an individual's level of creativity because creative individuals seem to possess qualities of flexibility (Dohr, 1982), originality, adaptiveness (MacKinnon, 1967), openness, and potential for growth (Kollen, 1984).

There is little agreement on which type of family environment is best. Literature has suggested that creativity is promoted by both a healthy, open, and positive family atmosphere as well as conflictual family relationships. Representing the first view, Torrance (1962) stated that "only in a friendly environment can we expect creative growth of a healthy kind to take place" (p. 185). In this view, parental concern should be focused on the creative child's openness to experience, values, interests, and enthusiasm. Srivastava (1977) added that the sense of freedom, the opportunity for experimentation with completion, and cooperation in the home environment are responsible for creative growth. Russell (1979) believed families that handle situational and developmental crises successfully will be higher in creativity than families that are less successful in handling crises.

Within the homes of those who become eminent, some have found a love of learning and a persistent drive toward goals by one or both parents (Goertzel, Goertzel, & Goertzel, 1978). The highly creative family may also be one in which individual divergence is permitted and risks are accepted (Getzels & Jackson, 1967). MacKinnon (1962) reported from his study of creative architects that they had been given freedom as children to roam and explore. Whitaker (1977) believed a healthy family is one that maintains inner unity as well as individuation. One should feel freedom to leave and return without family dissension and be able to belong to intimate subgroups outside the family. Although regular interaction with parents while growing up is related to creativity, physical separation from the family during college years also contributes to the creative potential of the student (Eisenman & Foxman, 1970).

Within a marital therapy context, Olson (1986) suggested that high levels of cohesion, high support, and high creativity are associated with smooth family functioning (cf. Russell, 1979). Olson et al. (1979) indicated that couple not in counselling are significantly more creative and more supportive than those seeking counselling.

Representing the second view, studies show homes of some eminent people are troubled by quarreling parents, inability to cope with a child's failures, and career choices (Goertzel et al., 1978). Brooks (1973) and MacKinnon (1962) found that the bond with parents is not strong, and frequent intrafamily conflict or indifference is felt (cf. Albert & Runco, 1986). The creative artistic male does not describe family discipline as always fair (Schaefer & Anastasi, 1968), but almost always as consistent and predictable (MacKinnon, 1962).

Expressed authoritarian child rearing by the mother has been related to lack of originality in the child (Nichols, 1964) and those receiving high control/low nurturance from their mother score lower in creativity (Heilbrun, 1971). Heilbrun and Waters (1968) suggested that high control/high nurturing mothers may foster dependency, an indication of low creativity.

Some have found that those who possess creative potential often report their parents to be rejecting, and having loving parents is frequently described by those with relatively low creative potential (Siegelman, 1973). Siegelman speculated that rejecting parents unconsciously encourage a rebellious attitude, resulting in independent thinking, but loving parents unconsciously encourage conformity by the child. This view is inconsistent with those of Olson (1986) and Torrance (1962), as previously quoted.

It is this dichotomous situation of perceived adaptability and cohesion in the family leading to both higher and lower creativity that has led, in part, to the present study. Perhaps creativity encompasses the spirit of adventure and chaos as well as high cohesion. The common denominator in this conflicting literature may be in the sense of freedom of expression and autonomy within a family structure, whatever degree of structure or flexibility the family might have.

The objective of this study was to assess the role of perceived family adaptability (rigid, structured, flexible, and chaotic) and cohesiveness (disengaged, separated, connected, and enmeshed) in relation to creativity levels in the respondents. It was of interest to determine if there was a relationship between creativity and family adaptability or cohesion, and to determine if creativity level could be predicted from perceived adaptability and cohesion scores.

RESEARCH DESIGN

The sample consisted of 80 freshman and sophomore college students at a large public university in the southwestern U.S. The median age was 19 years with a semi-interquartile range of 2.0. It was believed the freshman and sophomore status student had not yet been fully exposed to purposeful teaching of creativity (or noncreativity) as he or she was not yet fully into his or her particular academic major program which could accentuate or deemphasize the creative process. This sample included 36 interior design (ID) students (29 females, 7 males) and 44 hotel and restaurant administration (HRA) students (21 females, 23 males). All respondents voluntarily participated.

Instruments

Adaptability and cohesion scale

The Family Adaptability and Cohesion Evaluation Scales (FACES; Olson, Portner, & Lavee, 1985) were used as the measure of family environment. This instrument is based on the circumplex model and was selected because it describes underlying dynamics of a family system. The revised instrument used in this study was FACES III (Olson, 1986). It contains 20 statements with responses on a scale of 1 (*almost never*) to 5 (*al-*

most always). The 20 items of the FACES III were selected from those items used in a national survey of 1,000 normal families. The circumplex model is made up of two scales: adaptability and cohesion. Each of these is further divided into four dimensions. Family adaptability includes (from high–low) chaotic, flexible, structured, and rigid. Family cohesion includes (from high–low) enmeshed, connected, separated, and disengaged. The numerical answers to the odd numbered questions were added to obtain a score of cohesion, and the numerical answers to the even numbered questions were added to attain an adaptability score. Combining the dimensions allowed the identification of 16 distinct types of family systems. Olson (1986) reported that the scales were reliable, with internal reliability coefficients of .77 for cohesion and .62 for adaptability. The independence between the adaptability and cohesion scales ($r = .03$) was also established.

Creativity instrument

The How Do You Think (HDYT) Form E Adult (Davis, 1977) instrument consists of 100 statements with five point Likert-type rating scales. The HDYT asks for self-perceptions in such traits as artistic and aesthetic interests, curiosity, risk taking, self confidence, energy level, adventurousness, sense of humor, creativity and originality, and requests information pertaining to past hobbies and creative activities. Validity was established by Davis (1975) by correlating HDYT Scores with ratings of creative products, with an overall sample correlation of .42 ($r = .64$ for men, and $r = .36$ for women, both $p < .01$).

RESULTS

The Cronbach's alpha reliability coefficient was .87 for the cohesion scale, .71 for the adaptability scale, and .74 for the HDYT creativity instrument. Product moment coefficients were .26 between the HDYT creativity instrument and the adaptability scale of FACES III; .09 between the HDYT creativity instrument and cohesion scale of FACES III; and .47 between the adaptability scale and cohesion scale of the FACES II instrument.

Separate ANOVAs were conducted on the adaptability and cohesion scales of the FACES III instrument. The HDYT score served as the dependent variable and four categories of adaptability and four categories of cohesion served as independent variables. Significance was found for the adaptability factor ($F_{(3,76)} = 2.78$, $p < .05$) but no significance was found with the cohesion factor.

Persons from chaotic families had the highest mean scores, followed by flexible families, structured families, and those from rigid families (see Table 19.1). Tukey tests revealed a significant difference ($p < .05$) between the chaotic and rigid groups.

To gain additional insights into the relationship between adaptability, cohesion, and creativity, a 3×4 chi-square analysis was also conducted. In this analysis, two levels of adaptability (high vs. low) and two levels of cohesion (high vs. low) were cross-tabulated with three levels of creativity (high, medium and low). High adaptability included the chaotic and flexible groups, whereas low adaptability included the structured and rigid groups. A similar grouping by categories occurred for cohesion. Creativity groupings were created via a tertiary division of subject rank.

Table 19.2 demonstrates the resulting frequencies focusing on the significant findings for the high creatives (overall $M = 356.8$). The chi-squared analysis demonstrated that significant differences did exist in the number of high and low creatives as a function of family style ($p < .001$). The frequencies in Table 19.2 shows that in the combination of high adaptability with high cohesion, most of the subjects scored as highly creative. When high cohesion was combined with low adaptability, most subjects had low creativity scores.

Of concern was the small sample of males, but a *t*-test reflected no statistically significant differences between sexes in terms of creativity level.

Finally, correlational analyses indicated that the adaptability scores were significantly related to the HDYT scores ($r = .26$, $p < .05$), but the cohesion scores were not ($r = .09$). A multiple regression indicated that

Table 19.1. Means and Standard Deviations for Creativity (HDYT)
Scores as a Function of FACES III Groupings

FACES	n	Creativity Scores M	SD
Adaptability Scale			
Chaotic	31	324.0	41.0
Flexible	27	314.1	36.3
Structured	15	305.1	29.1
Rigid	7	282.7	27.8
	$N = 80$		
Cohesion Scale			
Disengaged	24	306.0	33.1
Separated	17	314.6	35.4
Connected	22	318.6	46.6
Enmeshed	17	316.2	34.6
	$N = 80$		

Table 19.2. *Distribution of Participants as a Function of FACES III Cohesion and Adaptability Groupings*

	Cohesion	
	Disengaged Separated Low	Connected Enmeshed High
Adaptability		
High		
Chaotic	n = 7	n = 15
Flexible	(sample N = 23)	(sample N = 35)
	(HDYT M = 318.1)	(HDYT M = 320.2)
Low		
Structured	n = 3	n = 1
Rigid	(sample N = 18)	(sample N = 4)
	(HDYT M = 298.7)	(HDYT M = 294.8)

Note. n denotes the number of highly creative individuals. N denotes the total number of individuals in a given quadrant. HDYT denotes How Do You Think Test.

the cohesion scores did not contribute significantly to the prediction of the HDYT scores, after the adaptability scores were entered into the equation (Betas = .28 [$p < .05$] and .04, respectively).

DISCUSSION

This study indicates that family adaptability is related to creativity. It also suggests that a sense of family cohesion is not a critical indicator of high individual creativity, at least as assessed by self-report instruments. Within the family, adaptability is evidenced through flexibility, freedom, and looseness (Olson et al., 1979). Perhaps within highly adaptable families, individuals are able to make their own mistakes as a learning process.

The major finding in this study is that the ability of the family to be highly adaptable (flexible or even to the point of being chaotic) seems to foster creativity. Previous research focused on issues related to cohesion only (i.e., rejecting or together families), with conflicting findings. In the present study, only the dimension of adaptability (i.e., freedom) seemed to be critical, with high and low creative subjects coming from connected or enmeshed families. This may help explain contradictions in the literature which have used retrospective studies and focused on variables akin to cohesion without the concomitant consideration of adaptability.

The need for highly creative people is more vital than ever, and adaptability appears to be growing in importance for reducing stressful living.

For the family researcher and therapist, creativity seems to be one method by which successful solutions for situational stresses might be obtained. Although there may be several other variables involved in creativity, having the ability to adapt to different situations might assist in lowering stress. Whereas previous studies have focused on the presence of stress in the family, this one addressed the family's ability to cope or adapt (thereby reflecting an influence on stress-level changes). The results from this study have positive and hopeful implications for those people who pursue professions that require a creative mind, as the traditional family unit evolves into new dimensions and restructuring.

REFERENCES

Albert, R. S., & Runco, M. A. (1986). The achievement of eminence: A model based on a longitudinal study of exceptionally gifted boys and their families. In R. J. Sternberg & J. E. Davidson (Eds.), *Conceptions of giftedness* (pp. 332–357). New York: Cambridge University Press.

Brooks, J. B. (1973). Familial antecedents and adult correlates of artistic interests in childhood. *Journal of Personality, 41*, 110–120.

Davis, G. A. (1975). In frumious pursuit of the creative person. *Journal of Creative Behavior, 9*, 75–87.

Davis, G. A. (1977). *How do You Think?, Form E, Adult.* Madison, WI: University of Wisconsin.

Dohr, J. (1982). Creativeness: A criterion for selecting a program development approach. *Interior Design Educators Council, 8*, 24–28.

Eisenman, R., & Foxman, D. J. (1970). Creativity: Reported family patterns and scoring methodology. *Psychological Reports, 26*, 615–621.

Getzels, J. W., & Jackson, P. W. (1967). Family environment and cognitive style: A study of the sources of highly intelligent and of highly creative adolescents. In R. L. Mooney & T. A. Razik (Eds.), *Explorations in creativity* (pp. 135–148). New York: Harper & Row.

Goertzel, M. G., Goertzel, V., & Goertzel, T. G. (1978). *Three hundred eminent personalities.* San Francisco, CA: Jossey-Bass.

Guilford, J. P. (1964). Progress in the discovery of intellectual factors. In C. W. Taylor (Ed.), *Widening horizons in creativity: Proceedings of the fifth Utah creativity research conference* (pp. 261–297). New York: Wiley & Sons.

Heilbrun, A. B., Jr. (1971). Material child rearing and creativity in sons. *Journal of Genetic Psychology, 119*, 175–179.

Heilbrun, A. B., Jr., & Waters, D. B. (1968). Underachievement as related to perceived maternal child rearing and academic conditions of reinforcement. *Child Development, 39*, 913–921.

Kennett, K. F. (1984). Creativity: Educational necessity for modern society. *Education, 105*, 2–6.

Kollen, P. P. (1984, August). *Creativity and critical thinking.* Paper presented at the Harvard International Conference on Thinking, Cambridge, MA.

MacKinnon, D. W. (1962). The nature and nurture of creative talent. *American Psychologist, 17*, 484–495.

MacKinnon, D. W. (1967). Identifying and developing creativity. In J. C. Gowan, G. D. Demos & E. P. Torrance (Eds.), *Creativity: Its educational implications* (pp. 227–235). New York: Wiley & Sons.

Nichols, R. C. (1964). Parental attitudes of mothers of intelligent adolescents and creativity of their children. *Child Development, 35*, 1041–1049.

Olson, D. H. (1986). Circumplex model VII: Validation studies and FACES III. *Family Process, 25*, 337–351.

Olson, D. H., Portner, J., & Lavee, Y. (1985). *Family Cohesion and Adaptability Evaluation (FACES III)*. St. Paul, MN: Family Social Science, University of Minnesota.

Olson, D. H., Sprenkle, D. H., & Russell, C. S. (1979). Circumplex model of marital and family systems: I. Cohesion and adaptability dimensions, family types, and clinical applications. *Family Process, 18*, 3–28.

Russell, C. S. (1979). Circumplex model of marital and family systems: III. Empirical evaluation with families. *Family Process, 18*, 29–45.

Schaefer, C. E., & Anastasi, A. (1968). A biographical inventory for identifying creativity in adolescent boys. *Journal of Applied Psychology, 52*, 42–48.

Siegelman, M. (1973). Parent behavior correlates of personality traits related to creativity in sons and daughters. *Journal of Consulting and Clinical Psychology, 40*, 43–47.

Srivastava, S. S. (1977). Creativity as related to birth order and number of siblings. *Indian Psychological Review, 14*, 1–4.

Torrance, E. P. (1962). *Guiding creative talent.* Englewood Cliffs, NJ: Prentice Hall.

Whitaker, C. A. (1977). Process techniques of family therapy. *Interaction, 1*, 4–19.

Chapter 20

Creativity in Old Age*

Gudmund J. W. Smith
Gunilla van der Meer

The present study is part of a larger project concerned with how people experience and come to terms with the advent of illness, aging, and death. As a starting point we have chosen to investigate elderly subjects around 70 years of age.

We have learned from previous research on creativity (summarized in Smith & Carlsson, 1990) that a person characterized by a generative view of life (i.e., by openness to new experience [McCrea, 1987]) is bound to

*The present investigation was initiated as a cooperative effort by the Gerotology Research Center in Lund, Sweden, and the present authors. We want to thank professor Bo Hagberg, head of the Center, for placing the facilities of the Center at our disposal. We are also indebted to Birgitta Liedberg, Bertil Nilsson, Karin Reinisch, Anne Skjaerris, and Lo Wirdheim for assistance with interviewing and testing; to Ingegerd Carlsson for supervising the scoring of the test protocols; to Göran Linde for carrying out the cluster analysis; and to professor Uwe Hentschel, University of Leiden, who made the original outline of the interview. The project was supported by a grant from the tercentenary foundation of the Bank of Sweden.

approach the basic questions of health and illness differently from an un-creative person. Very generally, we presume—partly in line with Erik H. Erikson (1959, 1963, 1964)—that those who have had a meaningful, cre-ative life are bound to treat the events of illness, aging, and death with more tolerance and equanimity than those who find their life empty and meaningless.

Pruyser (1987) argued that the ambiguities of old age may move some persons toward a late-life creativity. At that stage of life one is, above all, faced with the task of integrating life and death (Verwoerd, 1977). We can, then, further specify our view by stating that creative elderly people will be more likely than noncreative ones to handle these ambiguities in a constructive manner, as they have been observed to do in other prob-lematic and conflicting situations.

A central topic of this study is thus going to be creativity in the elderly. Little personality-oriented research on this topic has been done. More-over, the methodology on which the present authors rely for their analy-sis may be relatively unknown to many readers. An introductory outline of the planning was, therefore, deemed advisable.

To include a relatively broad spectrum of elderly people, we tested two different groups. One of them was made up of markedly active individuals, often eagerly talking about their busy life, youthfulness, and good health. To encourage them to serve as subjects, the original investigators at the Gerontology Research Center in Lund promised them free selenium tablets during the coming year. The other group was recruited among members of a pensioners' association. These people were probably more inclined than the former to let their activities be guided by others and to look for safety in the company of like-minded pensioners. We expected a considerable overlap between the two groups but assumed that they would differ in several ways regarding their attitudes toward illness and aging. Thus the subject pool was reasonably representative of elderly people.

The test battery consisted of a half-structured interview and three pro-jective, "percept-genetic" tests. The term "percept-genetic" refers to meth-ods of reconstructing and analyzing perceptual processes by means of special protracting techniques. Because the interview proved to be more useful for describing the subject group than for discriminating between subgroups, we concentrated more on the percept-genetic tests. Briefly de-scribed, the instruments were:

1. The Meta-Contrast Technique (MCT) uncovers anxiety and de-fense against anxiety by means of serial presentations, using suc-cessively prolonged exposure times and starting at subthreshold levels, of threatening picture themes (Smith, Carlsson, & An-dersson, 1989).

2. An Identification Test (IT) where the description of the picture of a face, rather vague and presented for very brief periods, so as to optimize the projection of the viewer's own self-image, was manipulated by the subliminal messages "I WELL" and "I ILL," specifically chosen to highlight the theme of the present study.

3. A Creative Functioning Test (CFT) including an ordinary and an inverted percept-genesis with a nonthreatening but meaningful picture. The inverted genesis is meant to determine if, as exposure times are gradually abbreviated, the viewer can free him or herself from the correct (conventional) meaning of the stimulus and entertain subjective interpretations (i.e., to break with the dominance of the objective world).

The choice of these particular instruments was steered by the necessity to learn in a general way how our subjects handled their anxiety (the MCT), to operationally define the rather vague concept of self-image, central in our analysis, specifically relating it to problems of health (the IT), and finally to illuminate our findings from the perspective of creativity (the CFT).

As mentioned already, the CFT was included because the dimension of creativity seems to be crucial for an understanding of how an individual reacts when encountering problems of health, illness, and death. As we see it, creativity is an attitude toward living, which may or may not be associated with artistic talent, scientific originality, or other typically creative endeavors (cf. Pruyser, 1987). The creative person is driven by an urge to look deeper than the surface of everyday living, to find the historical roots of his or her existence, and to let this insight form one's future prospects.

RESEARCH DESIGN

Subjects were obtained in collaboration with the Gerontology Research Center in Lund. The Selenium group (called S hereafter) included 33 subjects, 13 men and 20 women, who were 70 to 72 years of age. The Pensioners' Association group (called Pa hereafter) consisted of 27 individuals, 8 men and 19 women, between 67 and 86 years old. Twenty-two of these individuals were between 67 and 75 years of age.

Most of our subjects were typically middle-class. It is difficult, however, to assess their academic background in comparison with other age groups to which we would like to refer later. In their youth it was more uncommon, particularly among women, to obtain a higher education. If they had grown up today, probably more than half of the S group and less than half of the Pa group would have taken an academic degree.

The Interview

The interview was originally constructed to uncover the subject's attitudes toward various ailments and to elucidate his or her understanding of the possible causes of illness, somatic as well as psychic, his or her concept of life quality, and so on. The following aspects of the interview will be actualized in the differential analysis. Other aspects were used for descriptive purposes.

Fear of illness
Of 14 diseases listed, the subject was asked to estimate his or her degree of fear for each of them according to a seven-point scale. The fear scores could thus vary from 14 to 98.

Life after death
The subject had three possible alternatives to answer this question: There is no life after death; the possibility cannot be ruled out; and there is life after death.

Two Case Descriptions
Subjects were asked to consider two cases, the first describing *Martha*, a 65-year-old pensioner who had suffered from various ailments during her life but had, on the whole, preserved her health. Subjects were required to mark 4 out of 12 possible causes of her relatively good health. The alternatives were later divided in two groups; one group of active alternatives, where Martha had taken things in her own hands instead of leaving them for others to decide, and another group of more passive-deterministic alternatives. An example of an active alternative would be a case in which the doctor had wanted to operate on her stomach ulcer but she decided to decline; a passive-deterministic alternative would be one in which she had simply referred to her healthy family as the main cause of her good health.

The second case described *Erna*, a 65-year-old pensioner who had been sick and frail all her life. Twelve possible explanatory alternatives were again listed, and the subject was asked to choose four. The alternatives were later divided up into more or less psychological ones. An example of a psychological alternative would be Erna stating that the reason for her bad health was that she had never been able to feel real joy or sorrow; a less psychological and more deterministic alternative would be her referring to the doctor's inability to find a suitable medicine.[1]

---

[1]The case stories were originally written by Professor Uwe Hentschel, Leiden, the Netherlands.

One subject in the pensioners' association refused to take this part of the interview. This subject also happened to be the only one in this group whose score in the CFT reflected high creativity.

The Meta-Contrast Technique (MCT)

The MCT has been described in detail elsewhere (Hentschel & Smith, 1980; Kragh & Smith, 1970; Smith, Johnson, & Almgren, 1989; Smith & Danielsson, 1982). Both the MCT and the CFT utilize the same techisto-scope. Presentation of the former involves pairs of stimuli (A and B). Stimulus B depicts a young person sitting at a table with a small window in the background. Stimulus A in the version used here depicts a forbidding face. A is projected on the area of the screen occupied by the window in B. B was first presented with gradually prolonged exposure times (.01, .02, .04 s, etc). Once the subject had reported B correctly, the exposure time was reduced to a standard value (.06 s) which, unnoticed by the subject, continued into the main series, where A was exposed immediately before B. Although the exposure time of B was kept constant, that of A was gradually prolonged (.01 s, etc., as in the CFT described below) until A + B had been correctly reported in three consecutive trials (if possible). A + B was expose twice at each exposure step. Subjects were told to report everything they caught a glimpse of on the projection screen at each trial.

The scoring dimensions pertinent to the present study concern the subject's defensive strategies (i.e., the strategies used to ward off or distort the threat [stimulus A] directed at the young person in stimulus B) as well as the anxiety evoked by it. Here we only need to describe a few dominating defensive categories.

Repressive strategies

Highly transformed variants include: house, stone, wall, tree, bike, projector, or other well-defined objects. In clinical groups, the more transformed or stimulus-distant signs of repression indicate phobia or anxiety hysteria rather than primitive hysteria. Such signs are also often found in creative individuals.

Isolation and negation strategies

These various strategies have an important characteristic in common: The hero is separated from the threatening emotion. Even negation implies a distinction of perception and the conception of something threatening. *The threat is denied* ("no unpleasant man," "it is not a person"). *Transformations with streaks of repression* (the threat is turned away from the hero; the threat becomes a white object). *Genuine signs of isolation* (the threat becomes plain, whitened, empty; light, fully covering spot, white area, faceless figure; the threat is hidden by another protecting surface; protecting, often white curtains or light clouds; the threat is separated from the hero; a frame around the threat, a protecting cover, a wall obscuring the view). *Empty geneses* (no report of the threat before the correct one).

Sex-strengthening signs
The hero is reported to have a tie, a cigar, or the like.

Transitional objects
A doll, a teddy bear, a small friendly animal, or the like is reported close to the hero figure.

The Identification Test (IT)

The basic assumption underlying this test paradigm is that subliminal verbal tags presented on a face shown in front of the viewer affect the viewer's impression of the face. The more indeterminate the face, the more inclined the subject is to describe projected parts of him- or herself in the picture. By contrasting positive and negative messages, the experimenter should be able to manipulate the projected identification.

The picture was a black-and-white close-up photograph of an English actor (unknown to our subjects), a man somewhere in his 30s or 40s with rather feminine features. The picture was blurred using a soft pencil. Earlier research (Smith, Carlsson, & Andersson, 1989) confirmed that the picture shown briefly on a screen in front of the subject can be perceived as a man as well as a woman, as a small child as well as an adult, or even as an elderly person, and with many different emotional expressions.

The picture and either of the words "I", "I WELL" or "I ILL" were presented tachistoscopically on a screen in front of the subject. The size of the screen was 35 × 35 cm and its distance from the viewer was 1.5 m. The testing room was faintly illuminated with the Lux value at the screen surface being 1.2. When the face was shown this value increased only marginally.

Exposure times began at .01 s and were prolonged, step by step, with a quotient of $\sqrt{2}$. When the subliminal messages were used they were flashed immediately before the face b means of an independent projector.

Let us take the letter B to represent the picture of the face, the letters Ae for the word "I" when projected on the face, the letters Aw for the message "I WELL," and the letters Ai for the message "I ILL."

Starting with an exposure time of .01 s, B was then presented in the series of increasing exposure times. This series was continued until the subject recognized the picture as a face. Thereafter, the following four series were presented with the exposure time being .014 s for stimulus A (for exceptions, see below) and .057 s for stimulus B:

1. Ae + B   5 times
2. Aw + B   5 times
3. Ai + B   5 times
4. B alone   5 times

The order in which 2 and 3 were presented (called the *main series* hereafter) was randomized and unknown to the perimeter. The manipulation the experimenter had to make in order to switch from one series to the next was camouflaged by fake manipulations.

The instructions were as follows:

> I'm going to show brief flashes of pictures on the screen and will say "NOW" before each flash. These pictures will contain persons. I not only want you to describe them, but to give me your impression of them as well—what kind of people you think they are, whether you like them, what you believe they could be thinking and feeling. Also try to describe the atmosphere in the picture. Sometimes you may think that the pictures we show are very much alike; sometimes that they change from one exposure to the next. Please notice such changes.

There was practically no detection of stimulus A. In case the subject seemed to have suspected some extra stimulation in the form of extra lines or marks on the face, the exposure time for stimulus A (the verbal message) was cut back one scale step, and his or her report was excluded from the protocol. Two entire protocols were removed. When stimulus A in a backward masking paradigm comes close to the visibility threshold there is, above all, danger that its effect will be reduced compared with a truly subliminal stimulus (Spence & Holland, 1962).

The following scoring dimensions were used (Smith, Carlsson, & Andersson, 1989).

Sex

Gender was scored only when explicitly mentioned by the subject ("a man," "a woman," "he," "she"). References to the subject's own sex were counted separately from references to the opposite sex. Change of sex was scored both within and between series.

Age regression

Here we scored reports of "a child" (up to an age of 12 years) and "a teenager" (13–19 years, in reality 13–15 years) or "young people" obviously of that age, together with associations to children. Denials ("not a childish face") were not counted. Series where such reports were not interspersed with reports of adults should not be judged as "regressive." Change of age was scored both within and between series.

Defense

This scoring category included one or more of the following signs, designated in analogy with signs in the MCT: *Repression* (the subject shuts his eyes, yawns; the face is reported to do so; is seen as a statue or animal; as bits of a face; is continually reinterpreted). Reports of a photo and a person eating were counted as repressive tendencies. Two tendencies matched one full sign; *Extra Attributes* (a hat, a beard, or the like); *Projection* (the gaze is emphasized; the distance or position of the face changes); and/or *Isolation* (a completely white face; a veiled or covered face; and/or a silhouette). Intellectualizing answers were counted as tendencies towards isolation. Two tendencies matched one full sign.

Reaction-formation

The face appears to be happy, cheerful, contented, and so on, in the "I ILL" series.

Emotional involvement

The face is described as happy, joyful, angry, or the like. The main series was treated in the following way: One point was given for each presentation where emotion (positive or negative) was mentioned. The number of points was counted for the two main series together.

Youthfulness

The face is described as young, the hair as thick, the eyelashes as long and dense, and so on.

Activity

The face belongs to an active person, determined, angry, and the like.

Anxiety

The subject perceives nothing meaningful (zero-phases), reports that the face appears darker than before, that it is more diffuse, and the like.

Negative reactions and summing the scoring

The two main series are compared with respect to the following negative signs weighted in decreasing order: zero-phases (see above), darkness and diffuseness; negative expressions, denial of positive expressions, and reports of "the same" were also used in the comparison. If one series included signs of darkness and the other of diffuseness, the former was thus considered to be the more negative.

Validity of the IT

The previous version of the test, with two persons in stimulus B, has been validated in several investigations (Smith & Carlsson, 1988, 1990; Smith, Carlsson, Andersson, 1989; Smith, Carlsson, & Danielsson, 1985) of normal adults, children, teenagers, and psychiatric patients. These studies demonstrated that the subliminal tagging was indeed effective. In its present form, the IT has been tried successfully in groups of adult subjects with the messages "I GOOD" and "I BAD."

The Creative Functioning Test (CFT)

The tachistoscope used in the MCT and the IT was also used for the CFT, but with only one of its projectors. The stimulus motif was a black-and-white still life depicting a rounded glass bottle with a wide bowl beside it. This still-life was chosen among several alternatives because of its expressively "human" qualities. The illumination of the room was the same as that used in the IT.

Starting with .01 s, exposure times were arranged in a geometric series with a quotient of $\sqrt{2}$. The longest possible exposure time was 3.62 s. There were two presentations at each level, except for the very long exposure times. The increasing or straight series ended when the subject had described the stimulus picture correctly three times in a row. After the correct reporting, or C-phase, the inverted series with successively diminishing exposure times started one level below the one at which the straight series had ended. There were still two presentations at each level. The test ended when the subject ceased to see anything.

The instructions were as follows:

> This experiment concerns pictures briefly flashed on the screen in front of you. I'll say "NOW" just before presenting the picture. Please look at the screen then and tell me what you think you saw. Describe your impressions and what you believe it could have been, even if you don't feel quite certain.

Scoring dimensions

The following symbols were used to characterize the inverted series: XX, X, (X), O, S, '-'.

XX: The C-phase theme eventually disappears and makes room for a meaningful but "incorrect" interpretation, often directly matching a subjective theme in the straight series. Here is one example from a previous study: "it was a different picture now. I saw somebody looking out of a window." Similar themes were entertained by that person at the beginning of his straight series.

X: The C-phase give way to another interpretation but returns again at the next exposure, or it never really vanishes, but the subject plays with alternative meanings. One example is: "Now the old bottle looks like a statue again."

(X): The C-phase is retained but parts of the picture are given deviant interpretations: "Someone has drawn a bird on the bottle."

0: Fleeting impressions reported by the subject that some of the old impressions are coming back: "I'm not certain, the picture appears somehow different, like in the beginning perhaps, but I really don't know."

S: The C-phase is retained as far as its contents are concerned, but the form of the picture changes with respect to size, distance, depth, or perspective: "The bottle has grown much larger." According to previous studies, this sign is associated with sensitivity (therefore the S designation). The subject was scored for S when he or she had more than two S-reports.

'-' The description of the C-phase does not change until everything fades away: " The bottle and the bowl, just as before."

The scoring categories form a scale with XX and X representing high creativity, (X), O, and S medium creativity and '-' no creativity. The subject is allotted the highest of the scores given in the inverted series. Scores based on the straight series may also be interesting but reflect other aspects than creativity per se and are of marginal interest here.

Validity of the CFT

The CFT has been validated in a series of investigations against various kinds of independent criteria: originality and richness of ideas, in a study of researchers; an urge to create, in a study of amateur artists and poets; originality, expressiveness, renewal, and so forth, in a study of professional artists; and creative interests and occupations, in a series of studies of children and youngsters from 4 to 16 years of age (with the exception of high puberty, where the criterion correlations often broke down). Many correlations were .70 and higher. The most relevant studies are included in a recent volume (Smith & Carlsson, 1990).

Reliability of the Tests

The MCT, IT, and CFT have all yielded high interrater correlations in previous investigations. In the present study in which the authors independently scored the protocols, there were only minor differences between their scores.

Procedure

The S (Selenium) group was tested with the MCT more than one year before the other tests were taken. The Pa (Pensioners' Association) group took all tests on the same day in the following order: CFT, IT, and MCT. All subjects were tested by a person other than the present authors.

RESULTS

The interview results will be presented first, for they help to characterize the subjects.

Of the entire group, 78% considered their life as meaningful and only 20% claimed that their way of living could have involved health risks. Anxiety with respect to death and dying was admitted by 23% (a few more in the S subgroup). Intolerance toward side-effects of medical treatment was reported by 30%. Thirty-seven percent had a mainly positive attitude towards aging, 35% had a mixed attitude, and 25% had a solely negative one. In this respect we found a considerable difference between creative and uncreative individuals in the S group: Only 8% of the creative ones (all signs considered) were negative as compared with 35% of the uncreatives. Creativity scores, as shown in Table 20.1, were less marked in the Pa group.

Nine of the 33 subjects in the S group but only 1 of 27 in the Pa group reported no fear of illness (p = .02, two-tailed Fisher's Exact Test). Those scoring below 26 points were considered to have no fear.

In the S group 12 out of 13 creatives but only 11 out of 20 uncreatives did not wish to exclude the possibility of a life after death (p = .05, two-tailed Fisher's Exact Test). Only 5 out of 13 creatives in the Pa group did

Table 20.1. Creativity in the Two Subgroups

Group	XX/X	(X)	O/S	'-'
Selenium (S)	5	5	3	20
Pensioners (Pa)	1	7	5	14

Note. XX/X = highly creative; O/S = moderate; '-' = low creativity.

not exclude the possibility, whereas the corresponding proportion for un-creatives was 9 out of 14.

The MCT

The groups differed considerably with respect to their use of isolation strategies and stimulus-distant transformations of the threat picture. Pa was the more compulsive group. When all variants of isolation were added, the scores of 9 out of 33 in the S group and 20 out of 26 in the Pa group indicated that they used isolation strategies ($p < .001$, two-tailed Fisher's Exact Test). In contrast, 14 out of 33 S subjects were scored for transformed interpretations of the threat compared with only 1 out of 26 Pa subjects (with p being the same as above).

In the S group there was a difference between those who feared illness (more than 25 points on the scale) and those who did not (25 points or less). Those who said that they had little or no fear had more sex-strengthening attributes or reported more transitional objects in the MCT protocols ($p < .01$, Fisher's Exact Test, two-tailed). The frequencies are presented in Table 20.2.

The IT

A comparison of the use of young or active attributes (as defined above) between the two main series revealed the following: In the S group the face was reported as more young or active by 20 subjects in the "I WELL" series

Table 20.2. Number of Subjects in Fear of Illness and Certain Ego-Bolstering or Soothing MCT Signs

	Sex-Strengthening Attributes or Transitional Objects	The Remainder
Fear	5	19
No fear	7	2

Note. n = 33 (S group only)

and by 5 subjects in the "I ILL" series while 8 subjects showed no difference (z = 2.80, p < .01, one-tailed). Corresponding numbers in the Pa group were 9, 1, and 15 (z = 2.22, p < .05, one-tailed). The weaker contrast in the Pa group can be partly ascribed to the considerably smaller number of active-aggressive attributions (3) used by this more compulsive and supposedly more passive group of people. Incidentally, the use of active-aggressive attributions is generally more common in creative subjects without isolating defenses than in others (p = .02, Fisher's Exact Test, two-tailed).

A clear effect of the order in which the main series was presented is revealed in Table 20.3. There was no clear effect in the Pa group. In the S group the contrast is significant at the .01 level (Fisher's Exact Test, two-tailed) with the number of young-active attributions being greater in both series when the "I WELL" series was presented first.

What happens after the control series when a main series begins? Do subjects report "the same" or do they qualify their description at the very first exposure? There was a pronounced difference depending on the message presented in the S group, but not in the Pa group, where very few subjects use "the same" as an answer (p < .02, Fisher's Exact Test, two-tailed; see Table 20.4).

In the S group there was a difference between creatives and uncreatives with respect to reported mood. The mood was reported to be neutral in both series in 1 out of 13 creatives and in 10 out of 20 uncreatives (p = .025, Fisher's Exact Test, two-tailed). No corresponding difference in mood was reported by the Pa group.

The difference between the two main series with respect to the subjects' use of positive attributions and their denial of negative ones was also analyzed. Where both types of reactions were present, the positive attributions were considered first. In the S group no subject reported more positive attributes in the "I WELL" series; 16 reported more in the "I ILL" series; and 17 reported no positive attributes or the number reported was the same in both series (z = 3.75, p < .001, two-tailed). There were no such differences in the Pa group (i.e., there was no need for a reaction-formation type of defense when the message "I ILL" was presented).

Table 20.3. The Effect of Order on Young-Active Attributions

Number of Attributions in Both Series		
First series	>1	<1
I WELL	10(1)	5(10)
I ILL	3(4)	15(10)

Note. Outside parentheses = the S (Selenium group); inside = the Pa (Pensioners') group

Table 20.4. Type of First Answer in the First Main Series After
the Control (Selenium group)

Answer	I WELL	I ILL
"The same"	1	9
Other answer	14	9

The reactions in the Pa group were more direct reflections of the subliminal messages. The number of negative reactions (zero-phases–darkness–diffuseness, weighted in decreasing order, and also negation, denial, "the same") was summarized, and in the Pa group, four subjects showed more such signs in "I WELL" and 15 showed more in "I ILL." There was no difference between series or no signs at all for six subjects ($z = 2.29$, $p < .05$, two-tailed).

Smith, Carlsson, and Andersson (1989) demonstrated that creative people alternated between descriptions of adult and young faces in their IT protocols more often than uncreative ones (all series considered). Including both childish (up to 12 years of age) and youthful (here not above 15 years of age) faces we found such age regressions in 7 out of 13 creative subjects in the S group but in only 3 out of 20 uncreative ones ($p = .02$, Fisher's Exact Test, one-tailed). Although not significant, there was a tendency in the Pa group to move in the same direction as the S group. Including young people below the age of 30 in the description, 11 out of 12 creative people and 4 out of 11 uncreatives in the Pa group had such tendencies ($p < .01$, Fisher's Exact Test, one-tailed). Those Pa subjects not mentioning age were not considered in this comparison. The difference between the S and Pa groups can, as before, be partly ascribed to the greater number of highly creative individuals in the former group.

Uncreative people typically stabilize their age attributions. Among the 13 creative subjects in the S group only 4 kept within the age strata of 10 to 29 or 30 to 50 whereas 15 out of 20 uncreative subjects did so ($p < .02$, Fisher's exact test, one-tailed). The tendency toward the same direction in the PA group was not significant.

The Case of Martha

Because tendencies in both groups were similar, they were combined for the remaining analyses. Table 18.5 presents a breakdown of subjects choosing 3 to 4 active alternatives to explain the health history of Martha and those choosing only 0 to 2.

Table 20.5. Choice of Active Alternatives to Explain the Case
of Martha (Both Groups)

No. of Alternatives Chosen	Creativity Scores		
	XX/X	(X)/O/S	'-'
3-4 Active Alternatives	5	7	11
0-2 Active Alternatives	0	12	22

When comparing the left column with the two right ones using Fisher's Exact Test for 2 × 2 tables, a significant p value in relation to signs of creativity was found (< .02, two-tailed). In the cluster analysis described below, more attention was given to the choice of particular alternatives, which often differentiate the clusters.

Age Differences

A comparison was also made of the degree of creativity in the present group and two other groups. The first one was taken from Smith and Carlsson's (1990) study and contained one hundred seventy-one 10 to 16-year-olds, around 45% of whom had an academic background; the other group was tested by the present authors to form a reference group. It contained 59 subjects aged 23 to 61 years ($M = 34$), about half of whom had an academic education. The comparison yielded the following results. In the youngsters 29% scored XX or X and 37% (X), O, or S. Corresponding figures for the middle-aged group were 12 and 39, and in the combined elderly groups, 10 and 33 respectively.

CLUSTER ANALYSIS

The Selenium and Pensioner groups were jointly submitted to a (Ward) cluster analysis (Aldenderfer & Blashfield, 1984), a method designed to optimize the minimum variance within clusters. Based on squared Euclidean distances, the Ward analysis provided valid estimates of the connections in four-fold tables. Three solutions were tried: one with three, one with four, and one with five clusters. In the first five-cluster solution there were too many small clusters (6, 13, 13, 10, 17). The four-cluster solution was therefore chosen and is presented below. Fifty-nine subjects were clustered on the basis of 222 variables (89 from the interview, excepting two cases; 28 from the case histories; 37 from the MCT; 59 from the IT; and

9 from the CFT). One person who had not taken the MCT was deleted. A few other missing data were supplemented by the computer.

The variables mentioned in the cluster descriptions all yielded significant chi-squared values, those variables with p values < .01 being particularly emphasized in the text.

Cluster 1 (n = 6)

All individuals belonged to the Selenium group. All except one were creative according to the CFT, with four of them scoring XX, X, or (X).

Like other creative subjects studied by Smith, Carlsson, and Andersson (1989), there subjects were characterized by age regressions in the IT. Other age variations (most of them in the "I ILL" series) not only included reports of children and youngsters but of elderly people as well (in all subjects). It was only in this group (three subjects) that a change of sex in the "I ILL" series was found. This is of particular interest because other creative groups have been found to use a change to the opposite sex as a defense against negative subliminal messages (Smith, Carlsson, & Andersson, 1989).

The positive attributions in the "I ILL" series of the IT (see the scoring scheme) can also be seen as a defense of the reaction-formation variety and were, as has been pointed out already, common in the Selenium group. Other transformations of the face, interpreted as defenses (see scoring scheme), were also noted in this cluster.

The IT protocols were characterized by emotional empathy. It is typical that isolation types of defense are lacking in the MCT. In the case of Martha, these individuals preferred active, self-involved alternatives when trying to explain why she remained healthy; however, they did not choose the alternative primarily referring to control (mentioning her strong will, without concertizing). The case of Erna was interpreted in psychological terms.

Cluster 2 (n = 30)

Twelve subjects belonged to the Selenium group. Nineteen received creativity scores in the CFT but only 12 of them received XX, X, or (X) scores.

No anxiety, defensive signs, or age regressions were observed in the IT; still, a moderate number of other age changes did occur. The protocols were, however, characterized by emotional empathy. Eighteen subjects reported a clear fear of illness. Part of this cluster formed a small cluster within the five-cluster solution, characterized by isolation in the MCT (the whitewashing or making harmless variants of this sign considered less pathological than the screening-off variant).

All in all, the impression of the cluster must necessarily be divided, the heterogeneity being partly caused by the great number of subjects. A summary may, however, be feasible if the creative resources in this cluster are considered being inadequate for mastering the fear of illness in a constructive manner. The other side of this inadequacy was the lack of flexibility in the self-image. The isolating defense in part of the group may have contributed to this rigidity.

The split comes to the fore in the case of Erna. Twenty-two subjects chose deterministic explanations of why Erna remained ill. Yet among these a psychological variant (Erna was mentally unstable as a child) was preferred before the more somatic ones (e.g., a sick family). Compared with the choice of alternatives in Cluster 4 (where more deterministic alternatives were preferred) this tendency was particularly marked.

Cluster 3 (n = 13)

Eleven subjects were placed in the Selenium group. There were few themes in the straight CFT series and no scores indicating creativity. Consequently, no age regressions or other age changes were observed in the IT.

Positive attributions were rare in this test. Instead, anxiety scores were more numerous in both of the main series, even in the very first expositions of "I ILL" and "I WELL."

The MCT was free from screening-off isolation. The active alternatives were avoided in the case of Martha and the psychological ones preferred in the case of Erna. This was an anxious and vulnerable group that was not protected by constructive creativity nor by isolating defenses. Persons in this group were unable to take an active responsibility for their own health.

Cluster 4 (n = 10)

Three subjects were placed in the Selenium group. The cluster is clearly uncreative and can be seen as the antipode of Cluster 1. Thus positive attributions were rare in the IT as were defensive signs, age regressions, and other age variations. There were no sex changes in the "I ILL" series.

The lack of anxiety signs in part of the IT is consonant with the isolation in the MCT (the screening-off variant). As a result, these people did not admit any fear of illness. In the case of Martha they chose the active alternatives, especially the controlling one (in contrast to Cluster 1). This cluster was thus made up of compulsive people with a rigid, emotionally empty self-image.

DISCUSSION

Two distinctly different groups of elderly subjects were chosen for the present study: an active, partly health-conscious group, and a more passive-dependent one. The groups differed with respect to test results in the ways we had expected. Nevertheless, there was still a considerable overlap, as borne out especially by Cluster 2. This overlap allowed us to combine the groups in a cluster analysis. By using two groups, as said before, we hoped to increase the representativity of our subjects. Still, that recruitment may have been biased for a number of reasons (e.g., all subjects participated of their own free will).

In spite of their relatively great number, the items from the interview played a subordinate role in the cluster analysis. One possible reason for this was that many questions concerned previous work experience, general attitudes and opinions about society and health care, knowledge of various diseases, and so on, and these may not have been as close a reflection of their personality as were the test results. The most engaging part of the interview seems to have been the case descriptions, where the choice of alternatives was crucial for several cluster definitions.

One of the most striking results was that creativity, as scored in the CFT, was accompanied by age regressions in the IT. This association had been predicted on the basis of previous findings (Smith, Carlsson, & Andersson, 1989). The regressions were most pronounced in the more highly creative Selenium group. We interpreted these regressions as representing a highly flexible self-image in which the childish and youthful perspectives alternate with more adult ones. Such an interpretation agrees in a very general way with Kris' (1952) "regression in the service of the ego," being typical of creative functioning, particularly in its inspirational phase. Perhaps the return to childhood perspectives agrees even more with Niederland's (1973) "regression in the service of ego restitution," being the creative individual's way to reinstate a factual or fantasied condition prior to an object loss. In any event, it is consonant with our own observations that creative people have easy access to early memories and dreams (Smith & Carlsson, 1990).

As pointed out in another context (Smith & Carlsson, 1990), creative functioning does not necessarily entail deep regressions but may instead involve returns to "middle" periods in life in order to reactualize dormant ideas (Smith & Kragh, 1975). In our subjects, many age regressions concerned the teenage years and, in the pensioners' group, even young adulthood before 30 years of age. Shifts between middle age and old age were also more common among creative subjects. The self-representation of uncreative people in the IT was, on the whole, stable within the adult age stratum chosen from the beginning.

Among the differentiating factors in the MCT, two types of defense were most prominent: isolation and stimulus-distant reinterpretations of the threat. Isolating forms of defense are associated with compulsive character traits, as shown in the validation studies of the MCT (Smith, Johnson, & Almgren, 1989) and are relatively rare in creative people. The latter are characterized instead by reinterpretations of the threat or, as it has also been termed in the manual, repression at a high level of transformation (Smith & Carlsson, 1990). Typically, the Selenium group showed more of the just-mentioned defenses, whereas the pensioners' showed more isolation.

Furthermore, the Selenium group was characterized by reaction-formation in the IT when "I ILL" was presented (i.e., they reported more positive, cheerful faces). This may be part of a general trend to deny the negative aspects of aging (Bultena & Powers, 1978). Instead, they tended to regard "I WELL" as a provocation. In those series the face did not only become more youthful but also more active, even more determined and aggressive. The latter reactions are in line with the Selenium person's actively health-involved (counter-phobic) lifestyle. Their pronounced creativity may also make them more inclined to identify with an aggressor, as in a previous experiment (Smith & Carlsson, 1990), and their lack of compulsive defense mechanisms may render them less likely to deny aggressive impulses (Westerlundh & Sjöbäck, 1986). At the same time, the test protocols in the Selenium group were more empathic and vivid. The group of pensioners typically only reported more active faces in the "I WELL" series, and did so there only on rare occasions. Their rather indifferent face descriptions could also be regarded as part of the compulsive defense profile.

The correlation between various instruments was best illustrated by the cluster analysis. Clusters 1 and 4 are opposites in many respects, with the fear of illness and choice of alternatives in the case descriptions being among the key variables. It is not only interesting to note the choice of controlling alternatives in the case of Martha in Cluster 4 but also the nonacknowledgement of fear of illness. Those who claimed that they did not fear illness typically used either hero-strengthening or soothing interpretations in the MCT. Cluster 1 is obviously creative, and Cluster 4 uncreative. Cluster 3, with its anxious, vulnerable people, is also interesting.

Among the test instruments, the IT is fairly new; the messages "I WELL" and "I ILL" have not been contrasted before. Although there is an obvious subliminal effect, it is not a general one but is differential in character. That is, it depends on who is at the receiving end. The order between messages is also important, and even here the effect varies with the subject. It is, moreover, worth noting that "I" alone can have an effect, and some effects carry over to the final control series (without any subliminal message). The messages used here may be less provoking than those used before ("I GOOD," "I BAD") but on the other hand, we were dealing with people approaching the end of their lives for whom both "I WELL" and "I ILL" could be even more stirring.

Highly creative people can be found even among 70-year-olds. This agrees with the statement by Pruyser (1987) quoted in the introduction. Compared with 10- to 16-year-olds, however, not only the number of highly creative people but also the nubmer of moderately creative ones are considerably lower. We should not be overly surprised. As Zinberg (1976) pointed out, for instance, older people, because of negative social stereotypes about aging, often become isolated from their own emotions and filled with doubts about themselves, all of this being detrimental to creative functioning. It is more surprising that the change with respect to high creativity in the groups presented above is most noticeable between youth and middle age (from 29–15%). Because the middle-aged group still included a noteworthy number of moderately creative subjects, one could speculate that middle-aged people are already starting to grow uncertain about the value of their private ideas and fantasies. These figures should naturally be interpreted with caution because we do not know for certain that the groups are truly representative of their age strata.

Creativity seems to be a key factor in many important respects. Creative individuals have a less negative attitude toward aging and do not unequivocally close the door to a life after death. Their attitude toward illness appears to be less defensive, probably because they are able to handle their fears in a more constructive way. This was revealed in their being partial to active, self-involved alternatives in the case of Martha. On the whole, their self-projection in the IT was not only more flexible than in uncreative people but also more emotional, and consequently, less marked by boredom. To all appearances they lead an interesting life, even in old age. But creativity is not uninfluenced by associated personality features, particularly when it is of medium strength. In a compulsive context, for instance, as in Cluster 2, this kind of creativity may be inadequate for mastering conflict and fear in a constructive manner.

REFERENCES

Aldenderfer, M. S., & Blashfield, R. K. (1984). *Cluster analysis.* Beverly Hills, CA: Sage.

Bultena, G. L., & Powers, E. A. (1978). Denial of aging: Age identification and reference group orientations. *Journal of Gerontology, 33,* 748–754.

Erikson, E. H. (1959). Identity and the life cycle. *Psychological Issues, Monograph 1.* New York: International Universities Press.

Erikson, E. H. (1963). *Childhood and society.* (2nd ed.). New York: Norton.

Erikson, E. H. (1964). *Insight and responsibility.* (2nd ed.). New York: Norton.

Hentschel, U., & Smith, G. J. W. (1980). *Experimentelle Persönlichkeitspsychologie (Experimental personality psychology).* Wiesbaden, Germany: Akademische Verlagsgesellschaft.

Kragh, U., & Smith, G. J. W. (1970). *Percept-genetic analysis.* Lund, Sweden: Gleerup.

Kris, E. (1952). *Psychoanalytic explorations in art.* New York: International Universities Press.

McCrae, R. R. (1987). Creativity, divergent thinking, and openness to experience. *Journal of Personality and Social Psychology, 52,* 1258–1265.

Niederland, W. G. (1973). Psychoanalytic concepts of creativity and aging. Psychoanalytic approaches to creativity. *Journal of Geriatric Psychiatry, 6,* 160–168.

Pruyser, P. W. (1987). Creativity in aging persons. *Bulletin of the Menninger Clinic, 51,* 425–435.

Smith, G. J. W., & Carlsson, I. (1988). Depressive retardation and subliminally manipulated aggressive involvement. *Scandinavian Journal of Psychology, 29,* 186–193.

Smith, G. J. W., & Carlsson, I. (1990). The creative process. *Psychological Issues, Monograph 57.* New York: International Universities Press.

Smith, G. J. W., Carlsson, I., & Andersson, G. (1989). Creativity and subliminal manipulation of projected self-images. *Creativity Research Journal, 2,* 1–16.

Smith, G. J. W., Carlsson, I., & Danielsson, A. (1985). Identification with an aggressor or a victim and its relation to creativity. *Scandinavian Journal of Psychology, 27,* 252–257.

Smith, G. J. W., & Danielsson, A. (1982). Anxiety and defensive strategies in childhood and adolescence. *Psychological Issues. Monograph 52.* New York: International Universities Press.

Smith, G. J. W., Johnson, G., & Almgren, P. E. (1989). *MCT: The meta-contrast technique.* Stockholm: Psykologiförlaget.

Smith, G. J. W., & Kragh, U. (1975). Creativity in mature and old age. *Psychological Research Bulletin,* Lund University, *15,* No. 7.

Spence, D. P., & Holland, B. (1962). The restricting effects of awareness. *Journal of Abnormal and social Psychology, 64,* 163–174

Verwoerd, A. (1977). Training in geopsychiatry. In E. W. Busse, & E. Preiffer (Eds.), *Behavior and adaptation in late life* (pp. 328–348). Boston: Little, Brown, & Co.

Westerlundh, B., & Sjöbäck, H. (1986). Activation of intrapsychic conflict and defense. In U. Hentschel, G. J. W. Smith, & J. G. Draguns (Eds.), *The roots of perception* (pp. 161–215). Amsterdam: North-Holland.

Zinberg, N. E. (1976). Normal psychology of the aging process, revisited. I. Social learning and self-image in aging. *Journal of Geriatric Psychiatry, 6,* 160–168.

PART IV

SOCIETAL HEALTH AND CREATIVITY

Part IV

Introduction

Dean Keith Simonton has built some remarkable models of factors affecting individual creativity at the eminent level. The *Creativity Research Journal* asked him to address issues of pathology at the societal level. The goal was to identify political pathology that may influence creativity through its effects on eminent individuals. Now this is certainly not an easy task. One person's pathology may be another person's progress—just ask members of the major political parties at election time. But Dean Simonton took on the challenge, as did eight other people who provided insightful commentaries on this paper. Finally, there was a rejoinder by Simonton. The entire discussion is presented here.

Creativity and political pathology: Is the topic too value bound? A hopeless exercise? If one speaks only of factors that may help or hurt a society's creativity—of this and no more—one can perhaps move a bit away from the judgment of social health or unhealth. Or one may shift the question to whether creativity itself is intrinsically healthy for individuals and for cultures.

Surely creativity will not always be healthy. Suppose a terrorist succeeds with an ingenious plot and a nuclear explosion devastates a city. The lives of a great many are ended, and of many more changed irreversibly through the physical, environmental, and social deterioration that follows. Were there other healthier solutions? One might readily think so. How relative are the values rejecting mass murder by a capricious few; most people would strongly disapprove. As with intelligence, there is no moral qualifying test for the use of one's creativity. There are clearly questionable uses. Yet the present volume also addresses whether repeated application of creativity might, on the average, be good for one's mental health and one's greater connection with others—not entirely the same question. But we can hope that, on balance, the applications of creativity will further group as well as individual well-being.

By way of a preview for this section, one may note that there are three factors of political "disruption," if not "pathology," delineated by Simonton, which are said to negatively affect creativity. These include *international war*, which indeed also lowers integrative complexity of thought and raises arousal. *External threat* and *political instability* (anarchy) too have negative effects. A couple of other disruptions also show positive links with eminent creativity, this time as well with a generational lag—a delayed effect. This pattern may involve an experiencing in childhood with a later expressiveness as an adult. Overall, a greater creative diversity may be one social consequence. These two factors are *political fragmentation*, and *civil disturbance*. One sees in the commentaries that interpretation of such factors is not always simple. But their proposal, and the discussion they are already stimulating, represent a major advance of our thought in a tricky area.

Chapter 21

Political Pathology
and Societal Creativity

Dean Keith Simonton

A long and pervasive tradition holds that individual achievement of phenomenal stature must be associated with psychopathology of some kind (Becker, 1978; Lombroso, 1891; Prentky, 1980). "There is no great genius without some touch of madness," said Seneca, which Drydn seconded centuries later with "Great wits are sure to madness near allied,/And thin partitions do their bounds divide." Whether or not this judgment is true, however, is *not* the business of this essay to determine. Rather, the question to be addressed concerns whether a parallel association between genius and madness holds at a higher level of analysis—that of the society or culture. In order to boast an impressive mass of creative geniuses must a given sociocultural system be in some sense insane? Or is it possible that whatever the linkage between genius and madness at the individual level, the connection at the societal level is decidedly negative? Must a creative society be a healthy one?

There is no dearth of speculation on this question. The historian Arnold Toynbee (1946) speculated on the diverse factors that are associated with the rise and fall of world civilizations: Where the ascent is graced with both societal vitality and cultural creativity, the decline is plagued by political and cultural stagnation. For instance, the "nemesis of creativity" is found in the "idolization of an ephemeral institution," as when the culture becomes perversely committed to a political system that has long outlived its adaptiveness, whether that system be the city–state, monarchy, or the church. Likewise, the sociologist Pitirim Sorokin (1937–1941) investigated large cyclic changes in whole sociocultural systems, some "types of culture mentality" being more healthy and others more sick. A civilization displays creative élan when the political, judicial, social, economic, intellectual, and aesthetic subsystems all converge on a healthy condition, whereas the more pathological combinations spell creative decadence. For Sorokin, societal creativity goes hand-in-hand with a modal personality of supreme happiness and well-being, not madness. Finally, the anthropologist Charles Gray (1958, 1961, 1966), wishing to explicate the conspicuous "configurations of culture growth" documented by Alfred Kroeber (1944), proposed an epicyclical model in which the ups and downs in the appearance of creative geniuses are the ultimate consequence of underlying movements in political, economic, and social systems. When politics, the economy, and society are synchronized to reach their peaks, the civilization enjoys a creative fluorescence.

Notice that these theorists concur that, at the societal level, genius and madness are quite remote, even antithetical. Even so, none of these investigators, even the most empirically inclined of them, performed any direct tests of their theoretical hypotheses. Because these speculative schemes have not always survived close empirical scrutiny (Naroll, Benjamin, Fohl, Fried, Hildreth, & Schaefer, 1971; Simonton, 1976b), we cannot say for sure how pathology and creativity are related at the societal level. Therefore, my chief goal here is to bring together in one place the scattered results that may enlighten us on this subject. Later I will discuss what theoretical implications, if any, these findings have for our appreciation of the psychological processes that supposedly underlie the observed systematic effects.

THE EMPIRICAL RESULTS

Three limitations of the forthcoming review should be made explicit. In the first place, we will concentrate on *changes within* sociocultural systems rather than *contrasts among* separate systems. In other words, for a given nation or civilization, what happens to the aggregate production of creative products or persons when signs of pathology set in? Omitted from discussion are cross-cultural investigations which inquire whether the magnitude and properties of creativity vary across societal units according to the presence or absence of certain cultural traits, like socialization practices (cf. Barry, 1957; Martindale, 1976). The rationale for this neglect is simply stated: It requires more tenuous value judgments to discern contrasts in creativity and pathology across various cultures than it does to assess changes in the same attributes within a single society. Where the former condition invites ethnocentric bias, the latter at least has the virtue of adopting the society as its own control, so that a comparative baseline can be established within a given culture.

The second limitation concerns the class of pathologies on which we shall concentrate our attention. Although societies may be branded as unhealthy on all sorts of grounds, our focus will be on political ills. Most of the available quantitative research examines the repercussions of political events for creative expression, an emphasis that probably reflects: (a) the highly dramatic and intrusive nature of political phenomena and (b) the ease with which pertinent indicators can be quantitifed for subsequent statistical analyses. Hence, pathologies concerning accepted values and mores, the distribution of wealth, attitudes towards women and minorities, daily lifestyle, religious beliefs and practices, ecological disequilibrium, and a host of other critical possibilities will be ignored, albeit we will later find an excuse to speak briefly of economic malaise. Despite the obvious narrowness of this perspective, it can be argued that when something goes awry in a society, it does not take long for the problem to manifest itself in the guise of political difficulties of the type we will be discussing.

The third and last limitation regards the precision with which I can define the key concepts to be discussed in this essay. On the one hand, "societal creativity" is a fairly easy notion to comprehend, whether we consider it to encompass the total aggregate output of a culture or to entail the typical forms and content of the products that a creative society generates. On the other hand, what should count as "political pathology" is far less easily discerned. After all, we are dealing here with only a metaphorical concept—perhaps a useful one but not an idea that is highly isomorphic with individual mental sickness. One criterion could be that a society lacks equilibrium, yet this touchstone does not always work. An imperial state, for example, may exhibit a decadent and stifling stability, like some excessive neuroticism, whereas a revolution may, by creating a more just political system, represent a healthy state of affairs analogous to a therapeutic catharsis. In the absence of an optimal definition, the best procedure may be to follow a purely Baconian method, listing with as much grace as possible the raw facts in the hope that some consistent picture will eventually emerge. By so advancing, we may learn just as much about what might constitute political pathology as about the connection this elusive phenomenon has with societal creativity.

In any case, below we scrutinize how societal creativity responds to the coming and going of international war, external threat, political instability, political fragmentation, and civil disturbances.

International War

An especially ugly symptom that something's amiss is military conflict between sovereign states. Although one historian has ventured that "warfare usually tends to produce cultural and intellectual sterility" (Norling, 1970, p. 248), direct empirical tests of the supposed negative relationship have been in short supply. Even worse, many preliminary inquiries isolated no association whatsoever, whether positive or negative (e.g., Naroll et al., 1971; Simonton, 1976a, 1977a). Nonetheless, these studies suffered from unforeseen methodological problems, the most crucial being a generic conception of war and a reliance on time-series units of excessively long duration (e.g., generations or centuries). Yet different types of military struggles may influence creativity in contrary ways, and whatever impact war possesses may be transitory, lasting only for the duration of the conflict. In most instances, conflicts seldom endure longer than a half-decade. Hence, in one successful transhistorical time-series analysis (Simonton, 1980b), the appearance of scientific discoveries and technological inventions in European civilization was tabulated into yearly periods from 1500–1903 A.D., while war was differentiated according to a classificatory scheme employed by Wright (1965). Only balance-of-power and defensive wars drastically inhibit the annual rate of discovery and invention, whereas civil and imperialistic wars display no influence at all. Balance-of-power wars may indicate that the diplomatic constraints on the system of nations have broken down, one or more countries believing that the sword can win what the word cannot; defensive wars, which are those that involve the invasion of European culture by alien powers (such as the Ottoman Empire), hint of an internal weakness that welcomes exploitation from outside the cultural ecumane.

Despite the conjecture that "modern wars usually increase medical knowledge" (Norling, 1970, p. 248), the historical data show quite the opposite (Simonton, 1976d). Whatever gains are made by piling bloody bodies in hospitals fails to compensate for the far less hospitable aspects of military conflict, such as the massive waste of material and human goods. In addition, there is some reason to believe that the negative correlation holds in the arts as well as the sciences. To offer an instance at the individual level, William Shakespeare tended to write his best plays when England was at peace, whereas the dramatist's poorer plays tended to emerge when his country was entangled in military struggles with rival powers (Simonton, 1986b). The same effect holds for the dramatic output in the classical Athens of Aeschylus, Sophocles, Euripides, and Aristophanes (Simonton, 1983). Interestingly, an examination of the careers of 36 European monarchs indicated one possible basis for such inverse functions: Early in a reign, a king, queen, or sultan tends to succumb to military adventurism, but later in a reign the ruler is more prone to indulge in literary patronage, thereby diverting national resources from war to peace (Simonton, 1984b).

Far more fascinating, in my view, is the curious manner in which international war shapes the form and content of the creative products that somehow manage to surface despite the less than favorable political conditions. Such consequences have been most amply documented in literary creativity. Martindale (1975) showed that fluctuations in total war casualties per capita were associated with the content of English poetry, specifically encouraging the introduction of more secondary process imagery and the treatment of moral imperatives, but discouraging the handling of themes having to do with chaos. Literary content even seems vulnerable to whether the military news from the front is good or bad! A content analysis of 81 notable plays revealed that dramatists were more likely to discuss prudence when their nation was experiencing defeat but were less likely to do so when the war was proceeding more auspiciously (Simonton, 1983). In the particular case of Shakespeare, when England was under attack he became more prone to examine the theme of "conquest, empire, and political expansion as ends of war." Warfare has also been found to affect the level of integrative complexity to be found in the letters of British novelists (Porter & Suedfeld, 1981), an effect that we will return to later in this essay.

Influences have been observed for nonverbal kinds of creativity, as well. In the domain of popular culture, for example, women's dress fashions—especially the length and width of the skirt, waist, and neckline—to some extent are subject to the whims of European militarists (Simonton, 1977b; cf. Richardson & Kroeber, 1940). And in the domain of the *Hochkultur*, or at least within classical music, the melodic structure of thematic material has been shown to be responsive to the occurrence of military conflict (Simonton, 1987), an effect that is particularly aggravated when the composer has the misfortune of having to compose in the midst of a war zone (Cerulo, 1984).

Thus far this discussion has touched solely on contemporaneous side-effects of bloody disagreements among nations. Nevertheless, certain repercussions are long-delayed and therein are of longer duration. Winter (1973), for instance, examined the emergence of literary versions of the Don Juan motive since its first introduction by the Spanish dramatist Tirso de Molina in 1630. In England and France, the gain or loss of colonial territory was followed two decades later by the publication of new accounts of this legendary cynic and sexual conquistador. More immediately relevant is Winter's demonstration that the participation in war by 15 European nations from 1830–1959 was correlated with the appearance of Don Juan stories after about a decade lag. Because the Don Juan character symbolizes an entire worldview, we might suspect that warfare would deflect the course of intellectual history besides—and this is evidently so. A generational time-series analysis of thousands of philosophers spanning from Ancient Greece to modern times found that 20 years after a major outbreak of international war one can often observe a *decrease* in the number of thinkers who advocate empiricist epistemology, an ontology of unending change, philosophical nominalism and individualism, and ethical systems predicated on the pleasure principle (Simonton, 1976f). People are seemingly stimulated to scurry around in a quest for security, cohesion, permanence, and authority.

Oddly, there is some tentative evidence that the causal influence can sometimes run in the opposite direction: A few philosophical positions may establish an intellectual milieu more favorable to warfare, for a score of years after a resurgence in materialistic and skeptical thinkers, the probability of military conflict tends to increase (Simonton, 1976f). If we can link this result with what we have just learned about Don Juan theme, cynicism and Machiavellianism may be both an antecedent and a consequent of sanguinary disagreements among independent states. In partial support for this admittedly insecure speculation we might note Martindale's (1975) finding that the occurrence of aggressive imagery in English poetry was positively correlated with the hegemony of materialistic and hedonistic beliefs on the part of the larger intellectual community. Philosophical idealism, in contrast, was negatively correlated with aggressive imagery. This is one of the clearest examples of a pathological tie between politics and creativity that will be offered in this review.

External Threat

Changes sometimes take place so rapidly in a sociocultural system that its denizens must make equally quick adjustments in everyday living. Such mandatory coping may then have representations in the creative expression featured in a given time and place. Martindale's (1975) extensive study of English poetry provides an illustration. Taking a tabulation of scientific discoveries and technological inventions, he showed that timewise fluctuations in this index of "technological change" were *inversely* proportional to the amount of secondary process imagery present in concurrent English poetry. Hence, the rationality and reality orientation that demonstrably underlies technoscientific advance (Simonton, 1976d) does not receive endorsement from the passive recipients of these disruptive innovations—the sensitive poets of a society. A more universal and robust example, however, may be found in the rich literature on the linkage between external threat and authoritarianism. Building on the basic conclusions put forward in the classic studies on the *Authoritarian Personality* (Adorno, Frenkel-Brunswik, Levinson, & Sanford, 1950), these investigations have exploited historical data in order to show that authoritarianism expands in a society whenever the system must face some dangerous circumstances. Most often the threat is economic in nature (Sales, 1972), but occasionally the danger is more broadly defined to include political factors as well (McCann & Stewin, 1987).

This research began when Sales (1972) indicated that economic hard times favor high conversion rates to authoritarian churches, but economic prosperity encourages conversion to nonauthoritarian churches. Later Sales (1973) demonstrated that the state of the economy also affected other domains, such as the harshness of punishment mandated for sex crimes. For two reasons this body of research is germane to the topic at hand:

1. In line with the assertions of the initial research—which was, after all, largely inspired by then recent experiences of Hitler's rise in Germany—authoritarianism means a shift in the political climate toward an increasingly autocratic style of leadership. Specifically, the same threatening conditions that nurture authoritarianism also welcome American voters to cast their ballots on behalf of presidents who score high in power motivation (McCann & Stewin, 1987). Furthermore, power-hungry chief executives are more likely to enter the United States into military combat and to become targets of assassination attempts (Winter, 1987; Winter & Stewart, 1977). Such changes may be taken as hints of a substratum of political pathology, an inference that is strengthened by the argument that authoritarianism is a manifestation of an unfortunate personality disorder (Adorno et al., 1950). The concrete reality of this illness is illustrated in the second point.

2. Authoritarian times bring about distinctive modes of creativity in both popular culture and the more academic pursuits. To offer a representative sample from the first domain, in adverse circumstances: Comic strip characters exhibit more power and toughness, and magazine articles display more cynicism (Sales, 1973); television programs become more authoritarian in tone (Jorgenson, 1975); and books on superstitious topics like astrology and mysticism see improved sales (Sales, 1973). Closer

to home, external threat invites an increase in the popularity of parapsychological research in the professional journals (McCann & Stewin, 1984) and concomitantly lessens interest in psychology and psychoanalysis (Sales, 1973). Thus, it may have been no coincidence that the same political milieu that brought Ronald Reagan into the White House—and a First Lady who adhered closely to the daily horoscopes—also ushered in an era of drastic cuts in public funds to support behavioral science research!

Political Instability

As war is the most obvious hint of insanity in the sphere of international politics, so is political instability the surest clue that something is rotten within the national regime. By this condition I mean anarchy, albeit this latter designation may be a bit too judgmental. In any event, political instability is registered by political assassinations, coups d'etat, military revolts, dynastic conflicts, and conspiracies—all suggesting that the power elite of a nation is on the verge of moral and political collapse. Such events have a clear influence on the amount and magnitude of creativity that emerges in a civilization, even though the imprint tends to feature a generational delay. For example, in one generational time-series analysis the number of creators in generation g tended to be inversely related to the level of political instability in generation $g - 1$, the immediately preceding generation (Simonton, 1975).

It is important to recognize that this relationship, although holding across over a hundred generations of Western civilization, applied only to creativity in science, philosophy, literature, and music. Creativity in the visual arts, by comparison, tends to be largely immune from the detrimental effects of anarchy. Furthermore, it must be stressed that this negative function holds only when there is a time lag, for the contemporaneous association between creativity and anarchy is nil. Finally, not only does political instability affect the number of notable creators that emerge from each generation, but this factor is prominent at the individual level besides. In particular, an inquiry into the differential eminence of 2,012 philosophers observed that the more political instability in generation $g - 1$ the less famous the philosophers were prone to be in generation $g + 1$, or 20 years afterward (Simonton, 1976e). Lesser thinkers have little difficulty emerging out of a chaotic political milieu, but truly outstanding thinkers may be nipped in the bud.

Despite the evidence that political instability can inhibit the quantity of creators as well as the distinction to be achieved by the few creators who escape through the adversity, the data are nearly silent about whether anarchy determines the form and content of the creative products that highlight these dark times (cf. Simonton, 1976f). In fact, I can cite only one pertinent finding, and this concerns merely the career of a single creator, namely Shakespeare once again (Simonton, 1986b). Evidently, whenever the Elizabethan and Jacobean world in which this playwright worked was shocked by the disclosure of a dangerous conspiracy against the British crown—like the rebellion of the Earl of Sussex or the plot of Guy Fawkes—Shakespeare was stimulated to treat a telltale set of themes at some length in his plays. The Bard was specifically compelled to address such questions as "the duties of command and obedience in family life," "patterns of love and friendship in the family," "myth of the royal personage . . . and the burdens of monarchy," and finally, "the natural and the unnatural or monstrous."

This collection of issues may seem bizarre to those of us whose experience is narrowly restricted to democratic government. But this dramatist lived in an age of hereditary monarchy, an institution inextricably embedded in familial relationships and presumed to represent the natural order of human affairs, the life cycle of the monarch providing the very model for the historical ebb and flow of the whole nation. In this context, conspiracies against the sovereign were diabolically evil, or in more contemporary terms, politically pathological. The playwright evidently could not resist underlining this unnatural monstrosity in his dramatic output, and by this shrewd act, we can be sure, eliciting the appreciative applause of most of his audience!

Political Fragmentation

Unlike the previous three conditions, especially war and anarchy, whether one wants to count the current factor as an example of political pathology may require a difficult value judgment. Political fragmentation is the circumstance in which a civilization is divided up into a large number of independent states, where sovereignty is defined by the freedom to pursue an independent foreign policy (such as making alliances and declaring war). The city–states of Classical Greece and Renaissance Italy are prototypical instances of fragmentation, whereas the Macedonian Empire and Imperial Rome exemplify the opposing situation. Many philosophers of history, such Toynbee (1946), think that imperial expansion sounds the death knell of a political culture. Certainly large empires require the subordination of numerous minority peoples, an unfortunate consequence quite evident in Roman, Byzantine, Arabic, Ottoman, Russian, and Japanese empires. On the other hand, political fragmentation often brings with it internecine military struggles, and at the very minimum implies that a single people are split by arbitrary political divisions. For Bismarck the partitioning of 19th-century Germany was unnatural, as was the segmentation of Italy in the eyes of Garibaldi and Manzini. Perhaps only by reporting the repercussion of this factor for societal creativity can we get a more firm notion of whether political fragmentation is indicative of, or antiethical to, political pathology.

For one thing, it is fairly clear that splitting a culture into many autonomous units has rather beneficial consequences for the quantity of creative individuals that emerge. To start with, a generational time-series analysis of the origins of over 5,000 creative geniuses of Western civilization revealed a positive association between the number of creators active each 20-year period and the number of independent nations. This result also was found to hold for Islamic and Indian civilizations (Naroll et al., 1971; Schaefer, Babu, & Rao, 1977). This correspondence seems to endorse Danilevsky's "second law of dynamics of great cultures" that "in order for the civilization of a potentially creative group to be conceived and developed, the group and its subgroups must be politically independent" (quoted in Sorokin, 1947/1969, p. 543). Even so, we cannot necessarily infer that this principle applies to those imperial systems that are identified with a single language, culture, and people. Rather, the apparent regularity may apply exclusively to multi-ethnic, polyglot civilization areas in which the growth of the empire can only mean the oppression of the uniqueness inherent in any one people. Hence, political fragmentation fails to exert a positive impact on literary creativity in China (Ting, 1986).

Because political fragmentation does not change suddenly from generation to generation, it is not easy to discern precisely whether it operates contemporaneously or only after some generational delay (Simonton, 1976c). Nevertheless, the little evidence that we do possess seems to favor the latter alternative, particularly when we inspect the nexus between this political condition and philosophical creativity:

1. The proliferation of sovereign states tends to be more supportive of intense ideological diversity, as manifested in a plethora of distinct schools and positions (Simonton, 1976c). When a civilization is divided into so many political entities, it becomes far easier to "Let a hundred flowers blossom, let a hundred schools of thought contend" (to expropriate ironically a slogan from the 1957 campaign in China). Besides being a sure sign of intellectual vitality, and hence creativity, ideological diversity is strongly correlated with general creativity.

2. The most famous thinkers of Western intellectual history had a higher probability of emerging under times of political frag-

mentation than under an imperial age, an effect that operates with a generational lag (Simonton, 1976e). Hence, the same milieu that encourages a diversity of philosophical schools nourishes with equal force the appearance of the most influential intellects.

3. Political fragmentation provides a favorable setting for the development of a specific cluster of philosophical positions: A generation after an increase in the supply of autonomous states we are likely to witness an augmentation in those who advocate empiricism, skepticism, fideism, materialism, evolutionary change, nominalism, individualism, and hedonistic or utilitarian ethics (Simonton, 1976f). We may say that these beliefs represent the ideology of a politically diversified system of nations.

Perhaps it is now proper to surmise, from all that we have disclosed in this section, that an all-engulfing empire may reasonably be perceived as a manifestation of political pathology.

Civil Disturbances

When an imperial state has succeeded, perhaps over the course of several generations, to gobble up the bulk of its less powerful neighbors, the resultant drive toward cultural homogeneity—the "Russification" process—can eventually undermine the creative potential of the whole society. Matters are not hopeless, nonetheless, for some political events may serve to resuscitate the desired diversity. At least it is the experience of Western culture that revolts and rebellions in the context of imperial rule are inclined to raise the likelihood of creative activity two decades later (Simonton, 1975). These civil disturbances are more effective under political integration than fragmentation, for in the latter case such events may be mostly superfluous from the standpoint of rejuvenating the cultural heterogeneity of the civilization area. Anyhow, we must take care to distinguish between this positive effect and the negative effect previously noted for political instability. The latter variable concentrates on anarchy among those already in positions of high power, such as monarchs, dictators, and generals, whereas civil disturbances, properly speaking, involve the masses, those largely powerfulness in a political system. This distinction is obviously critical, given their divergent aftershocks. Civil unrest, unlike anarchy, may even be taken as a sign of political vitality.

We have just been talking of effects that operate only after a generational delay. Yet civil disturbances can certainly exhibit a more instantaneous impact. For example, an inquiry into the characteristics of 1,935 compositions in the classical repertoire found that those pieces created under conditions of civil unrest were more likely to become popular and to be more accessible to audiences (Simonton, 1986a). However, works that came to light under these exciting events also suffer from lower ratings of aesthetic significance at the hands of musicologists, and so the compositions are popular but shallow (Simonton, 1986a). Nor can we dismiss these artistic implications as mere subjective impositions, for the pieces conceived under conditions of civil turmoil objectively differ from those that issue under more stable domestic politics. Revolt and rebellion have a tendency to induce composers to create melodic material that is lower in originality and less variable in complexity (Simonton, 1986a), two aesthetic traits that were determined by totally objective computer content analysis of the transition probabilities between consecutive notes (Simonton, 1984c). Consequently, these works may be popular and accessible but aesthetically insignificant owing to attributes intrinsic to the composition; for some unknown reason composers are going for applause at the expense of profundity.

Civil disturbances leave an immediate impression on other forms of creativity. Like international war, intranational conflict deflects women's dress fashions in specific directions, whether we are inspecting the dimensions of the waist, skirt, or neckline (Simonton, 1977b). However, dress styles are not affected in the same manner by the two kinds of collective political violence. For instance, whereas international war narrows skirts, international war widens skirts! This divergence manifests itself in other domains as well, so we are not dealing with a fluke of just the superficial fashion scene. For instance, a content analysis of the correspondence of five British novelists found that war intensity caused a decrease in integrative complexity, a gauge of sophistication of thought. In contrast, civil unrest heightened the apparent richness of information processing (Porter & Suedfeld, 1981).

While we are on the topic of authors, we must mention, too, that of all forms of creativity, literature seems to be the most responsive to contemporaneous civil disturbances. Martindale (1975) discovered that aggressive imagery in English poetry declined during times of internal social stress. Similarly, an analysis of 81 classic plays indicated that the same political events elicited the treatment of particular themes, most notably the rather pertinent question of how to adjust the individual to social responsibility (Simonton, 1983). To return one last time to the career of Shakespeare, this playwright could evidently no more ignore the recurrent rebellions in Ireland than could the British monarchy. When such events became the news of the day he was provoked to examine "conflict in human life: opposed types of men and modes of life" (Simonton, 1986b).

But perhaps the most intriguing findings concern Sorokin's (1947/ 1969, p. 487) hypothesized "law of polarization," which he described as follows:

The overwhelming majority of the population in normal times is neither distinctly bad nor conspicuously virtuous, neither very socially-minded nor extremely antisocial, neither markedly religious nor highly irreligious. In times of revolution this indifferent majority tends to split, the segments shifting to opposite poles and yielding a greater number of sinners and saints, social altruists and antisocial egoists, devout religious believers and militant atheists. The "balanced majority" tends to decrease in favor of extreme polar factions in the ethical, religious, intellectual, and other fields.

Even if a careful analysis of Sorokin's (1937–1941) raw data suggests that he got the details wrong (Simonton, 1976f), Sorokin did capture an important truth with respect to how civil disturbances affect philosophical creativity. One generation after a massive outbreak of revolts, rebellions, and revolutions we witness in Western civilization a startling spurt in thinkers representing totally opposed beliefs and values with respect to all the critical philosophical questions: Advocates of empiricism rub shoulders with adherents of rationalism and even mysticism; materialists debate with idealists; those who believe that the fundamental ontological reality is eternal buck heads with those who think that all is in incessant flux; some version of the nominalist versus realist controversy is rekindled; individualists contend with collectivists and other proponents of the statist positions; determinists are countered by defenders of free will; and thinkers who broadcast happiness or pleasure as the foundation of moral decisions find themselves contradicted by intellectuals who maintain the ethical primacy of absolutes or love (Simonton, 1976f). The political turmoil of one generation that so divided a people becomes the intellectual unrest of the next generation. Does this succession exemplify an instance of political pathology breeding cultural effusion?

THEORETICAL IMPLICATIONS

Up to this point, the empirical literature has been reviewed with scant consideration of what these results tell us about individual creativity. What can we say about the creative process, person, and product from their diverse connections with political pathology? To address this question properly demands that we first lay down two useful distinctions that are implicit in the preceding discussion. To begin with, we must separate discussion of the *number* of creative individuals or products boasted by a society at a given historical time from the *form* that this creativity assumes.

Certainly counting the distinguished dramatists springing forth from each generation is not the same thing as assessing the thematic emphasis of the plays produced. The second distinction concerns whether we are dealing with short-term and immediate effects versus more durable effects that take years to be realized fully. Some creativity criteria, whether quantitative or qualitative, only display a transient response to political pathology, whereas other criteria require an appreciable amount of time to lapse, but once the cultural consequences of political events become tangible the impact may endure for decades. Needless to say, the psychological meaning of a given effect must take care to recognize both of these distinctions, because it is most improbable that one process underlies all observed relationships between political pathology and societal creativity. I would like to discuss briefly four principal possibilities:

1.   Some effects most likely provide clues about what sorts of political events inhibit or enhance the creative process. Thus, it is probably difficult to conceive genuinely innovative ideas when a person is under severe stress, given that many of the pertinent thought processes, such as intuition, depend on low levels of arousal (Simonton, 1980a). Granting this prerequisite, it should come as no surprise that international war lowers the output of creative products and even vitiates the actual quality of what works do get produced the adversity notwithstanding. This explains why the impact is so temporary, for political stressors provide only momentary annoyances in the majority of cases. In this interpretation, too, political pathology becomes but one of several other extraneous stressors that interfere with the individual's creative routine. For example, physical illness also tends to undermine creative output (Simonton, 1977a). This account receives further endorsement from the fact that we have some fairly direct evidence that warfare accentuates the emotional arousal of individuals (e.g., Cerulo, 1984; Porter & Suedfeld, 1981; Simonton, 1980c).

But why do civil disturbances project different consequences? The best answer may be that people respond quite differently to these two political conditions. Although one might think that collective violence is undiscriminating, its appearance is merely superficial. After all, in international war an entire political unit is at risk, and each citizen accordingly threatened, by some external power; but in intranational war the people are more directly engaged in the onrush of events, and may even experience a sense of exhilaration in the recognition that the political world is moving toward reforms that are long overdue. This differentiation is bolstered by the data suggesting that emotional arousal is actually *lower* in times of civil turmoil (Porter & Suedfeld, 1981; Simonton, 1986a). It may be naive for us to overlook the unrelenting tension associated with living in an unjust and oppressive system. Once the revolution, rebellion, or revolt has begun, the dissenters can in a sense "come out of the closet" and express to the world their long-suppressed accusations. In lieu of guarded whispers in left-bank coffee houses, citizens can take to the streets, shout from balconies, and raise up the barricades in an exciting anticipation of the forthcoming utopia!

2. Other effects may provide the raw material on which the creative process necessarily operates. This possibility is most obvious in the route by which political history supplies the content of literary products, such as plays and poems. Hence, it makes sense for poets to devote more words to moral imperatives in times of war, given how such conflict amplifies discussion of duty and obligation as part of the general call for individuals to make personal sacrifices for the public good. Yet the intrusion of exogenous events into the fabric of a piece may be more subtle and indirect. As a case in point, if "music sounds the way emotions feel," then the structure of a melody may mirror the internal emotional state of the composer at the time of the work's composition. From this linkage may arise the impact of international war upon the melodic style of a piece, an effect multiplied by the creator's presence in the midst of a war zone buzzing and booming with bombs and artillery shells. This consequence ties political pathology with a more inclusive collection of factors that, by affecting the emotional state of a creative genius, determines the form and content of an emerging creation. For instance, melodic structure is associated as well with physical illness, personal stress, and proximity to death (Simonton, 1980c, 1987, 1989).

3. Some unhealthy conditions may affect creativity even more indirectly. Rather than influence the creative process or the material on which that process operates, certain circumstances may have the most impact on those who represent the potential appreciators of creative products, whether those recipients be the intelligentsia or the masses. The zeitgeist, by affecting which avenues to social acceptance are most open, serves to elicit some forms of creativity at the expense of alternative forms. Such a contextual influence is most apparent in the research on the authoritarian response to external threat. Under adverse circumstances, psychologists with a bent toward parapsychology get encouragement to pursue their interests, whereas those of a more deterministic or natural science orientation may find themselves out of synchrony with their times. In popular culture especially, an authoritarian milieu provokes all sorts of marginal forms of creativity to come out of the closet, filling

bookstores with the occult and injecting machismo characters into mass entertainment. We do not have to subscribe to the notion that individual creators direct their creativity by assessing which way the wind blows in order to surmise that these incentives can deflect the course that creativity takes. Each creator may maintain his or her intellectual or aesthetic integrity, but some find themselves applauded while others experience the ignomy of being ignored. Nevertheless, even a playwright of the caliber of William Shakespeare was obliged to appease contemporary audiences; when material for costumes and sets must be purchased, space rented or theaters constructed, and actors paid, one cannot fuss overly much about the hypothetical tastes of remote posterity! Therefore, it should come as no surprise that Shakespeare modified the themes of his dramatic creations to acknowledge that his nation, glorious England, had to rally against the aggressors, to deal with the human issues evoked by nationalistic revolts close to home, and to handle the moral dilemmas spawned by conspiracies against the royal personage.

4. Because the preceding theoretical accounts only allow for contemporaneous and momentary influences, some other process must be recruited to explain how political pathology can sway societal creativity only after a wait of a score of years, and then more durably. To appreciate how such a mechanism can operate, we must first recall that the bulk of these lagged effects were isolated using generational time-series analysis (Simonton, 1984a). In this technique, the flow of history is sliced into consecutive 20-year periods, or generations, and a historical figure is assigned to that two-decade interval in which he or she attained the 40th year of life, a reasonable all-around estimate of the career peak (Simonton, 1988). Because a genius is 40 ± 10 years old in generation g, that person is 20 ± 10 years of age in generation $g - 1$. Accordingly, political events that take 20 years to materialize in the creativity of a nation or civilization may be deemed as developmental factors. That is, political events with causal delays a generation in length may be interpreted as environmental variables that determine the development of creative potential in adolescence and early adulthood. Hence, if political instability at generation $g - 1$ diminishes the number of illustrious creators in generation g, we can plausibly wonder whether this loss has something to do with the fact that creators in their productive phase in g were in their developmental phase at $g - 1$, and thereby had their early years distorted and twisted by the dramatic events. I have hypothesized that this adverse developmental influence reflects the necessity for creators in the so-called rational domains to acquire a strong sense that the world is fun-

damentally coherent, predictable, and controllable, enabling the individual to plan futures and conjure up ambitious projects. (Simonton, 1975)

Other generation-lagged factors work to enhance the level of creative potential in the forthcoming generation. Political fragmentation, by supporting cultural diversity, operates to nurture creative development as well. This fragmentation, by localizing politics, may equally establish that "internal locus of control" that anarchy does so much to destroy. Civil disturbances may also function by both of these mechanisms, each converging to generate the phenomena that demonstrate the law of polarization. In short, a special political milieu will endorse the growth of geniuses with the requisite capacities for self-actualization and the richness of experience that enables this drive to adopt the unique form of landmark creativity, the upshot being a creative society.

Naturally, because empirical conclusions in the behavioral sciences are always tentative, the theoretical implications just drawn are even more fragile. Nevertheless, it is very probable that some relationships exist in which, for the most part, the connections are antagonistic. Political pathology is very probably hostile to societal creativity. The only saving grace may be that whatever meager creative offerings sneak through the collective madness will probably pay some thematic homage to the tragic spirit of the times.

REFERENCES

Adorno, T. W., Frenkel-Brunswik, E., Levinson, D. J., & Sanford, R. N. (1950). *The authoritarian personality*. New York: Harper.

Barry, H. (1957). Relationships between child training and the pictorial arts. *Journal of Abnormal and Social Psychology, 54*, 380–383.

Becker, G. (1978). *The mad genius controversy*. Beverly Hills: Sage Publications.

Cerulo, K. A. (1984). Social disruption and its effects on music: An empirical analysis. *Social Forces, 62*, 885–904.

Gray, C. E. (1958). An analysis of Graeco-Roman development: The epicyclical evolution of Graeco-Roman civilization. *American Anthropologist, 60*, 13–31.

Gray, C. E. (1961). An epicyclical model for Western civilization. *American Anthropologist, 63*, 1014–1037.

Gray, C. E. (1966). A measurement of creativity in Western civilization. *American Anthropologist, 68*, 1384–1417.

Kroeber, A. (1944). *Configurations of culture growth*. Berkeley: University of California Press.

Lombroso, C. (1891). *The man of genius*. London: Scott.

Martindale, C. (1975). *Romantic progression*. Washington, DC: Hemisphere Publishing.

Martindale, C. (1976). Primitive mentality and the relationship between art and society. *Scientific Aesthetics, 1,* 5–18.

McCann, S. J. H., & Stewin, L. L. (1984). Environmental threat and parapsychological contributions to the psychological literature. *Journal of Social Psychology, 122,* 227–235.

McCann, S. J. H., & Stewin, L. L. (1987). Threat, authoritarianism, and the power of U.S. presidents. *Journal of Psychology, 121,* 149–157.

Naroll, R., Benjamin, E. C., Fohl, F. K., Fried, M. J., Hildreth, R. E., & Schaefer, J. M. (1971). Creativity: A cross-historical pilot survey. *Journal of Cross-Cultural Psychology, 2,* 181–188.

Norling, B. (1970). *Timeless problems in history.* Notre Dame, IN: Notre Dame Press.

Padgett, V., & Jorgenson, D. O. (1982). Superstition and economic threat: Germany 1918–1940. *Personality and social Psychology Bulletin, 8,* 736–741.

Porter, C. A., & Suedfeld, P. (1981). Integrative complexity in the correspondence of literary figures: Effects of personal and societal stress. *Journal of Personality and Social Psychology, 40,* 321–330.

Prentky, R. A. (1980). *Creativity and psychopathology.* New York: Praeger.

Richardson, J., & Kroeber, A. L. (1940). Three centuries of women's dress fashions: A quantitative analysis. *Anthropological Records, 5,* 111–150.

Sales, S. (1972). Economic threat as a determinant of conversion rates in authoritarian and nonauthoritarian churches. *Journal of Personality and Social Psychology, 23,* 420–428.

Sales, S. M. (1973). Threat as a factor in authoritarianism: An analysis of archival data. *Journal of Personality and Social Psychology, 28,* 44–57.

Schaefer, J. M., Babu, M. C., & Rao, N. S. (1977, March). *Sociopolitical causes of creativity in India 500 BC–1800 AD:* A regional time-lagged study. Paper presented at the meeting of International Studies Association, St. Louis, MO.

Simonton, D. K. (1975). Sociocultural context of individual creativity: A transhistorical time-series analysis. *Journal of Personality and Social Psychology, 32,* 1119–1133.

Simonton, D. K. (1976a). The causal relation between war and scientific discovery: An explanatory cross-national analysis. *Journal of Cross-Cultural Psychology, 7,* 133–144.

Simonton, D. K. (1976b). Do Sorokin's data support his theory? A study of generational fluctuations in philosophical beliefs. *Journal for the Scientific Study of Religion, 15,* 187–198.

Simonton, D. K. (1976c). Ideological diversity and creativity: A re-evaluation of a hypothesis. *Social Behavior and Personality, 4,* 203–207.

Simonton, D. K. (1976d). Interdisciplinary and military determinants of scientific productivity: A cross-lagged correlation analysis. *Journal of Vocational Behavior, 9,* 53–62.

Simonton, D. K. (1976e). Philosophical eminence, beliefs, and zeitgeist: An individual-generational analysis. *Journal of Personality and Social Psychology, 34,* 630–640.

Simonton, D. K. (1976f). The sociopolitical context of philosophical beliefs: A transhistorical causal analysis. *Social Forces, 54,* 513–523.

Simonton, D. K. (1977a). Creative productivity, age, and stress: A biographical time-series analysis of 10 classical composers. *Journal of Personality and Social Psychology, 35,* 791–804.

Simonton, D. K. (1977b). Women's fashions and war: A quantitative comment. *Social Behavior and Personality, 5,* 285–288.

Simonton, D. K. (1980a). Intuition and analysis: A predictive and explanatory model. *Genetic Psychology Monographs, 102,* 3–60.

Simonton, D. K. (1980b). Techno-scientific activity and war: A yearly time-series analysis, 1500–1903 A.D. *Scientometrics, 2,* 251–255.

Simonton, D. K. (1980c). Thematic fame and melodic originality: A multivariate computer-content analysis. *Journal of Personality, 48,* 206–219.

Simonton, D. K. (1983). Dramatic greatness and content: A quantitative study of 81 Athenian and Shakespearean plays. *Empirical Studies of the Arts, 1,* 109–123.

Simonton, D. K. (1984a). Generational time-series analysis: A paradigm for studying sociocultural influences. In K. Gergen & M. Gergen (Eds.), *Historical social psychology* (pp. 139–155). Hillsdale, NJ: Erlbaum.

Simonton, D. K. (1984b). Leader age and national condition: A longitudinal analysis of 25 European monarchs. *Social Behavior and Personality, 12,* 111–114.

Simonton, D. K. (1984c). Melodic structure and note transition probabilities: A content analysis of 15,618 classical themes. *Psychology of Music, 12,* 3–16.

Simonton, D. K. (1986a). Aesthetic success in classical music: A computer analysis of 1935 compositions. *Empirical Studies of the Arts, 4,* 1–17.

Simonton, D. K. (1986b). Popularity, content, and context in 37 Shakespeare plays. *Poetics, 15,* 493–510.

Simonton, D. K. (1987). Musical aesthetics and creativity in Beethoven: A computer analysis of 105 compositions. *Empirical Studies of the Arts, 5,* 87–104.

Simonton, D. K. (1988). Age and outstanding achievement: What do we know after a century of research? *Psychological Bulletin, 104,* 251–267.

Simonton, D. K. (1989). The swan-song phenomenon: Last-works effects for 172 classical composers. *Psychology and Aging, 4,* 42–47.

Sorokin, P. A. (1937–1941). *Social and cultural dynamics* (4 vols.). New York: American Books.

Sorokin, P. A. (1969). *Society, culture, and personality.* New York: Cooper Square. (Originally published 1947.)

Ting, S. -S. (1986). *The social psychology of literary creativity: An archival data analysis.* Doctoral dissertation, University of California, Davis.

Toynbee, A. J. (1946). *A study of history* (2 vol. abridgment by D. C. Somervell). New York: Oxford University Press.

Winter, D. G. (1973). *The power motive.* New York: Free Press.

Winter, D. G. (1987). Leader appeal, leader performance, and the motive profiles of leaders and followers: A study of American presidents and elections. *Journal of Personality and Social Psychology, 52,* 196–202.

Winter, D. G., & Stewart, A. J. (1977). Content analysis as a technique for assessing political leaders. In M. G. Hermann (Ed.), *The psychological examination of political leaders* (pp. 27–61). New York: Free Press.

Wright, Q. (1965). *A study of war* (2nd ed.). Chicago: University of Chicago Press.

Chapter 22

Societal Creativity: Problems with Pathology

Sharon Bailin

In his chapter, "Political Pathology and Societal Creativity," Simonton attempts to test the hypothesis that there is a connection between political pathology and societal creativity by surveying the empirical research which bears on this issue. He synthesizes a vast array of studies from a large range of sources and describes in intricate detail complex and sometimes contradictory relationships between political events and the quantity, quality, and content of creative outputs. It will not be the concern of this commentary to examine the validity of the alleged connections nor to question the research methodology. Rather, what will be of concern is the contention that these relationships reveal some connection between creativity and political pathology. This is a problem not because of any flaws in Simonton's research, but rather because of the difficulty inherent in applying the concept of pathology at the societal level.

The chapter describes connections between creative products and other cultural and social forces. And indeed, such connections would be precisely what would be expected given an understanding of the integral place of creative products in the social and cultural context. To demonstrate such connections is to reject the view that creativity is marked by radical novelty and hence a fundamental break with contemporary thought and practice and a total discontinuity between creative products and their antecedents (Hausman, 1984). This is a view which Simonton is right to reject. An analysis of creative works in various areas reveals influences on products with respect to both form and content from a range of intellectual, social, and political factors and reciprocal influences of the works on the society (Bailin, 1985, 1988; Gardner 1986, 1988). Simonton's essay describes with admirable comprehensiveness the complexities of such relationships in the political context.

The question remains, however, as to whether such connections can rightly be viewed in terms of a relationship between creativity and political pathology. The answer will, of course, depend to a considerable extent on one's conception of creativity and, even more centrally, on one's conception of pathology.

The hypothesis regarding the relationship between societal creativity and political pathology is suggested initially by a parallel to the individual case. Simonton states that there is a long and pervasive tradition that holds that individual creativity must be associated with psychopathology of some kind and that his essay is an attempt to discern whether a parallel association between genius and madness obtains at the level of the whole society or culture.

However, the alleged relationship between creativity and pathology is far from unproblematic even in the individual case. There is, as Simonton notes, another tradition which holds that creativity is associated with mental health rather than with mental illness (Maslow, 1971). This diversity of opinion rests, partially at least, on how creativity and mental health are conceptualized. If mental health is viewed in terms of adaptation to social norms, and creativity is seen as involving seeing beyond the accepted and thus violating the norms, then creativity will be pathological by definition. If, on the other hand, mental health is viewed in terms of personal growth and self-actualization, and such self-actualization is seen to require seeing beyond the ordinary, then creativity is by definition equated with mental health.[1] Thus it can be seen that even the notion of individual pathology is not unproblematic. Determining pathology is not a purely empirical matter. Rather, the notion of pathology presupposes

---

[1]An assumption which underlies both these views is that there is a distinctive process of thought which characterizes creativity. I believe that there are good reasons for rejecting this assumption (Bailin, 1988) and that there are, thus, no grounds for asserting a necessary connection between creativity and either mental illness or mental health.

some notion of health and hence of ideal functioning, and thus carries with it presuppositions regarding human nature and value judgments regarding human ideals.

Simonton does assert that it is not within the scope of his essay to determine the accuracy of the alleged connection between individual creativity and pathology. I do, however, believe that the individual case is relevant for several reasons. First, the hypothesis at the societal level is given its initial plausibility through the parallel to the individual case. Second, the same type of problems with respect to value judgments are apparent at the societal level as at the level of the individual.

As problematic as is the notion of pathology when applied to an individual, it is even more problematic when applied to a society as a whole. Indeed, if insanity is a psychological phenomenon, then one might wonder in what sense a society might be considered to be insane. Might this mean that the society is made up of a collection of insane individuals? This does not seem to capture Simonton's notion of pathology, however, because the mental health of individuals within the society is never at issue. The usage is more metaphorical, as Simonton himself notes, but it is a metaphor derived from individual pathology.

Simonton deliberately avoids offering a definition of political pathology. He does provide a list of symptoms, including international war, external threat, political instability, political fragmentation, and civil disturbances, but we are not offered an account of why or in what way these particular events constitute instances of pathology. The notion of political pathology presupposes some notion of political health, and it thus becomes necessary to ask what the standard is of political health from which these symptoms indicate a deviation. As a standard is never clearly stated, one must attempt to glean one from the various symptoms. Might the standard be the strength or vitality of the society? Yet a society may well prosper as a result of an international war. Might the standard be social cohesiveness? Yet an external threat may serve to pull a society together, and in addition Simonton is not sure whether political fragmentation constitutes pathology. Might social harmony be the standard for political health which underlies the various symptoms? Yet Simonton states that civil unrest might sometimes be a sign of political vitality. Is political stability the criterion? Simonton himself offers counter-examples to this proposed criterion. And one might further wonder in what sense a stable society which purchases its stability at the cost of repression is, in fact, healthy. It is not at all clear, then, precisely which criteria can be used for determining whether certain social phenomena are pathological. Indeed, in the case of political fragmentation, Simonton seems to conclude that an all-engulfing empire is a manifestation of political pathology on the basis of the effects that such an empire has on creative achievement—a clear case of begging the question!

The underlying problem here is exactly parallel to the problem previously described in the individual case, namely that the concept of societal pathology presupposes some notion of societal health, and the notion of what constitutes a healthy society rests upon views about the nature of society which depend ultimately on a political philosophy. A Marxist, for example, might view some forms of civil disturbances as signs of health, and might see a society in the throes of open class struggle as healthier than the society at peace, if peace is the product of capitalist oppression and compliance, the product of false consciousness. Similarly, an anarchist certainly would not view anarchy as a pathological, but might instead deem pathological a societal phase in which human beings are artificially constrained by institutions. And a democrat would likely view political instability as a sign of health in a society struggling against oppression.

There is a danger inherent in talk of pathology. In the case of an individual, the danger lies in defining mental health in terms of society's mores and then using the terminology of deviance to repress opposition. In the societal case, the danger lies in defining political health in terms of a particular political ideology. The problem is not in putting forth as desirable some particular political ideal. It is, rather, in making a value judgment regarding political ideals which is hidden in the guise of a strictly empirical claim. A judgment regarding pathology, in this context at least, can never be purely empirical.

Simonton is clearly aware of this problem regarding the tenuousness of value judgments at the societal level and attempts to avoid enthnocentric bias by not dealing with contrasts between cultures but only within one society. Nonetheless, as soon as one attempts to identify what is to be considered pathological and what is to count as healthy even within a society, one is squarely in the arena of political philosophy.

Is there any way in which this problem can be avoided in the type of analysis that Simonton offers? I think that his handling of the issue of political fragmentation points the way to a better approach. In dealing with political fragmentation, Simonton recognizes that there is a value judgment involved in making an assessment and thus does not initially commit himself to a judgment regarding whether fragmentation is pathological. Instead, he simply reports the repercussions of this factor for societal creativity. This mode of proceeding seems to avoid the type of problem previously described. The account offered in this essay of the connections between societal creativity and political phenomena has much to recommend it in terms of its detail, comprehensivess, and illumination of the issue. Framing the issue in terms of pathology seems unnecessary and unfortunate.

REFERENCES

Bailin, S. (1985). On originality. *Interchange, 16*(1), 6–13.

Bailin, S. (1988). *Achieving extraordinary ends: An essay on creativity.* Dordrecht: Kluwer.

Gardner, H. (1986). Freud in three frames: A cognitive-scientific approach to creativity. *Daedalus, 115*(3), 105–134.

Gardner, H. (1988). Creativity: An interdisciplinary perspective. *Creativity Research Journal, 1,* 8–26.

Hausman, C. (1984). *Discourse on novelty and creation.* Albany: SUNY.

Maslow, A. (1971). *The farther reaches of human nature.* New York: Penguin.

Chapter 23

Four Frames for the Study of Creativity*

David Henry Feldman

In Jean Genet's play *The Balcony*, the plot revolves around role reversal. Characters who were on the periphery of society, the pimps, whores, and thieves, all of a sudden find it necessary to assume roles as pillars of society. The basic point of the play is that roles are powerful determinants of behavior, and whoever occupies the role of, say, Chief Judge of the Supreme Court, will behave more or less as anyone else would behave in the same role. People who have watched from the balcony change their behavior when asked to move to center stage.

There is something of this quality in Dean Simonton's ingenious research about the powerful press of context on creativity. In Simonton's

*The title of this response is more or less stolen from an article written by my brother Jerome A. Feldman which appeared in the journal of *Brain and Behavioral Science*. Thanks go to the Jessie Smith Noyes Foundation, the Andrew Mellow Foundation, the Grant Foundation, and the Rockefeller Brothers Fund for supporting the work which give rise to the discussion presented here. Gratitude also goes to Ann C. Benjamin for reading an earlier draft.

world it seems as if people are interchangeable, more or less, and that large social patterns determine what kinds and what quality of work will be done in several realms of creative work. If there is a war, for example, then certain kinds of poetry and philosophy will appear. Different kinds of poetry and philosophy will appear during periods of territorial expansion.

This tack is evidently not taken to deny the importance of individual initiative, but rather to draw attention to the fact that there is much more to the process of producing important work than a lone creator expressing unique ideas. The problem is of course to see in what ways individuals and societies coinfluence each other.

Through efforts of the sort presented in the article under review, Dean Keith Simonton has almost single-handedly given the field of creativity research a new vitality with his fresh approach to research and spirited yet rigorous style of presentation. He has constructed a technique for analyzing large scale issues such as the relationship between war and creative output that is at once original, powerful, and compelling. Through "historiometric" analyses of products in various domains, Simonton has been able to shed new light on age-old questions. One of these, of course, is the long standing association between insanity and genius, a belief that goes far back into human history. This subject is explored with characteristic style and elan in "Political Pathology and Societal Creativity."

In this response, I will comment only briefly on the work presented in Professor Simonton's article. I have already made clear that I greatly admire the work and think it makes very significant contributions to the knowledge base from which we try to comprehend creative processes. I want to focus instead on a question that was stimulated by reading Simonton's article and is, alas, only tangentially related to it. But why it is only tangentially related is actually the key point I wish to make.

The question I wish to explore is: Why has the field of creative research come back from near oblivion to academic respectability and become one of the more interesting subfields of psychology? To answer this question, it is necessary to consider matters *intermediate* between the individual and the whole society, and it is in precisely these intermediate zones where I think much of the action resides, theoretically and empirically speaking, and contrary to Simonton's orientation.

CONCEPTUAL ISSUES IN STUDYING GENIUS AND INSANITY AT THE SOCIETAL LEVEL

The work presented in the present article rests on an assumption that bears closer scrutiny than it is given therein. That assumption is that the genius/madness connection for individuals is well captured in the kinds of events that are portrayed at the larger societal level. It is as if we were being asked to do an analogy problem with genius/insanity as the first element, and creativity/war as the second element. Genius is to insanity, so the reasoning goes, as creativity is to war (or disturbance or economic crisis).

Then we are being asked to accept that the first words in each element of the analogy are also analogous, that is, that genius and creativity can be considered similar. How far things are stretched in making this analogy becomes clear when data about skirt lengths and hemlines are introduced as evidence for the effects of war on creativity.

Finally, and most problematic, is the assumption that the *second* two terms, insanity and war, are also analogous. On the surface this comparison seems reasonable enough. As Howard Gruber has pointed out numerous times (e.g., Gruber & Davis, 1988), war, any war, is craziness. Still, it is difficult to cast all war into the bin of insanity. Consider the "just war" against the Nazi onslaught, or the "jihad" or holy wars of the Moslems. Were I to guess, I would bet that certain kinds of creativity (and perhaps genius—they are not the same) might in fact be catalyzed by the challenges and inspiration, if not the fear, of a war that is believed in.

Regardless of how destructive nuclear weaponry has been, it is no doubt true that the technology and knowledge base upon which nuclear weapons are built was one of the most startlingly original and successful additions to knowledge of the twentieth century. It is doubtful that the dramatic increase in knowledge brought about by concentrating resources in places like Los Alamos, N.M., would have happened in the absence of war.

It is an interesting and worthwhile effort to link changes even in such run-of-the-mill kinds of creativity as fashion shifts with changes in societal/political events. But the conceptual relationship between these sorts of events and genius in any meaningful sense is quite a stretch. For this reviewer the stretch is too much, and I find myself wishing that the comparison were simply dropped. The subject matter stands on its own without being tied to the ages old issue of genius/insanity.

I would simply reinterpret the work presented in the current article as dealing with relationships between broad scale political and social events, including war and political instability of various sorts, and various creative endeavors. Some of the most valuable insights in the reported work have to do with distinctions between different kinds of wars and different forms of political instability, and how each of these affects productivity, quality, and thematic selection in various fields like poetry, philosophy, and the visual arts. The resulting picture has the texture and complexity of reality, or at least seems closer to it than olympian universal generalizations of the Sorokin (1969) or Toynbee (1946) sorts.

Were Professor Simonton to be interested in further pursuing the question of the relationship between genius and insanity (and based on his omnivorous research appetite it is a good bet), I would urge him to look at more directly relevant data. For example, the number of cases of institutionalization for emotional breakdown among highly educated individuals in relation to political/social events might reveal interesting findings. All of this said, this work nonetheless represents a significant contribution to the effort to provide an empirical base from which to approach a complex and difficult topic. Perhaps less complex, though still a real challenge, is the topic to which I would now like to turn.

THE REJUVENATION OF THE FIELD
OF CREATIVITY RESEARCH

Few (other than die-hard creativity test devotees) would argue that the field was all but dead by the beginning of the 1970s (cf. Wallach, 1971; although see Guilford, 1970). Somehow, between then and now a field has come back to life. There are several important lines of research, new journals, books being well received, and what seems to be a critical mass of high-level scholarship likely to sustain high levels of activity for several years.

Perhaps the most dramatic recent sign of creativity's return to academic respectability was when James Greeno, known for taking a very hard line cognitivist position (and an antidevelopmental one at that), included work on creativity in his review on thinking for a special children's issue of the *American Psychologist* (1989). Greeno wrote:

> It may be that the extraordinary motivation for intellectual work that characterizes many exceptionally creative individuals is a version of the constructive epistemological position of individuals who believe that knowing and understanding are products of their intellectual processes. . . . How . . . preliminary intuitive connections can grow into full-fledged new systems of interaction with physical, social, or conceptual settings is a major question for future research. (Greeno, 1989, p. 140)

Another indication of renewed life from the same region of the academic landscape is in the recent work by computer simulators, who have been claiming that they can write programs that construct some of the scientific discoveries of the past, arguing in the process that creativity involves little more than the use of processes of problem solving common to all thinking (Csikszentmihalyi, 1988a, 1988b, 1990; Langley, Simon, Bradshaw, & Zytow, 1987).

Finally, when the mainstream journal *Cognitive Psychology* publishes a lead article on creativity (invention, specifically; see Weber & Dixon,

1989), it is clear that creativity research and theory have taken a major step back into the limelight. The solid center of cognitive science now recognizes creativity as a worthy topic of investigation. There can thus be little doubt that creativity research has once again arrived. What is much less clear is how and why it has done so. What can be learned about the social forces that led to the resurgence of creativity research by drawing from historiometric analyses? Is creativity research more likely to thrive in times of economic abundance? When there is external threat? When political fragmentation is relatively great?

I should mention at this point that I have a special interest in why creativity research has once again come into its own. Aside from the fact that I have been watching the field from the inside for more than 20 years, I have also been officially involved in stimulating the revival process. Since 1980 I have been chair of a committee of the Social Science Research Council (SSRC) that was charged with the task of helping to revive research on creativity and giftedness. With funding from the Mellon Foundation, a small group of fellow scholars and I have been actively trying to stimulate interest in these fields, not through direct promotional efforts but through scholarly activities that aim to show the importance and challenge of work in these areas.

During the decade of activities of the committee (members have included Jeanne Bamberger, Mihalyi Csikszentmihalyi, Yadin Dudai, Howard Gardner, Howard Gruber, Helen Haste, and more briefly Robert Siegler and Robert Sternberg), it appears that the committee's mission has been accomplished, at least in the area of creativity research.

In truth, however, it is not at all clear that the work of the committee has had much to do with the renaissance of the field. And so I am particularly interested in the question of just how the field has been brought back to life. I am, of course, happy to claim credit for the revival, and I am free to believe that the work of our group has been instrumental in bringing about the positive change. But I also know that the establishment of causal connections is always difficult, particularly when there is little control over the variables.

What must be acknowledged is that much of the work that has caught the attention of the scholarly community (and the more applied community as well) has come from sources outside the committee. Work by Amabile, Albert, Martindale, Perkins, Simon, Weber, and especially Simonton, among others, was not done with sponsorship or support from the SSRC. The most successful new efforts seem to have sprung up independently from any official sponsorship by the social science establishment. I should not overstate this: Work by Csikszentmihalyi, Gardner, and Gruber has been quite visible, and no doubt contributed to the present upsurge in creativity research interest. Still, the impression I have is that the critical mass needed for kick-starting the field came from sponta-neous individual efforts unconnected to any formal organized enterprise. Perhaps Dean Simonton, always ingenious, will think of ways to empiri-cally investigate these matters.

The first time (in the early 1950s) that creativity research became an important field was without question related to major political events. It was in the aftermath of World War II that the conditions emerged for a new set of tests that would better serve the survival of America than IQ tests had done. J. P. Guilford (1950) sounded the call for a major new ini-tiative that would help the U.S. win a future war. He called this work "cre-ativity" research because it involved innovativeness, leadership, originality, and quality of product. Guilford believed that this new "creativity" re-search was vital to the survival of the West. And, so must have the pow-ers that be, because federal support for the initiative was immediate, generous, and lasted for nearly 20 years.

So at least the first creativity research movement could be character-ized as following Simonton's 10-year delay following a "just" war. By the mid-1950s, creativity research on ability and personality was booming in several parts of the country. It was not until the antic 1960s, when cre-ativity research took a decisive turn to the left, that its support disap-peared and the fabric of a tight-knit research community began to unravel (Feldman, Csikszentmihalyi, & Gardner, 1990).

No such explanation can be straightforwardly mounted for the more recent return of creativity research to prominence. There is no war that has ended within the past 10 years, although Vietnam was "ending" about 20 years ago. In fact, the whole idea of trying to account for the changes in a field of research seems somehow too far from the action. That there may be *trends* to be identified, and that are associated with major politi-cal, economic, and social shifts, is well documented in Simonton's review. But if we are trying to comprehend a change in a field such as creativity research, it is clear that much more information is needed.

Essentially, the point I want to make about the framework that Si-monton uses is that it deals only with two polar ends of a continuum that should include other things besides individuals and broad social events. No one would want to dispute that individuals have something to do with creativity (although reading Simonton lulls one into forgetting about it), and the case is well made in Simonton's work for an association between war, political disorganization, and the like, and creativity. But as jazz singer Peggy Lee says, "Is that all there is?"

There are at least two other realms of analysis that must be brought into the picture if a plausible story about creativity research during the 1980s can be told. One of these has to do with the *domain* itself, that is, the body of organized knowledge that is represented in the work of creativity researchers and scholars (Csikszentmihalyi, 1988a, 1988b; 1990; Feldman, 1980, 1988, 1989). The other is the *field* of endeavor that provides the direct and specialized context within which the field evolves (Csikszentmihalyi, 1988a, 1988b; 1990).

When entered onto the continuum of factors that influence changes in quality and quantity of works, the domain and field fall between the individual and the broad social context. One could add other factors as well, no doubt, but these four should serve well as a framework for analyzing the process. Fewer factors lead to the unreal quality of interplay among events that I tried to convey with a reference to Jean Genet's play *The Balcony*. More factors might provide texture to the story, but tracking the relevant information through the four factors of individual, domain, field, and society, if done well, should provide a satisfying account.

To specify the domain and field shifts that have contributed to the recent surge in creativity research is beyond the scope of the present discussion, but a few points can be made to illustrate what kinds of things should be analyzed. As a domain, creativity research has shifted from working within its psychometric history and tradition to a cognitive and developmental psychology orientation. Rather than try to test for a creativity trait, researchers have begun to try to describe creative processes in cognitive terms (e.g., Gardner, 1982, 1988; Perkins, 1981; Sternberg, 1988) or developmental reorganizations (Bamberger, 1982; Feldman, 1982a, 1982b, 1982c, 1982d, 1988, 1989; Gruber & Davis, 1988). These recent efforts have opened up new areas of research and, more importantly, have reoriented the field. This reorientation has had much to do with the increase in research activity, and it is of course part of a much larger set of changes in the whole of psychology.

As for the field, several things should be noted. The involvement of the Social Science Research Council has for a half century been a sign of new or renewed interest in a research field. There are many instances when a SSRC committee proved catalytic to a focus of interest and resources; for example, the "cognitive revolution" was catalyzed, in part, by such a committee, as was the field of child language. The recent interest of the SSRC in giftedness and creativity began in 1975 and provided an arena within which the shift in the fundamental intellectual orientation of the domain was changed.

The MacArthur Foundation's so-called "genius grants" called more public attention to creativity and gave it greater status, spawning a number of similar programs in other foundations. Thus, private foundation support has increased, both in recognizing creative work and helping to energize the field of research, including research on the MacArthur Fellows themselves (Cox, Daniel, & Boston, 1985).

A final example is a combination of the domain and the field both contributing to a shift. Data have been accumulating for more than 20 years on the predictive validity of so called "creativity tests," and they have proven to be quite disappointing, I would even say devastating (although see Sawyers & Canestero, 1989). The promise that the creativity research movement made was to be able to produce psychometric instruments that would vitally improve on IQ. They have shown little ability to be of practical use in predicting real world creativity potential, and they are not being recommended for use in applied settings (Borland, 1989; Crockenburg, 1972; Feldman, 1970, Gardner, 1988).

At the same time, tests in general have come under increasing attack from policy and consumer groups. An organization called Fairtest has been particularly relentless in pursuing the testing industry. Although creativity tests have not been a particular target of Fairtest and other groups, they are affected by a changing climate in which testing in all forms is under attack (Fairtest, 1989). As testing has lost some of its hold on the public imagination and has proven, at least in the creativity field, to be of little use, the conditions for an alternative way of looking at and studying creativity have been enhanced.

These examples are, of course, brief and only sketchily presented, but the flavor of them should be clear enough. The point is that along with investigations of individual and broad social processes, those associated with fields and domains should also be pursued.

CONCLUSION

This discussion has wandered fairly far afield from the relationship between genius and insanity, or political pathology and societal creativity. Although there are worthwhile things to be learned from posing questions of that sort, and some of these are ably presented in Dean Simonton's article, my purpose has been to show that there are other aspects of creativity that should be simultaneously considered in any such effort. To look only at individuals and large social patterns is to invite a strange distortion of the effects of context on individual behavior, as in the example of the play *The Balcony*. Equally distorting is to see the individual as much more completely the master of his or her own fate than could possibly be the case, as in many previous accounts of creativity. Still, it is a vital step to move away from exclusive focus on either individuals *or* broad social causal variables.

By going two steps further and adding domains of knowledge and fields of endeavor to the overall picture, the dangers of distortion are vastly reduced. Although quite obviously not the whole picture, these four aspects of creativity are sufficient to prevent bizarre distortions of reality and offer as well ample opportunities for further research. Dean Simonton is a master practitioner at detecting subtle relationships between large changes in social, political, and cultural context and general rate and quality of creative output. As necessary as such efforts are, they should always be seen within an overall framework that also includes individuals, domains, and fields (Feldman et al., 1990). To do so will, I believe, insure a long and healthy future for creativity research.

REFERENCES

Bamberger, J. (1982). *Growing up prodigies: The mid-life crisis.* In D. H. Feldman (Ed.), *Developmental approaches to giftedness and creativity* (pp. 61–78). San Francisco: Jossey-Bass.

Borland, J. (1989). *Planning and implementing programs for the gifted.* New York: Teachers College Press.

Cox, J., Daniel, N., & Boston, B. (1985). *Educating able learners: Programs and promising practices.* Austin, TX: University of Texas Press.

Crockenberg, S. (1972). Creativity tests: A boon or boondoogle for education? *Review of Educational Research, 42,* 27–45.

Csikszentmihalyi, M. (1988a). Motivation and creativity: Toward a synthesis of structural and energistic approaches to cognition. *New Ideas in Psychology, 6,* 159–176.

Csikszentmihalyi, M. (1988b). Society, culture, and person: A systems view of creativity. In R. J. Sternberg (Ed.), *The nature of creativity.* Cambridge, England: Cambridge University Press.

Csikszentmihalyi, M. (1990). *The domain of creativity.* In M. A. Runco & R. S. Albert (Eds.), Theories of creativity (pp. 90–112). Newbury Park, CA: Sage.

Fairtest (1989). *Update on K–12 Testing.* Cambridge, MA: National Center for Fair and Open Testing.

Feldman, D. H. (1970). Faulty construction: A review of Wallach and Wing's "The talented student." *Contemporary Psychology, 15,* 3–4.

Feldman, D. H. (1980a). *Beyond universals in cognitive development.* Norwood, NJ: Ablex.

Feldman, D. H. (Ed.). (1982a). *Developmental approaches to giftedness and creativity: New directions for child development.* San Francisco, CA: Jossey-Bass.

Feldman, D. H. (1982b). A developmental framework for research with gifted children. In D. H. Feldman (Ed.), *Developmental approaches to giftedness and creativity* (pp. 31–45). San Francisco, CA: Jossey-Bass.

Feldman, D. H. (1982c, March). *Developmental science: An alternative to cognitive science: A colloquium.* Paper Presented at The Division for Study and Research in Education, MIT, Cambridge, MA.

Feldman, D. H. (1982d). Transcending IQ in the definition of giftedness. *Early Childhood Review, 23,* 15–18.

Feldman, D. H. (1988). Creativity: Dreams, insights, and transformations. In R. Sternberg (Ed.), *The nature of creativity* (pp. 271–297). New York: Cambridge University Press.

Feldman, D. H. (1989). Creativity: Proof that development occurs. In W. Damon (Ed.), *Child development today and tomorrow* (pp. 240–260). San Francisco, CA: Jossey-Bass.

Feldman, D. H., Csikszentmihalyi, M., & Gardner, H. (1990). *A framework for the study of creativity.* (manuscript in progress).

Gardner, H. (1982). Giftedness: Speculations from a biological perspective. In D. H. Feldman (Ed.), *Developmental approaches to giftedness and creativity.* San Francisco, CA: Jossey-Bass.

Gardner, H. (1988). Creativity: An interdisciplinary perspective. *Creativity Research Journal, 1,* 8–26.

Greeno, J. (1989). A perspective on thinking. *American Psychologist, 44,* 134–141.

Gruber, H. E., & Davis, S. N. (1988). Inching our way up Mount Olympus: The evolving-systems approach to creative thinking. In R. J. Sternberg (Ed.), *The nature of creativity* (pp. 243–270). New York: Cambridge University Press.

Guilford, J. P. (1950). Creativity. *American Psychologist, 5,* 444–454.

Guilford, J. P. (1970). Creativity: Retrospect and prospect. *Journal of Creative Behavior, 4,* 149–161.

Langley, P., Simon, H. A., Bradshaw, G. L., & Zytow, J. M. (1987). *Scientific discovery.* Cambridge, MA: MIT Press.

Perkins, D. (1986, May). Thinking frames. *Educational Leadership,* 4–10.

Sawyers, J. K., & Canestaro, N. C. (1989). Creativity and achievement in design coursework. *Creativity Research Journal, 1,* 126–133.

Sorokin, P. A. (1969). *Society, culture and personality.* New York: Cooper Square. (Originally published 1947).

Sternberg, R. J. (1988). A three-facet model of creativity. In R. J. Sternberg (Ed.), *The nature of creativity* (pp. 125–147). New York: Cambridge University Press.

Toynbee, A. J. (1946). *A study of history* (2 Vol. abridgment by D. C. Somervell). New York: Oxford University Press.

Wallach, M. (1971). *The creativity-intelligence distinction.* New York: General Learning Press.

Weber, R. J., & Dixon, S. (1989). Invention and gain analysis. *Cognitive Psychology, 21,* 283–302.

Chapter 24

The Origin of Creative Achievement: Spontaneity, Responsibility, and Individuals

Carl R. Hausman

Dean Simonton's "conjectures" about the relation of political pathology to societal creativity offer an intriguing discussion. From the perspective of one whose background is, I assume, fairly far removed from that of Simonton, I believe that his proposals in general make sense. In particular, I have in mind what he says in the last section in which he discusses the theoretical implications of his conjectures. He makes a necessary distinction between the literal number of creative persons in a society and the form their creativity may take. His suggestion that international war accentuates emotional arousal and that this accounts for the inhibiting of creativity deserves further attention, especially with respect to his own thesis that creative-yielding processes such as intuition "depend on low levels of arousal." Of particular interest in this connection is his additional statement that emotional arousal is lower during times of civil strife. For the purposes of his paper on political pathology, however, he does not pursue his thesis about emotional arousal and creativity, and the reader must take the responsibility of going to some of his other publications. In any case, the brief discussion of theoretical implications points us in the direction in which further study of Simonton's topic might usefully go. And, it is with this in mind that I turn to my comments. These will take the form of pointing to some of the problems that seem to me to be raised by Simonton's approach. I hasten to add here that I do not intend for my critical comments to minimize Simonton's evocative conjectures. I shall also suggest very briefly some of the ways in which future inquiry might be developed.

One problem, I think, is that the kinds of activities assumed to be creative are so varied that the stated purpose at the beginning is sometimes lost. Simonton's interest seems to be focused on determining how pathologies affect originality—which, incidentally, is not mentioned until well past the half-way point of his article—or, presumably, the creative achievement associated with genius. However, if the characteristics of women's fashions and philosophical positions, whether mediocre or great, are included as data along with the achievements of creators of the stature of Shakespeare, then the purpose of examining "successful," "phenomenal," and "distinguished" achievement, that of "genius," is submerged. Attention to what is to count as creative and created should be a preliminary consideration that could help bring the project under greater control. Surely it makes a difference whether the issue centers on correlations between political pathologies and the inhibition or enhancement of significant literary and scientific work or, instead, correlations concerning changes in tastes in hemlines—which might be the result of limits on quantity and kinds of materials available. I think it is essential to the kind of conjectures Simonton wants to make that attention be given to the criteria assumed for what is judged to be creative. Surely not just any production is creative. And, if not, what do we expect of those activities and outcomes that do exhibit creativity?

Another problem that deserves to be mentioned is that the focus of the study vacillates between relations between political pathologies and, on one hand, content, and on the other hand, the quality and quantity of achievement. It is not clear that the former relation is particularly significant. It seems prima facie evident that political conditions of all kinds would make a difference to what many creative persons select to be transformed as content within a poem or a painting. In contrast, it may not be evident what correlations there are between quality or greatness and

the kind of political pathologies that do not overtly and deliberately inhibit creativity. It is the second kind of correlation that seems to be of primary concern, and it is what I assume Simonton is most interested in
investigating. If so, his project could benefit from a narrower focus on
this issue. However, the issue is more complex because, at least in the
arts, there is reason to insist that form and content are inseparable and
interdependent. Even if Simonton thought it necessary to examine this
thesis before accepting it, it deserves consideration. And, if form and content are interdependent, then the correlations sought after must be quite
complex. Thus, it would help to include in Simonton's study some critical treatment of the role of the normative aspects of his subject. Correlations involving interactions of form, quality, and content, and matters
relevant to art criticism seem unavoidable.

The main question I would like to consider relates to another aspect
of the problem of defining the focus of study. On the one hand, Simonton seems headed toward hypothesizing about pathology and the amount
or kind of creativity that may characterize whole societies. On the other
hand, he seems primarily concerned with the ways in which social or political pathologies have impacts on individuals who might be creative. I
am not ignoring his initial description of his project, where he states that
he is concerned with both issues. However, he seems to waver or shift
attention, setting his sights on the two levels of human activity—sociocultural and individual. Moreover, the first level is apparently of interest
as a means to hypothesizing about individual creativity. And it seems to
me that the latter purpose emerges as fundamental for him. The project,
then, aims at determining how social-political conditions affect individuals with respect to their abilities or inclinations to be creative.

However, treatment of the first level, even as a means to understanding correlations relevant to individual creativity, raises an interesting
issue. What does it mean to pursue correlations at the level of whole societies? How can the locus, source, or agent of creative achievement reside in an aggregate or a group as well as in individuals? This question is
particularly significant for conjectures about the relation of conditions
identifiable in political contexts to creative achievement. In contrast to
uncreative changes, creative changes necessarily contrast in individualized
sources with respect to their uniqueness. If there is a difference between
creative and routine changes—and I think there is—then that difference
lies in the valuable newness, the uniqueness with respect to what was
known before, and that is exhibited in the created outcome. As new, the
achievement manifests at least one aspect that is individual, unprecedented, unpredicted. It is not a repeated product, and its character, or
part of it, is not of a sort that has been encountered before. I cannot take

space here to elaborate my reasons for saying this; I have done so elsewhere (Hausman, 1981, 1984, 1989).[1] Instead, I must take for granted that in the present context, the point that creations exhibit newness and thus uniqueness is at least recognized, if not agreed to and understood by everyone. Also, I take for granted that Simonton presupposed this characterization of created achievement—although he is not consistent in doing so—because, as noted earlier, he is concerned with phenomenal and original achievements and with genius. In any case, if there is something unique about a created outcome, then there must be a moment of uniqueness and a condition of spontaneity in the source of the outcome. It is in this condition that newness, the unprecedented outcome, originates. And such a condition or source must be individual, that is, it is something unique in the sense of being a single condition, the only one, which could satisfy what is necessary and sufficient for what is new in the result. If the condition is present in an individual instance, it is difficult to see how a whole society—although it certainly does provide a context of preestablished conditions—can be properly conceived as its fully responsible source.

It might be said that such a condition can be supposed for effects that are not regarded as creations. The condition for the mass production of a certain brand of shirt, for instance, is individual in being a single machine, or a single set of machines. Can it not be said, then, that all processes and products found in a society must be traced to individuals? This, however, is not the point. Rather, I want to say that there is a difference between the function of a source of creativity and the function of a source of routine processes. The difference is that in created outcomes, we have more than complex regularities or repeatable routines, such as performed by a machine, that are necessary and sufficient for the result. There is something that breaks out of the regularities that have prevailed up to the point of the creation. Thus, the source or condition seems to be something that cannot be understood completely or exhaustively with reference to features common to other sources or conditions. Is a unique source of creative achievement, then, properly resident in individual human beings or in groups such as whole societies? Individuals are the more appropriate locus of creative achievement. This is not to ignore the many factors that are contributed by communities and environment. However, it is to emphasize the singularity of certain moments and the

---

[1] I have argued for and discussed at length the problems of characterizing the expectations of creativity: *A Discourse on Novelty and Creation* (1984), and "Criteria of Creativity," in *the Concept of Creativity in Science and Art* (1981). Most recently, the issue has been raised in connection with the function of metaphors in language in my *Metaphor and Art: Interactionism and Reference in the Verbal and Nonverbal Arts* (1989).

condition that functions as the source of such moments when spontaneity occurs and creative achievement results.

In spite of this emphasis, there are ways in which it makes sense to regard whole societies as creative. We may attend primarily to the result insofar as it is manifest in the society as a whole. For instance, we may think of Hellenic Greek society as creative, as a society in which there was a rich outflow of accomplishments. We then might try to correlate the political conditions, including possible pathologies, with this manifestation of creativity. However, if we are aiming at more than simply describing what happened and we begin to examine the created outcomes with which political conditions are correlated, we begin to do what Simonton does, that is, pinpoint specific accomplishments and individuals who are responsible for these. This move from the whole to the agents that activate that whole seems necessary insofar as we are not merely describing but are looking for understanding of what can be merely described. The question behind the task of showing the correlations is: What are the conditions that are necessary and sufficient to account for diminished or enhanced creativity, for instance, in time of international war or civil strife? Thus, we look for the dynamic forces at work in the society, and these sometimes emerge in agents responsible for them.

The point just made, that the study of correlations of the kind in question leads to trying to identify the agents that are sources of the forces responsible for creative achievement, suggests another reason for assigning creative work to individuals rather than to society as a whole. This point must be developed briefly. Creativity is the potentiality of fundamentally new and valuable outcomes for which some agent takes responsibility. The concept of responsibility applies to agents in two ways. It may refer simply to them as the causes, or the necessary and sufficient conditions, for their actions, as it is sometimes said that the sun is responsible for growth, or that faulting, or shifting of the earth's tectonic plates, is responsible for some earthquakes. Responsibility may also be attributed to agents who are held accountable for what they do, as when a person is praised for good deeds on the assumption that he or she is accountable for thoŝes deeds, or as when Shakespeare is praised for some of his achievements because he was accountable for having accomplished them—he chose to create them and was responsible for doing so.

Now, we might ask whether a society as a whole can be an agent responsible and accountable for created outcomes. It seems to me that we may refer to societies in this way, but we do this with the assumption that there is something responsible for what the society does. And, if we ask how this is so, we move to the question: What is the locus of such an agency in society? Once we address this question as it pertains to creative accomplishment, it seems impossible to proceed without identifying individuals who are said to be responsible. Sophocles, Euripides, Socrates, Plato, Aristotle, and Pericles are some of the agents of those forces that made Hellenic Greek society an example of creative accomplishment. We are driven to identifying the individuals that may or may not contribute to those outcomes. These are the foci of responsibility for what happened and the sources held accountable and praised or blamed for what they did. With respect to non-creative accomplishments, the focus of responsibility may widen throughout the society—unless, perhaps, there is something destructive in the results.

I must sharpen the point that in cases of creativity, the agent is properly resident in individuals. Thus far, my reasons have been that individuals are the only loci of spontaneity and origin of newness and that individuals are the proper agents to be held responsible and accountable for what is manifest in society as a whole. The point might be interpreted as founded on the assumption that a whole society is nothing but the sum of its parts or individual members. This is not my intention. There are wholes that are not aggregates or summations of their parts. In fact, it seems to me that what in a created outcome exhibits newness is a gestalt character that is not reducible to its parts. However, the responsible agent of a gestalt, or a creative change in a complex of purposes that unify a society, is not identical with that gestalt. The point about the individuality of the phenomenon of creativity concerns the origin if a creation, not what it is in exhibiting that is created. And, I have suggested that the origin seems more properly located in individuals who constitute a society than in the society as a whole.

The point can be seen in light of comparing certain uncreative practices with creative activity. If we were concentrating on routine practice such as patterns of ceremony or ritual—for marriage, church service, manners—we would attend to what is common and repeated. We would be considering social habits. And, in these cases, the question of origin might not be readily focused on individuals responsible for the practice. Such a perspective might be taken, of course, if a ritual were thought to have originated with an individual, perhaps a charismatic person or a dictator. In this case, the origin might be regarded as a creative act, and the origination of a new ritual might well be an instance of a creativity. However, the study of correlations between routine, established social habits and political conditions, such as political pathology, might appropriately assume for purposes of the study that the society as a whole is the agency of these habits. In cases such as this, the outcome is central, and if attention were not directed toward identifying the agency of creative changes in these habits, individuals would not be of particular interest.

In cases in which individuals are effective in contributing creative activity to the character of the society, the society as a whole seems to take on a character that exhibits all or some characteristics of the individual created achievements. Political leaders such as Pericles presumably served such a function and helped to mold the habits of their society. And the dramatists and philosophers who affected their community were individuals who, we might say, helped to shape society. As a result, the society as a whole generated its own distinctive gestalt.

One upshot of the third and main issue on which I have spent the most time is the conclusion that the study of correlations between political pathologies and sociocultural systems must focus on individuals as the agents of these systems. It is not clear that the study proposes at the more general level is, after all, essentially different from studies of environmental, social, and political influences on creative individuals. However, there is, I think, a more important upshot, or, more accurately, an important consequence. This concerns a presupposition that underlies what I have said about attending to what is responsible and accountable for created outcomes. In distinguishing between what seems appropriately said of the practices of whole societies in contrast to creative acts of individuals, a normative consideration has been introduced. I suggested that creative acts invoke responses of praise—and sometimes blame when they are to shocking for all or some parts of society. This, of course, implies value judgments. And among those judgments are the values inherent in expectations of criteria of creativity. It seems to me, then, that a study of the correlations between creativity and any other condition presupposes norms, and these had better be made as explicit as possible. I think Simonton recognizes that normative considerations do enter his project. He makes this explicit in describing Shakespeare's work as poor or great. And he refers to value judgments at the beginning of his chapter in connection with minimizing them by omitting cross-cultural investigations. Yet his recognition is not extended to considerations of assessing what will count as creative and what norms in society are activated when creative acts propel the society toward new patterns of life.

In conclusion, I would like to make a final suggestion. The suggestion is not intended to call attention to a problem in what Simonton has done. Instead, it is a conjecture about what seems to me to be a fruitful direction to take. In other places, I have contended that metaphors can sometimes be creative (Hausman, 1989), and when they are, they exhibit characteristics of creative achievements in a relatively condensed form. A study that concentrated on possible correlations between shifts or changes in kinds of metaphors invented in various societies and stresses that appear when pathological conditions are present might serve in a complementary, perhaps supportive way, for the correlations considered by Simonton.

REFERENCES

Hausman, C. R. (1981). *The concept of creativity in science and art.* The Hague: Martinus Nijhoff. (Original work published 1979).

Hausman, C. R. (1984). *A discourse on novelty and creation.* Albany, NY: State University of New York Press.

Hausman, C. R. (1989). *Metaphor and art: Interactionism and reference in the verbal and nonverbal arts.* New York: Cambridge University Press.

Chapter 25

Innovation, Illegitimacy, and Individualism

Colin Martindale

It is always a pleasure to read one of Dean Simonton's articles. For the last several decades historians have of course been talking about clio-metrics or quantitative history, but still really have little to show for their talk. On the other hand, Simonton has single-handedly unearthed a huge number of historical regularities. I agree with Hippolyte Taine that "the basis of history must be scientific psychology." Taine did not have in mind the sort of thing that constitutes most of "psychohistory" and psy-chobiography. He envisioned exactly what Simonton does: genuinely sci-entific history firmly based upon psychological theories and methods. Many contemporary historians of art and literature (e.g., Rusch, 1985) have sunk themselves into a morass of confusion. Noting the obvious ne-cessity of interpretation and selection in writing history, they have jumped to the conclusion that objective historical studies are literally im-possible, that the historian constructs the past rather than being able to follow von Ranke's (1835/1906) prescription of finding out what really happened. Simonton's work offers a refreshing contrast to this pessimistic subjectivism. To quote Taine again, "there are facts here, as elsewhere." Simonton can be depended upon to dig out the most interesting of these facts and display them in a clear light.

When we ask whether creativity is related to pathology, we are confronted with an interpretive rather than a purely factual question. On the individual level, one could as recently as several decades ago have plausibly argued that creativity and psychopathology are unrelated because the latter does not really exist (Szasz, 1961). Advances in medical science have more or less completely obviated such an argument, and it is now rather well established that the two phenomena are indeed related. However, there is not—and probably cannot be—any such thing as objective political psychiatry. To speak of social or political pathology is to use a metaphor the meaning of which would seem to be almost completely relative. From our perspective, the late Ottoman Empire was classically pathological. Louis XIV would not have seen it as exuding any great vigor but would probably have seen it as more natural and hence healthier than modern democracies. We should recall that de Tocqueville came to America not to praise it but to diagnose what he saw as an advanced case of the terminal illness affecting all of Western society. It may seem reasonable enough to speak of war as pathological, but the trope breaks down if we examine it. A nation that has fought no defensive wars most probably has either never been attacked (because it was not worth the trouble) or does not exist any more. A dead nation cannot, by definition, be a healthy one.

Just as with wars, all sorts of excuses have been found for civil disturbances, dynastic conflicts, and military revolts. They may or may not indicate what we would want to call social pathology. As often as not one suspects that the pathology was invented after the fact by whichever side was victorious in order to legitimate its power. As Simonton notes, it is particularly questionable whether political fragmentation should be called socially sick or healthy. I don't think it should be called either, because one's attitude toward it depends almost entirely upon one's perspective. Many Americans seem to believe that Estonia has the right to secession and self-determination, but South Carolina most certainly does not. Once they are formed—from fragmented political entities—nations tend to resist fragmentation. Nations don't last forever, though. They eventually fragment again. If this is the natural course of affairs, it is a matter of taste which part of the rhythm we want to call pathological.

So long as we keep in mind how metaphorical the question is, it makes sense to ask about the relationship between social pathology and creativity. We need also to bear in mind that there may not be a single answer to the question. One of the virtues of Simonton's use of very long time series—often across several nations or civilizations—is that it reveals general, as opposed to local and particularistic, historical regularities. For example, his review suggests that political fragmentation per se is probably not related to creativity, but political fragmentation based upon ethnic divisions may be related to creativity. Use of short time series may reveal regularities that may or may not generalize well. A good example of this is some of my own findings cited in the review (Martindale, 1975). These concern the relationship between literary content and political and military factors. The relationships are certainly there for the sample of texts—from British 18th- and early 19th-century poets—that I studied. They tend to disappear, though, if we examine the course of British poetry from the time of Chaucer to the present (Martindale, 1990). There are several possible reasons for this. The less interesting is that the findings were purely fortuitous. The more interesting is that I happened—on purpose—to pick a time during which British poetry might reasonably be expected to mirror current social concerns. Before the 18th century, it tended to be the pastime or passion of courtiers and aristocrats. Since the mid-19th century, it has tended to be written not for an external audience but for other poets. Only in the 18th and early 19th century did British poets have an audience of much breadth. If the second reason is correct, then we should be able to replicate Martindale's (1975) findings in the poetry of other nations when such poetry lies within the boundary conditions mentioned above.

Some of my more recent findings are relevant to the question of the relationship between social "pathology," creativity, and literary content. I am currently concluding a study of trends in the context of texts by 170 British poets born between 1290 and 1949 (Martindale, 1990). In studying the relationship of these texts to extraliterary forces I have used a rather coarse-grained 20-year periodization. Of course, this aggregates over or averages out the effects of short-lived extraliterary phenomena. If we seek to explain the overall variability in content or word usage among the 170 poets, almost half of it seems best explained by evolutionary forces endigenous to the poetic system. This is in line with Sorokin's (1937) "principle of imminent change": So long as it remains intact, the main course of changes in any social system is the past history of that system. The rest of the variation can be attributed to individual differences in personality, social class, and so forth, and to external social forces. In regard to the latter, a quite consistent set of findings has emerged. Their discovery was quite serendipitous. In trying to relate literary content to sociocultural variables, I was not looking for anything special. Rather, I sought to investigate as broad a range of extraliterary time series as possible.

Most aspects of literary content are not consistently related to much of anything in the external society. However, one dimension of poetic content shows a consistent and meaningful relationship with extraliterary phenomena. The dimension has to do with references to the self ("I," "me," "my") and to the natural world versus references to social collectivities and to social actions such as leading, following, and controlling. It seems to be measuring the polarity between individualism and social solidarity or conformity. Following Lévi-Strauss (1964), we could say that the distinction is between "raw" (wild, natural, asocial) versus "cooked" (tame, civilized, socialized) poetry. It turns out that individualism in poetry (i.e., references to the self and avoidance of references to social actions) is correlated with a set of social phenomena that tend themselves to be interrelated. Poetic individualism is related to rate of scientific and technological innovation (Sorokin, 1937), a general index of Sorokin's (1937) sensate (empirical) emphasis in philosophy, industrial productivity (Mitchell, 1975), and rate of illegitimate births (Laslett & Oosterveen, 1973). All of these phenomena are positively correlated with one another and negatively related to economic prosperity (the ratio of wages to prices as measured by Phelps Brown, & Hopkins, 1956). The latter is also negatively correlated with individualistic content in poetry.

It is reasonable, but not certain, that poetic individualism reflects an individualistic or asocial attitude in society as a whole. Innovation is by definition a nonconforming and individualistic activity. One of the main traits characterizing creative people is disinhibition, nonconformity, and "poor socialization" (see Martindale, 1989). Innovation is, according to Schumpeter (1939), the main engine of economic growth. Schumpeter holds that the entrepreneur is an innovator just as much as is a poet or a scientist. Individualistic competition in a free market—as opposed to cooperation—is likely to foster industrial productivity. The illegitimacy rate has a number of causes, but one must certainly be a tendency to discount or ignore social and religious mores. Innovative ideas are quite literally like illegitimate children in that they arise from the mating of ideas that do not, except in the mind of the individual creator, belong together. Left-wing social theorists are apt to call the profits of the entrepreneur illegitimate, because the labor of many results in the enrichment of the individual. At extreme, right-wing theorists do not even deny this but, as with social Darwinism, offer an asocial equation of society with a state of nature where the distinction between legitimate and illegitimate has no meaning. Sorokin (1937) is clear that sensate philosophies tend to be individualistic and antireligious.

It would seem that poetic and social individualism go hand in hand. Furthermore, they are both negatively related to general prosperity. In eras when wages are high relative to prices, the content of poetry becomes less ego-centered and more prosocial, philosophy tends to be more idealistic and religious, and both innovation and illegitimacy decline. Industrial productivity also declines. It must if workers receive high wages for producing goods that are sold at low prices. Such eras may be socially healthy in the sense that they provide "the greatest good for the greatest number." However, they also seem rather complacent and boring. Of course, this is purely a matter of my own tastes. It is close to fact, though, that such eras cannot persist for any extended length of time. Without innovation, the economy winds down and becomes stagnant. Of course, low profits and high labor costs push it in the same direction. As a consequence, prosperity must decline. As it declines, individualism and innovation rise. One is reminded of Toynbee's (1947) assertion that at least a modest level of challenge is required for sociocultural development and, of course, of the old saying that necessity is the mother of invention.

Though international war is unrelated to the social variables described above, it too is correlated with an individualistic emphasis in poetry. This is consistent with McClelland's (1975) contention that war is more likely when a populace is more concerned with (individual) power and less concerned with affiliation and, by extension, other prosocial and cooperative motives. It should be noted that the long-term trend in Great Britain has been toward greater prosperity and economic vitality. The relationships described above refer to correlations from which such secular trends have been removed. In an "ascending" society, prosperity above what would be expected from long-term trends seems to stifle innovation and individualism. We might well find quite different results in nations where the long-term trend was in an opposite direction.

I find myself in agreement with some but not all of Simonton's theoretical explanations for the relationships he describes in his review. According to Simonton's (1988) chance configuration theory, one of the main determinants of creativity is the number and diversity of mental elements a person has. Clearly, the larger the stock of mental elements, the more likely useful combinations will be. Another determinant is the probability of "collision" of mental elements. There are a variety of theoretical reasons to expect that the rate of combination of mental elements should be higher in states of low arousal (Martindale, 1981; Simonton, 1980). There is also ample experimental evidence that stress of virtually any sort causes decreases in creativity (e.g., Martindale & Greenough, 1973). Of course, across the entire range, there is no doubt an inverted-U relationship between stress or arousal and creativity. Thus, maximal creativity is found with fairly low rather than extremely low levels of stress or arousal. Given this, Simonton's first principal possibility (stress decreases creativity) makes sense. It nicely accounts for why international war lowers both creative output and the quality of this output.

This explanation runs into trouble with civil disturbances, though. If war hurts creativity, then civil disturbances should hurt it more. However, the reverse seems to be the case. Simonton's explanation of this is unconvincing. His view of civil disturbances is rather rose-tinted. We need data to support the implication that civil disturbances in general do in fact lead to more justice or less oppression. I can think of many counterexamples. Some people may have felt "exhilaration" about the "exciting anticipation of the forthcoming utopia." Others were not terribly excited about the utopias that Lenin, Hitler, or Cromwell promised and, unfortunately, delivered. Rather than theory, we need more fine-grained data analysis. Whether civil disturbances lead to exhilaration (and more creativity) or stress (and less creativity) depends upon whether one's side is winning or losing. It may well be that civil disturbances produce effects that cancel each other. If a slight majority of creators is on the losing side—and becomes less creative—and slightly fewer are on the winning side—and become more creative—the net result will seem to be a slight decrease in creativity. There may also be threshold effects that, to make our job more difficult, vary from creator to creator. Large-scale civil disturbances, such as civil wars, affect almost everyone in a society. Many civil disturbances, even though they may be fairly severe or wide spread, may have quite different effects depending upon one's attitude. A present-day poet in London, for example, can be worked up either way about labor unrest in Wales or even London or may ignore it altogether. No matter how severe it gets, it is unlikely to bring down the monarchy.

Depending upon circumstances, war, civil unrest, and such phenomena may have their effects not via stress but via attention or distraction. This must certainly be the case with cross-national effects. The French revolution, for example, certainly put French creators under stress. However, until things got out of hand, it provided their British colleagues with an interesting spectacle that inspired some of them and merely distracted others. Even close to home, attention rather than arousal per se may be the crucial factor. Many European creators found the disturbances of 1848 *interesting* rather than either exhilarating or frightening. Because arousal seems to be the physiological *Anlage* of attention, this is a minor point. It is an issue, in any event, that cannot be resolved by examples such as those I have given, but only by systematic inquiry.

Simonton's second explanation (extraartistic phenomena provide the raw material for artistic content) seems reasonable. This is a standard "reflectionist" argument. As such, it is open to the main criticism against any such argument: It is not easily falsifiable. We can be sure of the content of Shakespeare's plays, and we can be sure that their content was correlated with political changes. We cannot, however, be sure that Shakespeare was appeasing his audience or reflecting their attitudes and values for the simple reason that we do not know what their attitudes and values were. No public opinion polls were, after all, conducted in Elizabethan England. It is plausible that Shakespeare and his audience may have felt the same way about conspiracies against the crown. It is far from certain, though. To be certain, we would need data about the composition of the audience and about their political sympathies.

Simonton's third set of developmental explanations seems plausible. Thus, it is reasonable that chaos induced by political instability should destroy the sense of security necessary for creativity. One wonders whether the mediating variable of "internal locus of control" is needed to connect political fragmentation with creativity. Political fragmentation, Simonton himself notes, leads to cultural diversity. This should cause any given creator to acquire a more diverse set of mental elements (Findlay & Lumsden, 1988), which is one of the causes of creativity in Simonton's (1988) own theory.

On a more mundane level, the relationship between political fragmentation (number of independent states) and number of creators may at least in part be artifactual. To simplify matters, let us say that each nation is "allocated" N eminent creators per generation. Of course, N is not a fixed number, but it must be a bounded one. If a nation produced 1,000 genuinely good poets in one generation, most would be forgotten, else the literary history of the period would be impossible to write or read. On the other side of the coin, there are nations that have never produced any poets who are very good in an absolute sense. Nonetheless, such nations have literary histories and some poets who end up being designated as eminent. If a nation splits in two, the new pair of nations now gets an "allocation" of $2N$ eminent creators. No one's absolute eminence has really changed. Some less eminent creators have merely received more notice if tabulations are being made on a nation-by-nation basis. We might ask who is the greatest Yugoslavian poet. Before Yugoslavia existed, such a question would obviously not have been asked. One would have asked about the best poet in Serbia, Croatia, and so on, and would have, in the process, come up with more names. I am not sure how to handle the problem that eminence is at least partly relative, but I imagine that Dean Simonton will come up with a good solution if he has not already.

REFERENCES

Findlay, C. S., & Lumsden, C. J. (1988). The creative mind: Toward an evolutionary theory of discovery and innovation. *Journal of Social and Biological Structures, 11*, 3–55.

Laslett, P., & Oosterveen, K. (1973). Long term trends in bastardy in England. *Population Studies, 27*, 255–286.

Lévi-Strauss, C. (1964). *Le cru et le cruit.* (*The raw and the cooked.*) Paris: Librairie Plon.

Martindale, C. (1975). *Romantic progression: The psychology of literary history.* Washington, DC: Hemisphere.

Martindale, C. (1981). *Cognition and consciousness.* Homewood, IL: Dorsey.

Martindale, C. (1989). Personality, situation, and creativity. In J. A. Glover, R. R. Ronning, & C. R. Reynolds (Eds.), *A handbook of creativity: Assessment, theory, and research.* New York: Plenum.

Martindale, C. (1990). *The clockwork muse: The predictability of artistic change.* New York: Basic Books.

Martindale, C., & Greenough, J. (1973). The differential effect of increased arousal on creative and intellectual performance. *Journal of Genetic Psychology, 123,* 329–335.

McClelland, D. C. (1975). *Power: The inner experience.* New York: Irvington.

Mitchell, B. R. (1975). *European historical statistics 1750–1970.* New York: Columbia University Press.

Phelps Brown, E. H., & Hopkins, S. V. (1956). Seven centuries of the prices of consumables compared with builders wage-rates. *Economica, 23,* 296–314.

Rusch, G. (1985). The theory of history, literary history and historiography., *Poetics, 14,* 257–278.

Schumpeter, J. A. (1939). *Business cycles: A theoretical, historical, and statistical analysis of the capitalist process.* New York: McGraw-Hill.

Simonton, D. K. (1980). Intuition and analysis: A predictive and explanatory model. *Genetic Psychology Monographs, 102,* 3–60.

Simonton, D. K. (1988). *Scientific genius: A psychology of science.* Cambridge: Cambridge University Press.

Sorokin, P. (1937). *Social and cultural dynamics.* New York: American Book Company.

Szasz, T. A. (1961). *The myth of mental illness.* New York: Paul B. Hoeber.

Toynbee, A. J. (1947). *A study of history.* New York: Oxford University Press.

von Ranke, L. (1906). *History of the popes, their church and state.* London: G. Bell. (Original work published 1835.)

Chapter 26

The Accidental Economist

Daniel L. Rubenson

As one who has been excited by many of Simonton's previous studies of creativity, I anticipated in this chapter a systematic treatment of the stated topic. Indeed, it provides a fascinating and wide-ranging review of the salient empirical literature. I was disappointed, however, not to find a consistent theoretical interpretation of these data. I did find that in many cases the empirical evidence he cites lends itself quite readily to an economic interpretation. And interestingly, the theoretical arguments that the article does advance are often economic in their orientation. After a few brief methodological quibbles, I will discuss the economic side of Simonton's analysis in greater detail, and propose alternative explanations, from the economic perspective, for some of the empirical findings he presents.

The main question addressed by Simonton's chapter is the possible relationship between societal creativity and societal mental health. The significance of this issue argues for careful methodology, and a crucial component of this methodology must be the measurement of these two variables. Simonton has, of course, blazed the trail with respect to measures of societal creativity, based on the historiometric approach. But his measurement of societal mental health seems to be unfortunately *ad hoc*, and based more on the ready availability of data than on their appropriateness. It is difficult to see, for example, how defensive involvement in a war provides evidence of societal pathology. And one can make a case for the position that civil disturbances or political unrest are indicators of mental health, with their absence seen as a sign of societal stagnation. To his credit, Simonton readily acknowledges these limitations of the available data. Still, the article's conclusions would be much stronger, and perhaps the empirical evidence more convincing, if based on more careful and sophisticated measurements of societal pathology.

Another concern involves the proper relationship between theory and empirical observation in scientific investigation. The basic organization of Simonton's article is to present an observation first, and then look for a theory to explain it. This approach seems to raise many more questions than it answers. Simonton observes, for example, that political instability leads to reduced societal creativity in some domains, but has no effect in others. Where is the theory to explain this difference? Are some creative processes more susceptible to this sort of interference than others, or is it the creators themselves who are affected? Without a logical reason for this difference, one might be tempted to pass it off as the result of measurement errors or purely random influences.

A similar issue arises in the discussion of warfare's effects on societal creativity. Simonton observes that imperialistic wars have no apparent effect on creativity, but defensive wars exert a negative influence. Again, where is the theory to explain why these different wars should have different influences on a society's creative output? Should one infer, as Simonton apparently does, that this observation provides evidence for the relative mental health of nations involved in imperialistic wars compared with the defenders? Some might find that conclusion profoundly troubling.

Although these minor complaints may limit the strength of any conclusions drawn from Simonton's article, they do nothing to detract from the impressive body of evidence he presents. A variety of theories are employed to explain these observations, but in fact most of the data are more coherently explained using elements of the *psychoeconomic theory* of creativity. Indeed, in several instances Simonton advances economic arguments without labeling them as such.

The psychoeconomic approach to creativity employs the economic paradigm in an attempt to explain many of the same phenomena of interest to psychologists, such as why some individuals are more creative performers is affected by changes in intrinsic and extrinsic factors.[1] Briefly,

---

[1]This approach is described more fully in Rubenson and Runco (1992).

this approach argues that an individual's creative activity is based, in part, on a consideration of the costs and benefits associated with that activity. Cost and benefit are used quite broadly in this context. Benefit, for example, includes consideration of the role of both intrinsic and extrinsic factors in the individual decision. The costs associated with creative activity are largely temporal and psychic costs, the latter based on any stigma or other emotional wear and tear resulting from creative thinking or enterprise. A major attraction of the psychoeconomic approach to creativity stems from its generality. This approach unifies the many intrinsic and extrinsic factors influencing the creative process within one logically consistent theoretical framework.

Creative activity can be described, then, using the supply and demand framework. The demand is both internal (based on intrinsic motivation) and external. The supply of creative activity comes from individuals, and depends in large part on the costs involved in being creative. With this in mind, along with the empirical data presented by Simonton, two aspects of the creative process should be explained. One is the development of creative potential in individuals, which will be described as the product of some initial endowments (such as heredity), active investments a person may make in his or her creative potential, and environmental influences such as the societal factors cited by Simonton. The other relevant aspect of the creative process is the production of creative activity, which takes place in distinct markets or domains (Csikszentmihalyi, 1997).

An important element of the psychoeconomic model is the role of external (to the creative individual) demands in the production of creative activity. In general, external demand is manifested in some incentives for creative output. The psychoeconomic model predicts that increases in external demand will cause increases in creative activity. The empirical results Simonton presents make a strong case for the importance of external demand in several different contexts. He discusses the role of a monarch's patronage, for example, as a factor causing changes in the creative quality and content of creative production. External demand is also key to his discussion of the effects of war on literary content, women's fashions, and musical composition. Similar arguments are advanced in his discussion of the effects of civil disturbances on musical composition and literary content, and the effect of authoritarianism on popular culture. The content of Shakespeare's plays is seen to be influenced by external demand, for Simonton argues that he "was obliged to appease contemporary audiences ... [and] ... modified the themes of his dramatic creations" (p. 362) in response to current political events.

In a similar manner, political fragmentation, by presenting increased opportunities for innovative solutions to societal problems, may increase the external demand for creativity. Indeed, Simonton cites evidence showing a positive relationship between political fragmentation and the quantity of creative output in a number of different historical and cultural contexts.

Another important element of the creative process is the cost of creative activity. The psychoeconomic approach predicts that reductions in the cost of creativity will tend to cause increases in the quantity or quality of creative activity. Again, Simonton provides ample empirical support for this proposition. He observes, for example, that civil disturbances are often associated with increases in creativity. A psychoeconomic explanation for these data is based on the psychic cost of creative activity. One of the important costs associated with creativity, psychic cost, is rooted in the emotional drain and possible stigma involved in being different. Simonton points out that civil disturbances are often characterized by increased openness of thinking, increased acceptance of new ideas, and reduced concern with external impressions. These changes in the social environment all serve to lower the psychic costs of creative activity, and would therefore be expected to increase creativity. In a similar way, psychic cost also provides an additional explanation for the observed connections between political fragmentation and ideological diversity, and creativity. Simonton argues that both of these are apt to be associated with increased diversity of thought and openness to new ideas, and therefore to reduced costs of creative activity.

The psychoeconomic approach also provides an alternative framework for examining developmental influences on creativity. An individual's creative potential is the result of a number of passive and active influences. Passive influences include the effects of genetic endowments; active influences include those steps an individual might take to intentionally increase his or her own creative potential. Examples of these active investments might be reading books on creativity, or taking courses designed to facilitate creative thinking. The individual's decision to make active investments in creative potential is based, in part, on a comparison of the incremental costs and expected future benefits associated with that investment. An assumption of this developmental model is that increased creative potential, by facilitating (lowering the cost of) creative activity, increases creativity.

Much of Simonton's data focus on the role of societal characteristics and events as developmental influences on creativity. In psychoeconomic terms, these environmental influences may directly influence the development of creative potential, or may influence the individual's decision to make active investments in creative potential. In this sense, the psychoeconomic model is consistent with the developmental model of Scarr and McCartney (1983), in which the individual is influenced by and also influences the developmental environment.

Civil disturbances, such as revolts and rebellions under imperial rule, and ideological diversity, are cited by Simonton as societal influences leading to increased creativity in the succeeding generation. The psychoeconomic explanation for these data is straightforward. As noted above, times of civil strife tend to be characterized by increased openness to new ideas, and reduced concern with external impressions. Indeed, Simonton points out that during civil disturbances, "dissenters can in a sense 'come out of the closet' " to express distinctive thoughts more freely. Ideological diversity is accompanied by a similar liberation of thought. In this environment, just as creative activity becomes more attractive, so does the expected future benefit from active investments in creative potential. The resulting increase in these investments manifests itself as increased creative potential, and therefore increased creativity, after a generational lag.

Similar logic applies to political fragmentation as a developmental influence on creativity. Political fragmentation increases the demand for innovative solutions to social problems, and as a result the expected returns to active investment in creative potential.

Psychoeconomic theory argues that, in considering the benefits resulting from creative activity, an individual will discount benefits accruing in the future. Like future income, future benefits are worth less than those received immediately. Individuals are likely to vary in terms of their discount rates, or the extent to which they are willing to defer current satisfaction for future gain. Further, it is likely that an individual's discount rate is the product of both developmental and contemporaneous influences.[2]

Simonton cites political instability as a developmental influence diminishing societal creativity in future years, under the hypothesis that this instability, coming during developmental years, reduces the ability of those creators in "rational domains" to see and appreciate the world as coherent and predictable. A psychoeconomic interpretation of these data, then, is based on the effect of political turmoil during the developmental years on individual's discount rates. To the extent that this turmoil lowers their confidence in the efficacy of planning for the future, or in future-directed activities in general, it will lead them to discount future benefits more heavily. This change in discount rate is by itself sufficient to reduce their incentive to make investments in creative potential or engage in creative activity. Increases in the discount rate can also help explain the observed attenuation of creative activity during wartime. Possibly more than any other external influence, war is apt to lower peo-

---

[2]Rachlin (1987) discusses a number of possible intrinsic and extrinsic influences on individual discount rates.

ples' confidence in their life prospects, and therefore focus their decision-making more on the current than that uncertain future.

Possibly due to conflicting empirical data, Simonton treats warfare differently from civil disturbances in analyzing their contemporaneous effects on creativity. He claims that warfare reduces creativity because it increases arousal, which is an inhibiting factor. Then, by this logic, because civil disturbances do not reduce creativity, they must not have led to the same arousal increases. But personal danger may be just as great, or even greater during a civil disturbance because of the latter's proximity. Wars are often fought at a considerable distance; it is hard to argue that residents of the mainland U.S. feared for their personal safety during World War II, for example. Yet many U.S. residents may have feared for their own safety during the many urban riots of 1965–1968.

The negative relationship between arousal and creativity is cited to explain the effects of war on that activity. But if this is true, then the data are inconsistent with the possibility that arousal may also be increased during civil disturbances. Under the psychoeconomic view, increased arousal may be interpreted as a factor raising the psychic cost of creative activity, because it is more difficult (costly) to be creative when under stress.

Different effects may then be observed for warfare and civil disturbance due to the potential for additional impacts on the psychic cost. A nation at war is likely to be more authoritarian and less tolerant of disparate views, and these societal traits increase the psychic cost of creativity. By contrast, civil strife is often characterized by increased openness of thinking. This increased freedom of thought may serve to reduce the psychic cost of creative activity, thereby countering the attenuating influence of increased arousal.

In his conclusion, Simonton observes that "it is most improbable that one process underlies all observed relationships between political pathology and societal creativity" (p. 360). Although not strictly one process, the psychoeconomic approach provides a unified conceptual framework capable of systematically explaining the observed variation in creativity across many cultures and historical epochs. Furthermore, the psychoeconomic framework is consistent with Simonton's discussions of developmental influences on creativity.

When viewed from this perspective, Simonton's article suggests additional conclusions. Because the empirical evidence reviewed is so supportive of the predictions of psychoeconomic theory, that approach to creativity research has received some additional validation. Further, much of his discussion of this evidence, in particular with respect to the importance of external demand, is beneath the surface terminology truly economic in nature.

REFERENCES

Csikszentmihalyi, M. (1997). The domain of creativity. In M. A. Runco & R. S. Albert (Eds.), *Theories of creativity* (rev. ed.). Cresskill, NJ: Hampton Press.

Rachlin, H. (1987). Economics and behavioral psychology. In J. E. R. Staddon (Ed.), *Limits to action: The allocation of individual behavior* (pp. 205–236). New York: Academic.

Rubenson, D. L. & Runco, M. A. (1992). The psychoeconomic approach to creativity. *New Ideas in Psychology, 10,* 131–147.

Scarr, S. & McCartney, K. (1983). How people make their own environments: A theory of genotype environment effects. *Child Development, 54,* 424–435.

Simonton, D. K. (1990). Political pathology and societal creativity. *Creativity Research Journal 3,* 85–99.

Chapter 27

Psychological Mediators of the Inverse Pathology–Creativity Effect

Winifred E. Stariha
Herbert J. Walberg

Simonton (1980) found that exceptionally innovative ideas are difficult to produce under duress; thought processes such as intuition, may function poorly under emotional stress. His chapter in the present volume reports on the analogous relation at the societal level.

Simonton's findings may be of interest to educators and policy makers trying to meet the intellectual, social, emotional, and physical needs of school-age children. This population includes not only children raised in democratic societies, but also those from countries experiencing international war, external threat, political instability, and civil disturbances described by Simonton. How can educators understand and serve students immigrating from these politically unstable environments? Consider also that disadvantaged, urban children, moreover, may suffer the effects of living in poverty stricken, gang-ridden, and drug infested areas. Is their creativity also affected by real or threatened violence of their social environments? Might the vicarious violence of television experiences by many children for long hours affect them similarly?

SOCIETAL PATHOLOGY AND LEARNING

Simonton reports a generational delay in the negative effect of societal pathology on creativity in science, philosophy, literature, and music. This appears plausible because childhood environmental variables determine learning and creativity development in adolescence and adulthood (Walberg et al., 1981). Reduction in adult creativity would occur if individuals develop in times of political stress.

Good beginnings often enlarge opportunities and enhance subsequent environments. Walberg and Tsai (1984) gathered evidence in the fields of communication, early childhood, cognitive psychology, and education showing that early advantages confer future advantages. This evidence corroborates Merton's (1968) "Matthew-effect" theory of "the rich getting richer" (from the Gospel of Matthew, in *The Bible*). He argued that in the sciences, initial advantages of university study, work with eminent scientists, publishing early, job placement, citation, and other recognition multiply and increase over time.

This process of cumulative advantage develops skills, habits, tastes, rewards, and opportunities leading to high levels of creativity productiveness in scientific work. Over time these characteristics and traits affect one another. The theory of the "Matthew-effect" is parsimonious and generalizable as it may be said that abilities develop during early environments and this early development affects future environments. Scientific creativity and educational development are examples of the general and pervasive phenomenon (Merton, 1968; Walberg & Tsai, 1984).

Suboptimal environments, on the other hand, may inhibit maximum development. Even talented, wealthy, educated individuals in violent or politically unstable environments might be affected if they are unable to insulate themselves from surrounding societal pathologies.

Creativity requires early encouragement, definite goals, clear attainments, constant effort, and high standards. These promote further effort and attract the attention of first-rate teachers and coaches, resulting in the positive-skew distribution of achievement and performance, creativity and eminence. One can view knowledge mastery and skill acquisition in school and society as foundations of creativity and eminence. All of these may be enhanced by natural and combined social environments, encouragement, concentration, and effort (Walberg & Tsai, 1984).

Inevitably, all these causes can be expected to be diminished by the stresses of civil disturbances, international war, and political pathology. Indeed, Simonton found that turmoil affects not only the quantity of creators emerging in each generation but also their individual productivity. Lesser thinkers might emerge from chaos but superior creativity may remain at a standstill. Under distraction and stress, moreover, teachers and mentors would have less time and energy for the new generation.

SOCIETAL PATHOLOGY AND SOCIALIZATION

Simonton's essay is appropriate given the events in the Peoples' Republic of China. If, in fact, political pathology reduces societal creativity, what will result from the violence to youth in Tiananmen Square?

What experiences, moreover, do immigrant children bring with them? Students in the Chicago Public Schools, for example, speak 150 languages or dialects and represent such countries as Afghanistan, Albania, Cambodia, Chile, Iran, Northern Ireland, and Lebanon—all of which are experiencing political turmoil. The stress students and the families have encountered may affect their prospects for learning and creativity, if Simonton's findings are generalizable.

There may, however, be exceptions to Simonton's generalization. As a case in point, the initial political reforms in Eastern Europe provide evidence that people may feel exhilarated by the prospects of constructive reforms. Czechoslovakian television newscasters, for example, report that actors and playwrights have turned their dialogues to freedom; newspapers portray throngs of rejoicing citizens. Can ecstasy produce creativity? Or does the prospect of stability under democracy enhance creativity?

Csikszentmihalyi (1988, p. 325) argued that creativity results from the interaction between three systems: social institutions that select the creations of individuals that are worth preserving; a stable cultural environment that saves and transmits original ideas to future generations; and the individual who initiates a change that society finds creative. Simonton corroborates the importance of the social and environmental contexts.

Such social and environmental effects are corroborated by studies of the childhoods of highly eminent adults. Walberg et al. (1981), for example, reported research that revealed family, educational, and cultural conditions of more than 200 highly eminent men born between the 14th- and 20th-centuries, including Lincoln, Mozart, and Newton. Their childhood environments and characteristics indicate distinctive intellectual competence and motivation, social and communication skills, general psychological wholesomeness, and versatility among with concentrated perseverance during childhood. Important factors include stimulation by the field of eminence and by teachers, parents, and other adults. Most had clear parental expectations for their conduct and also the opportunity to explore on their own.

We agree with Simonton (1980) that it is probably very difficult to conceive truly innovative ideas in an environment under the stress of international war or when political pathology is one of several other outside political negative influences interrupting an individual's creative processes. In view of the "Matthew-effect," political events of a decade earlier can be thought of as environmental variables determining creative potential in adulthood.

In our view, creative talent is composed of a rich and complex association of cognitive elements (Walberg, 1988). Achievement consists of the acquisition of these elements from the environment and the ability to retrieve them into conscious memory or recognize them in the environment. Creativity, which includes problem finding and solving, is the search by trial-and-error for new and useful solutions by combinations of stored and external found elements. This parsimonious account, following Aristotle, Simon (1981), and others calls attention to time for acquisition and association of elements, the importance of a rich environment, and to the natural continuity and linkage of creativity with achievement. This view is also consistent with Simonton's (1988) chance–configuration theory.

SOCIETAL CONDITIONS AND CREATIVITY

Political pathology and violence at the societal level can be expected to interfere with the psychological process of learning and creativity at the psychological level. Such pathology and violence can be expected to interfere with and distract from both prerequisite acquisition as well as reflective creativity. Time taken away from either can be expected to reduce the amount and quality of their products. To the extent that pathology and violence also affect parents, teachers, mentors, and others that stimulate potential creators, corresponding decrements in productivity can be expected. Such psychological processes appear to explain, at least in part, the societal linkages.

REFERENCES

Csikszentmihalyi, M. (1988). Society, culture, and person: A systems view of creativity. In R. J. Sternberg (Ed.), *The nature of creativity* (pp. 325–339). New York: Cambridge University Press.

Merton, R. K. (1968). The Matthew effect in science. *Science, 159,* 56–63.

Simon, H. A. (1981). *Sciences of the artificial.* Cambridge, MA: MIT Press.

Simonton, D. K. (1980). Intuition and analysis: A predictive and explanatory model. *Genetic Psychology Monographs, 102,* 3–60.

Simonton, D. K. (1988). Creativity, leadership, and chance. In R. J. Sternberg (Ed.), *The nature of creativity* (pp. 386–426). New York: Cambridge University Press.

Walberg, H. J. (1988). Creativity and talent as learning. In R. J. Sternberg (Ed.), *The nature of creativity* (pp. 340–361). New York: Cambridge University Press.

Walberg, H. J. & Tsai, S. L. (1984). Matthew effects in education. *American Educational Research Journal, 20,* 359–374

Walberg, H. J., Tsai, S. L., Weinstein, T., Gabriel, C. L., Rasher, S. P., Rosecrans, R., Rovai, E., Ide, J., Trujillo, M., & Yukosavich, P. (1981). Childhood traits and environmental conditions of highly eminent adults. *Gifted Child Quarterly, 25,* (3), 103–107.

Chapter 28

Anabolic and Catabolic Factors in the Creative Process

Morris I. Stein

For years I have been a fan of Simonton's. I read his books and (almost?) all of his articles. I looked forward to more. If it is possible, I was more than a fan. I was a devoted admirer in awe of his work.

Simonton could describe himself as a psychobiographer (when working idiographically with case studies); or he could describe himself as a historometrician (when working nomothetically doing large scale studies); but for me he was a "cliometrician"—a psychologist using statistics in carrying out the commands of Clio—the muse of history.[1]

---

[1]"Cliometrician" is a term coined by a historian (Fogel, 1989). "Cliometricians . . . are scientifically oriented historians who maintain that statistical analysis, based upon various records rather than human testimony, can take the guesswork out of the past. By contrast, traditional historians appreciate any kind of new evidence but consider modern techniques as merely tools; they believe that statistics alone cannot rebuild the complex house of history" (Mitgang, 1989).

More than once, in the midst of one of Simonton's articles, I found myself overwhelmed, so impressed was I with the vast range of his work. More than once I was intimidated by a sentence such as this one:

> A generational time-series analysis of thousands of philosophers spanning from Ancient Greece to modern times found that 20 years after a major outbreak of international war one can often observe a *decrease* (emphasis Simonton's) in the number of thinkers who advocate empiricist epistemology, an ontology of unending change, philosophical nominal and individualism, and ethical systems predicated on the pleasure principle. (Simonton, 1976)

Later he wrote, "People are seemingly stimulated to scurry around in a quest for security, cohesion, permanence, and authority" (Simonton, 1990).

In the face of this "powerhouse" of "thousands" of subjects "spanning generations" is it surprising that I should feel inadequate? My own empirical research on industrial research scientists took me "ages" to collect, and then I had studied only 34 "more" creative and 33 "less" creative subjects. What I would have done to get thousands! And the numbers of subjects was not the only factor I envied. The criterion was another. I used ratings by superiors, peers, and subordinates. But, I did not know and certainly would never know if my subjects' creativity stood the test of time. Simonton did.

As to research variables, one of my favorites in my work is a rather unique one in which I gather data on three generations—grandparents, parents, and subject. This, however, in no way compared to Simonton's "generational time-series analysis."

Feelings of awe and inadequacy receded only a short while ago when I read Simonton's (1989) "The swan-song phenomenon: Last work effects for 172 classical composers." In this article Simonton reported that shortly before composers died they composed a typical "swan-song score." Because of my long-standing interest in prediction, first with the Office of Strategic Services (OSS) Assessment Staff during World War II (OSS Assessment Staff, 1948) and later in empirical research in educational environments (Stern, Stein, & Bloom, 1956), I was intrigued with and attracted to the "swan-song phenomenon." Could the "swan-song score" be used for predictive purposes? Let us say that in the course of following a composer's work a swan-song appeared. Did this signal his or her imminent demise? Should one prepare for the composer's death? A macabre thought? No! A very humane one! If there was a characteristic swan-song that preceded a composer's death could it be used like an x-ray, alerting doctors to start treatment to prolong the composer's life? The composer could be rushed to the hospital and a creative life could be saved.

Imagine my surprise when I wrote Simonton and learned, much to my disappointment, that not only had no such predictions been made, but that he thought my standards were quite high. Was I asking too much? I do not think so. They were no higher than when colleagues and I undertook the research for what later became *Methods in Personality Assessment* (Stern et al., 1956) devoted to a series of successful studies in the prediction of behavior in educational environments. I still think some music lover ought to follow-up on the combination of Simonton's research and my suggestion. Just think of the number of composers whose lives might be saved.

One outcome of this experience was that it helped put my feelings about Simonton's work in perspective. Intimidation gave way to confidence. Awe was replaced by studied objectivity. With these new attitudes I approached the chapter under discussion.

Simonton starts his chapter with a model and set of assumptions that is basic to the remainder of the paper. He refers to, but does not question the validity of what he calls the "long and pervasive tradition (which) holds that individual achievement of phenomenal stature must be associated with psychopathology of some kind." He asks "whether a parallel association between genius and madness holds at a higher level of analysis—that of the society or culture." Inquiries are then made into the effects of "political pathology" on creativity in various areas. "Political pathology" at the societal level, Simonton tells us, is manifest in "international wars, external threat, political instability, political fragmentation, and civil disturbances." The discussion then focuses on how these pathologies affect the number, quality, form, and content of creative works. The effects of "political pathology" on the creative process at the individual level are discussed in the concluding section of the article.

Simonton's work is a major pioneering effort. The research surveyed is fascinating and thought provoking. Unfortunately space is limited so that it is impossible to discuss adequately the article's many positive points. I limit myself to comments and suggestions that I hope will serve as springboards for future studies.

THE VARIABLES

Simonton's variables, "international wars, external threat, political instability, political fragmentation, and civil disturbances," are broad multidimensional variables. They serve well for purposes of a first cut through the data. In the future, however, greater psychological specificity would be helpful. For example, under the conditions studied what are the effects of the redistribution of *power* and what are the psychological areas in which *threat* and *stress* are experienced? If psychological variables can be specified (and selections may well be made from Murray's [1938] collection of needs and press), a desirable measure of generalization can be obtained. One could then study the effects of the disruption and redistribution of power not only at the societal level but also in the microcosm of one's organization and work group.

There are points in the article when Simonton discusses results as if they were *causally* related to his variables when indeed only correlations have been demonstrated. Transgenerational effects, years apart, are related as if history followed a linear rather than a cyclical or other progression. When a politically pathological even is shown to be followed some 20 years later by certain primary process effects, could it be that these very primary process effects lay the foundation for the next politically pathological event? As some have said, the French Revolution led to freedom, but that very freedom was followed by the development and use of the guillotine.

I also wonder if further study of Simonton's multidimensional variables would not be helped by some specification of the kinds of roles played by creative individuals vis-à-vis the society in times of political pathology. At such times the creative person may be called upon (if one limits oneself primarily to the arts, as Simonton does) to be inspirer, prophet, sympathizer, and so on. The very existence of such roles and the opportunities that creative people may have to avail themselves of these roles could be critical in structuring the psychological environment in what might otherwise be a quite chaotic situation.

On occasion, Simonton himself is aware that he is making value judgments. Such judgments may be difficult to avoid because one person's "holy war" is another's "satanic crusade." Nevertheless, in scientific articles, value judgments must be avoided. Our enemies have also had poets (for a contemporary instance see Sachs, 1990), writers, painters, scientists, and so on. Are their creative processes, or primary processes any different from ours? Is the level of creativity they achieve different from or similar to the creative level achieved by our creative people? And, if so, in what ways?

Simonton's fascinating discussion of the effects of wars on medical knowledge and of the effects of different kinds of wars on the annual rate of discovery and invention should be pursued further to include wars in modern times. Attention should be focused not only on the relationship between political pathology and *content area* and the *rate* of discovery and invention but also on the relationship between political pathology and discoveries which vary in the degree to which they are capable of *destroying humanity* and are actually used against civilian populations as well as an enemy's soldier. To be included here would be those creative developments that can be and have been used against civilian populations directly (e.g., the Atom bomb at Hiroshima) and indirectly (e.g., the use of Agent Orange on the land during the Vietnam War).

Studies of the effects of political pathology on scientific developments in modern times should also focus on the behavior of scientists and the circumstances under which they work. One could begin with a study of the behavior of scientists in Hitler Germany during World War II. Consider Werner von Braun, who as a major in Hitler's SS (Storm Trooper) conducted his research in the underground facilities in Peenemunde. Bower (1987) wrote that:

> Despite the constant arrival of new labor, the number of workers never increased. On average, one hundred men a day died of exhaustion, starvation, and disease, or were murdered by SS guards, either on a whim or as punishment. Their emaciated bodies were usually disposed of in crematoria . . . those who were hanged as punishment were left at the end of the rope for days, successfully intimidating the survivors. Replacements supplied by the SS from other concentration camps arrived on demand from Rudolph or Werner von Braun. Neither scientist was directly responsible for these conditions, but they accepted the situation created by the SS without demur. (Bower, 1987, p. 112)

The crucial point is that studies of the effects of pathologies at the societal level are incomplete without investigating how they seep down to the individual level. And, then the question is, what are the psychodynamics of persons who implicitly or explicitly accept the values of their pathological societies and are willing to work in such environments? Contemporary research has focused on environmental factors that facilitate or obstruct creativity. Value conflicts, as between success and creativity, have been found in contemporary studies (Stein, Heinze, & Rogers, 1958). But conditions in current R&D organizations are not usually as intense as conditions encountered during wartime. We could learn much about environmental and psychological factors affecting creativity from studies of the Werner von Brauns and studies of those scientists who first were involved in the development of the Atomic bomb and then organized themselves as scientists concerned with its use.

Some specific questions to which answers could be sought are: To what extent do scientists have allegiance *only* to science and technology? And, as scientific and technological goals are pursued and attained, what role is played by an attitude that "lets the chips fall where they may?" Does it matter to scientists and researchers who their employers are—the United States or Hitler's Germany?

Then there is the related question, "Does it matter who works for us?" Reflect on the expedience of U.S. representatives during World War II when they became aware that the Germans were pioneering impressive developments in supersonic flight. Two of the German scientists presented their work to three Americans, an America Colonel who was also a test pilot, a scientific adviser to the U.S. Air Force, and Dr. Fritz Zwicky of the California Institute of Technology, who should be known to workers in the field of creativity.[2] In a report of this experience we are told that:

> Zwicky showed surprisingly little interest in the rumors that both Germans had been longserving members of the SS, were ardent Nazis, and had held daily rallies for their research team. . . . The three Americans began discussing how to make the best use of the German expertise and soon agreed that the most sensible solution was for the Germans to be transported across the Atlantic. . . . The Germans should be treated as fellow scientists, not as Nazis. They should be well paid and allowed to travel with their families, and critics who argued that the Germans were enemies should be told that 'pride and face-saving have no place in national insurance'. (Bower, 1987, pp. 89–90)

Studies of the effects of political pathology on creativity in both Germany and the United States during World War II are critical for the information they will yield for all students of the creative process. They are of unique significance because they represent a time in history when the political pathology discussed by Simonton was probably never so intense and so threatening both on the battlefield and in the traditionally "safe areas" of civilian life.

The recommended studies are critical because we look forward to scientific and technological advances to help with the greenhouse effect, the use and misuse of our physical environment, the development of biodegradable plastics, and the proper disposition of atomic and other waste materials. We also look forward to scientific contributions in the use of nuclear energy, genetic engineering and so on. Consequently, we need to learn more than we currently know about the matter of *social responsibility* and how it affects scientific creativity and scientists at work.

THE CREATIVE INDIVIDUAL AND THE AUDIENCE

The relationship between the creative individual and the audience (Stein, 1974, 1975) is not explicitly acknowledged in Simonton's article. Nevertheless, he does present several ideas about Shakespeare that should be

---

[2]Fritz Zwicky developed the *morphological cube* that has been used by many to stimulate their creativity. It was used very effectively by Guilford (1967) in his *The nature of human intelligence.*

noted. One that is most relevant for our purposes occurs when Simonton speaks of Shakespeare's work "in an age of hereditary monarchy." Simonton wrote:

> In this context, conspiracies against the sovereign were diabolically evil, or in more contemporary terms, politically pathological. The playwright evidently could not resist underlining this unnatural monstrosity in his dramatic output, and *by this shrewd act*, we can be sure, *eliciting the appreciative applause of most of his audience.* (Emphasis added)

The words I have highlighted may give the wrong impression. The impression they convey is that the creative individual is involved in some nefarious behavior in which people are purposely manipulated. I do not think that Simonton intended to give such an impression. Creative people do have to communicate with their audiences. (For a contemporary view on adaptations in Shakespearean work over time, see Taylor, 1989.) At times they do make "judgment calls" or else they will lose their audience completely. Creative persons like Shakespeare do this much less frequently than less creative persons or popularizers, and readers might get the wrong impression about the relationships between creative individuals and their audiences or clients if they limited themselves only to the behavior described in the quotation.

Awareness of the audience as an important ingredient in the creative process goes way back. Plato, in his dialogue with Ion (Warmington & Rouse, 1956) inquires whether Ion, when performing before an audience, behaves artfully or as a conduit for his muse's communications. Ion replies by saying that he attends to the audience's response because what he earns depends on their reactions. The relevant exchange between Socrates and Ion is as follows:

> Socrates: And do you know that you reciters make most of the audience . . .?
> Ion: Oh yes, indeed I do! I always look down from my platform, and there they are crying and glaring and amazed according to what I say. Indeed, I'm bound to pay careful attention to them. If I leave them crying in their seats, I shall laugh at my pockets full of money; if I leave them laughing, I myself shall cry over the money lost. (Warmington & Rouse, 1956, p. 20)

In the history of ballet we know that Nijinsky shocked his audience in *Afternoon of a Faun* with a masturbatory gesture close to the end of the first performance of the ballet (*The New York Times*, 1989b). The audience's reaction was so negative that the gesture was omitted in later performances. Kepler, the father of modern astronomy, took a "shortcut" in his work—deriving the movement of planets in ellipses rather than circles from theory rather than observation. The news item reporting this reevaluation of Kepler's contribution concluded with the following quotation from a Dr. Donahue:

> "He [Kepler] had a difficult time trying to convince people that the ellipse was correct," he said. "So he fudged a little. That doesn't take him down a notch. It was a small point in the argument." (Broad, 1990, p. C6)

PSYCHOPATHOLOGY AND CREATIVITY

I would be remiss in my responsibility as commentator if I did not reflect on the positive relationship between psychopathology and creativity set forth at the beginning of the article. Comments are in order especially because Simonton surprisingly is not concerned with the validity of his opening remarks. He said, "Whether or not this judgment ("that individual achievement of phenomenal stature (is) associated with psychopathology of some kind") is true, however, is *not* the business of this essay to determine."

There are *Pathographers of Genius* who claim they find something—psychologically, physically, socially, morally, and so on—seriously wrong with creative people. Early pathographers associated all kinds of physical and psychological "problems" and illnesses with genius or creativity. Later pathographers asserted similar claims and then, because their *zeitgeist* was different from that of those who came before them, they now claimed they had found new relationships between sex and creativity. Contemporary pathographers are more likely than their historical counterparts to cite sexual hyper- and hypo-activity, or heterosexual and homosexual preferences. In modern times, psychiatric diagnoses, especially manic-depression, is the psychiatric illness of choice.

Lombroso (1891), an early pathographer cited by Simonton, believed that genius "is . . . the manifestation of a diseased mind" and may have the following stigmata:

> smallness of body, rickets, lameness and other deformities, pallor, emaciation, strange and cretin-like physiognomy, lesion of the skull and brain, and pronounced macrocephaly (though 'microcephalic' skulls may also be found), stammering, left-handedness, sterility, absence of physical resemblance to parents, precocity, misoneism, and vagabondage. (Stein & Heinze, 1960)

Needless to say, many of these characteristics would hardly be considered pathological today. (Indeed, Lombroso included "left-handedness" as a pathological characteristic. This would probably not sit so well today with those who assign a critical role to the right side of the brain in the creative process.) Nevertheless, the alleged relationship between psychopathology and creativity caught the imagination of many people who came from different walks of life, and each got into the act in his or her own way. This is not the place for a thorough discussion in this matter. Let it suffice if I simply provide a sampling of the kinds of views expressed and the kinds of data cited.

Psychoanalysts (Sterba & Sterba, 1954) discussed the psychopathology of Beethoven's involvement with his nephew. Popular writers with a psychological bent (Naifeh & Smith, 1990) wrote about the "crippling effects" of Jackson Pollock's "emotional disabilities." A famous psychologist (Gleitman, 1981, 1984) referred to a person who made independent judgments as a "crackpot" (see Stein, 1984c, 1985).

Creative persons themselves participated directly and indirectly in fanning the flames of pathography. And sometimes they did so humorously. Members of the Royal Society called themselves *Lunatics* because they held their monthly meetings on the night of the full moon so that they could walk home by the way of moonlit streets. In the 18th century some writers referred to themselves as *prostitutes* (*The New York Times Book Review*, 1989a). Romantic painters of the 18th and 19th centuries became intrigued with the art of the insane and studied it in an effort to gain access to new ways of viewing the world. On the contemporary art scene, there is renewed interest in the art of the insane (MacGregor, 1989) and art works produced by the insane are selling for as much as $60,000 (Lipson, 1990).

Knowledge of the work habits of creative person's also feed the idea that creative people are insane. "Schiller kept rotten apples in his desk . . . Balzac wore a monkish working garb; Gretry and Schiller immersed their feet in ice-cold water. . . . The aesthetician, Baumgarten, advised poets seeking inspiration to ride on horseback, to drink wine in moderation, and, provided they were chaste, to look at beautiful women" (Levey, 1940, p. 286; reprinted in Stein, 1974). Before she started work, Dame Edith Sitwell lay down in a coffin; Colette started her work day by picking fleas off her cat; Poe wrote with his Siamese cat on his shoulder; and Victor Hugo and Benjamin Franklin said they did their best work while nude (Ackerman, 1989, pp. 1, 56, 57).

If one wants to, one can find much to cite in the work of pathographers. But let us look more closely at what else some of the persons cited said. We start with Lombroso, who said he found pathology to be strongly associated with genius. But a careful reading of his work indicates that he differentiates between the genius and the insane. He said:

> It is scarcely necessary to add that these great disordered minds must not be confused with the poor inmates, without genius, of our asylums. Although as diseased persons, they belong to the same category, and have some of the

same characters, they must *not* be identified with them. While ordinary lunatics are reduced to inaction, or the agitation of sterile delirium, these disordered men of genius are the more active in the ideal life because the less apt for practical life. (Stein & Heinze, 1960, p. 51, emphasis added)

Also, the Dryden cited by Simonton as saying "Great wits are sure to madness near allied" was the very same Dryden, who, while England's Poet Laureate, called Shakespeare "creative" after he wrote *Midsummer's Night Dream.* What is interesting about this is that according to Smith (1924), this was probably the first time the word "creative" had been used as an adjective describing a person's effort (Stein, 1983). Prior to this, painters and writers whose work was especially noteworthy were called "original." Dryden, however, felt that the *Midsummer's Night Dream* was better than just original, and hence he called it and Shakespeare "creative" (Stein, 1984b). Perhaps Dryden did believe that wit and madness were allied, but he saw and rewarded the positive aspects of Shakespeare's work and called it "creative."

Plato spoke of "divine madness" as a critical ingredient in creative works. But in the *Book of Ion* he differentiated between creativity achieved as a result of "divine madness" and when one is the conduit through whom the muse speaks and creativity that results from art (read art-ifice or training). The former is at a higher level than the latter. Some creative products are so mind-boggling that it is inconceivable that a mere human produced them. Such persons, it was thought, must possess divine powers and, if it be "divine madness," so be it.

The point is to caution the reader against quick and easy acceptance of what Simonton calls the "tradition" of the association between psychopathology and individual creativity. There is such a tradition, but in a scientific article it should not be permitted to go by unquestioned. It is especially crucial not to interpret the word "association" to mean "causal." Moreover, it is important not to underestimate the anabolic functions of a creative person's psychological characteristics and talent. It is these very anabolic functions that frequently enable the creative person to cope successfully with his or her psychological problems.

All of this is not to say that creative people are without their social or psychological difficulties or problems. They surely have them. They may even end up in mental institutions with psychiatric diagnoses, but it would be a grievous error to regard these diagnoses, in every case, as having the same significance as they might have in the case of noncreative persons.

In an effort to gain a more complete understanding of the relationships between psychopathology and creativity, the following hypotheses should be studied: (a) "'*Genius makes for insanity, but neither insanity nor the insane temperament makes for genius*'" (Jacobson, 1912). (b) The psychopathological state or experience may provide the creative individual with valuable insights to be used later in creative work. (c) Psychological stress and trauma may have devastating effects on nontalented persons, but when these happen to creative persons, their talent and creativity serve mastery and the trauma is brought under control. (d) The creative work, which may well be preceded by a depressive experience, serves an adaptive/reparative function. (e) The psychological significance of the symbiotic relationship between the creative person and the audience in which the former expresses unconscious anxiety provoking conflicts and makes them tolerable for the audience, and the audience, by accepting the creative work, absolves the creative artist of guilt. (f) The importance of separating out those instances where psychiatric diagnoses and hospitalization may be used for political reasons and convenience. (g) Symptoms similar to psychiatric ones that can be traced to materials used by creative persons (e.g., as in the case of the "Mad Hatter") need to be ruled out as is also true of the effects of physical illnesses contracted in the course of one's creative work.

The association between psychopathology and creativity is more complicated and more interesting than the pathographers and others let on. And it is these more complicated and more interesting associations that need study.

Basic to the above discussion is what is "normality" and, of course, there are many definitions. One is statistical—whatever the majority of people do is "normal" and anyone who deviates from the norm is likely to be at least a "crackpot," if not abnormal or insane. Another definition is that the normal individual adapts to his or her environment and becomes something of a conformist. Psychologically speaking, if one becomes a conformist and does not fulfill his or her potentialities or self-actualizing tendencies, then is that person "normal" or "abnormal"?

Let us close this section on something of a light note and recall an anecdote told about Paul Schilder, the famous psychiatrist. The anecdote has it that Schilder had been lecturing to his students on abnormal psychology. At the end of the semester the students turned to him and asked, "Dr. Schilder we now know a great deal about the abnormal person, please tell us about the normal?" To this request, Dr. Schilder replied, "When we find him, we cure him."

EXTRAPOLATIONS TO THE CONTEMPORARY SCENE

"Those who cannot remember the past are condemned to fulfill it," said Santayana (1905). Herein lies another valuable aspect of Simonton's article. Through his survey of the effects on creativity of political pathology at the societal level he has highlighted for us the enormous losses that we as a civilization have suffered.

All this becomes all the more poignant because of the political changes now taking place in Eastern Europe and elsewhere. Would that we were able to study the effects of this new-found freedom on creativity in our own time. In all likelihood it would reinforce our belief that creative persons need four freedoms "the freedom for study and preparation, the freedom for exploration and inquiry, the freedom of expression, and the freedom to be themselves" (Stein, 1963).

Extrapolating in terms of time is one value we can obtain from Simonton's work. Another is to extrapolate from it in terms of *place*. The same wasteful effects associated with political pathology at the societal level also occur in the microcosm of our universities, organizations, departments, and work groups. In these, we cannot even count on compensating generational effects, so we had better safeguard ourselves against any negative effects as best we can during our own lifetimes.

Consciousness also has to be raised about "political pathology" and power struggles in the realm of ideas. Most germane for our purposes is how they worm their way into creativity research. There are times when work in this area is not dictated by the demand requirements of the problem but by what power-group holds the research grant purse strings and the power-group's theoretical orientation. Witness for example variations in emphases on cognitive factors and psychodynamics; creativity versus intelligence; and divergent thinking as the sole measure of creativity versus a full battery of tests from the structure of intellect that apply to creativity.

No doubt with the passage of time and the appearance of generational effects, the fads and the variations will be seen as "paradigmatic shifts," but when one lives with them they feel more like "political shoves."

ANABOLIC AND CATABOLIC FACTORS

Years ago Henry Murray used metabolism as a metaphor to elucidate different kinds of personality functions.[3] In metabolism there are *catabolic* functions that break food down and *anabolic* functions that make for growth. In a complete study of a person one should look at both sets of functions. Any concentration on one to the exclusion of the other reflects

---

[3]The origin of this orientation can be traced to Sydenham, a physician in 17th century England, who said, "A disease, however much its cause may be adverse to the human body, is nothing more than an effort of Nature, who strives to restore health of the patient by the elimination of morbific matter" (Keele, 1974, cited in Altschule, 1989, p. 30).

a one-sided and partisan approach that distorts the complexity and richness of the system under study.

Variables in different areas contain both catabolic and anabolic functions. When a person is ill and running a high temperature, one may focus only on the fever or take heart in the fact that the patient is fighting the illness. In the social arena a crisis signifies dangers as well as opportunities. In the personality area anxiety can be disorganizing because of impending doom or stimulating because of anticipated psychological growth.

One can get the most out of Simonton's article by thinking of society as a system that has both anabolic and catabolic characteristics. Power relationships, or political pathologies, can operate catabolically to impede and obstruct creativity, or they can operate to stimulate and nurture creative developments. Power relationships are pathological and politically destructive when they are one-sided. As students of creativity, one of the ways in which we can serve society best is to sound the alarm when catabolism outweighs anabolism and the good in the creative process is threatened.

In this regard effective use can be made of Simonton's survey of the effects of political pathology. Martindale's (1975) work on primary and secondary process can serve as signs of where the society is or as prognosticators of things to come. It is also important to underscore the significance of role models for current and future generations of persons who fight for civil liberties and political freedom, like Lech Walesa in Poland, Vaclav Havel in Czechoslovakia, Nelson Mandela in South Africa, and Martin Luther King Jr., in the United States. Industrial companies that foster growth through creative research rather than by mergers alone need to be cited for their social contributions. Museums that function both as repositories of the society's cultural heritage and at the same time provide space for controversial works and ideas need financial support and encouragement. Educational institutions that nurture their students' self-fulfilling and self-actualizing tendencies are also part of the positive picture. These are only a sample of some of the symptoms of a society concerned with anabolism and whose creativity is not crippled by debilitating pathology.

CONTRICIPATION

When the historical effects of "political pathology" surveyed by Simonton are integrated with their contemporary effects, we can then see that we all *contricipate* in the creative process—some of us *contribute* creative works and others of us *appreciate* the process, the products, and the people. I coined the word, *contricipation* (Stein, 1984a, 1986) to call attention to the fact that everyone is involved in the creative process, and it is our responsibility to see to it that it endures regardless of pressures against it. All too often in our discussions of the creative process we focus our attention solely on problems of the creative individual—his or her difficult times, psychological difficulties, and other anabolic factors. These are noteworthy but they are incomplete. Problems with the creative process, like political pathology at the societal level, affect all of us. Just imagine that we might live at a time when we wanted to read a good book but no one wrote one because they were prevented from doing so. Just imagine you wanted to hear a symphony, but no one composed it because it was politically wrong to do so. Just imagine you wanted to go to a museum to see an exhibit of paintings or photographs, but the paintings and photographs did not exist because some powers objected to their content.[4]

When creativity is blocked by political or other forces, whose problem is it? The creative person's? It is a problem that each of us must help solve. Just as each of us *contricipates* in the creative process—by contributing to or appreciating it—so each of us must nurture it. When creativity is threatened by the kinds of pathological forces that Simonton alerts us to, we must each be prepared to protect it.

REFERENCES

Ackerman, D. (1989, November). O muse! You do make things difficult! *The New York Times Book Review*, pp. 1, 56–57.

Altschule, M. D. (1989). *Essays on the rise and decline and rise of beside medicine.* Philadelphia: Totto Gap Medical Research Laboratories.

Bower, T. (1987). *The paperclip conspiracy: The hunt for the Nazi scientists.* Boston: Little Brown.

Broad, W. J. (1990, January). After 400 years, a challenge to Kepler: He fabricated his data, scholar says. *The New York Times: Science Times*, C1 and C6.

Fogel, R. W. (1989). *The rise and fall of American slavery.* New York: Norton.

Gleitman, H. (1981). *Psychology.* New York: Norton.

---

[4]"These are not simple rhetorical questions. Consider the problems encountered by the exhibition of Mapplethorpe's photographs. At the federal level the National Endowment for the Arts is threatened with budget cuts. At the local level (Cincinnati) not only may the exhibit not be shown but "The museum's chairman resigned . . . amid boycott threats against his employer, a local bank" (Wilkerson, 1990, p. 1). In book publishing the emphasis on profits is so intense and cost of publishing so high that the quality of books produced are likely to be affected. Books and authors become more and more like commodities to be bought and sold just as long as they make money.

Gleitman, H. (1984). Some comments on Dr. Stein's critique of my account of Asch's social-pressure studies. *Perceptual and Motor Skills, 59,* 1003–1006.

Guilford, J. P. (1967). *The nature of human intelligence.* New York: McGraw-Hill.

Jacobson, A. C. (1912). Literary genius and manic depressive insanity. *Medical Record,* LXXXII, 937–939.

Keele, K. D. (1974). The Sydenham-Boyle theory of morbific particles. *Medical History, 18,* 240–248.

L'après-midi d'un faune. (1989b, December). *The New York Times: The Arts.*

Levey, H. B. (1940). A theory concerning free creation in the inventive arts. *Psychiatry, 3* (Summarized in Stein & Heinze, 1960, pp. 229–293).

Lipson, K. (1990, January). The art of madness. *Newsday.*

Lombroso, C. (1891). *The man of genius.* London: Walter Scott. (Summarized in Stein & Heinze, 1960).

MacGregor, J. M. (1989). *The discovery of the art of the insane.* Princeton, NJ: Princeton University Press.

Martindale, C. (1975). *Romantic progression.* Washington, DC: Hemisphere Publishing.

Mitgang, H. (1989, December). Books of the Times: Slaves' historian changes his mind. *The New York Times,* p. 20.

Murray, H. A. (1938). *Explorations in personality.* New York: Oxford University Press.

Naifeh, S., & Smith, G. W. (1990). *Jackson Pollock.* New York: Clarkson N. Potter.

Noted with pleasure: Kissing cousins. (1989a, November). *The New York Times Book Review,* p. 67.

O. S. S. Assessment Staff (1948). *Assessment of men.* New York: Rinehart.

Sachs, S. (1990, January). Poet seeks redemption in revolution: Romania's former laureate scorned for ties to dictator. *Newsday.*

Santayana, G. (1905). *Life of reason, Vol 1.* New York: Scribner's.

Simonton, D. K. (1976). The sociopolitical context of philosophical beliefs: A transhistorical causal analysis. *Social Forces, 54,* 513–523.

Simonton, D. K. (1989). The swan-song phenomenon: Last-works effects for 172 classical composers. *Psychology and Aging, 4,* 42–47.

Simonton, D. K. (1990). Political pathology and societal creativity. *Creativity Research Journal, 3,* 85–100.

Smith, L. P. (1924). *S. P. E. Tract No. XVIII four words: Romantic, originality, creative, genius.* London: Oxford University Press.

Stein, M. I. (1963). Creativity in a free society. *Educational Horizons, 41,* 130. (Also in Stein, 1974, 1984.)

Stein, M. I. (1974). *Stimulating creativity, Vol 1: Individual procedures.* Orlando, FL: Academic.

Stein, M. I. (1975). *Stimulating Creativity, vol 2: Group Procedures.* Orlando, FL: Academic.

Stein, M. I. (1983). Creativity in Genesis. *Journal of Creative Behavior, 17,* 1–8.

Stein, M. I. (1984a). *Making the point.* Buffalo, NY: Bearly Limited.

Stein, M. I. (1984b). A minority of one, a crackpot (?), in an introductory psychology textbook. *Perceptual and Motor Skills, 39,* 370.

Stein, M. I. (1984c). Creative: The adjective. *Creativity and Innovation Network, 10,* 115–117.

Stein, M. I. (1985). A reply to Gleitman. *Perceptual and Motor Skills, 60,* 10.

Stein, M. I. (1986). *Gifted, talented, and creative young people.* New York: Garland.

Stein, M. I., & Heinze, S. J. (1960). *Creativity and the individual.* Amagansett, NY: The News Press.

Stein, M. I., Heinze, S. J., & Rogers, R. R. (1958). Creativity and/or success: A study in value conflict. In C. W. Taylor (Ed.), *The second (1957) University of Utah conference on the identification of creative scientific talent.* Salt Lake City: University of Utah Press.

Sterba, E., & Sterba, R. (1954). *Beethoven and his nephew.* New York: Schocken Books.

Stern, G., Stein, M. I., & Bloom, B. S. (1956). *Methods in personality assessment.* New York: Free Press.

Taylor, G. (1989). *Reinventing Shakespeare: A cultural history from the restoration to the present.* New York: Weidenfield & Nicholson.

Warmington, E. H., & Rouse, P. G. (1956). *Great dialogues of Plato.* New York: New American Library.

Wilkerson, I. (1990). Trouble right here in Cincinnati: Furor over Mapplethorpe exhibit. *The New York Times,* March 29, A21 and A22.

Chapter 29

Monsieur Appends Reflections

Dean Keith Simonton

David Feldman opens his comments with a reference to one play by Jean Genet, but I would like to open my remarks by referring to another, Genet's *The Maids*. As an amateur Thespian in both high school and college, I was once recruited to perform the part of "Monsieur." Those who know this play realize that no such role exists, for Monsieur is a figure central but unseen; the drama is defined solely by the reflections and conversations uttered by two maids and their "Madam." My own part was choreographed: Monsieur danced about silently, miming worlds of fantasy, while the women so often spoke about him. By the end of the play I felt like screaming a few words to present my own reactions to the continuing commentary, but the director would certainly not allow any such insertions. Now I face a gathering of voices, all often talking about me "behind may back"—yet the editor has been gracious enough to allow me to mouth an epilogue.

Feldman uses Genet's *The Balcony* to spotlight what he sees to be a fundamental emphasis of my research. As a social psychologist by training, I am prone to focus on the external forces that shape the creator's life. To some undetermined extent an individual's career is the upshot of a whole inventory of environmental factors, and therefore persons placed in the same set of circumstances will end up having the same creative consequences. Although this may be a fair representation of my research program, my theoretical views are more elaborate. None of us can investigate every aspect of a phenomenon, and so each of us concentrates on that domain where we believe we can optimize our contributions to knowledge. Because the social psychology of creativity was practically nonexistent as a discipline, that is where I jumped in (Simonton, in press-b). Even so, I maintain in equal force that the individual represents the summation of a host of influences, many of which are highly idiosyncratic. Some inputs are genetic, producing personalities with a unique set of skills and curiosities that affect the way the developing individual incorporates the sociocultural milieu. In addition, each creator is certainly the product of distinctive events in childhood and adolescence that may motivate the peculiar preoccupations of adulthood. Hence, no matter how many extrinsic variables I list as determinants of creativity, an impressive residual will always remain that renders any single creator distinct.

If Feldman is astonished at the seeming interchangeability of my subjects, Stein is more amazed at the sheer size of my samples—subject counts running sometimes into the thousands. But in terms of the effort involved, I really must admit that these endeavors may not be much more arduous than his struggles to examine "only" 67 subjects. After all, when fewer than 100 persons make up a sample, it is usually because the number of variables investigated is very large and the difficulty of assessing those variables is immense. In contrast, for studies with big Ns, the number of variables may be just a dozen or so, and these few variables are easily quantified. For example, for a recent study of 10,160 creators and leaders in Chinese civilization, only four variables were necessary: eminence, floruit date, field of activity, and nationality, must the first requiring substantial psychometrics (Simonton, 1988b). So little data were needed simply because the individual information was eventually aggregated into a generational time-series analysis. Notice, too, that the "subjects" I favor never miss appointments, are available day and night, and ... well, indeed, I can carry hundreds of them around in my pocket on a floppy disk! Only introspective psychology has more convenient subjects of inquiry (for sometimes my luminaries refuse to respond to certain of my questions). Of course, there is a price to pay for this convenience, namely that such methods are geared solely toward "getting the big picture," and toward studying the worldwide distribution of forests rather than the fine pattern of tree bark. Hence, I often find myself studying smaller samples, even single cases, as in my work on Shakespeare and

Beethoven (e.g., Simonton, 1986, 1987). In such cases, it is Stein who boasts the impressive sample sizes!

Other commentators focus on more substantive matters. For example, Bailin challenges the utility of "political pathology," and both Bailin and Stein question my refusal to discuss how creativity and pathology connect at the individual level. These complaints are by no means devoid of justice: I have clearly opted for a metaphor that would allow me to survey some of the key features of what may be styled the "creative society." The heuristic value of this coordinating theme notwithstanding, numerous value judgments wait to ensnare the unwary in any such conversation. Still other commentators, such as Martindale, take issue with some of my theoretical interpretations of the data, pointing out explanatory deficiencies and offering some explanations of their own. Stariha and Walberg mention several psychological processes that might account for an inverse relation between creativity and pathology on the societal plane, and Rubenson sketches a "psychoeconomic" perspective that can subsume the diverse empirical findings under a unified framework. I welcome all of these efforts. Frankly, one reason for writing the target article was my dissatisfaction with how well my chance-configuration theory handled all the data on societal creativity (cf. Simonton, 1988c). In a sense, this chapter is an inventory of loose ends or residuals that are up for grabs by any adventurous theorist.

Nonetheless, a warning is in order as well. Established results regarding historical creativity are far richer than this chapter could convey, including numerous findings about developmental antecedents, individual differences in lifetime output, longitudinal changes in productivity, cognitive and motivational processes, and the phenomenon of multiple discovery and invention. A complete account would have to deal with these diverse relations all at once rather than provide post hoc interpretations piecemeal. For instance, although I am struck by the considerable power of economic explanations, there is reason to doubt whether this approach can provide useful interpretations for some of the fine features of a creative life, such as the unique patterns defining the developmental placement of career landmarks (Simonton, 1988a, in press-a). In addition, for economic explanations to become fully convincing, they must be integrated with the more complex picture of human thought, act, and affect that has been so exhaustively documented in psychology. Hence, for a scheme to become truly *psycho*economic, the image of the actor in the cultural marketplace must be made to mesh with the actual intricacies of the human self as it transforms over a creator's lifespan.

I must end by addressing Hausman's commentary, which applies a far more philosophical perspective to the issues raised in my chapter. Although I was stimulated by what he had to say, he makes two points on which I beg to differ. First comes his assertion that my "vacillation" between magnitude and content of creativity was unfortunate, for the content aspect is somehow less interesting, even trivial. Yet one of the chief debates in the history of any discipline is that between *internalist* and *externalist* explanations: Do observed innovations result from the endogenous working out of developments intrinsic to the discipline or do they emerge from exogenous inputs of events extrinsic to the field? One does not have to follow Marxist precepts to think that the second of these possibilities is both very real and important to our comprehension of societal creativity. To be sure, one could argue that often the influx of extraneous events produces content alterations that are so mundane as to be unworthy of discussion. But we should always be careful not to fall victim to a "hindsight bias" in which newly discovered correlations are dismissed as obvious on a post hoc basis only. That Shakespeare's thematic material was deflected in certain ways by the political and military headlines may seem uninteresting, yet notwithstanding centuries of Shakespeare scholarship, these reactions have never been noticed before. Indeed, I have amply documented elsewhere how humanistic speculations about possible trends have virtually no connection with the raw facts (Simonton, in press-c). These failed conjectures are especially likely when we are dealing with rather subtle content characteristics. For example, the manner in which military conflict shapes the melodic and harmonic structure of classical compositions can only be detected by a systematic content analysis followed by a sophisticated statistical analysis.

The second matter concerns whether creativity operates solely at the individual level, or whether it is meaningful to speak of creativity on the plane of the sociocultural system. Hausman offers some objections to the latter practice. For instance, he claims that only the individual can assume responsibility for creativity. Yet I would claim that quite the contrary is true. Although individuals are certainly responsible for any products that are offered as candidates for the designation "creative," the assignment of this tag depends on the larger society. I have documented at some length how creators are not necessarily the best judges of their own work, at least in the sense that often their reputations are eventually predicated on contributions for which they had relatively low regard. Hence, it is the culture in which creators work that is ultimately responsible for what counts as a demonstration of historically significant creativity. This is precisely where "value judgments" come into play. In truth, I have nothing against such assessments so long as they are used carefully. On one hand, I am opposed to imposing the standards of one culture upon the products and personalities of another, for such evaluations invite ethnocentrism. On the other hand, I see nothing wrong with looking at what a given sociocultural world takes to be its masters and masterpieces. Indeed, it must be manifest that according to my favorite operational definition of creativity, these "judgments of posterity" within a given heritage or discipline represent the fait accompli on which measures of merit are necessarily based. Furthermore, the notion of societal responsibility is often implicit in how we often view the phenomenon of creativity. When we say that so-and-so from an earlier era was a "neglected genius," we do not "blame the victim" but rather deride the myopia of a whole community that failed to appreciate properly the creator in its midst.

Let me close by drawing an analogy with the physical phenomenon of heat. There is nothing unscientific about measuring the temperature of a given body, even though the resulting number summarizes only the mean velocity of the millions of molecules that make up that body. By the same token, we can certainly gauge the creativity of a whole society despite the fact that his assessment only reflects the average creativity of the society's citizens. In some periods and places, a culture becomes "hot" whereas in other circumstances the culture becomes "cold." What I have been speculating about in the main article is whether political pathology, however defined, turns up the heat or blows out the flame.

REFERENCES

Simonton, D. K. (1986). Popularity, content, and context in 37 Shakespeare plays. *Poetics, 15,* 493–510.

Simonton, D. K. (1987). Musical aesthetics and creativity in Beethoven: A computer analysis of 105 compositions. *Empirical Studies of the Arts, 5,* 87–104.

Simonton, D. K. (1988a). Age and outstanding achievement: What do we know after a century of research? *Psychological Bulletin, 104,* 251–267.

Simonton, D. K. (1988b). Galtonian genius, Kroeberian configurations, and emulation: A generational time-series analysis of Chinese civilization. *Journal of Personality and Social Psychology, 55,* 230–238.

Simonton, D. K. (1988c). *Scientific genius: A psychology of science.* Cambridge: Cambridge University Press.

Simonton, D. K. (1990). Shakespeare's sonnets: A case of and for single-case historiometry. *Journal of Personality, 57,* 695–721.

Simonton, D. K. (in press-a). Career landmarks in science: Individual differences and interdisciplinary contrasts. *Developmental Psychology.*

Simonton, D. K. (in press-b). History, chemistry, psychology, and genius: An intellectual autobiography of historiometry. In M. A. Runco & R. S. Albert (Eds.), *Theories of creativity* (rev. ed.). Cresskill, NJ : Hampton Press.

Simonton, D. K. (in press-c). *Psychology, science, and history: An introduction to historiometry.* New Haven, CT: Yale University Press.

PART V

INTEGRATING PERSONAL PATTERNS AND SOCIETAL POSSIBILITIES

Part V

Introduction

Here we take another bold step. How can individual creativity serve to make us better, make the world better? A part of the message from Barron and Bradley, from Gruber, in this section, and from Richards in the next section, is that there's no one pattern—no single correct profile of a creative perfection. Creativity emerges unpredictably from the richness of our diversity—both within our own minds, and between all of us in this multipotentialled world. We should cherish this diversity, preserve, and enhance it, for it may help us in ways we cannot now imagine.

Such valuing is not automatic in a conforming world where difference may be more readily pathologized than celebrated, or in a competitive world, where difference may mean threat more than opportunity. Nor is it necessarily valued in an endangered world where suppression of certain contents of one's own mind, through defense, denial, consensual delusion (for example, poverty doesn't exist in this city, war has ended— no one is hungry tonight), may seem preferable to a painful awareness and an experience of hopelessness and despair. But after all, one may say, what can *I* do? Prince, the pop singer and composer, expressed one solution in song, "Two thousand-zero-zero party over—oops! Outta time—tonight I'm gonna party like it's 1999."

That's one approach.

Barron and Bradley take another perspective. We're all in a dialectic pushing and pulling, and can work together from our own unique perspectives, to forge new solutions. Among the mix, more highly innovative people may be marked by their particular ability both to participate in a process of change and to thrive from it. Here indeed is a way to address our major social issues—through sincere interest, shared concern, and a collaborative (if not always unified) effort. It can be done. Perhaps we can even enjoy doing it.

Consider this "creative" profile: a dash of originality, independence of judgment, and tolerance of ambiguity. Add a sprinkling of internationalism and trust in human nature—how interesting that these are tied in. Barron & Bradley's chapter looks at factors associated with a profreeze rather than pro-buildup position for nuclear weapons, but is not at all a position paper for a certain social policy. Rather, the chapter focuses on *process*, the process required for ongoing open inquiry, marked by "integrative complexity" or the complex integration of information.

Now, alternatively, one could stop this activity and use a bomb. When put so blatantly, it can hardly seem the healthiest solution. One might be reminded of Dudek and Verrault's chapter (this volume); the more creative the children the less they were preoccupied with aggression. Ah, libido—that's where the energy went instead.

Among the many memorable parts of Gruber's paper are two anecdotes. First, it seems, a lion and a lamb, when raised together, may in fact get along. The lion has more options than we might think. And so perhaps do we. Who is to say we are inevitably violent, overly self-concerned, and capable of no more prosocial behavior than we are now displaying, in trying to solve our social and environmental problems.

In a second anecdote, from Gruber's "Shadow Box" experiments, some people placed together in a problem solving task couldn't *help but cooperate*. What pleasure they had in breaking the rules of the study, and trading information to figure out the identity of an object from its shadows viewed from two different angles. Teamwork did it. Gruber also points out the obligation for exceptional creativity in what he calls the morally gifted person—but how this appellation can at the same time erroneously make it sound dull, guilt ridden, overly prescribed, and rigid. In fact, this work can be unusually demanding, complex and variable. It is also work that at its best can produce exceptional satisfactions and a profound joy.

Chapter 30

The Clash of Social Philosophies and Personalities in the Nuclear Arms Control Debate: A Healthful Dialectic?

Frank Barron
Pamela Bradley

Love and war, harmony and strife—these were the terms in which Heraclitus saw the basic cosmic principles of generation. In the clash of opposites lies the possibility of transcendence. Philosophers through the ages have chosen sides in their preference for one or the other of the polarities. William James summed it all up as a matter of temperament more than of rational choice—the tender-minded and the tough-minded always face one another, whatever the manifest content of what is at issue.

These same dichotomies may be discerned in attitudes toward nuclear arms control. And not only is policy opposed to policy and personality to personality, but even within each of us we can sometimes feel, however fleetingly, the tug of toughness versus tenderness, the desire for overwhelming power of arms for our side versus severe limitation of arms in the service of global security. The question is: Does one side of the attitudinal divide contain more healthful tendencies than the other? Or are both, reconciled, necessary for the solving of the global problem of nuclear arms? Is there a possibility of healthful reconciliation of these opposites? Or is one of them already the more healthy attitude psychologically? The present authors began with a prejudice in favor of an immediate nuclear freeze and curtailment of arms production, as our statement of hypothesis will suggest. But our gathering of evidence on the question seems to us to broaden the basis for discussion.

THE PLACE OF NEW RESEARCH

The relationships between personality and perceptual preferences, and political, philosophical, and social values concerning positions on nuclear arms policy have hardly been addressed as yet in the psychological literature. There are, of course, a number of studies that show how personal characteristics may influence social and political decisions. The relationship of aggressiveness to authoritarianism as both variables affect foreign policy stances has been the object of a number of well-known researches (Adorno, Frendel-Brunswick, Levinson, & Sangord, 1956; Christiansen, 1959; Eckhardt & Lentz, 1967; Etheredge, 1978). Personality correlates of political orientation have also been identified (Barron & Young, 1970; Constantini & Carik, 1980; Feather, 1984). Related psychological research on foreign-policy decision-making has focused on international conflict (Tetlock, 1983a, 1983b) and problems or miscalculations in such decision-making processes (Janis & Mann, 1977; Jervis, 1976; Suedfeld & Tetlock, 1977). But most of these studies are specifically peripheral to the topic of nuclear arms philosophy. The field stands in need of a new measure geared to issues confronting policy-makers and the public today. The present authors see this need as basic to the further study of the philosophic and personality determinants of behavior regarding nuclear arms issues. We therefore proceeded by first developing such a measure to serve as an anchor for our investigation of related values and personality attributes.

For this purpose, the senior author expanded the *Inventory of Personal Philosophy* (*IPP*, Barron, 1968, 1983) to include an a priori Nuclear Arms Reduction Scale (NAR) as well as several dozen additional items centered on attitudes towards nuclear age events, such as the population explosion, advances in molecular genetics and biotechnology, space exploration, the threat of ecological disasters as a consequence of technology, the computer revolution, social changes needed to ensure equal opportunity and social justice for minorities and between the sexes and other developments on a worldwide scale that have become increasingly important during the past four decades.

The NAR Scale, a 10-item scale written to hypothesize and then analyzed for internal consistency, eventually became the focus of the studies to be reported in this article. Relations between it and a variety of other measures, in samples of college-age adults of both sexes in the United States and in Western Germany, were analyzed. The hypotheses tested in this series of studies are as follows: (a) a favorable attitude towards nuclear arms reduction will be held by individuals showing a pattern of traits associated with creativity: greater complexity of our look, greater independence of judgment, more intuitive, and more disposed to express original ideas; (b) the well-known left-right dimension in social values will be strongly associated with attitudes toward nuclear arms, those opposed to a reduction in arms being more conservative and less internationally minded; and (c) personality traits associated with tolerance of others, trust in human nature, empathy sense of humor, and tendency to be expressive rather than repressive of affect will go along with a favorable attitude toward reduction of nuclear arms.

METHOD

Measures

Barron's (1983) revision of the *IPP* consists of 54 new items. Those related to nuclear arms control and superpower relations were chosen for analysis as a hypothetical subset, whose coherence, internal consistency, and singularity should be revealed by intercorrelating the 54 new items in the 1983 revision. Criteria used for defining the subset of nuclear arms reduction items and supporting its validity were, in addition to designed face validity, that the items: (a) should have a high average correlation with one another; (b) should generate a total score that would have a high correlation with each item separately; and (c) should show minimal gender differences in terms both of total scale score and individual items. It was further required that the part–whole correlation of each chosen item with total score from the subset of items should be greater than any of the 44 excluded items, and that, using a rationally contrasted group comparison method, the scale should discriminate groups as expected.

These rather stringent criteria were met for the 10 items eventually included in the NAR Scale, with the exception that 1 item of the 10 did show a gender difference (see Table 30.1 and Discussion). It was retained because of its other desired characteristics.

Two opposed political stances are· expressed in responses to the 10 items of the NAR Scale. On one side is what might generically be called the programs-reduction position. It is represented by these views (paraphrased from the items): we should have an immediate nuclear freeze; we should spend a lot less money for armaments; the Russians are unlikely to launch a first strike; a nuclear exchange could easily be precipitated by accident. On the other side is what might be called the probuildup position. It holds the following: deterrence through mutually assured destruction (balance of terror) is the best solution; all new homes should be equipped with bomb shelters; we should undertake more measures for civil defense; most antinuclear demonstrations are organized by Communists. Adherents of this second position also say they would "push the button" if they had to; and they would be willing to do anything necessary to survive a nuclear war.

The Adjective Checklist (ACL; Gough & Heilbrun, 1983) and the Campbell revision of the Strong Vocational Interest Blank (Strong, 1943)

Table 30.1. Item Content, Item Gender Differences, and Internal Coherence
of NAR Scale in Standardization Sample[1]

| IPP Item No. | NAR *Scale Items* | Gender Difference | | | | r *with Total score* |
| | | % *Agree* | | | | |
		M	F	ratio	p	
153	1. I think a nuclear exchange could easily be precipitated by accident.	62.2	75.0	1.68	.20	.60
152	2. The policy of "deterrence" through "balance of terror" is the best solution in the foreseeable future.	32.4	18.0	2.43	.12	.57
124	3. I wish we had more opportunity to participate in fallout shelter drills and other civil defense.	37.8	28.8	0.78	.38	.56
139	4. I would push the button if I had to.	33.3	11.5	6.50	.01	.56
156	5. I favor a nuclear freeze now.	81.1	88.5	0.93	.34	.55
140	6. Most anti-nuclear demonstrations in Europe are organized by Communists.	22.2	10.0	2.45	.12	.55
152	7. We should spend a lot less money for armaments if we want a strong economy.	70.3	84.3	2.51	.12	.53
119	8. I am willing to do whatever is necessary to survive a nuclear war.	58.3	38.5	3.43	.07	.49
137	9. The Russians would not hesitate to strike first if they had the chance.	51.4	40.4	1.37	.25	.45
134	10. All new homes ought to be equipped with bomb shelters.	32.4	33.3	0.01	.93	.44

[1]UCSC undergraduates, *N* of 95, 40 male, 55 female

were administered to the MBA Students. Two other standardized personality inventories were used in the assessment: the Myers-Briggs Type
Indicator (MBTI; Myers & McCaulley, 1985), and the California Psychological Inventory (CPI; Gough, 1957, 1987).

Subjects and Procedures

The subjects in this series of investigations were for the most part university students, of both sexes, in the United States and West Germany.
The educational institutions represented were the University of California
(Berkeley and Santa Cruz campuses), the University of Arizona, and the
University of Munich. Other samples of university-age individuals included enlisted men in the West German army, employees in a military
aircraft factory in West Germany, and members of the Green Party. A
study of the personality correlates of the NAR Scale, using the full-scale
assessment method, was carried out at the Institute of Personality Assessment and Research, University California at Berkeley, and employed as
subjects in two successive classes of graduate studetns in the Master of
Business Administration Program there. All but one of the university samples in the questionnaire study consisted of undergraduates in the social
sciences or education. The exception was a sample of medical students in
West Germany. The *IPP* was administered to these respondents in a group
setting and at a single sitting for each sample.

The NAR Scale was included in a battery of tests administered to 131
candidates for the Master of Business Arts degree at the University of California, Berkeley, in 1984 and 1985. The assessment format called for
three days of observation of the subjects in a variety of social situations
as well as group interaction procedures. Ten staff observers described
each subject at the conclusion of the assessment by checking adjectives
they considered descriptive of the subjects of the ACL. Each staff observer also described each subject using the California Q-sort (Block,
1961). Collation of observer data was achieved by averaging the observer
Q-sort item placements for each assessee, and by requiring that at least
60% of the observers checked a given adjective as descriptive of a subject
before it was considered consensually present.

RESULTS

Results are presented below under three headings: (a) development and
item content of the NAR Scale; (b) personality correlates of the scale discovered through its use in the IPAR (Institute of Personality Assessment
and Research) living-in assessments; and (c) its correlation with related
personality scales, drawn from such inventories as the ACL and the MBTI.

Consistency of the Nuclear Arms Reduction Scale

Data from the 1983 revision of the *IPP* were available for the five West German samples (who were tested in late 1983 and early 1984). These are incorporated in Table 30.2. Application of the contrasted group method on an independently estimated dimension from *very favorable* to *very unfavorable* vis-à-vis the West German government's position on the then-new NATO emplacement of Pershing II and cruise missiles showed that the scale, keyed in the direction of a nuclear arms reduction stance, was highly accurate in discriminating between the groups (Bradley, 1984). A one-way analysis of variance for the NAR Scores for the five West German samples was highly significant ($F = 12.74$, $p < .001$). Results of a Scheffe multiple comparison procedure, employed for pairwise comparison of the means, revealed two distinct homogeneous subsets whose highest and lowest means did not differ significantly: subset 1, soldiers in the West German army and West German civilians who were employed in military aircraft factories; and subset 2, West German university undergraduates, medical students, and members of the Green Party.

Correlates of NAR with Nonoverlapping IPP Scales

Because the 1983 revision of the *IPP* retained all the items and scales of the 1968 version, any new scale developed from the additional 54 items would not overlap with the previously standardized scales. This makes interpretation conceptually clear because it avoids the usual situation found in inventories in which there is considerable item overlap among scales.

Table 30.2 presents for all samples the correlates of the NAR Scale with the three empirically developed, creativity-relevant scales of the 1983 version of the *IPP*: *Independence of Judgment* (Barron, 1953a), *Complexity of Outlook* (Barron, 1963a), and *Originality*. It presents also the correlations of NAR with four factor scales of the 1968 *IPP*: *Religious, Conservatism, Ethnocentrism, Internationalism,* and *Trust in Human Nature.*

As Table 30.2 shows, NAR scored for proreduction correlated consistently, substantially, and positively with *Complexity of Outlook, Independence of Judgment, Originality, Internationalism,* and *Trust in Human Nature,* but negatively with *Ethnocentrism. Religious Conservatism* was negatively related to NAR in the American samples, but not in the West Germany samples.

Observer Adjective and Q-sort Descriptions

Each ACL and Q-sort item composite was correlated with NAR scores in the sample of 131 MBA candidates. Positive correlations significant at the

Table 30.2. Correlates of NAR with IPP scales

IPP Scale	United States (n = 95)	West Germany '84 (n = 122)	West Germany '85 (n = 63)
	r	r	r
Religious conservatism	−.32**	.07	.02
Ethnocentrism	−.21*	−.40*	−.28*
Internationalism	.41*	.40**	.17
Trust in human nature	.23	.32**	.26*
Complexity of outlook	.50**	.51*	.45**
Independence of judgment	.48**	.47**	.50**
Originality	.41*	.43**	.49**

*$p < .01$, two-tailed

**$p < .001$, two-tailed

.05 level of confidence are given below as characteristic of *High* on NAR; significant negative correlations are given as *Lows*. The data were analyzed separately for males and females.

The Q-sort correlates descriptive of high scoring males on NAR are, in order of decreasing magnitude: has *fluctuating moods* (.48); *initiates humor* (.41); tends to be *rebellious and nonconforming* (.40); is *facially and/or gesturally expressive* (.39); is *self-dramatizing; histrionic* (.30); *responds to humor* (.29); *thinks and associates to ideas in unusual ways; has unconventional thought processes* (.27).

Low scoring males, by contrast, are described as follows: favors *conservative* values in a variety of areas (.50); *does not vary roles; relates to everyone in the same way* (.37); is *emotionally bland* (.37); is *moralistic* (.32); *judges self and others in conventional terms* like "popularity," "the correct thing to do," and "social pressure" (.34); *tends toward overcontrol of needs and impulses; binds tensions excessively; delays gratification unnecessarily* (.34); is a *genuinely dependable and responsible person* (.28); has *high aspiration level* for self (.30; has a *clear-cut, internally consistent personality* (.28).

Low-scoring females were similar to low-scoring males: favoring *conservative* values (.51); *conventional* (.35); tending towards *overcontrol* (.32); *high aspiration level* (.30); *emotionally bland* (.30); *unvarying in role* (.29). In addition, however, they were distinguished for their *fastidiousness, pride in feeling objective and rational; keeping people at a distance*, and *handling anxiety and conflicts by refusing to recognize their presence; repressive or dissociative tendencies*.

High-scoring females, by contrast, were *expressive* (.33); *rebellious and nonconforming* (.31); *initiative of humor* (.29); *unconventional* (.28); *changeable* (.27); *tending to express their needs directly* (.28). In addition, they were described significantly more often as *sensuous, playful*, and *verbally expressive*.

The ACL descriptions (significant at the .01 level) gave much the same picture. High-scoring males were described most often as *progressive, rebellious, talkative, temperamental, self-centered,* and *uninhibited*; and significantly but somewhat less frequently as *original* and *high-strung.* Low-scoring males were described most consistently as *prudish, self-controlled, stable, steady, poised, conscientious, conservative* and *discreet.*

Low-scoring females were described similarity (at the .01 level of confidence) to low-scoring males: *prudish* (.66), *conservative* (.60), *narrow interests* (.48), *formal, discreet* (.42), *self-controlled* (.41), *cold* (.40). By contrast, high-scoring females were described as: having *wide interests* (.47), *informal* (.38), *courageous* (.35), *forgiving* (.35).

If one considers the total sample, both females and males, and accepts as very likely descriptors only those at the .01 level of confidence, high scorers on NAR emerge as *progressive, unconventional, rebellious and nonconforming, and moody.* Low scorers were *self-controlled, conservative, conventional, moralistic, prudish, inhibited, of narrow interests* and *having a high aspiration level for themselves.*

Oddly enough, all the correlations between the NAR and interest clusters on the Campbell revision of the Strong Vocational Interest Blank (Strong, 1943) were negative. The significant negative correlations were: Military Activities ($p < .001$); Conventional Investigative, Science, Mathematics, and Office ($p < .01$); and Athletics and Mechanical Activities ($p < .05$). The image of a practical, conventional, physically fit bureaucrat in a military setting that emphasizes mathematical and scientific thinking is hard to resist, and one should not be surprised that such a person would be opposed to nuclear arms reduction.

Finally, the NAR scale was correlated positively with *intuiting* (as opposed to *sensing* perception) and *feeling* (as opposed to thinking judgment) on the MBTI (both $p < .01$). Findings from the CPI show *empathy, tolerance,* and *flexibility* to be positively related to NAR ($p < .01$), with a new CPI scale, *v.2* (norm-favoring vs. norm-doubting) significantly negatively related to NAR. The picture is consistent with results from the interests inventory.

DISCUSSION

The basic generalization from all the above is this: The attitude in favor of strong efforts to reduce nuclear arms is embedded in a set of related social values organized around internationalism, trust in human nature, freedom from ethnocentrism, originality as a value, independence of judgment, and finally, perhaps central to all the above, a preference for complex rather than overly simple resolution of problems requiring integration of sometimes discordant elements.

Because this latter dimension has received much attention in the literature of personality and social psychology, from Barron's (1953b) original research on complexity-simplicity as a personality dimension to Suedfeld and Tetlock's (1977) recent work on integrative complexity, we shall begin our discussion by looking anew at the variable of complexity.

Complexity as a Dimension of Personality and Perceptual Organization

Complexity as a psychological variable has been distinguished for purposes of research in three aspects: complexity as a property of a stimulus field (particularly in visual displays); complexity as a personal characteristic of the human perceiver and actor; and complexity as an attribute of cognitive systems in primarily intellectual behaviors and behavioral products (such as integrative complexity in utterances and in the transformation of systems).

Attention was focused on the first of these aspects of complexity by Birkhoff (1933), Eysenck (1942), and Barron (1952). Refinements of the concept of stimulus complexity have been suggested by Berlyne and Borda (1968) and by Berlyne, Ogilvie, and Parham (1973). The idea of complexity as a personality dimension was put forward and supported by assessment-type research by Barron (1953b), and later was challenged by Welsh (1981), who sought to distinguish in personal complexity an active affective-cognitive components he termed *origence* and a more conventionally cognitive component he called *intellectence.* Early research on cognitive complexity was introduced into Guilford's (1968) structure of intellect model, with its concept of transformation of systems as one important intellectual operation. More recently, integrative complexity as a characteristic of behavioral products, particularly utterances and policy statements in negotiations, was identified by Tetlock (1983a) as a predictor of the course of events in foreign policy, particularly as between the U.S. and the former U.S.S.R.

The earlier work on complexity versus simplicity, linked respectively as well to asymmetry and symmetry, emphasized three things:

1. The preference itself is a perceptual *decision*, a *choice* of what to attend to or not attend to in the complex of phenomena that makes up the world we experience.

2. Either of these alternative perceptual decisions may be associated with a high degree of personal effectiveness—though also each may have an ineffective aspect.

3a. The personally effective decision in favor of a simple-symmetrical order makes for personal stability and balance, a sort of easygoing optimism combined with religious faith, a friendliness toward tradition, custom, and ceremony, a rational, healthy conservatism, and respect for authority.

3b. The decision in favor of a complex asymmetry makes for originality and creativeness and is associated with independence of judgment, personal expressiveness, and a constant effort to achieve a higher-order synthesis—something indeed like what has come to be called integrative complexity.

This article commends to your attention the possibility that just such choices lie behind opposed philosophies regarding nuclear arms in today's world. Could it be that denial and repression of the possible consequences of the use of nuclear weapons as instruments of international influence is the mechanism behind an eventually maladaptive simplicity? How does complexity of outlook relate to one's personal stance vis-à-vis issues of value in the nuclear age? If complexity does in fact embrace both originality and intellect, are we being as original and intelligent as we might be in trying to find solutions to the problems of nuclear arms control? Further, who exactly is the "we" in this question? Who is doing the thinking that controls national policy on nuclear arms in the U.S. and the former U.S.S.R.? What are their philosophies? How intelligent and original are they? How does one's personal philosophy affect one's assumptions regarding "the enemy"? How is intelligence affected by personal philosophy on specific issues? How is creativity affected? How do such factors as political loyalties, religious affiliations, ethnic roots, and socioeconomic class identification influence the range of possibilities one may consider if one thinks of changing the situation?

Is a reinterpretation of the earlier antitheses appropriate in view of these results? Consider, for example, the opposed factors in the *Barron-Welsh Art Scale* (Welsh & Barron, 1963). It has been suggested by some of the new work on geometrical forms known as fractals, an outgrowth of "chaos" theory, that "fractals find sense in chaos." Fractals stand between simple order and complex disorder; they are beautifully ordered within apparent disorder. Thomas Kuhn (1983) in his article "The Essential Tension" pointed out that the productive scientist must be at once a traditionalist and innovator. Now recall the positively toned adjectives associated with low scores on the Nuclear Arms Reduction scale: stable, poised, conscientious, conservative, and discreet. Can we do without such negotiators? And recall the negatively toned adjectives associated with high scores: rebellious, temperamental, self-centered, uninhibited. Is one "healthier" than the other? Might not a synthesis of the opposites be preferable, especially in leaders? Creative conservatives? Why not? Conscientious rebels and revolutionaries? Surely the best are just that. Might there not even be a place for stable and poised self-centeredness?

We think it would be a mistake to choose either alternative to the exclusion of the other. And because negotiations are necessarily collaborative, could not teams of diplomats be constituted to be inclusive, by both sides? C. G. Jung's Ultima Thule may be the answer: the conjunction of opposites.

REFERENCES

Adorno, T., Frenkel-Brunswick, E., Levinson, D., & Sangord, R. N. (1956). *The authoritarian personality*. New York: Harper and Row.

Barron, F. (1952). Personality style and perceptual choice. *Journal of Personality, 20*, 385–401.

Barron, F. (1953a). Some personality correlates of independence of judgment. *Journal of Personality, 21*, 287–297.

Barron, F. (1953b). Complexity simplicity as a personality dimension. *Journal of Abnormal Social Psychology, 48*, 163–172.

Barron, F. (1963a). Discovering the creative personality. In *College admissions 10: The behavioral sciences and education* (pp. 79–85). New York: College Entrance Examination Board.

Barron, F. (1968). *Inventory of personal philosophy*. Berkeley, CA: University of California Press. (Original work published 1952).

Barron, F. (1983). *Inventory of personal philosophy* (rev. ed.). Santa Cruz, CA: Laboratory for the Psychological Study of Lives, University of California.

Barron, F., & Young, H. B. (1970). Personal values and political affiliation in Italy. *Journal of Cross-Cultural Psychology, 1*, 335–367.

Berlyne, D. E., & Borda, D. M. (1968). Uncertainty and the orientation reaction. *Perception and Psychophysics, 1*, 335–367.

Berlyne, D. E., Ogilvie, J. C., & Parham, L. C. C. (1973). The dimensionality of visual complexity, interestingness, and pleasingness. *Canadian Journal of Psychology, 14*, 177–184.

Birkhoff, G. D. (1933). *Aesthetic measure*. Cambridge, MA: Harvard University Press.

Block, J. (1961). *The Q-Sort method in personality assessment and psychiatric research*. Palo Alto, CA: Consulting Psychologists Press (Originally published by Charles C. Thomas, Springfield, IL).

Bradley, P. (1984). *Dimensions of personality and attitudes toward the nuclear situation: A study of West German values*. Masters Abstracts. (University Microfilms No. E9791/1984/361).

Christiansen, B. (1959). *Attitudes toward foreign affairs as a function for personality*. Oslo: Oslo University Press.

Constantini, E., & Craik, K. H. (1980). Personality and politicians: California party leaders, 1960–1976. *Journal of Personality and Social Psychology, 38*, 641–661.

Eckhardt, W., & Lentz, T. (1967). Factors of war/peace attitudes. *Peace Research Reviews, 1*, 1–22.

Etheredge, L. S. (1978). *A world of men*. Cambridge, MA: MIT Press.

Eysenck, H. J. (1942). The experimental study of the "good Gestalt"—A new approach. *Psychological Review, 49*, 344–364.

Feather, N. T. (1984). Protestant ethic, conservatism, and values. *Journal of Personality and Social Psychology, 46,* 344–364.

Gough, H. G. (1957). *Manual for the California Psychological Inventory.* Palo Alto, CA: Consulting Psychologists Press.

Gough, H. G. (1987). *The California Psychological Inventory administrator's guide.* Palo Alto, CA: Consulting Psychologists Press.

Gough, H. G., Heilbrun, A. B., Jr. (1983). *The Adjective Check List manual.* Palo Alto, CA: Consulting Psychologists Press.

Janis, I. L. & Mann, L. (1977). *Decision making.* New York: Free Press.

Jervis, R. (1976). *Perception and misperception in international politics.* Princeton, NJ: Princeton University Press.

Kuhn, T. (1983). The essential tension. In F. Barron, & C. W. Taylor (Eds.), *Scientific creativity* (pp. 341–354). New York: Wiley.

Myers, I. B., & McCaulley, M. H. (1985). *Manual: A guide to the development and use of the Myers-Briggs Type Indicator.* Palo Alto, CA: Consulting Psychologists Press.

Strong, E. K., Jr. (1943). *The vocational interests of men and women.* Stanford, CA: Stanford University Press.

Suedfeld, P. & Tetlock, P. E. (1977). Integrative complexity of communication in international crises. *Journal of Conflict Resolution, 21,* 168–178.

Tetlock, P. E. (1983a). Policy-makers' images of international conflict. *Journal of Social Issues, 37,* 66–86.

Tetlock, P. E. (1983b). Integrative complexity of American and Soviet foreign policy rhetoric: A time series analysis. *Journal of Personality and Social Psychology, 49,* 1565–1585.

Welsh, G. S. (1981). Personality assessment with origince/intellectence scales. *Academic Psychology Bulletin, 3,* 401–409.

Welsh, G., & Barron, F. (1963). *Barron-Welsh Art Scale.* Palo Alto, CA: Consulting Psychologists Press.

Chapter 31

Creative Altruism, Cooperation, and World Peace*

Howard E. Gruber

In Geneva, a friend and I watched the Soviet film "Repentance" on television. It was made quite a few years ago but was then suppressed; it had been released in the climate of *glasnost*. The film is a surrealistic depiction of oppression under Stalinism. The central figure is a local Soviet-Georgian version of Stalin. There is great wanton destruction and, most significantly, the destruction of a great cathedral. At the end of the film, an old woman returns to the city and asks the way to the temple—the cathedral. Someone answers her, "There is no road to the temple." The woman replies, "Of what use is a road if it does not lead to the temple?"

In a larger sense, the struggle for peace is part of the wider struggle for the defense of our planet. I take it as a given that the concept of a greater self includes intense concern for issues that go beyond personal existence, issues that affect every living creature on our planet. The focus

*Adapted from a presentation at "The Greater Self: New Frontiers in Exceptional Abilities Research," a conference sponsored by the Institute of Noetic Sciences, Washington, DC, November, 1987.

of concern changes from year to year, from one global threat to another: nuclear winter, ozone layer, oil in the oceans, endangered species, Three Mile Island and Chernobyl, desertification, and so on. In the long run these will not turn out to be separable issues. They will have a cumulative effect of making the home planet less and less inhabitable. The plain fact is that our increasing ability to change our environment is also our ability to destroy it. Nuclear war, by far the most serious threat, even today, must be seen in its historical context of expanding technologies and frozen visions.

IS PEACE POSSIBLE?

Psychology and the other human sciences may have a special role to play in the search for an enduring peace. Their unique roles are to increase our understanding of the mental aspects of the arms race and the threat of war, and to improve our knowledge of positive human resources available in working for peace (Murphy, 1945).

It cannot be denied that the possibility of war depends on relatively durable aspects of human motivations, belief systems, and propensities for action. At the same time, the possibility of peace also depends on available human resources. The aim of this chapter is to examine some of these positive factors, particularly altruism, creative altruism, and cooperation.

Studies of animal behavior show that supposedly rigid instinctual patterns of aggression between members of different species are often quite variable and dependent on the animal's developmental histories. In his classic laboratory studies, Kuo (1930) showed that kittens reared with rodents did not kill them. However, other kittens reared in isolation who then saw their mothers kill a rodent eventually did so too. To simplify a complex series of experiments, the main factor is the development of rat-killing behavior was the kitten's opportunity to see its mother kill repeatedly. For the kittens who had been reared with a rodent, however, the potent stimulus was not effective. Similarly, in the Moscow Zoo, I have seen a cage inhabited by a lion and a lamb, living peaceably together.

When we turn to combat between members of the same species, it is by now an old story that for the most part it does not lead to killing. Such combat—the nearest analogue to war in infra-human species—is in general quite limited, ritualistic, and nonfatal. As Roger Johnson (1972) put it, "Nearly all animals are content to dominate or to banish conspecific rivals; only man, it seems, has a desire to injure his opponents and gain vengeance on them."

War-making, then, is not due to a rigid, unchanging instinct of aggression handed down to use from our evolutionary past. It is primarily the result of social and historical forces that produce a great variety of behaviors in different societies and in different epochs (Brown, 1987). Indeed, among Western nations, countries like Sweden and Switzerland make weapons but do not any longer wage war. Their war-related activities involve engineering skills and business acumen, not aggression. War is one of the most complex of all human activities, and to reduce it to an instinct of aggression is fatuous.

Anthropologists can tell us of so-called "primitive" societies, such as the Arapesh, in which there is nothing like an institution of war, and within which cooperation and sharing, rather than aggression and competition, are the norms. To be sure, warlike societies and norms of aggressiveness and competition can also be found. The point, however, is not that war is or has been a rare phenomenon, but that peace is possible.

Recognition of this key point—that peace is possible—simple though it seems, may turn out to be one of the chief contributions of the human sciences to human survival. When I was a student, before and during World War II, considerable energy was expended on arguing abut whether "human nature" makes war inevitable. On the whole, psychologists have argued against this idea. William James, a long-time pacifist, in his celebrated essay "The Moral Equivalent of War," written just before World War I, accepted the notion that there are certain admirable virtues characteristically associated with military life—for instance, sense of adventure, courage, comradeship in adversity, self-sacrifice, and altruism. James (1910) concluded that ways should be found to permit the expression of these traits in forms other than war. It should be added that the aspect of war has changed since James wrote, and the martial virtues he listed may no longer be possible to experience in war in quite the same way.

Later on, Otto Klineberg, among others, produced searching criticisms of the concept of an instinct of aggression, and pointed out the error of confusing the idea of individual aggression with the institutionalized aspects of military life and war. In our own times, as war becomes increasingly the creation of high technology, it comes to resemble an intellectual game rather than the muscular aggressiveness imputed to our cave-dwelling ancestors.

CREATIVE ALTRUISM

Ironically, the current fashion of sociobiology is to insist on the instinctual nature of altruism, a development which might be thought to simplify my task of examining the relationships among altruism, cooperation, and world peace. But jut as there are many forms of aggression, there are many forms of altruism. The kind I want to emphasize is very far from instinctual behavior. The concept of instinct relies upon and harks back to our evolutionary past. The concepts of creativity and creative altruism look forward to our future. They draw upon the exceptional intelligence and unique visionary capacities to be found only in the human animal.

There are some valid forms of altruism that serve to maintain the status quo and other valid forms that are designed to change it. The second kind is the main subject of this chapter. I will thus examine the distinction between conservative and creative altruism, and explore some of the relationships among cooperation, creative altruism, and creative work in general.

Most discussions of giftedness and high achievement neglect the topics of altruism, prosocial behavior, and extraordinary moral responsibility. They do so with good reason, for the definitional problems alone are formidable. Nevertheless, I contend that our understanding of creative work and extraordinary ability will remain fundamentally flawed and incomplete without careful attention to these matters.

The common sense use of the term "altruism" implies some unsolved problem in the disposition of human resources; it also implies that there may be something that ought to be done, which if done will eliminate the discrepancy between the actual and desired state of affairs.

The self-chosen task of the creative altruist, to work to bring such a change about, necessarily involves an exchange with others. In this exchange, there is a donor with available assets and a recipient with an unmet need. No matter how such exchanges begin, in the ideal case the long range outcome will be to reduce or eliminate the discrepancy. Moreover, appropriate planning and action will require cooperation among all the participants that is, both the donors and the recipients. Only through such cooperation can the desired change be brought about; indeed, such cooperation is not only part of the solution process but often part of the goal.

In a number of respects, creative altruism resembles other forms of creative work. Both require awareness of the possibility of something new, followed by the patient evolution of the understanding of the problem. Both require the translation of the inner life of desire and fantasy into forms of action in and upon the world. Both require prolonged, intentional search for adequate and harmonious solutions. Both require sensitivity to the impact of the innovation on some prospective audience or recipients. Especially in creative altruism, this takes the form of empathic awareness of the needs and feelings of the other.

In most research and discussions about altruism, the focus is on one individual helping another individual. There have been many ingenious, naturalistic experiments studying the way individuals choose between the role of bystander and Good Samaritan (and, of course, in the experiments as well as in history there are all too many passive bystanders). But in these experimental studies there is rarely an opportunity for dialogue or leadership to develop, although these are known to be important in other types of situations.

In my thinking about these matters, I have tried to focus attention in a somewhat different direction (Gruber, 1985). How does altruism work when there is massive danger and the victims are numerous, or potentially everyone? Individual survival requires species survival, and the integrity of one family's home requires the integrity of the home planet. In a sense, the difference between self-interest and human interest disappears when the perceived danger is very great. It might even be argued that if I have a vivid enough imagination I cannot be altruistic—whatever I do for others is really for myself!

But I believe that this line of reasoning violates the intent behind the ordinary language use of the term. Would we consider a person to be purely altruistic if he or she felt miserable when helping others? No, our thinking would take another tack. We should include the deep personal satisfaction that comes from being altruistic in our conception of the process. The highest forms of altruism will be just those that evoke the greatest joy. Which is not to say that there may not be some genuine sacrifices entailed, and some rue. As Shelley wrote in *To a Skylark*, "Our sincerest laughter with some pain is fraught."

OBSTACLES TO UNDERSTANDING CREATIVE ALTRUISM

Probably the major obstacle to understanding and undertaking creative altruism is that its ultimate aim is to make itself unnecessary; it is planned obsolescence on a grand scale. Since the goal is to eliminate the discrepancy between the actual and the desirable, altruists must work toward rendering themselves superfluous.

A second difficulty is that the actual conduct required inevitably demands the emergence of new forms of cooperation and reciprocity, and involves working together with victims and potential enemies. It requires taking the point of view of others in a way that goes beyond anything we are now taught to do. In other words, creative altruism requires simultaneous restraint of our needs for ego-aggrandizement and exercise of our visionary capacities—a rare and difficult combination.

A third difficulty reflects the enormous disparity that exists between the investment of resources in value-oriented research and investments in competence-oriented research. Almost the whole of modern scientific effort is aimed at increasing our power to change nature, while pitifully little is expended on improving our ability to decide which changes are worth making and which court disaster. All of life, including our species, evolved slowly. The series of changes that have made us what we are and fitted us for life on Earth include the way we have slowly appropriated and reconstructed our environment. The slowness of biological and early technological evolution permitted the mutual adjustments between us and our world that made us comfortable, at home. But with the advent of modern science and technology, environmental change goes forward at a pace that outstrips our ability to monitor it, or to nurture our own world with love and caring, and with a care for the future. While a few psychologists, notably Paul Baltes in Berlin, have recently discovered the possibility of studying "wisdom" as an aspect of human growth, we have yet to see a spate of research connecting the idea of wisdom with the fate of the Earth.

To take only one example—a relatively simple problem—the development of the consciousness and commitment necessary to save the disappearing ozone layer goes forward at an agonizingly slow pace. The discharge of destructive chemicals into our atmosphere is still increasing. To deal with this and a host of similar problems will require a new turn in world-consciousness, new ways of monitoring technological innovation, new social inventions, and new forms of creative altruism.

Within the human sciences, there is now considerable investment in research and development of "expert systems," whose aim is doing more faster. Relatively little time, energy, money or encouragement is given to the study of other aspects of the "greater self"—creativity, giftedness, wisdom, altruism, and moral responsibility.

A fourth difficulty is that, even within the sector of the human sciences relevant to the problems I am raising, there is an unfortunate fragmentation of effort. The study of creativity has, for the most part, been isolated from the study of giftedness; the study of creativity and giftedness has been, for the most part, isolated from the study of altruism and prosocial behavior. Even recent books on giftedness sidestep the issue of altruism and moral giftedness. Bloom (1985), in a comprehensive work on giftedness, noted that he wanted to study giftedness in the moral domain, but that he abandoned this aim because it was too difficult to define the concept. The subject was dropped, and other roads were taken. But I ask, what good is a road if it does not lead to the temple?

Ann Colby and William Damon (1987) have made an excellent start in studying very high levels of moral thinking and moral conduct. In particular, their work on solving the knotty problems of definition is exemplary. But they have explicitly excluded from consideration the criterion of creativity and innovation as part of the definition of high-level moral conduct. In the context of their research, this makes perfectly good sense, since the effective moral actor may conceivably borrow all of his or her ideas from someone else. But for the present purposes we cannot sidestep the issue of creativity.

Although I have been aware of these issues for sometime, my own work exhibits some of the same imbalance and fragmentation that I have been discussing. For example, my collaborator Doris Wallace and I edited a book, *Creative People at Work* (1989). The book has, as a coda, a final chapter on creativity and human survival. But in the case studies by the various contributing authors the issue of creative altruism and related matters is hardly even touched upon. Thus we have not yet found the way of integrating this topic into our research on creativity. We are devoted to the case study method both as a way of understanding creative people at work and as a way of getting a better grasp of what we might mean by a whole human being. As we go forward in our work we, too, must strive for new levels of integration.

PRINCIPLED ALTRUISM

What interests us here is not the altruism of everyday life, although there is such a thing and without it life would be poorer. Every time someone stoops to pick up a fallen object for another, he risks throwing his back to of joint, so some risk is involved. But that kind of everyday exchange is not what we have in mind. Here we are talking about how to be of some use in relation to difficult, deep, and seemingly intractable human problems. Let me propose three guiding principles:

1. *Morality and creativity.* When we say that something *ought* to be the case, we must mean that it *could* be so. To insist on the oughtness of an impossibility would not make sense. But what is possible? How do we know what we can do? We don't know unless we extend ourselves to our maximum capacity, in the most creative ways possible. So ought implies *can*, and in the search for the possible *can* implies creative work. Therefore, to fulfill our highest moral obligations we really have to search for pathways to creative altruism.

2. *Altruism and inequality.* When we speak of altruism we are speaking of inequality, of some disequilibrium in the distribution of human resources. Some people have something that others don't, and the ones who don't have it need it. It might be encouragement or security, it might be money or other resources.

From this inequality or disequilibrium the altruist has two somewhat different choices. One path is to eliminate or alleviate the immediate problem—the inequality—and then return to the status quo. The other path, creative altruism, is to try to eliminate the source of the problem. But destroying the roots of inequality effectively destroys the very situation that makes altruism possible. *Thus, creative altruism requires its own self-destruction.*

3. *Altruism and cooperation.* Creative altruism is not something you can do alone. You cannot simply do something *for* people, you must do it *with* them. That means you need them; that means you have to understand their point of view and their needs as they experience them. You have to have the humility to see what is good for them, not what you would like if you were in a similar situation. In the long run the goal is to replace your help with self-help by the people in question. They have to be engaged in the actual work that needs doing—the redistribution of human resources. *Thus, creative altruism requires cooperation.*

CREATIVE WORK

Most contemporary theories of creativity and giftedness treat the subject in an overly individualistic way. They do not provide for the movement between individual and social modes of functioning that characterizes real creative work. Our picture of creative work is quite different. We have discovered that, in various forms, some obvious and some not, collaboration, cooperation, and other intense social interactions are an inherent part of most, if not all, creative work.

We call our approach to creativity the *evolving systems approach.* It grew out of intensive case studies of a number of highly creative people. I will sum it up briefly, emphasizing four points: Uniqueness, purposefulness, collaboration, and the case study method.

Uniqueness. We are not discussing the creativity of everyday life (although that is an interesting and important subject). We are talking about unique individuals doing difficult things which others might think impossible. Usually these take a long time. We are interested in the long, purposeful, directed activity in which the creative process unfolds.

Purposeful work. We have found that the creative person develops a complex network of enterprises and purposes. They very difficulty of the tasks chosen mean that he or she is at the frontiers for a long time. At those frontiers, not only the limited problem that may have been the starting point is in question—everything is in question. So the creative person is always wrestling with several fundamental issues represented in this complex network of purposes.

Collaboration. Even in its most individual aspects, the creative process is an intensely social process. Collaboration is important in all creative work. The dreamer alone in bed, or sitting in front of the hearth and falling asleep, is thinking in a language that can eventually be shared with others. A full study of the social aspects of creativity would require us to consider not only collaboration but also the system of education and apprenticeship, the system of communication among creative people, the system of transmission and display of creative products, and the system of reward.

Case study method. In our work we emphasize the case study method, for three distinct reasons. First, the highest levels of creativity are simply not available for study under controlled laboratory conditions. The processes we are interested in take months and years, the time-scale of a creative life. Second, creative work involves the coalescence of a complex array of processes. To describe it well requires going beyond the necessary simplifications of experimental reports. The powerful tools of laboratory analysis are appropriate for casting an intense, narrow beam on a small number of variables, not for capturing the person at work. Third, we are interested in the whole person.

Nevertheless, there are certainly some aspects of the creative process that can be studied in the laboratory. We are finding that combining laboratory research with the case study method gives us the incontestable advantages of the narrow experimental beam without losing sight of the wider goal of understanding the unique creative person at work.

These points are illustrated below with a discussion of individuals exhibiting creative altruism under extreme conditions, and with a description of some of our experimental work on the cooperative synthesis of different points of view. Among the points that will emerge are these: First, the creative altruistic does not necessarily conform to stereotypes such as the self-abnegating saint. Second, creative altruism invariable requires collaboration. Third, cooperative work requires a balanced movement between individual and group effort.

The relations among these ideas may be summed up in a syllogism:

1. Creative altruism requires collaborative effort.
2. Collaborative effort requires movement between individual and social conduct.
3. Therefore, creative altruism requires the same kind of movement.

Thus, creative altruism expresses the highest development of the individual and at the same time depends on cooperation and mutual understanding.

CONFORMITY VERSUS COLLABORATION

The idea of creative altruism runs counter to the idea of conformity. Everyday altruism sometimes includes an element of conformity, but creative altruism works against it. Moreover, creative altruism is necessarily a rare event. Fundamental transformations in human relations cannot be an everyday matter.

Without conformity to social norms, war would be impossible. Much psychological research on conformity uses situations in which different people looking at the same scene from the same point of view see it differently. In such circumstances, there are only three alternatives—disagreement, compromise, or yielding by one party.

But there is another class of situations in which two observers are looking at the same scene from different points of view. In such cases, difference does not imply disagreement. The possibility arises of synthesizing the two perspectives in a new configuration not available to either participant alone. My colleagues and I use such situations in our experimental studies of cooperative synthesis of points of view.

In research on development of perspective taking, emphasis has been placed on the *individual's* ability to take the point of view of the other. Exchange between observers in different locations is usually absent. This model recalls the situation in the arms race where each power wants to understand the other just well enough to predict what the other will do, in order to take countermeasures. The ensuing conduct falls far short of the continuous and intimate exchanges necessary for synthesis of different perspectives into a new and shared vision of the real and the possible.

Our research goes beyond this basically individualistic model to a more fully interactive approach. Our subjects recognize that they see the world differently form their different perspectives and that their task is to work together to discover that reality—or, better, to construct the range of possible realities. In this work of synthesis the issue of compromise and yielding hardly arises. The task is difficult but both adolescents and adults can do it, although at different levels of sophistication.

There is a paradox in psychologists' present understanding of perspective taking. Many studies show that even young children can take the point of view of another. On the other hand, it is widely believed (and I believe) that, in the crucial situations that confront humanity, adults often do not do so. Is this a fatal gap between competence and performance? Perhaps the dilemma can only be resolved by going beyond the information "I" am given: Taking the point of view of the other is entailed in the superordinate task of constructing a livable and *shared* reality.

COOPERATIVE SYNTHESIS OF DIFFERENT POINTS OF VIEW

As noted above, if two people looking at the same thing see it differently, they don't always have to argue or decide who is right. They may realize that they are looking through different lenses, or, as in our experiments, from different angles. In such cases, the difference can lead to a creative result. By pooling their knowledge and helping each other the two observers can see the world more truly—more deeply and objectively—than if each remains locked into his or her own perspective.

This kind of creative sharing depends on give and take. Each must tell what he knows and each must listen to the other. It sounds simple but it's not always so easy. We devised the "shadow box" experiments in order to study this process of cooperative synthesis of different points of view under controlled laboratory conditions.

One of the ideas underlying this work is the notion that having a unique point of view is part of what makes each person special; no two individuals stand in exactly the same relation to the world. Yet the person doesn't come to the experimental situation with this specialness all set and unyielding. Being in a special situation, seeing things from a different place than one's partner's standpoint, opens the way to the individual's making a unique contribution to the partnership. That is the idea we tried to embody in our research with the shadow box.

The latter is literally a box, with an unknown object inside it. The object is lit from behind in such a fashion that it casts two different shadows on tow different screens, each of which may be seen by a different person. In the basic experimental situation, there are two people involved, each getting his or her own special view of this mircroworld. We ask them to talk to each other and try to figure out what is inside the box. In one problem, a triangular shadow is case on one screen, a square on the other. With some discussion, a team can arrive at the conclusion that the object inside the box might be a pyramid with a square base. We have used many variations on this basic experimental situation. For example, we compare two people working together with one person shuttling back and forth between the two observation points. Both situations are pertinent to understanding the process of synthesis.

Some of our results are as follows: First, considerable time may be needed, even by skilled adults, to solve what looks like a very simple problem. The partners have to develop a way of communicating with each other that is appropriate to this novel situation. They also have to develop trust, because a first reaction by many is what we have called the "you must be crazy" phenomenon: "How can you see a square? I see a triangle." Once they have communicated adequately on this first level, and can accept each other's point of view, they must engage in a more searching exchange. This is the collaborative problem-solving process that leads to a solution. If you were to watch some pairs of subjects for only 10 or 15 minutes, struggling to come to terms with each other about a relatively simple problem, some of your worst fears about humanity might seem justified. Fortunately, we watch them for longer than that. Often enough, the exchange becomes fruitful and the long-run results are more gratifying.

A second important result stems from the fact that a little geometrical analysis reveals that any one of these problems has more than one solution. Typically, only pairs of adults arrive at this idea of multiple solutions, although some adolescent pairs and occasionally some adult singles do so as well.

A third result deals with the relations between individual and cooperative work. In some of our experiments, we ask subjects only to tell the other person what they see on their screens, but then to work out the solution alone. We were interested in what happens when people behave in this way. But the important result is that they often don't. Many disobeyed us, even after repeated urgings to follow our instructions. The situation is one that evokes a quite spontaneous sharing of perspectives—cooperative work directed toward a goal. Now, it is clear that people don't always cooperate whenever they might, but it is pleasant to know that there may be some situations in which the cooperative synthesis of different perspectives is a natural and obvious thing to do—and, more, one that is difficult to avoid.

It should be added that, on the whole, we see the best performances in pairs that oscillate between working together and working alone. Incessant communication is not the most effective strategy. Each person needs some time to work things out for him- or herself. A related point is the comparison of the single subject with the pairs. There is not a striking difference in the number of problems solved. The important effect of working in a pair is the increased frequency of realizing the possibility of multiple solutions.

Almost 50 years ago, the Swiss psychologist Jean Piaget (Piaget & Inhelder, 1966) emphasized the importance of being able to take the point of view of the other: Given what I see in front of me, how does the same scene look to you, standing in another place? The shadow box work takes the next step. Once we get past the differences in our initial perspectives, we can translate them into opportunities to transcend our individual limitations. By overcoming our need to identify with a special position, we can put our knowledge together with that of another—not always an easy task—and arrive at a deeper, more penetrating and also more accurate grasp of reality than any one of us could achieve alone.

CASES OF CREATIVE ALTRUISM

The disaster of war do provide occasions to which some people rise. The Nazi persecution of Jews and other produced situations that people here and there confronted with courage, ingenuity, and compassion (Fogelman & Wiener, 1985). The percentage resisting the Nazis was all too few, but there were many who did so and their stories are instructive.

Oskar Schindler. Oskar Schindler was a self-serving German industrialist who, in Krakow, Poland, early in World War II, became a great creative altruist. He saved more than 1,200 Jews during the Holocaust, and was awarded the title of Righteous Gentile (a special title by which the state of Israel honors those who saved the lives of Jews during the Holocaust). In the beginning, Schindler was not what we commonly take to be a good person. Although he was often kind, he almost always acted from self-interest. He also committed dishonest acts and was a member of the Nazi party. It was his creative strength that enabled him to put his shortcomings, as well as his goodness and compassion, to the service of his greater self and to rescue as many persecuted beings as he could. Of particular interest are two dramatic changes he underwent. First, he moved from being an impulsive and sometimes opportunistic helper to being a compassionate person and finally a principled altruist. Second, he moved from being a man whose concern was limited to the people he knew to being someone whose concern included many people he did not know at all.

Schindler had many assets. One of them was his gambling skill. He could sit up all night playing cards with the Nazi officials he dealt with every day, and contrive to lose exactly the amount of money that would make them feel comfortable with him. The credibility he gained and maintained with the Nazis allowed him to go about his business of saving Jews. the most striking aspect of Schindler's case is that he did not start out with the idea of using his position as an industrialist to save people's lives. It began as an impulse which then grew on him—and grew and grew. At first he helped a few people with whom he was in direct contact, then his work expanded to the point where he was helping people he had never seen before.

Schindler didn't do this by himself, of course. He needed help from many people. One of these was Isaac Stern—not the violinist, but the chief accountant in a factory Schindler bought. It was Stern who really knew how to get Jews out, and he made many of the most helpful suggestions to Schindler. So Schindler the Nazi party member and Stern the Jew collaborated in order to accomplish this great work. In the process of working together, they experienced what people in our shadow box experiments feel. They had slowly to develop trust in each other. This wasn't easy, considering the distance that separated them at the beginning, but Schindler and Stern eventually became not only collaborators and allies but lifelong friends (see Keneally, 1983; Wundheiler, 1986).

Le Chambon-sur-Lignon. In this discussion I have emphasized unique people performing extraordinary acts aimed at transforming difficult situations, and finding ways of doing so in collaboration with others. This is a necessary task, in part because so much of behavioral science is focused on the average, the ordinary, or the universal. But I do not mean to exclude from consideration under the heading of creative altruism certain very modest acts, or certain actors who seem quite lonely and isolated. I will consider two instances. The first deals with a very modest act: opening a door to a stranger; the second deals with an extreme and fatal insistence upon principle.

In 1940, a Jewish refugee from the Nazis arrived in the French village of Le Chambon-sur-Lignon. She came to the Protestant pastor's house. He was away, but without hesitation, his wife Magda Trocmé said, "Naturally, come in." From this simple act grew a large-scale and complex rescue operation, that took place right under the noses of the Germans. Thousands of refugees were saved.

In this case, it is impossible to pick a point in time, the moment at which the simple act of responding to another's need became transformed into creative altruism. To begin with, the initial act did not just happen. It grew out of an old tradition in which the people of Le Chambon hid persecuted Huguenots from their pursuers. In 1940, it was Mme. Trocmé who took the first step. Then the pastor, André Trocmé, became the driving force, extending the rescue campaign to the point where the courage and ingenuity of the whole village was called upon.

There is a paradoxical turn of events here. This story differs from what we usually consider as high level creative work, in which the creative person recognizes his or her specialness and intends to do something that will change people's ways of doing and seeing. The villagers did not see their actions as very special. Apparently, for them it became "easier to open a door than to keep it closed." But as sometimes happens, the modest act became the starting point for something much bigger.

Without wanting to paint too rosy a picture of a grim period, it should be added that there were a number of similar episodes. In Italy, a group of Franciscan monks in Assisi also carried out a protracted, large-scale rescue operation (Ramiti, 1985). And the well-documented stories of mutual aid among the afflicted Jews are legion (Friedman, 1978). Feelings of admiration and sadness vie with each other as one reads this history.

Franz Jagerstatter. Franz Jagerstatter was a simple Austrian peasant from the region in which Hitler was born. After a somewhat undisciplined youth he experienced a religious conversion of great depth. In March 1943, he refused military service in the German army, contending that the war his country was waging was unjust. He spent the next months in prison, resisting considerable pressure to conform, both from the established Church and from political authorities. He was adamant in his refusal. On August 9, 1943, he was beheaded.

Apparently, he acted in an entirely individualistic way. Since he viewed the war as unjust, his moral principles left him no room for choice. While his actions were an expression of individual morality, they were deeply social in several respects. First, it is clear that he thought the principles he was defending were the proper expression of his Catholic faith. Second, he did not work out his ideas in isolation, or act on impulse. He had a record of stubborn anti-Nazism; he was the only person in his village to vote against Anschluss, the merger of Austria with Germany in 1938. He got some of his ideas from other resisters, discussed matters openly, and did his best to help his wife and children understand his behavior. Finally, even in the process of standing firm under pressure, his ideas developed and deepened (Zahn, 1968).

Was his act in any sense altruistic? On the one hand, it must be said, as it was often said to him, that his course of action leading to certain death was depriving his family of husband and father. To that, his answer was his simple conviction that they would have a joyous reunion in the after-life, and that it was better to give up a few years on Earth than to sacrifice eternity. He was aware of and did not reject the role of moral exemplar. Although he was a modest man, he did feel that his conduct might lead others to take steps that would benefit them spiritually.

The case of Franz Jagerstatter stretches our conceptions of creativity and altruism. The main motives for his actions were not those of helping others but those of personal principle and salvation. In absolute terms, his act was not highly innovative. Others have confronted illegitimate authority in similar ways; suitable occasions have presented themselves all too often in history. On the other hand, as indicated above, he certainly did have the spiritual welfare of others in mind. And certainly Schindler or the rescuers of Le Chambon and Assisi would not think of him as a stranger.

As for creativity—every confrontation with injustice has its special character and taxes the ingenuity of the dissident in new ways. In the context of his village, Franz Jagerstatter's conduct was unprecedented and unparalleled. I believe we can speak of creative work when an obscure peasant manages to write down his thoughts and beliefs, arguing his case with vigor and logical clarity, and sometimes with considerable subtlety. Consider only one example, a passage from his prison statement, written shortly before his execution:

For what purpose, then, did God endow all men with reason and free will if, despite this, we have to render blind obedience; or if, as so many also say, the individual is not qualified to judge whether this war started by Germany is just or unjust? What purpose is served by the ability to distinguish between good and evil?

This case, like the others, raises good and difficult questions for all who are concerned with transcending the immediate cares of ordinary life.

CONCLUSION

In this chapter I have explored the links among a group of concepts—the possibility of peace, altruism, creative altruism, creativity, collaboration, and the cooperative synthesis of disparate points of view. As a thought-experiment, I have written in a declarative vein, trying to set down and link up points that seem reasonably clear.

I now see that one could begin again, in a more questioning spirit, for there is so much that we don't know. As part of my reflections for this writing, I searched my own memories for episodes in which opportunities for altruistic behavior arose. Not surprisingly, I did not always come off well in this self-examination. But the exercise did produce what seems to me some promising questions as guides for next steps in the study of creative altruism. Some of these questions have partial answers in the psychological literature on altruism, but most of them have not even been posed. They are probably not even the best questions, but I set them down as a sort of new beginning:

What is the relation between self-consciousness and altruism? Does the person being altruistic have a conception of himself as such? What are the emotions associated with altruism, and how do they develop? How does the person choose the beneficiaries of his or her acts, or are these seeming choices really the outcomes of chance encounters? How do individuals or groups become sensitized to different issues and different needs? What are the differences between altruistic behavior conducted within definite institutional frameworks and that outside such frames? How are amounts of time, money, and other resources allocated? Does creative altruism develop out of conventional altruism, or does it follow a different developmental pathway? How does the collaborative effort necessarily entailed in creative altruism develop? What conditions favor the emergence of creative altruism, and what can we do to foster those conditions?

In spite of all these questions, one thing seems clear. The recent literature on giftedness and creativity shows that "gifts" are not so much given to their owners as they are devised and constructed through the person's own efforts. The same is true of the gift of creative altruism, which probably depends above all on a sense of the self expanding—expanding in our era, toward world-consciousness. This spirit is well expressed in *The Home Planet* (Kelly, 1988), a volume reflecting the experiences of 201 human beings who have actually traveled in space. As one of them, Sultan Bin Salman Al-Saud, put it: "The first day or so we all pointed to our countries. the third or fourth day we were pointing to our continents. By the fifth day we were aware only of one Earth."

REFERENCES

Bloom, B. S., ed. (1985). *Developing Talent in Young Children.* New York: Ballantine Books.

Brown, R. (1987), *Social Psychology.* New York: The Free Press.

Colby, A. & Damon, W., (1987), The Personification of Moral Values through the Designation of Moral Exemplars. Symposium presentation, Meeting of the Society for Research in Child Development.

Colby, A. & Damon, W. (1992). *Some Do Care: Contemporary Lives of Moral Commitment.* New York: Free Press.

Feldman, D. H. (1986), *Nature's Gambit: The Mystery and Meaning of the Child Prodigy.* New York: Basic Books.

Fogelman, E. & Wiener, V. L. (1985), The Few, the Brave, the Noble, *Psychology Today,* 61–65.

Friedman, P. (1978), *Their Brothers' Keepers.* New York: Holocaust Library.

Gruber, H. E. (1985), Giftedness and Moral Responsibility: Creative Thinking and Human Survival, *The Gifted and Talented: Developmental Perspectives,* Washington, D.C.: American Psychological Association.

Gruber, H. E. (1993). Creativity in the moral domain. In H. E. Gruber & D. E. Wallace, *Creativity Research Journal,* 6, 3–16 [Special issue on "Creativity in the Moral Domain"]

Holton, G. (1986), *The Advancement of Science and Its Burdens.* Cambridge: Cambridge University Press.

James, W. (1910), The Moral Equivalent of War, *The Writings of William James.* Chicago: University of Chicago Press.

Johnson, R. (1972), *Aggression in Man and Animals.* Philadelphia: Saunders.

Kelly, K. W. (1988), *The Home Planet.* Reading, Mass.: Addison-Wesley.

Keneally, T. (1983), *Schindler's List.* New York: Penguin Books.

Kuo, Z. Y. (1930), The Genesis of the Cat's Response toward the Rat, *Journal of Comparative Psychology,* Vol. 11, 1–35.

Murphy, G., ed. (1945), *Human Nature and Enduring Peace: Third Yearbook of the Society for the Psychological Study of Social Issues.* Boston: Houghton Mifflin.

Oliner, S. P. & Oliner, P. M. (1988). *The Altruistic Personality: Rescuers of Jews in Nazi Europe.* New York: Free Press.

Piaget, J. & Inhelder, B. (1966), *The Psychology of the Child.* New York: Basic Books.

Ramiti, A. (1985), *The Assisi Underground.* London Paperbacks.

Wallace, D. B. & Gruber, H. E. (1989), *Creative People at Work.* New York: Oxford University Press.

Wundheiler, L. N. (1986). Oskar Schindler's Moral Development during the Holocaust, *Humboldt Journal of Social Relations,* Vol. 13, 333–356.

Zahn, G. (1968), *In Solitary Witness: The Life and Death of Franz Jagerstatter.* Boston: Beacon Press.

PART VI

EVOLUTION OF CREATIVITY, INFORMATION AND OURSELVES

Part VI

Introduction

Is evolution good? Is it healthy? Understandable questions, perhaps, and we may hope the answer is *yes*. But the answer may also depend on what we mean by healthy. And on what we mean, first of all, by "evolution." One can refer not only to the evolution of biological organisms, of their *genes* and their phenotypes but, after Richard Dawkins, of *memes*, of units of information, from the broader world of transformation and imagination that we can so marvellously generate as individuals and cultures. The concluding paper, by Richards, presents a new view of issues of evolution, health, illness, and creativity, linking three biological models to analogous psychological phenomena in which health and illness are paradoxically intertwined. The discussion begins at the individual level, with extrapolations to the societal level. In so doing it also calls on the other papers in this volume.

Creativity may be defined in terms of an evolution of information: it is the ongoing recombination and transformation of the old to generate the new. Ideas, songs, equations, buildings, or the shaping of a young mind, are all a part of it. Where genes are concerned, organisms can mate biologically and create new combinations of genetic material. But with thinking and feeling and imagining, we can more readily and expansively combine sets of ideas.

By contrast with the creativity of genes, one finds more potential power in the creativity of ideas. Across time and space, millions of years, millions of miles, planets and galaxies, and universes of imagination, one can combine any and all information one wishes. This is no longer two al-leles on a chromosome seeking each other out but once in a generation. Here are limitless memes, all available together and in an instant, joining in endless and changing combinations, and co-evolving thoughts which a moment before might never have seemed possible. They may perhaps even be evolving new modes of consciousness and perhaps higher levels of existence even than that. There may well be some *chaos* in this mix, indeed some "edge of chaos" effects, as Richards suggests; this is the ordered chaos, and the new order, of creative insight— instantaneously reshaping the given to generate entirely new paradigms and possibilities.

Yet, if this is so, is it therefore also good, and is it healthy? Arguably yes, if one refers to the enhancing of life, and the enhancing of its diversity, complexity, and sustainability—all value judgments, to be sure. But this view is not without its problems. Consider, in the broad analogy, the person with sickle cell anemia who suffers severe crises and perhaps early death; meanwhile the more numerous carriers of sickle cell trait may show at worst only a mild anemia. At best, they all carry a *compensatory advantage*: resistance to malaria. How nice, one may think. But by what authority does evolution sacrifice the comfort and wellbeing of the sickle cell sufferer for the protection of the more numerous sickle cell carriers? Is this fair, nice, good, or even vaguely reasonable for the person in the hospital bed?

Richards' chapter begins with three such biological models in which illness and health seem paradoxically intertwined: *compensatory advantage, acquired immunity*, and evolution beyond *maladaptive genotypes*. Related psychological phenomena are then considered. Using a 2x2 format the discussion pursues four examples which are focused (for purposes of illustration) on issues of mood disorders, adversity, and creativity. Two illustrations involve the generation of new information (bipolar "overinclusion" and cultural diversity) and two involve its processing or manipulation (confronting individual adversity, and confronting global adversity). In each pair, the examples are at the individual and societal levels respectively.

In conclusion, it appears that if the situation is unfair, we creators can at least make it better. The paper highlights the importance of embracing our diversity while decreasing the tendency to call the deviant "pathological." We should also enhance our potential to treat whatever illness may arise, while at the same time embracing the creativity that may be associated with it. Thus, we may learn *consciously to evolve* to enhance the possibilities for ourselves and our world amidst the critical challenges of the 21st century.

Chapter 32

Conclusions: When Illness Yields Creativity

Ruth Richards

I. Preliminary Considerations and Three Biological Models
II. Related Psychological Phenomena and Illustrations
  A. Individual Level: Overinclusive Thinking—How Healthy?
  B. Social Level: Cultural Diversity and Preservation
  C. Individual Level: Confronting Personal Adversity
  D. Social Level: Confronting Global Adversity
III. Illness and Creativity: Some Overall Issues

In our artificially dichotomized world of good and bad countries, books, movies, and so on, people sometimes separate good health from bad, cleanly and without ambiguity, and focus largely on the latter. There are literally armies of professionals designed to identify and stamp out disease—mental or physical—who strive to replace it with some concept of *normalcy*. This assumes, in turn, that the norm is inherently healthy.

Yet the balance between sickness and health may be more complex. Here, I address the popular notion that creativity is connected with mental problems, one that dates back over two millennia (Becker, 1976; Jamison, 1990). Aspects of bipolar disorders will be presented by way of example with extrapolation to some important phenomena at the societal level. In so doing, I shall have occasion to touch on, to varying degrees, the other contributions to this volume.

As Dryden wrote (in *Absalom and Achitophel*): "Great wits are sure to madness near allied; And thin partitions do their bounds divide."

Many have heard of outstanding creative persons who suffered from mood disorders. Virginia Woolf and Ernest Hemingway were both manic-depressives, for instance, as most likely was Vincent Van Gogh. In looking at the validity of such creativity–psychopathology links it is essential not to romanticize these psychiatric findings. The suffering in mood disorders can be extreme, as expressed by the novelist William Styron (1990) in *Darkness Visible*:

> The pain is unrelenting, and what makes the condition intolerable is the foreknowledge that no remedy will come—not in a day, an hour, a month, or a minute. . . . It is hopelessness even more than pain that crushes the soul. (p. 62)

These are serious disorders with a high morbidity and mortality, when *untreated*—one out of five people will actually commit suicide (Jamison, 1993). This is particularly tragic because treatment can be so effective (Brent et al., 1988; Goodwin & Jamison, 1990). All three of the creative persons mentioned above—Woolf, Hemingway, and Van Gogh—eventually took their own lives.

PRELIMINARY CONSIDERATIONS AND THREE BIOLOGICAL MODELS

This chapter has three dominant themes. Bipolar mood disorders provide a major entryway into each of these, as well as representing in itself a clinical area of great concern—and at times perhaps of unsuspected opportunity. Before returning to issues of bipolar disorders, I will: (a) summarize these themes, (b) present for later reference three biological models of ways in which sickness and health may be intertwined, and (c) outline some considerations regarding creativity seen from an evolutionary perspective. The three themes:

1. *Creativity may be viewed as the evolution of information*—the evolution of *memes* rather than *genes*. Even as there are disorders of genes, there may be disorders of memes.

2. *We need to broaden our perceived limits of normality* to permit the rich diversity of sources necessary for this evolution of information—and, in so doing, to distinguish more clearly between the abnormal (unusual) and pathological (maladaptive). Such modification may ease the way for individuals whose deviancy includes personal suffering, as well as for others whose nonpainful and nonharmful behaviors have been pathologized.

3. *Creativity, as a key part of our conscious evolution,* will be increasingly important, if we're to move beyond our genetically influenced limitations in how we view the world, and increase our potential for adaptation and survival and in the 21st century and beyond.

Three Biological Models

Three biological models now follow of ways in which sickness and health may be intertwined. Later psychological phenomena will be related to these:

1. *Acquired immunity.* It is in getting sick, after all, that young children help temper their immune systems—that they acquire certain forms of *resistance.* Parents used to deliberately orchestrate certain exposures when a child was young, for instance to measles or whooping cough. One could often get off more "cheaply" at an earlier age. Yet whether one "pays" as a child or an adult, such immunity still has a price. Only more recently, with vaccines such as that for measles, mumps, and rubella, has the cost of certain types of protection gone dramatically down (Lawlor & Fischer, 1988; Smith, 1977).

2. *Compensatory advantage.* The effects of blood disorders such as sickle cell anemia (or the thalassemias) are mixed. The person with full-blown sickle cell disease, who inherits this from both parents (the homozygote), develops a serious anemia with risk of multiple medical complications and early death. Yet the larger number of genetic sickle cell carriers (the heterozygotes, who inherit from just one parent), may develop only a mild anemia, yet still show a positive *compensatory advantage*: resistance to malaria (Minkoff, 1983; Richards, Kinney, Lunde, Benet, & Merzel, 1988). Here too, a price is paid for a healthy result, but this time not everyone pays the same price. Indeed, some people pay very dearly. Significantly, such mixed results, these trade-offs of illness and health, are programmed into our genes.

3. *Maladapted genetic blueprints.* I now turn from individuals, and from groups of individuals, to the multiplicity of species that has populated the earth at different historical times. This diversity of organisms (of their genetic blueprints, or *genotypes*, and their real-life expressions as *phenotypes*) has provided a rich range of possibilities to meet changing environmental conditions. Yet not all organisms have been successful in thus perpetuating themselves, as described by Steven Jay Gould (1989), at the Burgess Shale, high in the Canadian Rockies. There, out of numerous creatures that evolved, only a relative handful survived. Also, consider the dinosaurs, thought by some to have perished after a meteorite, or perhaps a volcano, changed the earth's climatic conditions (Bak & Chen, 1991). Dinosaurs are now extinct in all but the movies. Taking a broad view, one might argue that this evolutionary process can at times reflect a form of ecosystem health—perhaps particularly if it moves toward a stable or increasingly diverse and interconnected life support system (e.g., Brown et al., 1992; Wilson, 1993). But just tell this to the dinosaur.

These situations may seem unfair to certain individual organisms. The person with sickle cell disease may suffer a terrible anemia "so that" the more numerous sickle cell carriers may thrive, and resist malaria. And what is good for the human being won't necessarily favor the malarial protozoan, the staphylococcus that can cause pneumonia, or the spirochete that causes the increasingly feared lyme disease. Much of life has been forged in conflict, both within and between species. Some solutions have "worked," at least on the average, but have left many victims.

The underlying principle in all this is biological *variability*—the creation of new and adaptable organisms—based on genetic material and its expression in a particular environment (the genotype and phenotype). This is surely a form of biological creativity. The point is to maximize adaptability to changing conditions (as for instance, with a staphylococcus that has developed resistance to penicillin). Species survival has been the ultimate goal. And reproductive (or genetic) survival, of individuals or of groups, has been an ultimate indicator of viability and health.

Our conscious awareness of individual or societal needs won't eliminate the underlying dynamic of conflict in this seemingly "unfair" struggle for survival. But it can at times help us reduce its costs to some of us.

This is one place where our own human creativity may enter: to broaden our environmental range of responses, to increase our options. We do immunize children against diseases like measles, and medically treat for sickle cell anemia. Challenging the status quo is what creativity is all about.

"Everyday creativity," in particular—involving *originality* and *meaningfulness* in the multitudinous activities of day-to-day life—has been conceptualized as a survival capability (Richards, 1990; Richards et al., 1988).

Creativity as the Evolution of "Memes"

In addition to *genes*, or units of heredity, we now speak metaphorically of *memes* or units of "cultural imitation" (Dawkins, 1976), and also look at their adaptive value (see also Csikszentmihalyi, 1988; Lumsden & Findlay, 1988; Richards, 1996a). Memes are transmitted from brain to brain (or book to book). Examples are an idea, equation, image, or melody; consider the powerful "meme-complex" comprising the English language.

Memes can be identified in other organisms but reach their highest development in human beings (Dawkins, 1976). As with genes, memes can be replicated, and can increase in frequency. But a "population explosion" of memes is unlike anything else. Memes can move at extraordinary rates, via published materials, video transmission, computer networks, and the like. Indeed, memes can do in ten minutes what it may take generations of genetic evolution to accomplish.

As with genes, the viability of particular memes or meme-complexes can be vastly influenced by environmental forces (consider the fate of last week's newspaper, compared to Shakespeare's sonnets). Sometimes the effects are widespread, dramatic, and nearly instantaneous, as with the news of President Kennedy's assassination.

In addition, memes can influence the viability of genes (as with prehistoric people who survived because they discovered fire), and such cultural and biological forces can continue to interact in a constantly changing dance (Lumsden & Findlay, 1988; Tooby & DeVore, 1987).

Creativity is most comparable to the "recombination of memes," to the putting together of information. This process is potentially more complicated than "genetic recombination"—than two mating organisms exchanging predetermined pieces of DNA, even though the biological offspring can be quite diverse. With memes, or information, one can put together anything at all that one wants. Memetic recombination can draw all at once, without limit, on multiple memes spanning thousands of miles and thousands of years. As its most *original* and *meaningful* (two widely accepted criteria for creativity, see Barron [1969]), this process is just what may of us mean by creativity.

This power of creativity is critical; it represents a different sort of "evolution," and evolution of information, and one which offers us—as purposeful, foresightful, and sometimes rational beings—a great deal of hope.

Table 32.1. Illustrations: Illness and Creativity

Generation of Information	
Individual	I. OVERINCLUSIVE THINKING Valuing broad and diverse conceptual modes
Social	II. CULTURAL DIVERSITY Preserving a multiplicity of styles and contexts

Use of Information	
Individual	III. CONFRONTING PERSONAL ADVERSITY Affective integration and creative courage
Social	IV. CONFRONTING GLOBAL ADVERSITY Affective integration and creative courage in groups

RELATED PSYCHOLOGICAL PHENOMENA
AND ILLUSTRATIONS

The discussion is framed in terms of four psychological illustrations, outlined in Table 32.1. Of these, the first and third illustrations deal with psychiatric phenomena related to bipolar mood disorders—although similar phenomena may occur in other circumstances as well. Issues involve, first, the *generation of information* (or "memes") and, second, its *use*. The second and fourth illustrations represent speculative extrapolations of these two informational processes to the societal level. Each illustration presents ways in which creative processes can help "seed change." Particular time is spent on the first example, because it has the most empirical support. In addition, two special topics are introduced here (involving chaos theory, and "cultural brainstorming"), which apply to other illustrations as well.

For each illustration, the following are given:

(1) Example
(2) Model(s)
(3) Pathology
(4) Potential Benefits
(5) Reducing our Costs
(6) Creativity and the Evolution of Information

This discussion is not meant to imply that creativity is *only* the result of illness or conflict. Other potential routes also exist (see Cropley, Rhodes, Runco et al., this volume; Richards, 1981, 1990, 1996b). Curiosity, challenge, mastery, the delights of beauty, and the joy of discovery can still be enough.

A. ILLUSTRATION ONE
INDIVIDUAL LEVEL: OVERINCLUSIVE
THINKING—HOW HEALTHY?

1. Example: Far-Reaching Manic Thoughts—John Ruskin

I roll on like a ball, with this exception, that contrary to the usual laws of motion I have no friction to contend with in my mind, and of course have some difficulty in stopping myself when there is nothing else to stop me. . . . I am almost sick and giddy with the quantity of things in my head— trains of thought beginning and branching to infinity, crossing each other, and all tempting and wanting to be worked out. (Ruskin in Jamison, 1993, p. 29)

2. Model: "Compensatory Advantage" and Creativity

As with John Ruskin's mania, one might ask if there is a positive side to the genetic risk for bipolar mood disorders—and might this include higher creativity? As with sickle cell anemia, could people who are carriers of a bipolar vulnerability, or people who have milder mood disorders or episodes, show a *compensatory advantage?* And could the diversity of information (memes) generated, this rich range of information—in its sometime eccentric entirety—have adaptive value for society, even apart from the individual?

3. Pathology: Widespread Mood Disorders That Cause Great Suffering

Among other psychiatric disorders, bipolar disorders have a particularly strong genetic component (e.g., Goodwin & Jamison, 1990; Wender et al., 1986). The genetics are likely more complicated than those of sickle cell anemia (e.g., Richards, Kinney, Benet, & Merzel, 1988).

The likelihood that there is some positive evolutionary advantage to this serious form of illness becomes all the more compelling when one hears that as much as 4–5% of the population may develop a mood disorder with an underlying bipolar vulnerability (Akiskal & Akiskal, 1992; Akiskal & Mallya, 1987). This is a very large group! Evolution may not only have avoided selecting against these illnesses, but may have favored them (Richards, 1993b; Wilson, in press).

a. A broad "spectrum" of mood disorders

Included here are *bipolar I* disorder (manic-depressive illness), *bipolar II* disorder (severe depressions, but milder mood elevations), *cyclothymia* (milder mood elevations and depressions), *hyperthymia* (a condition of more ongoing mild mood elevation), *bipolar III* disorder (a "masked" condition in which antidepressant treatment elicits a mood elevation), and, with some overlap, "pure" unipolar *depressions* or *dysthymias* with a bipolar vulnerability in the background. These conditions show other clinical features as well (e.g., Akiskal & Akiskal, 1992; Goodwin & Jamison, 1990; Keller, 1987). There are also evidently "healthy" people who carry a bipolar vulnerability without showing obvious symptoms—this group turns out to be quite important.

Indeed, if one were hypothetically to assume there was one relative without a mood disorder (but carrying a bipolar vulnerability) for every person who has one of the above mood disorders, it could even be that as much as 10% of the population carries the underlying risk for a bipolar disorder. This segment of society is so large as to raise serious questions about why it might exist (e.g., Richards, 1993b).

4.   Potential Benefits: Eminent-Level and Everyday Creativity

Before turning to these millions of people at risk, and the *everyday* creativity of all of us, it is useful to look at creativity and creators receiving *eminent* recognition. As Richards & Kinney (this volume) noted these are the creators with fame, notoriety, public recognition, or high professional regard, whom people often identify with the word "creative."

a.   Overall traits: How frequently are eminent creators mood disordered?

Significantly, the literature, including older studies that are individually flawed, all tends to point in the same direction: toward greater psychological difficulty among creative people who have reached eminence, in the arts in particular (Andreasen, Jamison, Ludwig, all this volume; Ludwig, 1992a; Ostwald, 1991; Richards, 1981, 1990).

Newer rates of illness among artists, using more thorough diagnostic and interviewing approaches, may seem truly startling. Consider Nancy Andreasen's (this volume) discovery that a full four out of five eminent creative writers had a major mood disorder (80% compared to 30% of controls). It was the rare creative writer who did *not* have a mood disorder. In addition, the majority of these writers had a bipolar disorder, often with mild mood elevations (bipolar II disorder). In support of this is Jamison's (this volume) finding that 38% of eminent British artists and writers had sought treatment for a mood disorder—a striking figure against the tragic fact that only about one out of three affected people even tend to seek treatment (Jamison, 1990). In addition, almost all (89%) of Jamison's sample had "intense creative episodes" sharing many qualities with the mild mood elevations of clinical hypomania. (See Richards & Kinney, this volume, for further discussion of these studies.)

Ludwig (this volume) found similar patterns for artists, using a totally different approach based on psychobiography. Ludwig actually looked separately at 18 professions, presenting illness rates both before and after age 40. Of great note, almost two-thirds (66%) of the poets had had bouts of depression noted after age 40. Expository and fiction writers, visual artists, and musical composers were also up there in the 40–50% range.

Although the methodology didn't allow inclusion of the bipolar "spectrum" of disorders, we do see full mania coming out before age 40 in 13–17% of poets, and 5–10% of architects, artists, business people, musical composers and performers, fiction and expository writers, compared to less than 1% in the population at large. (The rate of all bipolar-based disorders—including "pure" depressions—could therefore be several times higher than this.) We also see much early-onset psychopathology in general. This early illness can be seen (among other reasons) when the underlying vulnerability is bipolar.

It is interesting in itself that the psychopathology of scientists has been so little studied, compared to artists. But Ludwig (this volume) did in fact take a look, and found a much healthier picture than for artists. Or at least, Ludwig qualified it such that the illness of scientists was less obvious or less likely to be reported. For social scientists, for instance, rates of depression were in the low 20% range, about half that for artists. For physical scientists, numbers are in the low teens.

One study that we can compare is Juda's (1949–1950) extensive research on "highly gifted" scientists and artists, meanwhile noting that there are some methodological problems (Richards, 1981). Both the artist and scientist groups showed more than twice the population rate of psychosis (5–6%). (This could perhaps say something about the genetic vulnerabilities running in these families.) Yet nonpsychotic illness was about twice as frequent in the artists as the scientists (24% vs. 14%).

Thus, in both the studies by Ludwig (this volume) and Juda (1949–1950), scientists looked relatively more healthy than artists. Other non-artists Ludwig studied, including businesspersons, explorers, athletes, military figures, social activists, and social figures, also showed lower rates of depression. Granted that we still don't know who had a vulnerability to bipolar disorder running in their family, or who themselves may have had a more "silent" or subtle expression of this. But at the level of having an obvious and strongly remarked upon mood disorder, the key predictor, it seemed, wasn't being an eminent creative person. It was being an eminent creative artist.

*b.   Ongoing traits: How frequently are eminent creators
substance abusers?*

A startling figure cited by Rothenberg (this volume) is that five of the
eight Nobel Prize winners in literature as of 1983 in the United States had
at some time abused alcohol. Despite this, Rothenberg concluded that
drinking was more likely to hurt than to help creativity, based on biographical and autobiographical studies of 28 eminent writers and heavy drinkers.
Drinking was more likely to occur at the end of the working day than during it. Proposed functions were to help contain anxiety produced by the
creative process, and functions related to public image or self-concept.
Rothenberg also reminds us that alcoholism may be biologically based.

We should not forget that alcohol abuse can also be a response (and
certainly not the best one) to an underlying mood disorder. At least four
well-known authors mentioned by Rothenberg had a bipolar mood disorder (see Jamison, 1990, 1993): F. Scott Fitzgerald, Ernest Hemingway,
Robert Lowell, and Eugene O'Neill. Ludwig (1990) noted directly that
both Robert Lowell and Delmore Schwartz used alcohol to contain their
mania.

Indeed, almost one-third (30%) of Andreasen's (this volume) highly
mood-disordered sample of creative writers abused alcohol (vs. 7% of
controls)—and we have no way of knowing how many merely "used" it.
Ludwig's (this volume) creative writers showed comparable rates of
abuse. Things were worse yet for musical performers (40% before age 40)
and theatre people (60% after age 40). Although less severe than alcohol, drug abuse was an early problem among four of Ludwig's groups:
musical and theatre performers, fiction writers, and poets.

Another study by Ludwig (1990) provides further perspective; he
looked at 34 heavy drinking 20th century artists, performers, and writers
(including 12 of Rothenberg's 28 writers), using a modification of
Richards' (1981) typology of direct and indirect effects linking creativity
and psychopathology. It turned out that, for three-quarters of the sample,
drinking had directly and definitely hurt their creativity. Yet for another
9%, it had directly helped.

Furthermore, there had been indirect benefit of drinking for one-half
the creators, one example being E.B. White's single motivating martini
before writing. "Just one, to give me the courage to get started. After that,
I am on my own" (p. 955). And turning things around—consistent with
Rothenberg's (this volume) position—creative activity had in some way,
and at some time, driven almost a third (30%) of the writers to drink.

Yet before one reaches for a bottle (instead of a pen or a word-
processor), one should keep well in mind that: (a) these are eminent
writers chosen for their *drinking*, not their writing, that (b) many of these
writers also had a mood disorder—26% with a bipolar disorder in Lud-

wig's (1990) study—and possibly also a (c) familial predisposition to alcohol. The reasons for drinking, and its effects, may be complex indeed.

c. Overall traits: How mood disordered are everyday creators?
My research with Dennis Kinney and others at McLean Hospital and Harvard Medical School (Richards, Kinney, Lunde, Benet, & Merzel, this volume; Richards, Kinney, Benet, & Merzel, 1988), on *everyday* creativity speaks less to psychopathology per se, than to some more subtle qualities that may go along with it. (See also Schuldberg, this volume; Richards & Kinney, this volume, for issues of everyday vs. eminent creativity.) This suggests more of the *compensatory advantage* type of phenomenon. With sickle cell anemia, one recalls, it was the larger number of mildly affected "carriers" who showed the greatest advantage.

Everyday creativity may be a way of life. Our work on "everyday creativity" started with the millions of bipolar patients and their relatives, and not with a small handful of eminent creators, however interesting these may be. We looked at *original* accomplishment (just as long as it was *meaningful,* and not random) across the wide range of activities of everyday life, and not random) across the wide range of activities of everyday life, both at work and at leisure. We used our Lifetime Creativity Scales, which we developed and validated for this purpose on over 500 personally interviewed persons (Richards et al., 1988).

We are not talking here about the famous scientist or the eminent composer. I am talking about people who excelled in home landscaping, schoolteaching, repairing cars, raising their children, managing an office, and also about people who designed dangerous wartime resistance activities. We only required that they show *originality*, and this can be brought to just about anything.

We are also not talking about intelligence, or about special talents and skills, say in art or in music. These are certainly important to doing excellent work. However, being able to copy a painting perfectly is of no use if one can't do a new and original work. We are talking about a style of thinking, a way of reacting, perhaps a way of life—a dispositional dimension of personality (see also Cropley, Eysenck, both this volume). As Barron (1963a) said, "Originality is almost habitual with persons who produce a really singular insight" (p. 139).

Something very broad is running in these families. Interestingly, Andreasen (this volume) found, looking at relatives of her exceptional creative writers, that they too were more creative than relatives of her control subjects. But the writers' relatives weren't all writers themselves—they weren't necessarily even in related fields. Some were in music, mathematics, teaching; they were all over the block. What was running in these families wasn't a knack for writing, but something more a basic about liking to think in new and original ways. Our own family findings supported this too (Richards et al. this volume).

Consider what Eugen Bleuler said of manic patients (Jamison, 1990). It seems Bleuler was right:

> Because of the more rapid flow of ideas, and especially because of the falling off of inhibitions, artistic activities are facilitated even though something worthwhile is produced only in very *mild cases* and when the patient is otherwise talented in this direction. (p. 23)

Creativity in better-functioning persons.   When Richards et al. (this volume; also see Richards & Kinney, this volume) looked at manic-depressive, cyclothymes, and first-degree normal relatives, and controls with and without another diagnosis, they found it was not the full-blown manic-depressives who came out most creative on the average— although certain manic-depressives did excel. Rather, it was the individuals with less severe mood swings, the *cyclothymes*. But there was also one real surprise: Included as well were the psychiatrically *normal* relatives.

It is worth stressing that everyday creativity was assessed here by raters who knew absolutely nothing of the subjects' diagnoses or even their identities. Diagnoses were made by people who knew nothing at all about subjects' creativity. Thus the chance of even an unconscious sort of bias in these results was minimal.

Normalcy by itself wasn't the reason for heightened creativity, either; the normal control group didn't show this "creative advantage." For that matter, depression also wasn't the cause. In a small pilot study, we showed higher creativity among so-called "pure" depressives with a family history of bipolar disorder than in depressives who lacked this family history (Richards, Kinney, Daniels, & Linkins, 1992). Thus, the traces of a genetic *bipolar* liability may be subtle indeed.

In addition, the cyclothymes in our earlier work (Richards et al., this volume) may have included people who would now be diagnosed with a bipolar II disorder—meaning that the cyclothymes were potentially more heterogeneous at the depressed end than at the "higher" end of the mood spectrum. (This also puts this group closer to the eminent creative writers described by Andreasen [this volume], where bipolar II disorder was the most common diagnosis.) Findings by Akiskal and Akiskal (1988), Eckblad and Chapman (1986), Jamison et al. (1980), Schuldberg (this volume), and others (see Richards, 1990), support once again, with everyday samples, the importance of states of mild mood elevation, or of having a bipolar disorder in the family, for prediction of enhanced creativity.

d. States of mind: Can mood elevation benefit creativity?

Mood states can relate in different ways to creativity. Certain chronic or severe conditions may certainly be prohibitive of creativity (see Eisenman, this volume). But there are also reports, for instance, of depression increasing one's sensitivity (e.g., Andreasen, this volume; Jamison, 1990, 1993; Richards, & Kinney, 1990). I focus here, however, on that mood state most widely linked with creativity, the state of mild mood elevation or subtle "highs." I take two different perspectives: (a) styles of thinking linked with mood elevation, and (b) features of so-called bipolar "thought disorder." Several questions are asked:

When do patients feel most creative, and why?   Work with both everyday and eminent creators (Akiskal & Akiskal, 1988; Eckblad & Chapman, 1986; Jamison, Richards & Kinney, Schuldberg, all this volume) indicates that a state of mild mood elevation may be particularly important for being creatively productive—whether or not the creator also has more dramatic "highs" and "lows."

Jamison (this volume) broke this down further, finding a range of cognitive, affective, and behavioral changes during the hypomanic-like "intense creative episodes" of eminent writers and artists. Richards and Kinney (this volume) took this list and asked bipolar patients if they had experienced any of these features during their most creative mood states, along with asking what this mood state was.

Three types of phenomena were suggested in this initial exploration. The first was independent of subjects' preferred creative mood state, and might be called *tempered positive feelings* (e.g. sense of well-being, confidence, enthusiasm). The other two clusters applied only to subjects who liked creating when their mood was elevated (elevated either a little or a lot). One cluster suggested a *spontaneous exuberance* (expansiveness, impulsivity, euphoria), and another a *cognitive facility* (rapid thinking, association, fluency with new ideas).

Keeping well in mind that this is only one part of the picture, we turn to questions of cognitive style and creativity. A key question is *whether thought that appears "normal" in one context might be considered "abnormal" in another.* Very interestingly, Eysenck (1993; this volume) has come to a related position from the somewhat different direction of elevated *psychoticism*, as a dimension of personality, and its relationship to style of thinking. Below are put together several pieces of the puzzle.

What might mild mood elevation have to do with this?   One is not talking just about the mood disordered now, but about everyone (see Richards, 1993a, 1993b, 1994b).

Isen and others (e.g., Isen, 1985; Isen et al., 1987; see Richards, 1994b) have shown that even a very slight mood elevation across several forms of induction—after watching a brief comedy film, for instance—can increase all of the following: unusual word associations, overinclusiveness of categorization, and actual creative problem solving on specific laboratory tasks. Unusual associations and overinclusion have been associated with creativity in other contexts, as well (see Richards, 1981, 1990, 1996b).

Are there similarities in how mania affects thinking? Loose associations are characteristic of mania. Interestingly, so is overinclusive categorization, both *behavioral* (number of elements included in a category), and *conceptual* overinclusion (range of classification rules employed, including ones that are more vague, or distant, or developmentally primitive). The Object Sorting Test (Goldstein & Scheerer, 1941) is often used for this sort of study. It's worth looking in addition at two real-life examples:

> **Example.** Conceptual overinclusion (with primitive and shifting classification): A little girl, when she was one year old, happily thought several different things were a "cow," namely: (a) a chain saw (the buzzing sounded a lot like a "moo"), (b) a black and white patterned fish at the aquarium (it had the right markings); and finally (c) the domestic animal whose milk we often drink.

> **Example.** Behavioral (quantitative) overinclusion: An adult gave as instances of things with "wheels": a car, truck, watch parts, earth on its axis, wheels within wheels, Wheel of Fortune, wheeling and dealing, a wagon wheel used as a table (etcetera). One should note that this person could do well on an "Instances" test of creative thinking. (e.g., Wallach & Kogan, 1965)

How similar is the thinking of manics and creative writers? First, consider this report by a manic patients (Jamison, 1990):

> Thoughts chased one another through my mind with lightning rapidity. I felt like a person driving a wild horse with a weak rein, who dares not use force, but lets him run his course, following the line of least resistance. (p. 27)

Groundbreaking early studies by Andreasen and colleagues (Andreasen & Canter, 1974; Andreasen & Powers, 1974) help complete the circles. Creative writers, manics, and schizophrenics were compared on overinclusive thinking. As it turned out, there were many similarities between writers and manics, but not schizophrenics. The creative writers were also higher on abstract and cohesive thought, suggesting greater control of their so-called "deviant" processes. Indeed, with everyday creative persons too, Schuldberg (this volume) found that hypomanic traits and some unusual perceptual experiences and beliefs were counterbalanced by high *ego strength.* In creative children (Dudek & Verrault, this volume), high ego strength emerged as part of a picture of elevated primary process thinking and useful "regression in the service of the ego."

One is very much reminded of classic studies of eminent creative writers at the Institute of Personality Assessment and Research (IPAR), at the University of California, Berkeley (Barron, 1969), where the average writer, remarkably, was in the top 15% of the general population on *every* MMPI psychopathology scale. Yet writers once again showed the unusual combination of high ego-strength—and therefore appeared to be "both sicker and healthier psychologically than people in general" (p. 75).

e.   States of mind: Does this mean "thought disorder" is creative?

Taking another perspective (see Richards, 1994b), we look at examples of responses that can be called "disordered" on the Thought Disorder Index of Phillip Holzman and associates at McLean Hospital (e.g., Holzman et al., 1986; Shenton et al., 1989; Solovay et al., 1986). These descriptions were in response to projective materials such as the Rorschach Ink Blots—that is, responses to ambiguous stimuli that could bring about "thought slippage":

"It looks like a mastodon wearing shoes."	(incongruity)
"A beetle crying."	(incongruity)
"Because it's black, dark, darkness, lovemaking."	(looseness)
"Two crows with afros, and they're pushing two hearts together."	(fabulized combination)
"An evil witch doing a square dance . . . She had her dress like this and she was do-si-do-ing."	(playful confabulation)

How creative is manic thought?   These are colorful and lively responses. They relate to two dimensions that distinguished manic thought from schizophrenic thought in post hoc factor analysis of 22 scales from the Thought Disorder Index (Shenton et al., 1987)—namely *combinatory thinking* (marked by incongruous of fabulized combination and playful confabulation) and, in the middle example, *irrelevant intrusions* (looseness, flippancy).

But do these colorful responses mean the individuals who gave them are also more creative? If our criteria for creative are originality and meaningfulness, we may be in trouble on the meaningfulness part, particularly if the person is in poor contact with reality (e.g., psychotic individuals in Eisenman's sample, this volume). This doesn't mean creative potential isn't there. Consider the nature of manic thought. According to Holzman et al. (1986):

Manic thought disorder manifests itself as loosely tied together ideas that are excessively and immoderately combined and elaborated. Often, there is a playful, mirthful, and breezy quality to their production. . . . Schizophrenic thought disorder shows very little, if any, of the exuberant, jocular, frivolous elaborations of the manic patients. (p. 369)

Will "submanic" thought be creative?   Florid mania, one might think, would leave little room for controlled acts of creative exploration. One may recall that, even with fully manic-depressive individuals, it was not the extremes of elation or depression that are reported as best for creating (e.g., Goodwin & Jamison, 1990; Richards & Kinney, this volume). Rather, it was the states of mild mood elevation—and occasionally of normalcy. There are intertwined issues of idea-generation and idea-selection. What is needed is an appropriate balance of inspiration and control.

A great many questions remain. Is the creativity effect a "state" or "trait" phenomenon? Does this style of thinking just emerge when people are "up," or do they learn some tricks that "carry over" to other times of their lives? Is this thinking style largely genetic in origin, so that it's pre-programmed to happen, no matter what? Or does environment also play a role such that this thought style can be "picked up," maybe as part of a "family culture" or style—in the same way that college kids might get a little "loose" and silly at night, laughing in a dorm (see Eysenck, 1993; Jamison, 1990, 1993; Richards, 1990, 1994b, 1996b; Schuldberg, 1994).

And if this overinclusive and creative style can actually be taught, then shouldn't we perhaps be trying to do more of this—and not just for people with a mood-disordered background, but for people in general?

How does one explain higher creativity in "normal" relatives?   What can be learned from the psychiatrically normal relatives of bipolars, who also show an "everyday" creative advantage? For that matter, what about the bipolar III individuals, "pure" depressives or dysthymics with a bipolar family history who don't themselves show the signs of mild mood elevation.

It is fascinating that for manics, as well as for schizoaffective and schizophrenic patients, Holzman's group at McLean Hospital (Shenton et al., 1989) found thought disorder of the same general sorts in the first-degree relatives of patients, including relatives who are not themselves clinically ill. (Other evidence supports such patterns, both with schizophrenic families and with normal college students and their parents (see Richards, 1981, 1994b).

Thus the "dysfunction" of thinking, if it truly is one, may be subtle indeed. It could be an independent phenomenon, separate from mood (e.g., Eysenck, 1993; this volume, regarding a connection to *psychoticism*), or perhaps represent an undiagnosed condition of a *very* mild mood elevation (hyperthymia), as we have suggested (Richards et al., this volume; see also Schuldberg, this volume). This could also help explain certain patterns of thought found by Eysenck or Schuldberg (both this volume). This subtle state may even be optimal for creativity, providing a wealth of potential material along with the optimal controls to fashion it in creative ways.

Can people turn this "thought disorder" on and off?   One perspective, in general, is that creative persons are able to exercise flexible *choice* between conceptual *styles* of different developmental origin—and that more primitive modes of thinking become yet another tool in their conceptual toolbox (Richards, 1981). As with Andreasen and Canter's (1974) over-inclusive creative writers, during times of higher ego-functioning, some creators may have controlled access to this "thought disordered" type of creative tool.

f. States of mind: Creativity and addiction, and creativity as addiction

If mild mood elevation can stimulate creativity, earlier evidence suggests that chemical addiction may often hinder it. Rather than widening the periphery of one's field of vision, it may restrict one's vision and blur it from the center outward, through a deliberate distortion or anesthesia. Addiction, after all, involves compulsive stimulus-seeking behavior that can dominate all else and have adverse consequences for other parts of one's life. The flexible and subtle creative controls mentioned above may not have a chance.

But we may speculate for a moment about a more harmonious and intrinsic effect that could serve as both enabler and reward for creativity (Richards, 1990). After all, evolution might well have built in immediate or short-term chemical rewards to keep people pushing through the harder moments of creativity. Such a reward system certainly exists for parenting, where preprogrammed jolts of oxytocin, for instance, can help strengthen the rewards of attachment and caring, especially toward moments when children are frustrating or exhausting (Ackerman, 1994).

For some people, chemical concomitants of bipolar mood elevations may both enable and reward creative efforts. Also consider chemical mediators in the form of a small burst of *endorphins*, or *endogenous* opiate substances, which contribute to performance modulation in complex ways during peak physical accomplishment (Fobes, 1989). By somewhat similar mechanisms, our chemistry could perhaps provide the fuel to keep us striving, along with the ultimate creative reward—the joy, even exhilaration, that Flach (this volume) or Csikszentmihalyi (1990) have described (see Richards, 1990).

Here we're not talking abut a random abuse of diverse substances, but about an automatic and intrinsic doling out of special chemicals that are well deserved and useful, and would arrive at the most helpful times, almost by definition. This "worthiness" could even tie in with some of the physically beneficial effects previously attributed to creativity. This is an area that surely needs study—if an understanding of many aspects of substances, substance abuse, creative performance modulation, and health is to be achieved.

What sorts of substances might be involved? Interestingly, positive affect can lead to defocused attention, and to more complex cognitive content or configurations (Isen, et al., 1987; Simonton, 1988). Some stimulant drugs popularly linked to "highs" could tend, rather, to heighten arousal. Arousal pulls for the dominant, and not the unusual or original, response (Eysenck, 1993). Kyle (1988) suggested, on the other hand, the relevance of *exogenous* opiates to creativity, at least in the creator who is not drug dependent or addicted. He gives the example of Coleridge's famed opiate-inspired "vision in dream" when writing Kubla Khan. Kyle also noted support for a "sleep-like EEG" induced by opiates, along with behavioral alertness, and lessened hemispheric specialization. Various investigators (Bogen & Bogen, 1988; Hoppe, 1988; Hoppe & Kyle, this volume) have emphasized the importance of the latter for creativity.

Whatever the exact mechanism, a joyous creative experience can in fact intermittently occur—a "natural high," in the best sense. It gives many people added drive. Some creators do seem compulsively drawn to their work (e.g., Richards, 1990; Richards, et al., this volume), and it has also been said that some of these creators can go too far in their preoccupation, neglecting other people or their own basic needs (e.g., Gardner, 1993). If one aspect of this is chemical—involving learned behaviors tied to chemical response—it would be important to understand.

Yet, at the same time, one could argue that creative processing is an experience that many more people should "seek" if not actually become "addicted to." "Creativity-seeking" rarely involves the immediate gratifications of substance abuse. Creativity takes work, patience, intrinsic purpose and meaning, tolerance for ambiguity, and trust in oneself and the outcome. These are pleasant virtues indeed. Creativity-seeking could be a very worthy substitute for compulsive substance-seeking, its impulsive use, and the fragmenting experiences of escape, distortion, dyscontrol, and obliteration.

5. Reducing Our Costs: Treat the Pain—Don't Pathologize the "Differences"

For the sufferer of full-blown sickle cell anemia, one may offer medical treatment, yet this does not diminish the compensatory advantage in sickle cell carriers. The situation is improved for everyone. Can one do the same for bipolar mood disorders?

One shouldn't try too hard to "improve on nature," since we don't really know very much about nature. But there are at least two things we can do, as healers, to give people options and to ease their suffering. The first is to ease the pain of illness, and the second is not to imagine illness where it doesn't even exist.

a. Treating those who suffer

A Robot Man comic strip (Boston Globe,1–29–89) showed Vincent Van Gogh after taking an antidepressant. He threw up his arms, exclaiming, "I feel better already! I feel like painting happy paintings! Like rolling surf and sunsets and clowns on black velvet . . ." (Richards, 1990). Will treatment stifle creativity? This is a dangerous assumption (see also Andreasen & Glick, 1988; Jamison, 1990, 1993). In fact, treatment may not only decrease suffering but also *increase* creative potential. It is not the terrifying extremes of elation and depression that feed the most creative moments, as we have seen, but a more modulated state of mind (Richards, 1990, 1994b; Richards & Kinney, this volume).

Does treatment threaten creativity? Think of the high rates of mood disorders among eminent creative artists. Emotional extremes may provide content or process for such artists, which is useful at a later point as raw material (e.g., Andreasen, 1987; Jamison, 1993; Richards, 1981). Indeed they might do so, particularly if one is writing, acting, painting, or singing about mood disorders and the human condition. Yet one might ask how often one must go to Hades to describe it (and also how close one must get). Plus, what of satisfactions and, later, strengths that come from the *mastery* of great pain? (Krystal, 1981). There will be more on this question later.

There is tremendous potential in treating creative artists with conservative and carefully titrated doses of medication (e.g., Andreasen & Glick, 1988; Goodwin & Jamison, 1990). In one study, more than half the creative artists studied said treatment with lithium helped, or at least did not hurt, their creativity—and it did indeed help their pain (Schou, 1979). And who is to say, in any case, that creativity should be a higher priority than one's health? If anyone at all, surely it's the artist. Yet in view of the death rate of this illness (e.g., Brent, et al., 1988, Jamison, 1993), the only truly rational course is to give the medication a try and then decide.

When people don't want treatment. Clearly, no one should be forcing treatment on a person who doesn't want it, but treatment should at least be a realistic option. It cannot truly be an option until the average person is much better informed about mood disorders, the great effectiveness of treatment, and the tendency for a pervasive stigma based on ignorance to get in the way.

Some people, for instance, have the misguided belief that depressed people could just "snap out of it" if they'd only try a little harder. These critics would probably never speak this way to people suffering from pneumonia, gout, diabetes, or an ulcer. Yet, with an untreated bipolar disorder, as many as one out of five people may actually die—they commit suicide (Jamison, 1993). We are talking here about a highly fatal illness, and not a little case of "not trying." As previously stated, Van Gogh himself was one of the suicide victims.

Treatment, as mentioned, can be highly effective (Brent, et al., 1988). In some instances, even the knowledge of an alternative (other than suicide) can be of great help. Ultimately, the creator must decide what to do. But it seems possible, given the strong pull to create, and the adaptive value of the process and result, that the creativity linked with mood disorders may, under the best circumstances of options and support, take care of itself.

b.   *Expanding our perceived "limits of normality"*

Humans are not always great at valuing differences and diversity. We should strive to depathologize behaviors that may be considered "different" but are not at all harmful—and which may in fact be quite the opposite. These may be behaviors of the mood disordered, the traumatized, or the unaffiliated nonconformist (see also Martindale, this volume, on some unusual sources of divergence).

These individuals are not just repositories of "abnormality" to be "normalized" to look like "us." They *are* us. Theirs are the many forms of experience we share together. They also represent points along the colorful spectrum of response in an actively evolving culture. And in the 21st century, we will likely need a great deal more of this divergence! Did you hear an odd thought or comment? "How interesting. I'm glad you thought of it, because I wouldn't have seen it that way."

What is the source of the discomfort? Does something become abnormal simply because it's not the norm or not expected? Or is the issue one of context? A loose association is fine in a poem, but not in a business presentation? "It's black, dark, darkness, lovemaking" is a manic-type "thought disordered" response to a Rorschach inkblot (Solovay et al., 1986). Such description would not appear strange in poetry.

Is the issue fear of loss of control? We seem more comfortable with exceptional creators' very interesting high scores on multiple MMPI psychopathology scales (Barron, 1969), because these creators also show an above average ego-strength (see Dudek & Verrault, Schuldberg, both this volume). Are these creators painting from an optional palette that we feel they could put away if they wanted? Is such divergence then labelled "acceptable" if these creators can also "hold it together?"

We need to take our supposed respect for individual differences—along with respect for group and for species differences—and apply this just a little closer to home—to the biases engendered by our cliquish small-group orientation, which is a topic we will discuss presently.

6.   Creativity and the Evolution of Information

Three other, briefer, illustrations follow next, involving: a) cultural diversity and preservation, b) coping with personal adversity, and c) coping with global adversity. But before turning to these, one may speculate about what social good all this creativity is doing, how it may operate, and how it may influence both our memetic and genetic survival and progress. The discussion below is focused on bipolar mood disorders. But it can be applied to the other illustrations as well and is thus presented now. There are two focal areas:

(a)   Overinclusion, Chaos, and Creative (Memetic) Diversity

(b)   "Cultural Brainstorming" and Evolutionary Advantage

To be considered are: (a) an artificial intelligence model of mania that evokes images of overinclusion; (b) creative insight, through the lenses of chaos theory, and the "criticality" of naturally evolving complex systems, (c) the nature of "open" and "closed" minds, as a chaos phenomenon, and, following from this, (d) proposed phenomenon of *cultural brainstorming* in which adaptive creative thinking for society involves a division of labor—including groups of people devoted to the *transmission* and to the *reception* of new ideas (see Bak & Chen, 1991; Gleick, 1987; Hoffman, 1987; Lumsden & Findlay, 1988; Stein, this volume; Waldrop, 1992).

a.   Overinclusion, chaos, and creative (memetic) diversity

Speeding "overinclusively" between ideas: Hoffman's artificial intelligence model.   Picture an expanse of valleys and hills, a topographical system with contour lines representing the degree of elevation. Now let the valleys instead represent key concepts in memory. A car with a lot of energy could race among these valleys and hills before losing speed, going up one rise and then another, slowing down at the top a bit, but still making it over to the next valley. The course of the trip could be broad, varied, and complex. A car with a more limited amount of energy might travel a bit between two or three of these regions, but perhaps only briefly. A car with extremely low energy might simply wobble a bit in one neighborhood (whichever one it happened to start out in), and ultimately become stuck at the bottom (in energy terms, in a *local minimum*).

Now apply this model to mental processing during mania. Hoffman (1987) did a fascinating artificial intelligence simulation, based on Hopfield's neural net model, looking at associative memory and gestalt-seeking during cognition. The manic state corresponds to increased randomness of state adjustments of individual neurons. One might say that mania raises the temperature, or the energy level, of the system. This leads to jumps from one gestalt to another—jumps from one valley to the next in the picture. Thus, thoughts can range more widely over neural pathways, gathering in more distant gestalts and associations. But this accessibility has a price, namely instability and distractibility.

These "manic" cars are the ones that go too fast, go too far, and may even go out of control. For creativity, we need a compromise—a car that may not range as widely, but can be handled. Ideally, we might also give it a gas pedal and good brakes. Mild mood elevation, modulated by good ego strength (e.g., Barron, 1969), could fit this bill. This model is consistent with findings of overinclusive thinking, richer associations, cognitive complexity, and defocused attention in controlled states of mild mood elevation (e.g., Isen, et al., 1987; Richards, 1994b; Simonton, 1988).

In real life, however, we find a diversity of personal patterns and mood states, including ones that are "stuck" and that "go too far" (even in the same person at different times). We don't only get patterns that are optimal for creativity. Creativity may, indeed, be the *compensatory advantage* that makes up for a lot of the rest.

Creative insight: Action at the edge of chaos.   We turn from cars in motion to lofty sand dunes, and from speeding too fast to states of chaos. The issue: How *creative insight* may fit into the picture.

One has probably heard of impossible-to-predict natural events such as landslides, avalanches, or tornadoes, which can be started unexpectedly by just the tiniest particle—the critical grain of sand, snowflake, or puff of air. A flurry of changes then follows, readjusting things across some significant part of the system. This has also been called the Butterfly Effect, where a butterfly's movements in Peking might transform a storm system in New York (Gleick, 1987).

In fact, large systems built up from even very simple elements, when they interact with each other, can produce a totality that is much greater than the sum of its parts—a complex global picture with its own emergent structure (Forrest, 1991a, 1991b; Waldrop, 1992). In a simple sandpile, each grain of sand reacts locally and predictably with its immediate neighbors, based on simple rules. Yet the whole pile has an overarching configuration, appearance, history, and also potential, which too can be described. Further, such large interactive systems tend to evolve toward a chaotic state (Bak & Chen,1991; Gleick, 1987). In the case of a tall sandpile, this may mean major collapse.

And does such complexity built from simple beginnings apply to human beings? According to Forrest (1991), for certain problems such as modeling intelligent behavior, "it may be the only feasible method" (Forrest, 1991, p. 1).

Consider some "simple" neural models (e.g., Forrest, 1991a, 1991b; Hoffman, 1987, Lumsden & Findlay, 1988, this volume; Waldrop, 1992). Various *nodes*, all interconnected, represent specific memories (e.g., Hoffman, 1987, as above) or mental schemata (e.g., Lumsden & Findlay, 1988). The connections become stronger or weaker, depending on whether they are used more or less. The system thereby learns—and certain mental roads, as it were, become wider and better traveled. With a large number of strong, varied, and creative links (e.g., the person who was thinking of "round things . . . a car . . . the earth . . . Wheel of Fortune . . . wheeling and dealing . . .," and so forth), a single added association could reverberate widely throughout an extended mental system.

The human intellect is even more complex than this. At minimum, the evolving creative mind should lend itself to a chaos analogy.

Creative versus not-so-creative processing. Consider information arriving anew at this creative mind. The process works from the ground up. The arrival of some pieces of information will scarcely be felt. A new fact, like a grain of sand, may fall on a sand dune, and shift a few particles locally around it. Perhaps an overinclusive mind will be a little more responsive; the sand may shift a little bit more. But the changes won't be great. Taking a few descriptive liberties, we can apply this to simple, and to not-so-simple, problem solving.

Say that a person sees a new sign: "You can't park your car here." Registering this fact may result in a small and local reshuffling of information, mediated by braking counterforces for accommodation of this new information with the old (even as Piaget said). What will this person do? Probably review the memory banks and substitute a new mental hierarchy of places to park.

Yet if this shifting of hierarchies is sudden, dramatic, unexpected, and involves many interrelated consequences, it may, as Holland and associates have suggested, feel like an "ah ha" experience (e.g., Waldrop, 1992).

In this case, a key new concept may trigger a major cascade of mental shifts and accommodations, leading to a whole new mental reorganization, a reframing of one's experience (see Richards 1996a, b). Intricate networks of thinking, of assumptions, of interdependent beliefs, are shaken and shifted al at once, falling into new and perhaps even awe-inspiring configurations. "Eureka! I've got it!" said Archimedes, leaping from the bath, instantaneously certain that a submerged body displaced its own volume. And what about possible world view shifts consistent with a quantum mechanical view of reality, rather than that of classical physics (e.g., Goswami, 1993; Richards, 1994a). This dramatic coevolution of ideas may be just what we experience with creative insight.

Creativity and the "edge of chaos." The chance of rich mental possibilities should be greater the closer one gets to the so-called edge of chaos—but also the risks of "overdoing it." The latter may be particularly important for bipolar persons.

Now we mix metaphors again, by bringing in the now-classic physical model for the edge-of-chaos phenomenon (Waldrop, 1992): the phase transition between ice (which is rigid, inflexible, fixed) and water (fluid, dynamic, perhaps even chaotically turbulent). At this thin but richly portentous border of the "almost frozen," a range of possible new configurations exists. As the temperature drops even one-thousandth of a degree, whole new worlds come into existence, sudden complex crystallizations of water-turned-ice. Yet these new patterns still connect integrally with the old.

One might compare these shifting, freezing, melting, and joining molecules of water with the conceptual nodes in the examples above. The issue is how free these mental nodes are to connect, reconnect, disconnect, and holistically reconfigure with webs and systems of others. There had better be a little "ice," or resistance, in this mental system, or one's past experience could be swept away. Where do you live? What's your phone number? Who knows?

But with too much rigidity, a person's *new* experience could be effectively finished. There would be nothing else that could be linked in. The evolving creative mind should balance successfully between a baseline of fixed or frozen areas of mental rigidity, and the chaotic currents of unstructured and unanchored thought—to leave plenty of latitude for the big creative leaps while not getting swept away by the turbulence.

A fast and flexible system.   This position fits well with the model for odor recognition and discrimination of Skarda and Freeman (1987; see also subsequent commentaries), based on EEG data from the olfactory bulb. Chaotic electrical behavior is seen as the essential ground state for this perceptual apparatus—a background activity which collapses to more simple "attractor" states around each of a number of focal stimuli or smells. If so, it may literally be part of our mental job—and our pleasure—to bring order out of chaos (see also Krippner, 1994, and Krystal & Krystal, 1994, for other biological examples).

Such a system is fast, efficient, flexible, ever ready. As one would expect at an edge-of-chaos, small input changes can yield big results. Here comes the smell of an orange? Or is it a lemon? A lime? Sorry, not exactly. It is time to carve out a whole new holistic connectionist electrical gestalt for *kumquats.* But this new response need not be an agonizing electrical and mental feat. The proposed chaotic ground state insures that one is habitually and regularly throwing all the mental chips up in the air to allow even more complex or varied means of "self-organization" to emerge, just in the normal course of things.

How close is "bipolar processing" to the edge-of-chaos?   People at risk for bipolar disorder may conceivably have greater access to such a mental "edge of chaos." This could involve both proposed *structural* and *dynamic* factors (See Matthysse, 1991; Richards, 1994b). For bipolar disorder, these may be roughly comparable to certain *trait* and *state* factors. The structural (trait) factors could involve the rich associative connections between networks of ideas or "nodes"—connections which make a range of specific associations more likely, but also allow these ideas to be "used" and their linkages to be further modified. ("Round things . . . car . . . earth . . . Wheel of Fortune . . . wheeling and dealing . . .")

Dynamic (state) factors, such as the manic "temperature" factor in Hoffman's (1987) neural net model, may specify, more globally, just how far afield within—or outside of—a meaningful matrix of ideas one might go (". . . Wheel of Fortune . . . wheeling and dealing . . . wheels within wheels . . . plots and counterplots . . . spies and double-agents . . . John LeCarre . . . Great Britain . . . Prince Charles . . . Princess Di . . ." and the manic may loose-associate out of context, and out into mental space).

Yet this is not at all to suggest a rigid associative template with some dynamic movement within it. As we saw with odor (Skarda & Freeman, 1989), a "fixed" percept (or concept) in memory may, show itself only as an evanescent trace of mental activity, arising out of the flickering background of a chaotic electrical pattern. Take again, the olfactory signature of the kumquat, its fragrance now discriminated from that of other citrus fruits. As such, its mental "reality" is not that of a concrete object or even a fixed word or symbol, but exists as a dynamic pattern of information in time and space. It too, we suggest, may undergo sequential deformation—be redefined, modified—by the very process which is using it. (No, concludes someone, a kumquat is not really as bitter, as I first thought.)

It makes sense that (to some extent) the structural factors, as well as the dynamic factors, be transformed together as part of an integral mental flux. These are holistically interdependent, and can reconfigure together as part of a total transformation of one's understanding. This is supported by Stuart Kauffman's (1991) modelling of adaptive biological evolution or learning in complex information processing systems, based on random Boolean networks. Kauffman put in requirements for both heritability and variability—that is, for stability and change.

Adaptive change due to one mutant variant or another depends on the "fitness landscapes" in which each is embedded. These landscapes (where a low point is the most adaptive point—somewhat similar to our previous "car" example) can be smooth or rugged, and with many or few frozen components. But the key point there is that in coevolving (interdependent) systems, the *fitness landscapes themselves deform due to coupling between coevolving partners.* That is, your evolution and mine are interdependent.

Kauffman went on to suggest that optimal coevolution might include fine tuning for emergence of some barely frozen components, potentially at that most fluid of boundaries, the edge-of-chaos. Now, be this new biological information, or, as we've stressed, new physiological insights, their coevolving power could be such as to recontextualize all structures far and wide in the particular universe of meaning from which they came.

Indeed—a creative success.

Yet a great deal of the charm of our individual creativity—at our own individual edges-of-chaos—lies in its unpredictability. If we start an avalanche of new ideas, we may do so off in our own corner; we may have no idea how things will end. Thus, a creative-chaotic process will not always be "right on target," producing just what a program requires. There may be surprises aplenty—often as useful as unexpected—but there may also be irrelevancies, errors, and foolish pronouncements. How could it be otherwise?

In other words, with near-chaotic phenomena, a wide range of possibilities may be inevitable, in order to make more likely the desired ones in the middle. At certain times, and for certain people (and not just for bipolar individuals), the expected diversity of response may predictably "go too far." One has heard the reactions before. Someone seems "out to lunch," "off the wall," even "out in orbit." Anywhere but where one expected. How we value this as part of a total creative process is an extremely important question.

How chaos may play out in "open" and "closed" minds.   First, the "open mind" may tolerantly and cheerfully accept some of this jumbled diversity, even "weirdness." It is overinclusive, and it's all part of the price and the picture. England may do this rather well at times compared to the U.S. According to a British born radio personality, "The U.K. encourages eccentricity in its citizens—always has—it's quite acceptable to be odd, different, slightly batty. Here in the U.S. we encourage people to be "regular"—just look at how many TV ads want people to be regular people, just like everyone else . . . in business, the most eccentric thing you can do as a man is to wear a bow tie, and that makes you suspect" (V. Jones, in Hirsch, 1993, p. 3).

In the creatively open mind, there may be significant ongoing evolutions of systems of information across many aspects of personality, albeit still in small fits and starts. In more closed minded individuals, there may be little movement, and many unwelcome additions that simply disappear from consciousness until that moment of crescendo when they can no longer be avoided. (Then one abrupt action or another may result.)

Who is apt to be open minded? Certainly persons with more complexly organized associative mental structures (the static quality), and the energizing potential to access these (a dynamic quality) (see Matthysse, 1991; Richards, 1994b; Simonton, 1988). These people will also have fewer mental blocks or defenses to inhibit such exploration, and a true pleasure in this organization. Involved is the "deferred gratification" to seek and maintain temporary states of uncertainty and disorder, toward an ultimate joyous resolution. This is a description of the creative person and the associated cognitive style of *integrative complexity* (e.g., Barron, 1963a, 1963b). It is also a description of a number of bipolar persons (Richards, 1993b, 1994b).

b. *"Cultural brainstorming" and evolutionary advantage*

Cultural brainstorming. Not everyone is "wild" or eccentric, and not everyone should be. In this context, we would emphasize a potential division of psychological labor into *senders* and *receivers*. This is related to Barron and Bradley's (this volume) position on the necessity of divergent positions—complexly innovative and more stably conservative—in social policy discussions.

Creative senders: The "far out" people who can "seed change." Certain persons, including persons at risk for bipolar disorders—and perhaps also persons with an uninhabited versus inhibited reaction to novelty, as studied by Kagan (1989), or who show higher levels of psychoticism as measured by Eysenck (this volume), are rewarded for filling a necessary *cognitive niche* (Tooby & DeVore, 1987), or societal role. They are also motivated. In one way or another, these individuals are not comfortable within themselves or with the world around them and want to do something (e.g., Flach, Gedo, Richards & Kinney, Pennebaker et al., all this volume; Gruber, this volume; Richards, 1993, 1994; Runco, 1994). Some should represent the key individuals noted by Hausman (this volume) who initiate innovation, and who carry the initial responsibility for doing so. This initiator role involves the generation of new information or memes for the rest of society then to contemplate. These are the people who speak out, wake us up, and who "seed change."

Yet these persons will likely not have the final say. Society has a range of braking counterforces to select, modify, transmit, or just plain discard new information (e.g., Csikzentmihalyi, 1988; Feldman, this volume; Ludwig, 1992b; Richards, 1990)—and these operate at intermediate levels of domain and field of endeavor, as well as at the level of whole society (see Feldman, this volume). Stories reported, books published, papers read, pictures hung, compositions performed, complaints registered, votes counted. Certain bits of raw information, in addition, will be intrinsically more useful than others. For a healthy society, however, a significant ongoing "circulation" of new memes may be necessary.

Conventional brainstorming (Osborn, 1963) involves people or groups generating a wide range of ideas, including some very wild ones—indeed one cardinal rule is that "anything goes"—and judgment is deferred until later. By analogy, we propose the process of *cultural brainstorming* at a higher level of organization. A subset of the population generates all manner and sort of ideas. Some are useful and some are impossible. The major judgments are meanwhile deferred, at least in a whole-society sense. Subsequently, other parts of the population work to sort these ideas out, to decide which are the most useful in a given situation. Of course, they won't always be right.

Creative receivers: Some people don't want to hear the message. With creative ideas, reception is far from guaranteed, as Kuhn (1970) indicated in *The Structure of Scientific Revolutions*. One revolutionizing insight: "The sun, not the earth, is the center of the universe." This was Copernicus' heliocentric theory, and it had profound scientific, religious, and philosophical implications. The process of discovery can be pleasant for the creator (sometimes), but it may not be welcome at all to certain consumers. The psychoeconomic costs (e.g., Rubenson, this volume; Rubenson & Runco, 1992) may be too high. Consider the citizens who locked Galileo up for advocating the heliocentric view and related notions—persons who weren't ready for a mental avalanche of ideas for which they were unprepared and which they could not control. They preferred to deny, suppress, or avoid the information, and instead tried Galileo for heresy (Redondi, 1987).

Speeding up the reception of new ideas.   How can we make a society more open minded to new ideas? (see Gruber, 1989, this volume; Ludwig, 1992b; Lumsden & Findlay, 1988; Simonton, 1984, 1988, this volume). Perhaps, among other things, by insuring a certain critical mass of creativity processing persons at the everyday level—persons who receive, enjoy, transform, and integrate those new memes or creative insights they run into. In psychoeconomic terms, this could change the *demand* for creativity (Rubenson, this volume; Rubenson & Runco, 1992).

The schools can be a big help here—we're now talking creative styles and values (see Haste, 1993; Kreisberg, 1992). These creatively open people could help seed change at the level of reception, facilitating the major conceptual shifts that help bring about the societal changes of true innovation. The great many individuals at risk for bipolar mood disorders could certainly help fulfill such a role. Stein (this volume) goes further, indicating that we all have a special responsibility to participate in the social creative process, either as contributors or appreciators (Stein combines these in the term *contricipates*), and to help insure it remains healthy, open, and evolving.

Indeed, we need this process. If modern society is to change even faster—for some badly needed memetic evolution—then society should be seeded with a greater number of these creative change agents, both the senders and the receivers. The goal is more flexible, productive, risk-taking age—and there are certainly historical examples of Golden Ages for creativity in the past (Richards, 1990). Happily such transforming creative attitudes and methods can be taught. This should perhaps be a key aspect of what Ornstein and Ehrlich (1989) have called our *conscious evolution*.

Where's the genetic evolutionary advantage? Assuming these informa-tional phenomena are valid, does a genetic (reproductive) evolutionary advantage become clear, a survival edge that could maintain the gene(s) for bipolar disorders in the population down through the generations? After all, wouldn't one expect genotype to interact with this mimetic di-versity, to produce more viable phenotypes? (e.g., Lumsden & Findlay, this volume; Tooby & DeVore, 1987). Not necessarily—or at least not ex-clusively. The potential mechanisms are still many, and they may all be true at once.

Candidates for an evolutionary "edge" involve everyday creativity. Perhaps the advantage is not creativity at all, but, for example, the hypersexuality that can be found with bipolar disorders themselves. Creativity, the so-called compensatory advantage, could merely be a byproduct or an epiphenomenon. In whatever case, the evolutionary edge is likely to be a grass-roots matter, operating on the level of the everyday person. A few outstanding creative writers, however reproductively active they may be, just aren't going to make the difference (Richards, 1993b, 1994b).

Other possibilities for a reproductive advantage, found in connection with a personal/family history of bipolar disorders (e.g., Goodwin & Jamison, 1990) include personal appeal, leadership qualities, and in-creased socioeconomic status. Creativity could also play an indirect role as a health-producing activity—a bit like cardiovascular exercise—yield-ing more vigorous, in-control, and immune competent people. There is indeed some evidence consistent with this (e.g., Locke & Colligan, 1986; Pennebaker, Kiecolt-Glaser, & Glaser, this volume, 1988; Ornstein & Swencionis, 1990; Peterson & Bossio, 1991; Richards, 1990). Perhaps such people might also have higher fertility or reproductive success. This whole area badly needs study.

One evolutionary advantage: Filling a needed cognitive niche. The main hy-pothesis here has already been mentioned (but is not to exclude the oth-ers). I propose, based on the notion of *cultural brainstorming*, that persons at bipolar risk fill specific "cognitive niches" (Tooby & DeVore, 1987) and are rewarded by society for this. These are the colorful folks who can seed change at both the everyday and eminent levels—they propose, they argue, they try out the new, they export it to others. If society wants this, these creators may attain recognition, socioeconomic status, perhaps sex-ual appeal, and also the means to raise a family.

But if society has had too much, then some of these same people may perhaps be scorned, they'll be the ones who go too far, who are odd, ab-normal, and misfit, who should toe the line, behave in class, and con-tribute to society "like everybody else."

What is therefore proposed with the notion of cultural brainstorming is an open changing metabolism of novelty and reactive forces, in unstable equilibrium—and one which, at various times and in varying degrees, approaches the edge of chaos. But in this case, the process of challenging and responding, of creative mental evolution, takes place at the *interpersonal* rather than the *intrapersonal* level.

B. ILLUSTRATION TWO
SOCIAL LEVEL: CULTURAL DIVERSITY AND PRESERVATION

1. Example: The Disappearing Playwright—Aphra Behn

Dale Spender (1982) wondered why so many female thinkers have virtually "disappeared" from conventional historical records over the centuries, and in an 800 page documented book, she resuscitates a large number of these. Included is Aphra Behn, a highly popular playwright, as well as novelist, poet, adventuress, activist, abolitionist, feminist, and friend of John Dryden's in Restoration England, and who is buried not too far from Dryden, in Westminster Abbey. In a London that had only two theaters, Aphra Behn had 17 plays produced in 17 years. She also wrote thirteen novels. Spender wondered if Behn's typical outspoken advocacy from a woman's point of view, in plays like *The Forced Marriage*, had something to do with her relative disappearance.

2. Model: Maladapted Genotypes and Threatened "Extinction" of Memes

As once occurred with the dinosaurs, may we—with all our sophisticated wisdom—be losing a foothold on environmental conditions we need for survival? Here is proposed both an antiquated genetic program, and, partly in response to this, the equivalent of "diseases" among collections of memes. At issue is the loss, or retarded or distorted growth in our dominant culture of parts of certain domains of knowledge (e.g., history or literature). At worst, major meme-complexes could become "extinct." Malcolm X (1964) addressed this possibility with outrage, when he charged Toynbee with minimizing the contributions of Africa to mainstream history.

3. Pathology: Behaviors and Biases from an Earlier Environment of Evolution

At best, the richness of multiple cultures and viewpoints provides us a diversity of ideas, stories, sounds, visions, cultures, myths, remedies, traditions—gives us multiple memes to select from—and at a higher level of human organization than in the previous example of conceptual overinclusion. These are social experiments that have worked, at least in some context or setting, and have gone through their own mini-chaotic reactions to novelty, and had the rough edges removed. A certain amount of interchange and jostling among cultures and subcultures can broaden every one of us. When recast as political fragmentation, this diversity has proven to be a societal condition for increased creativity (Simonton, this volume).

a. Neglected, fragmented, and misinterpreted data

Yet, at times, we draw with great difficulty from the rich and varied sources around us. There is the isolation of geography and language, and unsuspected prejudices we may unknowingly assume from authority figures (consider the neglected wisdom of certain medical treatments considered unconventional in our society (Eisenberg, 1992), or, indeed, Spender's (1982) arguments about women intellectuals).

In addition, false dichotomies between fields (e.g., the current devaluation of the arts in an increasingly scientific society) or the language of feelings versus the language of logic, limit our potential to adapt to our world, and to accept all parts of ourselves and others (Richards, 1991, 1993a).

b. Forms of prehistoric bias

These problems, obviously, have complex environmental and genetic sources. Yet one worrisome genetic source derives from our evolutionary past, from our once necessary identification with small groups of kin or associates, in highly role-structured hunter–gatherer "bands." As strong as ties within the group could be, too, was the uneasiness felt about "strangers" from without (e.g., Glantz & Pearce, 1989; Tooby & DeVore, 1987; Wilson, 1993).

Today too, it is sometimes hard to think outside our accustomed roles or reference groups. Yet the ancient programming that still has us searching for our in-group, while nursing our xenophobia, will not lead us well into the global information age, or help us solve problems requiring global cooperation. We are left instead with the legacy of weapons—developed to defend against that ever-present stranger—that could easily destroy us all (Barron & Bradley, this volume; Gruber, this volume; Lifton & Markusen, 1989; Richards, 1993a).

Creative response is what's needed here now (Gruber, 1993; Richards, 1993a). Our genes can't fix this problem—they can't change fast enough. It is up to the memes, up to what Ornstein and Ehrlich (1989) have called, in their book entitled *New World, New Mind* our *conscious evolution.*

4. Benefits: Learning from Diversity and Evolving More Consciously

a. Political fragmentation as a model

Consider some consequences when we learn from diverse perspectives. In Simonton's (this volume) historiographic research on political fragmentation (as found with independent nation states in the ancient world), growth could occur from peaceful juxtapositions, but not if the picture included devastating war or internal anarchy (with overwhelming external threat or internal chaos). We might find a loose parallel to a compensatory advantage within the range of possible political disruptions, loosely comparable to the example with bipolar disorders. For enhanced creativity, political fragmentation can create some social disorder, but not too much, while keeping the strengths of the organism intact.

b. Early exposure to diversity can pay off later

Ideological diversity seems especially affected by political fragmentation—yet this occurs with a generational lag. Simonton (this volume) suggests these political events may be key environmental variables during the developing years. Stariha and Walberg (this volume) elaborate some potential early effects on learning, expectations, and motivations.

One may add to this, from the chaos and complexity perspectives (Gleick, 1987; Waldrop, 1992; Richards, 1996b), that a child might develop a richer mental connectivity, more fluid habits of movement within one's mind (static and dynamic factors), and fewer "frozen" mental areas of the in-group, out-group type (the in-group is right, the out-group is wrong) with the rich early exposure. This is consistent as well with the creative style of integrative complexity (Barron & Bradley, Richards, 1990, 1994b; Simonton, 1997, this volume). Conditions for creativity can come close to the edge of chaos.

In addition, Simonton (this volume) suggested that rich cultural diversity along with a localization of politics may nurture an internal locus of control, supporting greater creative initiative. This might be called the resilient position (e.g., Garmezy & Rutter, 1983; Richards, 1990; Gedo, Flach, both this volume), extended here to the societal level. This also fits at a cultural level with the flexibility and freedom of highly adaptable families of creative children (Gardner & Moran, this volume). And there is lowered arousal with political fragmentation; this is important for creativity (see Martindale, Simonton, both this volume), and is the opposite of the hyperarousal of international war. It seems appropriate that a personal creativity may result from conditions enhancing societal possibilities.

5. Reducing Our Costs: Attitude Change and Diversity of Resources

Rapid global access in the new information age—worldwide computer networks, data superhighways, and indeed the increased "externalizing" (Donald, 1990) of our own memories and thoughts, as we link more continuously into external data sources—will make huge quantities of data available (Dertouzos, 1992), and eliminate many barriers to other cultures. We are already seeing new "electronic tribes" (consider America On Line) that can make physical distance all but irrelevant. In addition there will be proliferation of cable channels, and interactive networks for special interests of all sorts (e.g., Kantrowitz & Ramo, 1993).

These issues may be compared to those in respecting and preserving biodiversity. Yet appreciating the richness of human knowledge and expression, including its multicultural sources, is not merely a matter of more and more information accrued, and arrayed in a row. An integrated valuing of the range of human experience is central, and this will require attitude change, in the schools, in families, in social institutions. Acknowledgement that "there are many ways to live," "there is no one right answer," "there is cooperation as well as competition," that "everything is interconnected," that "process is at least as important as outcome," will all be a part of this. Integrative complexity (Barron, 1963; Barron & Bradley, 1990; Richards, 1990, 1994b)—or the stylistic drive for complex integration of information—will be one essential quality.

6. Creativity and The Evolution of Information—and Ourselves

Our genetic, as well as memetic, survival is increased when we avail ourselves of the huge and richly elaborated libraries of human experience—and when we refuse to be burdened by "false memes" (or errors). If we honor personally a broader range of possibilities than we could ever conceivably even know or master, the ones we hope will be there, one day, will still exist. There is a parallel with species extinction, for we, in our shortsightedness, may well extinguish one-fifth of the species on this earth by the end of this century (Brown et al., 1991). Our conscious evolution needs to address the preservation of our heritage(s) as part of the preservation of ourselves.

C. ILLUSTRATION THREE
INDIVIDUAL LEVEL: CONFRONTING PERSONAL ADVERSITY

1. Example: Overcoming Personal Problems—Author, John Cheever

John Cheever was a son of alcoholic parents and himself suffered from alcoholism and depression. As a boy, he was expelled from prep school because of poor grades, and he never went to college. Yet even with his expulsion, Cheever was able to mold this into a successful short story—about an arbitrary dismissal for smoking a cigarette. It has been said that Cheever's writing helped him order a chaotic life and compensate for feelings of weakness and loss. His writing may also have provided at least one way Cheever could get his parents to listen to him. Indeed, a great many other people listened to this writer as well. John Cheever ultimately wrote more than 300 short stories and novels, and received numerous honors including the National Book Award and the Pulitzer Prize. (See Ludwig, 1990; Rothenberg, this volume.)

2. Model: Acquired Immunity and Coping with Psychological Stress

We turn to benefits from coping successfully with personal adversity. The biological model involves acquired immunity, through which an individual develops immune response to various threatening organisms and antigens.

The hypothesis here involves a form of psychic immunity, a creative stress-resistance developed under fire. The proposed benefits involve one's style of information processing—the integration and courageous use of one's experience. Freud (1908, 1920) was the prime advocate of creative transformation of internal, unconscious conflict. It is suggested that the historical decision to confront, rather than avoid, various internal or external adversities, when followed by successful results, can result in increased ability and motivation for a courageously confrontative and effectively integrated future response. Persons at risk for bipolar disorder may have particular opportunity for such confrontation. Yet, the difficulty is that many may be vanquished for the few that survive (see Richards, 1994b).

3. Pathology: Potential Adjustment Difficulties in Face of Adversity

It surely can't be an accident that, in one study of 400 eminent 20th century individuals, three-quarters had troubled beginnings (Goertzels & Goertzels, 1962). Many eminent creative persons have dealt with early adversities, including troubled childhoods, poverty, parental illness, traumatic loss, physical disability, or mental illness (Albert, 1971, 1983; Albert & Runco, 1986; Andreasen, 1987; Gedo, this volume; Goertzel & Goertzel, 1962; Ludwig, 1992; Ostwald, 1991; Richards, 1993b; Roe, 1963; Sandblom, 1989; Simonton, 1984, 1989). They have emerged competent and resilient, at least in the area of work performance.

Take as examples: (a) persons with bipolar mood disorders, and (b) survivors of trauma. Results could conceivably apply to many others facing unexpected and emotionally charged shifts, stresses, and challenges, coming from without as well as within (Richards, 1993a). This certainly includes the experience of having a depressed or bipolar parent. Mood disordered individuals can expedience sudden and unexpected shifts of mood that can disrupt their very sense of self, integrity, stability, and connection with others and their environment. Unlike some people, who can shut off bad moods or experiences and move on to something else, these people may find the shifts inescapable.

a. Achieving "affective integration"

Among other personal, interpersonal, and situational strengths that help people cope (e.g., Garmezy & Rutter, 1983; Rolf et al., 1990), I turn to different means people have for handling emotions, and once again to the example of bipolar mood disorders. Consider first how one creative actor establishes a mood:

> You start with something peripheral—the room, the smell, it's grandmother's house, and it always had a smell—bread or whatever. If you don't push, that smell will lead to something else—and something else. But you do it gently—and it all starts connecting. Use the senses, the color of the room, a little chain reaction—you get into that—and (then) you speak the lines. (see Richards, 1994b)

b. Ways we avoid affective integration

This fluid movement between different emotional states is neither easy nor common. Many people, in fact, have strong forces working against it. Their thoughts flow along more homogeneously in mood-congruent channels, as opposed to skipping readily from one affect to another (see Blaney, 1986; Bower, 1981; Richards, 1994a).

In addition, this flow is guided by principles of positive mood maintenance and negative mood repair. People tend to try to hold onto a good mood ("what a nice day," "everything's looking good," "I remember last year at the beach . . ." and to banish a bad one ("forget it!" "I'm not going to think about that"). (Isen, 1984, 1985; Richards, in 1994a). Whole areas of experience get emphasized and deemphasized, if not banished altogether. This might be said to create a certain amount of mood-linked dissociation.

These forces can limit the rich associative mental networks (e.g., Simonton, 1989) that favor creativity. Paradoxically, mood factors may also damp the motivation for creativity. Isen et al. (1988) have shown that mood elevation tends to lower willingness to take risks. As the saying goes, "Why take a chance with a good thing?" I suggest this creates a negative feedback loop that seems designed to discourage creativity (Richards, 1994b)!

4. Potential Benefits: Affective Integration Fueled by Creative Courage

a. Situations where affective integration may be favored

By contrast, persons experiencing bipolar mood swings beyond their control cold conceivably develop a qualitatively different mental organization. Through contiguity and sequential anticipation of swings between mood elevations and depressions, they could develop a more affectively integrated and complex mental organization (Richards, 1993a, 1994b).

The "flight from depression" may actually mix mood states. Of particular interest is mania, which has classically been described as "a flight from depression" (Eaton & Peterson, 1969). Hypomania too may have this quality. As one patient said, "I have felt infinitely worse, more dangerously depressed, when manic than when in the midst of my worst depressions" (Jamison, 1990, p. 27).

Whether or not such a manic defense actually succeeds, the alternation of mood states may also forge *directional* links between these affective conditions, that is, create associative pathways between diverse mood-linked schemas in memory storage. These could work against the more usual principles of mood-maintenance and mood-repair (see Richards, 1994b).

Action may seem the best response. Indeed, the bipolar person suspects that good moods won't last anyway, but neither will depressed moods. And it is in action, not inaction, that relief from depression may seem most available. This more resilient response might occur, especially for individuals with other personal strengths to support the effort, including intelligence, personal supports, and adequate ego-controls (Albert & Runco, 1986; Barron, 1969; Garmezy & Rutter, 1983; Jordan, 1990, 1992; Richards, 1994b). They could develop the ongoing stylistic conviction that negative material could be used toward positive purposeful ends (Blaney, 1986). Additionally, negative material could increasingly come to evoke positive affect, derived from the success of mastery (Krystal, 1981). On a neurological level, one is reminded again of the integrated hemispheric potential discussed by Hoppe and Kyle (this volume).

Thus, success could result from confronting and transforming the negative affect, rather than from banishing it. Lasting results could include a more complex cognitive organization, increasing creative capacity, through richer associative pathways between affectively charged material, and with greater confidence about, and motivation for, facing difficulties directly, in creative confrontation. Each subsequent success would build this capacity even further (Richards, 1993a, 1994b).

But the problem is, once again, the number that are vanquished by these events, for the few that survive.

Recovery from trauma involves courageous confrontation and integration. This process of mastery may also be applied to the treatment of psychological trauma. Yet trauma, in the form of early sexual or physical abuse of a vulnerable, trusting child, can leave in its wake major psychological and physical damage that may be altered only gradually and with difficulty (e.g., Peterson et al., 1991). In the current framework, such trauma represents the full-blown and devastating disease, rather than a more benign immunization against adversity and stress.

As the mind of the trauma survivor struggles somehow to cope with the inexcusable, it may alternate between periods of emotional numbing, with cognitive and affective distancing, and frank amnesia, and periods of intrusive and lifelike recollection with intense and overwhelming affect. Treatment of trauma can certainly change lives, and improvement can be dramatic, but progress often can be slow, and effects of that overwhelming experience hard to fully eradicate.

Notably, Horowitz's (1988) model for treating post-traumatic stress disorder (see also Peterson, Prout, & Schwarz, 1991) is directed precisely at the resolution of such "incomplete information processing." Success involves forging links between diverse cognitions and affects that may have been banished completely from consciousness, or dissociated from each other.

Rather paradoxically, we suggest the divisions and distortions of consciousness borne of trauma may, in certain cases—with a courageous processing of one's experience—serve not only to treat the trauma but even to reverse some of the "normal" fragmentation of consciousness due to the principles of mood maintenance and mood repair. In certain areas of experience, at least, a particular mental openness and creative flexibility may result. This could enhance creative courage and resilience, and could be a very hope-producing outcome indeed in the treatment of trauma.

5. Reducing Our Costs: A Learning Process of Stress Resistance and Creative Coping

Must one endure, and integrate, painful early experiences to have creative courage? Must one have a severe mood disorder and somehow live with it? No indeed. There are a range of alternatives between forced traumatic experience and sugar-coating the world. Life involves problems, and the solutions isn't to pretend that these don't exist. As we've said, one can treat the mood disorder. As for stress, one needn't erase it with high doses of positive mood maintenance but, rather, can learn to deal with it in measurable amounts.

a. Smaller successes in childhood

A child can be exposed advisedly to certain realities, and at the same time be taught to cope, through small creative steps, encouraging a more resilient, effective, and self-confident style. Risks can be taken when there's a good chance of success, both on the personal level (e.g., facing fears of the dark, jealousy of a sibling, parents' arguing) through games, question-and-answer sessions, drawings—fairy tales can also do this more passively, and on the social level (hunger, poverty, environmental deterioration) through concrete actions, including food collections, letters, student recycling programs. A sense of empowerment can also be built through group action.

A child can learn that there are problems, but that they can also be faced, made concrete and less frightening, and then manipulated creatively—and that it can feel very good to do so (Berman, 1991; Haste, 1993; Kohn, 1990; Kreisberg, 1992; Richards, 1993a). Furthermore, this child can become one of many who succeed. Very few need be left at the wayside.

b. The family as a training ground

The family is an important training ground indeed. It is seems significant that families of creative people—while more open and accepting of children's individuality (e.g., Gardner & Moran, this volume)—may also tend to be less harmonious interpersonally, with parents more capable of living with and expressing tension (e.g., Albert, 1971; Albert & Runco, 1986; Richards, 1981, 1990). A young person may therefore come to expect, and expect to deal with, such "complexities" (Albert, 1971), including realities that aren't always pretty. At times, this could be a mood-disordered family, where biologically influenced tensions and instabilities will resonate across the generations, along with, hopefully, some creative advantages for coping. This is a potentially complex sort of genotype–environment interaction (Richards, 1990).

But, again, one might think there could be better ways of building in this creative flexibility and coping capacity than letting it occur by default through dissent and family conflict. And once again, not all children will prevail.

c. The school as a training ground

The school can have a central role in helping children deal with conflict and adversity (e.g., Berman, 1991; Haste, 1993; Kreisberg, 1992). Consider two nine year olds. One grabs the other's bike without asking. The second hurls abusive names. "You jerk, you thief, you creep . . ." and so on. An adult can just separate them. But what if, instead, the children are helped directly to air their differences, work out their own alternative solutions, and perhaps more generally address such conflicts later through techniques including active listening and role-playing. They are able to feel heard, understood, more empathetic for the other, and can gain a sense of alternatives. They can also lay groundwork for future conflict resolution and cooperative problem-solving.

For both children and adults, programs like Stress Inoculation Training (Peterson, Prout, & Schwarz, 1991) provide another type of route to responsible coping, particularly when danger is real. Students learn and practice skills to conceptualize and respond to stress, taking steps that increase in difficulty. Poignantly, this program was used to help children in a wartime situation prepare for possible shelling raids. When an ultrasonic boom sent the school into the air raid shelter, other children panicked, but these children remained calm and organized.

d. Lifespan issues—psychological and physical health

Though never easy, it still may be somewhat simpler for a highly creative person to get old, to get sick, and even to face the inevitability of dying. In Smith and van der Meer's study (this volume), older people with higher creativity were less negative and defensive about aging, and also more flexible and emotional. This is very much reminiscent of qualities of children described by Dudek and Verrault (this volume). A key aspect could once again be "facing it." This may involve the empowerment and imagination to sense alternatives, but also the wisdom to respect and accept—as one may learn to do with one's own elusive creative mind—those grater forces which cannot be altered.

Indeed a great many healthy strengths may derive from a creative orientation, at any point in the life cycle. Cropley (this volume), a long-standing proponent of everyday creativity as an aspect of cognitive style, noted a range of personal qualities, such as openness, autonomy, playfulness, flexibility,risk-taking, perseverance, and humor, which are not only prerequisites for everyday creativity, but may equally be viewed as aspects of positive mental health. He suggested these are so intertwined that enhancing creativity should at once enhance personal well-being.

Integrated and harmonious function is underscored by Hoppe and Kyle's (this volume) descriptions of pathology when whole-brain integration through the corpus callosum is lacking. Contrast the complex and fruitful integrations of left- and right-brain function proposed in creativity as part of *hemispheric bisociation.* It is perhaps not surprising that creative activity (or the initiative, courage, optimism, or empowerment involved in the conviction that one can affect a circumstance creatively), may predict directly for improved physical as well as psychological health (see Langer, 1989; Locke & Colligan, 1986; Peterson & Bossio, 1991; Richards, 1990). The research that follows is particularly compelling.

e. But why not run away if one can?

Be there any doubt about the healthy effects of creative confrontation, consider a study (Pennebaker, Kiecolt-Glåser & Glaser, this volume) in which college students were asked to write creatively about some of their most traumatic experiences, ones they had discussed very little with anyone. Each writing session was only 20 minutes long. Meanwhile, a control group wrote about something more neutral. After only four days, not only did the first group end up feeling better psychologically, but showed evidence of stronger immune system function. Persons in this and two other samples also showed fewer subsequent outpatient medical visits than controls (Pennebaker, Kiecolt-Glaser & Glaser, 1988). Creative confrontation thus appears physically as well as psychologically healthier.

Why might this be? One woman who had been sexually abused as a child wrote first about her embarrassment and guilt. But with time, this turned into anger at her victimization, and finally yielded a broader perspective. "Before ... I'd lie to myself. ... Now I don't feel like I even have to think about it because I got it off my chest." (Pennebaker et al., this volume p. 300) This woman saved valuable psychic energy for a better purpose. She also built confidence, mastery, and coping skills that would help immunize her, psychologically as well as physically, against future adversity.

f. Will one naturally move toward self-actualization?

There are unending examples of creativity abused or misapplied—the ingenuity of the professional drug deal, the gang member planning a drive-by shooting, a tyrant conducting assassinations out of fear and insecurity, rather than face deeper issues within the self. There is no guarantee that creativity—any more than intelligence—will always be used to others' benefit, or will lead to personal growth and development (McLaren, 1993; Richards, 1993a; Runco et al., this volume).

Yet how hopeful indeed if such growth still tends to occur, on the average. If creativity, as an adaptive force, tends naturally to evolve in its purpose and motivation—growth, if you will—in the evolution of information through the self-actualization of individuals!

Rhodes (this volume) helps us visualize a potential movement of creative purpose from deficiency needs to self-actualization. Gedo (this volume), at one level, provides stirring evidence of "the healing power of art," based on the life of John Ensor. Expression was able to contain, reorganize, and give meaning to highly disruptive experience. Indeed, severe stress can be disorganizing; yet Flach (this volume) points out that just about any change or challenge can cause us—in our best moments—to reshuffle and reorganize a range of psychic structures. This is normal, healthy, and at best leads to great personal growth. *Resilience* or "the transit of stress-induced episodes of disorganization," is the key. Failures in this disruption–reintegration process can lead to varied forms of pathology.

One might compare the earlier analogy, from chaos theory, of how the arrival of new ideas might play out in open and closed minds. This includes the potential for widespread and frequent reverberations through rich creative connections, on the one hand—with a more integral and on-going series of reorganizations—and for rigidity and ultimate cataclysmic collapse on the other. (The first instance may be likened to the gradual shifting of land masses along the evolving contours of the earth's surface; the second is a devastating earthquake.)

How does creativity move from "deficiency" to "being" motives? Perhaps organically, in the absence of certain blocks. Rhodes (this volume) suggests, based on Maslow's needs hierarchy, that meeting deficiency needs (including love, acceptance, and self-acceptance) through creative work can also bring—and can teach—higher levels of intrinsic motivation and satisfaction through broader contributions that transcend these immediate ends. She cites the case of John Cheever, as described by Rothenberg (this volume) who, as a child, "felt helpless and unable to communicate with (his parents). . . . His turning to writing seemed to serve as a way to bring order into a chaotic, disorganized experience . . . a way to get his parents to hear him. . . . a means of compensating for his own feelings of weakness and loss (p. 91). From this child came the distinguished writer who gave so much to humanity.

Appearing almost as a happy epiphenomenon at first, the developing creator finds a new power to affect the external environment, and new joys in the creative process. Yet this discovery is driven, in the theory, not by chance, but by a fundamental need to become self-actualized, or to "become one's potentialities" (see Runco et al., this volume).

How commonly does this actually happen—that creative activity almost recursively generates greater personal and creative growth? If everyday creativity truly functions as an adaptive quality of evolutionary significance, one might hope this would occur frequently. However, there is a paucity of empirical research on connections between creativity and qualities of self-actualization. Furthermore, results are mixed and raise methodological questions (Runco et al., this volume). A subsequent study by Runco et al. (this volume) does show positive, if modest, correlations between aspects of creative personality and a measure of self-actualization. Although causality cannot be inferred, this finding is surely good news. We can at least hope that, with the right interventions and opportunities, such an association could be stronger yet.

g. Creative strengths for facing the future—Children and adults

Perhaps there are additional ways in which creativity points (in many instances) in prosocial directions. Dudek and Verrault (this volume) found that children who are creative are able to use richer primary process thinking, use more of it, and do so more effectively—through better use of regression in the service of the ego. Very interestingly, they also found a greater relative focus on libidinal than aggressive content.

How happy indeed if creativity not only enriches experience and possibilities, but inherently leads to more peaceful orientations. As the slogan from the 1960s goes, "Make love not war." Certainly, more alternatives can be seen by the more creative mind.

There are related results at the adult level. Barron and Bradley (this volume) found that traits such as originality, independence of judgment, internationalism, and trust in human nature were linked with a profreeze rather than probuild-up position on the Nuclear Arms Reduction Scale. The point here is not that creativity will bring one automatically and unerringly toward a particular social policy position. Most certainly not—and especially if diversity of viewpoint and of problem solving options are one's objective. The authors, who also found complexity of outlook correlated with this mix, were definite on this point. It is the openness of process, guided by the style of "integrative complexity" or the complex integration of information, that gives one the most hope for adapting to an unknown future. Related to what we have called "cultural brainstorming," Barron and Bradley (this volume) touted the virtues of also having the ordered, stable, conservative, and traditional modes of thought represented in a useful dialectic. There can, indeed, be many sides to a question.

h. Working together, and creative altruism

Creative altruism, what is that? Something for a few "selfless" people who are also capable of great amounts of pain and self-sacrifice? Something (unlike its name) that is really quite rigid and uncreative, dogmatic and guilt-producing? Altruism and moral creativity are burdened by such misleading stereotypes. (See Eysenck, 1993; Runco, 1993, for contrasting views). More likely, though, creative altruism is a process with which we all have some familiarity, as in, for instance, seeking ways to help a child, a friend, a spouse, a neighbor, at a difficult time.

If altruism is "one self helping another without consideration of personal gain" (Kohn, 1990 p. 266), then Gruber's (this volume) view calls on us to donate in addition exceptional intelligence, vision, and risk-taking to our efforts in order to challenge a status quo. This form of creativity can be the most demanding, Gruber tells us, but it can also lead to exceptional joy.

Significantly, the experience of joy does not preserve a subject-object distinction (Krishnamurti, 1969), and surely does not pit one person (or outcome) against another. Once again, this seems a sensible way for evolution to have designed it.

But will creative people tend to be more caring and giving? One might argue this, at least if personal growth and self-actualization can be results (see above). Yet the question is more complicated (see Richards, 1993a).

Consider, for instance, the creative terrorist. Or the all-too-creative white-collar criminal. Nonetheless, when creativity is turned to altruistic ends, it can be powerful indeed.

How "it feels" to do so may be critical indeed. Consider a Kantian view. "(If one acts) only from duty and without any inclination," says Kant, "then for the first time his action has genuine moral worth" (Kohn, 1990, p. 257). If it doesn't feel good, that is when it will really count, according to Kant. One is (or is not) self-sacrificing.

Along these lines, some popular game theories carry the assumption that we would not help our neighbor unless there were something in it for us. This is a self-serving, and adversarial position. Consider the Prisoner's Dilemma—You and your cohort are being questioned separately. Do you defect, or do you keep silent? A highly effective strategy in certain computer simulations has been the simple "Tit for Tat," AKA (either way) "Do unto others . . ." (see Barlow, 1991). One starts with a cooperative choice, and thereafter does what the other person does. One may ultimately cooperate because one can personally do better that way. There is now more going on than in a *zero-sum* game—you win, I lose.

Such decisions can become more complex, weighing in factors such as group size and length of outlook. (Things can be different if one must live with the outcomes in one's particular reference group over the long run). In hierarchical organizations, changes are sometimes particularly effective in the smallest units at the bottom, and can even lead to a happy escalation of cooperativeness; indeed there is an edge-of-chaos feeling to the possibility. Social systems analysts Glance and Huberman (1994) consider the unification of Germany or the breakdown of the Soviet Union as potential examples. ". . . cooperative behavior can indeed arise spontaneously in social settings, provided that the groups are small and diverse in composition and that their constituents have long outlooks. Even more significantly, when cooperation does appear, it does so suddenly and unpredictably after a long period of stasis" (p. 81).

But now, at what point might one move beyond an adversarial position, whether between individuals or groups. Or move beyond an ability to feel pleasure only if one's own individual (or group) situation is somehow bettered. Gruber (this volume) had to *stop* people from cooperating in his Shadow Box experiments. People viewing a boxed and shadowed object from different perspectives were desperately eager to share their unique viewpoints, and to put their common heads together.

The *process* of helping can feel good in itself, for instance, where a common goal is being achieved by people working together. The pleasure may indeed become focused almost on a disembodied goal, looming large above and bathed in feelings of accomplishment. The pleasure may become all the stronger where there is *empathy* for others, so that one's pleasure becomes mutually amplified and enhanced. Gruber (this volume) stresses the key role played by empathetic responsiveness in creative altruism.

Indeed, when helping behavior is based in empathetic caring—now going beyond Kantian principle, as a basis for morality, as one finds in relational theories of development (Gilligan, 1982; Jordan, 1991; Kohn, 1990)—it can produce fundamental satisfactions which can be described as existing "beyond altruism" (Kohn, 1990). This is akin to the feeling one can get from helping a child, a friend, a lover, taken to a higher level of generality, and even universality (Kohn, 1990; Richards, 1993a), as one human being helps another like oneself. It also reflects the vanishing difference between self-interest and human interest in the world today (Gruber, this volume).

While one can hope for this, we still have a great deal to do. A wide range of "mimetic" limitations (or "diseases") continue to obstruct us, and to challenge our *conscious evolution*.

But we've still got a lot to do. A whole new range of mimetic limitations (or diseases) still arise to obstruct us, and to challenge our conscious evolution.

6. Creativity and the Evolution of Information: Seeding Change

Progress involves overcoming difficulties. But these must first be seen, named, and accepted as part of our reality. In a rapidly changing world, we will have more of these conflictual memes to integrate into our awareness, in all of their emotional and intellectual complexity, if we're to cope and remain healthy as individuals and citizens. As things stand now, certain persons with problems are most apt to be forced into this creative awareness. Yet a healthy society in the 21st century will need more of this awareness in general, and also more key individuals to seed change. We all need to learn to point out the problems, not run away, and to be our own creative instigators. If we collude with each other, we might even get somewhere.

D. ILLUSTRATION FOUR
SOCIAL LEVEL: CONFRONTING GLOBAL ADVERSITY

1. Example: Becoming Aware—"The Silence of the Frogs"

This was the title of a *New York Times Magazine* cover story (Yoffe, 1992). Across the world, even in environments that seem relatively pristine, these familiar amphibians are disappearing. Their immune system have been weakened, and changes created by humans in our global environment likely have something to do with it. Indeed, frogs are broad samplers of nature in their complex life-cycles, moving from water to land, and from plant-eater to insect-eater. The immune system of the earth itself—the healing balance we depend on—may in fact be at risk. Frogs have been likened, on a global scale, to the "proverbial canary in the coal mine."

2. Model: Maladaptive Genetic Programming and Psychological Blindness

The main problem is that we don't confront global threats very well. For evolutionary reasons, we don't always even see them! When we finally take a look, we may put them quickly out of mind (Richards, 1993a). The biological model involves maladaptive genetic programming (and as before, there also remain issues of acquired immunity, or lack thereof). Bailin (this volume) asks whether true pathology in a society doesn't also imply pathology in individuals. That is very much the point. There are general psychological deficiencies we all share involving information processing, which need remediation: finding the "missing" process memes to increase our capacity for awareness, and then the *content* memes to warn us of approaching dangers. These tasks may be seen as part of our conscious evolution (Ornstein & Ehrlich, 1989).

3. Pathology: Potentially Hazardous Modes of Thinking and Being

The unprecedented threats we face include overpopulation, global warming, pollution, and decimation of natural resources (e.g., Brown et al., 1991; Ehrlich & Ehrlich,1991; Rifkin, 1990). Yet despite the fact that our own futures, and our children's futures, are at stake, it may take feature on the frogs to awaken us.

a. When we don't even see it
Our perceptual and conceptual apparatus was formed in prehistoric times (e.g., Glantz & Pearce, 1989). (The whole process may be likened to how the visual system responds to light [Guyton, 1976; Ornstein & Ehrlich, 1989].) Cells in our visual cortex are sensitive to edges and to dark–light changes.) Thus, we're out there in the grassy plain with out hunter–gatherer band, watching for the lion to attack us. Meanwhile, we're breathing poisons that we rarely even think about. Our systems are designed to respond to the sudden and spectacular—a good means no doubt to get out of the way of the animal before it pounces. But a steadily growing and lethal danger can be easily overlooked.

Meanwhile, the trivial, if sensational enough, will still draw our attention. As an illustration, we may be thinking about the marital separation of "Princess Di" on the cover of *Newsweek* while depletion of the tropical rainforests presses forward at a rate of 10 city blocks per minute, threatening the balance of life on our planet (Adler, 1991; Ornstein & Ehrlich, 1989; Richards, 1993a).

In many important ways, we are adapted to the wrong environment (Glantz & Pearce, 1989; Richards, 1993a).

b. When we close our eyes to it

We don't always feel hopeful or effective about problems on a massive scale, so at times, we may simply abolish them.

Very much in collusion with each other, we may experience "psychic numbing" (as used by Lifton and Falk (1982) in describing reactions to Hiroshima), numbing ourselves even to the misery even at our doorsteps, when it appears too overwhelming to address—the hunger, the poverty, the violence. We may read about this in the papers, we may give to a cause, we may even do some work (or we may not), but our actual human appreciation of the extent of the problem, or what it's like for that homeless mother and child, for instance, on a day-to-day basis, may be temporary or limited (Richards, 1993a).

And recently, the figures of persons who doubted that the Holocaust even occurred—a shocking one out of five people (Carroll, 1993)—was an unbelievable testimonial to the capacity to distort or deny reality.

The strategies of positive mood maintenance and negative mood repair stand people in good stead here. They enhance a collective and consensual *dissociation* from some of the most painful realities. They are certainly not psychological strategies we should simply take note of and accept. They are perhaps better indicators of the amount of trauma which we, as a society, seem to endure and tolerate.

4–6. Creativity and the Evaluation of Information: Our "Conscious Evolution"

We all need to see ourselves as trauma survivors (see also Freyd, 1991; Jordan, 1992), to work toward an enhanced mental openness and creative flexibility, so that we can better tolerate, and thus better confront, the problems in our world. Some of our most creative people will serve us well here as truth-tellers and instigators. But to hear what they say, and to act, we will also need to attend to the conscious evolution of every one of us, if we are truly to progress as a species.

ILLNESS AND CREATIVITY: SOME OVERALL ISSUES

Reducing the Risks While Respecting Diversity, and Extending the "Limits of Normality."

Jamison (1990, 1993) raised concerns that advances in genetic engineering may lead people to want to eliminate, or to select against, the gene(s) for bipolar mood disorders. This is a concern indeed.

It's not that simple with psychopathology and creativity. There are not clear-cut categories or prescriptions. The range of presentations we see with a bipolar vulnerability is one reflection of the diversity of which we're capable—and in a very real sense of the diversity that makes life possible. The border between the normal and abnormal is not only blurred, but it is shifting, depending upon a range of contexts and conditions. One genotype may produce this entire range—and we need this range.

The question is not one of eliminating a condition or an illness. This is simplified thinking about a complex and shifting spectrum. If one were somehow to stamp out bipolar mood disorders, for instance, it would endanger the diversity of our world, and every one of us. Indeed, with such a prevalent condition as this, it probably isn't even possible. The question, instead, is one of reducing the costs to allow people to make more subtle shifts within the phenotypic range to ease the fates of individuals. Some persons may still choose not to seek this. Creativity as they understand it has a strong adaptive pull. Thus, the true benefits of treatment and costs of abstention should be widely known and strongly stressed. Beyond that, it is up to individuals. Conceivably, the very choices made could further increase the diversity we see.

Viewing Creativity as the Evolution of Information—And as a Process that Can Be Less or More Healthy.

Creativity at once moves toward greater complexity, and an elegant simplicity in the organization of new forms. Memetic evolution can create more phenotypes, more options for us, and thus greater genetic viability. Unfortunately, creativity can also be abused, but it can most certainly be used in productive and adaptive ways. In this process may lie considerable hope for our growth and our future, beyond horizons we cannot currently see.

Our most helpful role here is to enable, to respect and to preserve diversity, and in some sense (with a few exceptions) not to presume to get in the way.

Such an evolution of information is not particularly new. It's how it has always worked! But we might go further and ask: "Which is more important, evolution of genes, evolution of information—or of both?" This question is not an idle one, for with the possible advent of sophisticated artificial life ("A-life") in the 21st century, the information may be able to forge some new evolutionary paths on its own. we may truly want to think—right now—as have Isaac Asimov and other science fiction writers, about the moral consequences of this possibility.

Evolving to Confront Dangers We May Not See, or Refuse to See

The above assumes we know what's going on and can choose. But there are many events in our environment we don't even see, including crucial global problems and threats. Here is a crucial place where genetic evolution may be not only be aided by memetic evolution, but saved. Our conscious evolution should, without question, be one of our highest priorities.

But we must deal first with the other side of this coin. When we're numbed to what we do see, we remain helpless and deceived. We have our own mini-distortions to keep our daily life running smoothly (or so that we can think it is). We act like trauma victims, and indeed we are dissociated from much of our human experience on the global level. Meanwhile, the whole system may be about to explode. It's our conscious evolution that can save us.

Cultural Brainstorming, and Optimizing Creative Results

The cultural context, and embedded social roles, may help determine the value of creativity versus thought disorder. A subtle shift in atmosphere may help shape whether innovative individuals will be rewarded or censured—that is, whether the creative heat will be turned up or down. Each individual will be rewarded according to individual efforts, as valued by society at a point in time. But the cumulative effect will give a portrait of a society.

At a higher level, there might be adjustments we can contemplate in a society, in both senders and receivers of innovation, adjustments in the proposed process of "cultural brainstorming," to further raise or lower the creative heat. This is another potential aspect of our conscious evolution. And here we are, not quite sure about what is sick and what is healthy, and missing a lot of other critical dangers in addition. At this point, it would appear, we had better turn the creative heat up.

REFERENCES

Ackerman, D. (1994). *A natural history of love.* New York: Random House.

Adler, W. Jr. (1991). *The whole earth quiz book.* New York: Quill.

Akiskal, H. & Akiskal, K. (1988). Reassessing the prevalence of bipolar disorders: Clinical significance and artistic creativity. *Psychiatry and Psychobiology, 3,* 29–36.

Akiskal, H. & Akiskal, K. (1992). Cyclothymic, hyperthymic, and depressive temperaments as subaffective variants of mood disorders. In A. Tasman & M. B. Riba (Eds.), *Review of psychiatry,* Vol. 11, (pp. 43–62). Washington, DC: American Psychiatric Press.

Akiskal, H. S. & Mallya, G. (1987). Criteria for the "soft" bipolar spectrum: Treatment implications. *Psychopharmacology Bulletin, 23,* 67–73.

Albert, R. S. (1971). Cognitive development and parental loss among the gifted, the exceptionally gifted and the creative. *Psychological Reports, 29,* 19–26.

Albert, R. S. (1983). Family positions and the attainment of eminence. In R. S. Albert (Ed.), *Genius and eminence,* (pp. 141–153). New York: Pergamon Press.

Albert, R. S. & Runco, M. A. (1986). The achievement of eminence. In R. J. Sternberg & J. E. Davidson (Eds.), *Conceptions of giftedness.* New York: Cambridge University Press.

Andreason, N. (1978). Creativity and psychiatric illness. *Psychiatric Annals, 8,* 113–119.

Andreasen, N. (1987). Creativity and mental illness: Prevalence rates in writers and their first-degree relatives. *American Journal of Psychiatry, 144,* 1288–1292.

Andreasen, N. & Canter, A. (1974). The creative writer: Psychiatric symptoms and family history. *Comprehensive Psychiatry, 15,* 123–131.

Andreasen, N. & Glick I. D. (1988). Bipolar affective disorder and creativity: Implications and clinical management. *Comprehensive Psychiatry, 15,* 113–131.

Andreasen, N. & Powers, P. (1974). Overinclusive thinking in mania and schizophrenia. *British Journal of Psychiatry, 125,* 452–456.

Bailin, S. (1990). Societal creativity: Problems with pathology. *Creativity Research Journal, 3,* 100–103.

Barron, F. (1963a). The disposition toward originality. In C. W. Taylor & F. Barron (Eds.), *Scientific creativity: Its recognition and development,* (pp. 139–152). New York: Wiley.

Barron, F. (1963b). The needs for order and disorder as motives in creative activity. In C. W. Taylor & F. Barron (Eds.), *Scientific creativity: Its recognition and development,* (pp. 153–160). New York: Wiley.

Barron, F. (1969). *Creative person and creative process.* New York: Holt, Rinehart & Winston.

Barron, F. & Bradley, P. (1990). The clash of social philosophies and personalities in the nuclear arms control debate: A healthful dialectic? *Creativity Research Journal, 3,* 237–246.

Bak, P. & Chen, K. (1991, January). Self-organized criticality. *Scientific American,* 46–53.

Barron, F. & Bradley, P. (1990). The clash of social philosophies and personalities in the nuclear arms control debate: A healthful dialectic? *Creativity Research Journal*, 3, 237–246.

Becker, G. (1978). *The mad genius controversy: A study in the sociology of deviance.* Beverly Hills, CA: Sage.

Berman, S. (1991). The real ropes course: The development of social consciousness. *ESR (Educators for Social Responsibility) Journal*, 1, 1–18.

Blaney, P. H. (1986). Affect and memory: A review. *Psychological Bulletin*, 99, 229–246.

Bogen, J. & Bogen, G. (1988). *Psychiatric Clinics of North America.* (Vol 2, No. 3). Philadelphia: WB Saunders.

Bower, G. H. (1981). Mood and memory. *American Psychologist*, 36, 129–148.

Brent, D. A., Kupfer, D. J., Bromet, E. J., & Dew M. A. (1988). The assessment and treatment of patients at risk for suicide. In A. J. Frances, & R. E. Hales (Eds.), *Review of psychiatry*, Vol 7, (pp. 353–385). Washington, D.C.: American Psychiatric Press.

Brown, L. R., Brough, H., Durning, A., Flavin, C., French, H., Jacobson, J., Lenssen, N., Lowe, M., Postel, S., Renner, M., Ryan, J., Starke, L., & Young, J. (1992). *State of the world, 1992: A Worldwatch Institute report on progress toward a sustainable society.* New York: Norton.

Brown, L. R., Durning, A., Flavin, C., French, H., Jacobson, J., Lenssen, N., Lowe, M., Postel S., Renner, M., Ryan, J., Starke, L., & Young, J. (1991). *State of the world: A Worldwatch Institute report on progress toward a sustainable society.* New York: Norton.

Carroll, J. (1993, July 20). The barriers obliterated by the Holocaust. *Boston Globe*, 15.

Cropley, A. J. (1990). Creativity and mental health in everyday life. *Creativity Research Journal*, 3, 167–178.

Csikszentmihalyi, M. (1988). Society, culture, and person: A systems view of creativity. In R. J. Sternberg (Ed.), *The nature of creativity*, (pp. 325–339). Cambridge, England: Cambridge University Press.

Dawkins, R. (1976). *The selfish gene.* New York: Oxford University Press.

Dertouzos, M. L. (1991). Communications, computers and networks. *Scientific American*, 265, 62–69.

Donald, M. (1991). *Origins of the modern mind: Three stages in the evolution of culture and cognition.* Cambridge, MA: Harvard University Press.

Dudek, S. Z. & Verrault, R. (1989). The creative thinking and ego functioning of children. *Creativity Research Journal*, 2, 64–86.

Eckblad, M., & Chapman, L. J. (1986). Development and validation of a scale for hypomanic personality. *Journal of Abnormal Psychology*, 3, 214–222.

Ehrlich, P. R., & Ehrlich A. H. (1991). *The population explosion.* New York: Touchstone.

Eisenberg, D., Kessler, R. C., Foster, C., Norlock, F. E., Calkins, D. R., & Delbanco, T. L. (1993). Unconventional medicine in the United States. *New England Journal of Medicine*, 328, 246–252.

Eisenman, R. (1990). Creativity, preference for complexity, and physical and mental illness. *Creativity Research Journal*, 3, 231–236.

Eysenck, H. (1993). Creativity and personality: Suggestions for a theory. *Psychological Inquiry*, 4, 147–178.

Eysenck, H. (1994). *Creativity Research Journal*, 7, 209–216.

Feldman, D. H. (1990). Four frames for the study of creativity. *Creativity Research Journal*, 3, 104–111.

Flach, F. (1990). Disorders of the pathways involved in the creative process. *Creativity Research Journal*, 3, 158–165.

Fobes, J. L. (1989). The cognitive psychobiology of performance regulation. *Journal of Sports Medicine and Physical Fitness*, 29, 202–208.

Forrest, S. (1991). Emergent computation: Self-organizing, collective, and cooperative phenomena in natural and artificial computing networks. In S. Forrest (Ed.), *Emergent computation*. Cambridge, MA: MIT Press.

Forrest S. & Miller, J. H. (1991). Emergent behavior in classifier systems. In S. Forrest (Ed.), *Emergent computation*, (pp. 213–227). Cambridge, MA: MIT Press.

Freud, S. (1908/1958). The relation of the poet to day-dreaming. In S. Freud, *On creativity and the unconscious* (collected writings) (pp. 44–54). New York: Random House.

Freud, S. (1920). *A general introduction to psychoanalysis*. New York: Boni and Liveright.

Freyd, J. J. (August, 1991). Memory repression, dissociative states, and other cognitive control processes involved in adult sequelae of childhood trauma. Paper given at the Second Annual Conference of the Program on Conscious and Unconscious Mental Processes, University of California, San Francisco.

Frijda, N. H. (1988). The laws of emotion. *American Psychologist*, 43, 349–358.

Gardner, H. (1993). *Creating minds*. New York: Basic Books.

Gardner, K. G. & Moran, J. D., III (1990). *Creativity Research Journal*, 3, 281–286.

Garmezy, N. & Rutter, M. (1983). *Stress, coping, and development in children*. New York: McGraw-Hill.

Gedo, J. E. (1990). More on the healing power of art: The case of John Ensor. *Creativity Research Journal*, 3, 33–57.

Glance, N. S. & Huberman, B. A. (1994, March). The dynamics of social dilemmas. *Scientific American*.

Glantz, K. & Pearce, J. K. (1989). *Exiles from Eden: Psychotherapy from an evolutionary perspective*. New York: Norton.

Gleick, J. (1988). *Chaos: Making a new science*. New York: Penguin.

Goertzel, V. & Goertzel, M. G. (1962). *Cradles of eminence*. Boston: Little, Brown.

Goldstein, K. & Scheerer, M. (1941). Abstract and conerete behavior: An experimental study with special tests. *Psychological Monographs*, 53, Whole No. 239.

Goodwin, F. K. & Jamison, K. R. (1990). *Manic-depressive illness*. New York: Oxford University Press.

Goswami, A. (1993). An idealist theory of ethics. *Creativity Research Journal*, 6, 185–196.

Gould, S. J. (1989). *Wonderful life*. New York: Norton.

Gruber, H. (1985). Giftedness and moral responsibility: Creative thinking and human survival. In F. D. Horowitz & M. O'Brien (Eds.), *The gifted and tal-*

ented: *Developmental perspectives* (pp. 301–330) Washington, D.C.: American Psychological Assoc.

Gruber, H. (1988). Creative altruism, cooperation, and world peace. In T. J. Hurley (Ed.), *The greater self: New frontiers in exceptional abilities research.* Sausalito: CA: Institute of Noetic Sciences.

Gruber, H. (1989). Creativity and human survival. In D. Wallace, & H. Gruber (Eds.), *Creative people at work* (pp. 278–287). New York: Oxford University Press.

Gruber, H. (1993). Creativity in the moral domain: Ought implies can implies create. *Creativity Research Journal,* 6, 3–15.

Guyton, A. C. (1976). *Textbook of medical physiology.* Philadelphia: W. B. Saunders.

Harrington, D. (1990). The ecology of human creativity: A psychological perspective. In M. A. Runco and R. S. Albert, (Eds). *Theories of creativity.* Newbury Park, CA: Sage Publications.

Haste, H. (1993). Moral creativity and education for citizenship. *Creativity Research Journal,* 6, 153–164.

Hausman, C. R. (1990). The origin of creative achievement: Spontaneity, responsibility, and individuals. *Creativity Research Journal,* 3, 112–117.

Hirsch, D. (1993). WRKO's Victoria Jones. *Talkers,* 43, 1, 3, 11.

Hoffman, R. E. (1987). Computer simulations of neural information processing and the schizophrenia-mania dichotomy. *Archives of General Psychiatry,* 44, 178–188.

Holland, J. H., Kolyoak, K. J., Nisbett, R. E. & Thagard, P. R. (1986). *Induction: Processes of inference, learning, and discovery.* Cambridge, MA: MIT Press.

Holzman, P. S., Shenton, M. E., & Solovay, M. R. (1986). Quality of thought disorder in differential diagnosis. *Schizophrenia Bulletin,* 12, 360–372.

Hoppe, K. (1988). *Psychiatric Clinics of North America.* (Vol. 2 No. 3) Philadelphia: WB Saunders.

Hoppe, K. & Kyle, N. (1990). Dual brain, creativity, and health. *Creativity Research Journal,* 3, 150–157.

Horowitz, M. J. (1988). Unconsciously determined defensive strategies. In M. Horowitz (Ed.), *Psychodynamics and cognition.* Chicago: University of Chicago Press.

Isen, A. M. (1984). Toward understanding the role of affect in cognition. In R. S. Wyer, Jr., & T. K. Srull (Eds.), *Handbook of social cognition,* Vol. 3, (pp. 179–235). Hillsdale, NJ: Erlbaum.

Isen, A. M. (1985). Asymmetry of happiness and sadness in effects on memory in normal college students: Comment on Hasher, Rose, Zacks, Sanft, and Doren. *Journal of Experimental Psychology: General 114,* 388–391.

Isen, A. M., Daubman, K. A., & Nowicki, G. P. (1987). Positive affect facilitates creative problem solving. *Journal of Personality and Social Psychology,* 52, 1122–1131.

Isen, A. M., Nygren, T. E., & Ashby, F. G. (1988). Influence of positive affect on the subjective utility of gains and losses: It is just not worth the risk. *Journal of Personality and Social Psychology* 55, 710–717.

Jamison K. R., Gerner, R., Hammen, C., & Padesky, C. (1980). Clouds and silver linings: Positive experiences associated with primary affective disorders. *American Journal of Psychiatry,* 137, 198–202.

Jamison, K. R. (1989). Mood disorders and patterns of creative in British writers. *Psychiatry*, 52, 125–134.

Jamison, K. R. (1990). Manic-depressive illness, creativity, and leadership. In F. K. Goodwin, & K. R. Jamison, *Manic-depressive illness*. (pp. 332–367). New York: Oxford University Press.

Jamison, K. (1993). *Touched with fire*. New York: Free Press.

Jordan, J. (1990). *Courage in connection: Conflict, compassion, creativity*. Wellesley, MA: Stone Center for Developmental Services and Studies, Wellesley College.

Jordan, J. (1992). *Relational resilience*. Wellesley, MA: Stone Center for Developmental Services and Studies, Wellesley College.

Jordan, J. V., Kaplan, A. G., Miller, J. B., Stiver, I. P., & Surrey, J. L. (1991). *Women's growth in connection*. New York: Guilford.

Kagan, J. (1989, April). Temperamental contributions to social behavior. *American Psychologist*, 668–674.

Kantrowitz, B. & Ramo, J. (1993, 31 May). An interactive life. *Newsweek*, 42–44.

Kohn, A. (1986). *No contest: The case against competition*. Boston: Houghton Mifflin.

Kohn, A. (1990). *The brighter side of human nature*. New York: Basic Books.

Kreisberg, S. (1992). *Transforming power: Domination, empowerment, and education*. Albany, NY: State University of New York Press.

Krystal, H. (1981). The hedonic element in affectivity. *Annual of Psychoanalysis*, 9, 93–113.

Kuhn, T. S. (1970). *The structure of scientific revolutions*, 2nd Ed. Chicago: University of Chicago Press.

Kyle, N. (1988). *Psychiatric Clinics of North America*.

Langer, E. (1989). *Mindfulness*. Reading, MA: Addison-Wesley.

Lawlor, G. J., Jr., & Fischer, T. J. (Eds.). (1988). *Manual of allergy and immunology*, 2nd Ed. Boston: Little, Brown, and Co.

Lifton, R. J., & Markusen, E. (1990). *The genocidal mentality: Nazi holocaust and nuclear threat*. New York: Basic Books.

Lifton, R. J., & Falk, R. (1982). *Indefensible weapons*. New York: Basic Books.

Locke, S. E., & Colligan, D. (1986). *The healer within*. New York: Dutton.

Ludwig, A. M. (1990). Alcohol input and creative output. *British Journal of Addiction*, 85, 953–963.

Ludwig, A. M. (1992a). Creative achievement and psychopathology: Comparison among professions. *American Journal of Psychotherapy*, 46, 330–353.

Ludwig, A. M. (1992b). Culture and creativity. *American Journal of Psychotherapy*, 46, 454–469.

Lumsden, C. J., & Findlay, C. S. (1988). Evolution of the creative mind. *Creativity Research Journal*, 1, 75–91.

Martindale, C. (1990). Innovation, illegitimacy, and individualism. *Creativity Research Journal*, 3, 118–124.

Matthysse, S. (1991). Mood disorders and the dynamic stability of the system of memories. In, J Madden IV (Ed.), *Neurobiology of learning, emotion, and affect*. New York: Raven Press.

McLaren, R. (1993). The dark side of creativity. *Creativity Research Journal*, 6, 137–144.

Minkoff, E. C. (1983). *Evolutionary biology*. Reading, MA: Addison-Wesley.

Ornstein, R., & Ehrlich, P. (1989). *New world, new mind: Moving toward conscious evolution.* New York: Touchstone.

Ornstein, R., & Swencionis, C. (Eds.). (1990). *The healing brain: A scientific reader.* New York: The Guilford Press.

Osborn, A. F. (1963). *Applied imagination.* New York: Scribners.

Ostwald, P. (1991). *Vaslav Nijinsky: A leap into madness.* New York: Lyle Stuart.

Pennebaker, J. W., Kiecolt-Glaser, J. K., & Glaser, R. (1988). Confronting traumatic experience and immunocompetence. *Journal of Consulting and clinical Psychology, 56,* 638–639.

Peterson, C., & Bossio, L. M. (1991). *Health and optimism: New research on the relationship between positive thinking and physical well-being.* New York: New York Free Press.

Peterson, K. C., Prout, M. F., & Schwarz, R. A. (1991). *Post-traumatic stress disorder.* New York: Plenum Press.

Redondi, P. (1987). *Galileo: Heretic.* Princeton, NJ: Princeton University Press.

Rhodes, C. (1990). Growth from deficiency creativity to being creativity. *Creativity Research Journal, 3,* 287–289.

Richards, R. (1981). Relationships between creativity and psychopathology: An evaluation and interpretation of the evidence. *Genetic Psychology Monographs, 103,* 261–324.

Richards, R. (1990). Everyday creativity, eminent creativity, and health. *Creativity Research Journal, 3,* 300–326.

Richards, R. (1991, August). Everyday creativity and the arts. paper presented at the Annual Meeting of the American Psychological Association, San Francisco, CA. Version in *Psychologie Heute,* (1992, December), 58–64 (German). Version in A. Montuori & R. Purser (Eds.). (in press). *Social creativity: prospects and possibilities* (vol 3). Creskill, NJ: Hampton Press.

Richards, R. (1993a). Seeing beyond: Issues of creative awareness and social responsibility. *Creativity Research Journal, 6,* 165–183.

Richards, R. (1993b). Everyday creativity, eminent creativity, and psychopathology. Commentary on "Creativity and psychopathology" by Hans J. Eysenck. *Psychological Inquiry, 4,* 212–217.

Richards, R. (1994a). "Acceptable" and "Unacceptable" Research. *Creativity Research Journal, 7,* 87–90.

Richards, R. (1994b). Creativity and bipolar mood swings: Why the association? In M. Shaw, & M. A. Runco (Eds.), *Creativity and affect* (pp. 44–72). Norwood, NJ: Ablex.

Richards, R. (1996a). Does the lone genius ride again? Chaos, creativity, and community. *Journal of Humanistic Psychology, 36*(2), 44–60.

Richards, R. (1996b). Beyond Piaget: Accepting divergent, chaotic, and creative thought. In M. Runco (Ed.). *New Directions for Child Development, 72,* 67–86. San Francisco: Jossey-Bass.

Richards, R. & Kinney, D. (1990). Mood swings and creativity. *Creativity Research Journal, 3,* 203–218.

Richards, R., Kinney, D., Benet, M. & Merzel, A. P. C. (1988). Assessing everyday creativity: Characteristics of the Lifetime Creativity Scales and validation with three large samples. *Journal of Personality and Social Psychology,* 54, 476–485.

Richards, R., Kinney, D., Daniels, H. & Linkins, K. (1992). Everyday creativity and bipolar and unipolar affective disorder: Preliminary study of personal and family history. *European Psychiatry,* 7, 49–52.

Richards, R., Kinney, D., Lunde, I., Benet, M., & Merzel, A. P. C. (1988). Creativity in manic-depressives, cyclothymes, their normal relatives, and control subjects. *Journal of Abnormal Psychology* 97, 281–288.

Rifkin, J. (1990). The global environmental crisis. In J. Rifkin (Ed.), *The green lifestyle handbook.* New York: Holt.

Roe, A. (1963). Personal problems and science. In, C. W. Taylor, & F. Barron (Eds.), *Scientific creativity: Its recognition and development,* (pp. 132–138). New York: Wiley and Sons.

Rolf, J., Master, A. S., Cicchetti, D., Nuechterlein, K. H., & Weintraum, S. (Eds.) (1990). *Risk and protective factors in the development of psychopathology.* New York: Cambridge University Press.

Rothenberg, A. (1990). Creativity, mental health, and alcoholism. *Creativity Research Journal,* 3, 179–201.

Rubenson, D. L. (1990). The accidental economist. *Creativity Research Journal,* 3, 125–129.

Rubenson, D. L., & Runco, M. A. (1992). The psychoeconomic approach to creativity. *New Ideas in Psychology,* 10, 131–147.

Runco, M. (1993). Creative morality: Intentional and unconventional. *Creativity Research Journal,* 6, 17–28.

Runco, M. A. (1994). Creativity and its discontents. In M. Shaw, & M. A. Runco (Eds.), *Creativity and affect* (pp. 102–123). Norwood, NJ: Ablex.

Runco, M. A., Ebersole, P., & Mraz, W. (1990). Self actualization and creativity. *Journal of Social Behavior and Personality* 6, 161–167.

Sandblom, P. (1989). *Creativity and disease: How illness affects literature.* Philadelphia: G. B. Lippincott.

Schou, M. (1979). Artistic productivity and lithium prophylzxis in manic-depressive illness. *British Journal of Psychiatry,* 135, 97–103.

Schuldberg, D. (1990). Schizotypal and hypomanic traits, creativity, and psychological health. *Creativity Research Journal,* 3, 218–230.

Schuldberg, D. (1994). Giddiness and horror. In M. Shaw, & M. Runco (Eds.), *Creativity and affect.* (pp. 87–101). Norwood, NJ: Ablex Publishing Co.

Simonton, D. K. (1984). *Genius, creativity and leadership: Historiometric inquiries.* Cambridge, MA: Harvard University Press.

Simonton, D. K. (1988). *Scientific genius: A psychology of science.* New York: Cambridge University Press.

Simonton, D. K. (1990a). Political pathology and societal creativity. *Creativity Research Journal,* 3, 85–99.

Simonton, D. K. (1990b). Monsieur appends reflections. *Creativity Research Journal,* 3, 146–149.

Skarda, C. & Freeman, W. J. (1987). How brains make chaos in order to make sense of the world. *Behavioral and Brain Sciences,* 10, 161–173.

Smith, D. W. (Ed.). (1977). *Introduction to clinical pediatrics*, 2nd Ed. Philadelphia: W. B. Saunders.

Smith, G. J. W., & Van der Meer, G. (1990). *Creativity Research Journal*, 3, 249–264.

Solovay, M. D., Shenton, M. E., Gasperetti, C., Doleman, M., Kentenbaum, E., Carpenter, J. T., & Holzman, P. (1986). Scoring manual for the Thought Disorder Index (revised version). *Schizophrenia Bulletin*, 12, 483–496.

Spender, D. (1982). *Women of ideas.* London: Pandora.

Stariha, W. E., & Walberg, H. J. (1990). Psychological mediators of the inverse pathology-creativity effect. *Creativity Research Journal*, 3, 130–133.

Stein, M. I. (1990). Anabolic and catabolic factors in the creative process. *Creativity Research Journal*, 3, 134–145.

Styron, W. (1990). *Darkness visible: A memoir of madness.* New York: Random House.

Tooby, J. & DeVore, I. (1987). The reconstruction of hominid behavioral evolution through strategic modeling. In W. G. Kinzey (Ed.) (1987). *The evolution of human behavior: Primate models.* (pp. 183–237). Albany, NY: State University of New York Press.

Wallach, M. A. & Kogan, N. (1965). *Modes of thinking in young children.* New York: Holt, Rinehart, & Winston.

Wender, P. H., Kety, S. S., Rosenthal, D., Schulsinger, F., Ortmann, J. & Lunde, I. (1986). Psychiatric disorders in the biological and adaptive families of adopted individuals with affective disorders. *Archives of General Psychiatry*, 43, 923–929.

Waldrop, M. M. (1992). *Complexity: The emerging science at the edge of order and chaos.* New York: Simon and Schuster.

Wilson, E. O. (May 20, 1993). Is humanity suicidal? *New York Times Magazine*, 24–29.

Wilson, E. O. (1992). *The diversity of life.* New York: W. W. Norton.

Wilson, D. (1992). Evolutionary epidemiology. *Acta Biotheoretica* 40.

X, Malcolm, & Haley, A. (1964). *The autobiography of Malcolm X.* New York: Ballantine.

Yoffe, E. (December 13, 1992). Silence of the frogs, *New York Times Magazine*, 36–38, 64–66, 76.

Author Index

Subject Index